Performing the Nation

Chicago Studies in Ethnomusicology

A series edited by Philip V. Bohlman and Bruno Nettl

Performing the Nation

Swahili Music and Cultural Politics in Tanzania

Kelly M. Askew

The University of Chicago Press

Chicago and London

The University of Chicago Press, Chicago 60637
The University of Chicago Press, Ltd., London
© 2002 by The University of Chicago
All rights reserved. Published 2002
Printed in the United States of America

11 10 09 08 07 06   2 3 4 5

ISBN: 0-226-02980-8 (cloth)
ISBN: 0-226-02981-6 (paper)

Library of Congress Cataloging-in-Publication Data

Askew, Kelly Michelle.
    Performing the nation : Swahili music and cultural politics in
Tanzania / Kelly M. Askew.
        p.   cm. — (Chicago studies in ethnomusicology)
    Includes bibliographical references, discography (p.   ), and indexes.
    ISBN 0-226-02980-8 (hardcover : alk. paper) —
    ISBN 0-226-02981-6 (paperback : alk. paper)
    1. Swahili-speaking peoples—Tanzania—Music—History and
criticism.   2. Tanzania—Cultural policy.   3. Taarab—Tanzania—
History and criticism.   I. Title.   II. Series.
ML3760 .A84 2002
306.4'84—dc21

                                                        2001008414

In memory of
Donald Ellis Askew
and
H. Leroy Vail

Contents

Illustrations

Maps

Figures

Tables

Acknowledgments

After three years in East Africa, I returned to the United States in 1995 to discover that an African saying had infiltrated popular American consciousness: "It takes a village to raise a child." This took me by pleasant surprise, because the Swahili equivalent, *Mkono mmoja haulei mwana*, "One hand cannot raise a child," is a saying that I hold dear in memory of the many hands and minds that contributed both to the raising of my son Christopher and the writing of this book.

First to appear in these acknowledgments, not surprisingly, are my parents, Leni Montilla Askew and the late Donald Ellis Askew, who together instilled and encouraged in me a twin love for learning and music. My mother is my beacon—she who independently left her home in the Philippines in her youth to discover and explore the richness and diversity of a world beyond her beautiful islands. I regret that my father, who passed away while I was in Africa, could not witness the conclusion of this long and arduous process, but I trust that he shares in my joy nevertheless. His mother, Mary Slick Askew, through her love for Native American and Australian cultures, introduced me to anthropology and—as the other musician in the family—gave me my first piano lessons. To my sister Christina Askew, my nephew Alexander Askew, my maternal grandparents, Luz and Napoleon Montilla, my Tito Rene and Tita Melinda Montilla, and my brother Mladen Mitic goes my gratitude for their love and support across the years and miles. And beloved of all is Christopher, whose existence and love never cease to amaze me.

From kin networks, I shift to academic ones. I extend my heartfelt gratitude to the many cherished colleagues who in reading all or parts of this manuscript gave so freely of their time, knowledge, support, and friendship: Ann Biersteker, Fred Cooper, Laura Fair, Ben Fortson, Susan Geiger, Werner Graebner, Michael Herzfeld, Tom Hinnebusch, Isaria Kimambo, Amandina Lihamba, Gregory Maddox, Joseph Mbele, Sheryl McCurdy, John Middleton, Deo Ngonyani, Pauline Peters, Hanan Sabea, Kay Kaufman Shelemay, Leroy Vail, Katherine Verdery, the students in my Winter 2000 "African Soundscapes" seminar, my editor, David Brent, the two anonymous reviewers, and my copyeditor, Nick Murray. Their comments and criticisms helped me tremendously and prodded my thinking into new directions. Special thanks go to Werner Graebner, whom I first met in a narrow alleyway in Mombasa, Kenya, in 1987. He remains a constant friend, ice cream collaborator, and font of information on Swahili music and culture. He mastered the CD that accompanies this book and did an amazing job, especially considering the poor quality of many of the original tapes. I also thank Werner, Matthew Lavoie, Leo Sarkisian, and Douglas Paterson for all their suggestions for the discography and their willingness to search their own collections for missing catalogue numbers and production dates. For help in editing the Swahili glossary and answering general language-related questions, I thank Deo Ngonyani, Suma Ngonyani, and Ben Fortson, all of whom have special places in my heart. For exquisite maps, and for his forbearance in suffering so many Swahili spellings, I thank David Kiphuth. Additional thanks go to Mwamoyo Hamza for double-checking the maps and offering advice on Tanga-related matters. And for assistance in producing high-quality photographs, I thank the staff at the University of Michigan Photo Services, especially Paul Jaronski.

In Tanzania, there are many whose contributions I would like to acknowledge and countless others whose names I cannot include here, but to whom I am no less grateful. Heading the list is Aisha Mabrouk, my dear friend and sister, who helped me translate songs and poems, taught me to cook Swahili cuisine, and mothered my son Christopher the many nights when I attended band rehearsals and performances. Her father, the late Ali Abrahman Ali Diwani, who served as a Minister of Parliament and Secretary of the National Union of Tanganyika Workers (NUTA), was a valued source of information. Her stepfather, the late Mwalim (Teacher) Pera Ridhiwani, an immensely well-respected local poet and scholar of Swahili history and language, introduced me to Tanga society and entrusted me to Aisha's care. To the three of them and to Aisha's mother, Mama Amina Anzuwani, go my heartfelt thanks and my enduring devotion. Special thanks go to Salim Pera Ridhiwani for painstakingly seeking the original sites of music clubs for the Ngamiani map, to Feisal Mabrook Omari and Fatime Diwani for assisting me with Swahili translations, and to Sadik Athman Mohamed, who helped me translate many Swahili songs. I also thank David Scheinman, Anthony and Ruth Ellman, Salim Kisauji, Nirmal Singh, and the family of Nirvanjan Pattni for their support throughout my time in Tanga. My roommates, both in Tanga and in the United States, have stood by me through thick and thin and constitute a treasured nucleus of social and academic support.

In Tanga, my roommates Hanan Sabea, Michael Beasley, and Tharani Sivananthan helped me in countless ways, as did Catherine Cockshutt Smith and Tracey Kaplan in the United States.

The familial support was complemented by scholarly support at the University of Dar es Salaam, most especially in the persons of M. M. Mulokozi and Louis Mbughuni. Many local scholars, musicians, and poets spent time patiently explaining things of various natures to me; they included Bi Pirira Athumani, "Chifu" Mohamed Ali Kiparisi, the late Waziri Kapalata, Rama Hamadi, Rashid Hamadi, Bi Shakila Saidi, Bi Sharmila Rashidi, Bi Lolita Hamisi, Ali Bakari "Boss," Sudi Hilal, Akida Jumanne, Hamisi Akida, "Babu" Akida Jumbe, Bi Kidude, and Mohamed "Bingwa" al-Ghassany. A special thanks goes to Mohamed "Kurupuka" Mzee, who transcribed more than a thousand songs from the tapes I never stopped collecting. Ministry of Culture personnel, both on the mainland and on the islands, gave freely of their time and knowledge. On the mainland at the national level, I thank Commissioner Ndagala, Louis Mbughuni, Godwin Kaduma, Mr. Maliwanga, Agnes Mandanda; at the regional level, Mohamed Majura, Nestory Mweta, Samuel Akile, Jeanstar Blandes, Mobali Muba, and Salimu Saidi; and at the district level, John Hizza, Ms. Rose, and Shabani Mshana. In Zanzibar, I thank Principal Secretary Hamad Mshindo, former Principal Secretary Osmond Duwe, Jumbe Said Ibrahim, and Iddi Farhan. I also received significant bureaucratic support and assistance from the office of the former Tanga Regional Commissioner, Azan al-Jabry.

For the financial support that enabled me to pursue my research and write this book, I thank the Office for the Vice President of Research and Office of the Provost (with special thanks to Lester Monts) at the University of Michigan, the Winkler Fund at Harvard University, the Ford Foundation, the Fulbright-Hays Doctoral Dissertation Research Abroad Fellowship program, Sigma Xi—The Scientific Society, the Harvard University Committee on African Studies, the National Science Foundation, the Yale Council of African Studies, and the Yale College Class of 1956. I also thank the Tanzanian Commission for Science and Technology and the Zanzibar Ministry of Information, Culture, and Tourism (now the Ministry of Information, Culture, Tourism, and Youth) for granting my requests for research clearance.

Finally, I thank all the musicians whose stories and music form the basis for this book, especially Babloom Modern Taarab, the Watangatanga Band, KIUBATA, Black Star Musical Club, Lucky Star Musical Club, Gita Ngoma, Msanja Ngoma, Saruji Cultural Troupe, Tanga Technical School, Golden Star Taarab, All Stars Modern Taarab, Tanzania One Theatre (TOT), Muungano Cultural Troupe, Culture Musical Club, Nadi Ikwani Safaa, JKT Taarab, the Tatu Nane Band, and the Kilimanjaro Band.

Common Abbreviations

ANC   African National Congress
ASP   Afro-Shirazi Party
BAKITA   Baraza la Kiswahili la Taifa (National Swahili Council)
BAKIZA   Baraza la Kiswahili la Zanzibar (Zanzibar Swahili Council)
Bandari   Harbours Authority
BASATA   Baraza la Sanaa la Taifa (National Arts Council)
BASAZA   Baraza la Sanaa la Zanzibar (Zanzibar Arts Council)
BIMA   National Insurance Company
CCM   Chama cha Mapinduzi (Party of the Revolution)
CUF   Civic United Front
DC   District Commissioner
DDC   Dar es Salaam Development Corporation
FRELIMO   Mozambique Liberation Front
GNP   Gross national product
IMF   International Monetary Fund
JKT   Jeshi la Kujenga Taifa (National Service Army)
JWTZ   Jeshi la Wananchi Tanzania (National Army)
KANU   Kenya African National Union
KIUBATA   Kikundi cha Utamaduni Bandari Tanga (Tanga Harbours Cultural
           Troupe)
NEC   National Executive Committee (of CCM)
NUTA   National Union of Tanganyika Workers
OTTU   Organization of Tanzanian Trade Unions
RC   Regional Commissioner
RCC   Regional Cultural Committee
RDC   Regional Development Committee
RDD   Regional Development Director
RTD   Radio Tanzania Dar es Salaam
Saruji   Tanga Cement Co.
SWAPO   South West Africa People's Organization

TAA	Tanganyika African Association
TACSO	Tanga Cultural Society
TANU	Tanganyika African National Union
TAPA	Tanganyika African Parents' Association
THA	Tanzania Harbours Authority
TLP	Tanzania Labour Party
TOT	Tanzania One Theatre
Tsh	Tanzanian shilling
TTACSA	Tanganyika Territory African Civil Service Association
TYL	Tanganyika Youth League
UWT	Umoja wa Wanawake wa Tanzania (Tanzania Women's Association)
VCC	Village Cultural Committee
VDC	Village Development Committee
Vijana	Umoja wa Vijana (CCM Youth League)
ZANU	Zimbabwe African National Union

1

ARTS OF GOVERNANCE

Art is not a mirror held up to reality, but a hammer with which to shape it.
—Bertolt Brecht

Policing the State, Performing the Nation

As we pulled up to the border an audible sigh echoed throughout the minibus. A long, clearly overloaded, forty-seater passenger bus was parked in front of the customs office with dozens of unloaded boxes stacked along its side. Customs officials were peering into the boxes and inspecting the interior of the bus. Clusters of weary passengers, including women in *buibui* (the full-length black veil worn by coastal Swahili women), men in *kofia* (embroidered caps worn by Swahili men), Asians of various denominations signified by the style and color of their garments,[1] along with unidentifiable others in Western-style clothing dotted the grounds surrounding the customs office. It did not bode well for a quick pass through customs for us, so after the driver parked to wait our turn I disembarked with the other twenty passengers on the minibus. We headed toward the makeshift shacks on the Tanzanian side of the border where we could purchase soda and *mishkaki* (grilled meat), *chips-mayai* (potato omelettes), or pan-fried chicken while waiting our turn for inspection. On a good day, one could pass through the border in less than an hour; but on a bad day such as today it could be a five- or six-hour ordeal.

We were en route to Mombasa, Kenya, from the city of Tanga, Tanzania, that was home to many of us on the bus. Mombasa and Tanga are two cities along the Swahili Coast of East Africa, a regional zone characterized by multiple forms of interstitiality: *geographic,* bridging land (the African continent) and sea (the Indian Ocean); *economic,* bridging mari-

1

time and agricultural activities; *religious,* bridging Islam, Christianity, and animism; *cultural,* bridging Africa, the Arabian Peninsula, and the Indian subcontinent; and *national,* bridging Kenya and Tanzania primarily, but also Somalia, Mozambique, and the Comoros Islands. National borders are key sites for the production, maintenance, delimitation, and reassertion of state authority. Our experience at the border—a common one the world over—temporarily transformed those of us who rode together on that bus. Variously on our way to visit family, pursue business opportunities, or (as in my case) attend a wedding, and coincidentally sharing a common bus to get there, we were suddenly witnesses to and participants in a performance of state power. As we watched and waited, waited and watched, Tanzanian immigration and customs agents asserted state authority to invade (the bus), interrogate (its driver and conductor), and inspect (its cargo and passengers)—an authority made tangible, a dominant ideology materialized *through its performance.*

* * *

On another road on another day in Tanzania, nightfall brought with it the 10:00 P.M. curfew that suspended all bus traffic in the country until the following morning. Buses en route to their destinations pulled off the road, and passengers bundled down as best they could in hard, unpadded iron seats to wait out the long night. In Muheza, the last stop before Tanga along the Dar es Salaam–Tanga road, travelers hoping to make it to Tanga before day's end gathered disconsolately at the silent bus stand. No amount of persuasion could convince a bus driver to risk the high fines that accompanied violation of the curfew. In desperation, someone turned to a lorry driver preparing to depart for Tanga. (Lorries, you see, were not subject to the curfew). The lorry, a *tipper* (dump truck), had ferried a load of construction gravel to a building site in Muheza earlier that day and was heading back to Tanga. The driver took pity and instructed his *turnboy* (helper) to let them board, charging each passenger a small fee. Old, young, male, female—people piled into the back of the tipper, as many as it would hold, too grateful for the lift to be bothered by the lack of seats. The tipper set off, descending Muheza's hills in the darkness. As the truck ambled along, murmurs of quiet conversation emanated from the truck bed as passengers grew acquainted with each other and discovered shared social ties. A few miles short of Tanga, however, to the driver's great dismay, a police roadblock arose in the distance monitored by several easily identified traffic police in their all-white uniforms. It spelled trouble for the tipper and its illegal cargo. The turnboy began banging on the back wall of the front cab to alert passengers of trouble ahead while the driver called out to them from his window. One passenger returned a reassuring response, telling the driver that his aid would not be rewarded with punishment. In the back, momentary panic was replaced with calm determination. One passenger was selected to lie down in the middle of the truck bed, and cloths borrowed off two female passengers were used to cover him from head to foot. Almost in unison, the crowd of passengers—who had not known each other prior to this journey—began wailing and crying, loudly bemoaning the loss of a loved one. As the truck neared the roadblock, an officer signaled it to stop. His companion peered into the back and mistaking (as intended) the covered passenger for a corpse and the surrounding strangers for its grieving kin, waved the funeral truck along. No fine was incurred, the tipper reached its destination in safety, and the passengers—through a spontaneous act of performance—outwitted an extractive and punitive state apparatus.

* * *

It was still a good two hours before the president's plane was scheduled to land, but already the rarely used Tanga Airport was teeming with people. District and regional cultural officers from the Ministry of Education and Culture scurried about from one performing group to the next, looking very busy and authoritative in their determinations over which group should be situated where. At the far end of the tarmac, Saruji Cultural Troupe dancers (sponsored by the local Tanga Cement Co., a government parastatal) rehearsed their numbers while the musicians warmed up their drums. To the right stood the Gita Musical Club, a mixed male/female dance society with Digo ethnic origins and a signature steel pan drum. They had given up attempting to rehearse over the heavy drums and insistent rattles of the Saruji troupe and instead stood by waiting patiently. To the right of Gita was placed Saruji's rival Kikundi cha Utamaduni Bandari Tanga (KIUBATA), the cultural troupe sponsored by the Tanga Harbours Authority. Completing the presentation of local cultural ambassadors stood a line of uniformed women (in matching *kanga*—printed cloths with Swahili sayings) and a line of uniformed men (in white, full-length, Islamic gowns called *kanzu*). They represented TAMTA (Tanganyika Muslim Teachers' Association), a prominent local mosque and religious academy, and had come to perform *kasida,* songs in praise of the Prophet Mohammed accompanied by drums and tambourines. Beside the TAMTA delegation stood a long row of Tanga's elite businessmen and politicians, who all wished to greet the president personally upon his arrival. Off to one side, members of the ruling party's CCM (Chama cha Mapinduzi, Party of the Revolution) Youth League stood at attention after having practiced a number of drills and formations. They were going to present the president with a new bandana with which to remember his visit to Tanga.

Close to the scheduled time, the presidential plane appeared on the horizon and soon thereafter set down on the tarmac. On cue from the district cultural officer, all four performance groups started performing at once. Musical confusion bordering on cacophony reigned, yet the goal of manufacturing a festive atmosphere was achieved. President Ali Hassan Mwinyi, second president of the United Republic of Tanzania, descended the stairs of his plane smiling broadly (figure 1.1). The Youth League approached in formation, and the president graciously received his gift, allowing one very young cadre to tie it around his neck. He ceremoniously walked down the line of performers, pausing momentarily and smiling his approval at each group, and then went to greet Tanga's privileged, bestowing his handshake on a lucky few. From there he was escorted to a waiting Landcruiser and whisked away to the Ikulu, the local State House.[2] The entire welcome from plane landing to car takeoff had lasted less than thirty minutes. Yet in those thirty minutes (and hours of preparation beforehand), the president, through his flaw-

Figure 1.1 President Ali Hassan Mwinyi at Tanga airport, September 13, 1993. Note the newly bestowed bandana encircling his neck. Photo by author.

less presidential performance, reinforced his political and social superiority, the cultural officers through their orders and general busy-ness had performed their authority over the musicians, Tanga's elite had performed their self-importance for each other, and—for those who wished to view it as such—the youths and musicians had performed their loyalty to the state.

* * *

"A construct such as the state," writes Timothy Mitchell, "occurs not merely as a subjective belief, but as a representation reproduced in visible everyday forms, such as the language of legal practice, the architecture of public buildings, the wearing of military uniforms, or the marking and policing of frontiers. The ideological forms of the state are an empirical phenomenon, as solid and discernible as a legal structure or a party system" (Mitchell 1999, 81). With the possible exception of public architecture, these "state effects" (Mitchell's phrase) all require performance, or rather "performative nonperformance" as Michael Herzfeld prefers to describe it (Herzfeld 1997, 31). While heartily agreeing with Mitchell on the palpability of performative processes, performance theorists will nonetheless tell you that a performance is anything but consistently "solid." As Edward Schieffelin notes, "genres of performance are . . . both fundamentally *interactive* and inherently *risky*. There is always something aesthetically and/or practically at stake in them, and something can always go wrong" (Schieffelin 1996, 60; emphasis in original). Indeed, the very tenuousness of performance—its susceptibility to modification, unrehearsed action, unanticipated response, and the contingencies of everyday life—renders it a powerful social force.

In this book, I follow Schieffelin's lead in showing "how a performative analysis can contribute to understanding the emergence of consequential realities in the historical world" (1996, 84). The reality under question here is the emergence of the Tanzanian state. Composed of two formerly independent entities, Tanganyika and Zanzibar, the United Republic of Tanzania is a state wracked by contradiction, fraught with multiple cleavages, and characterized by a condition of what can only be termed "consistent inconsistency."[3] In these respects, it is no different than any other state, for one trait deemed common, indeed fundamental, to states the world over is that they are "palimpsests of contradiction" (Lonsdale and Berman 1979, 491; also Herzfeld 1997, 2). Explains John Lonsdale, "States are a fabric of ordered tension between 'a variety of competing forms of authority,' each with different myths of legitimacy and principles of allegiance. Successive pragmatic rules of power which become norms, new layers of institutions to cope with new problems, get written into the historical structure, partially rubbed out and written over again, so that . . . nothing quite 'fits'" (Lonsdale 1981, 154). An increasingly dominant concern for state strategists then becomes how to smooth over the inconsistencies and present a unified national front that blankets dissension and masks diversity. Performance—in its many guises at customs outposts, high courts, state holiday celebrations, and government motorcades—offers a startlingly common recourse. Yet performance does not remain the exclusive tool of power-holders. As the vignette of the ad hoc funeral truck revealed, performance as readily constitutes a means of countering and destabilizing established power structures.

The relatively young state of Tanzania aptly exemplifies Lonsdale's assessment. The union of the Republic of Tanganyika (independent in 1961) and the People's Republic of Zanzibar (independent in 1963) created the "two countries in one nation" (*nchi mbili taifa moja*) that constitute today's Tanzania (see map 1.1).[4] It was surreptitiously signed into existence on April 26, 1964, by Julius Nyerere (first president of Tanganyika and subsequently Tanzania) and Abeid Karume (who assumed control over Zanzibar following the violent January 1964 revolution). Without forewarning and without their consent, Tanganyikans and Zanzibaris were summarily proclaimed national brethren, common citizens of the new state. The challenges, however, to this political marriage have been marked and many. As this book goes to press, the Union— fraught by competing agendas, visions, and visionaries—is very much under attack, and its continued existence open to question.

For three decades Tanzania's bifurcated identities of Tanzania Bara/ Tanzania Visiwani (mainland Tanzania versus island Tanzania) and Tanganyika/Zanzibar lay as discomfited but tolerant bedfellows under Nyerere's disciplining socialism. A two-government system prevailed: the Union (Muungano) government and the Zanzibar government (each with its own Parliament). An ongoing debate exists over whether or not a third government (for Tanganyika) is required.[5] The Zanzibar government controls its internal affairs, including agriculture, health, primary and secondary education, technical training, court system, communication, and (of particular significance for this analysis) cultural policy.[6] The Union government, situated on the mainland, concerns itself with all the same affairs with respect to the mainland plus Union issues such as defense, citizenship, treasury, foreign affairs, higher education, immigration, police, air travel/traffic, and the High Court.[7] Each "country" thus maintains its own government bureaucracy and internal judicial system but pays homage to an overarching entity that is rife with contra-

Map 1.1   Tanzania. Courtesy of David Kiphuth.

diction and conflict. The legality of the Union has been called into question and seriously contested by the argument that the Union Constitution was never ratified nor fully modified.[8] Tensions have mounted with
a series of events that placed Zanzibar in an independent position vis-
à-vis Tanzania, such as the 1992 decision by the Zanzibar government
to join the Organization of Islamic Conferences (OIC) without knowledge or approval from the Union government and in outright violation
of the Constitution. (Under intense pressure, it was forced soon afterwards to withdraw.)[9] In February 1995 (the year of Tanzania's first multiparty elections),[10] the World Bank recognized Zanzibar as an individual
country against the wishes of the Union government, which claimed

(and still claims) the exclusive right to represent Zanzibar internationally. The World Bank additionally recommended that donors negotiate with Zanzibar directly and separately in issues pertaining to grants and loans.[11] Soon thereafter, Zanzibari officials announced their intent to refashion Zanzibar into a duty-free enclave in the style of Hong Kong.[12] Finally, added to all this was the emergence of an opposition party called the Civic United Front, which has an island-heavy support base, endorses greater autonomy for Zanzibar, and argues against domination of the islands by the mainland. Small wonder that newspapers from that year on have overflowed with editorials questioning the status and viability of the Union and with charges lobbed both by islanders against the mainland and by mainlanders against the isles that each side benefits to the other's detriment.[13]

Thus in the wake of the transition from socialism to multiparty democracy (a process initiated in the 1980s), opportunities for questioning the received official representation of Tanzania as a united "nation" (in the sense forwarded by Verdery 1993 of a symbolic and ideological construct referencing the relation between a state and its subjects, and between a state and the international order of nation-states) have increased significantly. Subject always to debate (however much government officials pretend otherwise) from the date of its conception to the present, Tanzanian national identity is undergoing the latest in a series of dramatic transformations.[14] This book constitutes an attempt to map out these identities, analyze them for their novel and recycled elements, situate them in their broader political and economic context, and, most important, underscore how performance has been fundamental to both the active and reactive processes of transformation. Foucault's dictum that power is rendered efficacious only in the process of enactment supports the performative understanding of power that I seek to forward here (Foucault 1980, 89). "Power must be seen to be appreciated," goes the saying. Machiavelli understood this and secured his place in history by advising princes on precisely this fact. Emperors from Julius Caesar to Haile Selassie also understood this, as any decent biography discloses. Presidential handlers, image consultants, and royal advisors all understand this, thereby carefully choreographing their rulers' every interaction with citizenry. Power thus not only requires performance, but indeed is itself more often than not an act of performance.

Theories of Nationalism Reconsidered

Tanzania flies in the face of long-standing misconceptions of what constitutes a nation. Reigning paradigms contemplating the nature of the modern nation-state tend to assume congruence between the political and national and often the cultural unit (e.g., Gellner 1983), but such models do not apply to most modern states, much less postcolonies like Tanzania and Kenya, where boundaries were arbitrarily set without regard to the communities they sundered and within which a multitude of ethnic groups continue to maintain their respective social identities. Political/national congruence and cultural homogeneity—rare in our world to the point of being theoretically invalid—are formally undermined in Tanzania by the existence of two previously independent national units and the subsequent subdivision of each of these into multiple ethnic, "racial,"[15] religious, and socioeconomic constituencies. In the face of such diversity—including more than 120 ethnic groups—the notion of homogeneity is impossible to entertain.

And yet entertained it was in early policy documents and official speeches. Tanzania's politicians carved out an ideological and rhetorical space within which to construct first Tanganyikan and Zanzibari and then Tanzanian identities that would "cut across the barriers of tribe, race, and religion" (Taylor 1963, 172). In this respect, they conceived of "the nation" in terms set by Western nationalists and theorists that only recently have come under attack.

Theories of nationalism have progressed significantly since Ernest Gellner released his oft-cited *Nations and Nationalism,* which equated nationalism with the social conditions of industrial, late-capitalist Europe. While his model obviates the possibilities of cultural pluralism, of alternative economic progressions, and of non-Western circumstances for the establishment of nation-states, he nevertheless recognizes something he terms "will" as the social glue holding members of nations together (Gellner 1983, 54–55). It is this concept that Benedict Anderson elaborates, namely, the ability to think beyond one's immediate community to an "imagined community" that encompasses people whom one will never know personally. Although, like Gellner, Anderson presents a universalist interpretation that attempts to describe nationalism as a fundamentally singular (if not wholly European) phenomenon, he shifted attention away from national constructs to the processes of construction and highlighted "print-capitalism" as the primary medium of developing national consciousness (Anderson 1989, 46).

Anderson argues that nationalism is, in the end, a cultural artifact, yet he does not fully explore the ramifications of this—that nationalism would then be expected to take very different forms in accordance with cultural variation. Bruce Kapferer (1988) succeeded in establishing nationalism's cultural specificity through his comparison of the egalitarian ideology of Australian nationalism with the hierarchical ideology of Sri

Lankan nationalism. Similar in its attention to cultural variants but this time within a single state is the perspective on Greek nationalism offered by Herzfeld (1982, 1987, 1991, 1997). In Greece, two contrasting ideologies compete for symbolic dominance. *Ellinismos,* an ideology associated with the Classical past and bearing masculine connotations, is pitted against *Romiossini,* a more intimated, decidedly feminine ideology. This theme is echoed by Fox (1990a), who theorizes that national culture necessarily emerges from competing ideologies, an argument reinforced by research on Romania by Verdery (1990, 1991a) on Guyana by Williams (1990, 1991), on Quebec by Handler (1988), on England by Corrigan and Sayer (1985), and on India by Appadurai (1988) and Chatterjee (1986, 1993). Each of these case studies underscores the internally contested nature of nationalism: that within any single nation (Western and non-Western both), different ideologies compete for recognition and status as the dominant national ideology. Thus nationalism has evolved as a concept from being *(a)* a uniform Western construct, to *(b)* one that varies with cultural context, to *(c)* one that is strongly contested and highly negotiated with differing internal variants.

The negotiated nature of Tanzanian nationalism comes to the fore in an examination of its cultural policies and practices, specifically those relating to musical performance. An examination of policy documents reveals how policy shifted in accordance with the larger political/ economic/ideological transitions from pre-independence nationalism to post-independence nationalism to socialism and, most recently, liberalization. An investigation into the practices accompanying policy exposes the negotiation that occurred, and continues to occur, between the state and its citizenry. Three significant studies of music and politics in Tanzania precede and have informed my analysis: Susan Geiger's, Terence Ranger's, and Elias Songoyi's respective analyses of how *ngoma* (dance) societies served as potent vehicles for inculcating and mobilizing political consciousness during the late colonial and early post-independence periods.[16] The data they offer and the data I present here mark a radical departure from the exclusive emphasis on print media that pervades the dominant literature. Print media simply cannot prove as essential in situations where literacy is not widespread. The literate bias subsumed within the Eurocentric bias of Anderson and Gellner interestingly has not evoked criticism. I propose that attention to musical elaborations of nationalism can counteract this theoretical deafness.

"To understand the symbolic dimension of the effect of the state, and in particular what we may call the *effect of universality* [emphasis in original], it is necessary to understand the specific functioning of the bureaucratic microcosm and thus to analyze the genesis and structure of this universe of agents of the state who have constituted themselves into a state nobility by instituting the state, and in particular, *by producing the performative discourse on the state which, under the guise of saying what the state is, caused the state to come into being by stating what it should be* [emphasis mine]" (Bourdieu 1999, 71; see also Verdery 1991a, 3). This book is at heart an ethnography of Tanzanian nationalism, an examination—following Bourdieu's advice—of the agents and perceived enemies of the state, and of the battle they have waged over the construction of Tanzanian national identity. The war, however, is not one of words alone. Government documents employing words to bring a specific vision of Tanzania into being were often supplemented with government action, yet never was there a guarantee of success. In this case (and, I suspect, many others), "saying what the state is" did not always "cause the state to come into being." Indeed, as chapter 5 reveals, a high degree of failure was more often the norm. So here I would quarrel with Bourdieu for attributing as much unqualified success as he does to state constructions: "[T]he effects of choices made by the state have so completely impressed themselves in reality and in minds that possibilities initially discarded have become totally unthinkable" (Bourdieu 1999, 54). No, the situation in Tanzania resembles more that of Romania as described by Verdery, where "no one effectively controlled what was said: as people's words entered into a discursive field, they were instantly available for reinterpretation, to be seized and turned against their speakers" (1991a, 9). Aspiring hegemonies, be they imposed from the top or the bottom, are always subject to perforation. Latent possibilities and alternative visions can never be fully nor permanently eradicated, however imposing a state bureaucracy may appear (Gramsci 1971).

Yet some theorists persist in privileging the state and its constructions and in attributing to it a larger degree of success than is warranted. The "statist" or "state-centric" approach in political science presupposes the autonomy, coherence, agency, and effectiveness of the state. Evans, Rueschemeyer, and Skocpol's *Bringing the State Back In* (1985) has spawned decades of scholarship that champions the state as an autonomous agent, undiluted by either class or culture. Viewed unproblematically as occupying an oppositional relationship to "society," the state takes on human form as a rational individual, acting always in its best interests. All its many citizens are reduced to singular intent and purpose, and all cultural variation, competing visions, and socioeconomic differentiation are erased. Culture, when considered at all, figures primarily "as an effect and not a determinant of the state" (Steinmetz 1999, 17).

So, if my first point of critique of reigning state paradigms is that they exaggerate the effectiveness of state constructions, my second point of critique targets the very static perception they have of state identities. In this theoretical day and age when the fluidity and performativity of social identities (Butler 1990; Kondo 1990) is generally accepted, it is surprising why more researchers studying nation-states have not applied these same understandings to them. No less than individual or group identities do national identities wax and wane and undergo significant change. As the case in point, Tanzania, in its relatively short, thirty-seven-year life as a nation-state, has adopted and shed multiple political, social, and economic identities, which the following chapters explore in detail.

Finally, my third point of critique (applicable to both the state and nationalism literatures) relates to assumptions about where national identities originate. Early theorists of nationalism spoke at length about how nationalist constructs were created and imposed on ordinary citizens. Case studies drawn from Europe supported such paradigms, which located the power to imagine communities and invent traditions with elites, be they politicians or intellectuals (Hobsbawm and Ranger 1983; Herzfeld 1982; Handler 1988; Verdery 1991a). Producers of culture, so it would appear, must have access to resources that enable them to promote their particular vision of the nation. But the story I tell here is of how some of the least privileged citizens of one emergent African nation hijacked and reconfigured the process of nationalism. This case forces a reconsideration of existing theories of nationalism. Just as Foucault advanced our understanding of power as a diffuse resource available to everyone everywhere (albeit to differing degrees) and never the exclusive domain of some over others, so too should we view nationalism as something engaged in by people at all levels of the social matrix—even if their engagement takes the form of outright rejection or dismissive disregard. In discussing Anderson's analysis of nationalism, Herzfeld raises a similar concern: "[Anderson] does not tell us why this works so well and so often, nor does he tell us whether the actions of the converted exert a reciprocal effect on the cultural form of the evolving nation-state" (Herzfeld 1997, 6). Rather than an abstract ideology produced by some to be consumed by others, nationalism ought to be conceptualized as a series of continually negotiated relationships between people who share occupancy in a defined geographic, political, or ideological space. No amount of rhetoric can construct a nation if it fails to find resonance with the state citizenry. There must be some degree of mutual engagement for nationalism to flourish, but this very element of mutuality, of sharedness, of common participation, admits the possibility of dissension from those excluded from state activities. Citizens are not relegated to roles of passive observation and mute compliance. The mere fact that their endorsement (or at least the appearance of it) is key to any success-ful state enterprise forces every self-preservationist state bureaucracy to continually monitor the level of public support it commands.

The Production of Tanzanian National Culture

The waves of independence that swept across Africa beginning in the 1950s left in their wake a desire to recapture African culture and his-tory—the culture and history that had been mutilated and reinvented by colonial interests. Fledgling states, however, found themselves faced with enormous diversity and few unifying elements save the experience of colonialism (and even that was experienced differentially among and within the colonies). African leaders and regimes developed different approaches to the problem of internal unification, but almost all placed rhetorical weight on the construction of national cultures. One common strategy was to establish Ministries of Culture that were assigned respon-sibility for recovering and recuperating the past. Tanzania's leadership committed very early to this principle and embarked on a clearly articu-lated national project of social and cultural unification, one that explic-itly cited cultural homogenization as a goal (Mbughuni 1974). In his Republic Day speech of December 10, 1962 (the year following Tangan-yikan independence), Nyerere announced the establishment of the Min-istry of National Culture and Youth saying,

> The major change I have made is to set up an entirely new Ministry: the Ministry of National Culture and Youth. I have done this because I believe that its culture is the essence and spirit of any nation. A country which lacks its own culture is no more than a collection of people without the spirit which makes them a nation. Of all the crimes of colonialism there is none worse than the attempt to make us believe we had no indigenous culture of our own; or that what we did have was worthless—something of which we should be ashamed, instead of a source of pride. . . .
> When we were at school we were taught to sing the songs of the European. How many of us were taught the songs of the Wanyamwezi or of the Wahehe? Many of us have learnt to dance the "rumba" or the "chachacha" to rock-and-roll and to "twist" and even to dance the "waltz" and the "foxtrot." But how many of us can dance, have even heard of, the Gombe Sugu, the Mangala, the Konge, Nyang'umumi, Kiduo or Lele Mama? Most of us can play the guitar, the piano, or other European musical instruments. How many Africans in Tanganyika, particu-larly among the educated, can play the African drums? . . .
> So I have set up this new Ministry to help us regain our pride in our own culture. I want it to seek out the best of the traditions and customs of all the tribes and make them part of our national culture (Ministry of National Culture and Youth n.d., 3).

Musical performance, as one easily identifiable and highly emotive element of cultural practice, thus constituted an integral component in

Tanzania's cultural policy from its inception. Culture brokers within the government bureaucracy targeted "traditional" musical genres for appropriation and absorption in "Tanzanian national culture" (Mbughuni 1974).[17] Exactly what was envisioned as "Tanzanian national culture," however, proved and continues to prove elusive. Despite the confidence implied by continual references to "national culture" in policy statements outlining the means and strategies of its construction, conflicting and contradictory images reveal the fundamental ambiguity surrounding it. The process of selecting which musical traditions should represent the nation has been fraught with competing agendas. *Ngoma,* or "traditional dances," are valued for essentializing both "tradition" and the ethnic groups that perform them. At the same time, however, they are subjected to modification to accommodate nationalist goals and objectives.

Contradictions such as these at the level of cultural policy are reflective of larger problems concerning the "imagining" of the Tanzanian nation-state. Although the theoretical articulation of "imagined communities," "invented traditions," and "cultural constructions/productions" would seem to imply the existence of coherent final products, we are now well aware of the transient and un-final nature of social creations. In Tanzania, cultural objectives were deconstructed and reconstructed according to who wielded political authority. Colonialism, nationalism, socialism, and liberalization are all constructs that have informed the processes of imagining Tanzania, each one significantly altering the creations of the one that preceded it. And so we are left with two key questions: How does a nation come to be imagined? Who does the imagining?

Performance assumes center stage in this ethnography in two ways. First, it is employed as a vehicle for accessing the process of nation-building because it was consciously exploited by the Tanzanian state for that very purpose. As such, it perfectly supports my ulterior objective to highlight the imbrication of culture and politics and to level a strong rejoinder at those scholars who view popular culture generally and the arts in particular as tangential, discredited social domains of little or no relevance for the study of politics and government. Second, over the course of this book, I advance an understanding of power as embedded in performance. As Eric Wolf notes, "Ideas or systems of ideas do not, of course, float about in incorporeal space; they acquire substance through communication in discourse and performance" (1999, 6). "Performance"—whether or not Wolf realized it—is a loaded term. With it comes a significant corpus of theory exposing performance as a mode of social interaction that is contingent, emergent, undetermined, and susceptible to unrehearsed actions (Barber 1987; Coplan 1994; Drewal 1991; Schechner 1985, 1988; Schechner and Appel 1990; Schieffelin 1996, 1998; Turner 1986). This school of thought can be brought to bear on the related concept of power in fruitful and enlightening ways. Although I elaborate this argument most fully in this book's conclusion, the following story provides a microcosmic example of precisely this relationship.

Performing the Politics of the Personal

It was in 1987 during my first visit to the Swahili coast that I first came across the genre of sung poetry called *taarab*. New to my ears and with my fluency in Kiswahili yet in its nascent stage,[18] I found it difficult to understand not only the lyrics but the actions that accompanied its performance. I had been invited to a wedding. I knew neither the bride nor the groom but, as I was to learn later, these tend to be very open occasions to which the public—or rather, the female public—is welcomed. The celebration occurred in a rented hall with an elaborately decorated stage that was empty but for a couch and two chairs. Below the stage in front of the almost exclusively female audience stood the band and its key performer, the famous Juma Bhalo, or "the man with the golden voice." My close friend Zaina, who had brought me to the wedding, explained that he was the reigning king of *taarab*—that one's wedding wasn't nearly as successful a wedding if he didn't sing at it—and added with a smile that he was quite popular among the women.

My senses were overwhelmed. The women were dressed in the finest of materials—taffeta, satin, velvet, organza, and tulle in every imaginable color. The odors of perfume, rosewater (sprinkled on every guest by female attendants associated with the wedding party), *udi* (incense with which the women had infused their dresses), and perfumed hair ointments took my impoverished American olfactory senses by surprise. I had to adjust to the feel of sitting on woven mats and accommodating all the women in my immediate vicinity as we periodically changed position to avoid cramps. The *sambusas* (meat-filled pastries) I found delicious, but not so the overly sweet strawberry- and orange-flavored sodas that accompanied them.

Then there was the music: my first experience of *taarab*. This first impression was not all that favorable. Like many Westerners, I found the nasal quality of voice initially unpleasant to listen to and the melodies more Indian or Middle Eastern than my preconceived ideas of "African music" had allowed possible. I strove to understand the lyrics but my Kiswahili simply was not good enough, and I did not yet understand

that the Kiswahili utilized in *taarab* lyrics often draws upon archaic vocabulary and metaphoric references so as to disguise and hide meanings.
I took mental notes on the number of musicians (around five or so) and
the interesting mixture of Western, Indian, and Arabic instruments they
played: electronic keyboard, *nai* (a side-blown Middle Eastern flute),
tabla, bongos, and tambourine.

A special song announced the arrival of the bride:

Leo ni leo, leo ni leo	Today is the day, today is the day.
Mtauona mpambano kweli si uongo	You will see a contest, and that's no lie.
Jamali wa umbo, Na wajihi mwema	Exquisite in body and in appearance,
Mwingi wa urembo, Nawacha kusema	Beautiful throughout—I'll stop talking.
Wanitenda mambo, Bila ya huruma	You treat me without mercy.

She came down an aisle that opened up for her among us, preceded by
two ornately adorned young girls and some sisters/cousins to help arrange her and her exquisite green gown on the stage. According to local
tradition, Swahili brides here wear the color green on their wedding day.
If the celebration is held on several consecutive days (the ideal is to celebrate for three to seven days, but finances may not allow it), then she
must have a different dress for each event, one of which, in addition to
the mandatory green, is usually a Western-style, white bridal gown (figure
1.2). The bride ascended the stage and sat in state on the centrally posi-

Figure 1.2 A Swahili bride in Mombasa, Kenya, 1989. Photo by author.

tioned couch, the small girls perching themselves on the chairs to the bride's right and left. The bride kept her eyes permanently glued to her shoes and maintained a noncommittal, uninterested air about her. Packets of the *sambusas* with small cakes along with the red and orange sodas were distributed among the audience, and the *taarab* resumed in earnest.

As the musicians played, women would come up out of the audience to dance a bit and tip the musicians—generally the singer—with money. My eyes did not know where to settle between looking at the bride, the musicians, and the women dancing and tipping. Something happened that I missed. I only caught sight of one woman rushing out of the hall obviously upset. I wanted to ask Zaina, but she was busy discussing whatever had happened with the women seated beside her. Despite the commentaries humming around me throughout the audience, the music played on, and the dancing and tipping continued without pause. The bride never once looked up.

The answers I received to my questions both that night and over the next days and weeks coalesced into the following explanation. The song being sung when the altercation broke out was entitled "Hasidi." *Hasidi* translates as "an envious person," and in this context was used to refer to a woman envious of another's spouse. Juma Bhalo sang to his audience, "A *hasidi* does not want you to enjoy happiness. Envy and hatred she cannot ever leave. Nor is what she has ever enough. She will still look for more."[19] While these lines were sung, a woman in the audience rose to go tip Juma Bhalo. As she made her way to the front of the hall to give him the money and as she returned to where she had been sitting, she pointedly stared at another woman seated in the audience— directly yet indirectly, verbally (via the poetry) yet silently and nonverbally (through her body language) accusing that woman of coveting her husband, of being a *hasidi*. Having been publicly charged in so powerful a fashion (virtually everyone in the hall had recognized and understood the significance of the act except, of course, myself), the accused was reduced to tears and ran from the room. The significance of the act was self-evident. Social relations were being negotiated by means of musical performance.

This event initiated the process that would lead me to a career in anthropology. I was intrigued by the way this music was used and wanted to know more. The only distant equivalent we in the United States have to using music in this fashion is when individuals call up a radio station to make a special request and have the "dedication" announced. Although that could be perceived as a public act because of the countless listeners out on the radio waves, it nonetheless retains a strong element of anonymity owing to the lack of physical contact between the one making the request and the announcer, between the requester and the musicians (who are merely represented by a recording), between the announcer and the audience, and between the requester and the audience. Moreover, it is not dialogic interaction, as in the Mombasa case, because the act generally ends with the playing of the requested song. The immediacy of what I witnessed in Mombasa opened up to me a perspective on performance that directly related it to power relations at the interpersonal level. That opening would later widen to accommodate power relations at multiple social levels up to the level of the state, and lead to the development of the performative understanding of power that I present further on. The decade from 1987 to 1997 found me returning time and again to do additional research in Mombasa, then Zanzibar, Dar es Salaam, and finally Tanga on the northern Tanzanian coast to hear, observe, and document performances relating to the politics of the personal as well as the politics of the national.[20]

Toward a Theory of the Politics of Performance

The case described above of the Mombasa wedding and others analyzed in later chapters introduce several new insights on the study of performance. As shown, the genre of Swahili musical performance called *taarab* provides people (primarily, but not exclusively, women) with a context for airing and engaging in disputes. Individuals interact through the music, utilizing it as their communicative vehicle. Only recently has performance assumed a position alongside other forms of social interaction long deemed worthy of theoretical attention. Now begins the task of developing theories that specifically address performance head-on rather than seeing it simply as a component of some other social phenomenon (e.g., language, ritual, or theater). The recent studies by Bauman (1977), Schechner (1985), Schechner and Appel (1990), Fabian (1990), Cowan (1990), Drewal (1991), and Heath (1994) all focus on the phenomenon of performance. Yet they present a refracted image that contains few unifying threads. This section examines what little work has been done specifically on its political aspects in order to develop a theory of the politics of performance.

Performance as a focus of analysis has been approached from two major theoretical angles (following Drewal 1991; see also Carlson 1996 and Schieffelin 1998). One angle originates in language and communication theory, as well as sociolinguistics and folklore. Austin 1965, Searle 1969, Hymes 1964, and Bauman and Briggs 1990 characterize this perspective on performance as a means of communication. The second angle is that found, for example, in Goffman 1974, 1980; Turner 1974, 1986; and

Schechner 1985, 1988, which relates performance to an understanding of social life as enacted, as "social drama" (Turner), as a continual "presentation of self" (Goffman). Each perspective privileges a single metaphor for conceptualizing performance: in the first case, language, and in the second, theater.

As a representative of the first of these schools of thought, Richard Bauman attempts in *Verbal Art as Performance* (1977) to substitute a "performance-centered" approach to verbal art for the "text-centered" approaches that had previously dominated folklore scholarship. He defines performance as "a mode of spoken verbal communication [that] consists in the assumption of responsibility to an audience for a display of communicative competence" (Bauman 1977, 11) and he isolates the elements that pattern performance: genres, acts, events, and roles.

In focusing on performance as communicative interaction, Bauman shifts emphasis from the literal communication (the message being communicated, i.e., text) to the act of communicating (performance). He thus introduces process via performance to the communication models expounded by his theoretical predecessors. Bauman, however, grounds himself within a lingua-centric frame by postulating performance as verbal communication: "performance is a mode of language use, a way of speaking" (1977, 11). He recognizes the implicit interaction that occurs between the performers and the audience, but in the end performance is primarily a mode of text transmission: "[P]erformance puts discourse 'on display—objectifies it,' lifts it to a degree from its interactional setting and opens it to scrutiny by an audience" (Bauman and Briggs 1990, 73). One is then left wondering how nonverbal performance, or performance that communicates nontextual messages, fits into this paradigm. Royce 1984, Cowan 1990, and Heath 1994 attempt to redress this flaw—what Cowan calls "logocentrism"—by locating meaning in the nonverbal elements of the Western, Greek, and Senegalese dance they respectively study.

The approach advanced by Victor Turner is not bound by this insistence upon the primacy of language. Instead, he substitutes another lens: that of the agonistic paradigm of *social drama*. Social drama as a process consists of four distinct phases: (1) a *breach* of social relations, (2) escalation into a *crisis*, when the parties involved position themselves as antagonists in relation to each other, (3) *redressive action* to resolve the crisis, and (4) either *reintegration* of the contending parties or *schism* (Turner 1974, 38 ff.). In reevaluating this model some years later, Turner modified it to include performance in the phase of redressive action. The link between them lies in the reflexive quality of both performance and redress. Resolution of conflict requires reflection on the sources of the conflict and the weighing of potential solutions. Similarly, Turner views performance as occurring outside the regular flow of social life through special framing of time and place; it therefore constitutes a privileged site for invoking reflection. He moreover articulates a dialogic relationship between performance and social life such that each informs and is informed by the other:

> [S]ocial drama . . . results precisely from the suspension of normative role-playing, and in its passionate activity abolishes the usual distinction between flow and reflection, since in the social drama it becomes a matter of urgency to become reflexive about the cause and motive of action damaging to the social fabric. . . . The performative genres are, as it were, secreted from the social drama and in turn surround it and feed their performed meanings back into it. (1986, 90)

Richard Schechner follows Turner's lead but modifies it by highlighting performance as "restored behavior" or as "twice-behaved behavior," thus furthering the concept of reflexivity in performance.

> Restored behavior is symbolic and reflexive: not empty but loaded behavior multivocally broadcasting significances. These difficult terms express a single principle: The self can act in/as another; the social or transindividual self is a role or set of roles. Symbolic and reflexive behavior is the hardening into theater of social, religious, aesthetic, medical, and educational process. Performance means: never for the first time. It means: for the second to the nth time. Performance is "twice-behaved behavior." (1985, 36)

Goffman goes further than either Turner or Schechner in relating performance and social life by arguing that the self is always a performed self and social life always a stage. For Goffman, society determines the roles available to people and what matters is how well they carry them off. The theater metaphor acquires heightened significance when Goffman writes,

> A correctly staged and performed character leads the audience to impute a self to a performed character, but this imputation—this self—is a *product* of a scene that comes off, and is not a *cause* of it. The self, then, as a performed character, is not an organic thing that has a specific location, whose fundamental fate is to be born, to mature, and to die; it is a dramatic effect arising diffusely from a scene that is presented, and the characteristic issue, the crucial concern, is whether it will be credited or discredited. (1959, 252–53)

Both of these perspectives on performance, exemplified on the one hand by Bauman and on the other by Turner and Goffman, allow room for elaboration. As already discussed, Bauman's understanding of performance as a component of verbal communication ignores both the existence and effectiveness of nonverbal communication and the communication of nontextual messages. Turner and Schechner, on the other hand predicate their perspective upon a conflictual, agonistic view of social life that is articulated and at times mediated through performance.

With Goffman, they privilege theater as an analogy for social life without dealing adequately with the attendant problems of authenticity (if everything is enactment, then what is reality?) and instrumentality (by logical extension, if all roles are adopted, then none are intrinsic, and identity is thus purely instrumental). Queries Drewal, "Does performance need to be viewed primarily in theatrical terms, in this way removing it from everyday life except as metaphor? And what are the implications of such removal?" (1991, 9).

Nevertheless, combined insights from both of these perspectives offer the beginnings of a theory on the politics of performance: how performance is actively employed in the negotiation of power relations. To begin, the reflexive function of performance posited by Turner has political ramifications. The potential for political action exists if reflection constitutes "a process for creating critical consciousness and raising the awareness of a people, as a result of which they can then take action to solve their development problems" (Mlama 1991, 206). This philosophy spawned the influential "development drama" approach to problem resolution pioneered by Paulo Freire and articulated in his *Pedagogy of the Oppressed*.[21]

Schechner's delineation of the process of production underlying performance (training, workshops, rehearsals, warm-ups, performance, cool-down, and aftermath) affords multiple decision-making opportunities for performers—decisions that are necessarily affected by surrounding circumstances. As Drewal states, "Form is always in process, generated in the moment of production, sensitive to the politics of the moment," and "[T]he study of performance is especially political because it involves research on performers as they make choices and take action in particular historical and social situations" (1991, 17, 27).

An in-depth study of the processes of performance production has been done by Fabian (1990). Following the creation of a Zairean dramatic production from its inception (sparked by one of his own questions regarding a local proverb about power), through the brainstorming sessions of building a plot and developing a context, then through the initial rehearsals, final rehearsals, and its filming, to the viewing of the televised production in the company of others and the recording of their reactions, Fabian shows how every step of the process involves choices. Invariably, the choices are political ones on both a macro level (e.g., developing a plot that remains true to the spirit of the original idea but avoids including events that could be construed as veiled parody or resistance and thereby offensive to the powers that be) and a micro level (e.g., developing characters that accommodate the existing status hierarchy among the performers).

Beyond involving decisions that are linked to political circumstances, however, performance may contain an intrinsic element that makes it a particularly potent tool for political action. Bauman hints at this. Within his model are three characteristics that he deems essential to performance: (1) a display of competence, (2) a contribution to the enhancement of experience, and (3) susceptibility to evaluation (Bauman 1977, 23). These outline a relationship between performers and audience that appears weighted toward the audience, since performers are responsible for displaying their competence to the audience and are moreover subject to an evaluation of their performance. However, an "enhancement of experience" that he describes as "a heightened intensity of communicative interaction which binds the audience to the performer in a way that is specific to performance as a mode of communication" (1977, 43) ought to follow a "competent" performance that turns the tide in favor of the performers. "A not insignificant part of the capacity of performance to transform social structure . . . resides in the power that the performer derives from the control over his audience" (Bauman 1977, 16).

There is no doubt that Swahili individuals exploit *taarab* as a highly potent communicative medium. A key difference from Bauman's model, however, is that performers do not maintain a monopoly on the power of performance. They do not "control" the audience, nor is the audience's only power that of accountability, of evaluating the competence of the performers. In *taarab* performance, performers are not the sole agents doing the communicating. Audience members communicate as much or more, both with the performers and with each other. Meaning is located at the intersection of text, performance, embodied action (e.g., tipping audience members), and the intimacies of local knowledge that are possible in relatively small communities like Tanga, Tanzania, where people know a tremendous amount about each other's business. Communication in this case is very much a dialogic process between and among performers and audience members. This is true even in standard Western performance practice, albeit in a more constrained manner. Western audiences actively participate in a staged performance by adhering to or deviating from widely held expectations of appropriate audience behavior. They can applaud their support, cough their annoyance, or boo their disapproval. So even where the line between performers and audience is devoutly worshiped, audiences perform by upholding or undermining the role of engaged Western audience members. Bauman posits that "performance is a mode of language use, a way of speaking" (Bauman 1977, 11). I would like to further the notion by insisting that performance constitutes a *conversation*, not one-way speech directed solely from controlling performers to a passive audience.

Thus if, as I suggest, performance is best viewed as active dialogic interaction between and among performers and audience, then traditional emphases on the *product* (the text, the message communicated), plus recent performance theorists' emphasis on the *process* (Bauman, Turner, Schechner, Drewal), and concern for *form* and the *politics* of context (Cowan, Heath, Royce, Fabian) can be united and integrated into a single model. The interaction proves to be dialogic, and the distinction between the communicators and communicatees becomes highly fluid, not so easily glossed as "performers and audience." Moreover, it is an interaction that is contingent on the specifics of the temporal and spatial moment. Judith Butler, who prefers the term "performativity" to "performance" so as to further emphasize its nonfinite nature, describes performativity as having "its own social temporality in which it remains enabled precisely by the contexts from which it breaks" (1997, 40).

Within these many contributions to our understanding of performance, then, lie the seeds of an integrated theory on the politics of performance. To sum up, the elements of performance that directly relate to politics are the process of its production, its communicative function, the messages it communicates, its reflexivity, its capacity for an enhancement of experience (in Bauman's terms) or a transformation of being and/or consciousness (in Turner's and Schechner's terms), and the capacity for active power negotiation and contestation in local and national, private and governmental performances that the following chapters exemplify in case after case. These elements support three important conclusions. The first is a recognition of performance as a process actively engaged in by everyone in attendance as opposed to a product somehow owned by performers and transmitted for audience reception. The second is that *performative* necessarily means emergent and contingent—"a renewable action without clear origin or end" (Butler 1997, 40). The final conclusion relates performance unambiguously to the active construction of social life. Performance does not merely offer occasion to reflect on and perhaps rehearse "real" life. Swahili women who comment on each other's behavior and socially reposition each other through allegations and counter-allegations in *taarab* performance are not mirroring social reality or merely reflecting upon it but are *actively creating it*. The woman forced to flee the wedding auditorium left in a different social position from the one in which she arrived, as did her accuser. Here we see very clearly how performance constitutes a forum for reconfiguring social relations. As Schieffelin writes, "'Performance' deals with actions more than text: with habits of the body more than structures of symbols, with illocutionary rather than propositional force, with the social construction of reality rather than its representation" (1998, 194).

The Power of Performance and the Performance of Power

My focus on the imbrication of power and performance applies to multiple levels of social life, from individuals in a coastal town to party politics at the national level. It is not a strikingly new revelation that the two are intrinsically related. Power-holders have always known that in order for their power to be recognized and respected, it must be rendered palpable. Machiavelli's guidebook on the art of princely governance, for example, is an early text in the literature of the choreography of power, to be followed several centuries later by Corrigan and Sayer's (1985) exquisitely detailed analysis of the art of British governance and Kertzer's (1988) wide-ranging inventory of political pomp and ritual across the globe and throughout the centuries. Yet the connection between power and performance has yet to be clearly articulated, and this ethnography establishes a beginning toward that end.

Although wide-ranging in goals and implications, this book has the Tanzanian state as both its point of departure and return. Chapter 2 lays the historical foundation for understanding where this state originated and in what directions it is headed. Interwoven into that history is the history of one city—the city of Tanga—that held at certain times great political and economic significance and until recently remained a major musical center for the country.[22] Chapter 3 offers a musical ethnography of Tanzania, introducing the genres of *ngoma* (traditional dance), *dansi* (urban popular music), and *taarab* (sung Swahili poetry) that dominated the Tanzanian soundscape during the period of my research. Included in this chapter is a discussion of my field methodology with some limited speculation as to how my incorporation as a fellow musician in two bands influenced the course of my research. In chapter 4, I analyze in significant detail the genre of *taarab* and show how, in case after case of actual performances, it constitutes a powerfully effective mode of dispute negotiation.

In chapter 5, I refocus on the state by presenting the history of the Ministry of Culture, a migrant ministry rich in rhetoric but poor in resources, and how its original vision of the nation was forced to undergo considerable and continual revision in response to changing political and economic contexts. Its history and mixed accomplishments offer much food for theoretical thought on government involvement in cultural production. Chapter 6 presents an ethnographic analysis of the last National Arts and Language Competitions held in Tanzania in 1992— an event that encapsulated and foregrounded the process of nationalizing cultural forms. Serendipitously, the KIUBATA cultural troupe from Tanga secured first-place honors in the *ngoma* competition, thus enabling me to draw some conclusions about national cultural aspirations from my daily attendance at their rehearsals and the ultimate confirmation of these aspirations through the judges' approbation. Chapter 7 delves into the parallel yet divergent histories of two popular *taarab* groups—one private and one state-sponsored—and how state attempts to nationalize *taarab* (after excluding it from mainland cultural policy for decades) produced questionable results. The histories of these bands and their respective relationships to state policy expose all the contrariness, contradiction, and negotiation that underscore cultural production endeavors. Finally, I conclude with a partially fleshed-out performative theory of power that I encourage like-minded scholars to further. In my conclusion, I reexamine the Tanzanian state's contested relationship with musical performance vis-à-vis its attempts to generate a national culture and pose some questions about the nature of nationalism, governance, and power. It is the process of imagining the Tanzanian community that is under scrutiny.

The title of this introduction refers to governance as an art—a concept dating back at least to Machiavelli and elaborated by many theorists since. For Foucault, governance means "employing tactics rather than laws, and even of using laws themselves as tactics—to arrange things in such as way, that through a certain number of means, such and such ends may be achieved" (Foucault 1991, 95). Both Machiavelli and Foucault ground the term in its original meaning as "the regulation of conduct" (hence Machiavelli's discussion of the governance of a household) and apply this notion to the regulation of others' conduct. Why this should be considered an "art" begs consideration. The creative palette of the culture producer—whether farmer, teacher, wife, politician, musician, or intellectual—is limitless. How artists combine tones, melodies, shades of color, and different media to produce works of art mirrors how state agents and culture producers extract, modify, manufacture, and fuse together elements from history, performance practice, social values, and shared experiences to create a national identity.

> Thus, in the new nations, it is not just the regime that is in the business of cultural management, but all players in the political scene. Insofar as the concept of the nation is problematic, the need to create rituals to bolster or destroy it is politically crucial. It is a lesson to be learned from Ireland, from the Sudan, from the efforts to create an independent Quebec or an autonomous Punjab. No matter how culturally artificial or historically serendipitous the new national entity, it must be en-

dowed with a sacred unity and made to seem a natural social unit. (Kertzer 1988, 179)

Just as it is virtually impossible to fix a universal definition for what constitutes "art," so too is it virtually impossible to establish a fixed and finite version of national identity—however unified a nation may appear. It always and necessarily—in Tanzania and elsewhere—remains a work in progress.

2

TANGA, TANGANYIKA, TANZANIA

Kwa mapenzi, kwa mapenzi, mimi nakwenda Tanga
Wanawake wa kiTanga, ukicheka utatangatanga
Hata maji ya kuoga, huchanganywa na hiliki, abdalasini, uwa waridi,
na karafuu

For love, for love, I am going to Tanga. The women of Tanga—
laugh with them and you will be left helpless. Even bath water they infuse with cardamom, cinnamon, rose petals, and
cloves.

—from the song "Kijongolo," by the Chezimba Band (c. 1990)

Set between the shadows of the East Usambara Mountains and the
bay that connects it to the Indian Ocean and world beyond, Tanga
lies on the margins of Africa (map 2.1). It is part and parcel of both
the land that supports it and the water that sustains it. The setting
is one of incredible beauty. The East Usambara Mountains form the
tail end of a broken chain of forested mountains that further west
and north merge with the Congo River Basin rainforests. Sharing
traits with both their sister forests and the Indian Ocean environs,
the East Usambaras harbor a unique ecological marriage that has
produced an unusually high number of endemic floral and faunal
species—an amount akin to that of the Galápagos Islands.[1] For this,
and for being the recognized birthplace of *Saintpaulia ionantha* (parent
of the popular African violet), the East Usambara rainforest has acquired
international renown as one of the most valuable conservation areas
in all of Africa. It is considered one of the most beautiful as well,
with trees towering more than sixty meters high bearing vines that
hang down to a carpet of fallen leaves below, crosscut by many
streams and rivers. As a final virtue, it serves as a catchment forest,

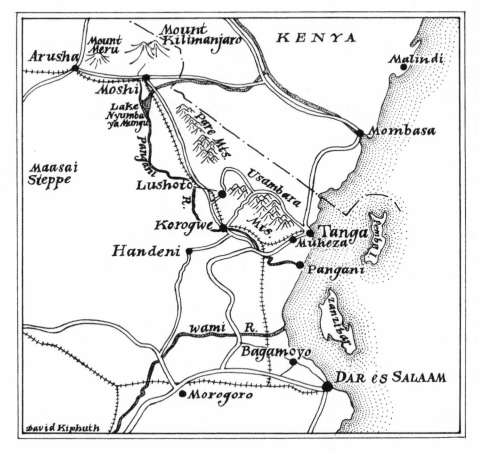

Map 2.1 Tanga Region. Courtesy of David Kiphuth.

collecting and providing water for the city of Tanga fifty kilometers away.

The slopes of the Usambaras merge and meld into loosely populated woodlands where citrus and kapok trees grow in abundance. During orange season, the roadsides are lined with children selling freshly woven baskets overflowing with oranges and tangerines for you to take home or savor on the spot. From the woodlands, one passes into an area of sisal plantations—sisal having once been the staple product of Tanga Region. A few decades ago, sisal was the source of the region's prosperity, making it the third most prosperous region in Tanzania, the "world's largest producer of sisal." However, that was all before the world demand for sisal plunged Tanga into the economic depression it continues to struggle against today. Passing rows and rows of neglected, overgrown sisal—often with the sisal plants indistinguishable from the weeds between them—one comes to signs of an urban center. A cement factory rises from the sisal-covered landscape, its plumes of smoke indicating that at least some Tanga residents remain gainfully employed. A prison behind stone walls is visible atop a small hill off to the right. After passing the 4H club headquarters, an army base, and a dairy farm, one comes to a large rotary that marks the boundary of Tanga municipality. On one side stands a soap factory and on the other, the deserted Saba Saba Grounds that come to life only once a year.

Saba Saba Day used to be a national holiday honoring the birth of TANU (Tanganyika African National Union), the political party that under Julius Nyerere's guidance channeled nationalist sentiment into a comparatively peaceful and successful bid for Tanganyikan independence. Literally meaning "Seven Seven" Day, in reference to the July 7 date, Saba Saba celebrations lasted a full seven days, during which these grounds and others throughout the country would teem with showcased pride in national products and services. In 1993, Tanga residents honored Saba Saba with stalls displaying prize animals and vegetables, booths enticing passersby with various games of chance, and exhibits by all the major industries, including arrays of cement and steel products by the cement factory and steel rolling mill, a nearly life-sized ship by the Harbours Authority, and a real miniature train by the Railway Authority that ferried excited children and adults back and forth on its one-kilometer course. With the formal announcement of multipartyism in 1992, however, opposition parties called for an end to the Saba Saba holiday, arguing that it unfairly promoted the ruling party. So in late 1993, Saba Saba was officially discarded in favor of Nane Nane ("Eight Eight," for August 8), an unofficial holiday honoring farmers. Confusion reigned in 1994 as to which holiday would be celebrated. Workers—pointing to unmodified government calendars that still identified Saba Saba as a national holiday—refused to go to work on July 7, taking their holiday by force. Some regions celebrated Saba Saba, others Nane Nane, and still others both. Editorials and opinions filled the newspapers,[2] and in 1995 a compromise position was reached that a single celebration would be held in the capital of Dar es Salaam on Saba Saba Day, but that the rest of the country would hold Nane Nane celebrations. Whether Saba Saba or Nane Nane, that one week of music, food, crowds, and entertainment strikes a sharp contrast to the other fifty-one weeks of the year when Tanga's Saba Saba Grounds lie empty and devoid of human activity save for one lone bar resolutely serving a small local clientele year-round.

Were one to continue straight through the rotary, one would pass the fire station, the railway station, and the Mkwakwani soccer stadium, and then have to choose whether to turn right or left. A turn to the right would take one across the railway tracks into Ngamiani, "the Place of Camels," the Swahili and African side of town. The place of camels is also the place of music, and Ngamiani is often mentioned in succeeding chapters. A turn to the left would take one to Tanga's business district (figure 2.1), site of expatriate offices and many Asian businesses. Its border is marked by another roundabout, in the center of which stands a large monument to the World Torch for Peace that passed through Tanga on October 26–27, 1986. It is flanked on one side by the former site of the Tanga School founded by the German colonial administration in 1892 (the oldest state school in the country), and on the other by the only working movie theater in town. Straight ahead is a market commonly known as *soko uzunguni* ("white persons' market"), and just beyond it—always calm and stunningly blue—lies Tanga Bay.

Despite its position as a trading center and port, Tanga never received the same attention in early travel logs and explorers' accounts as neighboring Pangani or other key coastal cities like Kilwa, Zanzibar, Mombasa, Malindi, and Lamu. Visitors to the coast have come to expect a certain distinctly Swahili form of architecture characterized by multistoried, stone coral structures bordering narrow, winding alleyways that display

Figure 2.1 Market Street, Tanga business district, c. 1950s. Photographer unknown.

arched doorways, patterned wood awnings, and intricately carved doors with geometric, floral, or Koranic script designs. Such visitors are generally disappointed when they walk through Tanga because although buildings of this style and era still stand in Pangani a mere fifty-two kilometers down the coast, none remain in Tanga, where the oldest buildings date to the start of the German occupation (1890s) and where an orderly grid of numbered streets replaces the more typical meandering alleyways.

There are at least two reasons for Tanga's architectural exceptionality. First, much of the town was destroyed in an 1888 German bombardment described at length further on. Second, although today's Tanga is situated on the southern side of Tanga Bay, this was not its original site. In the middle of the bay stands Toten Island (as named by the Germans) which, until the late 1800s, was where Tanga's main settlement existed. Now home only to snakes, spirits, tombs dating to the eighteenth and nineteenth centuries, and the discarded ruins of two mosques from the fifteenth and late seventeenth centuries, the island lies deserted. The physical erasure of Tanga through processes of migration and abandonment and a subsequent colonial demolition job parallels its narrative erasure from historical records. On the rare occasions when historians, explorers, and chroniclers mention Tanga in their narratives, they generally do so tangentially while discussing the affairs of other city-states such as Mombasa to the north or Pangani to the south, further relegating Tanga to the margins of history.

This chapter is subdivided into sections focusing respectively on Tanga, Tanganyika, and Tanzania. The historical narrative of Tanga—if one can be said to exist—is sparse, fragmentary, and heavy with silence. My intent in the first section is to offer an alternate account that resituates Tanga as a locus of meaningful, history-worthy activity in contrast to its current status as an ancillary settlement drawn into events and processes not of its own making. While I do not present much new information, my re-reading of existing materials with an eye to Tanga produces a revised narrative that reevaluates its significance in Swahili coastal history and sets the stage for understanding its position in contemporary Tanzania. In the second section, I present an outline sketch of the colonial history of Tanganyika. Because historical narratives continue to inform current politics in significant ways, it is necessary to be familiar with the key agents, events, and processes that helped create and define Tanganyika. Our discussion of Tanganyika lays the foundation for understanding how the ensuing United Republic of Tanzania came into being. This constitutes the focus of the third section, where I present a cursory history of the Tanzanian state and provide initial evidence for understanding how states enact and perform their existence—an argument elaborated in the second part of this book. Finally, the concluding section returns us to where we began: a discussion of Tanga and its position within the contemporary state.

In the Shadows of Mountains and Historical Neglect: Tanga

Identified as *Azania* by the anonymous writer of the *Periplus of the Erythraean Sea* (c. 40 A.D.), *Zingion* by Claudius Ptolemy (c. 150), and *Zanj* by Ibn Battuta (c. 1331), the East African coast has given rise to an extensive and multisited (Chinese, Arab, Portuguese, German, British) collection of early historical narratives.[3] These accounts resurrect from the mists of the past a lively, flourishing, and prosperous region that successfully mediated its position between land and water. Archaeological research supports these narratives in verifying the existence of ancient cosmopolitan cities and seaports and identifying a strikingly high degree of shared material culture—enough to justify interpretations of "the Swahili Corridor" (Horton 1987; Horton and Middleton 2000) as a distinct cultural region. From as early as the first century A.D., sailors and traders from the Arabian Peninsula, India, China, and Southeast Asia exploited alternating monsoon winds to navigate the Indian Ocean for travel to and from East Africa (Horton 1987; Freeman-Grenville 1962a, 1962b, 1988).[4]

> From the earliest times, before recorded history begins, the coast had belonged to the unity of trade of the Indian Ocean. The inland chiefs knew of their neighbours and of little beyond; the coastal folk looked across the seas and, by the coastwise traffic, were linked to each other, to the seaports of Arabia, the Persian Gulf and India, and beyond to Rome, Parthia and even China. There is no record of formal political unity, but common geography, trade and religion came to impose a common culture and a common language. (Freeman-Grenville 1962b,10)

What made the trade so profitable and thus historically laudable was not an exclusively outward orientation, as Freeman-Grenville would have us believe, but rather the confluence of two equally significant economic spheres. Sea-faring traders came to exchange products and knowledge with an equally extensive network of land-based traders who navigated caravan routes into the African interior (map 2.2). As the necessary mediating link, Swahili communities exploited both ocean and inland trade opportunities. The aggregation of ancient ports and settlements dotting the coastline between southern Somalia and northern Mozambique supplied ivory, gold, ambergris, rhinoceros horn, and ultimately slaves for export as well as markets for Indian and Middle Eastern imports. The exchange of material goods underscored an exchange of cul-

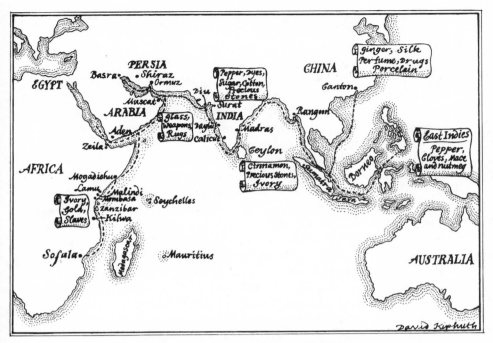

Map 2.2   Indian Ocean Trade Routes, c. 1000 A.D. Courtesy of David Kiphuth.

tural practices and beliefs, most noticeably the Islamic religion. Mercantile city-states developed along the entire coastal strip, every one of which was firmly grounded culturally, socially, and linguistically in its African context but marked by high degrees of cultural syncretism through such facets of social life as architecture, clothing, and expressive culture.

Thus it was from the meeting of diverse cultural influences, most predominantly African and Arab, that Swahili culture was born. The name *Waswahili*, which came to be applied to the communities that arose along the coast, is derived from the Arabic *sawahil*, meaning "coasts."[5] These peoples of the coast share kin and affinal networks, a common language (Kiswahili), religion (Islam), historical experiences, urban lifestyle, and cultural modes of expression such as musical performance. Swahili communities cannot, however, be said to have shared a common political or economic structure (not counting imposed colonial political frameworks), nor to fit any description of a corporate group. Allegiance to a common Swahili identity has been occasional at best. As Jonathon Glassman argues, "The boundaries separating Swahili townspeople from the supposed 'barbarians' of the hinterland were shifting, permeable, and extremely ambiguous, and they were kept that way by the constant challenges of slaves, villagers, and people from the interior who wished to cross them" (Glassman 1995, 266).

The earliest Swahili settlements found thus far date back as early as the sixth century along the Zanzibar Channel, and the eighth century on the Benadir coast (Barawa and Mogadishu in today's Somalia) and in the Lamu Archipelago (Shanga, Pate, and Manda of northern Kenya).[6] Archaeological and linguistic data confirm that settlers spread throughout the region to establish Malindi and Mombasa along the Kenyan coast, and Mafia and Kilwa on Tanzania's coast. The impressive ruined stone cities they left as evidence of their prosperity and sophistication collided head-on with assumptions about Africa held dear by colonial-era scholars and archaeologists. Unable to reconcile their social Darwinist philosophies with indisputable evidence of cultural parity, such writers escaped into a myth that these cities were the remnants of a foreign, non-African civilization, one that mysteriously died out many centuries earlier.[7] They found particularly incomprehensible the grandeur and renown of the city of Kilwa. Kilwa emerged in the twelfth century on an island off the coast of what is now southern Tanzania. Described by Ibn Battuta in 1331 as "one of the most beautiful and well-constructed towns in the world," Kilwa dominated coastal trade through its command of gold from Zimbabwe until the arrival of the Portuguese toward the end of the fifteenth century. The Kilwa Chronicle,[8] a local origin myth tracing the city's establishment to the arrival of a certain Sultan Hassan bin Ali from Shiraz (in ancient Persia) with his six sons in seven ships, fed colonial assumptions, as did the existence (even today) of entire villages along the coast with self-described "Shirazi" inhabitants.[9]

It was during the height of Kilwa's supremacy in the fourteenth century that settlers established a settlement some twenty kilometers south of contemporary Tanga. The area was called Mtangata, with Tongoni as its regional center, and it prospered during the fifteenth century. It was on a reef opposite Mtangata that Vasco da Gama ran aground on April 6, 1498, after being the first European to successfully circumnavigate the Cape of Good Hope. En route to India, da Gama's misfortune cost him a day's delay during which he was able to admire and take note of the Usambara Mountains and meet "Moors" (i.e., Swahili) who came out to his ship in two small crafts bearing a load of "fine oranges, better than those of Portugal."[10] He returned to Mtangata/Tongoni on his way back to Portugal in 1499, where he anchored for fifteen days, traded shirts and bracelets for fowl, and set fire to one of his three ships for lack of sufficient manpower to command them all.[11]

Mtangata along with the rest of the Swahili Coast experienced economic and political decline in the sixteenth and seventeenth centuries after the entrenchment of Portuguese control of the coast. Portuguese sources identify a powerful ruler of Mtangata as late as 1728, but following this there is no further mention, which likely indicates the shift of population away from and ultimate desertion of Tongoni. Today all that remains at Tongoni are a few scattered homesteads and significant ruins consisting of a mosque and nearly forty graves dating to the fourteenth and fifteenth centuries (the single largest collection of pillar tombs found along the entire coast) that testify to former glories and wealth.[12]

Between Tongoni and Tanga stands the ancient walled town of Ndumi. Tanga residents today carry a certain element of possessive pride with regard to Ndumi; many consider it to be an example of living history. Ndumi inhabitants speak a dialect not easily understood by Tangans, and the journey required to reach the town—namely, crossing an extensive tidal plain teeming with thousands of one-armed sand crabs, past two isolated graves standing side by side, and through an antiquated stone portal marking its entrance—impresses the senses with an overwhelming feeling of timelessness.[13] When I visited Ndumi perched on the back of a friend's bicycle, I was unknowingly repeating a journey made by the explorer Richard Burton a hundred years earlier. During his visit to the area, he was told of and urged to visit an ancient city that he assumed—typical of his time—to be of foreign origin.

> Knowing that Arab and Persian colonies had been planted at an early epoch in this part of the Sawahil, I accepted with pleasure a guide to one of the ancient cities. Setting out at 8 A.M. with a small body of spear men, I walked four or five miles S. West of Tanga on the Mtangata road over a country dry as Arabian sand, and strewed with the bodies of huge millipedes. The hard red and yellow clays produced in plenty holcus and sesamum, manioc and papaws; mangoes and pine-apples were rare, but the Jamli, or Indian damson (in Arabic Zám and in Kisawahili Mzambaráni), the egg-plant, and the toddy-tree grew wild. The baobabs were in new leaf, the fields were burned in readiness for rain, and the peasants dawdled about, patting the clods with bits of wood. At last we traversed a Khor, or lagoon drained by the receding tide: then, insulating the ruins, we sighted our destination after a walk of five miles over crab-mounds. From afar it resembled an ancient castle. Entering by a gap in the enceinte, I found a parallelogram some 200 yards long of solid coralline or lime, in places rent by the roots of sturdy trees, well-bastioned and loop-holed for bows and muskets. The site is raised considerably above the mean level of the country, attesting its antiquity: it is concealed from the seaside by a screen of trees and by the winding creek that leaves the canoes high during the ebb-tide; full water makes it an island. (Burton 1872, 2: 125f.)

Recent archaeological research has determined that although the walls of Ndumi date to the seventeenth and eighteenth centuries they enclose a mosque that was built in the fourteenth or fifteenth century on the site of a still earlier one (Allen 1993, 102; Mturi 1975, 9–13). Unique, mysterious emblems in relief surround the *mihrab* (wall niche indicating the direction of Mecca) of the mosque, yet its interior pillars resemble greatly those in the Friday mosque at Kilwa that date to c. 1277–94.

Swahili-speaking settlers from the northern coast credited with the establishment of Tongoni and Ndumi are also identified by local tradition as having founded Tanga,[14] although existing sources leave few clues as to when.[15] One of the earliest references to Tanga is in the chronicle of the *History of Pate,* which lists Tanga as one of the cities Pate conquered during its second invasion of the coast in 1392.[16] Popular among scholars and Tanga elders alike is a certain formulaic history whose elements can be applied to any of several Swahili cities: small fishing village turned trading center attracts wealthy, Muslim foreigners who in turn take local women (Bondei and Digo women, in the case of Tanga) as wives and over time assimilate local Swahili modes of behavior and language use (Chande 1998, 19; Nurse and Spear 1985; Middleton 1992, 33–35). This tale, found throughout the coastal region, often appears as an allegory for Swahili civilization, presenting it as the amalgamation of local (often cast as feminized and unempowered) elements and foreign (masculinized and powerful) elements.

Islands were the preferred choice for Swahili settlements. Lamu, Pate, Faza, Manda, Mombasa, Wasin, Jambe, Kilwa, Pemba, Zanzibar, Mafia, and the Comoros are all relevant examples. In this, Tanga was no exception. The reason, argues archaeologist Neville Chittick, was primarily one of security:

> These trading towns not only in the earliest period, but until quite recent times were sited for preference on islands; failing this the favourite position was on a spit of land almost encircled by creeks and mangrove swamps. This was for security; with a stretch of water protecting their wealthy towns from the poorer inhabitants of the hinterland, they had no need of defensive walls, which in the earliest period are seldom found. They would cultivate on the mainland if it was close, crossing to their shambas [farms] in boats, but did not venture into the interior. (Chittick, quoted in Chande 1998, 20)

Middleton, however, offers a different interpretation. He sees the Swahili preference for island settlements as a spatial representation of sociosymbolic differentiation: "The making of a canal between island and mainland creates a boundary, contrasted to the former lack of one and to formless spatial uncertainty. The definition of the island and its settlement by immigrant Muslim traders implies the creation of a town, a center of urbanity and religion. . . . The town of the island is now a 'founded' entity, with on one side the waste of the bush and on the other the waste of the Indian Ocean" (Middleton 1992, 33–34).

Local tradition in Tanga supports the claim that the islanders would commute to the mainland to cultivate. When questioned about the origin of the name Tanga, elders today in Tanga very often respond by describing how in the Bondei language, the term *tanga,* while literally meaning "outside," was commonly used for "farm plot" and that the islanders would often say in Kibondei, *"Naita tanga"* or "I'm going to the farm" when leaving the island to tend to their plots on the mainland. Hence the name came to be associated with the subsequent settlement that arose on the mainland.[17] An alternate etymological explanation draws upon the Swahili translation of the term *tanga* as the "sail of a vessel, of matting or canvas" (Johnson 1989, 452) and possibly refers to the sail-like shape of Tanga Bay (Chande 1998, 15). We are left to wonder why early Tangans chose to forsake their island security. In 1857 when Burton visited Tanga, the migration from island to mainland was nearly complete, with only a few huts and a fort remaining on the island (it was not completely forsaken until 1884). He described the mainland settlement as "a patch of thatched pent-roofed huts, built upon a bank overlooking the sea in a straggling grove of cocoa and calabash," and estimated the population at between four and five thousand, including twenty Banyan (Indian) merchants and fifteen Baluchis (Burton 1872, 2: 116). He also noted that two caravans a year departed from Tanga for the Usambara and Pare Mountains, Kilimanjaro, and Maasai areas.

> These caravans are seldom short of 400 to 500 men, Arabs and Waswahili, Pagazi or free porters who carry 50 lbs. each, and slaves. The imports are chiefly cotton-stuffs, iron wires (Senyenge), brass wires (Másángo), and beads, of which some 400 varieties are current in these countries. The usual return consists chiefly of ivory, per annum about 70,000 lbs., we were told—a quantity hardly credible. . . . [T]hey bring also a few slaves, some small mangey camels, and half-wild asses. (Burton 1872, 2: 117)

The ivory, slaves, and livestock mentioned above, plus other valued commodities of the time, such as ambergris, rhinoceros horn, rhinoceros hides, and hippopotamus teeth, were purchased inland, taken to the coast, and transported to Zanzibar for export.

The early history extracted and presented here closely relates Tanga to coastal patterns of migration and island settlement, to fourteenth- and fifteenth-century prosperity (as evidenced by the largest extant collection of pillar tombs), and to clear associations with Islamic and Swahili culture. But whereas the emphasis reiterated in coastal historiography is on the maritime and trading aspects of coastal economics, the very name of Tanga forces recognition of the continued involvement of coastal communities in agriculture. The strategy of diversifying economic activities to include agriculture, trade, and fishing is a long-standing coastal pattern. Swahili communities never were solely oriented to trade or maritime activities. The insistent theme in the literature that Swahili culture is more ocean-bound than land-bound, more oriented to the Indian Ocean than to Africa, leads by logical extension back to an all-too-familiar colonial refrain that Swahili civilization is ultimately more foreign than local in content. At a recent conference on East African arts,[18] the suggestion was made that we consider the Swahili Coast less part of East Africa than part of "Western Indian Oceania." The resurgent interest in divorcing Swahili society from its African roots can only be attributed to historical amnesia or, worse, to a disillusionment with Africanist interpretations. There is no reason why the coast has to be exclusively related to either Africa or the Indian Ocean and not firmly embedded—as has been shown throughout its history—in both.

Revisiting the early history of Tanga reminds us at a critical juncture in East Africanist historiography of the material and ideological grounding of Swahili culture in Africa. The move by early Tangan residents from island to mainland can be read as a response to declining economic opportunities following Portuguese disruptions of coastal trade or decreased concern with attacks from unwelcome outsiders. It may also, however, indicate a disavowal of isolationism and vigilant self-protection, and a rejection of social differentiation. Tanga society then as now was composed of a highly diverse mixture of local (especially Segeju, Bondei, and Digo) and foreign residents. Additionally, whereas international trade is subject to wider economic relations and processes that are too often couched within unequal power dynamics, having recourse to subsistence agriculture ensures a certain degree of economic security. A foot on land via a *shamba* or *tanga* on the mainland offered Tangans and Swahili communities elsewhere sustenance through critical times. In forsaking their stone houses, tombs, and ancient mosques on the island, Tangans clearly sought to guarantee that security, reaffirming and nurturing their mainland roots in the process. But the reasons why an island refuge would have posed an attractive option in the centuries predating its desertion in the early nineteenth century lie in the multiple struggles for dominance over the coast that Tangans and their neighbors faced, confronted, and lost in the subsequent emergence of an entity known as Tanganyika.

Competing Colonizers, Rival Residents: The Emergence of Tanganyika

> *Enda Manoel, ututukiziye*
> *Enda, na sulubu uyititiziye*
>
> Go away Manoel, you have made us hate you.
> Go, and carry your cross with you.
> —Swahili saying from the Portuguese period

Let us race through five hundred years of international relations in East Africa, less in search of Tanga's presence than of the embryonic state-hood that preceded contemporary Tanzania: its twin, truncated birth as the colonized territory of Tanganyika and colonized/colonizing territory of Zanzibar. Readers who desire more than the level of detail I provide here may consult the work of Nicholls (1971), Pouwels (1987), Sheriff (1987), Middleton (1992), Allen (1993), Willis (1993), and Glassman (1995).

Following Vasco da Gama's "discovery" of East Africa, Portuguese forces wasted no time in laying claim to the coast and its profitable trade networks. They succeeded by exploiting a fragmented local political terrain of independent city-states vying for power in the continual nego-tiation of inland and overseas trade routes. Pursuing a policy of divide-and-rule, they selected Malindi as their local headquarters, which sub-sequently defined for it adverse relationships with Lamu and Pate to the north, and Mombasa to the south. In 1528, a ruler of Mtangata sided with the Portuguese against Mombasa—marking the less than friendly position it held toward its powerful neighbor. Local rulers thus exploited connections to more powerful, often foreign, allies in attempts to im-prove their relative local standing. This strategy, however, which re-quired gambling local autonomy, often backfired, for Portuguese rule proved to be destructive and repressive to a previously unimaginable degree. Commercial desire for supply and watering bases for their ships en route to Goa combined with religious fervor for a crusade against Islam underscored Portuguese ambition for control of the coast. The stiff tribute they exacted[19] dealt a fatal blow to the fragile trade networks that constituted the economic underpinnings of coastal society.

The arrival of the Portuguese from the sea coincided with incursions of nomadic Oromo and mysterious Zimba on land, who instigated a long series of attacks on coastal settlements. The Oromo are considered responsible for having destroyed the Ozi kingdom and the cities of Luz-iwa, Malindi, Kilifi, Kilepwa, Mnarani, Gedi, and Ungwana.[20] Zimba forces attacked Kilwa in 1587 and Mombasa not long afterwards. Facing attacks from all sides and suffering heavily from a series of ill-conceived Portuguese decisions, coastal settlements entered a period of economic decline that lasted throughout most of the sixteenth and seventeenth centuries. As Sheriff describes,

Although the power of the Swahili merchant class was broken, the Portuguese lacked the resources for effective control of the whole coast and monopoly of trade. Their power north of Cape Delgado was restricted to the occasional collection of tribute, and the "Captaincy of Malindi" to serve as a centre of the Indian trade so crucial to Sofala. They tried to control sea traffic with a pass system, and granted a monopoly over certain commodities to the Captain of Malindi. They also tried to cut out Swahili traders from the Sofala trade. All these measures helped to kill the goose that had laid the golden egg. Trade in both gold and ivory declined. Although the Swahili merchant class, legally or otherwise, was able to circumvent these restrictions, it was embittered and felt oppressed, creating a fertile ground for disaffection and revolt. (1987, 16)

Upon the rise to power of a certain Mohammad Yusuf bin Hassan in Mombasa, the tide began to turn against the Portuguese. Born in Mombasa, he had been taken as a child to Portugal to be raised as a Christian, but upon his return to East Africa, he reverted to Islam and preached *jihad* against the Portuguese. Known to the Portuguese as Dom Jerónimo Chingulia, he entered the Portuguese stronghold of Fort Jesus on August 16, 1631 with a band of followers and killed Captain Pedro Leitão de Gamboa. A signal was given to waiting followers outside the fort, and the Portuguese houses in town were set on fire. Within two weeks, all the Portuguese in Mombasa were killed. His call for a coast-wide rebellion was heard in neighboring Tanga and Mtangata. There too all the Portuguese settlers were subsequently killed or routed. Portugal retaliated, meting out severe punishment, but the seeds had been sown and taken root. Rebellion soon flourished throughout the coastal region.[21]

Meanwhile, across the Indian Ocean, parallel events were taking place in the Arabian Peninsula. The people of today's Oman, who similarly suffered under Portuguese oppression, succeeded in 1650 in expelling the Portuguese from Muscat and, according to Chande (1991), "began to view themselves as the defenders of the Muslim cause in Africa" (53, n. 37). They received and offered to support a delegation of representatives from Mombasa, Wasin, Tanga, and Mtangata, who went to Muscat to request assistance against the Portuguese. The process of eradicating Portuguese control of the coast took exactly one century to complete. At times Oman gained ascendancy, while at other times Portugal appeared the victor. Yet Portuguese rule of the East African coast and quest for Christian converts did indeed end, ironically on Palm Sunday in April 1729 when all remaining Portuguese survivors relented and converted to Islam or escaped from Mombasa.

The coastal game of shifting allegiances and alliances did not end with the departure of the Portuguese. The loss of one demanding overlord simply resulted in the substitution of a new one: Oman. In 1741, Mombasa declared itself an independent state and laid claim to a large portion of the coast. Zanzibar, however, remained loyal to Oman and developed an intense rivalry with Mombasa that would last for decades. Concerned with its own internal affairs, Oman disregarded Mombasa's assertion of autonomy until Sultan Seyyid Said bin Sultan came to power in 1806. His increasing interest in Mombasa and the surrounding hinterland caused the Mombasa ruling elite (the Mazrui clan) enough concern that they repeated history and sought foreign protection, this time from the British. A short-lived convention placing Mombasa under the British flag was signed in Fort Jesus on February 9, 1824, but did not survive an economic embargo subsequently imposed by Oman. Oman's control of the Mrima coast—significantly of the towns of Wasin and Tanga, which had been exclusively supplying traders in Mombasa with ivory and rhinoceros hides in exchange for cloth and iron wire—cut the economic mainstays of Mombasa's elite. In 1826, the British withdrew their support for the Mazrui, and not long afterwards Seyyid Said shifted his capital from Muscat to Zanzibar so as to better control the trade that provided the bulk of his revenues. In February 1837, the sultan with little fanfare assumed control of Mombasa.

Coastal economics began a process of recovery and growth roughly around the time of the arrival of the Omani sultanate to Zanzibar. By the mid-nineteenth century, a vast commercial empire had developed under Seyyid Said's careful tutelage, featuring Zanzibar as its base and extending to present-day Mozambique, Malawi, Democratic Republic of the Congo, Tanzania, Kenya, and Uganda (Sheriff 1987, 190). A common phrase of the day, "When the pipes play in Zanzibar, they dance at the lakes" indicates the breadth of Zanzibari dominance throughout the region from the Indian Ocean to Lakes Victoria and Tanganyika. It was around this time, in the early nineteenth century, that Tanga shifted from being an island to a mainland settlement. One possible interpretation is that the population had grown to a point where the island could no longer comfortably accommodate everyone. More likely is that the security accompanying Zanzibar hegemony over key caravan ports like Tanga enabled residents to dispense with their island stronghold and live closer to the land that provided them agricultural produce.[22]

In addition to the increasing demand from Bombay for the "soft" ivory which only this vast East Africa network could provide, the 1830s and 1840s witnessed the start of "clove mania," which swept across Zanzibar and Pemba and constituted another highly lucrative source of revenue for the empire. International trade flourished far and wide, even attracting Americans seeking a share of the riches that the empire offered.[23] Slaves developed into a commodity of importance by the early 1800s for local clove plantations (Cooper 1977; 1980) as well as date plantations in Oman and French sugar plantations in the Mascarenes[24]—two hundred years behind the West African slave trade and just about the time that the British had decided slavery ought to be abolished. Despite growing antislavery sentiment from Europe and measures such as the Moresby Treaty of 1822 prohibiting the sale of slaves to Christians (signed between the British and Seyyid Said), slavery continued within the coastal region to meet local labor demands on the clove plantations of Zanzibar and the grain plantations of the coast. Thus, in contrast to West Africa, the East African trade in slaves was "metamorphosed from being primarily one dominated by the export of slave labor to one that exploited that labor within East Africa to produce commodities to feed into the world system of trade" (Sheriff 1987, 2; see also Glassman 1995, 81–82).

Germany, meanwhile, was making significant inroads into the interior regions of future Tanganyika. Unlike the British, Germany under first Imperial Chancellor Prince Otto von Bismarck did not hold a coherent master plan for colonial conquest. Bismarck, in fact, wavered considerably in his support for the undertakings of explorer Carl Peters, who established the Society for German Colonization and enthusiastically moved into the East African interior laying German claim to vast amounts of land. Bismarck nevertheless capitulated to the pressure to engage actively in colonialism and even went so far as to host the famous Berlin Conference of 1884 that ostensibly initiated discussion amongst European powers regarding rules to follow in the colonization of Africa.[25] In 1886, the boundaries of German East Africa and British East Africa were provisionally determined; they were finalized in 1890. Of the previously vast empire that he had once commanded, the sultan was allotted only a ten-mile-wide coastal strip plus the islands of Zanzibar and Pemba. A new colonial era had dawned in East Africa.

The beginning of colonial conquest would not prove to be a smooth one for Germany, however. No sooner had they announced their official presence than troubles began. As described by Glassman (1995), resistance movements emerged along the coast against the hegemonic ideologies and interests of both Germany and the residual representatives of the sultan who held nominal control over the coast. Revisiting the successful formula used to oust the Portuguese, coastal communities united in fighting the Germans. When Emil von Zelewski and his troops made a bungled attempt to assert German authority by storming a mosque full of worshippers on the Islamic holiday of *Eid al-Hajj* with their shoes on and accompanied by hunting dogs, armed resistance broke out in Pangani and spread throughout the coast within two months. Two men from very different backgrounds and purposes led the struggle: Bwana Heri bin Juma and Bushiri bin Salim. The people of Tanga (by this time a mainland settlement) joined in on September 5, 1888, by expelling both the few Germans who laid claim to their town and the sultan's representatives. Explains Glassman,

[B]y the end of September the Germans had been either killed or expelled from all but two enclaves on the Tanzania coast by a broad but brittle alliance of Shirazi patricians, lower-class townspeople, peasants and slaves from the surrounding countryside, and warriors from many parts of the interior. . . . The expulsion of Zelewski and his colleagues wounded German national pride and forced a reluctant Bismarck to commit the resources of the Reich to suppress the rising, thus turning German East Africa from a private venture into a formal colony, something the Iron Chancellor had hoped to avoid. Like many other imperial adventures of the time, this one was justified as a move against the slave trade. It became politically expedient for the Germans to characterize the movement against them as an "Arab revolt," engineered by Omanis and other Arabs in an effort to preserve their position as the region's premier slave traders, planters, and power-brokers. No serious observer believed this, largely because the few Omanis who at first supported the rising quickly switched sides as it became clear that the movement was directed against Arab rule as much as it was directed against the Germans. (Glassman 1995, 6)

With regard to Tanga, German forces were quick to retaliate. On September 8, 1888, the gunboat *Möwe* bombarded the town, leaving it nearly completely destroyed. The rebellion nonetheless continued to flourish until the May 1889 arrival of the German navy and an armed force composed of disaffected Sudanese mercenaries collected in Egypt and Nyamwezi caravaners whose trade networks (dependent upon access to the coast) were disrupted by the rebellion. German military subjugation of the coast was more or less achieved by July 1889. Describing the recapture of Pangani on July 8, 1889, Glassman writes, "Wissmann's troops plundered and raped indiscriminately, robbing even the Indian merchants who had 'joyously' welcomed the invasion. The rampage was allowed to continue for two full days" (1995, 256). Although the stone houses of Pangani's wealthy were spared, its African quarters were bombed. A few days later, Wissmann turned his attention to neighboring Tanga and made sure that its initial destruction the previous September was made complete. Very little was left of the town (Iliffe 1979, 92, 96; Glassman 1995, 220), which was later rebuilt under German supervision. The walled town of Ndumi, having provided shelter to Bwana Heri during the rebellion, met a similar fate (Glassman 1995, 256).

Germany would only have a relatively short involvement in East Africa. Following defeat in World War I, its colonial possessions were redistributed, and on February 1, 1920, *Deutsch-Ostafrika* became a "Class C Mandated Territory." Yet the Germans did build railway lines, roads, schools, hospitals, and a large part of the infrastructure that Koponen (1994) argues was necessary to exploit the colony. And after quelling the revolt in the coastal region, it was there—especially in Tanga, Pangani, and present-day Lushoto in the Usambara Mountains[26]—that the Germans based their colonial activities. Deutsch-Ostafrika's first governor, Julius Freiherr von Soden, founded the first state secular school against the wishes of the German state: the Tanga School. He reasoned that such a school was needed to prepare Swahili-speaking subordinate administrators who could help realize his goal "to restrict administration to the coast and establish commercial relations with the interior, using the coastal peoples and their Swahili language as his intermediaries" (Iliffe 1979, 208). But the school found it difficult to attract students in its early days, for upper-class Swahili families "regarded the new 'non-religious' school with suspicion, preferring to continue to send their sons to Koran schools. . . . To make attendance more palatable, a Koranic teacher was employed—a bold experiment which had to be abandoned when uproar was aroused by the missionary lobby in Germany and the Colonial Council intervened" (Koponen 1994, 505). It would nonetheless develop into a highly respected educational institution whose graduates would serve in high-ranking civil service and academic positions for years to come.

German administrators also selected Tanga as the terminus of the colony's first railway (the Usambara Railway). Construction began in 1891 along what had once constituted the northern caravan route to access areas designated for plantation agriculture—the focus of German agricultural policy (following Sultan Seyyid Said). The northern coast between Tanga and Pangani thus developed into the largest plantation area in the territory, producing coffee, sugar, sisal, rubber, tobacco, cotton, and coconuts (copra). Sisal was introduced in 1893 and by 1902 had become the third most valuable commercial crop in the country after coffee and coconut (Koponen 1994, 206).

Tanganyika officially received its name during the subsequent British colonial period. The British Colonial Office apparently had fun pondering possibilities:

> Smutsland [in honor of General Smuts who led British forces to final victory in East Africa] was dismissed as inelegant, Eburnea [from the Latin for ivory] and Azania as pedantic. New Maryland, Windsorland, and Victoria were vetoed by the Colonial Secretary's insistence on "a native name prominently associated with the territory." He considered Kilimanjaro and Tabora before settling on "The Tanganyika Protectorate" as proposed by his deputy undersecretary. (Iliffe 1979, 247)

But from where did the undersecretary get "Tanganyika"? One Tanga elder dates it to the German period and explained that from a German administrative perspective, they ruled Tanga and the *nyika* (lit., "bush" or "hinterland") beyond.[27] Another explanation positions Tanga as the point of entry into the territory and hence translates Tanganyika as "the land beyond Tanga" (Martin 1991, 80, n. 7). An alternative etymological possibility, however, could relate it to the verb *kutanga,* meaning "to go to and fro, go from side to side, dawdle, loiter, stroll about, wander"

(Johnson 1989, 452), thus lending itself to a colonial description of the territory as "to wander in the bush."

Beyond bringing the German colonial period to an end, World War I left behind other enduring social effects, not the least of which was the further spread of Kiswahili (the *lingua franca* of Zanzibar traders, the German army, and to a lesser degree, British forces as well), and a musical tradition called Beni characterized by military ranks and titles, uniforms, mock military drill steps, and the musical texture of military bands. Ranger's (1975) study of the Beni *ngoma* details the rise of this dance form in the 1890s and its demise in the 1960s. Already well-established in coastal areas by the time of the war, Beni dance societies expanded their networks to inland regions through the wartime movements of people and embraced with even greater enthusiasm naval and military themes in their dances (Ranger 1975, 47). "After the war, soldiers and porters returning to their homes from the Tanzanian front carried the Mbeni idea with them. Soon the dance was being danced in the garrison towns of Malawi and in the mining compounds of Southern Rhodesia; in the Katanga and on the Zambian Copperbelt; in northern Mozambique and even as far afield as Angola" (Ranger 1969, 177). Thus, off the battlefield, ancillary wars were fought between the dance associations of Marini (inspired by the German navy) and Arinoti, Kingi (named after England's King Edward) and Scotchi (complete with bagpipes). Swahili dance societies, including Beni, will constitute a focus of the next chapter, but it is important to note here that their existence, in particular the Beni phenomenon which spread so far and so quickly throughout the region, caused British administrators no small amount of concern.

> "There is no doubt that they form an encouragement to a certain class of native to keep in touch with their friends in different parts of the country," wrote the Assistant Political Officer, Dar es Salaam, in 1919. "They should in all probability evolve into a more formal social club and possibly with political importance. . . . The general question of the *Chama* [dance association] . . . is a matter worthy of investigation."[28]

British colonial administrators subsequently attempted to thwart the inherent potential for political organization in Beni by initiating a policy of discouragement, first by means of snubbing it and thus alarming elites, and second, by creating a new apparatus of control over all publicly held dances, consisting of mandatory fees and licenses (Ranger 1975, 91). As we shall soon see, this question of how to successfully monitor and contain the political potentialities of Swahili musical performance would trouble not only colonial administrations, but also the future Tanzanian state.

Portugal, Oman, Germany, and Great Britain: the last five hundred years have witnessed a shifting political terrain in which these colonial powers competed with local city-states and each other for access to and domination over the lucrative East African trade networks. All four foreign powers would discover that successful administration entailed subjugating or winning the cooperation of coastal communities who were long-established in the trade networks and essential to their maintenance. Although Indian Ocean networks would diminish in importance as economic attention during the turn of the century shifted inland to plantation agriculture, the mere access to global destinations offered by the coast secured its importance to any administration of the territory. Zanzibar, as seat of the Omani court for a century and gateway to the East, evolved in status from colonized to colonizer (under Sultan Seyyid Said) and back to colonized (under British "protection"). During the shift, it assumed a dual persona with strong cultural, religious, linguistic, and political affiliations to both the Swahili coast and Oman—a split identity that continues to pose significant problems in the present.

Yet understanding Tanganyika and Zanzibar's colonial experiences requires recognition of repeatedly demonstrated traditions of resistance and rebellion. Jockeying for power and status, coastal city-states held fractured relationships of fission and fusion with each other—sometimes uniting to face a common enemy but more commonly bound by brittle connections that broke easily under economic and political strains. External forces like Portugal and Oman could exploit these local tensions in the familiar tactic of divide-and-rule. But a century-long period of Zanzibari/Omani rule diminished the power of regional centers and focused political attention on the Sultan, then Germany, then Britain. Resistance to colonial rule took many decades to translate into a struggle for independence, but that struggle was made more efficient by the existence of widespread networks like the Beni *ngoma* network, and the existence of Kiswahili, which, through centuries-old trade networks, had developed into an East African *lingua franca*. Portugal, Oman, Germany, and Great Britain all laid claim to Tanganyika and Zanzibar. They faced challenges from each other and from within. And while the internal challenges may have appeared less than successful, the act of challenging—by sword and through song—set the stage for a successful bid for nationhood.

Independence and the Ongoing Creation of Tanzania

The growth of nationalist sentiment began in the 1940s with the Tanganyika African Association (TAA) as its loudest voice, an organization that developed from the Tanganyika Territory African Civil Service Association (TTACSA) that, in turn, was born of dance societies, football clubs, and mutual aid associations in Tanga.[29] TAA later became the Tanganyika African National Union (TANU) and adopted a platform for self-government and independence (Iliffe 1979, 512). Its eloquent spokesperson was Julius Nyerere—a British-educated Fabian sympathizer—who would become the first president of Tanganyika upon independence in December 1961. Zanzibar, on the other hand, still faced turbulent times. The island sultanate remained under Omani Arab leadership after receiving independence from Britain on December 10, 1963. A violent revolution on January 12, 1964, in which an estimated ten to twelve thousand "Arabs" lost their lives, put a swift end to Arab rule and resulted in a new government under the Afro-Shirazi Party (ASP) led by Abeid Karume. On April 26, 1964, Nyerere and Karume formalized an accord uniting their two nations into the United Republic of Tanzania. The ruling parties of Tanganyika and Zanzibar, TANU and ASP respectively, were later merged into Chama cha Mapinduzi (Party of the Revolution, or CCM), the party that continues to rule the republic today.[30] In 1967, Nyerere inaugurated the Arusha Declaration that set Tanzania on its own unique path of socialist idealism. Termed "African socialism," or Ujamaa, Nyerere's governing philosophy was an agriculture-based reinvention of communalism painted with shades of an idealized African past. Its primary vehicles were communal villagization and the nationalization of key industries.

Nyerere, a bright light in African politics whose death in October 1999 was mourned around the world, led his nation through the throes of birth and actively fought against the tendencies toward ethnic stratification that characterized neighboring states. With more than 120 distinct ethnic groups, his nation had much to fear from such processes. In an attempt to dull the edges of difference, he instituted social policies of unification such as the single-language policy that formalized Kiswahili's prevalence throughout the country by requiring it as the medium of instruction at the primary school level and the sole mode of political discourse. A second strategy was to systematically weaken localized social bonds and simultaneously strengthen national ones by moving and shuffling people throughout the country. Students admitted to state secondary schools are generally sent to schools far from their home regions, and the same holds true for national service cadets, army recruits, and teachers graduating from teacher's training college. In thus instituting continual movement, albeit within national borders, Nyerere consciously sought to create a sense of nation-ness and, in many respects, succeeded. To further the goal of national unity on a political level, he instituted a single-party state run by CCM and chaired the party for thirty years. His personal background as a teacher and his emphasis on education (resulting in, at one point, the highest literacy rate in Africa[31]) garnered him the title of *Mwalimu* (Teacher) by which he is still fondly known today.

It was in his economic policies that his critics found the most ammunition for their attacks. Ujamaa as a program of communal villagization was, by virtually all accounts, an abysmal failure (see chapter 7). Agricultural production declined, the country's foreign debt skyrocketed, and Tanzania acquired the ignominious title of "second poorest nation in the world" by the World Bank. During the early 1980s, the country suffered such severe shortages of basic items that people were commonly jailed on suspicion of hoarding food while others were summarily imprisoned for being caught idle and therefore not contributing to the development of the nation (the charge: economic sabotage). His nationalization policy effectively killed the emergent industrial sector and served as a strong deterrent to would-be investors. Political dissidents were jailed,[32] some with life sentences, and Tanzania—once the hope and prized jewel of socialist ideologues worldwide from China to Scandinavia to East Germany—began to fall from favor.

The government under President Ali Hassan Mwinyi (who succeeded Nyerere in 1985 after he voluntarily stepped down from office) formalized a withdrawal from socialist economics and the start of a transition from single-party socialism to multiparty democracy. The economic sector was the first to feel the effects of liberalization, with many suffering government parastatals relinquished to private ownership. Political liberalization was promised, and plans were laid for the first national multiparty elections to take place on October 29, 1995. Multiparty elections were to happen first, however, at the civic level on October 30, 1994, on the mainland. On Zanzibar civic elections were postponed until October 22, 1995 just before the national elections— the key contest being between CCM and the Zanzibar-based opposition party Civic United Front (CUF), an organization with overtones of Islamic reformism, Zanzibar separatism, and financial backing from the Middle East.

In the 1995 national elections, four candidates campaigned for the Union presidency: Benjamin Mkapa (representing the ruling party, CCM), the populist leader Augustine Mrema (Chagga-dominated National Committee for Constitutional Reform, NCCR-Mageuzi), Ibrahim Lipumba (Zanzibar-based, Islamic reformist CUF), and John Cheyo (a wealthy textile industrialist running on the United Democratic Party ticket—UDP). There were some irregularities noted in the electoral

process in the capital of Dar es Salaam,[33] though elsewhere on the mainland the electoral process was characterized more by a lack of organization, materials, and financing than widespread electoral fraud.[34] Some
polling stations opened late, others lacked a sufficient supply of ballots,
and still others did not receive ballots at all due to lack of transportation
for election officials. And although voting was extended into the night
to accommodate the masses of voters who turned out to exercise their
right to vote, it did not matter in some areas, where a lack of electricity
and funds to purchase candles effectively ended voting at sundown.[35]
Nevertheless, the clear winner proved to be CCM's Benjamin Mkapa,
who won 62 percent of the vote and ushered in the "Third Phase Government."[36]

The October 1995 elections have come and gone. Despite widespread
rumors of imminent ethnic slaughter, a notable lack of violence accompanied them. Numerous accusations of voting irregularities arose,
however, with respect to the elections on Zanzibar, where the two con-
tenders for the Zanzibari presidency were incumbent Salmin Amour
(representing CCM) and Seif Sharrif Hamad (running on the CUF ticket).
Salmin Amour was declared the winner, but only by a slim margin that
allowed lots of room for speculation and rumor: Amour 50.2 percent,
Hamad 49.8 percent, with 4,922 votes spoiled.[37] International observers
expressed their dissatisfaction with the results, and CUF immediately
filed a court case challenging the results, but the case has never (six years
later at the time of this writing) been resolved. Then in November 1997,
eighteen CUF officials were arrested on charges of treason. They lan-
guished in prison for three years despite considerable pressure from
international organizations like Amnesty International until the next
round of national elections on October 29, 2000, after which the newly
elected president, CCM's Amani Karume, son of Abeid Karume, released
them. Once again, voting irregularities were widespread, and CCM pronounced the winner by another suspiciously slim margin. On the mainland, President Mkapa handily won his reelection bid by an even larger
margin than his first win (70 percent of the vote).[38] Tensions and political violence in the isles are on the rise, and on January 27, 2001, they
reached a breaking point when the government violently responded to a
CUF demonstration, killing between thirty and seventy people, injuring
many more, and sending some two thousand islanders to seek asylum
as refugees in neighboring Kenya.[39]

Each change in leadership necessitates concomitant changes in the
symbolic accessories of governance. Within weeks of the 1995 elections,
a front page announcement in the government English-medium newspaper *Daily News* (November 28, 1995) read:

Mwinyi Portraits to Be Removed
All portraits of former President Mwinyi should be removed from public offices forthwith.

A government statement issued through the Tanzania Information Services (TIS) in Dar es Salaam yesterday said that the decision had been taken following the recent top leadership changes.

The government said in its statement that portraits of the Third Phase President, Mr. Benjamin William Mkapa, were being prepared and would soon be distributed.

Similar transitions had marked the shift from the First to the Second Phase governments. After relinquishing the presidency in 1985, Nyerere still retained his position as CCM Party Chairman for five more years before also imparting that title to his successor Mwinyi.[40] The titles beneath his picture, which by decree adorned every place of business, were subsequently modified from Rais wa Tanzania (President of Tanzania) to Mwenyekiti wa Chama (Party Chairman) to Rais wa Kwanza (First President) and finally to the title of Baba wa Taifa (Father of the Nation) to reflect his shifts in status. During the Second Phase, Mwinyi's portraits were similarly required for display in every public place and business, but it was the norm to display that of Nyerere as well. In fact, the Ministry of Culture issued a directive to government offices instructing them on the proper accommodation of both Mwinyi's and Nyerere's portraits: Mwinyi to be placed facing a room's entrance and Nyerere placed above the entrance for view upon departure.[41] This closely parallels what Corrigan and Sayer describe as the "sanctification of secular power" in England (1985, 61) wherein portraiture was contrived to further enhance and visually extend the power of the monarchy. Perhaps signifying a more pronounced break with its past, policy following the 1995 elections has been to display only the official portrait of President Mkapa.

As the Third Phase government kicked into gear, people and poets actively responded to the changes in their political leadership. Poetry, like music, is a very popular and highly utilized expressive medium in Tanzania with a well-documented history (Harries 1962; Knappert 1979; Shariff 1988; Mulokozi and Sengo 1995; Biersteker 1996). It holds special importance for the expression of political opinions. Virtually every major newspaper has a page or section devoted to poetry. In *Mwananchi* (Citizen), the poetry page is entitled, *Wasemavyo Washairi* (What the poets say). Soon after the 1995 elections, it featured the following poem by Khamis "Mwanchina" Laki Pashua, a poet from Tanga (*Mwananchi,* November 6–9, 1995, 11), who eloquently and metaphorically argued for political, social, and religious diversity in the appointment of the Third Phase Cabinet ministers.[42]

Baraza la Mawaziri ("Cabinet Ministers")

Bismilah naanza, Fatuma nipe kalamu	In the name of God, I begin. Fatuma, give me a pen.
Ni muhali kujibanza, mwanangu fanya muhimu	It is too difficult to suppress, my dear, hurry up.
Mengi tumeshajifunza, haziridhishi takwimu	We have learned much, yet the process was unsatisfactory.
Watoke kila mkoa, awamu hii ya tatu	Let them come from every region in this Third Phase.

- - -

Tusisahau wa Tanga, Rukwa Morogoro pia	Let us not forget those from Tanga, Rukwa, Morogoro also.
Watoke hadi Shinyanga, kuwepo na mizania	Let them come from Shinyanga to be the scales of justice.
Msiicheze pachanga, walahi ninawaambia	Don't dance pachanga[43]—I swear to God I am telling you,
Watoke kila mkoa, awamu hii ya tatu	Let them come from every region in this Third Phase.

- - -

Tuepuke "ukabila," ambao umeibuka	Let us avoid tribalism which has suddenly appeared.
Hii tuacheni bila, ambayo imepevuka	Let us reject it without allowing it to ripen.
"Mechi" ya kutoka bila, daima huwezi cheka	A match ending in a draw will never leave you laughing.
Watoke kila mkoa, awamu hii ya tatu	Let them come from every region in this Third Phase.

- - -

Damu mpya tunataka, wakale wawe wachache	We want new blood. Let the old be few.
Chungu kinapozeeka, kwa upishi ujichunge	Take care when cooking with an aged pot.
Ni rahisi kuvunjika, nachakula ukimwage	It breaks easily and spills the food.
Watoke kila mkoa, awamu hii ya tatu	Let them come from every region in this Third Phase.

- - -

Waganda walifaulu, mundo huu kuuweka	Ugandans have succeeded in changing their system.
Wakaepusha kukuru, uchumi ukatanuka	They escaped turmoil and expanded their economy.
Hilo nimelidhukuru, ni vizuri kulitamka	This I remember. It is good to tell.
Watoke kila mkoa, awamu hii ya tatu	Let them come from every region in this Third Phase.

- - -

Ubaguzi wa kidini, imekuwa DONDA ndugu	Religious intolerance has become a perennial wound.
Kila dini chagueni, hata wa miti miungu	Choose any religion, even the worship of tree deities.
Msilete tafurani, mambo mizungu mizungu	Don't bring chaos, agitation.
Watoke kila mkoa, awamu hii ya tatu	Let them come from every region in this Third Phase.

- - -

Kila pambe wamesoma, kilichokuwa "kitanzi"	They have learned every pretty speech to use as a noose.

Wagogo kule Dodoma, Wazaramo wa Chamanzi	The Gogo in Dodoma and the Zaramo of Chamanzi
Kumbuka na Kwa Diboma, imeshafika "kurunzi"	Remember the town of Kwa Diboma now in the spotlight.
Watoke kila mkoa, awamu hii ya tatu	Let them come from every region in this Third Phase.
- - -	- - -
Beti nane kituoni, risala hii someni	Eighth verse indeed terminus. Read this speech.
Amini usiamini, yangu ilani makini	
Kama mwataka amani, ibaki petu nchini	Believe it or not, my warning is true.
Watoke kila mkoa, awamu hii ya tatu	If you [pl.] want peace to remain here in our country,
	Let them come from every region in this Third Phase.

In this poem, Mwanchina warned his readers that although much was learned from the election process, still the way in which it proceeded proved to be less than satisfactory, fraught with problems. Tribalism and religious prejudice both raised their ugly heads during the campaign period in a country which—when compared to its turbulent and turmoil-ridden neighbors of Kenya, Rwanda, Burundi, Democratic Republic of the Congo, Uganda, and Mozambique—has been surprisingly tolerant of diversity. Our poet also argued for new blood in the political hierarchy, claiming that "aged pots . . . break easily"—a thinly veiled plea for multiparty representation. His continual refrain, "Let them come from every region in this Third Phase," appealed for cross-regional (and multiethnic, multireligious, multiparty) representation on the Cabinet as an antidote to the troubles witnessed during the electoral process.

When he subsequently announced his Cabinet, President Mkapa apparently heeded the warning of Mwanchina and others: of twenty-three Ministers appointed, only seven had ever served on previous Cabinets, while the remaining sixteen were new to party politics. Newspaper headlines that followed these appointments remarked,[44]

- "Mkapa atoa mpya: Mawaziri wengi wa zamani watupwa" (Mkapa surprises: many old ministers are thrown out; from *Nipashe,* November 29, 1995, including a follow-up section showing faces of the old guard who were thrown out)
- "Katika kuunda timu yake Mkapa hakuangalia "makunyanzi": Amefuata rekodi bora, umri na elimu, asilimia 73 wapya, 27% tu ndio wa zamani" (In forming his team, Mkapa did not consider "wrinkles." He considered good record, age, education. 73 percent are new, while only 27 percent are from before; from *Cheche,* November 29–December 5, 1995. Here the reference to "wrinkles" is to the old guard.)
- "Baraza jipya la mawaziri: Vigogo wawekwa kando" (The new presidential cabinet: logs are placed aside; from *Mfanyakazi,* November 29,

1995. Again, "logs" here refers to the old guard of Tanzanian politicians, heavyweights.)

- "Sura mpya zatawala baraza jipya: Mkapa awaengua vigogo wa chama tawala" (The new faces leading the new cabinet: Mkapa skims off the logs of the ruling party; from *Mtanzania,* November 29, 1995)
- "Mkapa ateua mawaziri wake: Sura nyingi mpya; Lowassa, Kolimba, Malecela, Msuya watupwa; Kikwete Wizara ya Nje" (Mkapa chooses his ministers: many new faces; Lowassa, Kolimba, Malecela, Msuya are thrown out; Kikwete is Minister of Foreign Affairs; from *Majira,* November 29, 1995)[45]
- "Mrema amsifu Mkapa: Asema mirija ya walaji imekatwa; Lowassa na Nyanda mko wapi?; 'Lakini hatuwaungi mkono' " (Mrema praises Mkapa: says the straw feeding the corrupt has been cut; Lowassa and Nyanda where are you?; "But we still do not join hands with them"; from *Heko,* November 30, 1995. This was a significant statement from one of the primary opposition party leaders.)
- "Dar hails Mkapa clean team" (*Guardian,* November 30, 1995). The article read as follows: "A team of 'clean faces.' A team which 'will sing a new political song.' A team 'dedicated to fight corruption.' These are some of the upbeat descriptions of President Mkapa's new cabinet coming from Dar es Salaam residents yesterday. And just as people were happy to see the new faces making an entry into the upper strata of Tanzanian politics, so too were they glad to se [*sic*] the back of so many of the CCM's old guard, the aging politicians who many had thought were responsible for the country's parlous economic state. . . ."

And so began the Third Phase of Tanzania's existence as a nation. Six years later, we find that political liberalization and multipartyism have had perhaps their deepest impact on island–mainland relations. The enduring legacy of a hastily conceived and ratified union is a political terrain dotted with rhetorical mines that now more than ever before threaten to disintegrate the United Republic of Tanzania. Financial backing from Middle Eastern sources for the CUF party in Zanzibar, which voices heavy criticism of the union and embraces an openly pan-Islamic, pan-Arab orientation, when coupled with the January 2000 (Zanzibar) government pardon for the Omani sultan deposed during the 1964 revolution, elicit whispered rumors of Zanzibari secession and possible return of the sultan. In addition, there is renewed debate over the possibility of formally resurrecting Tanganyika via establishment of a Tanganyikan government. In the current two-government system, mainland affairs are overseen by the Union government, which was established to deal with Union issues (such as international relations and defense), whereas Zanzibar has its own internal government to attend to non-Union, domestic issues (such as education and immigration). Thus the possibility of a three-government system is on the table.

The emergence of the united Tanzanian state parallels in certain key respects the emergence of Swahili civilization. Land and sea are intertwined, foreign and local elements find convergence, but this time the polarized opposition straddles a scant twenty-four miles of water. The islands of Zanzibar and Pemba may have been the stronghold of Arab sultans, but they have also been centuries-old homes to scores of Africans of both coastal and inland origins. They are repeatedly counterpoised to the Tanganyikan mainland, whence authentic Tanzanian Africans are said to originate, yet they are centuries-old homes to political and economic migrants from Arabian Peninsular regions, who began arriving in large numbers both along the coast and inland certainly by the 1520s (Pouwels 1987, 40) if not earlier.[46] Zanzibar and Pemba also widely signify the ocean, especially ocean trade, through their island status and monopoly on sanctified images of Indian Ocean dhow traffic—images that accordingly downplay the islands' equally strong economic associations with land-produced cloves, peppers, and spices. The Tanganyikan mainland, for its part, widely signifies the land (despite a long and active coastline) and the continent more generally due to its production of land-based ivory, rhinoceros horn, coffee, and sisal—items that could not, however, be obtained without certain ocean-borne products like cloth, weapons, beads, and wire. The obvious remaining trade in people that has received but passing mention thus far contributes significantly to this equation. Plantation-owning Arabs (especially in Zanzibar, Pemba, and Pangani) are most closely aligned with slavery. The caravans that traded in slaves taken from inland African populations may have been bankrolled by Asian financiers and the fruits of slave labor enjoyed by many a Western interest, but in the ideological language surrounding East African slavery, the onus of responsibility and culpability falls squarely on Arab shoulders. The actual reality of slavery was of course far more variable and complex than this (see Glassman 1995, 79–98) colored by shades of patronage, clientelism, patriarchy, and claims of membership in Islam's universal brotherhood, but the discursive formation of "overseas Arab slave traders" versus "inland African slaves" nonetheless continues to resonate today with Swahili identity occupying a contested terrain between the two.[47]

Thus we find that the all-too-familiar refrain of Swahili ethnicity debates[48]—the political elaboration of "Arab" and "African" (and related elaboration of "Muslim" and "Christian")—has found new and renewed currency in multiparty Tanzania. Increasingly Arabized islands are locked in tandem with an increasingly Africanized mainland. However much people might argue to the contrary, the problem is not so much conflict between supposed "Arabs" and purported "Africans" or between Muslims and Christians, but the existence of pressures and forces that sustain, bolster, and invigorate this prejudicial polarizing discourse.

Tanga—A Coastal Crossroads

To most people who have ever set foot in Tanga, it appears a rather unimpressive stop on the journey between Mombasa and Dar es Salaam— a crowded bus stand where the honking of hand-held bicycle horns distinguishes home-made frozen popsicle vendors from the peanut sellers who rhythmically shake tin can rattles (map 2.3). One might never notice that the bus stand is located between Barabara ya 11 (Eleventh Street) and Barabara ya 12 (Twelfth Street) in an area called Ngamiani (the Place of Camels) which, quite contrary to other urban layouts in East Africa, is a numerical grid in the style of New York City. Ngamiani has at least two traditions to its name. An aged female singer/poetess named Bi Abidjani shared one tradition with me.[49] She described how there once was an area of Ngamiani at the far eastern end of Barabara ya 7 where one used to find a large, stone, wheat-grinding mill powered by camels.[50] Harnessed to the mill, a camel would circle from morning to night, providing the Ngamiani inhabitants with finely ground wheat flour. The second tradition holds that the rival dance clubs that characterized not only Tanga but most cities up and down the Swahili coast in their efforts to outdo each other competed potlatch-style in the amount of animals they would slaughter for a dance event. Were one side to slaughter a cow, the opposing club, to continue the rivalry, had to slaughter two. A particularly unforgettable series of competitive rounds concluded with the slaughter of a camel and because that secured a clearcut victory for its club, the name Ngamiani remains to memorialize the event.

Ngamiani, like most of present-day Tanga, was designed and constructed by the Germans after their destruction of the original mainland settlement. It begins at the railway that neatly cuts Tanga into two halves—the Swahili/African half (Ngamiani) and the Asian/expatriate half. A century later, the social boundaries still exist, albeit more porous than before. Now, although you still do not find expatriates living or commonly setting foot in Ngamiani, you do find Asians, and conversely you find Swahili and other Africans living and working on the Asian/expatriate side of the tracks.[51]

Ngamiani is composed of rows and rows of tightly packed, single-

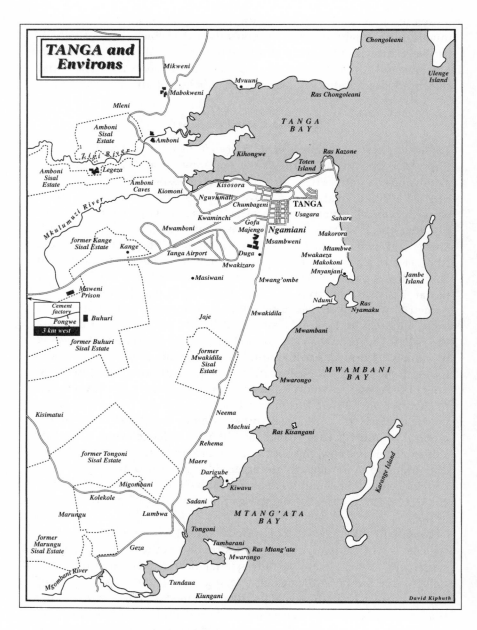

Map 2.3 Tanga and Environs. Courtesy of David Kiphuth.

story buildings with a few multistoried buildings. Most have rusty corrugated metal roofs, but many are thatched with dried palm leaf. This is the heart of Tanga. Barabara ya 1 (First Street) runs parallel to the railway tracks on its southern side. The streets continue to ascend in numerical value until Barabara ya 21 (the southern boundary of Ngamiani) and are grouped into neighborhoods or wards known as *mitaa* (sing. *mtaa*). As you walk around, you see vendors everywhere because nearly every household sells something, be it peeled and halved oranges, *kaimati* (Swahili-style sugar-frosted doughnuts), Turkish-style coffee, bottles of homemade pickled mango, peanuts, peanut brittle, or homemade popsicles called *askrimu* (from "ice cream"). Men can be seen pushing handheld carts collecting trash or bearing someone's burden for a fee (the closest equivalent to car rental Tanga has to offer). Bicycles are many. Children play soccer with homemade balls of cloth tied tightly with string. Elderly men play *dhumna* (dominoes) and *bao* (a now internationally famous game composed of a wooden board with a series of shallow holes into which beans are deposited and acquired according to a complex set of mathematical rules) while drinking coffee and arguing vociferously about politics. If it is a night without electrical power (an all-too-common occurrence), then kerosene lanterns and candles give Ngamiani a special glow and perspective. People gather around the *mishkaki* (grilled meat kebabs) and adjacent *chips* and *mayai* (french fries and scrambled eggs) vendors—a popular order being *mix*, a french-fry omelet. If there is electricity, then multiple musics waft and intermingle above the neighborhood: bands rehearsing, radios playing, *maulids* (long prayers recounting the birth and life of the Prophet Muhammad) being recited by children of local *madrasa* (Koranic schools), Sufi brotherhoods inducing trance through hypnotic *dhikri,* and wedding or initiation celebrations punctuating the night air with their distinctive rhythms and melodies. Some nights when distant drumbeats from an indeterminable direction are carried by an errant wind, I am told that they originate from gatherings of *wanga* (sing. *mwanga*)—mischievous female spirits whose social events—often cannibalistic festivities featuring dancing in the nude—hinge upon music-making. (These are the spirits blamed for causing you to sometimes wake up more exhausted than when you retired because they come in the dead of night to jump up and down on your body as you sleep—only one of their favorite pastimes.)

No description of Tanga would be complete without reference to Osale Utango, the Kenyan refugee whose flight from the Mau Mau rebellion (in which his brother purportedly played a significant role) brought him to Tanga in the early 1950s. Enticed by the availability of work on

Tanga's sisal plantations,[52] Osale found employment at the Amboni Company sisal plantation first as a sisal cutter, then at the sisal press (extracting the fiber from the leaves), and finally as an *uboi* (houseboy) for a wealthy Arab named Nassor Issa who owned a shop catering to the needs of Amboni's sisal workers. One day, so the story goes, upon seeing a large sum of money that Nassor Issa had set aside to deposit in the bank, Osale demanded an increase in his salary. An argument ensued during which Nassor pulled out a gun, but in the struggle he received a gunshot wound in the thigh. Osale fled unscathed, and a multiyear manhunt ensued. As a fugitive, he embarked upon a new career of robbing *wazungu* (expatriates) and distributing the wealth among poor peasants in the Tanga region—an East African Robin Hood. His exploits became famous, increasingly so as efforts by the British police to capture him continually failed.

Legends encircling Osale tell of how he would brashly warn expatriate farms of his imminent arrival. The police would be notified and lie in wait for him, yet through cunning and guile Osale would manage to enter the farm, tie up its inhabitants, seize all the money, jewelry, and arms he and his companion Paulo Hamisi (a Sambaa from the Usambara mountains) could carry, and escape without detection. His importance to Tanga lies in his having hidden for more than two years in the nearby Amboni caves, a series of as-yet-unexplored limestone caves roughly ten kilometers northwest of Tanga (see map 2.3). The details of his life that are remembered and recounted include his ownership of an Oris brand watch, his penchant for Enedu cigarettes, his thorough reading of the *Tanganyika Standard* every Sunday, and—with the exception of Paulo Hamisi—his avoidance of adults and preference for the company of children. Moreover, perhaps drawing on his Mau Mau experience, it is said that he required Paolo to take an oath promising never to kill, never to attack an African, a woman, or anyone poor, and to live a life of sexual abstinence.

In keeping with the general pattern of heroic legends, Osale's death has never been ascertained. Records at the Tanga Prison indicate that he was captured and detained but managed to escape after only a brief stay. It is said that the British colonial authorities, increasingly embarrassed by the situation, called for reinforcements from Kenya to come and aid in his arrest. Although it was well known that he lived in the caves, each time the police would attempt to penetrate the caves, he would move deeper within the maze of passageways and caverns and successfully elude capture. In the end, he was chased out of Tanga up into the Usambaras near Lushoto, where colonial authorities claimed to have shot him and summarily buried the body. Few Tanga residents believe it, however, arguing that as keen as the British were to capture him they would surely have made a public display of the body in Tanga to flaunt their success and warn others against similar transgressions. Thus rumor has it that the authorities killed someone they had mistaken for Osale and, rather than admit defeat, quickly buried the body and declared that they had gotten their man. Osale, in other words, lives on.

Tanga, a city rich in music and traditions, is made all the richer because of the many migrants like Osale who came to work on the surrounding plantations and contributed to the ensuing cultural mix. According to Ranger, Swahili urban culture was undermined in Tanga in part because of the economic demise following the 1888 German bombardment and in part due to the large number of immigrants that greatly outnumbered local Swahili (Ranger 1975, 39). Aristocratic lineages like those found in Lamu and Mombasa were unable to sustain their exclusivity in Tanga, where elite society included upcountry Christian clerks and civil servants—virtually anyone with wealth or education, irrespective of origin.

The Ngamiani grid used to contain ethnic neighborhoods whose boundaries were demarcated by musical performance (map 2.4). Between Ninth and Thirteenth Streets, a Nyamwezi group would perform Mkono wa Tembo (Elephant's Leg). Further down Thirteenth, one could see white-faced, feather-attired Manyema dancers hailing from the western edge of Tanganyika performing Kilua, while two rival Nyamwezi groups on the same block would vie for the largest audience with their Hiari ya Moyo (Heart's Desire) and Wingi Si Hoja (Abundance Is Not Necessary) *ngoma*. Kisonge (another Manyema *ngoma*) on Twelfth, Goma (a Digo *ngoma*) on Ninth, Gita (another Digo *ngoma*) on Eighteenth, Tukuranga, Katakata, and Kirumbizi (all coastal Swahili *ngoma*) on Fifteenth, and Tinge (another Swahili *ngoma*) on Sixteenth—these regular weekend events during the colonial period showcased Tanga's cosmopolitanism and cultural diversity.[53]

In the 1931 census, sixty-two ethnic groups were identified in Tanga Province and broken down into the two categories of "resident" or "immigrant." In Tanga District, the primary resident groups included (in order of numerical importance) Digo, Bondei, Segeju, Shambaa (Sambaa/Shambala), Zigua, Shirazi, and Swahili. The largest groups identified as "immigrant tribes" include Nyamwezi, Nyasa, Sukuma, Manyema, Fipa, Ha, Yao, and Makonde.[54] In that year, the resident population numbered 72,161, while the immigrant population numbered 32,289, constituting 30 percent of the district's population (table 2.1). Of the five districts in the province, Tanga and Pangani held the highest immigrant populations, a direct correlate of the higher concentration

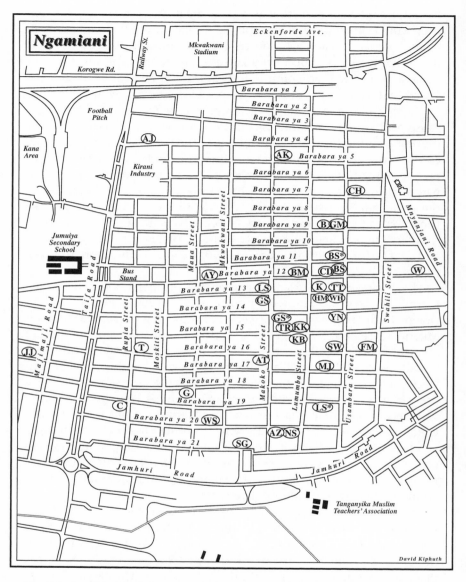

Map 2.4 Location of Musical Groups in the Ngamiani District. Courtesy of David Kiphuth.

Key

Name of Musical Group	Location	Abbreviation
Afro Taarab	Barabara 17 and Makoko St.	AT
Arab Young Club	Barabara 13 and Lumumba St.	AY
Arabia Kongo	Barabara 5 and Makoko St.	AK
Atomic Jazz Band	Barabara 4 and Moskiti St.	AJ
Azimio Musical Club	Barabara 20 and Makoko St.	AZ
Babloom Modern Taarab	Barabara 12 and Lumumba St.	BM
Bengwa Ngoma	Barabara 9 and between Lumumba and Usambara Sts.	B
Black Star Musical Club	Barabara 11 and Usambara St.	BS
Changani Ngoma	Barabara 7 and Usambara St.	CH
Chera Ngoma	Barabara 19 and Rupia St.	C
Freedom Modern Taarab	Barabara 16 and Swahili St.	FM
Gita Ngoma	Barabara 18 and Maua St.	G
Golden Star Taraab	Barabara 13, then 14, and Makoko St.	GS
Goma Ngoma	Barabara 9 and between Lumumba and Usambara Sts.	GM
Hiari ya Moyo Ngoma	Barabara 13 between Lumumba and Usambara Sts.	HM
Jamhuri Jazz Band	Barabara 17 and Maji Maji Rd.	JJ
KataKata Ngoma	Barabara 15 between Makoko and Lumumba Sts.	KK
Kilua Ngoma	Barabara 13 between Lumumba and Usambara Sts.	K
Kirumbizi Ngoma	Barabara 15 and Lumumba St.	KB
Lucky Star Musical Club	Barabara 13 and Makoko St., then 19 and Lumumba St.	LS
Moonlight Jazz Band	Barabara 17 and Lumumba St.	MJ
New Stars Band	Barabara 20 and Lumumba St.	NS
Shabaab Al-Watan	Barabara 16 and Usambara St.	SW
Super Gas Orchestre	Barabara 21 and Mkwakwani St.	SG
The Watangatanga Band	Barabara 12 and Mnyanjani Rd.	W
Tinge Ngoma	Barabara 16 and Rupia St.	T
Top Ten Taarab	Barabara 13 and Usambara St.	TT
Tukuranga Ngoma	Barabara 15 between Makoko and Lumumba Sts.	TR
White Star Taarab	Barabara 20 and Mkwakwani St.	WS
Wingi Si Hoja Ngoma	Barabara 13 between Lumumba and Usambara Sts.	WH
Young Novelty Musical Club	Barabara 14 and Usambara St.	YN

NOTE: When a musical group is included twice on the map, this indicates that it moved at some point in its history. The current, or most recent, location is identified with an asterisk by the group's abbreviation.

Table 2.1   Populations of Tanga Province by District: Residents versus Immigrants, 1931

	Tanga	Lushoto	Pangani	Handeni	Pare
Resident population	72,161	107,100	7,033	63,141	56,688
Immigrant population	32,289	4,677	10,833	789	1,223
Total district population	104,450	111,777	17,866	63,930	57,911
Percentage of immigrant population	30%	4%	60%	1%	2%

SOURCE: Adapted from Baker 1934, 108–9.

of plantations there. If we focus exclusively on the numbers of adult men, the differences become even more striking (table 2.2).

Nowadays, however, things have changed considerably. These same ethnic groups that used to draw upon each other for neighborhood companionship and support in times of need have dispersed throughout the district, making it now very difficult to pin down ethnically defined areas within Ngamiani. Ethnic enclaves still exist beyond the city center (for example the Makonde neighborhood of Magari Mabovu, or "Rotten Cars," the Pare neighborhood of Majani Mapana, or "Wide Leaves," and the large population of people from Pemba that dominate Makorora), but Ngamiani has become an urban melting pot housing an assorted population of people from different ethnic categories and economic positions.

Nyerere's policies of social unification are partly responsible for this. During the colonial period, British authorities passed the 1954 Societies Ordinance, "which required associations to seek government registration and obtain police permission before collecting subscriptions or holding public meetings" (Iliffe 1979, 553) as a move to monitor and tighten control over the growing nationalist movement. Originally designed to keep track of political associations, especially the many branches of TANU that were cropping up throughout the territory, the ordinance nevertheless forced associations of every variety to register and encouraged ethnic differentiation. Some of those registered in Tanga appear in table 2.3.

Table 2.2   Populations of Tanga Province by District: Adult Males, 1931

	Tanga	Lushoto	Pangani	Handeni	Pare
Resident adult male population	23,820	32,534	2,476	19,311	13,887
Immigrant adult male population	20,755	3,509	6,699	227	816
Adult male population for district	44,575	36,043	9,175	19,538	14,703
Percentage of immigrant adult men	47%	9%	73%	1%	5%

SOURCE: Adapted from Baker 1934, 108–9.

Table 2.3   A Sample of Registered Societies in Colonial Tanga, 1958–1960

Organization	Date of Registration	Objectives
Wapare Asili Union	6/26/58	Assistance with education, agriculture, trade, and in crisis times for all Wapare
Bondei Tanga Branch of the Bondei Cultural Union	5/26/59	A society formed in 1958 with 65 members, whose membership was restricted to Bondei, Shambaa, and Zigua
Up-Country Africans Organization	8/20/59	"To cement spirit of unity among us for if we do not hang together we shall hang separately and more-over we are far away from our mother-lands . . . being far away from our mother-lands we experi-ence a lot of difficulties such as being sick, work-less, and some other more uncountable difficulties . . . It is a true fact that a lot of up-country Afri-cans are living in these coastal areas and some of whom have completely settled and married here, now it often happens that when these poor fellows die, and there being no other relation by blood, some other men take possession of their properties with no preferential right of inheritance." To safe-guard and protect its members' properties and rights, and to help them in times of need.
Young Nyamwezi Sukuma Union	n.d.	[no information]
Wanyakyusa Union, Tanga	9/17/59	Membership restricted to Wanyakyusa only above 16; present membership: total of 29 members on 14th St.; its stated goals included providing members with relief in sickness or death, and repatriation of the destitute.
Chama cha Ukoo wa Wazigua	6/3/60	To increase unity/interaction of Wazigua, help in crisis such as sickness or death, enhance tradition by holding matches and *ngoma,* as at home.
Mahenge wa Ulanga Union, Tanga Province	applied 1/8/60	Membership limited to members of the Pogoro tribes (Mbimsa, Ndamba, Ngindo).
Warangi Union	6/4/60	[no information]
Sikh Union, Tanga	applied 7/26/60	To "promote social, moral, intellectual and physical ad-vancement of members . . . [and to] further the in-terests of the Sikh Community."
Wamakonde Association of Tanganyika, Tanga Pro-vince	4/21/60	[no information]

SOURCE: Tanzania National Archives, Tanga Region, accession 304, file no. A6/68 vol. 1, "Registration of Societies, Tanga District."

Yet immediately after independence in 1961, Nyerere announced that any association based on tribal affiliation would be refused registration on the grounds that it promoted tribal interests over national interests. Thus one finds in government files of "Registered Societies" notes regarding the refusal of applications from various groups on these grounds. The would-be Abagusii Sawyers Union, for example, which sought to "create social unity and better understanding between all tribes of South Nyanza" and "give advice to members regarding cutting and selling timber to increase wealth," was deemed unlawful and denied registration. The Union fought the denial, arguing,

> It is now well over 15 years since we Abagusii have all been known as the only African timber operators in all country [sic]. It would be hard to deny the fact today that the hard labor of our people has not also played a part in the development of this country. Our aim to register the Union was not based on trying to promote our tribal interest as the letter of refusal claims. This was a way to promote a close understanding among all different individuals whose trade in this Republic is timber sales. And on the other hand it could still give us a new respect in the eyes of our multiracial customers as well as the good government of this beloved land.[55]

The application for registration was denied all the same.

In another case, a group naming itself the Zanzibar Association, Tanga Branch applied for registration, stating that its objective was to "enhance unity of people from Pemba and Zanzibar in Tanga." The official response, however, was,

> As you are already aware of all the political events in our country, this idea at this stage looks quite out of date and contradicts the whole main objective and thesis of the aims and objectives of society. There is no more Tanganyika nor Zanzibar and Pemba as an autonomous Regime but a United Republic of Tanganyika and Zanzibar. Thus the aims and objectives have been achieved. Hence Zanzibaris living in Tanganyika must cease to be parochial and have to develop a great sense of belonging to the United Republic of Tanganyika and Zanzibar. TANU is capable of looking after and catering for the interest and welfare of all. Thus they should: acquire TANU membership and demonstrate their confidence in the Party and their support in the Union. Our aim is unity not factionalism. The same would apply to Tanganyikans living in Zanzibar and Pemba who would be requested to join the Afro-Shirazi Party for the same purpose.[56]

We can see in these cases how government policy worked to thwart and undermine the development of ethnic, regional, or religious affiliations that were considered dangerous to a nationalist project premised upon inclusivity. In Julius Nyerere's vision, a nation should strive to minimize social distinctions in favor of the common good. Although his vision ultimately proved too utopian to be fully realized in practice, it nevertheless laid some important cornerstones that have successfully stemmed the tendencies toward factionalism and fragmentation that typify Tanzania's neighboring states.

Wasemavyo Waswahili . . . (As the Swahili say . . .)

Tanga. Over the course of its history, its residents interacted and exchanged goods with traders from many distant ports, presented sublime oranges to welcome a Portuguese explorer, cultivated African roots by abandoning a socially and physically distanced island, and paid a heavy price for rejecting German authority. Tanga. Once a colonial administrative center, it housed the first state school for Africans and donated its name to an emerging state. Finally, Tanga—home to migrants from inland and overseas, it was a sanctuary for revolutionaries and a local Robin Hood, and birthplace of dance societies that spread music and politics to every corner of the territory, disseminating nationalist and anticolonial sentiment, and coalescing into a successful ruling party.

Because it constitutes a key coastal Swahili site, we can ask to what extent Tanga and Swahili culture more generally have contributed to the emergence of the Tanzanian state. The first and most obvious contribution is the Swahili language. More will be said later about language policy in Tanzania, but suffice it to say that the growth of nationalist sentiment was greatly facilitated by the existence of a language bridging a highly diverse ethnoscape.[57] Other common markers of ethnicity, such as dress, architecture, musical performance, and popular wisdom, however, have also been subsumed within a national process of Swahilization. Local discourse throughout the country on the streets, in the newspapers, and on the radio is peppered with Swahili proverbs (*methali*) often introduced by the phrase, "Wasemavyo waswahili . . ." ("As the Swahili say . . ."), such as "Anayechimba kisima, atatumbukia mwenyewe" ("He who digs a well will fall in it himself."), or "Nyota njema huonekana alfajiri" ("A lucky star can be seen at dawn."). Another forum for circulating *methali* are *kanga:* two-piece, colorful cloths with Swahili proverbial wisdom printed on them worn by and associated with Swahili coastal women.[58] *Kanga* use has spread so thoroughly throughout the country that a March 1993 "In Search of a National Dress" event voted an outfit composed of *kanga*s as the national dress.[59] Swahili male attire has similarly spread far and wide. The text accompanying the nineteenth-century picture of an inland ruler dressed in a long, white Swahili *kanzu* and bearing an Omani dagger explains, "Kingo of Morogoro, one of the trading warlords of the Mrima hinterland. Arab-inspired coastal fashions were considered a mark of prestige" (Glassman 1995, 49). Finally, the use of "Swahili" as a political term of reference further speaks to the Swahilization of the national agenda. Julius Nyerere, who hailed from the Zanaki ethnic group on the western edge of Tanzania, was quoted as announcing, "Mimi ni Mswahili" ("I am a Swahili") and even heard using Arabic expressions like "Wallahi!" which in this context denotes coastal Swahili culture. As summed up by one scholar, "[T]he process of Swahilization has played, and is playing, a vital role in the development of national consciousness in Tanzania" (Salim 1985, 219).

In the realm of musical performance, Geiger's (1997) research on female *ngoma* societies in Dar es Salaam and Ranger's work on Beni societies illustrate that although *ngoma* are often ethnically marked,[60] they did not always remain so. Beni as a social movement began from coastal points of origin yet attracted members from and developed branches in all regions within Tanganyika and beyond. Similarly, women's *ngoma* societies in Dar es Salaam diversified quickly; as Bibi Titi Mohamed, a famous *ngoma* singer and political activist in Dar es Salaam, described, "The *ngoma* groups . . . united people and included people from different tribes, Wanyamwezi and whoever and whoever. . . . You couldn't restrict. Anyone with interest could join, since we all speak Swahili" (Geiger 1997, 51). Reflecting their diverse populations, Dar es Salaam and Tanga *ngoma* societies incorporated people from a variety of ethnic backgrounds and created communal ties that nicely paralleled government objectives. In their inclusivity, then, *ngoma* associations exemplified a key Swahili trait: the continual accommodation of foreign elements.

Tanga provides ample evidence of the process of Swahilization. Mayor Salim Kassim Salim, now in his late fifties, was born and raised in Tanga and resettled there after having worked in Kenya as an aviation engineer for many years. He told me that he remembered as a child seeing different ethnic groups perform their *ngoma* in their areas of Ngamiani (which at that time only extended to Fourteenth Street).[61] But over time, he said, these performances slowly died out, and his recollections are of people mixing and sharing an increasingly common lifestyle, of children from every background playing together in the streets and attending school together, and of ethnicity losing the importance it had accrued during the colonial period when there were differential taxes, educational systems, food allowances, and other differential privileges and penalties.[62] If anything, said Mr. Kassim, the people of Tanga united as *watoto wa mjini,* or "children of the city" and looked down on their rural mountain neighbors, the Wasambaa. (We were discussing the increasing ethnicization of politics in the months prior to the October 1995 elections. His point was that the process of polarizing ethnic sentiment was something that had lain dormant in Tanzania since the end of colonialism.)

Swahilization is thus in many ways linked to the process of hybridization—an understandable connection given the fact that Swahili culture has always been predicated on the incorporation of diverse elements. More significant for our purposes here, however, it is tied in subtle, not always explicit, ways to the process of nation-state formation. And from women's *ngoma* to Beni to *taarab,* Swahili musical performance continues to act as an uninterrupted *ostinato* to both processes.

3

OF GINGER ALE AND ORANGE SODA

Sijaona manuwari ikipita barabarani.

I've yet to see a man-o'-war pass in the streets.
—Msanja song, Tanga

[T]he passionate spirit of rivalry and competition prevailing so openly throughout coastal society [is] a part of the coastal character and of the structure of the society itself. It shows itself in traditional dances, in modern football teams and dance bands, in relations between different quarters of villages, in some agricultural customs, in political parties, and often enough in matters of religion.
—Hasani bin Ismael, from the introduction to *The Medicine Man: "Swifa ya Nguvumali"*

On October 6, 1956, Britain's Princess Margaret arrived in Tanga for an overnight visit—one stop on a royal tour of British East Africa that culminated with the laying of the cornerstone for the new provincial hospital in Dar es Salaam. As her plane landed on the humble runway at Tanga Airport, a crowd of women in identical green and yellow uniforms sang their welcome to an accompaniment of drums and syncopated rhythms beaten on cow horns with wooden sticks. The historical significance of a royal visit was forever etched into local memory—less so by the actual visit than by its subsequent reenactment by Swahili women's dance societies in Tanga and elsewhere along the coast. Dance versions of the event (*kwini,* derived from "queen"—although she was but a princess) together with the procession of a fabricated man-o'-war (*manuwari*) through the streets of Tanga marked the climax of a furious rivalry that engrossed this coastal city for nearly a decade. What better signifiers of colonial experience than these—iconic monarchs and maritime might? Kanada and Fanta, the two warring women's dance societies in Tanga, enmeshed in an intense conflict over prestige, a historic display of one-up(wo)manship, offer yet another cultural illustration of anthropology's theoretical child: the potlatch. Taking their names from sister rival clubs in Kenya, who in turn found inspiration in the recently introduced soda beverages Canada Dry and Fanta Orange,[1] these women's societies formed a 1950s incarnation of a centuries-old pattern of competitive dualism along the Swahili Coast.

Kanada and Fanta performed *ngoma,* musical events encompassing music, dance, song, characteristic instrumentation, and a characteristic rhythm.[2] In the current mapping of Tanzanian musical performance, *ngoma* is juxtaposed most commonly with *dansi* ("dance" music, or heavily Zairean-influenced urban popular music), *taarab* (sung Swahili poetry), and *kwaya* ("choir" music associated primarily but not exclusively with church groups). According to local epistemologies, each of these genres subdivides into at least two significant categories. Within the rubric of *ngoma,* countless varieties are distinguished on the basis of ethnicity (e.g., *ngoma ya Wasambaa, ngoma ya Wadigo,* that is, Sambaa and Digo *ngoma*), region (e.g., *ngoma za Morogoro, ngoma za Tabora*); gender (*ngoma za wanawake,* "women," and *ngoma za wanaume,* "men"); and function (e.g., *ngoma za harusi,* "wedding dances," *ngoma ya shetani,* "spirit dances" performed in the context of spirit possession rites, and *ngoma ya daku* to wake slumbering Muslims for a midnight meal [*daku*] before Ramadan fasting begins anew). *Dansi,* the music that fills urban nightclubs and bars, is undifferentiated by region, being a pan-urban phenomenon, but is differentiated according to *mtindo* (sing.; pl. *mitindo*), or "style, a trademark that describes the music and characteristic performance of a band, as well as the dance associated with it" (Graebner 1994b, 359). Each band attempts to establish its own *mtindo,* and the extent to which it succeeds directly relates to its overall popularity.

In addition to *ngoma* and *dansi,* there is *taarab,* which subdivides into linguistic and regional categories. Unless specifically earmarked as *taarab ya kiarabu,* which is sung in Arabic, *taarab* constitutes sung Swahili poetry. (There are the inevitable exceptions. I have found a few examples of *taarab* sung in Kidigo and Kihaya.) Each major *taarab* center (Zanzibar, Mombasa, Tanga, Dar es Salaam) has a particular style (identified as "*taarab ya . . . ,*" e.g., *taarab ya Mombasa*). Some musicians describe a twofold division of "classical" versus "modern" *taarab:* the former, found primarily in Zanzibar and Dar es Salaam, exhibits large, thirty- to forty-piece clubs in the style of Egyptian film orchestras as compared to the "modern" clubs of Tanga, which rarely include more than ten or twelve members and whose heavily amplified sound reflects more Indian, Cuban, and Western musical influences.

Then there is *kwaya* (from the English "choir"), the musical consequence of Christian evangelism and African churches that traces its roots
to European choir music. *Kwaya* has since split into two very distinct
styles: sacred and secular. Sacred *kwaya* continues as an integral component of church services throughout the country, while secular *kwaya*, an
invention of government musicians,[3] disseminates political themes and
rhetoric during state-organized events. Finally, there are a variety of youth
musics that include Swahili rap, Swahili reggae, and a genre that emerged
during the early 1990s in Dar es Salaam called *mchiriku*. Described by
some as "protest music" and by others as *muziki ya wahuni* ("music of
hooligans"), *mchiriku* is performed by urban youths who employ a rudi-
mentary assortment of often self-made instruments to accompany their
songs about politics, poverty, abandonment, and life in the city.

Thus, the musical landscape Tanzania offers is as rich and diverse as
the population that lives within its colonially conceived borders. Musical forms are distinguished by numerous factors—region, ethnicity, gender, class, urban/rural settings, religion, performance context, and performance style being the predominant ones. In my research, I sought
to document the range of musical performance of the city of Tanga and
the nation as a whole more generally. Toward that end, I collected data
not only on the types of performance, but the contexts in which they
are performed, for what purposes, who performs them, how they are
performed (performance practice), for whom, and the meanings attributed to and constructed through the act of performance. In this chapter,
I will map out a part of this musical terrain through an analysis of three
genres: *ngoma, dansi,* and *taarab.*[4] The chapter is accordingly divided into
three sections. Each one is devoted to a genre and outlines its history,
describes current performance practice, and relates its history and practice to the active construction of social and political realities. Because
the anthropologist is never an invisible or inaudible entity in the social
reality under scrutiny, my own shifting identity as ethnographer, musician, and town resident receives some limited attention here as well.

Royal Visits and Honored Guests: *Ngoma* Performance

In the 1950s, Tanganyika and Zanzibar prospered. The war and its rav-
ages were receding from memory, a process aided by an economy on
the rise. Tanga Region in particular thrived because it produced the bulk
of Tanganyika's favored export crop, sisal (see Sabea 2000). During this
period, Tanganyikan sisal commanded both a high price and a near
monopoly of the world market. In 1956, Tanganyika produced a total
of 185,762 tons (Hitchcock 1959, 7), and production peaked in 1960–

Table 3.1 Estimated Marketed Production, Annual Basis, Thousand Metric Tons, 1962–1972

Crop/Product	1960–62	1970–72	Increase or Decrease, Percentage 1970–72 over 1960–62
Sisal	208.9	180.0	−13.8
Cotton lint	34.5	73.8	+113.9
Clean coffee	24.4	49.0	+100.8
Cashew nuts	46.5	123.5	+165.4
Tea	4.2	10.6	+152.4
Tobacco	2.2	12.4	+463.6
Pyrethrum	1.7	3.4	+100.0
Groundnuts	16.5	3.4	−79.4
Other oilseeds*	37.3	25.8	−39.8

SOURCE: Aldington 1975, 59.
*Sesame, Castor and Sunflower.

62 at 208,900 tons, sold at the price of 1,417 shillings per metric ton (Aldington 1975, 59, 63). The northern railway line ending in Tanga was built to transport sisal. Cotton and coffee, the other primary export crops, came nowhere close to the scale of export attained by sisal: total production figures for 1960–62 were 34,500 and 24,400 tons respectively (Aldington 1975, 59). The higher prices they commanded, however, narrowed the difference in generated income, as illustrated in tables 3.1 and 3.2. A decade later, competition from synthetic fibers, among other problems, would result in a declining demand for sisal— a contrast to the growth to be experienced in both the cotton and coffee sectors. The decline of sisal would hold severe consequences for Tanga,

Table 3.2 Export Prices of Major Agricultural Commodities, Shillings per Metric Ton, 1962–1972

Commodity	1960–62	1970–72	Index (1960–62 = 100)
Sisal (fibre and tow)	1,417	888	63
Cotton lint	4,482	4,161	93
Clean coffee*	5,400	6,474	120
Cashew nuts	938	1,355	144
Tea	7,887	6,233	79
Tobacco**	3,182	3,182	100

SOURCE: Aldington 1975, 63.
* This is a weighted average of sales of mild and hard *arabica* and *robusta* coffees.
** This is a weighted average of flue- and fire-cured tobaccos.

bringing it to the brink of economic collapse, with repercussions even into the present. But in the late 1950s, that was a still unknown, unforeseeable future.

It was during the years of plenty that Princess Margaret came to visit. Across the channel, Zanzibar too was experiencing a period of growth, its clove production not yet seriously challenged by the soon-to-dominate Indonesian industry, so the entire East African Protectorate had much to celebrate. The economic climate enabled the expenditure of exorbitant amounts of resources on the acquisition of prestige through *ngoma* activities.

Competitive Dance Societies and Competing Social Claims

By the 1950s, the rage for women's Lelemama *ngoma* had already swept through the coastal region, having peaked in the interwar years (Strobel 1979), and men's Beni *ngoma* had firmly established itself throughout the Protectorate having spread westwards from coastal Swahili points of origin (Ranger 1975). The fascination in these *ngoma* with uniforms, brass instruments (in Beni), ships, railway, royalty, and colonial military ranking was comfortably interpreted by colonial authorities as adaptation to absolute colonial power—"proof" that their attempts to foster "civilization" among local populations were succeeding.[5] In fact, however, coastal musical performance predating the colonial era adhered to an ideology of exploiting difference wherever difference could be found. As explained by Ranger,

> Coastal dance associations had always been sensitive to the possibility of dramatizing divisions and contestations in dance. Thus in 1824, at Pongwe town, Lieutenant Reitz saw a dance expressing the rivalry of the Mazrui family of Mombasa and the Sultan of Zanzibar; in 1861 in Magugu village von der Decken saw a dance combat between the "French" and the "English" factions. Now in the 1890s there was a search for the right rival to balance Kingi. Kingi came to be thought of as representative of King Edward of England. In Malindi it was balanced by Sultani. In Mombasa it was first countered by the Kilungu band. . . . Then a satisfying dichotomy was found.
>
> The new rival to Kingi was named from the one observable division among the British of Mombasa—the division between English and Scots. . . . The division between English and Scots in Mombasa may not have been so sharp as that ancient hostility had been in other colonial times and places. But it was good enough for the rivals of Kingi. By at least 1910 the great dance rivalry of Mombasa was the competition between Kingi and Scotchi. Every weekend the trumpeters of Kingi confronted the bag-pipers of the Scotchi in a contestation that was as new as colonialism and as old as Swahili urban culture. (Ranger 1975, 24–25)

And this brings us back to the story of queens and ships, of ginger ale and orange soda. Soda beverages could be opposed in the same manner as colonial regimes and provide rhetorical fuel for contestation via *ngoma* performance. Anything dichotomous or contradictory could be appropriated for translation into local musical practice. Kanada and Fanta, active in Tanga in the 1950s after the demise of Lelemama, were women's dance societies (*chama* sing., *vyama* pl.) dancing Ngoma ya Ndani (inside dance). This *ngoma* drew its name from its performance practice, namely, having to dance indoors away from male view because of the erotic and sensual dance moves that characterize the style. It was and continues to be performed in the context of weddings and female initiation ceremonies. Male drummers who provide the necessary instrumental accompaniment are the only men permitted at a performance. Yet over the course of my research, male friends of mine would admit to having surreptitiously peered at Ngoma ya Ndani through not-entirely-covered windows or over neighboring walls as children. What they would see both then and now would be a circle of women moving in a clockwise rotation—each woman facing the back of the woman ahead of her—around drummers seated in the circle's center. The general dance movement—a slow, sensual rotation of the hips and pelvis called *kukata kiuno*—is performed in synchronization to the slow 6/8 pulse of the drums—a rhythm called *kumbwaya*. Performers agree that the dance mimics sexual intercourse and constitutes practice sessions for women young and old to develop or display their personal skills while demonstrating the art of love-making to the bride-to-be. Kanada and Fanta each registered roughly thirty *wanachama* (members), some of whom variously described the *raison d'être* of female *ngoma* to me thus: *enzi za bibi zetu* (our grandmothers' legacy), *raha ya moyoni* (happiness of the heart), *sio kukaa na mawazo tu* (to avoid sitting only with worries), *kazi zetu ni kutungana* (our work is to compose songs about or against each other).[6]

Piecing together the story from its many variants, I was told by former members of Fanta that it was through their organizational skill and political clout that Princess Margaret visited Tanga and, very importantly, that she did so by plane. When her plane set down at the Tanga airport, Fanta was there to greet her in uniform and in song. One might question the self-ascribed role of Fanta in this royal visit, but it resonates loudly in the minds of those who claim the honor and prestige such a coup would have conferred. To the women of Fanta, therefore, the honor of having brought a real British "queen" to Tanga by plane translated into a decisive victory over their opponents Kanada.[7]

This perspective is disputed by former members of Kanada, not in detail but in the claim of a final Fanta victory. No one denies that Her Royal Highness came to Tanga, and Kanada are even willing to concede Fanta a role in the affair, but they claim final victory for having set

Figure 3.1 *H.M.S. 1st Canada Dry Tanga,* c. 1958. Photo supplied by Sharuu Majura; photographer unknown.

the town's population agog at seeing an enormous man-o'-war parade through the streets of Ngamiani and neighboring Makorora. In fact, it was a seven-ton Bedford lorry elaborately decorated as a man-o'-war float bearing Kanada members in matching uniform singing their own praises and deriding Fanta members for their numerous faults (the primary one, of course, being membership in the wrong group). One member of Kanada produced a picture of the famous man-o'-war to dismiss any doubts I may have been harboring (reproduced here). It shows an impressive "ship" cruising a typical street in Ngamiani lined by thatched-roof dwellings, its bow adorned on both sides with the painted title: *H.M.S. 1ST CANADA DRY TANGA.* Although the year of its passage is disputed, 1958 is the year most often cited. Parades of fabricated man-o'-wars and steamships had already been introduced by *ngoma* associations in Zanzibar and Mombasa (Ranger 1975, 23, 34; Farrell 1980, 74, 76, 80) and thus were not new to the region, but this was nevertheless a new sight to the somewhat marginalized city of Tanga. Perhaps my random sample population represented more Kanada aficionados than Fanta, but people who purportedly stood outside of the competition (although in a city as closely knit as Tanga, links are easily traced between most individuals, creating *de facto* alliances with one *chama* or the other) pronounced Kanada the victor over Fanta. Setting aside the determination of victor versus vanquished, the visit nonetheless reverberated throughout local musical practice for years to follow.[8]

Disputing Social Status through Song

The 1950s rivalry between Kanada and Fanta constitutes yet another chapter in an ongoing story of rival dance societies well documented by other scholars.[9] The pattern revolves around *vyama,* whose membership roughly corresponded to different halves (moieties) or neighborhoods within a town whose songs posited inter-*chama* differences as ones not merely of geography but of ancestry and social status: long-established residents versus relative newcomers. Each society drew its membership from a wide social spectrum, and yet "the songs exchanged by the clubs exploited long-standing contrasts in social rank, opposing people of 'ancestry' to those without, natives to newcomers, 'people of the coast' to 'people of the hinterland,' and so on" (Farrell 1980, 15; see also Fair 1994, 270). *Vyama* would vie for opportunities to perform at weddings, where they would insult and deride their rival group through song. With each event, the conspicuous consumption ante would be raised one notch: if a goat had been slaughtered at an event associated with one *chama,* two goats or a cow would be the requisite response at the rival *chama*'s next event (Bakari 1981, 84).

Dance societies served and continue to serve as mutual aid societies for club members contributing labor to the work and tasks associated with weddings and loans of *chama*-owned cooking pots and utensils. Song and dance make the mountainous preparations required for a proper Swahili wedding less onerous, as do the many extra hands. Lavish displays of extravagant amounts of food and luxurious clothing, however, also provide opportunities to accumulate and enhance the prestige of the *chama* and its members. They often work in cooperation with secret and not-so-secret women's societies that perform specialized dances at wedding celebrations and, in some groups like the Bondei and Makonde, *unyago* (female initiation) and *jando* (male initiation) ceremonies. At such functions, women's *ngoma* societies overlap with *makungwi* (sing. *kungwi*) a.k.a. *masomo* (sing. *somo,* "instructress")—women responsible for preparing and guiding the bride, groom and/or initiates through marriage and puberty respectively.

The main Beni rivalry in Tanganyika—Marini versus Arinoti—originated in Tanga as a variation on the preexisting Dar-i-Sudi and Dar-i-Gubi rivalry (Ranger 1975, 37). Ranger argues that in Tanga, dance associations articulated their differences not on the basis of neighborhood (as was the typical coastal pattern elsewhere) but of social status:

> In Tanga, where Swahili urban culture was much less secure, the *Marini* at first claimed a monopoly upon it. But even this did not last for very long. Soon the *Marini* became the society of the élite, the educated, the smart—no matter what their origin. By 1914 Christian clerks from upcountry and Ngoni *askaris* [soldiers] shared the leadership of *Marini* with young Swahili of good family. *Arinoti* remained essentially the

society of the unskilled labour migrant, 'the unclean ones,' even though it had its own quota of literate men with bureaucratic skills. (Ranger 1975, 40)

A relic of communal memory, Beni was no longer performed in Tanga at the time of the Kanada-Fanta rivalry. But interestingly enough, Kanada and Fanta manipulate neighborhood distinctions for their membership, not restricting membership in terms of ethnic identity. This was an unusual policy. Ngamiani constituted a very fragmented social space—its enumerated continuity notwithstanding. As described in the last chapter, streets originally were identified with specific immigrant communities and the public weekend performances of their respective *ngoma*.[10] Ngamiani is conceptualized and officially demarcated into three sections: Northern Ngamiani (Ngamiani Kaskazini), Central Ngamiani (Ngamiani Kati), and Southern Ngamiani (Ngamiani Kusini). Kanada drew its members from Central Ngamiani (Streets 8–14), while Fanta drew its members from Southern Ngamiani (Streets 15–21). The groups may have constructed each other through their songs on the basis of ancestry, rank, and status, but in reality each *chama* represented a broad social spectrum, in relation not only to ethnicity, but to the socio-economic diversity necessary for the lavish displays so integral to *ngoma* practice. Not long after the passage of the famous *manuwari*, Kanada and Fanta—like Beni—died out, eclipsed by the rise of another *ngoma* sensation: the Msanja *ngoma*. However, the newness of its dance, rhythm, and songs were not matched by newness in membership. The same networks of affiliation that had supported Kanada and Fanta reconstituted themselves into Scouti (former Kanada members) and Kenya (former Fanta members). As Farrell (1980) found for *ngoma* competitions in Kenya, the same lines of affiliation were exploited time and again in the construction of "new" *vyama* and the performance of new *ngoma*.

Some other features common to *ngoma* performance—whichever *ngoma*, whichever society—emerge from both textual and musical analysis. For one thing, *ngoma* songs, like *taarab* songs (as will be shown) and like the meaning-laden sayings printed on the *kanga* worn by coastal women, draw on a long tradition of subtlety in language. Heavily saturated in metaphor and double entendre, *ngoma* song lyrics express a Swahili predilection and talent for verbal ingenuity. According to one scholar, such ambiguity serves the necessary purpose of veiling instructive and admonitory messages without upsetting local social relations.

> Linguistic sophistication is no perquisite of wealth or aristocracy. The use of language is often most consciously subtle and playful among the outwardly simple people who live in the villages, where society is intimate and people are even more concerned than in town society with each other's characters and business—things they could not avoid if they would. (Lienhardt 1968, 4)

The following examples illustrate the use of metaphor in *ngoma* songs.

Msanja Song, Tanga

Kwa mafuta, mimi natumia ya uto
Ukitaka ya uzuri, utakuja chapwa na
   fimbo
Fimbo—"fimbo spesheli"
Bakora ya babu, eeh—"bakora spesheli"
Kijaluba cha babu jinga—"kijaluba
   spesheli"
Mkwaju wa babu, eeh—"mkwaju
   spesheli"

For body oil, I use low-grade coconut
   oil.
If you desire better quality, you will be
   hit with a stick.
A stick—a special stick,
Grandfather's cane—a special cane,
The idiot's tobacco tin—a special
   tobacco tin,
Grandfather's tamarind paddle—
   a special paddle.

In the above Msanja song, the singer offers women one route out of poverty: prostitution. For the woman desirous of a better life (exemplified by high-quality body oils), being "hit" by the metaphorical stick, cane, tobacco tin, or paddle of undesirable men (old men or idiots) constitutes one strategy for material advancement. In the following song, members of Gita Musical Club, a mixed-gender Digo dance society in Tanga (figure 3.2), deride their rival society, Chera Musical Club, by comparing it to a donkey. Some event must have accorded Chera a public success (the metaphorical "horns"). Gita, however, points out that Chera's success is but a facade for inherent, long-term failure and moreover equates itself with a patient and resourceful farmer who is sure to succeed in the long run (track 6 on the accompanying CD).

Punda wa Tanga ("Donkey of Tanga")
Mwinshehe Zongo, Gita Musical Club, Tanga

Punda wa Tanga
Mwaka uno waringa kuota pembe
Na pembe nzakubandika

- - -

Mkulima mwenye moyo
Akikosa mwaka huno anangoja mwakani
Na jembe halitupi mtu

- - -

Larawarawa goma laingia mkongwe
Larawarawa Gita laingia mkongwe naja

- - -

Chorus
Hazina uaminifu
Zitaanguka njiani
Nasema punda wa Tanga

Donkey of Tanga,
You are proud of having grown horns
   this year,
While the horns are artificial.
- - -
A determined farmer,
If he suffers loss this year, he waits for
   the next year.
A hoe will not let one down.
- - -
With a slow motion the big dance is
   coming (to you), old man.
With a slow motion Gita is coming, old
   man, I am coming.
- - -

They are not reliable;
They will fall along the way,
I am telling you, Donkey of Tanga.

Figure 3.2 Mwinshehe Zongo of Gita Musical Club performing for an airport reception to welcome Prime Minister Rashid Kawawa (wearing the hat and military uniform, immediately to the right of Mwinshehe Zongo), date unknown. Photographer unknown.

A final common feature relates to rhythm. Many *ngoma* rhythms feature triple meter—either a slow 6/8 called *kumbwaya* or a fast 6/8 called *chakacha*. Other rhythms found in *ngoma* practice share the name of the *ngoma* with which they are associated, for instance, Goma and Vugo (a slow 12/8 rhythm). The deceptive simplicity of the basic triple beat nonetheless allows for inexhaustible variations, each of which can spawn a new *ngoma* style. Costumes add another layer of signification, although along the coastal strip local *ngoma* place less emphasis on this element of performance than do those of other regions.

Table 3.3 Coastal Swahili Dichotomies

Sheria/sunna (Islamic Law)	*Mila* (Tradition/Custom)
Islamic	Non-Islamic
Male	Female
Patriliny	Cognation
Hierarchy	Egalitarianism
Cash economy	Subsistence economy
Women secluded	Women productive
Women dependent	Women autonomous

SOURCE: Caplan 1982, 40.

Power, Swahili Identity, and Ngoma Performance

Throughout the Swahili coast, identity is articulated within, between, and around multiple sets of dichotomies, such as Arab/African, maritime/mainland, literate/oral, foreigner/indigene, slave/free, and coast/hinterland. Scholars of the 1970s and 1980s, well-equipped with structural models, took great care to record this ethnographic realization of Lévi-Straussian binary oppositions, as shown in tables 3.3 and 3.4.

Seemingly trapped in dual oppositions (further reverberations of the Arab-African debate), both scholars and coastal individuals have emphasized one or another pole in relation to reigning power structures. In the colonial period, for example, racist policies discriminated between "natives" and "non-natives," conferring economic and political benefits on the latter. Coastal people who could document or fabricate Arab ancestry could elevate themselves to "non-native" status, and census figures show that many did so (Fair 2001, 28–55; Salim 1976). During the same period, scholars conceptualized the coast largely in Arab terms, as discussed earlier, due to their inability to reconcile the sophistication of

Table 3.4 Swahili *Ngoma* Dichotomies

Our club (*chama chetu*)	Your club (*chama chenu*)
Native-owners (*wenyeji*)	Strangers (*wageni*)
Coast (*pwani*)	Hinterland (*bara*)
Known origins (*asili*)	Unknown origins (*utovu wa asili*)
Wealth (*mali*)	Poverty (*umaskini*)
Islamic piety (*ki-Islamu*)	Paganism (*ki-kaffiri*)
Intelligence (*akili*)	Stupidity (*ujinga*)
Dignity (*makini*)	Agitation (*kuhangaika*)
Modesty (*haya*)	Shamelessness (*uhayawani*)

SOURCE: Farrell 1980, 128.

coastal culture with their evolutionary, racist frameworks. After independence, however, strong antiforeigner sentiment developed in the new states that encouraged coastal individuals to emphasize, perhaps rediscover, African ancestries and allegiances, and similarly provoked nationalist scholars to rewrite their histories and locate the source of and inspirations for coastal culture in its African context.

Recent efforts to recast the debate over Swahili identity argue instead for agreement on the essential open-endedness and permeability of Swahili identity wherein such oppositions constitute complementary elements, not conflicting essences, of that which is Swahili.[11] David Parkin argues as follows:

> The tension is, then, between the outward-looking sense of identity and the inward focus on a particular community, between centrifugal and centripetal tendencies. This often takes the form of a conflict between maritime and mainland pulls and claims. These can never be resolved, for peoples from the mainland are constantly "becoming" Swahili just as coastal Swahili influence what happens inland with the result that what constitutes the Swahili cultural and linguistic complex is always in a state of development and of flux. (1994, 2–3)

Willis similarly argues that a practice-theory approach to the question of Swahili identity (ethnic identity as dynamic, "created and recreated constantly through negotiation" [Willis 1993, 12]) frees us from the tautological ramifications of previous opinion. For him, "There is no single 'definition' of the Swahili. Different people, in different situations, may appropriate this ethnonym or apply it to others, according to their perception of their own advantage. The Swahili are not a discrete, enduring unit—but neither are the members of any other tribe" (Willis 1993, 12). The "elusiveness" of Swahili ethnicity (Salim 1985), then, boils down to a fundamental precept of ethnicity that is simply made more obvious in the Swahili setting: that "internal and external boundaries constantly shift, and ethnicity has to be constantly redefined and reinvented" (Yelvington 1991, 165).

In coastal society, as described in the previous chapter, the nature of the coastal trade generated much intermingling and a certain predilection toward the assimilation of newcomers. The cosmopolitan strip of city-states became havens at various points in history to groups external to the coast—people from the Arabian Peninsula as well as from inland regions of Africa—and for others marked the final African soil they would see before being sent abroad as slaves. Whatever the route that brought them there, every group of newcomers contributed to the development of Swahili town life.

> A crucial aspect of the development of many coastal settlements was the persistent, frequent necessity of integrating groups of . . . newcomers (*wageni*) with the estab-

lished social order within them. One thing, then, which characterized the coastal town was that it institutionalized change introduced by such immigrants, and, furthermore, the internal structures created to institutionalize such change reflected the fundamental ambivalence townspeople felt toward the outside world. The basic problem for the Swahili town was that of maintaining order and continuity in town life while creating unity out of diversity, one society out of many. (Pouwels 1987, 33)

The diversity was and is even greater than the dualistic arguments would imply. In practice, a large variety of finer distinctions exists within the binary oppositions that make for neat theoretical cases. For instance, the label "African" ignores locally perceived differences among the Swahili based on locale (Bajuni from the Lamu Archipelago, Amu from Lamu town, Unguja from Zanzibar, Mvita from Mombasa, Tangata from Tanga, etc.). It also ignores differences between these Swahili subgroups and hinterland Mijikenda groups (Kauma, Giriama, Chonyi, Jibana, Kambe, Ribe Rabai, Duruma, Digo, Segeju), whose economic and political associations with coastal Swahili communities and Arabs stretch back into history (Spear 1978; Parkin 1989, 1991; Willis 1993). Finally, it disregards distinctions between all of these groups and noncoastal Africans, recent immigrants from upcountry, many of whom were brought as slaves to work on coastal plantations (Cooper 1977, 1980; Sabea 2000). Similarly, the term "Arab" overlooks distinctions drawn between Omani Arabs (who came to the coast in large numbers following the relocation of the Omani Sultanate to Zanzibar in the 1830s), the two time-differentiated groups of Hadrami Arabs from the Hadramawt in Yemen, the first of which was a migration of Islamic crusaders on *jihad* in the 1520s (Pouwels 1987, 40) and the second a migration of mostly peasants, artisans, and merchants escaping chaotic conditions in southern Arabia following 1870 (112–13). Moreover, it does not reference those who identify themselves as Shirazis from Persia (treated by historians as a largely fictive claim; see Pouwels 1984, 1987, 34–37; Nurse and Spear 1985, 64–67; Spear 1984; Glassman 1995; Fair 1994, 242–49). These successive migrations from both outside and inside Africa contributed to the aforementioned characteristic of Swahili towns: high rates of immigration and settlement. So, although some scholars would perpetuate a series of binary oppositions and characterize local ideology as such, these break apart into a multitude of affiliations and subcategories, to reveal the nature of Swahili identity as inconstant and permeable, receptive to the incorporation of all of these groups of outsiders.[12] "The binarism belongs to the code itself; it does not describe the heterogeneous and shifting social world in which people [scholars especially] nevertheless use it to establish their own claims to power and distinction" (Herzfeld 1997, 14, my insertion).

It has been argued that the competitive dualism embedded in *ngoma* performance paradoxically provides a mechanism for the smooth incorporation of newcomers: "[M]odern scholars agree in regarding this factionalism as a basic integrative device for urban settlements which had constantly had to absorb new elements over the centuries" (Ranger 1975, 19);[13] "Rivalries . . . tend to draw in others who are members of neither, thus producing a binary opposition which is in a sense more unifying than the opposition of many different fragments" (Lienhardt 1968, 16; see also Farrell 1980, 80). And yet, "far from serving as mechanisms for the mediation and resolution of conflicts, [*ngoma* events] became impregnated with tension, and often turned violent." *Ngoma* constituted "important sites for the contestation of power" (Glassman 1995, 163, 161).

For one thing, *ngoma* associations provided a power-laden mode of social organization within the community at large. Writing in the nineteenth century, Swahili ethnographer Mtoro bin Mwinyi Bakari commented,

> In the old days there were on the coast many competitions. For this they said, "Let us form a society of one quarter of the town to challenge another." They chose their leader, a vizier, a counselor, and a messenger. All affairs were referred to the leader—if a man died, or was going to be married, or was bereaved, the leader took charge. The vizier's business was that if any matter arose in the town, it was referred to the vizier, and he reported to the leader. The counselor was consulted on every matter, and the messenger summoned the people, going to every house to tell them, "Tomorrow there is a meeting at the leader's at nine o'clock, because somebody is dead," or "We are going to a funeral," or "We are going to condole." Then the society acted as one man. (Bakari 1981, 83–84)

However, beyond simply mirroring existing power structures and conflicts, the work of Strobel (1979) and Farrell (1980) demonstrates the capacity within *ngoma* performance to exert pressure for the redistribution, or at least realignment, of power. Strobel describes how in Mombasa, street warfare broke out during Lelemama performance, causing elders and the government to impose a 1934 ban on all *ngoma* performance—a ban subsequently lifted and then reimposed in the late 1940s.[14] She argues that Lelemama did more than provide women with a means of "express[ing] rebellion against their restricted lives" (1979, 172). Refused access to the mosques, denied public positions of authority, excluded from the formal job market, and forced to maintain some adherence to the Islamic practices of veiling (albeit a loose interpretation) and seclusion, women used *ngoma* performance to transform dissent into political action. *Ngoma* associations spawned the repoliticization of women. Women activists manipulated the preexisting organizational structures of the associations to construct new political organizations that lobbied for and succeeded in acquiring voting rights for Muslim women in 1958. Moreover, the disregard for status and ancestry that characterized women's *ngoma* associations "suggests that women, because of their position in Mombasa society, have been important agents in the integration of different elements into Swahili culture" (Strobel 1979, 21). In other words, women's *ngoma* societies took a highly proactive role in redefining social relations in Swahili society.[15] The same proved true elsewhere along the coast. Ranger (1975), Glassman (1995), Fair (2001), and Willis (1993) all argue that while nineteenth-century *ngoma* performance constituted a medium for the exertion, affirmation, and articulation of elite authority and position, the escalating nature of the competitive displays created such a drain on elite resources that it resulted both in their demise and in an opening of *vyama* membership to anyone with the financial wherewithal to participate. Thus, membership became increasingly accessible to segments of society previously relegated to lower positions, especially to those with the means to purchase their upward mobility. Strobel's point thus holds true that remarkable shifts in coastal power structures were effected through *ngoma* performance. As Ranger succinctly states, "These 'traditional' dance societies . . . are very inadequately described as *just* dance societies. They were a way of recasting the network of relationships within a moiety or quarter; they were an expression of most of the existing values of Swahili urban society; and they were also mechanisms of innovation" (1975, 19–20).

A century later in Tanga and surrounding areas, modern dance societies perpetuate these traditions of competition and cooperation. The primary shift that has occurred since the time of Mtoro relates to gender: while the societies he describes had both male and female members, by the colonial period dance societies were segregated into distinct women's and men's *vyama* (Ranger 1975; Strobel 1979), and by the time of my research in the late 1980s and early 1990s, men's *vyama* had ceased to exist, while women's *vyama* continue, each urban center having its own signature style: Msanja in Tanga, Vugo in Mombasa, and Kibao Kata in Dar es Salaam. Although there were abundant memories of men's societies from the not-too-distant past (within the previous decade), none were still performing (although a few men's *vyama* are reputed to exist in the Lamu Archipelago). There are, however, two functioning and somewhat (if rarely) active rival *vyama* in Tanga that have mixed-gender memberships: Gita and Chera. No longer popular choices for entertainment at weddings, these societies now perform almost exclusively for official government functions, especially at national holiday celebrations or presidential visits.[16]

Although Kanada and Fanta live on only in the form of memories and remnants of half-forgotten songs, Ngoma ya Ndani continues to be performed in Tanga. And although these two associations ultimately dissolved at the end of the 1950s/early 1960s, the tradition of organized female *ngoma* groups did not die with them. Whether motivated by Islamic fundamentalism, which disapproves of such performances, or, contrarily, by a desire to move out of seclusion into a more public arena, women in Tanga outgrew their loyalties to Kanada and Fanta and around 1955 created something new and slightly less erotic to fill the gap. One woman, formerly a member of Fanta, explained, "The dance movement we dance in Ngoma ya Ndani cannot be performed outside. We wanted to perform an *ngoma* that many could see, so we began dancing Msanja."[17]

And so from the roots of these *vyama* grew two new groups performing a new *ngoma* but with loyalties remaining more or less in place: Scouti, drawing membership from what was Kanada and geographically covering Streets 8–14 in Ngamiani, and Kenya, covering Streets 15–21, drawing its members from what was Fanta. Membership figures for all four associations averaged roughly thirty members, further indicating continuity. The *ngoma* they dance features the same slow 6/8 rhythm called *kumbwaya,* and the women perform in the same Ngoma ya Ndani formation: a circle around the male drummers. The primary difference is a shift in emphasis away from dance to supplemental rhythmic accompaniment on cow horns with wooden sticks (figure 3.3). Dance movement is not entirely displaced, however. While beating the horns in intricate syncopated patterns that change according to cues both in the song texts and from the drummers in the circle's center, Msanja performers sway from side to side and follow the group leader in beating the horns alternately high above their heads or low near their knees. The presence of an audience seated around the circle of performers marks another significant difference from Ngoma ya Ndani, in which virtually everyone in attendance joins the dance. The signature hip movement, *kukata kiuno,* that characterizes Ngoma ya Ndani is officially absent in Msanja, and yet it is not uncommon for audience members to show their enthusiasm for the performance by momentarily joining the circle to display their skill in *kiuno* (to a lot of ululation) before returning to the sidelines.

Ngoma performance continues to excite and engender a sense of community irrespective of ethnic and class differentiation. And yet, in a distinct reversal of performance practice at the local level along the coast, *ngoma* performance at state-sponsored events emphasizes and reinforces ethnic identities in seeming opposition to state rhetoric for a non-

Figure 3.3   Women performing Msanja *ngoma,* 1994. Photo by author.

ethnicized, homogeneously Tanzanian nation. States are consistently full of contradictions. One grows accustomed to finding a lack of fit between rhetoric and practice, and in the case of Tanzanian *ngoma,* there is decided disparity between state rhetoric, state-sponsored performance practice, and local practice. I came to recognize the contradictions during my intensive involvement with a state-sponsored cultural troupe in Tanga as an *mgeni rasmi,* or "honored/official guest."

The Ethnographer as Honored Guest

When I first arrived in Tanga in September 1992, I came as a resolute researcher with laptop computer in hand and visions of the mountains of fieldnotes it would surely produce in mind. Immediately, I began the process of establishing (in some cases reestablishing) contacts with the poets, musicians, elders, cultural officers, and city residents whose ideas and accomplishments would guide my research. By the end of that first month I had found the focus of those early months of fieldwork. A local cultural troupe under the aegis of the government-owned Tanga Harbours Authority had reached the final round of the National Arts and Language Competitions. Known as KIUBATA, the acronym for Kikundi cha Utamaduni Bandari Tanga (Tanga Harbours Cultural Troupe), the group rehearsed every morning and, as the November competitions approached, in the afternoons as well. Seeing this as a perfect case study for local-national intersections and interstices at the musical level, I religiously attended these daily rehearsals; in the evening I explored other musical genres, contexts, and groups, and wrote up detailed notes on every event and interaction. September and October passed in this fashion.

This period of intensive involvement with KIUBATA and the flurry of preparations for the competitions provided me the opportunity to establish close relations with officers from the district and regional offices of the Ministry of Culture who, like me, had been attending the rehearsals regularly. Their self-described role was to ensure that performances suited "national interests." Interest in KIUBATA united us and I found myself treated as an honorary cultural officer: a chair for me was regularly placed alongside their chairs and I was included in the conversations and discussions that preceded, accompanied, and followed rehearsals. Since my research proposal and permit had passed through the various culture offices, the *ofisa utamaduni* (cultural officers) knew of my training in music. From the age of six, I had trained as a classical pianist and subsequently won a scholarship to attend a performing arts high school. There, I underwent rigorous training in Western music theory and performance practice. I continued my training in college, opting to pursue a dual major in music and anthropology. Thus, from time to time prior to the national competitions, questions of a musical nature were referred to me. This role of "honorary cultural officer/ foreign consultant" was assigned to me not merely in the context of KIUBATA rehearsals but in the rounds we made to the rehearsals of the three other groups preparing to represent Tanga at the national competitions.[18] These comprised students from two Tanga secondary schools— Tanga Technical School (formerly the Tanga School) and Usagara Secondary School—performing *mashairi* (poetry) and *tamthiliya* (drama) respectively, and the Saruji Cultural Troupe (affiliated with another government parastatal, the local cement factory) performing *muziki wa ala* (instrumental music) and *ngonjera* (dramatized poetry).

I look back on this period as the *mgeni rasmi* ("honored guest") stage of my fieldwork. Our arrival at any rehearsal was met with the same general patterned reaction: chairs would be found (not often an easy task) and arranged for us from a privileged vantage, and sodas were often presented to us. Some days would find us visiting all or most of the four groups and the flow of pre-lunchtime sodas often left me feeling slightly the worse for the display of generosity and respect it signified. In early November, I accompanied all the groups from Tanga to the national competitions in Arusha, which I documented in text, photographic image, and video (the focus of chapter 6). The Ministry did not have funds for the cultural officers to go to Arusha, foreshadowing the general lack of funds for cultural activities that would become an all-too-obvious trend over time. But most of them came anyway on their own funds.

Upon our return to Tanga, KIUBATA triumphant as the first-place winners in the *ngoma* contest and Saruji bearing the first-place honors from the instrumental music contest, anticlimax set in. Missing a new *raison d'être*, KIUBATA stopped rehearsing. In December 1992, circumstances compelled me to move temporarily away from Tanga's urban locus to an outlying rural area, the now defunct Amboni Sisal Estate.[19] Unable to make it into town for evening rehearsals and performances, I refocused my attention toward music production in the area surrounding me. Great numbers of Makonde live on and around the estate, having been recruited from southern Tanzania and northern Mozambique in the 1920s to cut and process the sisal. Throughout Tanzania, the Makonde are touted for their skill in musical performance. Of particular renown are Ngongoti, an elaborate dance performed on stilts, and Sindimba, easily the most popular Makonde *ngoma* and one that now figures prominently in official conceptions and articulations of Tanzanian national culture. I was fortunate to have been invited to several Makonde initiation ceremonies during my time on the estate. These ceremonies used to span the period of a year but are currently reduced to a month of isolated instruction.[20] As the period of instruction draws to a close, celebrations are staged in anticipation of the return of the *wari* ("initiates"; sing. *mwari*) to communal life. At these celebrations, elaborately masked and costumed *vinyago* (pl.) dance at a furious pace to driving, interwoven polyrhythms, frightening young women and children with occasional bolts into the crowds (figure 3.4). Rival circles composed of different local Makonde communities, each with its own *kinyago* (sing.) and drummers at its center, compete to attract the largest crowd. Then, on the final day, the *wari* are released from seclusion and perform *guaride*, militaristic songs and dances involving the synchronized execution of intricate movements and maneuvers with carved wooden rifles.

Amboni—the name of the sisal estate, the company that owned it, and the local village constructed adjacent to it—was where I spent my first Ramadan. The weeks preceding it were fever-pitched with musical activity as people quickly got married and initiated, since you cannot have a proper wedding or initiation without music, and music is almost entirely banned during Ramadan (music being denied as part of the regi-

Figure 3.4 Makonde *kinyago* (masked dancer), 1993. Photo by author.

men of strict abstinence). The one exception is *ngoma ya daku*: music performed by roving gangs of youths who wander from home to home in the dead of night drumming and singing songs to wake you up to eat. When successful or appreciated, they are tipped with coins; thus, the practice constitutes a means of earning some pocket money. During those nights, I used to arise at the sound of the drums, dress quietly, and slip out into the night air heavily scented by flowers whose perfume is only activated after the sun's retreat: *yasmini* (jasmine), frangipani, *langi-langi* (night queen). I usually asked one of the Amboni night watchmen to accompany me, which they readily did to break their boring routine and humor this odd *mzungu* (foreigner) with the penchant for local music.[21] Off we'd go in search of the music, following the sound of the drumming, treading carefully to avoid army ants on the march, occasionally startled by a burst of maniacal laughter from an arboreal bushbaby somewhere high above our heads, our path lit only by the moon whose phases determined the duration of this holy month of Ramadan.

In my six months at Amboni, I was thus treated to local practices of some of the more popularized *ngoma* that have attained "national" stature. One of the three *ngoma* performed by KIUBATA in the national competition was a Makonde *ngoma*. Having had the opportunity to see Makonde perform their *ngoma* at their own events, I had a basis for comparison, a yardstick for measuring change during the translation to a national level of music performance. I view this first stage of my fieldwork (September 1992–June 1993) as an immersion in *ngoma* practice. In all, I attended 102 *ngoma* events ranging from initiations to weddings, 43 KIUBATA events (including both rehearsals and performances), and, of course, the national competitions. I was not, however, devoted to *ngoma* to the exclusion of other genres. Affiliation with KIUBATA—a full-fledged cultural troupe encompassing a variety of genres—offered immediate access to a *dansi* band and a *taarab* band. I also attended a few weddings and a few rehearsals. At all events, I wore the *mgeni rasmi* label, or, slightly better, *mtafiti* (researcher). That would soon change.

"Jazz" in the Cities of East Africa: *Dansi* Performance

In many ways the side-by-side existence of *ngoma* and the popular urban jazz form is symbolic of the peculiar paradox of contemporary African urban society—the juxtaposition of new and old. Reflecting the old, yet timeless traditions of Tanzanian society, the *ngoma* symbolizes the stabilizing force of tradition—a force which has endured the process of urbanization while still maintaining the most fundamental aspects of African traditional life. The popular jazz band, on the other hand, is reflective of Tanzania's ability and desire to change, to be innovative, to be a part of the modern world. (Martin 1982, 157)

The all-too-common alignment of *ngoma* with tradition and *dansi* with modernity exemplified in the preceding quotation (see also Bender 1991) requires serious rethinking. *Dansi,* or "urban jazz," the music resonating throughout the country in the bar-halls of Tanga, Dar es Salaam, Morogoro, Arusha, Tabora, Moshi, Korogwe, and elsewhere is all too easily represented as a genre of change in contrast to purportedly frozen-in-time *ngoma*. One author even went so far as to place *ngoma* and *dansi* on the opposite ends of a Marxist, historical-materialist, evolutionary schema in which *ngoma* relates to precapitalist modes of production, Beni and *kwaya* represent the incursion of colonialism, and *taarab* and *dansi* correlate with the experience of urban capitalism (Donner 1980). While one can see why the heavily syncretic montage of musical elements as far-ranging as Western ballroom dancing (waltzes, fox-trots and swing), Afro-Cuban rhythms (rumba, samba, cha cha cha, *pachanga*) and, more recently, Congolese *soukous* guitar style that jointly constitute *dansi* might lend itself to such interpretations, they ultimately cannot be substantiated. The mutability, adaptability, and innovative borrowing already shown to be the essence of *ngoma* practice deny such neat polar oppositions. *Dansi* admittedly is a more recent development in the history of Tanzanian music and therefore more "modern" in terms of its placement in time, but it is no more a reflection of "modernity" in its being characterized by "Western mass consumer culture—fragmentation, heterogeneity, decentering, suspension of judgment, mixing of genres" (Barber and Waterman 1995, 242) than *ngoma*. As Barber and Waterman have demonstrated in their deconstruction of a strikingly similar opposition between supposedly static, traditional *oríkì* praise poetry and purportedly innovative, modern *fújì* popular music (1995), *ngoma* and *dansi* represent not two poles but two points on a spectrum of East African musical practice and performance.

The Emergence of Dansi

Colonialism, as one of several historical moments heralding great change, did introduce new musical practices, of which some were adopted and absorbed and others discarded. Despite the aspirations of would-be colonial culture-brokers, European musical practices were not in fact transplanted in wholesale fashion. This may have been the intent, but it certainly was not the result. Inculcating "proper" musical behavior was viewed as a productive strategy in the colonial "civilizing" project, and considerable effort was made in this regard. "European music represented a world of order to the inexplicable monotonies and sudden passions of African drumming; musical ability was taken as a sign, a promise of potential for civilization" (Ranger 1975, 13). As already described, the first state school in Tanganyika was founded in Tanga in 1892 (Koponen 1994, 505; Hornsby 1962). A school band was established early on, and one author notes that, at the time of World War I, "the school band remained in Tanga, and when the British forces captured Tanga, the band was taken over by them" (Hornsby 1962, 150). Scattered throughout various documents in the National Archives are many references to the Tanga School Band—to its success and resultant performances both in Tanga and beyond. On May 18, 1939,

---

The King's Birthday 1950

Programme of Music

By

Tanga School Band

1. Introduction

2. Entertainment March

3. Blue Bells of Scotland

4. Two Lovely Black Eyes

5. Selection

6. The Wearing of the Green

7. Cock of the North - Scotch March

8. A Hunting

9. The Farmer's Boy

10.Oh Shout! Winter Leave is Taking

Prepare the Foe is Coming

Men of the Harlech

Drums

Retreat

Tanga, June 8th, 1950

Figure 3.5   Musical program for the King's birthday, 1950. Recreated by author.

the Fife and Drum Band of the Tanga School performed with the King's African Rifles in the King's Birthday Parade.[22] The program of events for the King's birthday celebrations in 1950 is shown in figure 3.5. Even the famous Beni *ngoma* has been linked to the Tanga School Band. In his *Report on Social and Economic Conditions in the Tanga Province*, District Officer E. C. Baker describes the Beni *ngoma* as "a modern *ngoma* which was originated in Mombasa by an ex-bandsman of the German Government School at Tanga" (Baker 1934, 99).

At the time of Baker's report, *dansi* was already emerging as a popular form. He wrote,

It has frequently been suggested that the Beni *ngoma* might be used to control the urban population as a substitute for the lost tribal organisation. . . . But in my opinion it is moribund and its place is being taken by the dance-hall run on European lines.

The detribalised native with social aspirations dances the fox-trot or waltz in preference to performing the Beni *ngoma* in the public streets, and uses his club or one of the dance-halls rented for the purpose. One of the difficulties connected with this form of recreation is that no Mohammedan will dance with his wife or with his female relations, while the non-Mohammedan natives are also generally unwilling to allow their womenfolk to attend the dances. Consequently the family is split up, and the movement may even be retrogressive since the wife and husband could both attend the *ngoma* as spectators, even if one of them did not take part, whereas the fact that dancing takes place in a room prohibits the presence of onlookers in any numbers. These dance-halls, however, are innovations which have been brought about by the impact of Western civilisation, and must be looked upon as a form of social recreation which requires judicious direction. If developed on wise lines they may by advancing the status of women do a much greater amount of good than it is possible to visualize at the present time. (Baker 1934, 99)

Thus as early as 1934, *dansi* was gaining popular support—significantly, pan-ethnic support—in Tanga, Dar es Salaam, and elsewhere. Equally significantly, Tanga was an early locus of its performance and popularity. Iliffe (1979) describes *dansi* as

the international, individualistic ballroom dancing whose personalised sexuality shocked the elderly. Like Beni it apparently originated around Mombasa and entered Tanganyika through Tanga, whence it was probably brought to Dar es Salaam in the early 1930s by the *avant-garde* of the Tanga Young Comrades Club and was popularised by branches of the New Generation Club formed in several towns later in the decade. With their "kings" and "queens" adopted from the Beni societies, their female sections composed chiefly of nursemaids, and their insatiable thirst for tea and soft drinks, New Generation Clubs epitomised the *dansi* mode. (392)

Thus *dansi* clubs were popular in Tanga and Dar es Salaam in the 1930s and eventually gave rise to major *dansi* bands whose influence would spread the genre even further afield. The Dar es Salaam Jazz Band played to enthusiastic crowds in Dar es Salaam by 1939 (see Iliffe 1979, 392), and 1944 saw the establishment of the Morogoro Jazz Band in Morogoro. Its famous guitarist/singer/composer Mbaraka Mwinshehe (b. 1944) became one of the country's most influential and celebrated musicians throughout the 1960s and 1970s, its brightest star until his untimely death in a car accident in 1979. Other famous bands of the era included the Cuban Marimba Band (originally named La Paloma, est. 1948), Jamhuri Jazz Band (a Tanga band, est. 1955), Atomic Jazz Band (a Tanga band, est. 1956; see figure 3.6, and listen to "Tanzania Yetu," track 5 on the accompanying CD), and NUTA Jazz Band (organized by the National Workers Union in 1965), which continues to perform today

Figure 3.6 Atomic Jazz Band record cover, early 1970s. Actual record cover supplied by Leo Sarkisian. Image courtesy of University of Michigan Photo Services.

under the name of OTTU (Organization of Tanzanian Trade Unions) Jazz Band—the oldest surviving band in the country.

Swahili Musicians and Poets as Organic Intellectuals

In the decades when yearnings for independence and self-rule germinated in the minds of those who would constitute the elite in an independent Tanganyika and Zanzibar, *dansi* provided one way for African men and women to appropriate symbolic power and cultural capital from colonialists to "'prove' their equality and ability to govern themselves along European lines" (Fair 1994, 317). It constituted an investment in social distinction (Bourdieu 1984), a claim to the upper levels of a socially recognized hierarchy of the arts. Paralleling the origins of Belizean beauty pageants studied by Richard Wilk, *dansi* constituted a strategy to fight the *political* issue of independence and self-government, within the *cultural* arena of respectability, education and "taste." Their strategy equated the foreign with the upper-class British and thereby with respectability; the local could not be a source of culture in these terms. For some participants there was an underlying and unspoken goal of continuing the privileged position of a small, educated middle class. . . . But for many the issue was one of "uplifting" the masses with a respectable spectacle. (Wilk 1995, 122)

On a more pragmatic level, African political activists in pre-independence Zanzibar strategically exploited the popularity of *dansi* to attract youth to dance clubs for the underlying purpose of educating them in radical economics and politics.

Like earlier dance traditions . . . disenfranchised members of the [African] community were able to appropriate the symbolic tools of the ruling powers and to transform them into a medium which simultaneously granted power to the under-class while undermining the exclusiveness and hegemony of the ruling class. . . . Dancing to fox-trots and wearing fancy gowns provided them with a cover for political education and organizing and a very effective means for attracting younger and less politically minded individuals into their organizations. (Fair 1994, 319)

Such covert political uses of *dansi* were not the exclusive domain of the islands, however. On the mainland, *dansi* played the same role of serving as a cover to political organization. Werner Graebner interviewed Ally Sykes, a founding member of TANU and prominent musician with the Merry Blackbirds Band, who explained,

We often played for the "Freedom Fighters" mainly at Msimbazi Hall in Dar es Salaam. There were charities for TANU, ANC, ZANU. Many times the band's performances acted as a cover for political meetings of TANU whose members met in the backrooms when there was a dance. The band also raised money for the political fight, for peoples' travelling money or for the printing of pamphlets. (Graebner 1992a, 228)

In addition to using musical contexts simultaneously as contexts for political discussion and organization, musicians voiced political sentiment in their songs. Sometimes they would camouflage their political messages with the same subtle wordplay that characterizes *ngoma* songs. At other times, however, pretense and subtlety would be thrown to the wind, as in the following song from the Tanganyika Boys (1960):

We want our freedom!
The time is ripe,
So we can get our country.
We are not content with just anything.
We ask God in prayer.
All of Africa is ours!
All of us have to get their independence,
Especially we Tanganyikans.
(Quoted in Graebner 1992a, 223)

Music and politics thus combined to create a potent mix of political action and agents. Through music, Africans could appropriate European symbolic and cultural capital for themselves, voice their political agendas in song, and use musical events as opportunities for education and organization. More than this, however, the social networks that sustained musical practice constituted ready pools of political agents. Just as Lelemama structures in Mombasa were mobilized to lobby for women's voting rights, Beni structures in Tanga—so casually dismissed by Baker—formed the nucleus of the TTACSA (Tanganyika Territory African Civil Service Association), which was established in Tanga on March 24, 1922 (Iliffe 1979, 267). The first African political association in the territory, TTACSA set an example that was soon embraced in urban centers throughout the country with the emergence of multiple TTACSA branches, and its founding "can be taken as symbolic of the flight of the civil servants from Beni" (Ranger 1975, 94). Nevertheless, its growth fed upon preexisting *ngoma* networks and drew strength from men who had developed leadership skills in the Beni associations. In 1929, the Tanganyika African Association (TAA) was established; by the 1940s it would supplant the TTACSA, drawing on similar networks (Ranger 1979, 94–96). It was from TAA that the Tanganyika National Union (TANU), established on July 7, 1954, subsequently evolved—the party that would lead the territory to independence. Clearly, politics and music were very much aligned, to the point where Ranger noted that "indeed, it was sometimes hard to distinguish between a branch of the African Association and an élite dance club" (1975, 96).

As exemplified by Ally Sykes, a strong core of TANU activists consisted of musicians, poets and dancers.[23] The founder and leader of TANU for Tanga Region was the famous nationalist poet Mwalimu Mwalimu Kihere (1903–1974), who also served as a district commissioner for many years. Other politically active poets were Ghulam Mabondo bin Mwinyimatano (d. 1972/3?; musician, poet, and teacher at the Tanga School, born in Mnyanjani, Tanga); Swalehe Kibwana (1887–1966; poet, politician, TANU secretary, mayor of Tanga); Mahmoud M. Hamdouny bin Khalfan (b. 1920 near Bagamoyo; poet, Qur'anic teacher, trader, CCM branch chairman in Dodoma); Issa Kitenge (b. 1929 near Kigoma; poet, fisherman, TANU leader, CCM chairman, and most recently the branch leader and national congress delegate for one of the new opposition parties, UMD); Mathias Mnyampala (b. 1919 in Dodoma, d. 1969; nationalist poet and Dar es Salaam court magistrate); and the most famous Swahili poet of all, Shabaan Robert (b. 1909 near Tanga, d. 1962).[24] Appealing to people to join and strengthen the TAA (prior to TANU's establishment), Shabaan Robert composed the following:[25]

Tabu zilizo kali, wajibu kuelezwa	The terrible troubles must be explained
Ifahamu serikali, dola ya Kiingereza	With regard to this British government.
Waume wenye akili, na wake wanaowaza	Intelligent men and women,
Kazi hii halali, kimya kinaangamiza.	It is right to struggle. Silence will destroy
Tuungane kwa sauti bila mtu kuiza	us.
Ifike kiliko kiti, Dola iwe yawaza	Let us unite as one voice without dissent,
Kuwa uko umati, mashaka yawaumiza	That it reach the chair, so the govern-
Kando mtu asiketi, mwendo unafuliza	ment may ponder this.
	There are crowds full of doubt.
	Let no one sit aside. Time is quickly
	passing.
- - -	- - -
All come on, kila mwenyeji aweza	All come on, every resident can
Do his turn, Tanganyika kiukuza	Do his turn, to make Tanganyika great.
Know each grain, uzito inaongeza	Know each additional grain increases the
African Association, naam mwangaza	total weight.
	African Association, yes, it is the light.

There were some significant female figures as well. Moza Ali Suleiman (1935–1969), a Zanzibari poet and composer of *taarab* songs, was a prominent political activist aligned with a political party that was eventually banned. Mwashamu Yange (b. circa 1934) is a political poet in Tabora who has worked closely with both TANU and CCM. Bi Pirira Athumani (b. 1920s) in Tanga was until her death in June 2000 commissioned periodically by cultural officers to perform her poetry for political events; her notoriety was strongly linked to her prowess as a *ngoma* singer. Not coincidentally, TANU's first female member, Bibi Titi Mohamed,[26] was the lead singer of a women's *ngoma* group in Dar es Salaam called Bomba. She alone is credited with having increased the TANU membership of two thousand in March 1955 by an additional five thousand female members by September of that same year. Her success stemmed from effective mobilization of support from *ngoma* networks:

> To mobilize the women, I went to the *ngoma* groups. First of all, I went to their leaders. The leaders [agreed to] call all their people so I could come and talk to them about TANU—what it does, what it wants, where it is going. For example, I talked to Mama Salehe Kibuyu, leader of the "Bombakusema," and she called together all of the "Bombakusema" women. I met them at Livingstone Street at the corner of Kariokoo [*sic*] Street where Mama Binti Salehe Kibuyu stayed. She said, "Titi is calling you, and I have called you for the sake of Titi. Here she is and she will tell you what she wants." . . . Then I went to Mama binti Makabuli. She was a leader of "Warumba." She lives in Narumg'ombe [*sic*] Street near Lumumba Street. She is still alive, but very old. She called the "Warumba." And that's how I went to "British Empire" and to "Ratusudan" and to the "Safina" group, "Submarine" and "Ratulail." I went to all these groups. (From a 1984 interview with Susan Geiger; see Geiger 1997, 58)

By 1961, when Tanganyika acquired its independence, Bibi Titi Mohamed—a woman from a modest background with a total of four years of formal primary school education—occupied a position of political prominence second only to that of Julius Nyerere himself (Geiger 1987, 2).[27]

Substantiating Antonio Gramsci's propositions that every social stratum produces its own "organic intellectuals" to direct the ideas of, organize, and educate its constituency, and, moreover, that political parties constitute the domain of organic intellectuals (Gramsci 1971, 15, *passim*),[28] we thus find that Tanganyika's (and Zanzibar's) most prominent organic intellectuals were its poets, its dancers, and its musicians, whose "directive" political role found voice through the party (and post-1992 parties). These organic intellectuals could easily mobilize support from preexisting musical networks to further their political activities. Musical, primarily *ngoma*, networks have figured so prominently in coastal culture that virtually every historian documenting coastal culture has had to devote considerable attention to the topic (see Ranger 1975; Strobel 1979; Willis 1993; Fair 2001; Glassman 1995). Writes Willis,

> Individuals could use a network created through one institution to break into another institution, and through this create new networks. So a migrant to Mombasa might seek out and stay with a family member already living in the town, and through them join one of the urban dance societies. Through this, in turn, they might acquire a new patron, and find work and other housing. Life in Mombasa was a question not just of who you knew, but also of how you knew them. . . . Because these institutions were thus involved in daily life and survival, it is impossible to discuss ethnicity, or dance, without considering the daily exigencies of life in and around Mombasa. Conversely, it is an incomplete analysis which seeks to understand life in Mombasa without looking at these institutions. (Willis 1993, 7)

Beyond coastal society, however, *ngoma* networks served the same purpose of drawing in people from diverse backgrounds and forging new affiliations. Geiger's richly detailed history of TANU women locates the roots of Tanzania's nationalist movement in *ngoma* societies: "If the goals of nationalism include a sense of larger community beyond parochial groups, whether 'tribes' or other presumably bounded entities, women in Dar es Salaam, through their *ngoma* and other dance/singing organizations, were already engaged in a form of nationalism. As Bibi Titi recalls, these groups were open to all, regardless of tribe or place of organization: 'All people are mixed up together just like this . . .' " (Geiger 1997, 63). Musical networks—whether of *dansi* or *ngoma*—thus constituted, and continue to constitute, vibrant and potent social forces implicated at multiple levels of political action.

The Congolese Sound

If *dansi* began with the taint of colonial elite society, as a form of Europeanized cultural capital and a source of distinction (Bourdieu 1984), it certainly did not remain so for long. Current descriptions of the genre never mention "fox-trots," "swing," or "waltzes." Today, *dansi* is considered by some to be a weak imitation of Congolese rumba and *soukous* (the successor style of Congolese rumba). Ballroom dancing as an entry into elite society was not unique to Tanzania. Throughout Africa, similar developments were taking place. In the Belgian Congo, "early highlife, swing and Afro-Cuban music were the staples of the first bands to play at formal dances where the few members of the elite 'evolués' could mix with Europeans" (Ewens 1994a, 315). Afro-Cuban rhythms struck a particularly resonant chord in the 1950s and spawned a musical movement quickly embraced and directed by non-elites. This new movement, the Congolese rumba, fused a variety of local and global elements to create something decidedly new. Perhaps its signature characteristic was the adaptation of the local style of playing the thumb piano to the newly introduced electric guitar, accented against a musical background featuring such global ingredients as French cabaret or *variété* music, vocal harmonic skills learned at church, and brass-band religious fanfares (Ewens 1994a, 315). The likes of Joseph "Le Grand Kalle" Kabasele, leader of African Jazz (est. 1953), and Franco, leader of OK Jazz (est. 1956), formed their bands two decades *after* the formation of the first *dansi* bands in Tanganyika. Yet owing to the existence of a far superior musical infrastructure in Zaire—including the powerful transmitters of Radio Congo Belge (formerly Radio Free France) that began broadcasting African music in the 1940s, and major record labels that provided support for the artists they signed (Graham 1992, 109; Ewens 1994, 315)—and the mass influx of Zairean musicians into Tanzania following the 1961 assassination of Prime Minister Patrice Lumumba, the Congolese sound was injected deep into the Tanganyikan musical scene. Artists who emigrated to Tanganyika alternately came as complete bands (Orchestre Makassy, Orchestre Maquis—see the discography at the end of this book) or as individual artists (Remmy Ongala) who subsequently joined local *dansi* bands and contributed their Congolese flair. Despite meager economic payoffs and a dearth of recording facilities and companies (a significant hindrance to aspirations for international renown), Tanganyika nevertheless offered a climate more conducive to music-making. Thus, it became permanent home to a great number of Zaireans who went on to play an active role in the development of *dansi*.

Certainly, this is not to say that *dansi* is essentially Zairean. While some musical elements can be viewed as characteristically Congolese, such as the intricate melodic and rhythmic guitar-work shared among multiple electric guitars that traces its roots to thumb-piano performance style, *dansi* also contains elements drawn from a variety of local sources, most noticeably local *ngoma* rhythms. Moreover, the Zairean bands in Dar es Salaam term their music *dansi,* not *soukous,* thus acknowledging the distinction. Like Congolese rumba, and like the Yoruba *fújì* music described by Barber and Waterman (1995), *dansi* constitutes a mixture of diverse traits drawn from multiple sites and multiple time periods, and like *ngoma* it is continually adapting to the historical contingencies of the moment. All too often dismissed by outsiders as a weak reverberation, a poor imitation of first European ballroom music and then Zairean *soukous, dansi* draws on a rich local repertoire of Swahili proverbs and sayings, local *ngoma* rhythms, local dance styles, and the local rivalries that are so rarely absent from Swahili performance.[29]

Another point of convergence between *dansi* and *ngoma* is their shared emphasis on dance. In both genres, the fundamental goal is to incite audience members into joining the dance. The extent to which this goal is achieved constitutes the standard for evaluating the success of any given performance. The two genres differ, however, in their performance settings, with *ngoma* found primarily in the context of life-cycle rituals such as weddings and initiations but also frequently in state celebrations (national holidays, political rallies, etc.), and *dansi* found primarily in urban nightclubs and at the rare elite wedding or state celebration. Also, whereas in 1993–94 it cost more than Tsh. 50,000 (roughly $100) to hire a *dansi* band for a private function, it cost between Tsh. 5,000 and 10,000 to hire *ngoma* performers. This is another reason why *dansi* remains linked to elite identity formation, whereas *ngoma* is associated with rural traditionalism.

To sum up, although the forces that united to produce *dansi*—colonialism, urbanism, political turmoil in Zaire, and developments in broadcast, recording, and instrument technology—lend support to the view of this genre as a "modern" phenomenon, it should be clear that both *dansi* and *ngoma* are steeped in and shaped by similar sets of social and historical forces. In common parlance, the varieties of *ngoma* are frequently linked to ethnic identities, whereas *dansi* is considered a pan-ethnic activity and marker of urban, and often elite, status. Yet the studies by Ranger on Beni, by Strobel on Lelemama, and by Geiger on women's *ngoma* networks all support the parallel role of pan-ethnic *ngoma* in constructing urban identities. Other elements shared by both genres include a rich verbal repertoire of Swahili proverbs, sayings, and metaphors; common rhythms; common dance movements; a common propensity toward rival factions; and, in some cases, common performers. Both genres also share a common "modern" orientation—the fragmentation, heterogeneous references, extended networks of allusion, and transcendence of the here-and-now that Barber and Waterman (1995) identified in their examination of Yoruba popular music and praise poetry.

Finally, *ngoma* and *dansi* share a history in which they have served political purposes and quite directly enabled political action. In reflecting upon the nature of class differences, Gramsci notes,

> One of the most important characteristics of any group that is developing toward dominance is its struggle to assimilate and to conquer "ideologically" the traditional intellectuals, but this assimilation and conquest is made quicker and more efficacious the more the group in question succeeds in simultaneously elaborating its own organic intellectuals. (Gramsci 1971, 10)

That is to say, class distinctions are elaborated in part by the intellectuals who direct the ideas and aspirations of each class; furthermore, since no class is without its intellectuals (even if not of the "traditional," i.e., literary, scientific, educated, brand), a successful strategy in the political struggle of a dominated class is for its own organic intellectuals to confront and "conquer ideologically" the traditional intellectuals of the dominant class. Musicians and poets in Tanzania have frequently served the role of organic intellectuals, actively challenging the status quo and vigorously pursuing alternatives. My discussion of political activism via music could easily have been placed in the context of my discussion of *ngoma*—as the examples from Lelemama, Beni, and TANU's early dependence on women's *ngoma* networks illustrate. The timing of decolonization in the 1950s and 1960s, however, coincided perfectly with the rise in popularity of *dansi*. Viewed as a modern urban genre indicative of widespread social change by those guiding the fight for independence (who aspired to positions of power in an independent Tanganyika and Zanzibar), *dansi* played a slightly more prominent role in the struggle for independence. As might be expected, however, once the tables had turned, with Africans assuming a position at the table's head, the use of music for political purposes was suddenly questioned by those who had benefited from this very strategy. But that remains to be explored in later chapters.

"On the third day, give her a hoe . . ."

When housing back in Tanga proper became available in the summer of 1993, I bade farewell to Amboni, and my research entered another phase. There is a Swahili saying: *Siku mbili mgeni, siku ya tatu mpe jembe,* "Two days a guest, on the third give him/her a hoe." If my initial time in Tanga was marked with *mgeni* status, I was now presented with a musical hoe, the keyboard. From sideline observer, I became first a musical apprentice, then a performer in two bands—one *dansi,* one *taarab*—for which my training as a classical pianist proved useful.

In June of 1993 I attended my first rehearsal of a *dansi* band called the Watangatanga Band (The Wanderers). At that time, there were only two *dansi* bands in Tanga—Watangatanga and a band affiliated with the Tanga Harbours Authority (therefore an affiliate of KIUBATA) called Bandari Orchestra. It was no secret that the general manager of the Harbours Authority was a great fan of music, especially *dansi* music. This in part explained the commitment by this particular parastatal to music, for certainly there was considerable expense in maintaining KIUBATA, a troupe numbering about forty performers and covering the genres of *ngoma, sarakasi, dansi,* and *taarab,* who were paid monthly salaries plus allowances for every rehearsal and performance attended, and who were provided with transport on the Harbours Authority buses when they performed. Proceeds from the performances did little to offset the expenses, especially since a significant proportion of KIUBATA's performances were unpaid performances at government-sponsored events (such as national holiday celebrations). Although I attended a few Bandari rehearsals, I discovered that they performed only rarely due to the poor condition of their musical equipment. Watangatanga, however, held permanent contracts at two Tanga venues, guaranteeing them income twice weekly.

During that first rehearsal of Watangatanga, I found the band listening to a cassette of the popular British artist Elton John in an effort to learn the song "Sacrifice." It is common practice for *dansi* bands to pepper their performances with "covers" (reproductions) of popular hit songs—from the West (e.g., Elton John, Lionel Richie, Ace of Base) and from other parts of the world such as the former Zaire, West Africa, Jamaica (reggae), South Africa, and Brazil (the at-that-time ubiquitous *lambada*). In attempting to imitate "Sacrifice," they found parts of the chord progression new and difficult to reproduce and asked for my assistance. After deciphering that particular progression and rehearsing the song with them several times, I was asked to play keyboards on another song, the famous "La Bamba." Although the band owned two keyboards, they had long since lost their keyboardist—hence the request for me to perform these songs with them at their next show. Little did I know that this would mark an irreversible shift in my status in Tanga. No longer the passive observer, I was included on stage from that day forward as part of the act of performance.

According to my field records, between June 1993 and April 1994 I attended rehearsal on a daily or weekly basis in addition to a total of thirty-six Watangatanga public performances. Of these, thirty-three were regular weekly performances at one or the other of the two venues where Watangatanga constituted a house band. Every Saturday night, they performed at the Mkonge Hotel, the most upscale hotel in Tanga, on the shores of Tanga Bay, from 10:00 P.M. until 3:00 A.M.; every Sunday night, they performed at the Splendid View Hotel, a venue on the border of Ngamiani with a splendid view of little more than the railway tracks that define the border between Ngamiani and the business district. Splendid View attracted a more mid-range clientele, as reflected in the drop in entrance fee to Tsh. 800 ($1.60) from the Tsh. 1,000 ($2.00) charged at Mkonge. The only time the band did not perform was during the month of Ramadan when, in keeping with the overall tenor of this Islamic city, they took a month of vacation.[30]

As my days and evenings grew increasingly structured around rehearsal and performance schedules, I faced growing constraints on my time to write fieldnotes. Matters only worsened when my concurrent participation in a *taarab* band began, necessitating *two* daily rehearsals and multiple performance engagements in the evenings, especially weekend evenings (often two or three in a single evening). What I lost in terms of detailed description was more than compensated for by the perspective I gained on Swahili musical performance from the vantage of the stage. I had the opportunity to document interactions on stage and off, in social relations, in performer-audience relations, and in musical interplay. In my career as a *dansi* musician, I presided over the keyboards (which were always at the back of the stage layout), playing mostly non-Swahili hits. (In all, I played keyboard on a total of seven songs: three Western pop hits, one Zairean hit, two Afro-Cuban/Latin hits and one popular Swahili song from Kenya.)[31] When the band discovered I could also sing, I was asked to sing backup vocal on a few songs and the lead vocal part on one Zairean cover.

In the year I performed with the Watangatanga Band (figure 3.7), I learned a tremendous amount about the uses, practices, economics, and politics of *dansi* performance. *Dansi,* as an integral and ubiquitous component of Tanzanian urban existence, offers those who partake of its performance one strategy for reasserting and maintaining their urban, "modern," often but not exclusively Christian (due to the associations with alcohol consumption), identities. It is to the creation and maintenance of "modern" Muslim identities via an urban musical alternative, that we turn next.

More Local/Global Interstices: *Taarab* Performance

Taking its name from the Arabic abstract noun *tarabun,* meaning "joy, pleasure, delight, rapture, amusement, entertainment, music" (Wehr

Figure 3.7   The Watangatanga Band, 1994. Photo by author.

1976, 555), or "ecstasy, a complete engagement with music,"[32] the genre of musical performance known as *taarab* is a form of sung Swahili poetry associated distinctly and uniquely with the coastal region of East Africa. The distinguishing feature of *taarab,* commonly separating it from both *ngoma* and *dansi,* is its strict adherence to poetic structure.[33]

Taarab: Its Structure and Defining Characteristics

Taarab is only *taarab* if it follows certain poetic conventions of rhyme (*vina*), meter (*mizani*), and extensive use of metaphor. The typical *taarab* song is strophic, composed of verses (*mabeti*) sung to the same music and interspersed with a common refrain or "chorus" (*kibwagizo* or *kii-tikio*) and instrumental interlude (*muziki*). In terms of composition, it is not uncommon for these elements to be created by different compos-ers, with one excelling in poetry and another in its musical accompani-ment. Thus songs often have multiple composers; some recent cassettes in the local music industry credit one person for composing the poetry (*shairi*), another for the musical accompaniment (*muziki*), and a third as the singer (*mwimbaji*).

In *taarab* poetry, as in most Swahili poetry, rhyme occurs midway through the line and again at the end of the line. The most common poetic structure consists of four verses of three lines each with sixteen syllables per line, and rhyme occurring at the eighth and sixteenth syllables creating an 8 + 8 poetic structure. Its ubiquity led another scholar, Jan Knappert, to declare this "*tarabu* metre" (Knappert 1977). The examples he collected in 1969 and 1973 illustrate that *taarab* poets used to follow the general principle of Swahili poetry of maintaining a single rhyme scheme at the end of the line from start to finish throughout all the verses, even while sometimes varying the mid-line rhyme. Nowadays, however, *taarab* composers no longer abide by this rule and freely change rhyme schemes from verse to verse—all the while, however, staying strictly within a constant metric structure to facilitate the strophic musical structure. The following verse from a song entitled "Nimezama" ("I am Drowning") illustrates the 8 + 8 structure with a -*za* and -*zi* rhyme scheme (track 1 on the accompanying CD):[34]

Wenzangu nawauliza, Nini dawa ya ma-penzi?	My friends I ask you: what is the medicine for love?
Waganga nimemaliza, Wa makombe na hirizi	I've tried all shamans with their potions and talismans.
Bilahi Mola Muweza, Ataniafu Mwenyezi	Oh Almighty God, deliver me.

The following verse continues with a new -*zi* and -*ka* rhyme scheme:

Nimezama kwa mapenzi, Sijui kama tazuka	I am drowning in love. I don't know if I'll emerge safely.
Kujikwamua siwezi, Taabani nateseka	I cannot extricate myself. I am in great distress.
Bilahi Mola Mwenyezi, Ataniafu Rabuka	Oh All-Powerful God, deliver me.

Another example of the 8 + 8 structure, this time maintaining a constant end rhyme throughout all the verses but a varying midpoint rhyme, is "Aliyejaliwa" ("The Favored One"; track 8 on the accompanying CD), performed by the National Insurance Corporation (BIMA) *taarab* troupe:

Aliyejaliwa ("The Favored One")
Ally Star, BIMA Modern Taarab, Dar es Salaam

Tachukia kila siku, Mimi siko sawa nawe	Every day you'll despise the fact that you and I are not alike.
Fanya mchana usiku, Bidii ufanikiwe	Keep persevering day and night so that you succeed.
Hilo lako dukuduku, Utajishinda mwenyewe	This bitterness of yours will be your downfall.

- - -
- - -

Wasema kama kasuku, Mengi watu wakujue	You talk incessantly like a parrot so that people know you.
Ulipiga marufuku, Nilipo niondolewe	You demanded that I be removed from where I was.
Hilo ni dua la kuku, Juwa halimpati mwewe	Know that the prayer of the chicken does not affect the hawk.

- - -
- - -

Wanipangia tuhuma, Wataka uthaminiwe
Kunipachika lawama, Unataka usifiwe
Mtoaji ni Karima, Kipi upatacho wewe?

You accuse me hoping you will be
    believed.
In laying the blame on me, you seek
    praise.
Only God can save. What have you
    achieved?

- - -

- - -

Si kama nakukashifu, Tulia nikuzindue
Panapo maji marefu, Nataka upaelewe
Nawe ni hali dhaifu, Utajitosa mwenyewe

It's not as though I am slandering you.
    Calm down. Let me set you straight.
I want you to understand where deep
    waters lie.
You are in desperate straits, yet you will
    plunge further into this yourself.

- - -

- - -

Chorus
Aliyejaliwa, Wewe usishindane naye
Utajisumbua, Mola ndiye ajuaye

Don't try to compete with the favored
    one.
You'll only trouble yourself. Only God
    knows.

This is by no means the only poetic structure possible. An example of 6 + 6 construction in which the rhyme at the half line is *-ia* and at the end of the line *-na* follows in a verse from the song "Pendo Raha Yake" ("The Joy of Love"), by the Young Novelty Musical Club of Tanga (track 2 on the accompanying CD):

Sitovumulia, Pendo la hiyana
Pendo ni tabia, Zenye kufanana
Nakutia nia, Hamtogombana

I refuse to suffer a mean-spirited love.
Love blooms between similar personalities
And elicits a determination never to fight.

There can also be hemistichs of unequal length, as in the following 4 + 8 example:[35]

Ufahamu, Mtu hajui la kesho
Hutadumu, Ungatumia vitisho
Maadamu, Lenye mwanzo lina mwisho

Understand that no human knows what
    tomorrow brings.
You will not last forever even if you re-
    sort to scare tactics,
Because every beginning has its end.

Poets also experiment with lines of varying length, as illustrated by the next excerpt, which follows an 8 + 8 format for both the first and third lines, but an 8 + 4 format for the second line:[36]

Fahamu haijanisha, Hamu ya kilicho chema
Ambacho menionjesha, Muadhama
Kidogo menirambisha, Kishae unaninyima

Know that my desire for this beautiful
    thing has not ended
That you gave me to taste, my love.
You gave me but a taste, and then with-
    held it from me.

- - -

- - -

Sasa unanitabisha, Moyo wataka lazima
Hamu haijanitosha, Naungama

Now you aggravate me, yet still my heart
    insists.
Desire has not satisfied me, I confess.

Mbona wanibabaisha, Nataka nawe wa-
  goma
	Why do you tease me? I want but you
	  hold back.

Finally, although the three-line stanza is the single most prevalent form, stanzas of two, four, and sometimes even five lines exist as well. For an example of a song consisting of four four-line stanzas in a straight 8 + 8 structure, see "Nyuki" ("Bee") in appendix A. Below is an example of a song with two-line verses following an unusual 8 + 7, 8 + 8 structure. It begins with a single-line introductory chorus:

Muhibaka ("Darling")—excerpt
Rashid Hamadi, Babloom Modern Taarab, Tanga

Ewe muhibaka, Usinitese mwenzio	You, my darling, please do not hurt me.
- - -	- - -
Nateseka duniani, Sinapo pakushika	I suffer much in this world and have
Tafadhali niauni, Ujuwe naadhirika	nowhere to go.
	Please tend to my needs. Know that I
	embarrass myself.
- - -	- - -
Nakupenda si dhihaka, Umo mwangu	I love you—it is no joke. You are in my
moyoni	heart.
Huba zako nazitaka, Wangu mwana	I want your love, my dear, do not refuse.
sinikhini	
- - -	- - -

Chorus

Aaaaa, Usinitese mwenzio	Aaaaa, don't hurt me.
Hali mimi nakupenda nawe, Usinidhulumu	I am in love with you. Do not treat me unjustly.

The standard context for the performance of *taarab* is weddings. Thus, not surprisingly, many songs revolve around the theme of love. Knappert (1977) deciphered ten themes in the *taarab* songs he collected:

1. The nature of love
2. The pangs of love
3. Separation
4. Parting (the cause of separation)
5. Reunion
6. Desertion
7. Unrequited love
8. The fickle woman
9. Infidelity
10. The love for a child

I would add a few more themes to this list drawn from the more than twelve hundred songs I have collected. These would be general insult songs (see "Aliyejaliwa" above), insult songs aimed at a former lover, songs of lamentation and hardship, and political songs (often in praise of political leaders). Although often characterized and casually dismissed as uncomplicated love songs, *taarab* proves itself to be much, much more. One of the most common features—in fact a defining characteristic of the genre, analyzed in depth in the next chapter—is the use of metaphor, innuendo, and double entendre, within which lies the power-laden potential for political maneuvering. By means of *taarab* performance, messages are communicated that local protocol prohibits otherwise.

Because the poetry receives the greatest emphasis and attracts the most audience attention, lines are often sung twice or even four times to ensure that the text is heard and understood. A common melodic structure is to have the first and third lines sung to the same melodic motif and a different motif for the second line, resulting, with repetition, in an AA-BB-AA structure. Although common, this is by no means the only melodic format, another popular one being AA-BB-CC.

Musically, *taarab* constitutes a dynamic expression of cultural cross-fertilization drawing upon disparate elements from local *ngoma* and from musical exchange through interaction in long-standing Indian Ocean networks and, more recently, the global economy. *Taarab* incorporates select Arabic and Indian instruments, melodic structures, stylistic devices, and aesthetics that, when united with local *ngoma* rhythms and the Bantu language Kiswahili, meld into a single mode of cultural expression aurally reflecting its diverse, multicultural, social setting. Although the degree and source of foreign influence vary considerably depending upon geography and historical circumstance, the predominance of *ngoma* rhythms such as *kumbwaya, chakacha, vugo, goma,* and *mdurenge* in *taarab* performance throughout the region grounds it firmly within its local African setting.

In both Arabic and Indian aesthetics, music is divided into the two primary elements of melody and rhythm, although some scholars would add *fioriture* (the art of vocal and instrumental ornamentation) as a third element (Farmer 1957). This strikes a marked contrast with Western musical traditions, wherein harmony is accorded as much importance as melody and rhythm. This melodic/rhythmic aesthetic applies as well to *taarab* performance. *Taarab* songs rarely have more than four or five supporting harmonies, and instruments like the keyboard and accordion, which serve to provide harmonic support in Western music, are played as melodic instruments in counterpoint with the vocalist's melodic line. The same holds true for the lead string instrument be it an *udi* (a.k.a. *'ud,* a lute) or electric guitar.

Taarab performance practice also reflects the importance of ornamentation (in Swahili termed *nakshi*) found in Middle Eastern music, something else that is fundamentally at odds with Western musical practice. In Western music, ornaments serve to accentuate the melody and sometimes, the harmony. In Arabic music, however, ornamentation serves as a

> vehicle for expression . . . the Arab artist has made his goal that of expressing himself through the manipulation of abstract and stylized motifs. From these he creates compositions conveying a sense of never-ending design. . . . Ornamentation for the Arab artist, therefore, is not an addendum, a superfluous or extractable element in his art. It is the very material from which his infinite patterns are made. (al-Faruqi 1978, 18)

Types of ornamentation that emerge in *taarab* performance include sequences, shifts of accent, grace notes, slides, *appoggiatura,* vibrato or tremolo, turns, accents, and a heavy dose of *melisma*—extending one syllable of text over a series of pitches. This emphasis on embellishment, on *fioriture,* relates quite directly to training in Qur'anic cantillation. On this point, Lois Ibsen al-Faruqi writes,

> Even the kindergarten student "sings" his religious lesson in imitation of his teacher's cantillated example. No daily prayer or social event fails to provide "lessons" in Qur'anic cantillation and, thereby, in musical expression or performance. Though the Muslim would never regard such customs as performer or musical training, the effect of these religiously determined customs on the musical tradition is significant. Even in recent years some of the most famous of professional performers are known to have been trained in Qur'anic recitation. (al-Faruqi 1981, 68)

But whereas Arabic art music is "composed of musical formulae, of a conjunct string of short motifs or motif conglomerates in varied repetitions," (al-Faruqi 1978, 26), *taarab* is not an improvisatory genre. The strophic Swahili *taarab* songs are very clearly composed as structurally unified statements and are reenacted from one performance to the next in largely similar fashion. If changes are made, they often result from the vocalist's reading of the politics of the moment.

Finally, another Arabic musical element that carries over to a limited degree into *taarab* ideology is the use of melodic scales known as *maqamat*. There are countless *maqamat* throughout the Islamic world from Egypt and northern Africa to the Gulf states, Turkey, India, Central Asia, and beyond. "Each of the *maqamat* is based on a theoretical scale, specific notes of emphasis, and a typical pattern of melodic movement, in many instances beginning around the tonic note of the scale, gradually ascending, and finally descending to the tonic" (Racy 1984, 12). *Maqamat* are utilized in the *taarab* of Mombasa and Zanzibar, but they appear to have undergone some modification in practice in the movement to

East Africa. Names of *maqamat* used in East Africa resemble some of those recorded in other parts of the Arab world (Rast, Bayaat, Sikka, Nahwandy, Hijaz, Hijaz Dukka, Jirka, Kardaan, Swabra, Shuri, Rast Hussein),[37] but the musical reenactment varies. The same holds true for Western scales that have also been imported, often in form and not content, for use in *taarab* performance.[38]

To sum up, although *taarab* is often erroneously thought of as a direct musical/poetic importation, in fact it is decidedly local in origin. Concepts and terminology such as the name *taarab* or the musical concepts of Arabic *maqamat* and Western scales have been borrowed to apply to uniquely Swahili practices. Like both *ngoma* and *dansi, taarab* exemplifies the Swahili talent for assembling transnational musical bricolages.

Divergent Histories of Taarab

According to the overwhelming consensus on its history,[39] *taarab* dates to the reign of Sultan Seyyid Barghash of Zanzibar (1870–88). Following a failed attempt to overthrow his (then Sultan) brother, Barghash was sent into exile and spent a number of years in India and Egypt, where he was exposed to and greatly impressed by magnificent palaces and court life. Upon his return to Zanzibar and subsequent succession to the sultanate, he embarked on an active mission to construct his own court culture, of which a key element would be music. He sent a Zanzibari identified as Mohamed Ibrahim to Cairo to study Arabic music in order to establish a similar musical tradition in Zanzibar upon his return. Mohamed Ibrahim did so, organizing and training an initial group of six or so musicians, who gave their premier performance at the newly built palace named Beit al-Ajaib (House of Wonders). So pleased with the results was the sultan that he ordered the group to perform for him every evening after dinner at the Beit al-Ajaib, where the music would waft down to crowds of listeners below. Sung in Arabic and performed on imported Egyptian instruments such as the *udi* (lute), *nai* (flute), *dumbak* (drum), *daf* (tambourine), *kamanja* (single-string relative of the violin), and *qanun* (trapezoid zither with seventy-eight strings), *taarab* as elite Zanzibari court music was born.

As with the phenomena of *dansi* and *ngoma,* however, the process of expropriating elite symbols and practices occurred again with *taarab*. The rise to prominence in the 1920s of Siti binti Saad, a woman of slave ancestry who became the single most famous *taarab* singer to date, facilitated the process through her compelling voice and compositions.[40] Siti made *taarab* accessible to the general public not only linguistically by singing in Kiswahili, but also socially by penetrating its elitist veneer and opening her home to the practice of music-making and to all who enjoyed it (Fair 2001, 128, 169–225). She took *taarab* "out of the palaces and into the hearts of ordinary kiSwahili-speaking Zanzibaris" (Fargion 1993, 116) and thus brought to life the true meaning of *tarabun*. Her example inspired other women to unite and form women's *taarab* clubs to continue singing her songs even after her death in 1950. The most popular of these clubs were Royal Air Force, Royal Navy (another famous pairing inspired by colonial experience), and Sahib el-Arry, which performed for the female celebrations of Swahili sex-segregated weddings. Over time, local rhythms drawn largely from women's *ngoma* both locally and from the mainland (e.g., *kumbwaya, chakacha, vugo*) replaced in popularity the original Arabic rhythms introduced by Mohamed Ibrahim. Janet Topp Fargion analyzed the blurred boundaries between "ideal" *taarab*, women's *taarab*, and *kidumbak*, an offshoot syncretic tradition blending elements of both *ngoma* and *taarab*. She emphasized the need to recognize all three forms in order to make sense of *taarab*'s ubiquitous popularity in Zanzibar (Fargion 1993, 124).

These, then, are the main outlines of the history of *taarab* as presented in the available literature, a literature marked by remarkable unanimity. With the one exception of Graebner (1991, 1999), *taarab* historians have limited themselves to discussions of *taarab* in Zanzibar and argued that *taarab* performed on the mainland represents a diffusion of the genre from Zanzibar outwards in temporal and geographic space. This is a highly Zanzibar-centric perspective. *Taarab* is not, in fact, the exclusive product of a sultan's aristocratic affectations. At the same time that a highly formal approach to its creation was occurring in Zanzibar, a more casual, more organic process of *taarab* development was occurring on the mainland.

The Indian Ocean trade network that sustained the region economically did not merely entail the exchange of commodities. Accompanying the trade in material goods was a concurrent trade in cultural practices. Arabian dhows constituted the primary mode of transport, and seamen entertained themselves on these long journeys with music of their own making. A voyage was never complete without an instrument or two; thus instruments and musical traditions from Arabia and India traveled in this manner to East Africa to be incorporated within and influenced by local musical practices. Ports like Lamu, Mombasa, Tanga, and Zanzibar thus became focal points for the production of music (Fair 2001, 173–74, takes note of this).

Sayyid Ali Basakutta (born c. 1919) is recognized as one of the first people in his home town of Lamu to play the *udi*.[41] He accompanied Siti binti Saad when she came to Lamu in 1944 to perform for the district commissioner—only one event in an illustrious, highly acclaimed career as one of the premier musicians of his time. Born in Lamu, he had been working at the port as a young man in his teens (1930s) when he met seamen from Kuwait who had brought an *udi* with them and would perform occasionally on the dock. Enchanted, he sought them out and asked them to teach him. They did so for the duration of their stay in Lamu and, as a parting gift to their talented student, left him the *udi* to continue playing. He practiced on his own and in a few years' time was skilled enough to perform in public, primarily for weddings and other celebratory functions. His reputation spread, and soon people from Mombasa began hiring him to perform for their weddings. In time, he settled in Mombasa but because a more heavily Indian style of *taarab* took over the Mombasa aesthetic and because he felt a strong calling to religious devotion that he considered incompatible with his immersion in musical performance, he eventually stopped playing altogether.

In Tanga, from which Beni and *dansi* began their encroachment on the territory's musical consciousness, *taarab* proved to be another musical genre that developed and accrued significant popularity from an early point in its history. Hamisi Akida was born in the Chumbageni neighborhood of Tanga on November 22, 1914, and was very active in a Beni association called Tanganyika. He recalls that *taarab* groups were performing and already quite popular in Tanga before he moved to Dar es Salaam in 1939.[42] He dates the emergence of *taarab* in Tanga to the 1920s and identifies a group called Tanga al-Watan as Tanga's first *taarab* group,[43] composed of Hatibu bin Hatibu (who played the *udi* and *gambusi,* another variety of lute related to the Yemeni *ganbus*), Mrs. Mwana Peponi (a singer), Malao (who played violin, known in Kiswahili as *fidla*), Akida Abdulrahman, and others who filled out the music with tambourine (*rika*), flute (*nai*), clave (*timing*), and an instrument he called the "ukelele-banjo" (likely, a *tashkota*). Another organization he linked to *taarab* performance was the Chumbageni Social Club. Developments in Tanga thus paralleled developments in Dar es Salaam, where *taarab* was first associated with social clubs like Shuban li Arab and the Citizens Club (Graebner 1991, 189) also in the 1920s. By 1939, the two major *taarab* orchestras in Dar es Salaam were Egyptian Musical Club and Al Watan, and not surprisingly they were intense rivals. (After his move to Dar, Hamisi Akida served as leader [*kiongozi*] of Egyptian for seventeen years.)

Despite its importance as a principal East African port, it clearly was not only at the dock that the Tanga tradition of *taarab* was born. In addition to the standard *taarab* ensemble and social setting exemplified by Tanga al-Watan (with the imported *udi* and *nai*) and men's organizations such as the Chumbageni Social Club, *taarab* was embraced and popularized in Tanga by a group of independent-minded women. In the 1940s, nine women formed a group called Raha til Fuad (Happiness of the Heart) headed by a strong-willed divorced woman, Mama Akida, a.k.a. "Mama Lodi" (from the English "lord"). They sewed matching uniform dresses (*sare*) and prepared a repertoire comprising their favorite Siti binti Saad and Indian film songs but modified by the substitution of their own Swahili lyrics (Swahili contrafacta, if you will—vocal compositions "in which the original text is replaced by a new one").[44] They sang without instrumental accompaniment and did not charge to perform, since it was enjoyment—the happiness of their hearts— that inspired them in the first place. After some time, one of the members introduced the tambourine (*rika*) to the group's sound, and the group grew in popularity to the point of being invited to record some of their songs at the Tanganyika Broadcasting Corporation (TBC). Eventually, men joined, first as instrumentalists, then as composers and singers, and, perhaps as a reflection of its changing membership, the group's name changed to Special and later again to Young Novelty. Akida Jumbe, son of Mama Akida,[45] joined Young Novelty in 1962 as an accordionist and singer. By that point, Young Novelty's instrumental ensemble consisted of: *fidla* (violin), *udi*, accordion, harmonium (Indian keyboard instrument operated by bellows), *tashkota* (a hand-picked stringed instrument), *tabla* (Indian drums), mandolin, string bass, and clarinet. It soon developed a rivalry with another *taarab* band named Shabaab al-Watan. As in *ngoma* history, one rivalry led to another, spawning a history of competitive *taarab* clubs in Tanga that continues even today.

Fission and fusion define *taarab* club membership, both now and in times past. Financial arrangements regarding club expenses and income frequently bring discord, often to the point of division. This caused a breakaway faction of Young Novelty to establish the Black Star Musical Club in June 1963. Black Star would become an internationally recognized group, but it too fell subject to the same processes that brought about its birth. In 1970, a breakaway faction left Black Star to found Lucky Star Musical Club, and so it continued. Every decade from 1950 onward is remembered in terms of a dominant rivalry born of the previous rivalry: Young Novelty and Shabaab al-Watan in the 1950s–60s, Black Star Musical Club versus Lucky Star Musical Club in the 1970s, Golden Star Taarab versus White Star Taarab in the 1980s, and Babloom Modern Taarab versus Freedom Modern Taarab in the 1990s.

Figure 3.8   Mama Akida ("Mama Lodi") and her son Akida Jumbe of Young Novelty Musical Club, c. 1960s. Photo supplied by Akida Jumbe; photographer unknown.

Taarab and the Reiteration of Regional Styles

By the time Sayyid Ali Basakutta was learning the *udi* in Lamu, *taarab* as Zanzibar's court music was already well established, and Siti binti Saad was already well on her way to Africanizing the genre. And by the time that the women of Tanga's Raha til Fuad had sewn their uniforms and begun singing at weddings, Siti binti Saad had passed away, and Sayyid Ali Basakutta had rejected his life in the material world. As produced on the Kenyan mainland by dockworkers and on the Tanganyikan mainland by male social clubs and women's cooperatives, however, *taarab* never attained the same associations of high culture that it did in Zanzibar, originating as it purportedly did in the sultan's palace. While it is true that Dar es Salaam *taarab* groups reflect stronger Zanzibari influences (of what Fargion terms "ideal" *taarab*) in the selection of instruments, use of Arabic rhythms, and adherence to ideals of Arabic melodic scales (*maqamat*), *taarab* groups in Tanga, Mombasa, and Lamu developed along significantly different lines, eschewing strict adherence to Arabic rhythms and *maqamat*. I would suggest that the differences in style—one that musicians today label as the difference between "classical" (i.e., Zanzibar) and "modern" (i.e., Tanga/Mombasa) *taarab*—relate to different origins (palaces versus docks, social clubs, and women's cooperatives) and relative proximity to or distance from the sultan's sphere of influence. I would also suggest that these differences have coalesced and hardened into regional styles such that the trained ear can easily distinguish *taarab* of Mombasa from that of Zanzibar and *taarab* of Mombasa from that of Tanga. Thus, through musical performance, the age-old regional personalities associated with the formerly sovereign city-states once again find expression in a modern setting.

Certain musical features distinguish the regional varieties of *taarab*. "Ideal" Zanzibari *taarab*, as performed by groups such as Nadi Ikhwan Safaa and Culture Musical Club, still pays homage to its Egyptian roots by utilizing the *maqamat* and various Arabic rhythms, and by sporting large orchestras (20–40 members) that resemble the large orchestras found in Middle Eastern classical music. They comprise full string sections (multiple violins, cello, and double bass), *qanun, udi, dumbak, nai,* accordion, and lately various electric instruments such as electric guitar, keyboard, and electric bass. A full mixed female and male chorus sings the refrain. Performance practice retains a formal aristocratic air enhanced by the Western-style suits worn by male instrumentalists and fancy gowns worn by female singers. Paid-admission *taarab* concerts are common and generally begin with an instrumental prelude called a *bashraf* that displays proficiency in Arabic musical technique. *Taarab* songs in Zanzibar revolve around the same themes of love and social relations, but are longer than songs on the mainland due to the extended instrumental interludes that precede each verse of poetry. An average Zanzibari song lasts 15–20 minutes, whereas songs from Tanga last about 5–10 minutes.

This description by no means describes all the *taarab* groups in Zanzibar. As the research by Fargion and Fair illustrates, "ideal" or "classical" *taarab* falls at one end of a diverse spectrum of musical practice that also encompasses smaller groups. The all-female groups perform their own brand of *taarab* in the same general style as the classical groups but with decreased adherence to *maqamat* and more inclusion of local rhythms. Moreover, the smaller groups tend to perform more commonly in wedding celebrations than paid-admission concerts, yet they are no less popular. A recent arrival on the Zanzibar *taarab* scene is a group called East African Melody Modern Taarab that forcefully represents itself as "modern" like mainland groups (e.g., BIMA Modern Taarab and All Stars Modern Taarab in Dar es Salaam, and Babloom Modern Taarab and Freedom Modern Taarab in Tanga) in distinction from "classical" Zanzibari *taarab*. This particular group has its own unique, heavily amplified and very electric sound due to a long, two-year performance contract overseas in Dubai that provided it access to the latest in electronic musical equipment. They are the first group to utilize an electric drum machine, eschewing the typical drums found in *taarab* performance—*bongos, dumbak, tabla,* and even modern drum-kits.

In the Tanga tradition of *taarab* performance, groups are small, consisting of no more than ten members, and the primary instruments are electric guitar and keyboard for melodic counterpoint, electric bass for harmonic reference, bongos, and (recently) Western drum-kits for rhythm, and various additional percussion instruments like the tambourine, rattles, and timing sticks. This characterizes current groups that define themselves as performers of "modern *taarab*." Although also "modern" in the sense of having readily adopted technological advances such as electric instruments, they do not differ in fundamental makeup from the famous *taarab* bands of the 1960s and 1970s. Today's electric bass, guitar, and keyboard substitute for the stringed double bass, *udi,* and accordion of Tanga's yesteryear or Zanzibar's today, serving the same musical functions outlined above. Reliance on local *ngoma* rhythms such as *chakacha* and *kumbwaya,* as well as Afro-Cuban rhythms drawn from *dansi* music, such as *samba, rumba,* and *pachanga,* occurs in all varieties of *taarab*—classical and modern both. But in Tanga, interest in composing within Arabic rhythms or melodic modes (*maqamat*) died out long ago.

Indian influence is strongest and most obvious in the *taarab* tradition of Mombasa, where the practice of appropriating Indian film songs and applying Swahili lyrics originated. Mombasa's sound is less amplified than Tanga's, but the smaller group structure dominates there as well, the difference being the inclusion of Indian instruments such as the *tabla* and *harmonium* to better approximate Indian rhythms and melodic styles. Song length approximates that of Tanga rather than the lengthy format followed by Zanzibar songs. Several of Mombasa's leading *taarab* performers have toured in Europe and released CDs on Western recording labels. These include: Malika, Zein l'Abdin Musical Party, Zuhura Swaleh and Maulidi Musical Party (see the discography).

Finally, in Dar es Salaam, culturally and geographically situated between the two poles of Zanzibar and Tanga, both influences can be found in the larger orchestras like Egyptian Musical Club, Muungano Cultural Troupe and the recently established Tanzania One Theatre as well as the much smaller All Stars Modern Taarab. Dar es Salaam, because of the large number of national corporations based there that have sponsored cultural troupes, has developed a standard performance practice encompassing *ngoma, kwaya,* drama (*tamthiliya*), acrobatics (*sarakasi*), *dansi,* and even magical acts (*mazingaombwe*)—a "variety show" format. The increase of *taarab's* popularity brought about its inclusion to the standard program, and some groups that failed to include it died out as a result.[46] More significant, during my years in Tanzania, *taarab* was always reserved as the final act in a cultural troupe performance since, as it was explained to me, it constituted the show's crowning and most popular element. Were it placed at the beginning, said Captain Komba, director of Tanzania One Theatre, a considerable portion—if not vast majority—of the audience would leave immediately afterwards.[47]

This sums up some of the primary differences in *taarab* styles found along the coast. Musical practice evolves in historically specific ways, and the multiple histories of *taarab* enhance our understanding of coastal society as teeming with cultural possibilities. An abundance of musical elements were selectively harvested to produce—within Swahili aesthetic parameters—this distinctive poetic form. And while *taarab* styles reflect regional cultural preferences, they also reinscribe them and thus contribute to the sense of cultural particularity that coastal communities so highly value now as in centuries past.

From Practice to Performance: The Participant Observed

> Performing is in essence "giving form to"; it occurs whenever communicative exchanges are initiated that involve all participants, including, of course, the ethnographer.
>
> —Johannes Fabian, *Power and Performance*

Not long after I began performing with Watangatanga, I accompanied Tanga's Babloom Modern Taarab band on a trip to Kenya to appear on Kenyan television. It was July 1993, and the weekend trip afforded us many opportunities to talk and learn about each other during the long bus ride and many delays at the television studio. In the context of one of our discussions, the question arose: Why was I so interested in their music? Upon discovering that I was also a musician, one response was,

"Ndiyo maana!" ("That's the reason!"), while someone else produced the band's keyboard so that I could demonstrate my skill and introduce them to "my music." I played for them one of my favorite Chopin nocturnes—somewhat difficult to do without the full keyboard range (their keyboard had sixty-seven miniature keys, as opposed to a piano's eighty-eight full-sized keys). Then I switched traditions and played a popular jazz piece inspired by Rimsky-Korsakov's "Flight of the Bumble Bee." This elicited intrigue with and admiration for the independent movements of my right and left hands, because in the *taarab* keyboard tradition, the left and right hands play the same melodic motifs separated by one or two octaves. Classical piano music is a tradition unto itself, dependent upon no other instrument. Rhythm, melody and harmony are all produced by manipulating the keys in time and in tonal space. In *taarab* music, however, the keyboard is only one of a necessary complement of instruments in which each pursues its own musical and acoustic role. It serves as a melodic instrument, "singing" accompaniment to the melodies sung by the singer and the lead guitar (or *udi* or *fidla*). Rhythm is provided by the percussion section (bongos, drums, timing sticks, tambourine, rattles), while harmony is generated from the interplay of instrumental and human voices.

With my performance, my musicianship was established and with it the beginnings of a fraternity among us. My status experienced a sudden shift, for the rest of the afternoon was consumed with teaching me the keyboard accompaniment to one of their songs. It was not an encounter with romantic *communitas,* however. We did not suddenly experience harmonic convergence and go singing and playing off into the sunset. Contrary to popular belief in "music as a universal language," it was immediately obvious that we approached music-making from fundamentally different perspectives, and the following two years constituted our shared attempts to bridge those perspectives and their inherent assumptions. One assumption became apparent within moments after my delivery of the Chopin and "Bumble-Bee Boogie," because the initial request made of me for "my" music was repeated. Confusion must have reigned on my face, for I was suddenly interrogated:

Babloom member: ". . . *your* music. Surely you have composed your own music, have you not?"

K. A. (in weak protest): "But I am a trained *performer,* not a composer. I perform *others'* music."

Babloom, almost in unison: "What kind of musician are you then?"

Although that conversation impressed upon me the idea that every Swahili musician composed as well as performed, I would come to learn over time that the difference posited between our respective traditions did not constitute a difference in essence but one of degree. In *taarab,* as in Western classical music, there exists a division of musical labor whereby some individuals (*mpigaji,* "instrumentalist"; *wapigaji* pl.) are recognized as particularly adept at playing certain instruments,[48] while others (*mtunzi,* "composer"; *watunzi* pl.) are noted for their skill in composition—either of the *mashairi* (poetic texts that serve as song lyrics) or *muziki* (the instrumental interludes between song verses) or both. There is, nonetheless, in the Tanga *taarab* tradition a much greater element of communal composition and communal performance practice than exists in the West and, moreover, an assumption that no one individual can or should monopolize any single aspect of music production.[49] Certain tendencies toward specialization may be identified, but rarely do individuals lay exclusive claim to musical skills. In all the groups with which I worked, there were always multiple composers, multiple vocalists, and multiple instrumentalists for each instrument. In part, it was explained to me, this constitutes a necessary adaptive strategy to an environment in which 100 percent commitment to a group cannot be expected—music being largely a secondary activity. Because of the uncertain composition of the group at any given performance, there have to be alternate performers for all the instruments so that the performance can go on.

To my Western sensibilities, however, the continual exchange of musical roles came as quite a surprise. After attending my first Babloom rehearsal back in September 1992, I commented in my fieldnotes that "one notable feature of the rehearsal was that the musicians invariably switched instruments, and did so with obvious ease." I still remember the care I had taken during the rehearsal of the first song that night to note who was playing what, even drawing a diagram in my notebook of the instrument layout with what names I could remember indicating the performer of each instrument. And I remember my disappointment when, with the next song, everyone got up and, in the manner of "musical chairs," changed positions and instruments thus rendering my diagram totally irrelevant.

Upon discovering my musical capabilities, Babloom set to work transforming me into a colleague. That very day they taught me the keyboard part for one of their songs, and I performed it with them two days later at a wedding in Mombasa. On our return to Tanga, I was presented with a surprise—a formal marker of my new status within the band. In Mombasa, which has more shops than Tanga and a greater selection of goods, members of Babloom had shopped for cloth for new band uniforms. Two weeks later on the day of my official Tanga debut with the band, they also debuted the new uniforms. When I went to the band's club earlier in the day to confirm the time of the performance, some musicians and fans of the group were playing a board game called *keram*, while others were gathered in small groups talking. The band's director asked me to wait and disappeared inside the living quarters of the building. He returned with a brown paper package that he ceremoniously presented to me. It contained a uniform—the same shirt sewn for the other band members but sewn with the buttons running down the opposite side (which he carefully explained defined it as a woman's shirt). The gratitude that overwhelmed me must have shown on my face, because everyone seemed pleased.

That evening, I arrived at the hotel dressed in my new shirt and a black skirt (they had told me that they would be wearing black pants). As I went to sit as a member of the audience to wait for the one song I knew, I suddenly was struck with the glaring statement on how the band viewed me. They looked quite smart in their new uniforms, ten men all wearing the same shirt as my own. There were two female members of Babloom, however, one lead singer (the band's star Fatuma) and one back-up singer. Significantly, they wore a different uniform. While our shirts boasted multicolored, geometric designs against a lime green background, the two women wore identical yellow dresses with black polka dots. There was no other possible interpretation: I had been incorporated as a classificatory male. After the performance (in retrospect one that I'd just as soon forget because of my dismal execution of the keyboard accompaniment), I raised the uniform issue with the band's director, lightheartedly asking why I wore the male uniform. He explained that as a keyboardist, I was rightly presented with the uniform worn by instrumentalists, reminding me again that the placement of my buttons defined it as a female uniform. Thus, he preferred to identify *role* as the distinguishing factor as opposed to gender, but it just so happens that roles within the band are gendered: instruments are played only by men, whereas singing constitutes both a male and female task. When my role within the band progressed and I was taught to sing, the female members insisted that I wear the same uniform they wore since my role as vocalist (*mwimbaji*) elevated me in their eyes from instrumentalist (*mpigaji*) status.

As others have found before me, the shared act of music-making catapults one into a new set of relations with musicians of a different musical tradition. In seeking to solve the mystery of the Bulgarian bagpiper's fingers, for example, Timothy Rice (1996) found himself in a liminal experiential plane that ultimately proved very rewarding both personally and theoretically.

The perspective I had acquired in the process of learning to play competently (not necessarily well) was neither emic nor etic. It was my own. I could now supply from my own self-understanding verbal explanations of the complex mental processes necessary to generate this music. . . . If emic understandings are located in other people's heads and given to us in their language reports, then my understanding wasn't emic. On the other hand, if etic understanding involves applying objective analytic methods to sounds without regard for their cultural salience, then my understanding wasn't etic either. I felt as if I had achieved a mediation between these two theoretical categories, these two ontological conditions, and that this mediation challenged fundamentally one of the most important theoretical foundations of our discipline. . . . Although I wasn't Bulgarian, I could act like a Bulgarian in the production of a complicated musical form, and when I acted like a Bulgarian in this particular way, they did too; that is, if the occasion were right, they danced. (1996, 110–11)

By the end of my fieldwork two years after my Babloom debut, I had been carefully inculcated in *taarab* performance and privileged with an insider's vantage on its practices, politics, and contexts. My repertoire of Babloom songs grew to thirty for which I played keyboard and fourteen that I sang—all from memory as I had been taught. In total, I attended more than 350 *taarab* performances, of which roughly one-third were weddings. I participated either as a keyboardist or vocalist in nearly 300 performances and accompanied bands on tour to Korogwe, Zanzibar, Mombasa, Dar es Salaam, Muheza, and Pangani. In 1994, Babloom released a cassette of the songs I sang with them, and between 1994 and 1995, various music videos were produced of performances in which I participated that are still aired occasionally on Zanzibari, Tanzanian, and Kenyan television. The anthropological lens was refocused from my observation of others' participation to others' observation of my participation (figure 3.9). After one year of dual participation in both *taarab* and *dansi,* I spent my last year ensconced primarily in *taarab* performance. Watangatanga collapsed as a result of an internal dispute in the middle of 1994, eleven months before the end of my research. It reappeared as Les Watanga Stars later that year with slightly different personnel and a new patron, but by that time I was fully engrossed in the world of *taarab.*

My mode of research, having been thus transformed from observation to participation, engendered an unavoidable shift in ethnographic practice. The demands of my role as performer, with its accompanying social and temporal obligations, made it ultimately impossible to pursue the rigorous note-taking regimen that had marked the first year of my fieldwork. Any loss of detail, however, was more than compensated for by the experiences, knowledge, and mutual trust gained over the course of my shifts in status from *mgeni* (guest) and *mtafiti* (researcher) to *mwimbaji/mpigaji* (singer/instrumentalist) and finally to *mwenyeji* (local resident).

Figure 3.9 The author performing with Babloom Modern Taarab. Taarab composer, singer, and violinist Issa Matona of JKT Taarab came to tip (it was a joint Babloom—JKT Eid Mosi concert), March 14, 1994, Tanga. Photo by Ezekiel Mazengo.

Conclusion: Musical Action, Social Action, Political Action

In this chapter, my aim has been to provide a limited musical ethnography and social history of three musical genres—*ngoma, dansi,* and *taarab*—that permeate coastal Swahili society. Each of these genres constitutes a form of cultural expression and a resource through which social and political identities are constructed, contested, reshaped, and manipulated. These histories and descriptions profoundly implicate music in the processes of defining gendered, ethnic, regional, urban/rural, political, religious, and socioeconomic statuses. Individuals can utilize music to diminish or augment social distance, reinscribe or subvert hierarchies. The type of music one hires for an event can signify socioeconomic status or mark an attempt to alter a prescribed or widely attributed status. It also can mark ethnic and regional identities, as when individuals hire *ngoma* from their perceived home region to maintain and confirm linkages, or when coastal Swahili seeking to construct Arab affiliations hire *taarab* groups singing in Arabic for their events. Music can serve as an indicator of religious affiliation and degree of devotion, as the alcoholic associations of nightclubs and bars taint *dansi* for pious Muslims, and conversely mark urbanites who hire *dansi* bands as "modern," well-to-do, and generally Christian.

> Social performance, following writers such as Bourdieu (1977) and de Certeau (1984), is . . . seen as a practice in which meanings are generated, manipulated, even ironised, within certain limitations. Music and dance . . . do not simply "reflect." Rather, they provide the means by which the hierarchies of place are negotiated and transformed. (Stokes 1994, 4)

Musical performance, in other words, can thus serve as a tool, a strategy for laying claim to specific social labels and political objectives. It is a time-proven social resource and effective mode of political action that continues to play a vital role in daily life, as the following chapter reveals.

4

WEIGHTY GESTURES, SIGNIFICANT GLANCES: *TAARAB* PERFORMANCE AND THE CONSTITUTION OF SOCIAL RELATIONS

> The theoretical benefit that is to be derived from making performance a guiding idea is a conception of relationships between texts and interpretation which is neither static nor hierarchical but processual. The burden of such an approach is to show the essential openness of that process.
>
> —Johannes Fabian, *Power and Performance*

> An ethnography of musical communication which concentrates on musical meaning and interpretation should be concerned with explicating some of these lived epistemologies, these intertwinings of form and substance, these practices full of potential or realized coherence and contradiction.
>
> —Steven Feld, "Communication, Music, and Speech about Music"

Case 1: "A Lover Does Not Need a Divorce"

We were gathered outside under a translucent, indigo sky where a host of stars had already made their appearance. Stars in the night sky scattered points of light across the mantle of Tanga Bay, which stretched out before the audience and vanished into the purple silhouette of the distant Usambara Mountains. But the stars on the ocean's surface were in fact kerosene lamps hanging off the bows of small wooden boats to attract the seasonal *dagaa* (small fish resembling sardines) to fishermen's nets. As the last of the sun's aura faded from view, the band began in earnest to entertain its audience of well-dressed Swahili, African, and Arab adults and children seated on the hotel lawn in the growing darkness.

A popular song about tea (the complete lyrics appear in appendix A) elicited quite an audience response. A number of women rose from their seats to cross the invisible boundary that demarcated the stage area and tip the musicians with bills, coins, and much flourish.

Tamu Ya Chai ("The Sweetness of Tea")—excerpt
Rama Hamadi, Babloom Modern Taarab, Tanga

Japo wamejaa tele, wazuri wa kusifika	Although there are many praised for their beauty,
Wa rangi hizi na zile, ambao wameumbika	Of these colors and those, who are nicely shaped,
Mimi wangu yule yule. Siwezi kumuepuka	Mine is the same one. I cannot resist her.
- - -	- - -

Chorus
Tamu ya chai sukari	The sweetness of tea is the sugar.
Sihadaike na rangi	Do not be attracted by the color,
Hata iwe ya maziwa	Even if it has milk

Tea, sweet and good to drink, prevails over more expensive soda as the most common beverage along the Swahili coast. Served either dark as *chai ya rangi* (literally, "tea with color"), heavily spiced with ginger, or light, *chai ya maziwa* ("tea with milk"), spiced with cardamom, cinnamon and cloves, tea in this song is equated with a metaphorical woman whose beauty is not determined by the color of her skin. The song's composer challenges local conceptions of beauty, shifting emphasis away from external appearance to inner goodness, and critiquing an unfortunate aesthetic predilection common to both his society and ours.

As the song came to an end, a young, well-dressed Swahili woman approached the band from the side of the stage to make a special request: the song "Hawara."

Hawara ("Live-in Lover")
Khalid Akida, Babloom Modern Taarab, Tanga

Kwani utune mafunda, Na maneno kuropoka	Why is it that your cheeks are puffed out and you rant and rave?
Mimi wewe kukupenda, Mwenyewe ulinitaka	I only loved you after you loved me first.
Kama umeshindwa nenda, Hawara hana talaka	If you can't take it anymore, get lost. A lover doesn't need a divorce.
- - -	- - -

Moyoni hayanichomi, Ondoka sina udhia	My heart does not pain me. Leave, I'm not bothered.
Na wala sikutazami, Njia unayoendea	Nor will I watch which way you go.
Haiwi nipende mimi, Huku vyangu wanilia	How can I accept loving you when you only love the gifts I give you?

- - -	- - -
Sipendi ya kubishana, Wako wengi kama wewe	I don't like to quarrel. There are many others beside you
Wajuao pendo sana, Wafuatao wenyewe	Who know love well and who pursue me themselves.

Hidaya ni kupeana, Si peke nikupe wewe	Real love is shared by two—not given only by me to you.
- - -	- - -
Heshima kuwekeana, Ndio utu na usawa	To respect each other is both human and
Kuropoka yaso maana, Ni lipi la kushauwa	right.
Kama umepata bwana, Nenda usije chelewa	To babble nonsense—what makes you do this?
	If you've found another man, go. Don't delay.
- - -	- - -

Chorus

Wewe acha kuropoka, Kama menichoka nenda	You—stop babbling! If you are tired of me, go.
Hawara hana talaka, Nenda mwana kwenda	A lover does not need a divorce. Go, woman, leave.

Hawara is one of many words in Kiswahili meaning "lover," but it specifically indicates a lover with whom you live but to whom you are not married. As the song was being performed, the woman who had requested it, "Asha,"[1] repeatedly entered the stage area to tip the singer and other musicians with stylized, elegant movements. She remained within the stage area for the duration of the song, dancing, gesturing with her arms in tandem with the lyrics, and mouthing the lyrics, making it clear to all that this song held special meaning for her. Occasionally, other women would come to tip, but they did not dance for long and would return to their seats. Before the end of the song, a second young woman, also Swahili and equally well-dressed, whom I will call Rukia, made a request of her own: the song "Semeni Semeni," which accordingly was performed next and to which she now tipped enthusiastically and frequently.

Semeni Semeni ("Talk All You Want")
Khalid Akida, Babloom Modern Taarab, Tanga

Semeni semeni, Wala hayatonikera	You can talk, talk all you want but it will never disturb me.
Huyo muhisani, Kwangu mimi ndie bora	He, my lover, is perfect for me.
Nitamthamini, Mpaka kesho akhera	I will cherish him till tomorrow in Heaven.
- - -	- - -
Lilo la maudhi, Yeye sitomtendea	I will never offend him.
Taichunga hadhi, Yake kwa kunyenyekea	I will give him honor, show him reverence,
Sipate maradhi, Au jambo la udhia	So that he will not suffer illness or vexation.
- - -	- - -
Na analotaka, Naahidi nitampa	And whatever he wants, I promise to give him.
Simweki na shaka, Bure katoka mafupa	I won't give him reason to doubt me nor grow thin with worry.

Kwangu amefika, Mughibu sitomtupa	He has settled with me, my lover. I will never throw him away.
- - -	- - -
Kweli nampenda, hadharani nabaini	I love him truly—publicly I make it known.
Penzi talilinda, Sitolitoa thamani	I will cherish this love. I will never consider it worthless.
Litaponishinda, Nami siwi duniani	When it does overcome me, it will be when I am no longer of this world.
- - -	- - -

Chorus

Semeni, Mchokapo acheni	Talk until you tire, then stop.
Muhisani, Simwachi asilani	I will never leave my lover.

The innocent observer who might interpret tipping (*kutunza*) as an act of appreciation for the musical quality of the song or the musical technique of the performers would be sorely mistaken. As it was later explained to me, Asha had recently split from her lover, who subsequently entered into a relationship with Rukia. He was in attendance that night as Rukia's escort. The meanings and motivations suddenly become clear: Asha used the song "Hawara" to send him the message that she did not care that they had broken up—a lover, after all, does not need a divorce. He was free to go. Rukia responded with a message to Asha that, unlike Asha, she would cherish her lover and never throw him away.

* * *

Taarab, often blithely characterized as "Swahili love songs," permeates East African social life. One hears it while passing shops in the street. One hears it at wedding celebrations. One hears it played daily on the radio, and until 1996 one heard it every Sunday evening performed under the stars at what used to be Tanga's only tourist hotel.[2] Yet upon closer inspection, *taarab* proves to be much more than a genre of uncomplicated love songs. Beneath sometimes banal declarations of romantic love lie layer upon layer of social critique, political positioning, gender debate, identity contestation, and dispute negotiation. One of the most common features—indeed, a defining characteristic—of this sung poetry is the heavy use of metaphor, innuendo, allusion, and double entendre. Metaphor produces multivalence and transforms the songs into power-laden weapons commonly exploited in the negotiation of social relations. By means of *taarab* performance, coastal women (and, less frequently, men) convey messages that local protocol prohibits otherwise; it thus constitutes a very potent and highly gendered mode of communication. What in chapter 1 I termed the "politics of the personal" provokes considerable underscored attention in *taarab* poetry as well as powerful underscored action during *taarab* events.

Taarab thus presents a particularly enlightening example of the imbrication of power and performance. According to Foucault, power "is neither given, nor exchanged, nor recovered, but rather exercised, and . . . it only exists in action" (Foucault 1980, 89). It is in its performance, therefore, that power is realized. Work on political ritual and rhetoric (Moore and Meyerhoff 1977; Kertzer 1988; Hobsbawm and Ranger 1983; Herzfeld 1988), and on the active construction of nation-states (Steinmetz 1999; Herzfeld 1997; Coronil 1997; Verdery 1991a; Handler 1988) contributes to a perspective on power as essentially performative. On the other hand (as reviewed in chapter 1), developments in the study of expressive culture have evoked increased understanding of the political nature of performance. Its ephemeral quality means that performance exists "in the moment" in a way that texts do not. Performances are always subject to split-second decisions involving differentially weighted obligations to people, desires, expectations, societal factions, identities, worldviews, and so on. An ever-growing literature on the politics of performance attests to this: Ranger 1975 on the Beni *ngoma;* Strobel 1979 on the Lelemama *ngoma;* Coplan 1994 on Basotho migrants' poetry; Fabian 1990 on Swahili popular theatre; Cowan 1990 on Greek dance; Vail and White 1991 on poetry and song in southern Africa; Drewal 1992 on Yoruba ritual; Erlmann 1996 on Zulu migrants' *isicathamiya* songs; Barber, Collins, and Ricard 1997 on West African popular theater; and recent edited volumes by Gunner 1994 and Parkin, Caplan, and Fisher 1996. Taken together, these overlapping bodies of scholarship give rise to a conclusion promoted throughout this book: that as politics are predominantly performative, so too is performance predominantly political.

In this chapter, I offer a series of *taarab* case studies that forward this argument and two related theoretical claims. To begin, each case forces reconsideration of dominant performance paradigms that posit a unidirectional process of communicative flow from performers to audience. As discussed previously, such models acknowledge the latent power within a performance event but locate it primarily in the actions and decisions of performers. Audiences are powerful only insofar as they evaluate a performer's "competence" (Bauman 1977). Depending on perspective, the balance can be skewed in favor of performers (seen as wielding considerable control over their audiences) or audiences (to whom a performer is ultimately beholden). Data culled from *taarab* performance, however, reformulates the relationship in an intriguing way. In his introduction to *The Politics of Cultural Performance* (1996), David Parkin relates "cultural performance" to Turner's "social drama" paradigm and that, in turn, to the methodological focus on societal conflict and contradiction forwarded by Manchester School theorists Max Gluckman, Clyde Mitchell, and Abner Cohen. He argues for an understanding of cultural performance as people's "non-explicit or diversionary, and therefore ceremonialised, ways of resolving the contradiction that comes from having to co-operate with neighbours and kin with whom they necessarily diverge, sometimes fundamentally, in their interests" (Parkin 1996, xix). I echo this position because *taarab* is a highly utilized, highly effective means of negotiating disputes and social relations in Swahili society. In literally taking their disputes and social claims center stage, female audience members like Asha and Rukia relegate performers to the sidelines and thus undermine the ubiquitous "performers-audience" opposition so central to mainstream performance theory. Their actions, moreover, prove Foucault's dictum that power is a widely dispersed resource that can be commanded by many, not restricted to the few.

Secondly, while Abu-Lughod's (1986, 1990) analysis of Bedouin love poetry was significant for drawing attention to another highly gendered and equally metaphorical form of expression at a time when female perspectives were largely unexplored, she positioned it as a "discourse of defiance" and a "discourse of rebellion" that offered women poetic release from the challenges of patriarchal life. I argue here that *taarab* poetry goes beyond the reflection on and articulation of emotions and sociopolitical positions. It extends beyond discourse. *Taarab* performance constitutes a power-laden mode of social action that is deeply implicated in the ongoing constitution of social relations.

Taarab Performance as Dispute Negotiation

The following case studies drawn from performances I attended between 1992 and 1997 survey a variety of meaningful actions and reactions. The potent combination of allusive song texts, multilayered performance practices, and shared local knowledge provides all the necessary ingredients for negotiating social relations Swahili-style. Participants manipulate song texts—a practice called *kumpasha mtu* (to send a message to someone), *kumwimbia mtu* (to sing about someone), or *kumaanisha* (to imbue with meaning)—to reposition each other in the constellation of their social universe. There are a host of uses to which *taarab* poetry is put, but among the most common are affirmations or rejections of love relationships (as illustrated in the case of Asha and Rukia) and denouncements of moral character. All three objectives emerge in our second case study.

Case 2: The Battle over Salim

Back at Tanga's Mkonge Hotel at a regular Sunday evening performance, Naima pulled aside the band's director to request a song.[3] He started to apologize, explaining that the band had not performed that song in over a year because the singer who sang it had left to join another group, but she merely responded by pressing more money into his hand. She insisted that—irrespective of how well or poorly it was performed—the song *must* be performed. So, with a few mistakes that no one aside from the musicians appeared to notice or care much about, the following was sung:

Mwana wa Mwenzio ("Someone's Child")
Khalid Akida, Babloom Modern Taarab, Tanga

Jamani isiwe tabu, Kufanya mapenzi nae
Mkatafuta sababu, Ili nimuache yeye
Kwani mwendo taratibu, Atazowea mjue

Ah, it shouldn't cause trouble that I am in love with him.
You search for reasons for me to leave him.
Isn't it true that slowly, slowly, he will grow accustomed to my love? You should know this

- - -

- - -

Udogo ni lake umbo, Ni mazito mambo yake
Lipi utafanya jambo, Hata yeye asumbuke
Lolote kwake ni pambo, Jueni msidhurike

He may be small in stature, but he is great in other things.
What can you do to cause him worry?
Anything I do for him is great. Know that you will not be able to disturb him.

- - -

- - -

Kama mwamona hafai, Awakera nini nyie
Huba zangu za kurai, Zitamfanya apowe
Na ikiwa hatambui, Nitamfunza mwenyewe

Even if you don't consider him suitable, why does it concern you?
My satisfying love will make him settle.
And if he isn't very experienced in love, I will teach him myself.

- - -

- - -

Acheni jama acheni, Maneno mnayosema
Mwajitia shughulini, Kutafutana hasama
Mdogo takuwa lini, Nacheni nikuze jama

Stop it, you people. Stop saying these things.
You keep yourselves so busy looking for trouble.
For how long will he be too young? Leave it to me to bring him to maturity.

- - -

- - -

Chorus
Nasema yenye ukweli, Walimwengu
    watambue
Mwana wa mwenzio, Mkubwa mwenzio
Mwana wa mwenzio, Chako kitoweo

What I say contains the truth. People of the world, recognize this.
Someone's child is another's adult.
Someone's child is savory for you.

As the song was performed, Naima repeatedly came up to the musicians to tip them with large-denomination bills that she waved about with much flourish before depositing them on the singer's forehead, in his shirt pocket, or in his hands. After each tip, she would exit the stage area and wend her way back through the audience, nearly reaching the table she shared with a man and a few other women before turning around to return to the stage and continue tipping. Occasionally, she chose to tip the other performers arranged behind the primary singer: two guitarists (one lead, one bass), two drummers, one playing a drum kit and another on bongos (these all being male instrumentalists), a foreign female keyboardist (myself), and three back-up singers (two women and one man). All the instruments were electric but for the drums, clavé (called "timing"), and a tambourine played by backup singers. Poor lighting focused exclusively on the stage area reduced everything else to dusky shadows with only the moon's pale light available to aid visibility. From time to time, when caught by the stage lighting in the liminal space between musicians and audience, Naima would cast pointed looks off to one side away from the area where her table was situated. Although she was not alone in venturing on stage to tip, other women tipped far less frequently—usually once, at most twice. Naima left no room for doubt that she was sending someone a message.

Local gossip confirmed that Naima was considerably older than Salim, the boyfriend with whom she shared her table. The significant looks she cast in the other direction were aimed at his former girlfriend Fatima, who also happened to be there. The song came to an end, and Naima disappeared from view. A little while later, the band started playing a song called "Kubwa Lao" ("The Toughest One"). Fatima immediately rose and began to tip in earnest.

Kubwa Lao ("The Toughest One")
Seif Kassim Kisauji, Babloom Modern Taarab, Tanga

Nimeshaji-prepare, Kwenye shughuli ya leo *Tena niko so sure, Vishindo hapa ni kwao* *Uwanja umetulia, Ainuke kubwa lao*	I have already prepared myself for today's event, And I'm sure all challenges end here with me. The floor has cleared. Let the toughest one stand up.
- - -	- - -
Hatutaki muamuzi, Nasema leo ni leo *Watangaza sikuwezi, Tutaona mwishilio* *Ukishindwa hukatazwi, Waweza timura mbio*	We don't want a referee. I say today is the day. You announced that I cannot beat you—we'll see in the end. And if you lose, there's nothing to stop you from running away.
- - -	- - -

Si kama nakushitua, Kukweleza ya bayana	It's not as if I shock you to tell you openly
Nataka kulichimbua, Lile zizi la fitina	I want to dig up the roots of discord.
Kibwebwe nakufungia, Tena wasiwasi sina	I tie on *kibwebwe*[4] because of you and am not at all worried.
- - -	- - -
Asonijua ni nani? Ni bora akatulia	Who doesn't know who I am? Better that person keep quiet.
Tena nawapa ilani, Mimi siwakuchezea	And I'm giving you a warning: I'm not someone to play with.
Kacheza na hayawani, Kiwango uliopangiwa	Go play with animals—that's more your grade.
- - -	- - -

Chorus

Kwa utulivu sipati kifani	For calmness, I have no match.
Na kwa uovu mimi namba wani	And for evil, I am number one.

This song provided Fatima the poetic and social space she needed for her public, if indirect, response to Naima. She tipped repeatedly and tried to outdo Naima in the amount of embellishment she performed with her body as she moved between audience and performers, sometimes only half-disguising an arm gesture in Naima's direction during passages of poetry that resonated with her concerns. Her challenges (*vishindo*) via the poetry were met as Naima rose from her seat to countertip. Neither one betrayed any overt hint about the fierce contest over a man and their identities in which they were engaged. Smiles remained on their faces except when they mouthed the song's poetry along with the singer to emphasize an especially relevant line of poetry, and the closest physical contact they had was when the hem of one ornate dress brushed against that of the other. Nevertheless, for some of the audience members with whom I compared thoughts afterwards, the conflict escalated to an anxiety-inducing level because the performance area was at one end of the hotel swimming pool (with tables and chairs for the audience arranged around the pool), and people worried that one woman might push the other into the pool!

Yet despite the intensity of sentiment on display in an albeit obscure and camouflaged manner, emotions suddenly were blanketed when taken outside the context of performance, or rather when placed in a new performance context. Passing and politely greeting each other on the way to the soda and snacks vendor, one would never have guessed that, just moments before, these women were engaged in a heated battle over their status both within the community at large (as "cradle-robber" on one hand, and rejected, undesirable woman on the other), and in relation to each other: an enmity publicly revealed exclusively in the context of *taarab* performance. As the evening drew to a close, Salim took the unusual step of entering the female-dominated tipping area to tip the singer during a love song: "She is loved. I cherish her and have no other beside her."[5] As conspicuous as he already was being male and tipping, he garnered even more attention by timing his movements not only for this particular song, but also during a point in the song when no one else had gone to tip. Only then—when he had exclusive access to the singer, the sung text, and the audience's attention—did he tip and turn to glance meaningfully at Naima before returning to take his seat beside her.

Despite the apparent *coup de grâce,* the battle was not concluded that evening. At the following Sunday's performance, Naima and Salim were again in attendance, and, although Fatima was absent, her relative Mariam had come with a friend. That evening, the battle continued no less vehemently between Naima and now Mariam acting on behalf of Fatima. At the time of this performance, I was far from well-versed in *taarab* protocol and practice. I knew enough to recognize the signs and actions of a dispute between Naima and Mariam, yet I mistakenly interpreted it as their own, personal feud. When I inquired about the source of the feud and why Naima appeared to be involved in so many public feuds, the unanimous opinion among the band members and various audience members was that this was a reprise of last week's dispute, with Mariam acting on behalf of her relative. Midway through the evening, the band's director chose to perform again—this time without a request from Naima—the song "Mwana wa Mwenzio." When band members began to complain, reminding him of how poorly they had performed it the week before, he silenced their opposition with a wave of his hand and proceeded to announce the song over the microphone. The song was performed, and Naima once again tipped frequently. Mariam tipped during other songs—any song that could be interpreted as an insult or challenge—accompanied by her friend. The two would wait until no one else was in the open dancing/tipping area between the musicians and audience, and then go and at the same moment (bringing to my mind images of synchronized swimmers) cast pointed looks in Naima and Salim's direction.

That night after we had all returned to the home of the director, which also served as the band's administrative headquarters and rehearsal space (the "club"), the lead guitarist Masoudi asked Seif, the director, why he had forced the performance of that song over their objections. He explained that he knew it would undoubtedly elicit a response from Naima with counter responses from Mariam. Such a dynamic benefits the band because it always generates more money in tips. Then, to my dismay, he further explained that he knew I would want to see the *vishindo* (challenges, provocations, insults) again—this being my research—so let them go at it for me to watch. (I subsequently asked him to refrain from sparking battles in the name of my research.)

The Ascendance of Mipasho and Twilight of Mafumbo

This use of *taarab* for airing and engaging in disputes I have witnessed countless times, often without recognizing it for what it was. Understanding the actions within these performances requires current knowledge of the local gossip (of which there is a continuous, never-ending stream), which in turn reflects the strength of communal ties in communities such as Tanga. As noted by Bauman and Briggs,

> [P]erformances are not simply artful uses of language that stand apart both from day-to-day life and from larger questions of meaning, as a Kantian aesthetics would suggest. Performance rather provides a frame that invites critical reflection on communicative processes. A given performance is tied to a number of speech events that precede and succeed it (past performances, readings of texts, negotiations, rehearsals, gossip, reports, critiques, challenges, subsequent performances, and the like). (Bauman and Briggs 1990, 60–61)

In these first two case studies (Asha versus Rukia, Fatima versus Naima), love politics finds expression through *taarab* love poetry. Yet by no means are disputes and hidden messages (*mipasho*) limited to matters of the heart. Nor, as evidenced by Salim's actions, is deployment of song lyrics restricted to contests and struggles. Although he was the source of their dispute, Salim was in a sense external to the dispute negotiated that evening between Naima and Fatima. He decided nonetheless to affirm publicly his relationship with Naima through the predominantly female mode of action, tipping. Similarly, Mariam's resumption of a dispute that was not ultimately her own constituted a public affirmation of loyalty to her relative. Thus, these events illustrate the potential within *taarab* performance for the exchange not only of insults and devaluations of social standing, but of positive affirmations of friendship, loyalty, love, and kinship.

Three terms that inevitably arise in discussions about *taarab* are *mafumbo, mipasho,* and *vishindo. Mafumbo* means "riddles" or "hidden meanings"; *mipasho* means "messages"; and *vishindo* encompasses "challenges," "insults," "affronts," "boasts," and "attacks." *Taarab* songs are characterized by these three elements, although it is not necessary to have all three in every song. *Mafumbo* enable multiple meanings, meanings which may be considered *mipasho* that can be used as challenges or insults (*vishindo*) in the context of performance. A popular song, for example, about a woven mat upon which strangers/visitors rest, "Jamvi la Wageni,"[6] hides a second meaning in which the mat refers to a promiscuous spouse/lover upon whom various visitors rest (see case 9). Another popular song sung from the perspective of a woman who has become a man's second wife directs the following to her co-wife:

Figa moja haliweki chungu	A single stone will not support a pot
Alo wako na mimi ni wangu	The one who is yours is also mine[7]

The lines refer to *mafiga,* the three stones set in triangle formation around hot coals to support a pot in the common East African cooking arrangement. In another song, copper is denigrated for its attempts to resemble gold: "You will polish and scrub, but they are not the same even for the scrubbing. Know that copper is not gold."[8] And a song from one of the older and most famous groups from Tanga, Black Star Musical Club,[9] praises *halua,* a sweet, gelatinous, cardamom-suffused confection served at weddings with bitter, Turkish-style coffee. Despite being served, sometimes over the course of several days, on a single platter from which everyone pulls a piece (this contrary to Swahili culinary do's and don'ts, which generally forbid serving food that has been touched by someone else), *halua* is nonetheless a prized delicacy, forever sweet and good to eat. It is contrasted in the song with *makombo,* leftover food that must be discarded. The poet uses *halua* as (once again) a metaphorical woman who, even after having been touched by one man, does not lose her sweetness and remains "good to eat" by another.[10] This relates to the metaphor of "eating from one plate" used in more than a few songs with an underlying meaning of unwittingly sharing a lover (the food on the plate) with someone else (see Sahani Moja, "One Plate," in appendix A).[11] This aesthetic of *mafumbo* (metaphoric allusion) parallels the aesthetic of *heliaki* (indirectness) described by Adrienne Kaeppler for Tongan poetry: "The composer manifests *heliaki* in metaphor and layered meaning, skirting a subject and approaching it repeatedly from different angles. Hidden meanings must be unraveled layer by layer until they can be understood . . ." (Kaeppler 1993, 497).

Interviews with older *taarab* musicians, poets, and composers, however, reveal a common complaint. They argue that the current period of *taarab* performance is only concerned with *mipasho* (hidden messages) that are paradoxically less and less hidden in the texts and that strike a great (to their minds) contrast with *taarab* performed two decades ago and earlier that adhered more strictly to a *mafumbo* aesthetic. Songs like "Kubwa Lao" ("The Toughest One"), which challenge, insult, abuse, and defame in baldly explicit language with sparse use of metaphor, are seen as fundamentally distinct from songs of a previous *taarab* generation. Contemporary songs are often described as laden with *ma-*

Table 4.1 *Mafumbo* Songs: Black Star, Lucky Star, and Babloom

Band	Total Number of Songs Reviewed	*Mafumbo* Songs	Percentage of *Mafumbo* Songs
Black Star Musical Club	142	33	23%
Lucky Star Musical Club	259	22	8.5%
Babloom Modern Taarab	136	8	6%

tusi or "foul language" and thereby divergent from ideals of respectable behavior. Older songs, by contrast, are remembered as being very indirect, correspondingly more discreet, and utilizing a much higher degree of metaphor than today's songs. Reigning opinion dates the shift from a *mafumbo* to a *mipasho* aesthetic to the emergence of self-defined "modern" *taarab* in the early 1990s.

I tested this idea by comparing the repertoires of Black Star Musical Club (est. 1960) and Lucky Star Musical Club (est. 1970)—two of the older *taarab* clubs in Tanga—and Babloom Modern Taarab (est. in 1990), taking note of the number of songs built entirely around a single metaphor. The results are displayed in table 4.1. This cursory overview indicates a substantial decrease in the number of *mafumbo* songs over the past four decades. Surprisingly, however, the decrease occurred much earlier than contemporary discourse would indicate. The lower percentage of *mafumbo* songs in the repertoire of Lucky Star Musical Club is striking, given that they were once the preeminent club in Tanga and represented the ideal form of Tanga-style *taarab* to many. Another aberration in the Lucky Star repertoire is the comparatively higher number of explicitly political songs (presidential praise songs, songs honoring national holidays and foreign presidents, and so on; see table 4.2). Lucky Star members repeatedly reminded me of how committed they had been to singing the government's praises, serving as *de facto* government praise poets. The vast majority of their songs, however, revolve around love—love lost, love gained, love desired.

Despite slight disparities in social memory and social practice, as

Table 4.2 Explicitly Political Songs: Black Star, Lucky Star, and Babloom

Band	Total Number of Songs Reviewed	Political Songs	Percentage of Political Songs
Black Star Musical Club	142	2	1.4%
Lucky Star Musical Club	259	26	10%
Babloom Modern Taarab	136	5	3.7%

evidenced in these repertoires, a nostalgia for *mafumbo*-style *taarab* remains. People young and old pointed me to the notorious dispute between Black Star and Lucky Star Musical Clubs, sung through the following series of songs, as an example of the former glory of *mafumbo*.

Case 3: Black Star versus Lucky Star

The Swahili say, *Nyota njema huonekana alfajiri,* "A lucky star can be seen at dawn." It means that luck or talent can be identified early on . . . and so it was with a band of the same name in coastal Tanzania during the 1970s and 1980s. In 1970, a group of malcontent musicians left the fold of Tanga's nationally celebrated Black Star Musical Club to start their own band. They called themselves Nyota Njema (Lucky Star) Musical Club (figure 4.1) and quickly rose to a position of prominence not only in the Tanga musical scene but at national and international levels, as evidenced by invitations to perform for Presidents Jomo Kenyatta of Kenya in 1973 and Samora Machel of Mozambique soon after Mozambican independence in 1975. Their success, however, caused bitterness

Figure 4.1 Lucky Star Musical Club on tour in Kenya in the 1970s. Photo supplied by Shakila Said; photographer unknown.

among Black Star members, who subsequently launched a musical attack armed with metaphorical allusion and innuendo. The two bands engaged in a dispute over which was the better band—both musically and in the moral character of its members.

Prior to the birth of Lucky Star, the renowned songstress Shakila (born Tatu Saidi in 1944) had animated Black Star with her widely praised voice and recorded a number of songs with the group in Mombasa (see the discography).[12] After she and her husband Hatibu Akida (another Black Star musician) left Black Star with several other members in a dispute over the band's financial management to found Lucky Star, another female singer named Sharmila (born Jalala Rashid c. 1954) arose to fill the gap left by Shakila. Lucky Star's success threatened Black Star's position and generated an enmity between them articulated and enacted through song.

One of the first songs directed against Lucky Star by Black Star was "Mnazi Mkinda" ("Young Coconut-Palm"), composed by Black Star's lead composer Kibwana Said and sung by Sharmila. The song describes a young coconut-palm whose short height makes its branches and fruits easily accessible to thieves:

Walinda wewe walinda, Mali inateketea	You protect yourself, yet your wealth is
Mnazi wako mkinda, Werevu wauchezea	destroyed.
Kwa hila wamekushinda, Wevi hao	Your young coconut palm—wily people
wamezea	toy with it.
	They beat you in cunning, those thieves
	who desire it.

Shakila is a woman of short stature. The song plays upon this characteristic, drawing a parallel with the young coconut palm and indirectly charging Shakila with promiscuity in the sharing of her metaphorical "fruits" with many "thieves."

The song did not pass without a response from Lucky Star. Their reply, sung by Shakila, equated Black Star's famous composer Kibwana Said with a monkey who, although the recipient of good fortune, is nevertheless doomed to failure (see the excerpt below). The refrain indirectly accuses Black Star of not being satisfied with its own success and position, coveting that of Lucky Star as well (track 3 on the accompanying CD).

Kitumbiri ("Monkey")—excerpt
A. S. Jinamizi, Lucky Star Musical Club, Tanga

Hata nawe kitumbiri, Kitumbiri majaliwa	Even you, monkey, favored monkey,
Umejifanya hodari, Miti kutaka nyanyuwa	You thought yourself so great, wanting to
Hali tawi na tambiri, La kushinda kupasua	uproot trees
	When you are incapable of breaking
	branches.

- - -   - - -

Kaditamati kwa heri, Kitumbiri majaliwa	Good-bye, favored monkey.
Kama ujile kwa shari, Naona umeghumiwa	I think you are confused if you come looking for a fight.
Utaipata athari, Jiti likikwangukia	If the mighty tree falls on you, you will be injured.
- - -	- - -

Chorus

Kitumbiri majaliwa	Favored monkey,
Wala kwenu na kwetu wajajaliza	You eat at your home and then come to eat again at ours.

Kibwana did not let the insult pass in silence. He composed a response likening Shakila to a fox:

Mbweha ("Fox")
Kibwana Said, Black Star Musical Club, Tanga

Mbweha nakupa hakika, Sinitafute undani	Fox, let me assure you, do not test my anger,
Ovyo ovyo kuropoka, Kama mtu afukani	Babbling nonsense like a fool.
Kamba uliyotamka, Na wewe imo shingoni	The rope you mentioned encircles your own neck.
- - -	- - -
Usisahau watani, Kwenu ulikozalika	Do not forget joking relations from your birthplace.
Si mtu mwenye thamani, Wala mwenye kusifika	You are someone of no value worthy of no praise.
Sinitafute undani, Kesha wajakasirika	Do not test my anger. Tomorrow you will be angry.
- - -	- - -
Kuumbua ukitaka, Ukashifu mshindani	If you want to embarrass or insult your competitor,
Uwe umekamilika, Hunalo doa mwilini	You had better be perfect, your body free of defect.
Hayo uliyotamka, Mbona nawe ukundini	Are you not a member of the very group you criticize?
- - -	- - -
Mbweha ninakuusia, Maovu usiyaombe	Fox, I warn you. Do not ask for evil.
Utahadhari dunia, Ina hatari kumbe	Be careful of the world. It is full of danger, human being.
Ajabuni ya ngamia, Kucheka nundu ya ng'ombe	It is a wonder that the camel laughs at the cow's hump.

In the second verse, Kibwana implies that Shakila transgressed the rules of acceptable insult and went too far, forgetting "the joking relations of her birthplace." He recognizes that rivalry (*upinzani*) exists and, when controlled, is not necessarily a bad thing. This makes explicit the fact that, although primarily disputing the relative musical and popular standing of their respective bands, Shakila and Kibwana were contesting the boundaries within which their dispute could occur.

The Politics of Tipping

This pattern of dueling composition, called in Swahili *kutungana* (literally, "to compose to/about each other"), predates the emergence of *taarab* by several centuries and constitutes a defining characteristic of Swahili performance practice, as demonstrated by both the Beni and Lelemama performance traditions (see Bakari 1981; Harries 1962; Mulokozi 1975, 1982; Ranger 1975; Strobel 1979; Shariff 1988; Biersteker 1996). Song texts directed at specific individuals or groups, however, constitute only one way in which *taarab* music is implicated in the airing and negotiation of disputes. The musicians are not the only disputants. On the contrary (as in the first two cases), it is common for members of the audience to lay claim to song texts in the negotiation of their own personal disputes. They do so through the act of tipping.

The Swahili term for tipping musicians with money or other forms of gift is *kutunza*. Tipping is common practice primarily during musical events; that is, one does not tip at restaurants or hair salons, and only recently have people begun tipping attendants at petrol stations. The Swahili dictionary published by the University of Dar es Salaam defines *kutunza* as "the act of giving a gift to someone after they have successfully accomplished something, e.g., dancing a *ngoma* or singing."[13] Over the course of my fieldwork, I attended over four hundred musical performances in various contexts, including weddings, initiation ceremonies, state celebrations, and paid-admission concerts. And although the practice is more common to *taarab* performance than *dansi* and *ngoma,* a musical event without at least some tipping was rare. Nor is the practice engaged in only by elites. An implicit sliding scale operates, so that tips at events in urban halls or at upper-class homes are often in the form of high-denomination bills, whereas in rural villages, coins or even flowers constitute the bulk of tips.

There is a definite art to the act of tipping—as much performance as anything on stage. In *taarab* contexts, where close attention to the poetic texts creates a primarily seated (i.e., not dancing) audience, women dominate the tipping scene. The uninitiated or very shy may unceremoniously walk up to the singer to hand him or her some money, but the vast majority will make their way from the audience to the stage with a stylized, elegant dance that enables them to stand among the seated and thus show off skill in dancing or perhaps a new dress. People perform the act of tipping with varying degrees of flourish in accordance with their own presentation of self. Some wave money in circles around the singer's head before depositing it in a hand, in a pocket, on the head, on the forehead, or even sometimes in the singer's mouth. (I have expe-

Figure 4.2 Women tipping Khadija Kopa with Culture Musical Club, Zanzibar, 1990. The brass urn below her is where she deposits the tips. Photo by author.

rienced this on more occasions than I'd prefer to remember; it makes singing rather difficult.) Dancing occurs but rarely is openly acknowledged, for proper Muslim female decorum demands modesty at all times, and dancing is considered by many to be an immodest activity. Thus when approaching the musicians to tip, women will often deny that they are going to dance (*kucheza*) and insist instead that they are going to tip (*kutunza*). As further evidence of this, they frequently wave the money they plan to tip or their pocket-books conspicuously in the air for all to see, thus signifying unambiguously the motivation behind their entrance into the public eye.

When combined with lyrics that speak to a particular personal issue, tipping provides people with the means of appropriating those lyrics and claiming them for personal use. Someone angered by a friend's lack of loyalty, for example, in choosing to tip during a song about a disloyal friend appropriates the text for a personal dispute and, without transgressing local protocol, makes public a private grievance. The message can be further magnified with an ambiguous wave of the hand or a pointed look in the direction of the targeted friend. The sending of messages via tipping is called *kumpasha mtu*. The verb *kupasha*, related to the word *mipasho*, is the causative form of the verb *kupata*, "to get." Another term for the act of sending a message is *kumaanisha*, literally, "to make meaning" (the causative form of *maana*, "meaning"), in the sense of communicating a specific meaning to someone. As illustrated in the case of Naima, Fatima, and Salim, tipping is utilized as much to affirm as to contest social relations. Another way of affirming friendships is the very common occurrence of two women going together to tip (e.g., Mariam and her friend), often wearing matching dresses that they had sewn for the occasion. Tipping is the audience's medium of participation. Herein lies the flaw in the strict "performers-audience" opposition found in much performance theory for *taarab* performance clearly is not limited to those situated on stage.

In the case of Naima, Fatima, and Salim, a battle was waged between two women over a man and over their social identities. Naima sought to construct for herself a public identity as a fulfilled, satisfied, and fulfilling, satisfying lover, regardless of the age difference between her and Salim. With embodied action, her significant glances toward Fatima communicated the charge that Fatima had been unsuccessful in fulfilling and satisfying Salim—hence she was now alone. Fatima disputed both messages by selecting and tipping during a song that claimed for herself status as "number one," that is, "the best," interpreted here as the best lover. She thus contested Naima's characterization of her as rejected or undesirable.

Proper conduct as locally defined would not allow these individuals to say these things to each other privately, much less publicly. People emphatically asserted that to engage in such disputes outside the context of *taarab* is considered *aibu*, "shameful." Honor dictates engaging in disputes in a culturally defined manner. *Taarab* poetry provides disputants with the words they cannot voice while abiding by codes of proper, respectful behavior (*heshima*). The act of tipping provides a socially sanctioned opportunity to confront an opponent face-to-face and air grievances within a liminal physical space (between musicians and audience) that allows room for much impromptu elaboration. It was explained to me that women often harbor their offenses, resentments, and feelings of injustice, saving them for expression at the next *taarab* performance, where they can give full reign to their disputes in a culturally prescribed manner.

Although this use of music and poetry as a means of dispute negotiation within Swahili communities has never been fully explored, neither has it gone unnoticed by researchers. The use of *ngoma* songs for the exchange of insults and challenges has been well-documented in Ranger 1975, Strobel 1979, Farrell 1980, Bakari 1981, Glassman 1995, Campbell 1983, and Franken 1986 and 1994. In the context of her discussion of *sheria* (law) and *mila* (custom) as interchangeable and often intertwined means of resolving disputes on Mafia Island (an island off Tanzania's southern coast), Caplan (1995) makes passing but significant reference to music as an alternative medium for dispute negotiation:

> Another point is that women have other means of prosecuting quarrels than taking them to a forum. The singing of songs at rites of passage (circumcision, girls' puberty ceremonies, and weddings) or at the preparations for them is a customary way of scoring points off opponents. The songs never mention people by name, but everyone present, including very often members of the "other side" know to whom they refer. (Caplan 1995, 209)

Anthropological Approaches to the Study of Disputes

In his 1979 treatise *Disputes and Negotiations: A Cross-Cultural Perspective,* generally accepted as a landmark contribution to the anthropological study of disputes, P. H. Gulliver drew a sharp theoretical boundary between two processes of dispute resolution: negotiation and adjudication. By *negotiation,* Gulliver refers to the process by which "people attempt to reach a joint decision on matters of common concern in situations where they are in disagreement and conflict" (xiii), a process he posits as fundamentally different from that of *adjudication,* whereby the decision-outcome is determined by a third party: "a single individual or set of persons [who] hold[s] the acknowledged right, that is the legitimate authority and responsibility, to reach and enunciate a decision that is the outcome of the dispute and is in some degree binding on the disputing parties. Compulsorily or voluntarily, the disputants surrender the ability to decide for themselves" (4). Although credited with an innovative shift away from earlier models that had defined disputes by the application of legal codes, Gulliver nevertheless has been criticized for grounding his analyses within the notion of equilibrium that characterized the anthropological theory of his day. His analysis of disputes tends to focus on reconciliation and resolution, that is, the restoration (even if only temporary) of social harmony.

> Once begun, negotiations produce some outcome. . . . The point of importance, however, is that the outcome is marked in some form or other, and there is an expression of collaboration and agreement. The negotiations have been concluded, and there may be a good deal of amity. On the other hand, a persisting antagonism and a number of disagreements may remain; the parties may be bitter rivals still. For the moment, however, there is agreement, whether limited or broad, and a mutuality in the achievement of an outcome. (Gulliver 1979, 169)

Taking issue with the assumption that disputes necessarily result in resolution, Elizabeth Colson writes, "The handling of disputes settlements as though these were rituals of reconciliation . . . masks the realities of the social coercion that maintains some semblance of peaceful co-existence despite on-going antagonisms" (1995, 70). Yet despite undertones of an equilibrium model, Gulliver brought theoretical attention to processes of negotiation that previous normative analyses privileging the application of legal norms had ignored.

Gulliver defined *power* as "the endeavor by the parties to use the resources available to them that afford each some negotiating strength and a means of exercising persuasion and coercion upon the other," and *norms* as the "rules, principles, morals, values—oughts which are claimed to set standards by which disputed issues can be assessed, and indicate the proper allocation of rights, obligations, and objectives" (1979, 187). In drawing attention to the play of power in dispute negotiations, Gulliver provided "a much more instrumental interpretation of the invocation of norms and legal ideas than had been put forward by the others" (Moore 1995, 25) and thus "contributed toward a theoretical move away from structural-functional models and toward processual analyses" (Moore 1995, 27). As Caplan points out, however, in her analysis of *sheria* (law) and *mila* (custom) as two sometimes conflicting, sometimes complementary sets of norms in Swahili communities, "[N]orms . . . not only may be counterposed to power, but are themselves also contested and therefore changing" (Caplan 1995, 220).

I learned about dispute negotiation within coastal Swahili society through hearing about and documenting, witnessing, and even participating in disputes. Both processes of adjudication and negotiation are found in common practice. Persons in the role of adjudicators range from respected elders within a family or clan to the ten-house cell leader (a remnant of the socialist era), the *kadhi* (an Islamic religious authority), the neighborhood police sergeant, and the various levels of courts. (For a particularly rich and comprehensive analysis of discourse and adjudication in Swahili Islamic courts, see Hirsch 1998.) My experiences with adjudicated disputes, however, are few in comparison with the numerous cases I saw being negotiated. A characteristic practice that I noted time and again was the deployment of indirection, camouflage, subterfuge, and pretense, of which the veiled gestures and allusions in *taarab* performance are but one illustration. Having witnessed so many covert negotiations in *taarab* events, I nearly misunderstood it as a characteristic unique to *taarab*. It was only after I had the practical misfortune (but in retrospect, theoretical fortune) to be accused of a traffic violation, bringing me into direct confrontation with two segments of Tanzanian police forces, that I recognized the wider existence of a protocol of pretense.

Case 4: Mama Gari Bovu (Lady with the Rotten Car)

About midway through my research, I acquired an ancient, 1970s Toyota pickup—the result of a barter arrangement made with an expatriate in town in exchange for tutoring him in computer skills. The vehicle fit nicely with my research because it sounded like a traveling orchestra, what with the chorus of clangs, knocks, and rattles that constituted its normal, on-the-road audio accompaniment. It frequently broke down, but that kept me at a happy distance from the expatriates of Tanga who would speed by in brand-new, air-conditioned Landcruisers and Pajeros. And, being a pickup, it provided (when functioning) handy transport for a complete band—instruments, equipment, band members, and all. It also doubled well as transport for a crowd of veiled women to and from weddings.

Although the truck had acquired for me the name Mama Gari Bovu, "Lady with the Rotten Car,"[14] it suited me and my needs but for one thing: I became a target for the traffic police. In a seeming reversal of the situation here in the United States, where it is the fast and fancy cars cruising along at illegal speeds that are often targeted by police for traffic violations, in Tanzania the unfortunate targets of police attention are the slowest, most decrepit vehicles to brave the pot-hole-ridden roads. Such vehicles are sure to exhibit one violation or another, and the lack of proper taillights, a working emergency brake, and a decent coat of paint all constitute violations invoking fines. A little negotiation and self-deprecation, however, goes a long way toward reducing fines. A common strategy for reducing or bypassing the negotiation process is to insert a bill of money into one's folded drivers' license and hand it to the officer before a word is spoken and before a violation is identified. The situation represents underdevelopment in stark relief because it is the poor and weakest who suffer the most; those with the least resources are subject to the most exploitation.

My truck was a popular target. The original taillight covers had long since disappeared and I had replaced them with painted plastic. The bed of the truck had several gaping, rusted holes that matched the holes in the cab's floor though which mud splattered my legs and clothing during the rainy season. It was a vehicle that would long ago have been relegated to a junkyard in the United States, but it afforded my colleagues and me the luxury (?) of long-distance travel. And so, keeping the truck alive and on the road became a constant preoccupation among my circle of friends, and doing so entailed assigning someone on every outing the role of lookout for the all-white uniforms of *trafiki* (the traffic police).

On the unlucky days when I was sighted, I was invariably cited, and negotiation ensued as to the amount of fine I would have to pay. According to common knowledge, such fines for traffic violations constitute supplementary income for *trafiki,* who purportedly receive very low wages.[15] The goal is always to negotiate a fine payable on the spot, because the consequence of *not* reaching settlement is the confiscation of one's drivers' license and a trip to the traffic police headquarters for more negotiation and the return of the license. After I experienced several unpleasant inspections and lost a significant amount of money to fines, a friend of mine, Saidi, whose family owns a bus line servicing various routes to and from Tanga, advised me to come find him should I ever experience another run-in with the *trafiki*. His line of work kept him in good stead with them thanks to a standing agreement involving the regular exchange of money in return for infrequent arbitrary stops and bus searches.

One morning as I drove the truck on an errand, I stopped before turning a corner onto one of Tanga's main thoroughfares. Tanga may be a city, but it is a small one that benefited greatly from a Chinese aid project introducing massive numbers of inexpensive Chinese-made bicycles. Bicycles have become the dominant form of local transport, with buses filling the need for longer trips. Cars are few and far between. Thus despite being one of the main thoroughfares, the street was empty but for one lone car a considerable distance away that morning as I made the turn. As it turned out, however, that lone car was in fact a police car full not of white-uniformed *trafiki* but brown-uniformed *polisi* (police), and it was moving at high speed. So by the time my old truck had made the turn, the police car was upon me, its inhabitants visibly impatient with my slowness. To accommodate their urgency, I quickly turned off onto the nearest street, and they sped on past. As luck would have it, four hours later, on my way with some band members to collect some borrowed furniture for a wedding celebration, we had the misfortune to run into the same car of *polisi,* who recognized my *gari bovu* and ordered me to the side of the road. When I inquired why I was being stopped, they only responded that I knew my violation and demanded my license. I eventually handed it over (reluctant because it is *trafiki* who issue traffic violations, not *polisi,* who are concerned with criminal activity) and was told to meet them at the *trafiki* headquarters. Instead of going straight there, I first collected my friend Saidi and together we made our way to the *trafiki* headquarters.

At the headquarters, the police sergeant immediately demanded an apology. I asked again for an explanation of my supposed violation and was told that I had pulled out into oncoming traffic without looking. I attempted to explain that plenty of space had been available and that it was due to their speed—something I could not have guessed from the distance—that the space so quickly diminished. I also argued that had I truly been at fault, they should have stopped me immediately rather than wait until they happened to see me four hours later! I refused to concede fault—in part because I truly did not consider myself at fault, and in part because I worried about worse consequences were I to admit to the violation. After my continued refusal to apologize, the brown-uniformed *polisi* decided to leave and open an official case (*kesi*), which would mean continued confiscation of my license until the matter was resolved. As they stalked off towards their car, a *trafiki* captain urged me to go and apologize. He said, "You are in our country now and this is the way we do things," but I still worried about potentially worse consequences following an unwarranted admission of guilt to authorities that did not have the authority to issue traffic violations in the first place. After more discussion, the *trafiki* told Saidi, "It is clear that she will not apologize, so you have to do it for her. Go to *polisi* headquarters with her. Have her stay in the car so that she can be seen, and go talk on her behalf. That will end the matter." We did exactly that. We drove to the *polisi* station, and Saidi conspicuously parked the truck right outside the main entrance. I waited in the truck in plain view of all inside, while Saidi argued for clemency, pointing out that I was, after all, "a foreigner who didn't know any better." After about ten minutes, he returned with my license, the sign of settlement. The case had been dropped.

In a similar set of relationships to those found in *taarab* performance, an unrelated third party assumed the task of articulating my dispute with the *polisi*. Saidi, like a *taarab* singer, provided the words I could not bring myself to say in the negotiation of my personal dispute. Although the constraint on my ability to speak was my own sense of justice rather than adherence to local rules of social protocol, there nevertheless arose strikingly similar structural relationships to those in a typical *taarab*-articulated dispute. My visual presence in the car constituted a *mpasho* (sing.; *mipasho*, pl.), a message of apology that was verbally communicated by Saidi. A definition of communication focusing on the sending of messages and their interpretation has been outlined by Feld:

> Communication is not, in other words, a "thing" from which people "take" meanings; it is, rather, an ongoing engagement in a process of interpreting symbolic forms which makes it possible to imagine meaningful activity as subjectively experienced by other social actors. Communication is a socially interactive and intersubjective process of reality construction through message production and interpretation. (Feld 1994, 78–79)

It was the acceptance by the *polisi* of Saidi's role as mediator, as interlocutor, that facilitated a settlement to the situation, but we were led to believe that settlement would have been hampered or impossible had I not submitted to the pretense of being apologetic by allowing my presence to be freely interpreted as such.

Gulliver analyzes the role of third-party mediator in a variety of social contexts and offers a typology of mediators: (1) disinterested, (2) interested, (3) partial, and (4) linked to both parties. The change in relationship from the initial dyad of a dispute into a triadic interaction is thus accounted for. But how can we accommodate the relationships within *taarab*-enacted disputes in which there is at least a *quadripartite* relationship encompassing disputants (at least two) plus the singer and the audience? The disputants provide the dispute, the singer provides the information and argument, and the audience represents the communal norms and moral authority to which the disputants appeal. The cases to follow will make clear these relationships.

Finally, Gulliver stresses the importance of information exchange and learning in the process of negotiation: "The course of negotiation . . . involves the exchange of information: alleged facts and proffered interpretation of them, argument, appeals to rules and values, threat, promise, demand, offer, counteroffer, and so on. The flow of information permits a continuous process of learning by each party about the requirements, preferences, expectations, perceptions, attitudes, feelings, strengths, and weaknesses of both the opponent and himself" (Gulliver 1979, 5–6). In fact, he posits that

> [t]he crucial distinction then, between adjudication and negotiation is that the former is a process leading to a unilateral decision-making by an authoritative third party, whereas the latter is a process leading to joint decision-making by the disputing parties themselves as the culmination of an interactive process of information exchange and learning. (Gulliver 1979, 6–7)

It should now be clear that *taarab* constitutes one such process of information exchange, a form of musical communication providing alleged facts and their proffered interpretations, arguments, appeals to rules and values, and so on, via the *combination* of sung poetry and participants' actions. Meaning is located at the intersection of text and performance. Heard or viewed in isolation, the texts and performances would lack reference, thereby negating the process of negotiation. As the following case studies reveal, *taarab* performance is characterized by multiple voices, multiple agendas, multiple interpretations, and multifarious relationships between disputants, singers, and audience. In highlighting the dialectical dynamics of Swahili musical performance and the negotiation of social relations, I join Feld in his attempt "to redress the imbalance common in analytic perspectives that equate musical communication with the extent to which a listener receives a composer's or performer's intentions" (1994, 94). The idea that music can only convey a single variety of meaning—that of the composer—to a passive audience, cannot be accepted in the case of Swahili *taarab,* nor is it likely to hold true for many other genres. Rather, "[m]eaning . . . is momentarily changeable and emergent, in flux as our interpretive moves are

Figure 4.3   Fatuma Kisauji with Babloom Modern Taarab, Tanga, 1994. Photo by author.

unraveled and crystallized" (Feld 1994, 88) and, in the context of the Swahili coast, constitutes a powerful, contested social resource.

Case 5: An Incident of Violence

Another night at Mkonge Hotel. During the song "Kubwa Lao" ("The Toughest One"), a woman, Zakia, was dancing and tipping, waving a single finger in the air during the song's refrain: "Kwa utulivu sipati kifani na kwa uovu mimi namba wani," "For calmness I have no match, yet for evil I am number one" (see case 2). Another woman was similarly inspired to dance with notable enthusiasm to the song, and, perhaps sensing the growing antagonism, other tipping women exited the stage area, leaving behind only Zakia and this other woman. Both were waving the single finger, each claiming to be number one. Since you can't have two number ones, angry looks were exchanged, they got a little too close to each other while dancing, one of them shoved the other, and that was that—clothes ripping and all. The singer stopped singing in order to try to pull them apart. A few men rushed forward to hold them back, because they both wanted to keep on fighting. A friend of Zakia's later told me that Zakia didn't know that woman but had seen her on several occasions at *taarab* performances and noticed that she frequently sent challenges her way (*"alinifanyia vishindo"*) through tipping, meaningful looks, and dancing. As news of the fight circulated through town the following day, a neighbor of mine subsequently forbade his wife from attending future *taarab* performances, saying that they only breed *fujo* (trouble, violence) and no longer evoked *ustaarabu* (gentility) and *heshima* (respectful behavior).

Case 6: An Unsuccessful Attempt at *Vishindo*

The following case recalls Bauman's emphasis on the display of communicative competence, for it constitutes a case of communicative *in*competence on the part of one tipping audience member.

* * *

Babloom was invited to Dar es Salaam to perform at a wedding with All Stars Modern Taarab, Babloom's sister-band. The wedding was to begin with a *kesha* (an all-night musical celebration) at someone's home. Beforehand, as we were whiling away the day, preparing the instruments and talking with our hosts, the discussion turned to a video of a recent All Stars performance that was playing in the background. On the tape, there was a woman who repeatedly tipped and demonstrated *vishindo* during a song, announcing: "I have your man. Now you are alone." Fatuma (Babloom's lead singer) and Swabah (All Stars' lead singer) derided her for her actions because her husband had recently left her for another woman, and apparently the other woman was in the audience at that performance. The rejected wife wanted to show strength before the other woman, but made a completely inappropriate choice of song for doing so. Everyone agreed that she had simply shamed herself further by not knowing when to tip and when not to. "Hajui kutunza," "She doesn't know how to tip," was their final conclusion.

Case 7: The Cultural Officer and His Wife

While the previous cases all focused on disputes between individuals within the audience, the following case involves a prominent band member.

* * *

A cultural officer (*ofisa utamaduni*), Idirisa, working for a regional office of the Ministry of Culture was formerly married to a now famous *taarab* singer. Theirs had been an arranged marriage, and she had been a young, fourteen-year-old bride from a well-established urban family with a business in transport, whereas he was from a nearby rural village associated primarily with fishermen. His education and career as a civil servant had made him a suitable match, but after many years of marriage and the birth of several children, the marriage ended. He remarried, and only after she had been divorced for quite some time did she begin to engage in singing for a *taarab* band run by her brother. She never remarried.

As *ofisa utamaduni*, one of Idirisa's jobs was to make the necessary arrangements when an outside band wished to perform in his region. On one occasion, a touring *taarab* ensemble requested permission to perform there. Because of the intertwined relationship between text and performance and the fact that *taarab*'s "communicative competence" (Bauman 1977) depends upon effective comprehension of the poetry, audiences must know the texts to *taarab* songs well in order to participate. Outside groups do not always fare well when the audience is unfamiliar with their songs because listeners are unable to employ the song texts for their personal concerns and are reluctant to engage in tipping. Moreover, the practice of tipping is central to performance not only as a political tool but as an indicator to performers of how they are being received. When audience members remain glued to their seats and do not tip, *taarab* performers are left wondering if their music falls on contextually deaf ears, and the potential for interpersonal political maneuvering remains untapped. Performers do not merely tolerate a certain degree of performance from the audience but *expect* it, and when it fails to occur they often find themselves unprepared to bear the full weight of the performance on their own. Idirisa thus approached the band run by his former brother-in-law to request that they perform a joint show with the visiting group in order to ensure an audience. The brother-in-law agreed, and the necessary preparations were made.

This occasion occurred early in the career of the emerging star who formerly had been Idirisa's wife. In fact, it was the first time that he would see her in her new role as *taarab* singer. Idirisa described having felt publicly shamed and humiliated when she sang the song "Kisebusebu" ("Pretensions"), including veiled gestures and glances in his direction throughout the performance. He said that he had to creep out of the performance venue in embarrassment. He ended the story with a bitter and oft-heard denouncement of today's *taarab* (*taarab ya leo*) as being only concerned with *mipasho* as compared to *mafumbo* songs of the past *(taarab ya zamani)*.

Kisebusebu ("Pretensions")
Seif Kassim Kisauji, Babloom Modern Taarab, Tanga

Nimekutoa Sahare, Nikakuleta mjini   I took you from Sahare (a rural area) and brought you to the city.

Sikukutoa kwa ndere, Ni hiari ya moyoni
Leo wanicheza shere, Ulitarajia nini?

It was not with a love charm but your
   own heart's desire.
Today you mock me. What was your
   original aim?

- - -

- - -

Walikuonea gere, Jinsi ulivyonawiri
Chakula hukula pure, Samaka kwa mahamri
Leo mekuwa mwerere, Kula bada wa hiyari

They were jealous of you, of how you
   became so attractive.
You did not eat bean porridge. You ate
   fish with biscuits.
Today you've become worthless. Eat the
   cassava porridge you now desire.

- - -

- - -

Wa wapi walosifika, Kwa huba na
   taadhima
Wamebaki wazunguka, Wanaposhika
   wakwama
Huko ni kuadhirika, Hebu kumbuka ya
   nyuma

Where are those who became famous for
   love and honor?
They are wandering around. Wherever
   they settle they lose out.
What they do is shameful. Just remember
   the past.

- - -

- - -

Checheku checheko hizo, Ujuwe wachekwa
   wewe
Sio kwa zako pambizo, Tuwa usijifutuwe
Wakuona hamnazo, Kwa hicho chako
   kiwewe

The laughter you hear—know that they
   are laughing at you.
Not for your good looks, so do not think
   highly of yourself.
To them you seem crazy because of this
   confusion of yours.

- - -

- - -

Chorus
Kisebusebu, Kiroho papo
Wajionea adhabu, Kila ushikapo sipo

You pretend you don't want me, your
   heart's secret desire.
You feel as though you are being
   punished. Whatever you attempt to
   grasp escapes you.

Case 8: Quarreling Housemates

Since the costs of building a house lie beyond the means of the majority
of Tanga's residents, most adults—married or single—rent a room in
someone else's house. Munira had come from a family with some wealth
and owned her own house. She was divorced and supported herself by
renting out two rooms of her house. Juma, a colleague of Munira's from
work, rented one room with his wife. After a year, the relationship
started to break down between Munira and her renters. An altercation
broke out, and, without warning, Munira filed a lawsuit against Juma
and his wife in the local Islamic court, seeking damages for verbal abuse.
Juma clearly was taken aback by this action, since they all had been close
friends not long before. He was of the opinion that however angry Munira was, she should have attempted to resolve the dispute through discussion and perhaps mediation through shared friends before taking it
to court. One evening, after appearing in court and receiving a judgment
in Munira's favor from the Islamic judge (*kadhi*), they all found them-

selves at the Mkonge Hotel at the weekly *taarab* performance. The song "Shoga" ("Friend") filled the air:

Shoga ("Friend")—excerpt
Khalid Akida, Babloom Modern Taarab, Tanga

Shoga yangu nakupasha, Usinifanye mjinga	My friend, I'm informing you: don't make a fool of me.
Cheko na bashasha, leo hii nazipinga	Today I will put a stop to the laughter and charm
Ambayo wanionyesha, Yananitia uwoga	That you display in order to intimidate me.
- - -	- - -
Njama yako meijua, Ni kufanya mageuzi	I know your goal is to upset things and bring change.
Ilani natoa, Ukaapo maizi	I'm issuing you a warning to consider.
Nitakuja kuumbua, Yakuingie majonzi	I'll come to disgrace you and make you sad.
- - -	- - -

Chorus

Shoga leo nakwambia	Friend, today I'm telling you.
Ukome kumzoea shemejio	Stop flirting with your brother-in-law.

Although Juma did not avail himself of the opportunity to tip, he nevertheless co-opted the song's message by loudly singing along from his table within earshot of Munira. Although the rest of the song chastises someone who covets her friend's spouse/lover, these verses aptly suited his underlying purpose of questioning Munira's abrupt switch from loyal friend to pseudo-enemy.

Case 9: The Wronged Wife

Actions sometimes do speak louder than words; and inaction—or, more precisely, tactful self-management—may be deafening.

—Michael Herzfeld, "Rhetoric and the Constitution of Social Relations"

Once the wife of a *taarab* singer, hearing rumors of her husband's wandering ways, packed up her children and belongings while he was away on tour and returned to her familial home. He returned to an empty house and a town full of gossip. Life went on, he continued to perform with the band, and his wife remained with her family and the couple's children. One evening, his band was hired to perform at a wedding near her familial home, and his wife attended along with some of her closest female friends. The estranged couple, separated but not divorced, ignored each other for the most part. But then the song "Jamvi la Wageni" ("The Visitor's Mat") was sung:

Jamvi la Wageni ("The Visitor's Mat")
Rama Hamadi, Babloom Modern Taarab, Tanga

Hakika nimeamini, Mtu ni yake tabia
Sikujua asilani, Mwenzenu nikarukia
Kumbe jamvi la wageni, wanalo pumzikia
	Truly I believe that a person's character is
	   revealed through their behavior.
	I never would have believed it. I, your
	   friend, was taken by surprise.
	In fact he is a visitor's mat on which
	   many have taken rest.

- - -	- - -

Nilitia maanani, Moyoni kuniingia
Nikamuweka nyumbani, Yote kumtimizia
Ametoka barazani, Ndani hakuvumilia
	I reflected on this, pondered it in my
	   heart.
	I cherished him at home, taking care of
	   his every need,
	But he wandered outside. He couldn't
	   endure staying inside.

- - -	- - -

Kaniona hayawani, Na mjinga wa dunia
Hakuzoea ya ndani, Kwani anayachukia
Hutokea barazani, Wapate kumkalia
	He considered me a dupe, the world's
	   biggest fool.
	He could not get used to being inside
	   since he hated it so.
	He went out seeking others to sit on him.

- - -	- - -

Amenishinda jamani, Sio ninamchukia
Ni kwamba hawezekani, Kwa mmoja
   kutulia
Yeye jamvi la wageni, Nnje wanalokalia
	I've had enough of him, my friends. It's
	   not that I hate him,
	It's that it's not right for just one person
	   to remain true.
	He is a visitor's mat on which outsiders
	   sit

- - -	- - -

Chorus

Sasa naliweka kando *Nimeliacha hilo jamvi la wageni, nimeliacha* *Kanichochea karaha* *Nimeliacha hilo jamvi la wageni, nimeliacha* *Laniudhi moyo wangu* *Nimeliacha hilo jamvi la wageni, nimeliacha*	So I am putting it aside. I have left this visitor's mat, I have left it, Which stirs up feelings of disgust. I have left this visitor's mat, I have left it. It pains my heart. I have left this visitor's mat, I have left it.

The wife, normally a regular tipper at taarab events, had been notice-ably distanced from the evening's entertainment, remaining in her chair the entire time, conversing quietly with her friends. Suddenly, during the final verse of the song, she rose from her seat. "I've had enough of him, my friends. It's not that I hate him, it's that it's not right for just one person to remain true. He is a visitor's mat on which outsiders sit," intoned the singer. Those in the know watched with interest as she slowly, deliberately, and without flourish or any dancelike movements walked to the stage area and, instead of tipping the singer, turned abruptly to tip her husband, who was playing keyboards. Keeping her eyes downcast, she placed the money on the keyboard and silently re-turned to her seat. He studiously avoided looking at her, the band played on, but her public reproach resonated for weeks to come.

This case is rare in that the wronged wife's actions may have contributed to a resolution of the conflict. Furthering Colson's critique of approaches that presuppose resolution in their analysis of disputes, I have emphasized here the role of *taarab* performance in dispute *negotiation*. If disputes aired in *taarab* contexts reach resolution, they rarely do so within that context. Yet in this case, the wronged wife appealed to the audience that night as upholders of Swahili ethics and the moral standard against which her husband's actions could be measured. She successfully shamed him by publicly accusing him of adultery ("welcoming many visitors"), and her action increased public pressure on him to seek her forgiveness. Although it would be impossible to accurately weigh the impact of her *taarab*-mediated accusation, the level of discussion between the elders in their two families did rise considerably shortly thereafter, and less than a month later, they were reconciled.

Taarab and the Constitution of Social Relations

In taking dispute as the point of departure in my analysis of *taarab* politics and performance, I seek to uncover one of the "hidden levels" of negotiation alluded to by Moore (1995, 27) and highlight *taarab* performance as both a mode of dispute negotiation and a "resource of potential power" in the sense offered by Gulliver:

> Potential power exists in a wide variety of resources, depending in the particular case on the nature and context of the dispute, the relationships of the disputants with each other and with other people and their position in the society. As suggested previously . . . it is neither necessary nor useful to make any primary distinction between resources of a non-normative kind (economic, physical, political [I would add musical], etc.) and those of a normative kind (rules, standards, values). The dividing line between the two is often unclear; in any case, all resources offer potentials for power that combine or can be combined, in the actual attempt to exercise persuasive strength against the opponent." (Gulliver 1979, 202)

The disputes—whether between individuals, bands, communities, or between state and citizenry (see chapter 7)—revolve around social relations. Resolution is rarely achieved (or at least rarely publicized—it's often difficult to know), but social statuses can undergo profound transformations in the blink of an eye or nod of the head. Power here reflects the capacity to constitute, negotiate, and transform social relations— relations that, following Herzfeld, are constituted in part through their expression:

> Social relations are not the same thing as their expression; but we can intercept and understand them only when they are expressed, so that representing them as static and immutable is far more of an intellectualist illusion—and far more reductive—than acknowledging their constitution *through* expression. Our very

perception of them is part of the process whereby they are so constituted. (Herzfeld 1988, 7–8)

Some may take issue with the idea that social relations are in part constituted through their expression. The suggestion is not that *all* social relations are so constituted or that they are *only* so constituted. There is no denying the inequities and rigidity of power in certain types of social relations. My run-in with the police in Tanga provides one example of a social relationship that was fundamentally unequal and allowed little room for negotiation. The performance in that event (the exhibition of their power to confiscate my license and initiate a case against me, my stubborn refusal to concede fault, and my mediated apology) resulted only in the performed maintenance of a very unequal power relationship. My interlocutor Saidi, however, clearly had a different relationship with the traffic police that he could exploit in order to assist me. As the owner of a fleet of buses that regularly travel roads monitored by *trafiki,* he had negotiated a relationship with them that benefited everyone involved. Although still situated in a less powerful position than the state-authorized police, Saidi nevertheless commanded a position more powerful than my own. His performance as mediator confirmed this. Our performances did not change our respective positions in relation to each other, but in communicating them, the performances reconstituted them and thereby reinscribed them. The event involved the negotiation of a settlement to our dispute. It did not involve the negotiation of our social relations.

In the cases of *taarab* performance presented above, however, social relations are clearly being negotiated. Relationships among participants tend to be more equal and more fluid than the relationship between myself and Tanzanian police. A woman making public the claim that another woman is interfering in and attempting to destroy her marriage opens to negotiation among a community of relatively equal peers the social positions of both women. It is also significant that she makes the claim through words not her own, because this provides her with a means of eluding responsibility should the situation take a bad turn— *she* didn't say anything to instigate trouble, she could argue, and in that way highlight the ambiguity and ephemerality of her act of tipping.

Throughout the many years of my involvement in Swahili social life, people have told me time and again how *taarab* provides an opportunity for communicating certain messages that cannot be communicated otherwise. As a medium for the negotiation of certain types of dispute, therefore, *taarab* is unparalleled. And unlike gossip, which serves as a private (though no less successful) medium of social control, *taarab* takes the intimacies of local knowledge possible within a community whose members come into frequent contact with each other into the public domain. Tanga may be an urban environment, but a sense of the local remains strong.

In her study of Bedouin love poetry, Lila Abu-Lughod found a discourse similarly imbued with power like that of *taarab* poetry: "Love poetry, as a discourse of defiance, is seen as a discourse of autonomy and freedom. . . . Love poetry as a discourse of rebellion is used to assert this freedom and is credited by others with tremendous power" (Abu-Lughod 1990, 36). But she goes on to postulate that defiance and opposition to norms and ideals is characteristic of all poetry: "There is plenty of evidence that poetry is in general associated with opposition to the ideals of normal social life" (Abu-Lughod 1990, 35). In local uses of *taarab*, defiance and opposition are poetically articulated less against community ideals than against the actions of locally known individuals. Through poetry, Swahili women (and, to a lesser extent, men) appeal to and thereby *uphold* community ideals by disputing each other's moral and social standing. Multivalent texts enable different agents to employ songs for their own personal situations. Societal ideals, however, remain largely unquestioned, and disputes frequently remain unresolved.

Researchers who would privilege text over performance would miss much of the information exchanged during *taarab* performances. This ethnographic example provides a forceful argument against text-centric models that place exclusive analytic emphasis on the message communicated—the perceived product—while turning a deaf ear and blind eye to the process of communication. While it is true that certain *taarab* songs may contain specific messages that can be apprehended exclusively through the song's poetry (as when composers engage in song-dueling), the vast majority of messages sent and information exchanged during *taarab* events are only related to the text *by means of* performance, and often performance by audience members. *Taarab,* I thus argue, is a multivalent social practice encompassing the poetry, the poetics, and the performance of—the "giving form to" (Fabian 1990, 11)—social relations.

5

CULTURAL REVOLUTION IN TANZANIA?

[T]he nation-state's claims to affixed, eternal identity, grounded in universal truth are themselves, like the moves of all social actors, strategic adjustments to the demands of the historical moment.

—Michael Herzfeld, *Cultural Intimacy*

Watanzania tudumishe Utamaduni (Tanzanians, let us perpetuate Culture.)

—Lyrics commonly sung to the Chikocha *ngoma*, a Mwera *ngoma* from southern Tanzania

State formation is cultural revolution; that is its supreme (if never final) achievement, and the essence of its power.

—Philip Corrigan and Derek Sayer, *The Great Arch*

Letting a Hundred Flowers Blossom . . .

On the fourteenth of May in the year 1966, a delegation of five Tanzanian officials ended a two-week tour of China.[1] Their tour included visits to the Peking Ballet, Peking Opera, an open air theater in Canton where they were treated to a puppet show, a Workers' Commune, and, most impressive of all, given the description they gave upon their return, the May Day celebrations held in Tiananmen Square. I quote at length from their final report:

We saw May 1, 1966 in Peking in a large arena called Tiananmen Square. At 9:00 AM despite bitter cold and light rain, the Square was filled with crowds of people, elderly, youths, workers, students, and visitors from around the world.

School children greeted everyone who entered with shouts of joy, hand salutes, papers, leaves and flowers. It was indeed the school children who made the arena a spectacular sight with their dancing, singing, military marching, etc.

A large area of the Square was filled with various elements of Culture, not from the Ministry of Culture but from the people themselves. . . .

There were traditional dances (for example, Sinkiam Dance, Mongolian and Minority Nations traditional dances) . . . plays . . . acrobatics and songs. The army also performed . . . and there was one woman who sang praises of the Communist Party, of its achievements since the revolution. The people of China were very happy to hear stories of its ruling party; everyone watching expressed their happiness with applause. Those performers used a special stage, traditional instruments and many weaponry.

The Square was filled with many decorations, countless people, beverages, breads, candies and fruits for sale. In the evening, we went again to the Square around 7:00 P.M. and found people singing, dances being danced, and musical bands being listened to by the entire arena. Because we stood high above the Square, we were amazed to see millions of students and soldiers dancing, passing each other and milling around without any disturbance or strife.

After about half an hour, there began the fireworks display. They showed 180 different fireworks in designs of stars, flowers, and crops like wheat, filling with exceptional beauty the skies above the country of China.[2]

Two days after the Tanzanian delegation departed, Chairman Mao Tse-Tung released his infamous May 16 Circular that unleashed a decade of turmoil and violence now known as the Chinese Cultural Revolution.

Although the Tanzanian Ministry of National Culture and Youth issued a pamphlet entitled *Cultural Revolution in Tanzania* (n.d., 1975?) indicating an affinity with Chinese objectives, and although there were significant cultural exchanges between the two countries throughout the period of 1966–76, Tanzania's cultural revolution (thankfully) developed along a different trajectory. In a comparison of Chinese and Soviet cultural revolutions, Maurice Meisner explains that "[h]aving achieved power in countries burdened not only by economic backwardness but also by the persistence of old feudal traditions and habits, both Lenin and Mao insisted that the modern cultural transformation of the masses was no less pressing a post-revolutionary task than that of modern economic development. For Lenin in the early 1920s, as for Mao three decades later, a 'cultural revolution' was essential both for the industrialization of the largely agrarian lands they had come to rule and for the realization of . . . promised socialist goals" (Meisner 1985, 279). This was no less true for Julius Nyerere in Tanzania, who, in constructing his own political philosophy, drew considerable inspiration from Mao Tse-Tung. Like Mao and unlike Lenin, Nyerere located the source of proletarian culture and consciousness in the rural peasant (as opposed to the urban worker), and argued that cultural transformation constituted a prerequisite of modern economic development (not its product—an inversion of orthodox Marxism).

Yet there was one fundamental difference that unequivocally distinguished Tanzanian cultural policy from that of either China or the former Soviet Union. According to Meisner, Lenin rejected Western capitalism without rejecting its modern and technologically superior culture.

Figure 5.1 Pamphlet cover, Ministry of National Culture and Youth, c. 1975. Courtesy of Ministry of Education and Culture, United Republic of Tanzania.

Although subject to the Marxist view that society inherits the cultural as well as material accomplishments of the past, Lenin sought to use modern culture to overcome a Russian cultural heritage steeped in feudalism. Mao similarly viewed the cultural heritage of his people from a purely negative standpoint, yet unlike Lenin, he found little of value in Western culture. Instead, as Meisner describes, he argued that China was "a land which labored under the twin burdens of the 'slave ideology' of an 'imperialist culture' imposed from without and the persistence of the decadent Confucian values of its indigenous feudal culture. Unless both were 'swept away,' Mao maintained, 'no new culture of any kind can be built up. There is no construction without destruction" (Meisner 1985, 283). And so his Red Guards, invested with the authority to cleanse China's culture, went about "smashing recordings of Beethoven and old Buddhist relics with equal abandon" (285). In short, neither Lenin nor Mao found anything worth emulating or worth preserving from their respective cultural pasts and thus pursued policies of eradication, erasure, and new construction.

Nyerere, on the other hand, developed his political, economic, and cultural program of African Socialism upon the premise that the past held the keys to the future. African Socialism predicates a return to the proto-socialist, communal villages of a romanticized, politicized past. Whereas Mao and Lenin feared and consequently rejected the past, Nyerere embraced it—even as he rewrote it.

The aim of this chapter is to document the progression of ideas and policies that have circumscribed "cultural development" in Tanzania (and former Tanganyika and Zanzibar) from the colonial era through the nationalist and socialist periods leading into the present transition toward political and economic liberalization. We will chart how Tanganyikan/Zanzibari/Tanzanian culture was deconstructed and reconstructed according to reigning political paradigms. The political history provided in chapter 2 informs and is informed by the ideological elaborations presented here. Far from being a stagnant domain, as might be inferred from stasis-tainted terms like *tradition* and *custom,* the idea of culture evokes rich discourse from Tanzanian citizens, scholars, politicians, and philosophers alike. Tanzanians have participated vociferously in global debates on "cultural estrangement," cultural recovery, and the necessity of rejecting neocolonial cultural paradigms with as much force and vehemence as colonial forms. Nyerere's writings, alongside those of Frantz Fanon, Aimé Césaire, Amilcar Cabral, Léopold Senghor, Wole Soyinka, and Ngugi wa Thiong'o, contribute to a florescence of thought that continues to influence, inspire, and incite.

Having made the theoretical leap of recognition that states as "imagined communities" do not reflect naturally existing, temporally and spatially bounded entities, we can now shift attention to the processes of imagination involved. Colonialism, nationalism, socialism, and political/economic liberalization are experiences and constructs that shaped processes of cultural production in Tanzania. Each one significantly altered the creations of the one that preceded it. Each one also retained some of the concerns and practices of the one that preceded it. A central problem in the production of Tanzanian nationness alluded to earlier is its bifurcated Tanganyika/Zanzibar, mainland/islands identity—the dilemma of creating a sense of wholeness from historical halfness. This paradox—resulting in two National Museums, two National Archives, two sets of National Arts and Language Competitions, and two Ministries of Culture espousing varying articulations of "national culture"— adds a layer of complexity to an already fraught terrain of competing social visions.

In their analysis of English state formation, Corrigan and Sayer argue that "state formation necessarily is cultural revolution; that is its supreme (if never final) achievement, and the essence of its power" (1985, 180). My analysis focuses precisely on the un-final nature of would-be cultural revolutions. The process of imagination is always subject to interruption and on-the-spot reconfiguration. Attention to the polyphonic discourses surrounding cultural development specifically relating to nationalist ideals of music, clothing, and art, and the production of national symbols (e.g., national anthem, national language, national holidays, national monuments, national cultural troupes) exposes the cacophony that continually threatens to deafen state attempts at harmony. We begin with a review of cultural policies devised and implemented by colonial authorities and proceed through Tanzania's nationalist and subsequently socialist periods. Discussion of the current phase of political democratization and economic liberalization is reserved for the next two chapters.

Cultural Production in Tanganyika and Zanzibar: Colonial Constructions

Colonial involvement in Africa ushered in new economic, political, and social formations while simultaneously ushering the continent out into a significantly different position in the world economy than it had previously occupied.[3] Terms of trade determined by colonial metropoles (England, France, Germany, Portugal, Belgium) consistently placed Africans and African products in disadvantaged relations to Europeans and their products. Africa was perceived as both a wellspring of exportable raw materials and a captive market for European-processed finished products—an economic equation that promised unlimited profits for Europe and underdevelopment for Africa. The European dominance upon which this relationship rested was constructed and maintained by a number of factors: (1) military might enabled by technologically advanced weaponry; (2) advanced modes of transportation; (3) medical breakthroughs in the realm of tropical disease control, treatment, and prevention; (4) the capital to purchase and distribute these arms, means of transport, and medicines among colonial forces; and (5) a high degree of political instability in many areas of Africa that inopportunely coincided with European arrival and mitigated against united efforts to drive out the colonizers.[4] Nonetheless, however much power European colonizers wielded, it would never prove hegemonic enough to fully appropriate and commandeer all African initiative and creativity.

While it is true that colonial agents were no more united in thought and action than colonial subjects (Cooper and Stoler 1989), one theme in arguments vindicating colonialist ventures focused on the "civilizing" mission. Unadulterated economic extraction was sparsely camouflaged in obeisance to Social Darwinism and its categorization of the world into superior versus inferior cultures—discourses framed in scientific arrogance and profound Western ethnocentrism. A widely circulated belief among colonial agents held that for Africans, "'cultures' did not so much define their unique ways of life as constitute an obstacle to their modern future" (Cooper and Stoler 1989, 619).

Colonial administrators selectively protected or tolerated African cultural practices, filtering out what they considered "acceptable" traditions from those deemed offensive and incompatible with "civilizing" interests. In Tanganyika, *ngoma* (traditional dances) constituted a prime target of the Native Authority. This arm of the British colonial administration compiled a list of twenty "acceptable" *ngoma* (Martin 1982, 158) out of hundreds regularly performed. As discussed earlier, the timing of Beni's growth during the German colonial period and resulting perception of Beni dance societies as "Germanophile" (Ranger 1975, 54),[5] together with its tremendous expansion throughout the Tanganyika Territory, evoked alarm and concern among British colonial administrators. Although it was more or less freely allowed in Kenya, in Tanganyika Beni was subject to outright prohibition in some regions and heavy bureaucratic controls everywhere else (Ranger 1975, 91). Colonial administrators devised and implemented a complex apparatus of licenses, permits, and fees during the 1920s that transformed local "custom" into a source of state revenue—one still exploited in the postcolonial present. The following two cases—one drawn from the mainland and one from Zanzibar—depict the emergent regulation of *ngoma* with all the multiplicity of opinions and agendas it encompassed and subsequently quelled.

From the Tanga Regional Archives: Ngasu ya Mshitu

A six-year exchange of official correspondences from 1948 to 1953 in Tanga Region concerned an *ngoma* associated with the Ngasu ya Mshitu initiation ceremony of the Mbugu ethnic group. In 1920, the requirement of licenses and levying of fees for publicly performed *ngoma* had been introduced in the territory (Ranger 1975, 91): one license, one fee per *ngoma*. On September 15, 1948, the political officer of Lushoto sent the following telegram to his counterpart in Same:

> Reference your letter No.11/6/65 of 11/9/48 I agree that there can be no objection to a fee charged for an ngoma. But the rate of Shs. 2/= per head sounds to me very high even though it is for an initiation ceremony. The Wambugu, as you know only come into your district for this specific purpose once in every few years, owing to their ancestral route of arrival in Lushoto district. They bring the youths between certain ages and teach them something of their traditional origins.
>
> Personally I have never heard of a charge made per head for any sort of ngoma and I shall be grateful if you will confirm that it really is Shs. 2/= for each boy

initiated, as you are not definite on that point. Do the others have to pay also, or only initiates?

I presume it is a revenue measure for the treasury and if so it would seem reasonable to allow a reduced rate for strangers who get no benefit whatever from the native administration and indeed only spend a few days in the district every few years.[6]

The Pare (Same) district commissioner responded on September 21, 1948:

> I confirm that the prescribed fee is 2/= per each boy initiated. Of this amount 1/50 goes to the Native Treasury and =/50 goes to the Wazee ("elders") who conduct the ceremony i.e. in this case to the Wambugu Wazee. No other fees are payable.
>
> I am told that these fees have been levied under written rules more than 20 years, and that when South Pare was part of Lushoto District, i.e. up to 1928, similar fees were payable in the Usambaras.
>
> I am at present having all the rules relating to ngomas re-written and consolidated, and the Pare Council is considering a reduction in the 2/= a capital fee for the Ngasu ya Mshitu ceremony. Until then I am afraid the Pare Council is not prepared to allow any reduction for the Wambugu and unless otherwise instructed I do not propose to intervene in the matter.[7]

The response to the disagreement was to call upon the "senior sociologist," Mr. H. A. Fosbrooke, to investigate the matter and make recommendations. In his report, submitted three years later in 1951, Mr. Fosbrooke first disputed claims that the ceremony was objectionable by arguing for cross-cultural moral comparability.

> The factor which seems to have influenced Government most is [Sir Charles] Dundas' dictum that the *ngashu* is responsible for frequent infanticide. The basis for this statement is that those who failed to live up to the teachings of the *ngashu* that procreation should be avoided before full adult[hood] had been assumed, would do away with such illegitimate offspring.
>
> It would be equally logical to argue that the concept of Christian marriage is responsible for suicide and infanticide when an unmarried mother in a fit of remorse does away with herself and her child, or that our laws of property are responsible for the overcrowded state of the gaols in the territory. . . .
>
> When so many Africans and Europeans alike lament the deterioration in manners and discipline, so noticeable today, it appears to be a retrograde step to prohibit any institution which contributes in any way to the encouragement of these virtues.[8]

He then took a strong stand against the imposition of fees on similar grounds: "The only aspect of the situation which appears indefensible is the levying of fees in respect of *ngashu*. If payable in respect of this Pagan ceremony why not then on the Islamic *jando*,[9] or even the Christian baptism or confirmation?"[10] His final recommendations were

1. That entry into the *ngashu* should be entirely voluntary.
2. That no fee should be payable to the Native Authority for the ngashu *per se*.

3. No prohibition should be placed on the instructors accepting their customary fees.

4. That any brewing should be subject to the existing Native Authority rules and others, if in fact such exist, for the control of brewing other than for sale.[11]

The response of the Pare district commissioner, however, was to forward the Fosbrooke report to the Tanga provincial commissioner, endorsing all the recommendations except for the elimination of fees. Clearly, economic factors (specifically, a potential loss of revenue) influenced his thinking and that of the Council; another influence, however, was a very conscious concern with control. He wrote,

> There remains the question of a fee. The Senior Sociologist recommends that there should be no fee. The Council has carefully gone into this point and recommends a fee. From the administrative point of view I would recommend a fee, because I think that this will give more control. If it can be held merely with permission, then there will be less control, and Barazas [Councils] may be more inclined to give permission without due thought. The fee collection means that they must in any case take *some* action, and therefore will think before taking *any* action. It will also serve to underline the fact that the ngoma is being held under the authority and supervision of the Native Authority.[12]

The final correspondence in the matter came from the acting provincial commissioner in April of 1953. He supported the Pare district commissioner in the continuation of fees, but expressed a new concern "that there must be no question of a 'Secret Society' emerging."[13] This statement reveals a realization that *ngoma* networks, as effective mediums of communication and social mobilization, could potentially harbor subversive action. As history would later prove, this concern was well-founded.

In sum, this debate over one *ngoma* unveils the fractured face of colonialism and its competing internal agendas. Social science, a commonly used tool for facilitating colonial administration, did not in this case support the repressive intervention sought by high-level officials. Nor were high-level officials united in thought over how to approach the issue. The concerns and parties in conflict—some discernible only by implication—are outlined below:

1. *Inequity in ngoma procedure* wherein the standard "fee per ngoma" policy applied to other *ngoma* is in this case supplanted by a "fee per participant" policy (political officer, Lushoto, versus political officer, Same)

2. *Jurisdiction* over *ngoma* participants who do not constitute resi-

dents of the district where the *ngoma* is performed (political officer, Lushoto, versus political officer, Same)

3. *Fee amount*—considered exorbitant by some and appropriate by others (political officer, Lushoto, versus political officer, Same)

4. *Fee distribution* between the Native Authority and the elders who perform the ceremony; Fosbrooke's third recommendation implies that despite official allocation of one-fourth of the fees collected to the elders, the elders are somehow prohibited from accepting it (political officer, Same, versus Fosbrooke)

5. *Voluntary participation* in the *ngoma;* the fact that Fosbrooke makes this his first recommendation implies that it is not always voluntary, although it is left unclear as to whence force originates: from Wambugu elders and/or a bureaucracy that stands to gain increased revenues from increased participation

6. the continued transmission of *moral knowledge* (Fosbrooke) versus the claim that this "moral knowledge" was in fact immoral (in perpetuating infanticide—Sir Charles Dundas)

7. *Racial/religious discrimination* in the extraction of fees and licenses from African ceremonials and not the ceremonials of other (Arab, Christian) social categories (Fosbrooke)

8. *Custom as a source of revenue* (Fosbrooke versus District Commission, Pare, and acting provincial commissioner, Tanga)

9. *Clear demarcation of administrative concerns* in the application of regulations regarding the brewing of alcoholic beverages independent of *ngoma* regulations (Fosbrooke)

10. *Control* by the Native Authorities over "native" assemblies, customs, and life in general; the exercise and maintenance of colonial state power (district commissioner, Pare, and acting provincial commissioner, Tanga)

From the Zanzibar Archives: Raz'ha

Similar concerns and similar conflicts emerged across the channel in Zanzibar. The Ngoma Regulation Decree, drafted and enacted in Zanzibar in 1934, decreed that *ngoma* and *maulidi* (Islamic religious recitations accompanied by tambourines and drums) were not to be held without acquisition of a permit and payment of a fee. A list of five prohibited *ngoma* accompanied the ruling. Although no explanation is provided for why those particular *ngoma* were prohibited, further correspondence reveals continued negotiation over the addition of other *ngoma* to the "prohibited" list, as well as the extension of permits and fees to more practices through a widening of the definition of the term *ngoma*.

The conflict over a performance practice of Arabic origins called Raz'ha illustrates debate over what constitutes *ngoma*. This *ngoma* was described by one anthropologist in 1917 as "a war-dance practised by the Arabs . . . prior to starting out on a raid" performed by men holding aloft swords that they rotate ever so slightly so as to reflect light in a dazzling manner while they dance (Skene 1917, 413). First evidence of colonial concern over Raz'ha appears in a letter dated July 23, 1936, authored by the acting provincial commissioner of Zanzibar:

> With reference to the attached minute from D. C. Zanzibar I suggest the A. G. be asked to advise whether or not the Raz'ha Dance comes within the purview of the Ngoma Decree Cap.36. For his information I would mention that the dance consists of a number of persons standing in a circle with unsheathed swords which they flicker rhythmically in the air by a wrist movement accompanied by a beat of the foot, slapping or in some cases a chant, while two in the centre of the circle perform a mock fight. As the D. C. states this dance is not always accompanied by music, drumming or singing and therefore he is in some doubt if it could be termed as "Ngoma" under Cap.36.
>
> The point is that hitherto no permits have been taken out to perform this dance and the Manga Arabs wish to continue to be allowed to perform without obtaining a permit, for as they say, the dance is not necessarily an organized affair but usually quite spontaneous.
>
> It is not recommended that the dance as such should be prohibited, which could be done by order of Ex. Co., but if the A. G. considers the dance to be outside the provisions of Cap.36 it is recommended that Sec.2 Cap.36 be amended to bring it within the meaning of the term "Ngoma" as suggested by D. C. Zanzibar. This would then enable the D. C. to require a permit to be taken out before the dance is performed. Under Sec.5 such permits may be issued free of charge at the discretion of the D. C.[14]

As a result of this correspondence, the official definition of *ngoma* in the Ngoma Regulation was revised to read, "'[N]goma' means any Arab, African, Indian or other oriental entertainment or dance whether accompanied or not by music, drumming or singing."[15] Raz'ha indisputably fell within the bounds of the new definition and became subject to its required permits and fees. The commissioner's observation that "the Manga Arabs wish to continue to be allowed to perform without obtaining a permit, for as they say, the dance is not necessarily an organized affair but usually quite spontaneous," indicates an antagonism toward state intervention by Raz'ha participants. This antagonism took a more active and more public form a few months later. The record is incomplete, but a later document confirms that at some point between August 1936 and February 1937, the Zanzibar district commissioner issued a directive that no Raz'ha permits should be issued until further notice. It would appear that Raz'ha performers somehow expressed their resistance to state involvement and thereby evoked a more hostile stance from the state. This, in turn, provoked outright rebellion.[16] In flagrant violation of both the order from the D. C. as well as the newly amended

(1936) Ngoma Regulation, performances of Raz'ha were held in the very public Mnazi Mmoja grounds during the Eid holidays of February 1937 in plain view of the police and various constables.[17] No mention is made of a police response, and the notable silence supports speculation that no action was taken.

This act of defiance against colonial control and against *ngoma* regulation bears witness to the constant negotiation over cultural production both among and between colonial administrators and colonial subjects. In the early 1960s, the Ngoma Regulation would again emerge as the topic of debate, this time on grounds similar to those voiced in the Fosbrooke report on Ngasu ya Mshitu. Certain factions of the colonial bureaucracy targeted racial language in the Regulation and demanded its removal. In sympathy perhaps with the apparent inaction displayed by his own forces two decades earlier, it was the commissioner of police who wrote on October 19, 1959,

> Although this Decree discriminates in no way against the class of person who may obtain a Ngoma permit, it is certainly discriminatory regarding the type of dance or religious ceremony to be held. Whereas a fee must be paid for a permit to hold an Arab, African, or Asian dance accompanied by drumming and dancing, no fee could be charged if say Scottish Dancing were held in the midlle [*sic*] of Mnazi Mmjoa [*sic*] accompanied by bag-pipes, etc. Similarly an Arab religious celebration accompanied by music would be fee paying, whereas a meeting of the Salvation Army accompanied by tambourines, drums and trumpets would not.
>
> Ngomas held in Zanzibar are frequently the scene of brawls, assaults and drunkeness [*sic*] and it is most desirable that some control should be exercised over the holding of Ngomas. Setting aside the question of payment of fee, adequate control could be exercised under Section 36 of the Police Decree (I assume that an Ngoma comes within the definition of "assembly"). However, this might result in an appreciable loss of revenue.
>
> If it is considered desirable to retain the Ngoma Regulation Decree, the suggestion of discrimination might be overcome by deleting the words "Arab, African, Indian or other Oriental" from the definitions of "Ngoma" and "Maulidi" in Section 2 of the Decree.[18]

In making this statement, the police commissioner did not stop at criticizing the racial distinctions perpetuated in the Ngoma Regulation. He questioned the regulation's necessity and continued relevance even while acknowledging the loss of income that would result were it to be eliminated. In the colonial files on *ngoma* preserved in the Zanzibar Archives, this document is followed by a series of proposed drafts and revisions to the Ngoma Regulation from other sectors of the colonial bureaucracy dating to 1962. All expressed the same concerns as the police commissioner: dispensing with racial categories and ascertaining the amount of control over *ngoma* performance to be asserted or relinquished.[19] Before a final version could be enacted, however, independence came to Zanzibar the following year.

Although these materials expose the range of opinion over cultural production within the colonial administration, the timing of the relaxation of *ngoma* regulations deserves comment. According to Prof. Elias Songoyi of the University of Dar es Salaam, the year 1948 marked a notable policy switch on the part of British administrators in Tanganyika (1988a, 18). Citing the work of another scholar, E. N. Hussein, Songoyi argues that while colonial cultural policy prior to 1948 proscribed traditional dances due to the widespread opinion that they would encourage tribalism, after 1948 colonial administrators decided and directed that such practices should be permitted and encouraged. Rather than interpret this as diminishing cultural oppression, Songoyi argues that this was in fact a conscious response to the growing tide of Tanganyikan nationalism following the end of World War II. Song, already in use as a way of expressing desire for independence and mobilizing the masses, had to be moved into an arena where it could be monitored and contained. The rhetorical justification, however, was that this constituted a charitable gesture, a way of "brightening . . . the lives of the people of the colonies" (E. N. Hussein 1974, as quoted in Songoyi 1988a, 19).

The data presented here on Ngasu ya Mshitu and Raz'ha—two examples of increasing (even if contested) colonial control and regulation—date to 1948–53 and 1934–37 respectively. The evidence from Tanga Region displays continued concern for expanding rather than reducing the scope of *ngoma* regulation, and the same can be said of Zanzibar as late as 1956. During that year, at least one colonial agent was interested in prohibiting additional *ngoma*. Attracting particular attention was the *ngoma* called Shambe, described by the district commissioner (Urban) of Zanzibar as "vulgar," "obscene," and "objectionable" because of the way its male participants dressed as women: "And it is this 'effaminancy' [*sic*] in the open by immoral men which is abhored [*sic*] or resented by the public. Their congregation is the attraction of many evils although in fact the evils are there in their hearts before."[20] Although the final 1962 exchange of opinion over the regulation's racial language does suggest a shift in emphasis, it ironically arose just as colonialism was confronting its increasingly apparent lack of relevance.

The themes that echo across these case studies in colonial-era cultural production are many, yet dominant ones concern the desirability and appropriateness of indigenous cultural practices/products, the authority of cultural producers, the economic and political benefits to state power of establishing a bureaucratic apparatus for regulating cultural production, and the exercise of control. Cultural practices were evaluated in terms of the degree of repugnance to European idea(l)s of decency and perceived threat to colonial power. Curiously, although the imposition and implementation of regulations, permits, and fees stemmed from decidedly colonial concerns with exercising control (social, cultural, economic, and political) over Africans and their cultural practices, this bureaucratic apparatus did not disappear with the end of colonialism. If anything, the apparatus was enlarged and strengthened after independence. It is to this seeming contradiction that we turn next.

Cultural Production in Tanzania: Post-Independence Inventions

> It is the intention of Government to substitute the beating of drums for the firing of guns on all important occasions in future.
>
> —Permanent secretary, Ministry of National Culture and Youth, February 7, 1963

Following independence, many African regimes placed the reconstruction of their cultures and histories at the top of their list of priorities. The cases presented above of colonial intervention in cultural affairs extended far beyond musical performance into colonial education, language policy, the rewriting of history, bureaucratically enforced racial distinctions (for instance, in the realms of taxation, access to education, and the distribution of food rations during the war), and religious proselytization to Christianity. Just as colonial authorities imposed prohibitions against and increased fees for *ngoma* deemed offensive, so too did they enforce adoption of colonial languages (English, French, German, Portuguese) and actively discourage magico-religious practices (e.g., ancestral spirit offerings, spirit possession activities), local modes of knowledge transmission and socialization (puberty rites), and traditional medicine. These various trajectories of colonial intervention combined to create a praxis of colonial control that, although ridden with internal contestation and inconsistency, nevertheless constituted a formidable obstacle to African empowerment during and after the period of colonialism.

Thus, one finds that soon after being bequeathed or forcibly seizing the mantle of political power, African elites often cited the cultural devastation of colonialism as a symbolic and ideological deterrent to development, one requiring immediate correction. Soyinka applied the phrase "race-retrieval" to this domain of nationalist concern:

> "[R]ace-retrieval" . . . involves, very simply, the conscious activity of recovering what has been hidden, lost, repressed, denigrated or simply denied by ourselves— yes, by ourselves also—but definitely by the conquerors of our peoples and their Eurocentric bias of thought and relationships. . . . It is only part of the unworthy game of placing entire peoples outside of history. Their existence as participants in a historic process, it is claimed, did not commence until the descent of the imperial yoke. Yet, for a people to develop, they must have constant recourse to their

own history. Not uncritical recourse but definitely a recourse. To deny them the existence of this therefore has a purpose, for it makes them neutered objects on whose tabula rasa of the mind the text of the master-race—cultural, economic, religious, etc.—can be inscribed. A logical resistance counterstrategy therefore develops; the true nationalist finds himself, at one stage or other, and on varying levels, confronted with a need to recover that history and culture. (Soyinka 1991, 35)

The force of such rhetoric, of placing a heavy and pronounced emphasis on the cultural consequences of colonialism, took many political forms, from Léopold Senghor's *Négritude* to Mobutu Sese Seko's *Authenticité,* and continues to resound today in critical analyses of colonialism and neocolonialism. The Kenyan playwright and scholar Ngugi wa Thiong'o expounds on this theme while infusing it with the idea of cultural hegemony:

> The entire economic and political control is effectively facilitated by the cultural factor. In any case, economic and political control inevitably lead to cultural dominance and this in turn deepens that control. The maintenance, management, manipulation, and mobilisation of the entire system of education, language and language use, literature, religion, the media, have always ensured for the oppressor nation power over the transmission of a certain ideology, set of values, outlook, attitudes, feelings etc., and hence power over the whole area of consciousness. . . .
>
> By thus controlling the cultural and psychological domain, the oppressor nation and classes try to ensure the situation of a slave who takes it that to be a slave is the normal human condition. If the exploited and the oppressed of the earth can view themselves and their place in the universe as they are viewed by the imperialist bourgeoisie, then they can become their own policemen, no longer able to see any significant contradiction between their own condition and that of the oppressor nations and classes. (Ngugi 1993, 51)

Yet not all African leaders felt equally strongly about combating the cultural consequences of colonialism. Faced with formidable social, economic, and political challenges plus the general unevenness of inherited infrastructure, newly independent African nations pursued widely divergent approaches to their internal development. Ghana's Kwame Nkrumah initiated the slogan, "Seek ye first the political kingdom and all else will be added unto you," indicating his emphasis on political development. His position has been contrasted with that of other African leaders who instead prioritized the *economic* kingdom (e.g., Jomo Kenyatta and Danial Arap Moi of Kenya; Jerry Rawlings of Ghana) on the strength of the argument that political independence without economic independence produces only hollow victories.[21] According to Ali Mazrui, however, overemphasis on economic development results in neocolonialism—both internally and in relation to the world at large—wherein the divide between haves and have-nots deepens and widens.[22] He thus argues instead that African leaders should seek first the *cultural* kingdom from which all else would follow. Julius Nyerere can be described as a leader who, in the words of Mazrui, sought first the cultural kingdom.

Traditionalism, Would-Be Cultural Committees, and a New Civilizing Mission

Initial attempts to recapture African cultural heritage focused on the collection of customs deemed "traditional"—a venture pursued in true colonial fashion. From independence through the implementation of Ujamaa socialism in 1967, Tanzanian cultural production revolved around the reconstruction and collection of local traditions and customs. In his Republic Day speech to Parliament on December 10, 1962, Nyerere announced the formation of the Ministry of National Culture and Youth and his reason for creating it:

> Of all the crimes of colonialism there is none worse than the attempt to make us believe we had no indigenous culture of our own; or that what we did have was worthless—something of which we should be ashamed, instead of a source of pride. Some of us, particularly those of us who acquired a European type of education, set ourselves out to prove to our colonial rulers that we had become "civilized"; and by that we meant that we had abandoned everything connected with our own past and learnt to imitate only European ways. Our young men's ambition was not to become well educated Africans, but to become Black Europeans! Indeed, at one time it was a compliment rather than an insult to call a man who imitated the Europeans a "Black European." . . .
>   So I have set up this new Ministry to help us regain our pride in our own culture. I want it to seek out the best of the traditions and customs of all the tribes and make them part of our national culture. (Ministry of National Culture and Youth, n.d., 3)

This conscious turn toward traditionalism entailed a sudden rejection of modernization, the modernization to which Nyerere—like so many African elites in the struggle for independence—had at one time aspired. During the pre-independence nationalist movement, elites by and large adopted certain European manners as an appropriation of European cultural capital. They symbolically sought to convince colonial powers of the cultural parity between Africans and Europeans. If parity were established, it would strike a fatal blow to the foundational "civilizing" mission justifying colonialism and establish Africans as "a less distinctive category of being" (Cooper and Stoler 1989, 610). With effort, this rhetorical crack could potentially be widened to make the case for self-rule. Nyerere, schooled at the University of Edinburgh and translator of several Shakespearean plays into Swahili, ultimately proved suitably convincing.

In establishing the Ministry of National Culture and Youth, Nyerere created a unit within the state structure that would be responsible for ensuring the recovery, promotion, and development of the nation's culture. In his own words, this would be the most important Ministry of his administration. In certain respects, most notably in the realm of language policy, it was accorded a significant degree of power to pursue its objectives. In other respects, however, the disjunction between its rhetorical importance and its actual position as the least funded, least stable of all ministerial divisions highlights one of the many contradictions to beset the young Tanzanian state.

On February 26 and 27, 1965, the Second Vice President R. M. Kawawa addressed the Regional Commissioners' Conference and outlined the government's policy objectives with regard to national culture:

> The main objective of National Culture is the development of Tanzanian nationalism and personality through the promotion of our own cultural activities. The political importance of developing this national cultural personality cannot be over emphasised. Tanzania is a new nation and has to establish herself beside older States. It is also important that we preserve for posterity what remains of our traditional culture in the face of rapid economic and social development.[23]

In this speech, he laid out specific guidelines for the formation of Cultural Committees at the village, district, regional, and national levels whose responsibilities were "to promote activities in fields (a) Swahili language and literature, (b) music, singing and dancing, (c) drama and theatrical performances, (d) traditional arts and crafts."[24] The committees were directed to draw their membership from national organizations, for example, TANU, NUTA (National Union of Tanganyika Workers), UWT (Umoja wa Wanawake wa Tanganyika, the National Women's Organization), TYL (Tanganyika Youth League), TAPA (Tanganyika African Parents' Association), government representatives, "and a few interested individuals."[25] A key element emphasized throughout the memorandum was that competitions held at each of the four levels should constitute the primary means of promoting the arts. He did not skirt the issue of finances, but neither did he provide much by way of actual funds. He later directed that funds should be raised by

1. Charging entrance fees to competitions
2. Donations from individuals or organizations (e.g., employers, NUTA, Cooperative Societies)
3. Contributions from Local Authorities (Town Councils and District Councils)
4. Special exhibitions and sales
5. Small ad hoc subventions from the Ministry of Community Development and National Culture[26]

This speech authorized the Ministry to apply pressure on regional and district commissioners to establish cultural committees. Thus, government files at all levels from 1965 to 1968 are replete with requests for progress reports on cultural committees from the National Ministry to the regions, from the regions to the districts, and from the districts to the villages, as well as requests for more time and money from the villages to the districts, from the districts to the regions, and from the regions to the National Ministry. In Tanga Region, Handeni District was one of the first districts to comply with the order and form a cultural committee. On December 23, 1965, twenty individuals were elected to the District Cultural Committee, and thirteen ideal members approved for the village level.[27]

Handeni District Cultural Committee
1. Area commissioner (chairman)
2. Executive officer (vice chairman)
3. District chairman, TANU
4. Deputy district secretary, TANU
5. Chairman, Handeni District Council
6. District chairman, U.W.T.
7. NUTA section secretary
8. TAPA district secretary
9. Chairman, Chanika Mgambo Coop.
10. Chairman, Nguu Farmers Coop.
11. Chairman, Kwamsisi/Kwasunga Coop.
12. District chairman, T.Y.L.
13. District education officer
14. Community development officer
15. Leader of the United Republic National Service at Mkuyu
16. Mr. D. Killo: arts and crafts experts
17. Mr. M. Petro: arts and crafts experts
18. Mr. M. Somboja: drummer/theatrical experts
19. Mr. A. Gumbo: drummer/theatrical experts
20. Mr. Y. Ulenge, poems expert

Ideal Membership of Handeni District Village Cultural Committees
1. Chairman, Village Development Committees (chairman)
2. Village executive officer
3. TANU branch secretary
4. Teacher of local school
5. Local chairman of U.W.T.
6. Local chairman of T.Y.L.
7. Expert in arts and crafts
8. Expert in drumming, local *ngomas*
9. Poems expert
10. Community development worker

11. NUTA representative
12. TAPA representative
13. Cooperative Societies representatives

As exemplified in these committee rosters, representation of key national organizations (TANU, UWT, NUTA, TYL, TAPA, etc.) would be present, thus mirroring the structure of the Regional, District, and Village Development Committees. The idea was to relate the central administration to the villages via a chain of relationships "between national leadership and regional and district level leadership; between the national leaders and the basic village units . . . between the various regional, district, and branch organizations, both vertically—as orders flow down and information and requests flow up—and horizontally— as different geographic units meet at the same level of the hierarchy" (Bienen 1967, 81). Yet, the dominance in these committees of representatives from the ruling party (including the youth league and women's section), local government, and other political organizations (NUTA, Cooperatives) indicates that, contrary to rhetoric emphasizing their purported role as vehicles for popular participation, these committees would simply replicate existing government positions.

Of the other districts in Tanga Region, only Pangani and Korogwe formed committees.[28] Yet the committees of all three districts existed primarily on paper paralleling the situation in the country at large. On November 5, 1966, the national office of the then Ministry of Community Development and National Culture issued a report of the regions and districts that had made progress in establishing their cultural committees. Only three (Ruvuma, Dodoma, and Mtwara) of the twenty regions on the mainland had established Regional Cultural Committees; at the district level, a mere sixteen districts had formed committees and met at least once; an additional seventeen districts (including Handeni, Pangani, Korogwe, and Lushoto) established committees in theory but had yet to hold a single meeting; and twenty-seven districts (including Tanga District) were cited as not having formed a committee nor made any progress whatsoever. From 1964 to 1967, the Culture division shared a ministry with Community Development. Hence it is not surprising that the Cultural Committees should have resembled the Development Committees in more ways than one. Not only borrowing the same membership structure, RCCs (Regional Cultural Committees) and VCCs (Village Cultural Committees) remained a "paper phenomenon" in the majority of cases, just like the RDCs (Regional Development Committees) and VDCs (Village Development Committees) (Bienen 1967, 350). The following description of the problems faced by the VDCs applies equally well to the VCCs (Village Cultural Committees):

[T]he lack of trained community development personnel hindered the rapid creation of a network of VDCs. And after committees were formed, it took time to explain the tasks expected of them. They were creations of central government and regional administration, not spontaneous expressions of local initiative; and there was little pretense about this. All the speeches made by national and regional/district leaders notwithstanding, little real attention or encouragement was paid by leaders after the VDCs had been established. Early members were sometimes even mocked by villagers for having been drawn into the arrangement. (Bienen 1967, 350)

The record is replete with indications that the second vice president's vision of an interlocking web of Cultural Committees was not shared by his citizenry. Lack of funds and lack of trained personnel were among the primary reasons cited by district and regional officers to their superiors when forced to explain the lack of progress in forming Cultural Committees. In November 1965, the Tanga area secretary explained to the commissioner for culture that "while we all want very much to preserve our traditions, our problem is that even if we establish Cultural Committees, it will be difficult for things to go smoothly without person(s) to guide the process, because meetings alone will accomplish nothing." Moreover, he pointed out, "The problem of money to pay personnel is an obvious one, but I fail to see why personnel in the Community Development distance themselves from National Culture as though they were not part of the same Ministry? Certainly, had they been told that they do this work, Cultural Committees already would have been established and successful in their work by now."[29]

Foreshadowing developments to come with regard to the forced implementation of the Ujamaa villagization program a decade later, government officials in frustration resorted to various measures of coercion. Ruvuma Region, one of the three regions celebrated for having successfully formed RCCs, utilized the strategy of sending out letters addressed to "Dear Sir/Madam" informing people that they had been "elected" to the Regional Cultural Committee. Meanwhile, the national headquarters decided to allocate funding on the basis of how successful a region/district was in establishing RCCs, DCCs, and VCCs. In June 1966, the ministry's principal secretary wrote, "[O]ur financial resources are not yet healthy and therefore, whatever small amount you may get from this Ministry should be taken as a symbol of paternalism to those who have already given up their time for the sake of developing and promoting our cultural talents. . . . I would like to stress that because of the inadequacy of funds Government contributions will be made only to those regions where Cultural Committees, District or Regional—have been established and can show signs of being active."[30] In particular, the Ministry requested the completion of standardized forms five pages in length describing the RCCs', DCCs', and VCCs' meetings, attendees, activities, progress on the organization of competitions and shows, problems encountered, research on traditions deemed worthy of preservation and those inappropriate for inclusion in National Culture, and reasons for arriving at these positive and negative assessments. The Ministry ordered that these forms should be completed four times a year. Furthermore, it directed that a second standardized report form for the description of active cultural groups, traditional and nontraditional, should be submitted by every district—a cultural census, if you will.

Such demands, made in the absence of financial and or personnel support, proved unreasonable and were simply ignored. Although Korogwe, like Handeni and Pangani, had succeeded in producing a theoretical Cultural Committee, the Korogwe area secretary explained to the Tanga regional secretary on October 21, 1966, "A Cultural Committee was appointed by the District Development Committee in 1965 but up to this date it has not taken trouble to meet. Efforts have been taken to persuade the Committee to hold meeting [sic] but in vain. It has now been resorted to bring this matter before the District Development Committee so that it appoints another Committee to replace the present one which is not active."[31] In short, the anticipated wellspring of popular involvement in reviving, promoting, and preserving Culture failed to materialize.

In all of Tanga Region, only one report was ever submitted by a Cultural Committee, and it was by the Cultural Committee of Handeni District. In its five-page report dated December 12, 1966, the committee targeted five practices noted in Handeni District that were deemed offensive, and then followed their discussion with agreed action to be taken. First, the fashion among young females to wear tight and short (ending above the knees) dresses was pronounced disrespectful and not in accordance with African tradition. Barmaids, in particular, were seen as notable perpetrators of this offense. The committee decided to forbid the wearing of tight and short dresses in contexts of government functions and meetings, and by employees in bars run by the TANU Youth League. Secondly, the committee discussed the rising prevalence of divorce and the attendant problems of women and children left without adequate support. Blame was placed on the increasing trend for youths to select their own spouses against the wishes of parents who know better, a further show of disrespect toward elders. It was decided that divorce should be discouraged heavily and made more difficult by means of increased bureaucratic regulations.

The last three items to receive committee attention all concerned the Maasai, who constitute a significant, if marginalized, portion of the Handeni population—specifically their marriage practices, clothing, and funerary practices. After discussing divorce in the general Handeni population, committee members commented that divorce was a particular problem among the Maasai, who, as nomadic pastoralists, do not register their marriages nor divorces via normal bureaucratic procedure. Someone presented the case of a woman abandoned by her husband who, after a long period of time, met and settled with another man to whom she bore five children. Because there had been no formal divorce, the former husband succeeded in having a court recognize his claim on the woman as his wife and the five children as his property. The committee did not make any recommendations with regard to this issue. The second item concerned Maasai clothing, or rather lack of underclothes, a common male Maasai practice. "The committee members have claimed that the time has come for Maasai to discard this mode of dressing."[32] It was suggested that the area commissioner call a meeting with the Maasai to explain to them the necessity of change. Finally, the committee took issue with the lack of burial practices among the Maasai, who, it was claimed, leave their dead in the bush to rot and be eaten by wild animals. The debate was framed as a public health concern, the questionable argument being made that "animals who eat the corpses then pollute human water supplies."[33] Whereas the British had romanticized the Maasai, these concerns of the Handeni Cultural Committee confirm the view that Nyerere and TANU saw them instead as an embarrassment, saying that they had to be "taught a lesson" and "brought into the twentieth century" (Coulson 1979, 8).

There was an attempt in 1966 to generate popular support for the government's cultural development initiatives. A newspaper editorial in *Nchi Yetu (Our Country)*, written by a Mr. Munseri, addressed the perceived need to rework local cultural practices. The article was subsequently disseminated to all regional and district cultural offices by a Ministry official with a cover letter applauding Mr. Munseri's careful thought and argument on the topic of national culture (even if not wholly agreeing with every point he made). Mr. Munseri tackled the question of selectivity, arguing that there were certain customs that were either bad, laughable, or shameful and thus in need of elimination. He cited as his first example the practice of screaming during Buhaya funerals, screaming that he considered so extreme that outsiders would think the mourners crazy or drunk. This, he argued, "is not right at all for today's Tanzania that wishes to take its seat among the nations of the world."[34] Secondly, Munseri targeted artistic practices/products that to his mind brought shame on the nation and should be stopped—practices like the Sukuma *ngoma* where snakes are placed in dancers' mouths, and products like sculptures depicting the lame or poor in torn, ragged clothing. "The work to encourage people to stop practices to which they are accustomed is undeniably hard and difficult, but we have no recourse than to do so with a strong heart to make our nation respected."[35]

Cultural Production in Tanzania: Socialist Revisions

The year of Tanganyika's independence coincided with the release of Frantz Fanon's *Les damnés de la terre (The Wretched of the Earth)*. His forceful arguments, borne by "the winds of change" that were blowing across the continent, took root in many a government official and university intellectual's mind. African intellectuals and nationalists found particularly relevant his essay "On National Culture," in which he derided attempts to create a national culture from an assortment of customs. Culture, he argued, is predicated upon a national consciousness that in turn is achieved only through the struggle for liberation. It is "not folklore, nor an abstract populism that believes it can discover the people's true nature. . . . A national culture is the whole body of efforts made by a people in the sphere of thought to describe, justify, and praise the action through which that people has created itself and keeps itself in existence" (Fanon 1963, 233).

As described in chapter 2, Nyerere ushered in Tanzania's experience with African Socialism in 1967 with the Arusha Declaration. Just as his political and economic agendas progressed from less to more radical in tone and action, so too did his theories relating to cultural development and those of his Ministry find increasing resonance in revolutionary socialist principles, especially those articulated by Fanon, Bertolt Brecht, and Ernst Fischer. Nyerere's original vision of national culture as a collection of customs was abandoned in favor of "all that which marks out a nation as a nation and helps it to continue developing as a nation" (Mbughuni and Ruhumbika 1974, 275). A new variety of selectivity was introduced regarding cultural practices: only those considered progressive in an overtly socialist sense would be retained.

> In a socialist society all art is seen as a servant of society. A tool to help man better understand and shape his society according to his collective needs. Divorcing art or the artist from society is another sin of the decadent bourgeoisie society, inseparable from the commercialisation of art, which all socialist societies have to fight. . . .
> The art which, therefore, our Division of Culture and its organs should promote in our rural communities, *ujamaa* villages and urban centres is that which will help us to better understand our environment and transform it according to our needs. (Mbughuni and Ruhumbika 1974, 280)

As summarized in 1974 by Louis Mbughuni, a former director of arts and language in the Ministry of Culture, Tanzania's cultural policy was organized around six points:

1. A selective revival of our traditions and customs
2. Promotion and preservation of our cultural heritage
3. Our culture as an instrument of national development and unity
4. The development of our tribal cultures into one national culture
5. The contribution of our culture towards the development of mankind and the contribution of other cultures to our own development
6. The necessity of overhauling the educational systems inherited from the former colonial powers and the need for all Tanzanians to remove the influence of the colonial mentality from their minds (Mbughuni 1974, 18)

This list makes evident a number of relevant items: first, an express intent to be *selective* in cultural recovery (Point 1); second, the intent to use culture as a tool for nationalist—which from 1967 on meant *socialist*—development (Points 3 and 5); third, hints of *homogenization* vis-à-vis the desire to unify all groups into a single national culture (Point 4); fourth, a stand against cultural isolation in the express desire for *cultural exchange* with other countries (Point 5); and, finally, *anticolonialist* rejection of colonial residue in education specifically, but in all things generally (Point 6).

The Colonized as Colonizer: Uniting Traditionalism with Socialism

Even if the Cultural Committees never caught on, popular debate did continue over Tanzanian Culture. In a 1981 monograph entitled *National Culture*, Yusuf Halimoja devotes a chapter to customs and traditions, subdividing the chapter into two sections with disturbingly familiar headings: "Appropriate customs and traditions" and "Inappropriate customs and traditions." He begins the first section as follows:

> Let us begin by asking ourselves which customs and traditions are appropriate to the development of our nation: The answer is short. It is those customs and traditions that help to forward the objective of our nation. . . . Those customs and traditions that assist people to live a life in accordance with the politics of socialism and self-reliance are indeed the ones that should be promoted and, when necessary, modified to ensure that they correspond to our present condition. All customs and traditions in accordance with unity, stability, cooperation, good health, etc. should be developed. (Halimoja 1981, 20; translation mine)

In the ensuing discussion, Halimoja identifies the following as "appropriate" customs: hard work, cooperation, generosity, mutual respect, traditional education (education, however, in line with socialism and self-reliance), long-term planning, proper discipline in raising respectful and obedient children, protection of society and the environment, the preservation of historical records, mutual assistance (for example, preparing food during funeral services to help the family of the deceased feed mourners), and non-competitiveness. Alternatively, those deemed "inappropriate" include customary food prohibitions (that inhibit healthy diets), oppression of women, lack of long-term planning that results in unnecessary poverty, and belief in the evil eye, curses, and black magic that causes some people to greatly modify their behavior to their detriment. A notable target for reform is bridewealth payments. Halimoja explains that in traditional practice bridewealth served as a symbolic token of conjugal unity between two individuals and two families. Today, however, greed has caused increasing inflation of bridewealth payments so that the practice resembles the business of slavery, for after having paid such a substantial sum, the groom feels that he has truly "bought" his bride and is entitled to treat her as he wishes. Moreover, because a divorce would entail the return of the money, women find themselves without recourse in bad marriages because the sum of money paid in bridewealth is often too great a sum to be raised easily by her family. In all, Halimoja argues, it has resulted in increased oppression of women.

These arguments for selectivity demonstrate reigning concerns with socialist development as well as concerns to appear modern. The theory has come full circle. From emulating modernization during the struggle for independence to valorizing "tradition" (albeit certain ones over others), Tanzanian intellectual trends demonstrate a return swing of the pendulum to the side of modernization with the writings of Halimoja. Leaving behind those practices that reinforce negative, essentially colonial, perceptions of Tanzanians as backward and steeped in unhealthy, unprogressive tradition constitutes a primary objective of this cultural producer. But, so goes the counterargument, "tradition" does not in and of itself presuppose backwardness. Indeed, some intellectuals argued that tradition and modernity are not necessarily mutually exclusive categories. As former Director of Arts and National Language Godwin Kaduma noted, "Too often tradition and progress are treated as if they were deadly enemies. Tanzanians do not see it that way, and they are bent on dancing their way to self-reliance" (Kaduma 1971, 17). Nyerere found inspiration for his unique brand of socialism in African tradition, or at least in what he conceptualized and propagated as "African tradition"— a "tradition" of communalism, cooperation, and self-reliance. He wove together elements of a somewhat altered past with elements of a contemporary political philosophy for the purposes of producing a national identity and national culture at once socialist yet African, internally oriented yet modern. An agenda such as this would have to accept the inevitable contradictions as par for the course.

Language Policy, BAKITA, and BAKIZA

> Among the preconditions for establishing regimes of colonial
> power was, must have been, communication with the colonized
> . . . needed to maintain regimes, military, religious—ideological
> and economic.
>
> —Johannes Fabian, *Language and Colonial Power*

A key domain since its inception and one of the few undisputed successes of the Culture Division is its language policy. Kiswahili, spoken by more than fifty million people worldwide (Mvungi 1980), is the national language of Tanzania, the primary mode of governmental communication, and a powerful symbol of Tanzanian unity. Although the language is also widespread in neighboring Kenya and Uganda, in neither country does it constitute the primary medium for governmental communication. English prevails in both those countries.

Kiswahili commands a position of historical and continued preeminence in East Africa. Its grammatical structure is undeniably Bantu, but its vocabulary contains a large percentage of adopted words. As described in chapter 2, Kiswahili was the *lingua franca* utilized along the trade routes to and from the coast whence it originated (Whiteley 1969). The fact that more trade routes traversed Tanganyika than Kenya explains, in part, why it became more prevalent in Tanganyika than Kenya. During the period of German colonial rule, German was introduced in 1894–95 as the medium of administration and education but was quickly discarded in favor of Kiswahili. One scholar argues that German administrators worried that German language skills would provide access to politically dangerous reading materials (namely, Marxist literature) that could incite revolutionary consciousness in the colony (Gibbe 1983, 48). Kiswahili usage was already widespread and therefore a ready vehicle for colonial administration in Tanganyika, as confirmed by Wilfred Whiteley, historian of the Swahili language:

> By 1914 the Administration was able to conduct much of its correspondence with village headmen in Swahili. . . . This was one feature of German Administration which proved of great value to their successors, the British, and evoked a good deal of approval in later years. The Report on the Territory for 1921, for example, stated ". . . the late German system has made it possible to communicate in writing with every Akida and village headman, and in turn to receive from him reports written in Swahili." Such advantages could be shared by administrators and administered alike. For the former it was convenient to have a single language in which high standards could be imposed on officers and maintained throughout their service. For the Education Department it meant that problems of staffing were minimized and those of textbooks simplified. . . . It also meant that the Junior Service, staffed by Tanganyikans, was not restricted to regional postings; and members could be transferred without difficulty from one part of the country to another. . . . There is also some evidence that it engendered a sense of belonging to a unit larger than the tribe. (Whiteley 1969, 60–61)

During British colonial rule, Kiswahili suffered a minor setback when Indirect Rule was introduced, for the policy encouraged use of indigenous languages (Gibbe 1983, 49). Administrative ease won out in the end, however, and by the final decade of British rule, Kiswahili had expanded considerably via the compilation and publication of dictionaries, and the printing and distribution of as many as forty Swahili newspapers (Whiteley 1969, 62). The continued use of English, however, as the medium of communication for the highest levels of administration, the higher courts, and secondary and university education perpetuated the stereotype of Swahili as an inferior language. Broken English became a source of social stereotyping and social differentiation. A popular song from the 1950s, sung by "Frank Humplinck and Sisters" in the style of the Andrews Sisters, played on this theme:

> I greet my girl friend, "How do you do?"
> She's startled and swings round.
> She asks why I'm calling her an *mdudu* [insect].
> I'm amazed, stupefied.
> I explain to her it's an English greeting.
> That's how one greets one's friends when one meets them.
> - - -
>
> **Chorus**
> Listen, my good friend, I don't want any jokes, eh eh.
> Don't annoy me, my friend, I don't want to be called an *mdudu*.
> Even you're an *mdudu*, even you're an *mdudu*.
>
> - - -
> There are many fools like this one,
> Claiming they don't know English.
> When they're drunk, they just rattle it off.
> "How, *mdudu*, how do you do?"
> Listen how they speak English.
> It's not "broken," nor is it the real thing.[36]

Despite latent negative associations between Kiswahili and its role in the slave trade, TANU chose Kiswahili as its language for mass organization and recast it in a positive light as the language of revolution, the language of unity. There is no doubt that it enabled and facilitated the spread of nationalist consciousness and sentiment. Its greatest strength lay in its lack of association with any single ethnic unit. This "supra-tribalistic component" (Gibbe 1983; Whiteley 1969) enabled its adoption without generating charges of favoritism of one group over another, and its tremendous diffusion throughout the Territory facilitated political organization and TANU's development. It is said that Julius Nyerere once boasted that he had to refer to interpreters on only two occasions during his tours of the country (Whiteley 1969, 65).

Another instance of the bureaucratic divide shadowing the twenty-five-mile channel between Zanzibar and the mainland is the coexistence of two Swahili language councils: BAKITA (Baraza la Kiswahili la Taifa), the National Swahili Council serving the promotion and development of Swahili on the mainland, and BAKIZA (Baraza la Kiswahili la Zanzibar), serving in the same capacity on the islands. Zanzibar, however, has different linguistic antecedents (Arabic and English) than the mainland, owing to its differing colonial history. Secondly, whereas a multitude of languages color the linguistic map of the mainland, on Zanzibar Kiswahili is the dominant language, sharing the field only with the language spoken in Makunduchi on the island's southernmost tip. The objectives of the two councils are compared and contrasted in table 5.1.[37]

Many credit the impressive sense of Tanzanian national unity in large

Table 5.1 A Comparison of BAKITA and BAKIZA Objectives

BAKITA	BAKIZA
1. To promote the use of Kiswahili throughout the United Republic of Tanzania	To ensure that Kiswahili is used in all government activities
2. To cooperate with other government agencies engaged in the development of Kiswahili (e.g., the university and mass media) and to endeavor to coordinate their activities	To ensure that all educational and governmental texts are written in or translated into Kiswahili
3. To encourage the use of Kiswahili in the conduct of government affairs and public life in general	To advise various agencies on the use and promotion of Kiswahili
4. To encourage the achievement of high standards in the use of Kiswahili and to discourage its misuse (e.g., censor Kiswahili publications for impure, or "bad," Kiswahili)	To incorporate dialectical differences in the research and promotion of Kiswahili
5. To cooperate with the authorities concerned in establishing standard Kiswahili translation of technical terms	To research all the various forms and traditions of Kiswahili
6. To publish a regular journal for the promotion of Kiswahili and Swahili literature *(Lugha Yetu)*	To select which foreign language should be taught that can assist in Zanzibar's economic and cultural development
7. To provide services to the government, public agencies, and individual authors writing in Kiswahili	To emphasize use of Arabic and English because of their importance to Zanzibari economic and religious domains
8.	To promote Swahili literature by publishing books, newspapers, and journals, and to ensure proper usage of Kiswahili in these various areas.
9.	To revive the use of Kiswahili as the National Language in various fields of expertise

part to Nyerere's decision to institute and enforce Kiswahili as the national language as well as the sole instructional medium in primary schools. Although the unfortunate consequence of this policy is the decided decline of Tanzania's other 120 or so indigenous languages (some to the point of near extinction), it nevertheless greatly facilitates communication throughout the country. If conversant in Kiswahili, one can travel anywhere in the country and communicate without hindrance. The same cannot be said of Kenya, where, despite its position as the secondary national language, Kiswahili is still associated almost exclusively with the coastal region. There is perhaps no other element that so forcefully symbolizes Tanzanian national unity, a unity that, in this domain, even supersedes mainland-island distinctions and provides rhetorical justification for the Union.

A Migrant Ministry: Cultural Revolution in Retreat

The years immediately following the 1967 Arusha Declaration witnessed a sudden efflorescence in cultural production. Poets, musicians, dancers, and playwrights all rallied behind the government's ambitious program to eliminate social inequality and evenly distribute the nation's resources. They produced art that extolled the party and its leaders and sang the praises of socialism. Yet despite this "unleashed energy hitherto untapped, the production and development of cultural expressions after 1967 . . . did not develop to their envisioned dynamic potential" (Lihamba 1991, 270). Lihamba attributes the failure to three factors: (1) a vaguely defined, incoherent cultural policy, (2) weaknesses in the cultural administration, and (3) lack of moral and material investment.

The Ministry's weak administration and critical lack of resources resulted in a pattern of it being bounced from one Ministry to another— a pattern continuing even to the present day. When Nyerere established the Ministry of National Culture and Youth in 1962, he appointed Mr. Lawi Sijaona as its first minister, and Mr. Joseph Nyerere (his brother) and Bibi Titi Mohamed (the same Titi Mohamed who led the drive for TANU registration in the years before independence) as deputy ministers (Geiger 1997). In 1964, two years after its establishment, the Ministry of National Culture and Youth was disbanded and reconstructed as the Ministry of Community Development and National Culture. Changes in ministers accompanied the changes in ministry. As one official wrote, "The Culture Division . . . had known by 1965 four different ministers and four different principal secretaries, all within a period of less than three years. These constant changes were not conducive to planned development, particularly in an area as sensitive as culture" (Mbughuni 1974, 20).

In 1967, the same year the Arusha Declaration was announced, Culture was demoted from ministerial status to that of a department within the Ministry of Regional Administration and Rural Development. That same year, the tone of official correspondence shifted back again to the issue of responsibility for cultural development that had previously been raised by the Tanga area secretary. Letters to the national office from Mara, Arusha, and Iringa Regions (dated February 8, 22, and 27, 1967, respectively) complained about the onus of the forms and requested that responsibility for cultural affairs be transferred to the regional and district development officers. In a partial admission of defeat, the national office responded that Cultural Committees should be conceptualized as subcommittees of the Development Committees. A year later, the national office was still demanding forms that, at least from Tanga Region, were not forthcoming. Only Handeni District ever completed the five-page progress report, and it did so only once. Handeni, Pangani, and Lushoto all completed their cultural census reports. Interestingly and ironically, Tanga District, the seat of regional government, never once produced a committee nor a report of any kind. Its sole contribution was a draft constitution for the Tanga Cultural Society (TACSO) that never again would reappear in the official record.

By 1969, government insistence on the formation of Cultural Committees diminished to the point of silence, indicating a cultural revolution in retreat. The final reference to the topic was in a letter dated February 12, 1969, from the commissioner of culture to all district commissioners, in which he requested general information on cultural activities (significantly, without any reference to or request for the standardized forms and reports), but then admitted that "[w]e understand that this work should be accomplished by regional and district cultural officers, but that cultural officers at the district level do not exist and that there are only five cultural officers for every region. But this work cannot wait another year or two."[38]

The wanderings of the Culture Division were far from over. In 1969, it was demoted to a unit within the Ministry of National Education and remained there for five years. In 1973, a presidential commission was appointed to inquire into the status of the Culture Division and hired a team of professional consultants, McKinsey & Co., Inc., to produce concrete recommendations (Mbughuni 1974, 22). Action taken upon the McKinsey report resulted in the promotion on February 11, 1974, of the division back to the status of a full ministry: the Ministry of National Education and Culture. This ministry only existed for one year, however, for when the final McKinsey report was published in 1975, a new home had been identified for Culture in the newly reestablished Ministry of

National Culture and Youth. In 1980, ministerial reorganization occurred again, resulting in the emergence of the Ministry of Information
and Culture. In 1984, the Culture Division was once again deprived of
its ministerial status and placed under the Prime Minister's Office. In
1985, it was annexed to the Ministry of Social Welfare, Culture, Youth,
and Sports, which subsequently was reconfigured in 1988 as the Ministry
of Labor, Culture, and Social Welfare. In 1990, the Ministry of Education and Culture was revived and Culture continues to abide there today. The history of its wanderings is depicted in table 5.2.[39]

When I arrived in Tanga in 1992, there was a striking discordance
between the theoretical placement of Culture and its day-to-day functioning. Tanga's regional cultural officers still worked in cooperation
with social welfare, youth, and sports officers. They all continued to
share the offices of the former Ministry of Social Welfare, Culture,

Table 5.2 A Migrant Ministry: The Tanzanian Culture Division, 1948–Present

Date	Swahili Title	English Title
1948	Idara ya Maendeleo	Development Department
1957	Wizara ya Serikali za Mitaa na Utawala	Ministry of Local Government and Administration
1959	Wizara ya Vyama vya Ushirika na Maendeleo	Ministry of Cooperative Societies and Development
December 10, 1962	Wizara ya Mila na Vijana	Ministry of National Culture and Youth
1964	Wizara ya Maendeleo na Utama-duni	Ministry of Community Develop-ment and National Culture
1967	Wizara ya Tawala za Mikoa na Maendeleo Vijijini	Ministry of Regional Administration and Rural Development
1969	Wizara ya Elimu ya Taifa	Ministry of National Education
February 11, 1974	Wizara ya Elimu ya Taifa na Utamudini	Ministry of National Education and Culture
1975	Wizara ya Utamaduni wa Taifa na Vijana	Ministry of National Culture and Youth
1980	Wizara ya Habari na Utamaduni	Ministry of Information and Culture
1984	Ofisi ya Waziri Mkuu na Makamu wa Kwanza ya Rais	Office of the Prime Minister and First Vice President
1985	Wizara ya Maendeleo ya Jamii, Utamaduni, Vijana na Michezo	Ministry of Community Develop-ment, Culture, Youth, and Sports
1988	Wizara ya Kazi, Utamaduni na Ustawi wa Jamii	Ministry of Labor, Culture, and So-cial Welfare
1990	Wizara ya Elimu na Utamaduni	Ministry of Education and Culture

Youth, and Sports that had officially ceased to exist as of 1988. More important, however, cultural officers and social welfare officers claimed to share their work and assist each other as necessary. The functional head of the entire office was a sports officer. I was told that although Culture had officially moved to Education, the Education ministry maintained its own office elsewhere in Tanga, and that there was little interaction between the two. The primary reason for communication appeared to be negotiations over a vehicle utilized by the sports officer yet also earmarked for educational purposes. For most of my first two years in Tanga, a sign hung over yet another building identifying it as the regional office of the Ministry of Labor, Culture, and Social Welfare. By the time I left in 1995, however, that sign had been taken down. Not so the sign for the Ministry of Social Welfare, Culture, Youth, and Sports. It continues to identify the *de facto* base for cultural administration in Tanga Region.

Cultural officers have long complained of a lack of direction and lack of understanding of their assigned roles. In her research on Tanzanian cultural policy especially relating to theatrical performance, Amandina Lihamba noted, "In all the areas visited during the research for this study (1983/84), cultural officers complained about lack of moral and financial support as well as lack of seriousness and interest on the part of Regional and District political functionaries. Only a few of the officers knew what they were supposed to do and all harboured frustrations and helplessness towards their responsibilities. . . . While most of those interviewed (2 out of 3) thought there was a national cultural policy, few could formulate the nature of the policy or what their role in it was" (Lihamba 1985, 357).

The story of one cultural officer's recruitment into the Culture Ministry is quite revealing.

> It happened one day that I went to Kikuyu to teach in the school when I met one relative who said, "Congratulations!" I was surprised and said, "Congratulations for what?" He said we have heard on the radio this morning during the *Majira* show that you had been named to be Culture Officer for Dodoma Region. I told him I did not have any news. We parted and I continued on to school. When I arrived at the school I saw the teachers smiling in happiness as they came to meet me and all of them shook my hand and said, "Congratulations! Congratulations!" I remained speechless. I asked them, "Congratulations for what?" They said it was announced last night and this morning on the show *Majira* that you have been named to be Cultural Officer for Dodoma Region and that this work will begin at once and you should report to your RDD [Regional Development Director]. Then I realized that this news could well be true. I took leave from my people to go wait at the Boma for the RDD to ask him, and I went to the Boma where I found RDD Ndugu James Gwagilo. When he saw me he shook my hand with happiness and said, "Hongera sana." I was invited to use a car to go to the school to get my things. Then I sat down. He gave me a big ledger for me to sign. Then he took me to the

room that had been prepared early that morning. He took me inside and said, "This is to be your office." Inside were one table and one chair only. He said, "So start to work." He left me there without files—there were no records. I had to start where? What culture? Ah, the whole day I was in the office without one person to explain to me what to do or where to start. At four-thirty I closed the office and returned home the same as always.[40]

This excerpt is taken from the autobiography of Ernest Musa Kongola. Kongola served as the Dodoma Region Cultural Officer from 1974 to 1976 and then was transferred to the Ministry headquarters in Dar es Salaam to be assistant to the Secretary for Arts and Languages until his retirement in 1977 at the age of fifty-five. Kongola tells a rich tale of how in the complete absence of any direction or directives, he developed his own theory of and approach to culture. On his second day on the job, he jotted down a list of those practices most linked to culture in his mind: dance, games, art, music, language, clothes, hair styles, cooking, and work culture. Upon developing this guiding framework, he then very systematically went about documenting these practices for every village in his region—all of which he visited on foot because no transportation (not even a bicycle) was provided him. He also sent a copy of his framework to the Ministry headquarters, and "they were happy to see this arrangement and said continue and they in the Ministry began to use the structure which I had sent them."[41] His is a rare success story. Through his own initiative and passion, he took an originally empty title and filled it to the fullest, even to the point of influencing the Ministry itself. "Continuing this work was not easy," Kongola admits, "but because I loved it I did it."[42]

Cultural activities continue to receive little or no government funding. The phone in the Tanga regional office was disconnected in 1993 and never reconnected due to lack of payment. The disputed vehicle was eventually confiscated by the Education Ministry for its exclusive use, leaving the Culture Division with access to nothing but public transportation. The cultural officers with whom I worked declined in number over my three years' research period as some were retired early (with minimal severance pay) due to government cutbacks. Those that remained never knew when they would be paid their "regular" salaries. The lack of regular salaries legitimized lack of regular work for many who subsequently helped themselves to days off to pursue other more economically beneficial activities. Once when I stopped by the office to check in and say hello, I found a cultural officer at her empty desk knitting. By way of response to an unasked question, she explained with a somewhat bitter laugh that knitting was, after all, a cultural activity, was it not? She then went on to share with me her plans of applying for one of the many small development loans that were particularly accessible to female entrepreneurs to open a tailor shop and "forget this business of Culture."

In Zanzibar, where cultural policy remains under the jurisdiction of the Zanzibar Government, the Culture Division has experienced only slightly more stability than it has on the mainland. As with TANU on the mainland, the ASP (Afro-Shirazi Party, Zanzibar's ruling party prior to the consolidation of TANU and ASP into today's CCM) directed cultural affairs until the government assigned the task to a proper ministry. Sources vary on the exact history of its movements, but the Culture Division appears to have followed the itinerary outlined in table 5.3.

It will require more research to determine the justifications behind each move of the Culture Division on both the mainland and the islands, but the pattern indelibly marks these parallel histories with inconsistency, disjuncture, evasion of responsibility, and contested visions. The practice of Tanzanian cultural development clearly has occurred at a significant distance from its articulated rhetoric. One policy document, entitled *National Cultural Policy Guidelines* (1988), however, claimed the following:

> Culture encompasses all aspects of society that enable the community to struggle against its environment while balancing humanitarian and social needs; this treasure includes all domains such as faith, bravery, traditional beliefs, laws, art, customs and traditions, technology, religion, preservation, communication, business, education, security, nutrition, entertainment, and oral literature. In other words, Culture is everything and constitutes a compass or stick for measuring the whole community within its environment. Culture is the sole foundation of all community activities. According to this philosophy, cultural matters concern all Party and Government sectors. There is no sector of the Party of Government that does not involve Culture in the fulfillment of its day-to-day responsibilities.[43]

Can we attribute the Culture Division's many movements to a literal interpretation of the above guideline? I think not. What appears more

Table 5.3 Another Migrant Ministry: The Zanzibari Culture Division, 1964–Present

Date	Swahili Title	English Title
1964	Wizara ya Elimu na Mila	Ministry of Education and Customs
1975	Wizara ya Mila, Utamaduni na Michezo	Ministry of Customs, Culture, and Sports
1976	Wizara ya Utamaduni na Michezo	Ministry of Culture and Sports
?	Wizara ya Habari, Utamaduni na Michezo	Ministry of Information, Culture, and Sports
?	Wizara ya Habari, Utamaduni na Utalii	Ministry of Information, Culture, and Tourism
1992	Wizara ya Habari, Utamaduni, Utalii, na Vijana	Ministry of Information, Culture, Tourism, and Youth

likely is that the hoped-for Tanzanian Cultural Revolution never materialized beyond the written page and thus was forced into an early retreat. As Lihamba argues,

> Government and Party rhetoric on cultural promotion and development have continued but have not been matched by genuine practical efforts to actualize objectives and activities. The Arusha Declaration ushered in an era where the State was to have control over cultural production. The inability of the State to become a cultural producer has been underlined by its ineffectual organs operating without a coherent policy or programme. (Lihamba 1991, 275)

A national language, a national anthem, national holidays, national monuments, and a national dance troupe together substantiate and legitimize the nation's existence. They jointly imply a sense of agreement upon what constitutes the nation, and yet constitute a thinly veiled effort to mask continuing debate and negotiation over what Tanzania is, what it isn't, and what it is yet to become. Clearly sacrificed in practice, early official concern with authenticity and tradition was never wholly consistent at the ideological level either. The key symbolic markers of national identity listed above were all overseen and organized by the Ministry. The national anthem, "Mungu Ibariki Afrika," however, hailed from South Africa, the National Dance Troupe performed (as many troupes continue to do today) acrobatics learned in China, and the national arts competitions include a *kwaya* competition (from "choir"— the musical consequence of interactions with Western Christianity). Thus even during the early traditionalist phase of national cultural production, it was not the perceived "indigenousness" of something that rendered it acceptable to official post-independence nationalism, but how well it fit with reigning political paradigms and objectives. Alignment with China, one of Tanzania's most generous socialist patrons, and with the continued fight against colonialism (apartheid) in South Africa allowed for some bending of the authenticity mandate that otherwise dominated Tanzanian cultural policy of the time.

Traditionalism came to be replaced by the new ideological template of socialism. This constituted the dominant frame of reference during the three decades of attempted cultural revolution that followed the Arusha Declaration. Socialism provided the scales on which customs were weighed for selection or repression; it projected the development goals to be echoed through artistic production; it mandated cultural as well as social equality that resulted in much standardization of cultural form; it engaged in intercultural exchange, most often with other socialist countries (China in particular); and its anticolonial rhetoric was often cast in socialist vs. Western capitalist terms. In short, socialism determined both the "object" (a young nation struggling out from under the weight of an oppressive colonial past) and the "objectives" (a truly egalitarian, self-reliant socialist society) of national cultural production.

Of Permits, Fees, Licenses, and Constitutions: Neocolonial Cultural Administration

After independence, it was a stated objective of TANU to transform or abandon altogether colonial structures (Bienen 1967, 308), yet it was another objective stated by the president himself to borrow when necessary from other cultures: "I don't want anybody to imagine that to revive our own culture means at the same time to reject that of any other country. A nation which refuses to learn from foreign cultures is nothing but a nation of idiots and lunatics" (as cited in Ministry of National Culture and Youth, n.d., 4).

Cultural exchange with other countries, primarily other socialist countries, provided one resolution to this apparent contradiction between the rejection and acceptance of foreign influence, for it would entail borrowing from fellow socialists or nations sympathetic to Nyerere's goals. China, Guinea, and Zambia all sent cultural troupes to Tanzania to perform and introduce Tanzania to their socialist take on artistic and cultural production. Pan-Africanist ideology provided a bridge of fellowship to other African nations, whether socialist or not. Hence, in an act of unity with neighboring countries as well as unity against the regime of South African apartheid, Tanzania, Zambia, and Zimbabwe all adopted the music of "Nkosi Sikelel'i Afrika," the ANC's anthem, as their national anthem, but each one substituted its own song lyrics (see figure 5.2). TANU (Tanganyika African National Union), KANU (Kenya African National Union) and ZANU (Zimbabwe African National Union) shared names, as well as histories of resistance and rebellion against their respective colonial regimes. And Dar es Salaam in the 1960s and 1970s provided safe haven to virtually anyone with a cause: SWAPO, ANC, FRELIMO, even exiled Black Panthers. Che Guevara and Malcolm X are among those rumored to have talked political shop over Tanzanian coffee.

Cultural exchange with China took precedence. This followed from the fact that Tanzania received tremendous amounts of economic assistance from China. The following describes the situation as of 1976:

> From the outset, the Chinese seemed determined to tailor their aid efforts specifically to prime Tanzanian needs. One of their first aid projects was a $4 million textile mill designed to utilize Tanzanian cotton. A new brewery and police training programs followed. So, too, did a high-powered long-range radio transmitter designed to beam broadcasts to southern Africa. Next followed the Chinese take-

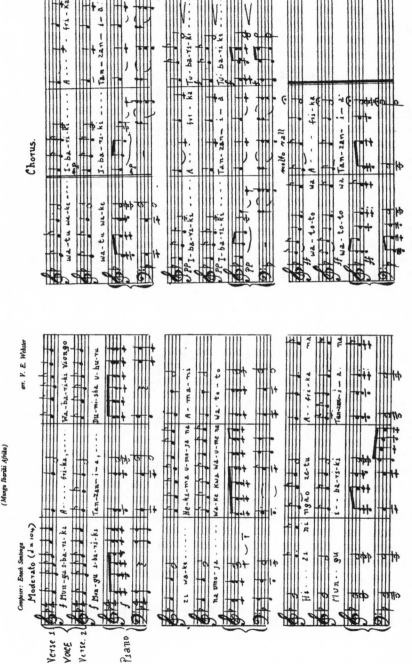

Figure 5.2 Mungu Ibariki Afrika: The Tanzania National Anthem (translated lyrics in appendix A).

over of military training programs previously supervised by the Canadians. (The extent of this Chinese military aid effort, including the supply of arms, has never been clear.) Finally, and most important of all, has been the Chinese financing, engineering, and building of the railway between Tanzania and Zambia. Associated with this effort have been Chinese-directed programs training Tanzanian rail workers and related health facilities for workers and populace along the railroad right-of way. Given all these, it is evident that the Chinese aid of $450 million plus to Tanzania has been by all odds the largest aid program for a black African state from a Communist nation. (Duggan and Civille 1976, 153–54)

Also by 1976, Zanzibar had received upwards of $12 million in Chinese aid. When the Chinese cultural troupe toured Tanzania, its members suggested that talented Tanzanian youth be sent to China to be trained in acrobatics. A total of twenty youths between the ages of twelve and fourteen were selected (eight were from Tanga) and sent to China in 1965 for four years of training. An additional ten were sent in 1968 to be trained in the performance of musical accompaniment for acrobatic shows. Upon their return in 1969, these youths were incorporated into the National Ngoma Troupe, alternatively known as the National Dance Troupe and National Drama Troupe. When the Tanzanian delegation visited China in 1966, they were taken to visit the Tanzanian youths and assess their progress. The transformed youths greatly impressed the delegation, and many of China's socialist practices and ideas provided sources of inspiration and emulation.[44] As has been demonstrated, however, despite government efforts to incite a cultural revolution along the lines of the Chinese example, such a revolution was not forthcoming.

The materials presented here show the creation of a cultural administrative bureaucracy that duplicated the socialist bureaucratic structure found in virtually every other domain of Tanzanian governance. The model from which they were all derived was the party structure, beginning with the central TANU (later CCM) offices and expanding outwards to the regions, districts, villages, and branches down to the ten-house cell. Yet in the domain of culture, such an unwieldy and overbearing structure proved incommensurate with cultural practice and failed utterly to materialize.

Moreover, this postcolonial, socialist structure married colonial practice, and herein lies the reason for the lack of mass involvement in the Tanzanian Cultural Revolution. Government administrators may have demolished the more obvious colonial apparatus of cultural production (the Native Authority, etc.), but they did not root out colonial concerns. Postcolonial administrators, like colonial administrators, assessed local cultural practices to determine whether or not such practices should be promoted or prohibited. The standards of measuring good versus bad customs, appropriate versus inappropriate traditions, may have changed along with the change in government personnel, but selectivity as a goal and practice remains.

Regulation of cultural performance and production constitutes another residual colonial practice that, rather than experiencing anticolonial repression, has expanded and flourished under postcolonialism. The concern with permits, with fees, with licenses, and most recently with constitutions continues into current cultural administration and in fact dominates it. Today, every cultural group is required by law to register as a society under the "Societies Ordinance CAP 337" with the Ministry of Home Affairs and as a cultural group with BASATA (Baraza la Sanaa la Taifa, the National Arts Council)[45] on the mainland and with BASAZA (Baraza la Sanaa la Zanzibar, the Zanzibar Arts Council) in the islands. All requests for registration must be accompanied by a group constitution indicating its administrative structure, the handling of finances, selected bank, elected officials, goals, and intents. Performance groups that would like to perform outside their home region are required by law to apply both for a permit to leave their region and a permit to enter the region of the planned performance. Registration must be up to date for any group to be granted a license to perform, and a license is required for each performance within or beyond the home region. From the proceeds of each performance, 5 percent goes to the district cultural office, 10 percent to the regional cultural office, Tsh. 20 for each ticket sold pays the entertainment tax, another Tsh. 10 for each ticket sold pays the mandatory contribution to the local Festivals Committee, and an additional 1 percent of the total income pays the stamp duty. Small wonder that the majority of Tanzanian performers consider the state an exacting, oppressive institution that, for all its rhetoric on the promotion of Tanzanian arts, is actually the primary reason for the declining fortunes and increased precariousness of Tanzanian artists. Corrigan and Sayer cogently argue that state formation entails placing restriction on "all forms of 'making public'—printing and publishing, dramatic performance, singing, speaking and/or reading aloud, preaching, graphic and other visual depictions, and so on" primarily by means of "*licensing* approved individuals or places (and often examining and registering their products before they are made public), thereby criminalizing the unlicensed, and *regulation* by the criteria required if the status of proper, approved, acceptable and/or legalized was to be granted" (1985, 23, emphasis in original). Apparently, this proves no less true for the colonial and postcolonial Tanzanian states.

Finally, above and beyond the financial demands made on artists by the cultural bureaucracy, they are required to provide their artistic talents for state celebrations. On every national holiday, cultural officers send a standard letter to all performing groups notifying them that their services are requested. In theory, funds are set aside to pay the performers a token payment, but pressure is applied in terms of their "duty" as citizens to volunteer their artistic services for such functions. Every group must develop and negotiate its personal relationship with the cultural officers in its home district and region. Some groups opt to collaborate, often bargaining on the amount of money paid to the Ministry after every performance. But there are also groups that resist, that refuse to register and refuse to pay the amounts demanded of them. In general, one finds that performers combine the two approaches, incorporating some resistance in their acts of collaboration, some collaboration in their acts of resistance. We examine some actual examples of the negotiations between performers and the postcolonial state over cultural production and analyze the effects of postsocialist transition to multiparty democracy on state cultural policy in the following two chapters.

The evolution of cultural policy in colonial and postcolonial Tanzania explains the lack of revolution. The top-down approach to cultural production, irrespective of who wields political power, has had mixed results with largely negative consequences for Tanzanian artists. Colonial administrators initialized construction of an unwieldy and extractive apparatus that was subsequently completed and reinforced after independence despite vehement denouncements of colonial cultural oppression. Present-day cultural officers continue the colonial tradition of passing judgment on local practice and continue to view cultural performance as a source of state (and, unfortunately, often personal) revenue. In effect, the putative Tanzanian Cultural Revolution has been reduced to petty fee collection.[46]

But, as case after case of defeated totalitarianism demonstrates, people display creative repertoires of strategies to circumvent and undermine aspiring hegemonies. Culture policymakers may hold certain conceptions of both the object and the objectives of national cultural production, but these ultimately were and continue to be subject to public approval.

6

COMPETING AGENDAS: THE PRODUCTION OF TANZANIAN NATIONAL CULTURE

Tradition is the living art of the dead. Traditionalism is the dead art of the living.

—Jaroslav Pelikan

[A]ll states are theaters of power. . . . [T]he rulers' need to categorize people in order to know how best to dominate them gives to their subjects an inexhaustible resource of (mis)information to manipulate—either to protect themselves from or to gain a purchase on the intervention of the state. Rulers on stage are continually plagued by mimics, understudies, and false cues.

—John Lonsdale, "States and Social Practices in Africa"

The National Arts and Language Competitions: An Introduction

My early affiliation with KIUBATA made me a regular visitor to the Harbours Club, a building overlooking the Tanga Harbor that was designed to support leisure and entertainment activities for Bandari (harbor, port) workers. As described earlier, there were three musical groups sponsored by the government-owned Tanga Harbours Authority (THA): (1) KIUBATA, (2) Bandari Orchestra (a *dansi* band), and (3) Bandari Taarab. All the Bandari bands rehearsed at the Harbours Club. It consisted of a bar open throughout the day and most of the night, a squash court used primarily by non-THA expatriates, a small rehearsal room for the Harbours Authority *taarab* and *dansi* bands, a large room that doubles as an auditorium and meeting hall, and an outdoor paved basketball court. Virtually every major industry or company in Tanzania once set aside such a building for its workers. In local parlance, they are called Social Welfare Halls and administered by the company's "social welfare officer." Standard workers' benefits also included company housing, subsidized food rations, and medical benefits.[1] Although agriculture had constituted the political cornerstone of Tanzanian socialism, the government promoted a few select industries. Industrial enterprise was approached very gingerly for fear that it would invite foreign domination of the economy or, equally bad, create a new class of African entrepreneurs to disrupt the ideal of the classless socialist society (Duggan and Civille 1976, 192–94). A very active process of proletarianization nonetheless was (and to some extent still is) facilitated by company infrastructures like that of THA that were designed to inculcate strong worker identities.

THA (Bandari) competes with the Tanga Cement Factory (Saruji) for workers—the dyad composing the two industrial giants of Tanga. Other major companies include the railway, various soap factories, a nonproducing fertilizer factory (now only distributing imported fertilizer), a steel rolling mill, some sawmills producing parquet flooring, a couple of soda beverage plants, and a number of sisal estates. Of them all, however, only Bandari and Saruji still invest in the arts, and an intense rivalry—yet another musical dualism in true Tanga style—exists between KIUBATA and the Saruji Cultural Troupe. KIUBATA performs *ngoma, sarakasi* (acrobatics), and *tamthiliya* (theatrical plays); Saruji performs *ngoma, sarakasi, tamthiliya,* and also *mazingaombwe* (magical acts) and *ngonjera* (dramatized poetry focusing on political or social themes). Saruji does not, however, have a *taarab* or *dansi* band like Bandari. The artistic domains of the two companies thus overlap while allowing for some differentiation. Where they most often collide is in the genre of *ngoma* performance.

Prior to 1995, the Ministry of Culture (and whichever ministerial bedfellows it had at the time) had been responsible for organizing Arts and Language Competitions throughout the country in two-year cycles composed of four rounds: district, regional, zonal, and national. Following independence, Tanga Region was redistricted into six districts: Tanga, Lushoto, Korogwe, Handeni, Muheza, and Pangani. In no other district outside of Tanga is there a performance group that can successfully compete against Bandari or Saruji. These two troupes would traditionally alternate years in capturing the honors at the district and subsequently regional level arts competitions because whoever won the district honors automatically secured the regional honors for lack of competition. In the competitions leading up to the 1992 national competitions, KIUBATA, district and regional champion, also managed to capture the honors in both the *ngoma* and *sarakasi* competitions at the zonal level: the Northern Zone encompassing Tanga, Arusha, and Kilimanjaro (Moshi) Regions. Although Saruji lost to Bandari in the *ngoma* competition, it nevertheless won the right to represent the Northern Zone at the national competitions in the categories of *muziki wa ala* (traditional instrumental music) and *ngonjera.*

My initial attendance at a Bandari Taarab rehearsal in September 1992 introduced to me the breadth of THA's artistic production. The groups, although independent entities at the start of my fieldwork, often performed together—KIUBATA, Bandari Taarab, Bandari Orchestra—as a unit; thus, the musicians of Bandari Taarab let me know about the other groups and invited me to sit in on their rehearsals as well.[2] After hearing that KIUBATA was engaged in intensive daily rehearsals in preparation for the upcoming national competitions in November, I instantly decided to seize this as a case study for understanding the dynamics of state involvement in cultural production. Here was a state-sponsored troupe due to perform at the national competitions—the nation on display—where groups from all over the country (private and public) would present their interpretations of national culture. So beginning on September 30 and continuing through November 2 of 1992, I attended the daily rehearsals and performances of KIUBATA and then accompanied them to the competitions in Arusha.

The National Arts and Language Competitions: Rehearsals in Tanga

The guidelines of the *ngoma* category at the national competitions dictate that competing groups must perform a total of three *ngoma:* two from the group's home region, and one from a distant region (so as to inculcate a sense of inter-regional unity). Each group is limited to a total of thirty minutes of performance time that can be distributed among the three *ngoma* as wished, and a maximum of twenty performers is allowed per group (including both dancers and instrumentalists). KIUBATA had selected three of its most popular *ngoma* for the competitions. Their two local *ngoma* selections, Mbuji and Ukala, both hail from the Zigua ethnic group of Handeni District in Tanga Region. The Zigua are one of a handful of Tanzanian ethnic groups praised for their musical prowess. (Conversely, stereotypes abound of other ethnic groups famous for the *lack* of musical ability, one example being the Chagga of Kilimanjaro Region.) The third selection, Liungunjumu, represented the Makonde ethnic group from the southern region of Mtwara.

As discussed in chapter 3, I was welcomed to KIUBATA rehearsals as an honorary cultural officer. A chair was always set aside for me next to KIUBATA's leadership that consisted of

mwenyekiti (chairman)
katibu (secretary)
mjumbe (representative)
mwalimu mkuu (head teacher)

mwalimu msaidizi (assistant teacher)
mwalimu wa mashairi (poetry teacher)

The *mwenyekiti,* Mr. Lamek Tandika, explained to me that KIUBATA was formed in 1976 and that he joined it in 1978 as a teacher of *kwaya*—a genre the group rarely, if ever, performs today. He explained that they have a repertoire of thirty-eight *ngoma* representing various regions throughout Tanzania, although they translate the majority of song texts into Swahili so that everyone can understand. The group has more than sixty performers, but the continually changing nature of group member-ship makes it difficult to identify a reliably constant total.

KIUBATA performers encompass both THA workers and nonworkers. Whereas many of the men held jobs with THA as dock workers or security men, the majority of women had no employment beyond KIUBATA except for two who worked as Mama Ntilie ("Mama Serve-Me-Some-Food"), selling home-prepared food items, coffee, or tea in an informal capacity to workers down at the docks. KIUBATA performers were paid a minimal monthly salary that was padded with rehearsal and performance allow-ances, as well as overnight allowances on occasions when the group toured outside of Tanga municipality.[3] Yet, the financial gains are minimal; most performers justified their involvement more in terms of the personal en-joyment it brought them. *Ngoma* performers, more so than *taarab* and *dansi* performers, are marginalized in society. For many observers, the erotic nature of some *ngoma* dance movements extends to those who per-form them, thus invoking a reputation for sexual and moral laxity.

The process of producing three *ngoma* for national consumption at the competitions entailed considerable negotiation. As an observer and occasional participant in KIUBATA's rehearsals prior to the competi-tions, I was well-situated to take note of the many issues raised and con-tested by KIUBATA performers, leadership, and visiting cultural officers alike. Each *ngoma* elicited different concerns; thus what follows is an *ngoma* by *ngoma* account of these concerns and the corresponding deci-sions that, in the end, resulted in a winning performance.

Mbuji

In the written explanation submitted to the judges at the 1992 competi-tions, KIUBATA's leadership described Mbuji, named after a variety of rattle worn wrapped around the ankle, thus:[4]

> This ngoma is danced during various celebrations like puberty rituals, offerings to the spirits, celebrations of the Party and Government, and especially during har-vest time when it is performed for entertainment. This ngoma is danced in the Tanga Region, Handeni District, by the Zigua ethnic group.

The KIUBATA version of the dance begins with men and women entering the stage in sex-differentiated lines, dancing to a moderate, polyrhythmic duple meter played by an assortment of drums (track 4 on the accompanying CD). The women wear plain white cloths adorned with beaded chains across their chests, black head wraps, patterned cloths tied around the hips (to emphasize hip movement—a general characteristic of East African female dancing), and hold miniature wooden spoons. The men wear purple grass skirts, beaded chains across otherwise bare chests, elaborate hats made from black-and-white colobus monkey skins with matching shoulder adornments, *mbuji* rattles wrapped around their ankles, and they hold cow-tail fly-whisks and rattles. The black-and-white colobus monkey skins were specially ordered from Handeni district at considerable expense—an expenditure justified on the grounds of emulating "authentic" and "original" costume for this particular dance.

KIUBATA performs the dance as a set of choreographed formations. Sometimes the lines of men and women face each other; at other times they face the audience. The moderate duple meter that characterizes the first section is interrupted by a very brief section of unaccompanied song and then a sudden switch to a considerably faster tempo. During the final, faster section, the female dancers perform the hip-rotating dance

Figure 6.1 Rupia of KIUBATA performing Mbuji *ngoma* at the National Arts and Language Competition, Arusha, Sheikh Amri Abeid Stadium, November 7, 1992. Photo by author.

Figure 6.2 KIUBATA performing Mbuji *ngoma* at the National Arts and Language Competition, 1992. Photo by author.

movement called *kiuno* that is associated primarily with puberty and marriage dances. KIUBATA ends the dance with the exit of the two lines of male and female dancers minus one performer each. A mini-comedy is enacted as the solitary female dancer continues to perform *kiuno* to the exaggerated astonishment of the remaining male dancer—in this case the head teacher (*mwalimu mkuu*), Rupia.

The song element consists of a single line performed in call-and-response pattern. Rupia initiates the call with the Swahili term, "Utamaduni, eh" ("Culture, eh"), that he repeats three times in a descending melodic line. The other performers then respond, "Utamaduni wajenga nchi," or "Culture builds the country." This single line of lyrics that KIUBATA sings to Mbuji clearly reflects the influence of Tanzanian political discourse. Sung not in Zigua but in Kiswahili, it strikes a chord of dissonance with the great concern with accuracy and authenticity (especially in their costumes and movements) that otherwise exemplifies the troupe, a concern explicitly voiced to me by the *mwenyekiti* (chairman). Such lyrics—reverberating with recent and current political rhetoric—clearly undermine this effort. When I asked about this, the poetry teacher and chairman together launched into a speech about how culture and customs build the nation—how they form its foundation, without which it would crumble and fall apart.[5] On another day, however, when the same topic came up in conversation, they explained that, "those were the days of CCM," referencing a period of more active party involvement in artistic production.[6]

This line of text was the end result of considerable and significant negotiation, an illustration of changing sensibilities in accordance with changing national politics. When I first began attending their rehearsals, these were the lyrics they sang. Yet, a week later, I noticed that they occasionally alternated it with a different text, "CCM builds the country." I was told that this was indeed the "original" text honoring CCM for taking initiative to expunge and reject colonial culture and revive local culture.[7] Due to the initialization that year of Tanzania's transition to multiparty democracy, however, it had accordingly been changed to "Culture builds the country." The group was keenly aware that it would be performing for an audience with mixed politics and decided against any display of partisanship. At one point, during rehearsal on October 13, 1992, the troupe experimented with changing the lyrics yet again, this time to "Tanzania ajenga nchi" ("Tanzania builds the country"). This struck me at the time as being problematic and redundant, even nonsensical, for how can the country build the country? The same thought must also have occurred to the group's secretary, for he interrupted the rehearsal at one point to inquire of the chairman, "Chairman, what is the meaning of 'Tanzania builds the country'? What is 'Tanzania'? And what is the 'country'?" The chairman explained that "Tanzania" in this case was an abbreviated form of "Watanzania" ("Tanzanians"), thereby rendering the line's meaning into the much more intelligible, "Tanzanians build the country." So the secretary then argued that this was not clear and that the prefix *wa-* should thus be included for clarity, but the chairman responded that it included too many syllables for the melodic line. When I pointed out that it contained as many syllables as "Utamaduni," he replied that they had been dropping the *U,* leaving it to be implied by the remaining syllables, "-tamaduni." In the end, KIUBATA's leadership decided to revert to "Utamaduni" (or, rather, "-tamaduni") and leave it at that. Thus, this is what was sung at the national competitions.

For all the expressed concern over authenticity, I was somewhat surprised to come across a communication dated June 27, 1966, in the Tanga Archives from the area secretary of Handeni District addressed to the Tanga regional commissioner with a strikingly variant description of Mbuji.[8] The communication was a list of *ngoma* commonly performed in the district, a list headed by Mbuji.[9] Under the category of Mavazi (Dress), however, the accessories listed were bells, beads, and ostrich feathers. There was no mention of grass skirts, cow-tail fly-whisks, nor colobus monkey hats and shoulder gear. It was not so much the notable differences that caught my attention, for one expects practices to change with time. Rather, I was struck by KIUBATA's insistence on emulating authenticity and by their search for a static tradition rendered illusory by the historical record. Performance is by nature a process, and yet KIUBATA was in search of an objectified thing.

In his analysis of the construction of Québécois national culture, Richard Handler discovered a very similar process, one he terms "cultural objectification":

> Like a thing, the nation or ethnic group is taken to be bounded, continuous, and precisely distinguishable from other analogous entities. Moreover, from this perspective, what distinguishes each nation or ethnic group is its culture, which provides the "content" of group identity and individuality. And if culture is pressed into service to distinguish one bounded collectivity from another, it too must be bounded: that is, culture must be analyzable and identifiable, such and such a "trait" belonging to this nation or originating in that region. Dancing folk, for example, can be "recorded," that is, abstracted from an ongoing social milieu; their activity can be redefined as a thing (a dance) which is part of the cultural content unique to a bounded social entity; then . . . the thing (and the people) can be represented, in the frame of a theatrical stage, as authentic pieces of national culture. This is cultural objectification. (Handler 1988, 13–14)

In its self-conscious drive for accuracy and authenticity, KIUBATA creates a finished product that it presents to its audiences as "tradition" and "national culture." Whereas the histories of *taarab* and *dansi* highlight cultural production as an activity engaged in by a wide range of social strata including the upper echelons of society (aristocrats, colonists, intelligentsia), the case of KIUBATA provides us with a case of cultural production pursued by manual workers, low-ranking government officials, and marginalized women. This is a situation paralleling that of Yoruba popular culture, as described by Barber and Waterman, "where not just the elite, but also masses of the urban poor and the intermediate classes, self-consciously valorise local practices as 'our traditional heritage'—seeing them simultaneously (as it were) from within and from without, with sincerity but also with ironical self-consciousness" (Barber and Waterman 1995, 243). The self-consciousness of cultural production is revealed to an even greater extent in the second *ngoma* KIUBATA performed in competition, named Ukala.

Ukala

Ukala is another *ngoma* associated with the Zigua ethnic group of Handeni District. The dance is one of several performed in the context of the Ukala ritual—a ritual organized around the presentation of offerings known as *tambiko* to the ancestral spirits (Maguluko 1991, cited in Lange

1994, 67). This particular dance enacts a hunt. Dancers mime a protracted search for animals followed by the hunt and slaughter. In the second half of the performance, the successful hunters call for women to come collect the meat to carry back to the village. The dance was taught to KIUBATA by their poetry teacher, Mzigo wa Ndevu, who is himself Zigua.

Mzigo wa Ndevu claims that this *ngoma* is quite different from others for the reason that it teaches something, "Ukala inafundisha." It is for this reason that the group devoted a full twenty of the thirty minutes allotted for the competition to this *ngoma,* leaving only five minutes each for the other two. They also presented an extensive description/explanation to the judges, a portion of which follows:

> This dance is performed in Tanga Region, Handeni District by the Zigua ethnic group. It is performed to accompany offerings to the spirits, for Party and Government functions, and especially when hunters wish to go hunting in the bush. This dance is performed at night when the hunters are receiving advice from a senior hunter and his wife who advise them in the Zigua language. In [English], it is:
>
> "This is a hunting talisman. Go safely and kill.
> There are animals here and there."
>
> After this, the grandfather hands over their weapons and again advises them: "You are the head hunter. Take this gun. If it fails you, take this medicine, blow it on the animal so that he sleeps and then call the others, your younger brothers who are learning the art of hunting. Let them be the ones to kill the animal. In the wilderness, there are lions and leopards; there are thorns and bees. Do not be afraid."
>
> After this, the young hunters are told to grasp their bows and arrows and prepare themselves while their older brother enters the bush.
> This dance is divided into three traditional sections:
> (a) The grandfather and grandmother make offerings on behalf of the hunters
> (b) The head hunter together with his brothers enters the wilderness to hunt
> (c) Taking away the animal from the bush

I watched this *ngoma* go through numerous variations and modifications in the rehearsals leading up to the competitions—a process that illuminated many of the concerns with authenticity, nationalism, and cultural production. The first section was performed by Mzigo wa Ndevu himself with a female dancer as his wife. He advises his grandsons, provides them with magic sleeping dust, and then sends them off with a blessing. This section remained relatively uniform throughout, with only minor variations in Mzigo wa Ndevu's speech.

The second and third sections underwent the most alteration. In the hunt, the lead hunter begins alone and encounters various trials along the way. He first steps on a thorn, injuring his foot, and grimaces with exaggeration as he pulls it out. At one point during the rehearsal process, he also ran into a hive of bees. Then he spots his prey, blows some of the magic powder on it, and calls his brothers to come help kill it. His rifle misfires and the younger brothers ultimately kill the animal with their bows and arrows. After that, they divide it up into several portions and call the women, who come to bear the meat away in baskets held atop their heads. There is no singing until the arrival of the women and additional rifle-bearing hunters to fill out the line so as to have one male for every female performer. At this point, the lead hunter sings in Kizigua, "Na ukala ee, na ukala ndima" (translated by Mzigo as, "Hunting, hunting is traditional work"). The women and other hunters sing the same line back in response. The lead hunter then sings, "Akomile mwingaile" (translated by Mzigo as, "It has been killed. Come collect it"), a theme which he elaborates further, to which the chorus of women and lesser hunters sing their same response: "Na ukala ee, na ukala ndima."

During the rehearsal process, there was much experimentation with the thorn and bees motifs. They were alternately included, removed, and shifted from one hunter to another. The bees, in particular, first attacked the lone lead hunter, then all three hunters, and then, in the version settled upon for the competitions, only one of the younger hunters. Tremendous attention was paid to minute details. A hunter was invited from Handeni District to come demonstrate to KIUBATA exactly how he butchers the animal after having killed it, in particular how the skin, head, and internal organs are removed. It was also pointed out that large leaves would be cut from nearby trees on which the meat would be placed to protect it from dust; so accordingly, a new scene was introduced wherein one of the young hunters cuts leaves down for this purpose. Another added scene inserted between the hunt and butchering portrayed the three hunters relaxing and congratulating themselves by taking snuff and smoking cigarettes. Finally, in a contradictory move against the goal of accuracy, it was decided that the women should dance the erotic *kiuno* movement of the hips (a dance element not typically associated with this *ngoma,* but with *ngoma* affiliated with puberty and marriage rites) to increase the element of excitement among the performers and audience alike.

Not only can the Ukala elicit excitement among the audience, it has the power to attract other-worldly visitors. During one rehearsal, I noticed that a female dancer was sitting off to the side and not participating. When I inquired after her health, Mzigo wa Ndevu responded, "She has a problem with this *ngoma.* This *ngoma* involves spirits, and she is prone to possession." He further explained that the particular rhythm utilized in this *ngoma* was also common to spirit possession *ngoma* (*ngoma ya shetani*). Thus, "Every time they perform this Zigua *ngoma,* someone always gets possessed."[10] Performing it invokes supernatural forces that cannot be controlled once unleashed. According to local understanding, certain persons have closer relationships with the spirit world than others. Sometimes there is a monogamous relationship with a regular spirit, often one inherited from a deceased family member who had previously supplied the spirit with a bodily home. In other cases, a person may be receptive to not one but many spirits, often of various types. (The spirit world parallels the human world in its social groupings—Maasai, Arab, European, etc.)[11] Whatever the degree of involvement with the spirit world, people either witnessing or participating in spirit possession *ngoma* run a higher risk of possession during its performance. It can even be dangerous for persons who have not exhibited any predilection for possession, for such a predilection can lie latent, not manifesting itself until the spirit sees fit to impose itself—not uncommonly, in the context of such *ngoma*.

As the competition neared, cultural officers from the local district and regional offices of the Ministry of Culture and Education made more regular appearances at KIUBATA's rehearsals to pass judgment on the group's efforts and offer their "expertise" to make any necessary modifications. On October 16, 1992, four regional cultural officers, one district cultural officer, and a visiting cultural officer from the Arusha office attended rehearsal. An officer was also expected from the Moshi office, since KIUBATA would be representing the Northern Zone (Kanda ya Kaskazini) that included both Arusha and Moshi, but that officer did not turn up. KIUBATA ran the three *ngoma* back to back as though in actual competition, while the cultural officers timed them to certify that they stayed within the allotted thirty-minute time limit. Following the *ngoma* performances, the KIUBATA *sarakasi* performers ran their acts.

Following the run-throughs, I was invited into the bar with the cultural officers and KIUBATA leadership for the assessment and critique of what we had just seen. Initial criticisms concerned timing (the *ngoma* having utilized twenty-five minutes *without* costume changes, coming dangerously close to the limit), and a request that the sung text of Mbuji not alternate between "Utamaduni" and "CCM" but rather be restricted exclusively to "Utamaduni" so as not to offend members of opposition parties. Then the discussion turned to Ukala. The following is an account of the ensuing discussion as recorded in my fieldnotes.

The discussion revolved around Ukala, with cultural officers X, Y, and Z arguing that every action (*kila kitendo*) needs to be meaningful (*kuana maana chake*). They were arguing about the choreography of male *wasanii* (performers) dancing with *bunduki* (rifles) instead of *upindi* and *mishale* (bows and arrows), since the hunted animal is ultimately killed with these and not the rifle, which fails its owner (*inaka-*

taa). Officer X even turned to me to make sure that I understood the discussion and said in English that bows and arrows "are more traditional." Everyone agreed with them, adding that the rifle was a remnant of *ukoloni* ("colonialism") and therefore undesirable. The chief cultural officer told KIUBATA's secretary to call in the *ngoma* teachers to request this immediately. I was telling Officers X and Y that previous rehearsal utilized spears (*mikuki*), but as I was speaking the teachers entered . . . and, after some thought, they agreed to exchange the rifles for bows and arrows.

The discussion then moved on to other Ukala issues. It was questioned why the hunters, after successfully killing their prey, sat down to sniff tobacco, sneeze, and smoke a cigarette. Officer Z exclaimed that "*hana maana*" ("It is meaningless"). It was expressed that this took up precious time for seemingly little reason. But the teachers staunchly defended this inclusion, citing the authority of Zigua who were consulted on this and who said that hunters always relax in this manner after a kill. In the end, they won. Discussion turned to the spreading apart of imaginary foliage to impress upon the audience that this was an *msitu kweli* (a real jungle), not just any *porini* (wilderness). The question arose that, if this is the *msitu kweli*, then the performers need to wear shoes like Maasai hunters, but this was shot down, and the compromise was to reintroduce the part where the hunter gets a thorn (*mwiba*) stuck in his foot. Rupia (KIUBATA's head teacher) was somewhat persistent about this, and I wondered if he was trying to get more out of the guests (i.e., shoes), but the cultural officers successfully argued that it would require more precious time to put the shoes on than to act out the part about the thorn.

This discussion and the previous ones foreground a great variety of theoretical concerns: meaning (contested and negotiated); colonialism (rifles versus spears versus bows and arrows); accuracy/authenticity (the fine points of butchery); "tradition" (to smoke or not to smoke); authority (of Zigua hunters versus cultural officers); narrative (thorns, bees, jungle); patronage (the hope of acquiring shoes); and audience satisfaction (adding *kiuno* to the women's portion of the dance). Above all, it again draws attention to the fact that cultural production in this particular domain is very *actively* pursued. Nor is it controlled by any single agent or agency. The teachers, the leadership, and the cultural officers all partook of the process of defining the KIUBATA version of Ukala. Although the performers constituted the conduit for presentation, they were less involved, although the presence of their *mjumbe* (representative) meant that they were not excluded from the discussion.

The end product that emerged from these rehearsals and negotiations was lent added authority by KIUBATA's correlation with Zigua regions. Siri Lange, a researcher from the University of Bergen studying *ngoma* troupes in Dar es Salaam, also attended the competitions. She wrote afterwards,

In the dance drama [of Ukala], the women come to collect the meat from the game their husbands have hunted in the woods. They enter singing the songs, and then sit down on their knees, miming the movements of putting meat into their baskets. The way the College of Arts and Muungano Cultural Troupe dance it, the emphasis is on the arm-movements, the rest of the body softly bouncing. When they are finished, they put the baskets on their heads and rise to a signal from the drums.

Having seen the dance being performed in this way many times, I was surprised to see . . . the KIUBATA group dancing it with vigorous hip-movements at the point when they are on their knees. My friend . . . from Tanga, the place where the dance originates from, . . . told me that this was not the way the Zigua dance it themselves. "They have added this to increase the sweetness (*utamu*) of the dance," she said. Judging from the movements of the girls, the dance was no longer a dance about hunting and food, but more in the category of initiation/fertility dances. Ironically enough, the KIUBATA group is from Tanga. This fact made a fellow on-looker, an employee of the National Arts Council, insist that what they performed was the *original* Ukala, it was the other groups which had got it wrong. (Lange 1994, 70; emphasis in the original)

Thus, as representatives of Handeni District by virtue of representing Tanga Region, KIUBATA are viewed as the most qualified agents to present this "tradition." Authenticity is thus twice evoked—as valuation of both the cultural product and its producers.

Ukala has come to be remembered as one of KIUBATA's signature performance pieces—even though they have rarely performed it since the competitions. Ukala was also performed by the National Ngoma Troupe (1963–1979) when it existed and, as such, was objectified early on as an element of Tanzanian national culture. Although a major thrust of troupe (national or otherwise) performance practice is *standardization* through continual, repetitive rehearsal, there is no agreed-upon version of this *ngoma* (nor, for that matter, most *ngoma*), as the above negotiations illustrate. A central, minimalist structure composed of a characteristic rhythm, the hunting theme, and the element of drama allows for much flexibility and reinterpretation. Lange discovered that Ukala is an *ngoma* performed by the vast majority of troupes in Dar es Salaam (eight out of eleven groups canvassed) and, moreover, that it is one of the ten most commonly performed *ngoma* overall (Lange 1994, 44–45). She found a description of the "original" Ukala ritual (Maguluko 1991; again, assumed to be a static entity) against which she compared other troupe performances (lyrics and movements). She found only marginal uniformity. Moreover, when she inquired into the meaning of the lyrics, she discovered that "[t]he artists performing Ukala do not know the exact meaning of the words they sing, but they know that the songs are about hunting" (Lange 1994, 68). She attributes this to both the multi-ethnic nature of troupe performance (wherein members, by mandate, are drawn from a variety of ethnic groups), and the oral tradition. The Zigua language is unfamiliar to most performers, which creates a high potential for the inaccurate transmission of lyrics.

Literature has traditionally been transmitted orally in Africa, and this is the way the dance-songs are taught and learned in contemporary society too, in commercial dance-groups, as well as at the College of Arts. In the multi-ethnic situation however, this oral transmission has a weak point. Artists who do not know the current local language will pass the song on in their own personal interpretation. After the song has gone through a few such transmissions, it may be completely incomprehensible to a speaker of the language which the song originally was composed in. One specific case where I have been able to document this process is the Ukala dance. (Lange 1994, 66)

Thus, despite attempts by both private and government troupes to create standard versions of *ngoma*, change continually creeps into practice, indeed *defines* practice. Standardization is relegated to ideological conceptions of *ngoma* performance, not its actuality. KIUBATA performed Liungunjumu, a Makonde *ngoma* from the southern region of Mtwara, as their final entry in competition in fulfillment of the required *ngoma* from a different region. Considerable and noteworthy effort was expended in attempts to standardize this *ngoma*, a process continually undermined by a desire for distinction.

Liungunjumu

Liungunjumu is a dance performed during the elaborate initiation rituals of the Makonde, an ethnic group that straddles the border between Tanzania and Mozambique. Makonde were recruited in the 1940s to work as wage laborers on the sisal plantations of Tanga region as an alternative labor force, since local people displayed little interest and were reluctant to work. The work of a sisal cutter is extremely strenuous, involving many dangers from unusual stinging and often poisonous insects and snakes that nest among the sisal plants, and from the sharp leaves of the sisal plant itself. Large numbers of Makonde came to Tanga—often on foot—from Mozambique lured by recruiters' promises of wealth and comfort (free housing, free food, etc.). The promises rarely fulfilled, they nevertheless settled and formed their own communities in the greater Tanga area. In the last national census to record ethnic information (1964), the Makonde ranked the most populous by far of immigrant communities in Tanga District. In table 6.1, the five indigenous populations of the region (Bondei, Shambaa, Digo, Zigua, and Segeju)[12] top the chart immediately followed by the Makonde population, which nearly equals that of the Segeju:

Not surprisingly, then, KIUBATA selected a Makonde *ngoma* as their third entry. It fulfilled the demands of the foreign *ngoma* requirement without being truly foreign. Several of KIUBATA's performers are Makonde. Moreover, the *ngoma* has the added benefit of riding on the popularity of another Makonde *ngoma* named Sindimba, the single most popular and commonly performed *ngoma* of the troupe performance circuit.

Table 6.1   Ethnic Populations of Tanga District, 1964

Tribe	District Population
Bondei	31,629
Shambaa	30,234
Digo	26,471
Zigua	13,042
Segeju	11,810
Makonde	10,763
Ngoni	5,813
Rundi	4,563
Bene	4,540

SOURCE: Adapted from Lucas and Philippson 1973, 165.

Sindimba, like Liungunjumu, is an *ngoma* associated with Makonde initiation rites. It is enormously popular, with its driving beat and erotic *kiuno* movements by both men and women alike. Not formally encouraged by cultural policymakers, it was even condemned by some government officials for inciting promiscuity and being a bad and corrupting influence. Yet of the eleven Dar es Salaam troupes surveyed by Lange, it was the only *ngoma* common to all the groups (Lange 1994, 44). One scholar of Tanzanian cultural policy writes,

> For this reason, I do not see why our schools or the National Ngoma Troupe cannot perform *ngoma* without performing Sindimba. I am not opposed to the performance of Sindimba. Not at all! SINDIMBA is a Makonde *ngoma* that has won over people's ears and eyes.
> If people do not see this *ngoma* of Sindimba, they will say that the show was not exhilarating. And truly, the Sindimba *ngoma* has become the characteristic way of ensuring that a show is exhilarating. What I contend is that, because we have so many *ngoma,* they should always be performed and danced by those who are chosen to entertain our people. (Omari 1981, 14–15; my translation)

I was once told a story that illuminates the contradictions of nationalist endeavors. Apparently, there had been some severe criticism emanating from government quarters of the perceived immorality of certain *ngoma* (reflecting colonial concerns). An *ngoma* troupe had been invited to perform a Makonde *ngoma* (quite possibly Sindimba) for President Mwinyi and his wife Mama Siti, but was later un-invited by personnel in the Ministry of Culture because the practice of wearing *kanga* (Swahili printed cloths) tied around the breasts leaving the stomach exposed was deemed inappropriate in the presence of Mama Siti. Mama Siti clearly had been designated the national personification, the national embodiment of moral, chaste domesticity. To the Ministry's shame, however, a journalist later caught on film the image of some of these same disapproving cultural officers attending and obviously enjoying a performance of a foreign (European?) cultural group in which the women wore only bikinis. The journalist published his picture with a heading to the effect of, "Our traditional *ngoma* are not permitted but performances with women dressed like this are."[13]

That tolerance has come even if unbidden. When I interviewed Mr. Godwin Kaduma, the director of arts and national language, in July 1993, he referred to Sindimba as one of the *ngoma* that had captured national attention, that—by virtue of its ubiquitous popularity—had earned the right of inclusion as an element of "national culture."[14] He used it as an example of how "national culture" is determined not by policy, but rather "by the people."[15]

The tremendous popularity of Sindimba makes it easier to "sell" an *ngoma* based on the same precepts of movement, context, meaning, and ethnicity. Makonde *ngoma* are extremely popular overall. The Makonde, even more than the Zigua, are famous for their dancing and musical prowess. Hence, it is not surprising that of the fifty-five dances that encompass the *ngoma* repertoires of the eleven troupes surveyed by Lange, a full thirteen (24 percent) are of Makonde origins (see table 6.2)—a highly disproportionate percentage, given that they are one of twenty-seven ethnic groups represented in the sample (Lange 1994, 44–45). Liungunjumu was one of the thirteen Makonde *ngoma* included in the study and was found to be performed by six of the eleven troupes.

It thus becomes apparent that the selection of Liungunjumu for the national competitions was a highly strategic choice. Having Makonde performers in the troupe implied that they could contribute their intimate knowledge of the *ngoma* to the other performers and then jointly convey that knowledge with greater conviction to both the judges and audience. Moreover, it could scarcely fail to evoke the response of *moto-moto* (literally, "extreme heat" or excitement) that, according to Omari (1981), always accompanies performances of Sindimba, since it entails the same types of dance movements and a similar rhythm that combine to excite an audience. The following anecdote from Lange, who danced with an *ngoma* troupe as part of her research methodology, reveals this relationship.

> In July 1992 the Muungano Cultural Troupe were recruiting new dancers to the group. Four girls aged between 16 and 20 years were trained, and I was in their class as I was going to perform too. When we were learning Ukala, our teacher, who was a Zigua, complained that the girls overdid the hip movements. The girls had problems in refraining from what they believed the audience would like, and the teacher finally told them: "This is *not* Sindimba, stop that wriggling!" (Lange 1994, 71)

Table 6.2 Popular *Ngoma* by Ethnic Group, 1992

Zone	Ethnic Group	Number of *Ngoma*
South	Makonde	13
	Makua	1
	Yao	1
	Mwera	4
	Ngindo	1
	Ngoni	4
	Nyasa	1
East	Kutu	1
	Pogoro	1
	Wadde	1
	Zaramo	3
	Zanzibar	1
Highlands	Manda	1
	Nyakusa	1
	Safwa	3
West	Gogo	1
	Ha	3
	Iramba	1
	Manyema	2
	Nyaturu	1
Lake	Kerewe	1
	Nyamwezi	1
	Sukuma	2
North	Digo	1
	Masaai	1
	Sambaa	2
	Zigua	2
Totals	27 ethnic groups	55 *ngoma*

SOURCE: Adapted from Lange 1994, 44–45.

The description of Liungunjumu presented to the judges at the competition follows:

This ngoma is danced when initiants are released from seclusion, during various Party and Government celebrations, and also after the harvest. It is performed for entertainment. It is performed by people from Mtwara Region by the Makonde ethnic group.

This *ngoma* is sung in the Makonde language. Its translation follows:
- Normally, a child is carried by the mother who is preparing to go to the ngoma. The mother tells her child, "Sleep. I want to go to the nice *ngoma*."
- If I die, who will the young girls marry? [Response]: "The one who digs the grave."
- At the end of the *ngoma*, the song lyrics are: Young girl, you are called to leave early in the morning to say good-bye. I go to learn our customs. [Response]: "Yes, yes."

Unlike the Zigua *ngoma,* Liungunjumu exhibits a musical accompaniment domineered by a single, tall drum called *msondo.* The rhythms played on the *msondo* dictate the dance movements, whereas in both Mbuji and Ukala dancers get their cues to shift from one dance movement or formation to another from a whistle blown by the lead dancer. In Swahili terminology, the *msondo* "drives" the dance (*inaendesha*). In Liungunjumu as performed by KIUBATA, there is no lead dancer. The men and women dance in lines, executing tightly constructed formations while maintaining the constant *kiuno* hip movement that mark this as a puberty/fertility *ngoma.*[16] All of these elements—driving rhythms, fast-paced dancing, and the syncopated improvisations of the *msondo* drum—unite to create a relentless sense of excitement in the audience.

During my time out at the Amboni sisal estate, I was invited to several Makonde performance events. I attended six initiation events that were often spread out over several days. In the initiation process, Makonde children are sent away for a period of seclusion, during which time they are taught Makonde customs, sexual matters, the execution of military formations, and Makonde values such as respect for elders. According to elderly men I knew well who had made the trip to Tanga region as already initiated youths, the "true" initiation proceedings back in Mozambique required a full year of seclusion. Today, however, initiates (*wari* pl.; *mwari* sing.) are rarely kept in seclusion for more than a month.

The majority of musical events associated with initiation occur the day of and the day before the *wari* are released from confinement. The return of the children, marching in formation in high step and bearing crudely carved wooden rifles, strikes one immediately with the militaristic thrust of the training. This is a common stereotype of the Makonde: that they are a warlike society, particularly adept at killing. So widespread is this belief that the majority of night watchmen hired at private homes are Makonde, the idea being that Makonde-ness alone guarantees a fierce and stalwart guard. The tradition of facial scarification—no longer included in the initiation process due to heavy government pressure against it—further reinforces the stereotypes.

At these initiations, I saw Sindimba and several other *ngoma* performed. With the exception of Guaride (the *ngoma* performed in militaristic formations by the initiates), participants in all the other *ngoma* dance in a large circle around the drummers. The common performance practice was for the circle to maintain uniformity of movement, often *kiuno,* and for individuals to take turns entering the middle of the circle to demonstrate their skill. There was an overriding sense of spontaneity and improvisation, with the circle sometimes attracting more than one individual, sometimes engendering a mini-competition between individuals, and sometimes remaining empty when *motomoto* had not yet been achieved or had died out.

What a contrast, then, from the performance of Liungunjumu perfected by KIUBATA over the course of seemingly endless rehearsals, with only a modicum of spontaneity and improvisation reserved for the *ngoma*'s conclusion. Strict formations define KIUBATA's Liungunjumu, the desired product being the precise execution of perfectly synchronized movements. During rehearsal on October 6, 1997, I heard the *mjumbe* (representative) call out to the dancers, "Mbona maembe?" ("Why mangoes?"), which made little sense to me. He later explained that the feet of the dancers were not executing their formations in sync, "falling" without precision as mangoes fall off the tree (*bila mpango*, "without a plan"). At another point in the rehearsal, the head teacher told the female dancers to "silence" their feet ("Miguu kimya"), that is, to keep their feet stationary so that only the hips move in *kiuno* style. At another rehearsal, the teacher once yelled out, "Tarabu! Tarabu!" equating their lackluster performance with the perceived calmness and sedateness of *taarab* performances.

Improvisation was allowed only at the *ngoma*'s ending. The final formation presents a line each of male and female dancers, facing each other to form male-female pairs. Two couples at a time step aside from the rest of the lines to dance as a quartet, ending their dance with a final, highly suggestive thrust of the hips toward their partners in very close proximity. After a moment of holding the position, the dancers exit. In this manner, two quartets exit leaving behind a final quartet composed of KIUBATA's Makonde performers. Here, the experts, the original "owners" of the *ngoma,* improvise with a wild abandon quite distinct from the precision and exactitude displayed up until that point. In rehearsal, they experimented with an ending in which the women jump on the backs of the men, who then exit by running offstage bearing their captives piggyback style. It was explained to me that this was the overall theme of the dance: *kutorosha mabibi* ("to capture women," what the THA chief secretary explained as, "They are raping the women").[17] In competition, however, the ending was modified for even greater effect: roles were reversed with the women bearing the men offstage on their backs to the audience's great astonishment and delight.

In having access to Makonde *ngoma* performed in both ritual and troupe contexts, I could document, to a limited degree, transformations in meaning and practice. Although Liungunjumu was not performed during the initiation rites I attended, there was enough uniformity of general performance principles among the other Makonde *ngoma* to draw some initial conclusions regarding differences in performance practice between these contexts. For troupes, lines replace circles because, according to one cultural officer, "Circle formations are not good because you only see a small part of the whole, mostly backs."[18] Orientation toward an audience thus constitutes a principal concern, especially when the audience includes judges. Moreover, a context of initiation was replaced with one of competition. In the former, children are reintroduced to society as classificatory adults graced with the knowledge necessary to act as adult Makonde should. In the latter, it is the performances rather than the people, the *ngoma,* that are reintroduced to society paradoxically as both relics of cultural excavation and modern expressions of the nation. Considerable effort is spent on synchronization and standardization, on denuding *ngoma* of spontaneity and improvisation for the sake of constructing polished performances. And in Tanzania, the ideological justification for introduced/induced change or introduced/induced stasis in cultural practice is related in many instances to its socialist agenda.

Uniformity and conformity. Socialism through synchronization and standardization. Encasing difference in a palatable veneer of if not resemblance, then at least parity. These may have been the intended axioms of Tanzanian nation-building, but as the national competitions showed, such goals were sometimes undermined, subverted, or only partially implemented in actual practice.

The National Arts and Language Competitions
November 6–8, 1992, Arusha

Louis Mbughuni, former director of arts and languages, designed and implemented the national competitions. The objectives and rationale behind holding them have been described thus:

1. To provide entertainment for the people and build a spirit of appreciation which wants to see, buy, and value art.
2. To build a spirit of cooperation and competition among artists as well as give them an incentive to develop skills. At the same time the artists will learn from each other.
3. To provide a venue for cultural officers to meet and exchange views.
4. To advertise, develop, as well as preserve cultural heritage. (Lihamba 1985, 367)

The 1992 competitions began unceremoniously with the poetry competition at 8:30 A.M. on the morning of November 6. A group of secondary students from Tanga Technical School represented the Northern Zone in this event, singing their poem in praise of socialism, "Nguzo Ni Sisi Vijana" ("We, the Youth, Are the Pillar"), with all its thirty verses (see appendix B for the complete text). Following the poetry competition was the traditional instrumental music competition, and again Tanga represented its zone with the Saruji Cultural Troupe. In all, Tanga represented the Northern Zone in six of the ten competitive events. The events, in the order they occurred, and the representatives for the Northern Zone (Kanda ya Kaskazini) are presented in table 6.3. Only after the story-telling competition and a break for lunch did the official opening ceremonies take place, replete with speeches from various officials from the Ministry of Education and Culture, including Director of Arts and National Language Mr. Godwin Kaduma.

The entire three-day event was suffused with assertions of and references to "taifa letu" ("our nation"). Moreover, the structure of the competitions supports the potentially paradoxical expression of ethnic diversity within national unity. According to Herzfeld, "Nationalism is directly predicated on resemblance, whether biogenetic or cultural. The pivotal idea is that all citizens are, in some unarguable sense, all alike" (Herzfeld 1997, 27). In Tanzania, state culture brokers make a claim for cultural unity in the face of tremendous cultural diversity. By enforcing unity of genre with specific unilateral requirements of time allotment, number of musicians, and geographic representation, competition organizers from the Ministry of Education and Culture create resemblance across an otherwise widely differentiated sociocultural landscape. It standardizes the form of expression while still allowing for differences in content. It contains and circumscribes variation without mandating

Table 6.3 Entries in the 1992 National Arts and Language Competition, Northern Zone

Event	Translation	Region	Performers
Mashairi	Poetry	Tanga	Tanga Technical School
Muziki wa Ala	Instrumental music	Tanga	Saruji Cultural Troupe
Hadithi Simulizi	Story-telling	Kilimanjaro	—
Nyimbo za Asili	Traditional song	Arusha	—
Ngonjera	Dramatized poetry	Tanga	Saruji Cultural Troupe
Kwaya	Choir	Arusha	—
Sarakasi	Acrobatics	Tanga	KIUBATA
Sanaa za Ufundi	Handicrafts	Kilimanjaro	—
Ngoma	*Ngoma*	Tanga	KIUBATA
Tamthiliya	Drama	Tanga	Usagara Secondary School

homogeneity. Amidst the multiplicity of ethnic representations and the multiplicity of expressive genres resonates a sometimes underlying, sometimes directly stated message: Tanzania is a nation whose wealth lies in its diversity.

If we measure the success of the competitions by audience turnout, then this was only a mildly successful event. The stadium was far from full (in fact, it felt quite empty); most of Arusha was seemingly oblivious to this event. But if we measure its success by performance quality, then a much better assessment is in order. "Quality," as defined by the performative characteristics emulated by KIUBATA during their rehearsals, entailed synchronized precision of movement, execution of interesting formations, accurate representation of "tradition," "modern" orientation to an audience, and an ability to elicit a sense of *motomoto* (exhilaration) in performers and audience alike. In these respects, the *ngoma* performances were generally successful—some more so than others. Table 6.4 lists the zones, their respective *ngoma* entries, and information on the regional and ethnic affiliation of each *ngoma*.

Despite the diversity of cultures, ethnicities, and traditions on display in these performances, there was a nagging sense of uniformity. As the competition progressed, certain dance formations grew familiar, reappearing, as they often did, in the performances of different groups.

Table 6.4 *Ngoma* Entries, 1992 National Arts and Language Competitions

Zone (*Kanda*)	*Ngoma*	Region (*(Mkoa*)	Ethnic Group (*Kabila*)
Southern (*Kusini*)	Msewe	Zanzibar	Zanzibari
	Sindimba	Mtwara	Makonde
	Ngongoti	Mtwara	Makonde
Western (*Magharibi*)	Muheme	Dodoma	Gogo
	Nindondumila	Dodoma	Gogo
	Sekei	Arusha	Maasai
Eastern (*Mashariki*)	Mganda wa Kikutu	Morogoro	Kutu
	Sangula	Morogoro	Pogoro
	Mganda wa Kimanda	Nyasa	Manda
Highlands (*Nyanda za Juu*)	Uyeye	Rukwa	Konongo
	Mitete	Rukwa	Fipa
	Bugobogobo	Shinyanga	Sukuma
Lake (*Ziwa*)	Lilandi	Musomo	Kuria
	Bongonyosi	Mwanza	Kerewe
	Lingondo	Mtwara	Makonde
Northern (*Kaskazini*)	Mbuji	Handeni	Zigua
	Ukala	Handeni	Zigua
	Liungunjumu	Mtwara	Makonde

Also, the styles of entering and exiting the stage area showed little variation. The limits on spontaneous improvisation and emphasis on group
precision precluded individual artists from distinguishing themselves or
showcasing their talent. In occasional performative spaces such freedom
was allowed, but always framed within the broader context of uniformity and group participation—the whole being greater than its parts.
This standardization of performance practice indicated a successful Ministry strategy to solve the perceived "problem" of uniting more than 120
groups into an imagined and socially enacted nation.

Two notable breaks in the standard, however, exposed the diapha-
nous nature of Tanzanian nation-ness. Interestingly enough, the two
incidents both concerned a single ethnic group, the Maasai—the same
group that elicited such concern among the Handeni Cultural Committee. The Maasai have a long history of conflict with the state: not recognizing national boundaries, not remaining stationary so as to participate
in communal agriculture (during the Ujamaa years), impeding conservation efforts, and not being easily available to receive state-distributed
resources and services such as water supplies, schools, and dispensaries.[19]
The first incident related to the Traditional Song competition. Arusha
was to represent the Northern Zone in this event, and it is in Arusha
Region that the vast majority of Maasai live. Without informing the
other regions in the zone, Arusha's cultural officers decided to replace
the winners from the zonal competition with a group of newly selected
Maasai. It was reported that Arusha cultural officers simply drove out to
Maasai areas, selected a group of ten Maasai on the basis of the elaborate-
ness of their beadwork and dress, and presented them in competition
without determining whether or not they could sing. They may have
been singing the same song, but there was no concordance in starting
or ending the song, nor in their actions during the song's performance.
In stark contrast to the other entrants, they had no organized choreography; it appeared very arbitrary and unrehearsed. Moreover, at the song's
conclusion, there was obvious hesitation as they clearly were unaware
of the competition protocol of bowing in unison before walking offstage
in an orderly fashion. Instead, there were looks of confusion, a few
bows, and a disorderly exit. "Hawana mpango" ("They have no plan," or
"They are disorganized") was a common remark heard by both myself
and Siri Lange, the University of Bergen researcher. The entire incident
evoked no small amount of amusement from the audience and angry de-
nunciations from both the Kilimanjaro and Tanga cultural officers for
the "breach in procedure" in not presenting the expected zonal winners.

The incident provided further fuel to a growing inter-zonal conflict between Kilimanjaro and Tanga on the one side and Arusha on the other. Apparently, the Arusha cultural office claimed an unfair portion of the funding provided by the national office to help the regions cover the expenses of bringing performers to the competitions. An officer from the Tanga regional office told me that the Ministry of Culture had allotted room and board allowances for a total of 52 performers per zone, regardless of whether or not this met actual expenses. Tanga alone, between KIUBATA, the Saruji Cultural Troupe, and the students from both Tanga Technical School and Usagara Secondary School, had sent a total of 67 performers, so clearly the limit of 52 was insufficient for the expenses of all three regions. Nevertheless, Arusha succeeded in appropriating 30 of the 52 allowances despite the fact that, as the city hosting the competitions, it was home to many of their performers. Tanga ended up with a total of 21 allowances, while Moshi received an allowance for only a single performer.[20]

In addition to the unrehearsed, unpolished Maasai singers, there was a second incident regarding the performance of a Maasai *ngoma* by another region. The requirement of having to perform one *ngoma* from a distant region was not instituted until 1983. Prior to that, competitive groups generally performed *ngoma* only from their immediate area and experience. The goal of invoking a sense of inter-regional unity was clearly expressed by Mr. Maliwanga, chief officer of the performing arts at the national office of the Ministry of Education and Culture, who served as master of ceremonies for the *ngoma* competition. He told an endless stream of invented anecdotes about the *ngoma:* for example, "When former American President, Jimmy Carter, saw the Maasai Sekei *ngoma,* he loved it so much that he now plays a videotape of it every morning before he begins work." A slew of such tall tales constituted a narrative *ostinato* to the event, continuing even during the performances—stories about Queen Elizabeth and Mganda wa Kikutu, F. W. de Klerk and Sangula, and Queen Victoria and Bugobogobo. Maliwanga concluded his narrative, however, with an affirmation of the "unity through diversity" motif. He commented on how unusual it was for a country to have groups performing other groups' *ngoma* and how it simply was not possible in other places. He remarked that people from other nations, upon seeing this Tanzanian competition with a group from Bukoba performing a Maasai *ngoma,* would be quite surprised.

Well, it was that very performance of the Maasai Sekei *ngoma* that elicited strong reactions from performers and audience members alike. The group had greatly pleased the audience with its performance of Gogo *ngoma,* the Gogo being yet another ethnic group praised nationwide for their musical abilities.[21] Their first *ngoma* entry, Muheme, evoked much admiration. It was unusual in that it was led musically by a group of eight female drummers in impressive costume supplemented by two male dancers playing rattles—a reversal of the more typical musical hierarchy in which men play drums and women play rattles (if they play anything at all). Their third entry, however, of the Maasai *ngoma,* struck a marked contrast to the professionalism of their previous two performances. Whereas before their costumes had been elaborate and well-designed, they now appeared on stage in fake wigs, cardboard cutouts worn around the neck to represent beaded necklaces, and faded tan cloths for the men with pale pink cloths for the women—a considerable deviation from the colorfully rich reds, deep purples, royal blues, and elaborate beadwork that characterized the visually compelling if musically unsatisfying Maasai singers. Again, the audience was vociferous in its response with a groundswell of muttering, undisguised laughter, and calls of "Ovyo ovyo" (meaning something haphazard or carelessly pursued). What also struck me as I watched the performance was how the artists performed a caricature of stereotypes about Maasai performance practice: occasionally, a male performer would jump up and roll his eyes with exaggeration, letting out startling whooping calls or shrieks, and creating a general sense of wildness and untamedness. I could not help but wonder how Maasai assessed this representation of themselves. It was not a wholly positive representation.[22]

Thus KIUBATA, fortunate to have been given the final competitive slot, arrived on the scene in the glory of THA-provided costumes that verified THA's economic status more than anything else. Yet costumes do not make a performance. The artists themselves performed a perfect performance. The air-hostess smiles never left their faces. The precision of their footwork, dance formations, and the manner in which they held their respective props (wooden spoons, baskets, bows and arrows, etc.) was flawless. Their head teacher, Rupia, elicited much laughter for his antics and exaggerated expressions while performing the hunting scenes of Ukala—a performance that won for him the Best Individual Male Artist award. KIUBATA's message of cultural and national unity, "Culture builds the nation," was heard and reinforced by its equally perfect execution of Zigua and Makonde *ngoma*—the Makonde *ngoma* evoking considerable delight as the women ran off bearing their men. KIUBATA won the first-place honors in the competition, their intensity of rehearsal and their oft-repeated work mantras coming to fruition: "Kazi iko?" "Arusha!" ("What's our job?" "Arusha!") and "Kazi yetu ni moja tu . . ." "Kuleta ushindi!" ("We have only one job . . ." "To win!"). After two unsuccessful bids for the national title in previous years, KIUBATA finally won recognition as Tanzania's national *ngoma* champions.

The Performance of National Identities

In the above cases of *ngoma* performance, a quite contradictory situation revealed itself in which changes were introduced—often for nationalistic purposes—within an overriding discourse of "authenticity." "Authenticity" as a discursive tool, a means of claiming social position and a mode of asserting social power was invoked in some of the preceding circumstances and silently bypassed in others. It distinguishes those who know (e.g., a dance troupe with Zigua and Makonde artists performing Zigua and Makonde *ngoma*) from those who don't, and thus constitutes a technique of differentiating people and bestowing symbolic capital on a select group. As one scholar points out, "[W]e should see 'authenticity' [as] a discursive trope of great persuasive power. It focuses a way of talking about music, a way of saying to outsiders and insiders alike 'this is what is really significant about this music,' 'this is the music that makes us different from other people'" (Stokes 1994b, 7).

In the building of a national culture, authenticity is contested at various levels and alternately exploited to suit differing and at times opposing ends. In Tanzania, this trope is used to distinguish internal groups from each other, thus strengthening and maintaining certain ethnic boundaries, while concomitantly used to distinguish indigenous Tanzanian culture from foreign-born culture, thus erasing or sublimating those same ethnic boundaries.

A political tract published by the Ministry of National Culture and Youth expressed concern over the need to preserve and promote "indigenous Tanzanian Music" (note the use of the singular form denoting a unified entity) in the face of an onslaught of foreign influences:

> The indiscriminate spread of European musical values brought striking alterations and deformations to the character of indigenous Music in Tanzania. . . . As a result these types of music scarcely suited our customs and language, instead it turned over an awkward page in the Tanzanian music history. . . . For this reason our projected task in the field of music is twofold: (a) to bring indigenous Tanzanian music into the normal curriculum of Tanzanian schools, Colleges of National Education, and eventually into University; (b) to bring the study of Tanzanian Music into line with that of other musics of the World, ensuring its continued usefulness as a social Art within its proper present day context, while giving credit and encouragement to the gifted Tanzanian composers and musicians. (Ministry of National Culture and Youth, n.d., 14–15)

This passage draws attention to a third concern with authenticity that marks the domain of state efforts at cultural, specifically musical, production: the determination of "indigenous" as also "social" or "socialist." The authors of this text follow Nyerere in his project of revising

Figure 6.3   Ngongoti *ngoma* performed at the National Arts and Language Competition, 1992. Photo by author.

history to support his claims of an authentic, indigenous communalism, a proto-socialism on which he predicated his program of Ujamaa socialism. In the same manner, they view "indigenous" through a socialist lens and thereby value only those traditions and customs that support the perspective outright or would only require minor modification. Authenticity made an uncomfortable bedfellow with socialism insofar as it was accorded respect only when it provided rhetorical fuel for socialist revisions of history.

To sum up, musical performance proves an effective tool for "consolidating" identities (Barber and Waterman 1995) at a variety of levels, as evidenced by the 1992 National Arts and Language Competitions. It can be used to assert identities in support of state nationalist projects as well as identities against. The polyphonies of ethnic identity in Tanzania can sound harmonious or intensely dissonant. In a world region where ethnic dissonance reigns supreme (Hutu–Tutsi conflict in neighboring Rwanda, Burundi, and the former Zaire; Luo–Kikuyu conflict in neighboring Kenya; and the conflicts in Somalia and Mozambique that are tainted with ethnicity although framed in other terms), Tanzania stands alone in its lack of overt ethnic conflict. Ethnic stereotypes abound of the economically privileged Chagga or administratively privileged Sukuma abound, but they rarely receive more than passing attention. On Zanzibar, however, there are greater tendencies toward violence, and a checkered history with regard to ethnic relations. Significantly, the only mention of Zanzibar or acknowledgment of its existence during the competitions—despite all the many references to "our nation," of which Zanzibar constitutes a major part—was the Msewe *ngoma* from Zanzibar performed as the very first *ngoma* in competition. It was the foreign *ngoma* entry by the Southern Zone competitors, who followed it with two Makonde *ngoma:* Sindimba and Ngongoti—perhaps the two most famous Makonde *ngoma* (the second being recognizable for being danced on stilts; see figure 6.3). Aside from that one glimpse of an essentialized Zanzibar, performances in Arusha consolidated mainland identities and a fragmented national identity. Zanzibar's own Arts and Language Competitions and Festivals, meanwhile, celebrate and consolidate Zanzibari identities and another fragmented national identity. Thus, one finds underneath, alongside, and superscripting the competitions in *ngoma*, poetry, and so forth an equally vigorous contest between alternate views of the Tanzanian nation. "National" Competitions and "National" Festivals constitute one way of approaching the problem in practice. How the problem has been approached from the level of ideology constitutes the focus of the next chapter.

7

OF MWANYAS AND MULTIPARTYISM:
TAARAB PERFORMANCE AND
THE TANZANIAN STATE

Musical innovation is full of danger to the State, for when modes
of music change, the laws of the State always change with them."
—Plato, *Republic* IV, 424

Taarab, as I have already shown, is a highly popular musical form in
East Africa and a vibrant practice for negotiating and constituting social
relations. Yet its foreign—in particular, Arabian—taint (with colonial
and slave-trading overtones), excluded it from inclusion in dominant
theoretical constructions of Tanzanian national culture. Mainland cultural policy documents consistently categorize *taarab* as "nontraditional" music along with "school bands," "brass bands," and "choirs."
Contradictions—an all-too-typical characteristic of state enterprises—
once again abound. In practice, *taarab* bands were, in fact, often called
upon to perform for state functions and visiting foreign dignitaries.
Lucky Star Musical Club, in particular, featuring the acclaimed voice of
Bi Shakila Said, performed for Presidents Jomo Kenyatta of Kenya and
Samora Machel of Mozambique. Yet *taarab* has never been included as
a competitive category at the National Arts and Language Competitions.
On the islands, moreover, in stark contrast to mainland policy, *taarab*
is considered the national genre, well accepted by all as intrinsic to Zanzibari identity, and long supported with state and party (CCM-Zanzibar)
funding.

In 1992, however, a move toward merger occurred in CCM theories
of cultural development. The possibility that this genre, a known vehicle
for alternate discourses, could easily turn a critical eye/voice from personal to metapersonal concerns was not lost on mainland party officials,
and a decision was made to embrace it within the national cultural fold.

The undeniable growth in *taarab*'s popularity throughout the country and beyond (even as far as Burundi)[1] undoubtedly added another factor for consideration. Thus, in tandem with the official establishment in 1992 of political pluralism and the announcement of multiparty elections to be held in October 1995, mainland CCM officials established a new cultural troupe named Tanzania One Theatre, the primary feature of which was its *taarab* performers. In so doing, CCM attempted to exploit the Swahili women's art of musical critique.

In this chapter, I outline the fall of Tanzanian socialism and the consequent rise of multiparty democracy.[2] What emerges is a shifting Tanzanian imaginary in the years 1992–95 when it shed its socialist mantle and adopted political pluralism. I then trace the transformations in meaning and practice that accompanied the recent full-scale incorporation of *taarab* into official Tanzanian mainland cultural practice and policy. That it previously had been excluded on the basis of being defined as "foreign" exemplifies the ambiguity and contradictions that, in the cultural politics of modern Tanzania, accompany all things Swahili. As described in chapter 2, the long-established position of Swahili communities within Indian Ocean trade networks cast them in a borderland between agricultural, maritime, and mercantile economies, African and Arab ethnicities, and "native" versus "non-native" status—all the while bearing the postcolonial burden of association with the slave trade. Whereas prepolitical liberalization (pre-1992) *taarab* performers had occasionally been called upon to perform the role of praise-singer, from 1992 onward official use of the genre increased in sophistication, approaching yet not fully commanding the communicative potency it engenders in coastal contexts. We begin with the description and analysis of a *taarab* performance that foreshadowed political liberalization, a case of resistant collaboration, or, better yet, collaborative resistance.

The 1991 Presidential Visit and a Band of Rebels

In the guise of promoting national cultural identities, the arts have been turned into political mouthpieces of government or party policies, exhorting people to abide by government plans and to be grateful to the leaders for their independence and whatever development has come their way. The airport or state banquet dances fashionable with many African countries is one manifestation of such art.

—Penina Muhando Mlama, *Culture and Development*

In 1991, President Ali Hassan Mwinyi made a visit to Tanga. The city's cultural apparatus temporarily awoke from its slumber to organize the traditional grand welcome at the airport, ensure that strings of small multicolored flags and large palm branches would line the streets lead-ing to the State House (which so rarely received guests—presidential or otherwise), and plan the musical entertainment for the culminating din-ner that promised to be the highlight of the visit. Roadwork crews began repairing potholes in the streets on which the presidential motorcade would pass, poets associated with CCM set to work composing new praise poems, and schoolchildren found it difficult to concentrate on their lessons knowing that in a matter of days their normal routine would be set aside in favor of a march to the stadium to see one parade after another of cars, dignitaries, party members, and fellow school-children, and hear songs, poems, and speeches, including one from the president himself.

The Municipal Council met to decide upon the program of events. At the dinner, there would have to be music. What was the state of Tanga's bands? Only the *dansi* band Watangatanga had new and fully func-tioning equipment, thanks to assistance from a German development agency. They were accordingly placed on the program. It was well known, however, that Zanzibari-born President Ali Hassan Mwinyi was particularly fond of *taarab*. Tanga, a traditional *taarab* stronghold, no longer could boast its former musical ascendance. Bereft of material as-sistance and plagued by mismanagement, its *taarab* bands had fallen from their once-dominant position. The famous rival pair of Black Star Musical Club and Lucky Star Musical Club now rivaled each other only in their respective states of disrepair. Lucky Star had lost its star singer, Bi Shakila, to the JKT Taarab (National Service) band in Dar es Salaam at the personal request of former Defense Minister Salim Ahmed Salim (another *taarab* devotee), who did not want to have to travel to Tanga to hear her voice.[3] A flood of desertions had followed, with singers and instrumentalists leaving to seek better fortunes with *taarab* groups in Zanzibar, Dar es Salaam, Dodoma, Mbeya, and even Burundi. Black Star had fared no better. It may have retained its star singer, Bi Sharmila, but its equipment was irreparable after so many years of nonmaintenance due to corruption and theft among a leadership that lacked the foresight to invest in the band's continuation.[4] Black Star could not be relied upon to perform a straight half-hour of music without its amplifier blowing out or some other electronic disaster. Certainly it would not do to have an embarrassing blow-out before the president of the nation. (It wasn't an idle fear. Once during an earlier presidential visit that featured Black Star, an impaired amplifier suddenly started blasting out the national news broadcast midway through a song!)[5] The other two possible groups, Golden Star and White Star, were not considered because Golden Star seemed to be based out of Mombasa these days rather than Tanga, and no one knew very much about White Star.

Someone suggested the new group that called itself Babloom Modern Taarab, a breakaway faction from Black Star. Their equipment appeared relatively reliable and their tremendous popularity after their recent debut the year before indicated that something of interest was happening. The district cultural officer objected, pointing out that the band was so new that they had yet to register with the authorities as required by the Societies' Ordinance, and moreover that they were currently breaking the law by performing as an unregistered group. Were Babloom to perform for the president, it would be in outright violation of the law.

In point of fact, the cultural officer was in a bit of a bind. He could dissent but not argue his point too strongly, for ultimately he was at fault for allowing an unregistered Babloom to perform in public. Furthermore, the group had become undeniably popular. The Council considered his objections, but without an alternative *taarab* option, decided upon Babloom with the proviso that someone be dispatched to investigate the matter and see if arrangements could be made to register the band in time for the visit.

In the end, a deal was worked out whereby the fee that the Council would pay Babloom to perform (a mere Tsh. 5,000, at that time roughly equal to US$10, a quarter of what Babloom ordinarily charged then for a typical wedding gig) would be put toward the costs of registration, leaving Babloom the additional tasks of applying for registration with BASATA (the National Arts Council) and drawing up a group constitution (*katiba*), a stipulation of the Societies' Ordinance issued by the Ministry of Home Affairs. The BASATA form was duly completed, and the Council agreed to wait for the constitution until a later date. An official program was drawn up listing Babloom and Watangatanga as the dinner entertainment.

The president arrived amidst as much pomp and circumstance as could be mustered in this tropical and declining city. At the dinner, the two bands were set up side by side on the stage area. Watangatanga performed first, two songs lasting roughly twenty minutes in all. The music provided a background to the dinner conversation, appreciated yet not the object of much attention. After they stopped, they yielded the stage to Babloom. It had been prearranged that the bands would take turns playing two songs each turn. Seif Kisauji, Babloom's founder and director, took the microphone and began by singing a song of praise for Augustine Mrema, the very popular and populist Minister of Home Affairs. Although Mrema would later desert CCM to join a series of opposition parties and launch an unsuccessful bid for the presidency, in 1991 he was well ensconced in CCM's upper echelons and had garnered for himself a "hatchet man" reputation—blowing the whistle on corruption among those in his own rank and below. It was Mrema who instituted the nationwide neighborhood watch program called Sungusungu, in which a male member of each ten-house cell would take a weekly turn staying up all night to guard the area of his cell.[6] The program succeeded in greatly reducing crimes of theft nationwide, but it grew increasingly obvious over time that not everyone was taking his turn as conscientious socialist citizens should. Instead, some avoided the responsibility altogether, while those with financial means hired private guards to do the task for them.

Framed though it was by the opening chorus and final verse in typically laudatory praise-song style, Kisauji's song nevertheless offered a scarcely concealed critique of local leaders.

Mrema ("Mrema")
Seif Kassim Kisauji, Babloom Modern Taarab, Tanga

Kwa sote Watanzania, Kusema tuna uhuru
Twaona na twasikia, Wapo wanaotudhuru
Mbele tayahadithia, Msiseme nakufuru

All we citizens of Tanzania are free to say what we want.
We hear and see that there are people who are not good to us.
I am about to tell you, and don't say that I am blaspheming.

- - -

Sahare kubwa mfano, Viwanja tumeuziwa
Huu ni mwaka wa tano, Njia hatujachongewa
Tatizo kama hilono, Nani wakulaumiwa?

Sahare is a good example, we were sold many plots,
But it is now more than five years and roads have not been paved.
For problems like this, who is to blame?

- - -

Ukipanda mshahara, Na forodha kadhalika
Kwa sisi tulofukara, Twaona twadhalilika
Twaomba uwe imara, Tuweze kunufaika

If you raise salaries, the taxes and duties also increase,
For us, the poor, we find ourselves even more oppressed.
We ask that you be strong so that we may benefit.

- - -

Jukumu la sungusungu, Wengi tumejitolea
Kubwa nikuomba Mungu, Lipate kuendelea
Jigeuze nungu nungu, Choma wanozembea

Many of us uphold our Sungusungu responsibility.
We ask God that this continue.
Transform yourself into a porcupine and attack those who evade it.

- - -

Chorus
Fichu fichu, fichua wazi, Mrema twakuombea
Pumu zimepata mkohozi,[7] Wahujumu wanalia

Reveal them for what they are, Mrema, we pray for you.
The job has found the right person.
Corrupt leaders are crying.

Sahare is a neighborhood in Tanga that not long ago was barren of habitation. The municipality decided to open the area to construction and began selling plots accompanied by promises of paved roads, schools, and sewage systems. As of today, however, many years later, the roadwork and basic services have yet to materialize. Resentment runs high among Sahare residents on account of the dirt tracks that serve as roads during the dry season but become impassable muddy rivers during the rainy season. The song, in typical *taarab* fashion, cloaks a critique of local government within the acceptable format of a praise song. The thin veil of praise bore tremendous symbolic power that protected the band from possible repercussions; Mrema was exceedingly popular at the time, and in criticizing corruption, the song upheld everything for which Mrema stood. Following the song, Babloom performed one of their standard repertoire and then ceded the stage once again to Watangatanga.

Rather than consider "Mrema" their political act of the day, Babloom ascended the stage the second time with an even sharper weapon: a song entitled "Ubaya Hauna Kwao" ("Evil Has No Home")—another of Seif Kisauji's compositions. The song's title is a Swahili proverb meaning that evil has no home, no single location, but is everywhere; hence, one must continually be on guard. If "Mrema" implicated local leaders only indirectly via the reference to Sahare, there was no mistaking that they were once again the target of Kisauji's poetry in "Ubaya Hauna Kwao." The "evil" of corrupt local government officials, whose greed and theft worsens the situation of already struggling and impoverished Tanzanians, needs to be checked. But if "Mrema" passed with little reaction, not so "Ubaya Hauna Kwao." The band had only reached the end of the third verse when a high-ranking cultural officer surreptitiously disconnected the main power line to the band's equipment.

***Ubaya Hauna Kwao* ("Evil Has No Home")**
Seif Kassim Kisauji, Babloom Modern Taarab, Tanga

Ukialikwa ziara, Njia zinateuliwa *Zinachongwa barabara, Ambazo utapitia* *Nyingine zimedorora, Mashimo yameenea*	When you come for a visit, certain roads are selected They are paved, the ones on which you will pass The rest are left as they are ridden with potholes
- - -	- - -
Usipite njia hizo, Walizokuchagulia *Chagua uzitakazo, Upate kujionea* *Mengi ni malimbikizo, Nchi inateketea*	Do not travel those roads they chose for you Choose your own that you may see their condition Many things have been delayed. Meanwhile the country rots
- - -	- - -
Hebu amua ziara, Ya ghafula kuvamia *Wananchi tutakerwa, Hawakuitegemea* *Utayaona madhara, Nchi inavyodhuria*	Come, make a surprise visit without warning. The citizens will be distressed, not expecting it. Then you will see the damage, how the country has been ruined
- - -	- - -

Wao haswa ndio chanzo, Vyama vingi kuliliwa	They are the real reason behind the cries for multipartyism
Hasira wengi tunazo, Kwa nini mali yaliwa	Many of us are filled with anger: why is our wealth eaten?
Hawatovipa mkazo, Tumeshawagutukia	They will not support multipartyism, but we already know them for what they are
- - -	- - -
CCM Msimamo, Vyama vingi hatuhofu	CCM prevails, opposition parties do not frighten us
Wasanii nasi tumo, Tuimara mara dufu	Even we performers belong to CCM, we support it twice as much
Bali kuna milalamo, Ya watu waharibifu	Yet there are complaints about the corrupt ones in the Party
- - -	- - -
Mkutano meamua, Sisi twaukubalia	At the meeting you decided upon multipartyism, we accept that
Hao wanaotumiwa, Kwa hamu twawangojea	We wait for those to come to determine their true intentions
CCM imetua, Wasiwasi imetoa	CCM has settled upon this, we are not worried
- - -	- - -

Chorus

Ali Mwinyi, Ubaya hauna kwao	Ali Mwinyi, evil has no home
Waondoe watu hao, washindwe tena kutamba	Remove those people, stop their boasting
Manufaa yao, Kwetu sisi ni msiba	They benefit themselves while we are in mourning
Viongozi hao, Twendeni nao sambamba	We should follow those leaders step by step
Watatudhuru	They will destroy us

I interviewed Seif Kisauji on several occasions about this particular performance for the president because the ramifications of that event were to pursue Babloom from 1991 into the period of 1992–95, when I participated as a member of the band. The following is a translated excerpt from one of these interviews.

Interview with Seif Kassim Kisauji—November 6, 1993, Tanga

K.A.: So, you sang this song "Mrema" first?

S.K.: Mmm hmm [affirmative]

K.A.: But there were no bad reactions to this one?

S.K.: They laughed a bit at first. They thought it was good. But the municipal officers they . . . When we sang the part about Sahare, they also got angry.

K.A.: Of course.

S.K.: Don't you recall when we met the Municipal Director that day when we performed at Raskazone Hotel? His name is. . . . He was there. He said, "It was only one month before that I had come to Tanga,"—he was transferred from another city. "To arrive and after only one month hear a song like this, I thought, 'Am I already being forced to leave my job?' I was so surprised! Yet it is true what you say. For that reason, I did not care too much because it is true. The city is no good. And you are right to say what you see because you are an artist."

K.A.: So, first you sang this song and then you rested? Or did you immediately begin "Ubaya Hauna Kwao"?

S.K.: We then played one of our regular songs. We were performing in turns with Watangatanga. In our first turn, we performed "Mrema" and another song. In our second turn, we began with that.

K.A.: "Ubaya Hauna Kwao"?

S.K.: Hmmm.

K.A.: I would like to know at what point they stopped you—do you remember?

S.K.: When we had finished the third verse. These others we did not sing. But the chorus is very long, and we began with the chorus, then this verse, then the long chorus, then this verse, then the long chorus, then this verse, then the chorus and then they cut the electricity.

K.A.: They were very angry?

S.K.: [The district cultural officer] came after me, "What kind of song are you singing?!" [Laughter]

K.A.: And afterwards, did you see how President Mwinyi reacted?

S.K.: Hah?

K.A.: Mwinyi? Was he listening closely? Or . . . Because you know that at events like this, people are talking and not listening much at all.

S.K.: Haaaa! He was with Mama Halima [the regional commissioner]. He was leaning back in his chair like this, you see? He was leaning back in his chair at the table, see? Now you know this song begins with a chord [he sings the chord note by note]. You see? It begins like this and then we sing the chorus: "Ali Mwinyi, ubaya hauna kwao." So, he and Mama Halima looked at each other. Now Mama Halima, you know, is a great fan of *taarab*. She told him—I saw her!—she said to him, "Listen and you will hear something special." Mwinyi laughed and then he leaned forward in his chair. Before he was leaning back like this, right? He moved the chair and then sat like this with his arms on the table. He was positioned like he was really going to listen well. [Laughter]

K.A.: Eeh.

S.K.: And that's why they were filled with anger to see this—*Lo!*

K.A.: Anger?

S.K.: Yes, those [cultural officers]. They were very angry.

K.A.: OK, wait. So he, Mwinyi, was listening closely—until you were cut short?

S.K.: Hmmm! And also the journalists, they were transcribing what we sang. In shorthand—you know how they write? If you say something he writes it in double time—*dju dju*—and he has caught everything you said. They were very worried.

K.A.: Who?

S.K.: [The cultural officers].

K.A.: Was it published in the newspapers?

S.K.: It was not published.

K.A.: Why?

S.K.: I don't know. Perhaps they followed the journalists and talked them into not publishing it.

K.A.: But if Mwinyi was happy to hear it? Did you truly see his face? How was it?

S.K.: He was laughing! He was happy. He was talking with Mama Halima. You could not hear what they were saying but his face showed that he liked the song.

K.A.: So then why did he order that the song be cut off? Why did they pull the plug?

S.K.: The president did not know. He understood that it was only a power outage.

K.A.: Oh.

S.K.: As for me, you know that audience had many people—many, many people were invited, famous people here around town. There were [lists some of the important businessmen in Tanga]. The big important people. Many of them! It was a dinner. It was packed with people. The people were scared. My uncle was there. He was frightened! He was shaking. He said, "Seif, why do you sing this song?" Anyway, people were talking [imitates the sounds of lots of people talking]. You know how in a dinner, this one speaks to that one. . . . But when the band began, all the people stopped talking. Waa! And they filled me with fear! I was trembling! [Laughter] Aye yai yai yai!

K.A.: I'm sorry.

S.K.: Tsk tsk [shaking his head]. I was singing while playing the keyboard, and I was shaking. I was grateful to [the cultural officer who pulled the plug] [Laughter] because I thought, why was everyone suddenly listening to this song so seriously? I started wondering, why did I do this?! [Laughter]

K.A.: And then that ended Babloom's part? Or did you sing again? Was there a third turn?

S.K.: They did not make us sing again. [Laughter] They told Watangatanga to perform until the end of the dinner.

From that day forward, Babloom Modern Taarab discovered that it
had a most bitter enemy in the district cultural officer who had originally objected to the idea of their performing for the president, for it
was upon him that all blame for the event fell. Municipal Council
members castigated him for having failed in his duty to inspect and if
necessary censor ahead of time the songs that the bands would be performing. The band, on the other hand, suffered no repercussions aside
from not being asked to perform for the president the next time he came
to Tanga.

Kisauji's memories clash somewhat with those I collected from Watangatanga band members, who also performed that evening. Their version did not differ substantially except in one regard: whereas Kisauji
portrayed the Regional Commissioner Mama Halima's original reactions
as, if anything, positive ones, Watangatanga members remember her being very ill at ease. "How could she not be embarrassed in front of her
boss," said one, "with this guy singing about how local leaders (possibly
implicating her) are bad and should be carefully monitored?!"[8] They
passed judgment on Babloom, arguing that the song was highly inappropriate. Watangatanga, however, as I was to learn over the course of
time, had a very different relationship with Tanga's cultural officers than
Babloom, which never did register in Tanga. (Although it had been
agreed that Babloom's payment for that performance should be applied
to their application fee, the cultural officer later denied this arrangement
and demanded the fee while withholding their payment. Babloom resolutely refused to pay it and continued to perform unregistered for five
more years, only registering when the band moved to Dar es Salaam in
October 1996.) Watangatanga, on the other hand, was not only a properly registered band but also one that regularly contributed a percentage
of its weekly income to the same disgruntled cultural officer who would
forever remain Babloom's enemy. When called to perform for national
holiday celebrations and the like, Babloom maintained its maverick
aloofness and generally managed to find an out-of-town wedding for
which to perform (managing, somehow, to acquire the necessary permits) while Watangatanga dutifully appeared with few complaints on
the designated days. But I only discovered these subtleties in each
group's relationship with the cultural office over the course of several
years.

On another occasion in 1995, the topic of the 1991 visit came up
in a post-rehearsal Babloom conversation about the conflicted relations
between musicians and the government with the cultural officers in be-

tween. This time, Kisauji provided more information on how he came to compose "Ubaya Hauna Kwao." He explained that the visit had occurred in the heart of wedding season. The order to perform for the dinner came from the Municipal Council after Babloom had already accepted the deposit on a wedding performance scheduled for the same day as the visit. (Babloom's policy on accepting a performance is that half of the agreed-upon fee be paid at the initial booking with the balance to be paid upon the band's arrival at the wedding.)[9] Owing to the president's visit, Kisauji was forced to go to the wedding organizers to return their deposit and ask that they find another band. Following this, however, the district cultural officer notified the band that the presidential visit had been postponed to another date for which Babloom had been booked. The band had already lost one paid performance with no compensation and now had to cancel a second wedding, again returning the deposit. The presidential visit, however, was postponed yet again. Kisauji claims that in the end, the band lost four weddings for the sake of the visit, and that the last time, they not only lost the wedding revenue, but Kisauji personally paid for Lucky Star to perform, so embarrassed was he at having to cancel at the last minute. That final time, the district cultural officer appeared only one day before to announce that the visit had been moved again and was confirmed for the following day. Said Kisauji, "That was insulting to the band! Certainly the people planning the event know in advance. Why then do they treat us like children, arrogantly assuming that we will drop everything else without complaint?" That day, as Kisauji worked his day job transporting truckloads of sand and gravel to construction sites, he composed the song: "With each trip going and coming, another verse would come to me. It came from anger, it was composed with anger."[10]

One of the many ironies attached to the story is that the event called into question Babloom's loyalty to CCM when the final verses that were never sung proclaim their continuing allegiance. It cast Babloom in a negative light from the perspective of the local government, but time heals all wounds, and when the party and local government found itself in need again of a *taarab* band, they were quick to forget history—although not so soon as the next presidential visit in September 1993.

At the time of the 1991 visit, Tanzania faced its final year of single-party socialism and the impending multipartyism that Kisauji spoke of in "Ubaya Hauna Kwao" was soon to be an official reality. Through song, Babloom illuminated and analyzed some of the problems that plagued Tanzanian socialism, critiquing in particular the inefficacy of a parasitic bureaucracy best represented by corrupt local government leaders. As both intellectuals and artists, Babloom performs the role described by

Katherine Verdery as "producers of meaning." She argues that "Social-ism's intellectuals are . . . both necessary and dangerous: necessary be-cause their skills are implied in setting social values, and dangerous be-cause they and the political center have potentially divergent notions of what intellectual practice should consist of. When—as often happens—these notions do not agree, a conflict emerges over who has the author-ity to define intellectual work: those who *do* it, or those who *order* it" (Verdery 1991b, 429; emphasis in original). Babloom's performance dur-ing the 1991 presidential visit vividly exemplifies this type of conflict.

The year 1991 was a turning point for Tanzania. It marked the tension-filled transition from socialism to something as yet undeter-mined. The immediate history underlying the composition of "Ubaya Hauna Kwao" reflected a much longer history grounded in disappoint-ment, poverty, and unfulfilled visions. To comprehend fully the signifi-cance of Tanzania's move toward economic and political liberalization, we need to understand what went wrong with its experiment in Afri-can socialism.

Ujamaa: Yet Another Failed Socialism

For all the hopes placed by socialist ideologues worldwide in Tanzania's experiment with African Socialism, Tanzania emerges economically scarred and struggling under the weight of its $8 billion in foreign debt. As recently as 1997, Tanzania faced severe shortages in food, particularly in grains—a striking indicator of the failure of agriculture, the rhetorical backbone of Tanzania's economic policy.[11] While it once boasted the highest primary school enrollment rate in Africa at 85 percent, Tanzania now sends only 60 percent of its children to school and has tremendous difficulty convincing teachers to continue working for little or no pay.[12] Inflation, unemployment, and urban migration remain high, and the country's per capita GNP has fallen from its 1961 figure of $200 to about $130 in 1996 (Joel 1996). Frequent shortages of water and electricity mark everyday life, medical personnel and school teachers often go on strike for better pay, and the continuing influx of refugees from neigh-boring Rwanda, Burundi, and the Democratic Republic of the Congo place additional pressures on an already overburdened government ad-ministration.

Socialism in Tanzania has reached and moved beyond its zenith. The myth of returning to a proto-socialist past was proven to be just that, a myth. The failed Ujamaa agricultural scheme of communal villagization is a microcosm of the fate of Tanzanian socialism. Voluntarism was one of the basic principles of Nyerere's vision of Ujamaa, a vision whose truth and benefits, he thought, would become so self-evident that citizens themselves would take up the cause:

> [S]ocialist communities cannot be established by compulsion. . . . [L]iving together and working together for the good of all . . . depends on a willingness to co-operate, and an understanding of the different kind of life which can be obtained by the participants if they work hard together. Viable socialist communities can only be established with willing members; the task of leadership and of Government is not to try and force this kind of development, but to explain, encourage, and participate. (Nyerere 1968, 131)

Paralleling events in the concurrent and equally unsuccessful cultural revolution, the absence of strong proletariat response led the government to announce in 1969 that it would take a more active role in the organization of *ujamaa* villages. As with the monetary enticements offered only to active Cultural Committees, the government declared that *ujamaa* villages would be given priority for the provision of basic services such as schools, dispensaries, and water supplies (Miti 1982). Yet whereas the cultural revolution simply fizzled out into silence, the national decline in agricultural production and productivity caused great alarm amongst party leaders. Rural development in the form of villagization was the basket into which the government had placed the majority of its economic and rhetorical eggs. The party consequently severed the final thread with ideals of voluntarism and began engaging in a series of "operations" that consisted of "the concentrated use of persuasion, inducements, and compulsion to move large numbers of people into villages" (McHenry 1979, 44).[13]

By the end of 1972, 5,556 villages had been established, housing 1,980,862 people, or 15.6 percent of Tanzania's rural population (Hyden 1980, 102; Shao 1982, 38; McHenry 1979, 43). This was not satisfactory. Operations accounted for the bulk of these villages, and the figures concealed high rates of failure owing to a variety of factors, including general mismanagement, theft, and the false pretenses of some putative *ujamaa* villages that were, in fact, organized solely to further someone's political ambitions or to attract the resources offered by the government. Finally, involvement in communal agriculture remained a low priority in those villages that did emerge, the bulk of attention being directed toward private, family-based agriculture as before (Abrahams 1985, 7). A clearly frustrated Nyerere publicly recanted his policy of voluntarism during a 1973 inspection tour of *ujamaa* villages:

> His speech . . . reminded the audience about all the things that the TANU Government had done for the people after the Arusha Declaration. . . . He then went on to ask what the peasants had done in return for these favours. In answering the question, President Nyerere suggested that they had done virtually nothing. They

had remained idle and evaded their responsibility to make a contribution to the country's socialist development. He concluded his speech by saying that he knew he could not turn people into socialists by force, but what his government could do was to ensure that everybody lived in a village. He said he wanted that to be done before the end of 1976. . . . Nyerere stressed the moral obligation of the peasantry to contribute to the successful implementation of the *ujamaa* policies. His tone was sterner than usual, barely hiding his anger. He was talking as a teacher upset with the behaviour of his pupils. (Hyden 1980, 130)

Rather than admit defeat, the president and party embarked on an even more coercive engagement with a reluctant peasantry: Operation Tanzania. Between 1973 and 1976, millions of people were moved into villages, their previous homesteads physically destroyed, and their possessions forcibly moved to designated sites. By 1976, between 85 percent and 91.3 percent (estimates vary) of the rural population had been resettled into villages (see tables 7.1 and 7.2), making Operation Tanzania the largest resettlement effort ever carried out on the continent.

Operation Tanzania succeeded in placing the peasants in villages that were subsequently provisioned with basic social services. It failed, however, to instigate the agricultural revolution deemed necessary for self-reliant socialism. In a scramble to retain his legitimacy and that of his government, Nyerere engaged in rhetorical sleight-of-hand by distinguishing "*ujamaa* villages" (voluntary and based on communal work) from "development villages" (compulsory but not necessarily based on communal work), positing the latter (hence Operation Tanzania) as a stepping stone to the former. But by the early 1980s, economic decline reached the crisis proportions described in chapter 2. Food imports sus-

Table 7.1 Movement of People to Villages

Year	Number of Villages	Total Population
1968	180	58,000
1969	650	30,000
1970	1,200	500,000
1971	4,484	1,595,240
1972	5,556	1,980,862
1973	5,631	2,028,164
1974	5,008	2,560,474
1975	6,944	9,140,229
1976	7,658	13,067,220
1978	7,768	13,847,000
1979	8,200	13,905,000

SOURCE: Shao 1982, 38.

Table 7.2 Percent of Rural
Population Estimated to be in Ujamaa
Villages, 1969–76

Year	Percent
1967	0.0%
1968	0.7
1969	1.7
1970	4.4
1971	12.5
1972	15.6
1973	15.5
1974	19.1
1975	66.6
1976	91.3

SOURCE: McHenry 1979, 43.

tained the population, and store shelves lay barren of even the basic ne-
cessities like salt and sugar. Individuals discovered with a sack or large
basket of maize meal or beans or found idle were tried in special "economic sabotage" courts for the crimes of hoarding and not contributing
to the improvement of the nation. Others feigned hypoglycemia, lining
up at dispensaries in the hope of getting some sugar. The situation was
compounded by a number of coinciding external factors: the dissolution
of the East African Community in 1977 (resulting in large investments in
infrastructure), the inflation of oil prices (1979–80), and war with Uganda
(1978–79) that required tremendous defense expenditures (Gibbon 1995;
Hyden and Williams 1994). After a drawn-out battle in the early 1980s
with the IMF and World Bank over structural adjustment and conditional
aid (Havnevik 1993), President Nyerere conceded that change was inevitable. He stepped down from office on November 5, 1985 (a very uncommon act at the time for an African head of state) and set the course for
economic liberalization by welcoming Ali Hassan Mwinyi, a supporter of
free market economics, to the helm. Summed up by one Kenyan journalist, "Tanzania's spell under Socialism proved to be the longest road to
Capitalism. . . . All the political and economic pillars which plunged the
country to where it is, have finally crumbled" (Joel 1996).

Locating Lost Legitimacy

The failure of socialist regimes worldwide continue to generate much
food for thought. In *What Was Socialism and What Comes Next?*, Kather-

ine Verdery locates the problem in part in a lack of state legitimacy that, she argues, results in internal resistance and sabotage at all levels.

> Against an official "cult of work" used to motivate cadres and workers toward ful-filling the plan, many workers developed an oppositional cult of nonwork, imitating the Party bosses and trying to do as little as possible for their paycheck. Cadres often found no way around this internal sabotage, which by reducing productivity deepened the problems of socialist economies to the point of crisis. (Verdery 1996, 23)

She further argues that since socialist logic rests not on the accumulation of profits, as in capitalist systems, but on the accumulation of the means of production, it generated unwieldy, ultimately parasitic, state bureaucracies. Control became the nature of the game. "In short, these systems had a basic tension between what was necessary to legitimate them—redistributing things to the masses—and what was necessary to their power—accumulating things at the center" (Verdery 1996, 26).

Analysts of Tanzanian political economy locate similar problems in their attempts to understand the failure of its experiment with socialism. The rise of a bureaucratic bourgeoisie (Shivji 1976; Cliffe and Saul 1973–74), the development of state capitalism in lieu of state-monitored so-cialism (Coulson 1979, 15), and the opposition between increasing cen-tralization and imposed "development from above" (Havnevik 1993) versus continuing rhetoric of participatory self-reliance and "planning from below" (Max 1991, 41; Saul 1979) all combined to embed one set of contradictions within another and undermine the state's legitimacy.

> Tanzania has had to deal with a paradox. There, African socialism is conceived as a form of egalitarian self-government by The People, but the historical fact is that socialism has been imposed from above by a central government and by the party organization that controls it. The puzzle of legitimation in Tanzania is thus a dou-ble one of continuing to associate the party and the government with the notion of the democratization of power from below, while at the same time acting to increase the efficiency and effectiveness of those directing matters from the top. The problem is one of leading while appearing to follow, of directing while giving voice to immense rivers of rhetoric about the commitment to populism. (Moore 1988, 155–56; see also Osaghae 1990)

The Tanzanian bureaucracy missed few opportunities to increase its control over virtually every sector of life from culture to economics. It left few social stones unturned. In the cultural domain, as we saw in chapter 5, it attempted to penetrate and transform people's everyday practices of dress, marriage, funeral rites, performance style, and so on. Politically, the state sought to replace existent structures of local gover-nance with the penetrating, omnipresent party apparatus that reached down and outward from the president and NEC (National Executive Committee) down through the regions, districts, municipalities, and vil-lages to the ten-house cell. And in the economic domain, "The state was taking over private industry and starting new industrial enterprises; the state was taking over large-scale agriculture and setting up agricultural enterprises of its own; the state was taking over external and internal trade, transport, banking and insurance. The state controlled prices and wages, imports and credits and used all the levers available to it to enhance the state economy and to nurture it with surplus drained from the private sectors" (Freyhold 1979, 118–19).

Without adequate financial and social resources to maintain and manage, plan and direct this enormous and all-encompassing apparatus, and lacking compatibility with local conceptions of cultural, political, and economic practice (see Hyden and Williams 1994), the state bureaucracy walked into the crisis of the 1970s and 1980s. Paradoxically, however, while continually reorganizing itself economically and politically to increase control and maintain legitimacy, the Tanzanian state has remained stable within a region characterized by instability. It does so while continuing to champion the same old rhetoric of populism and self-reliance, albeit with different twists as the situation demands. Sally Falk Moore surmises that "the disjunction between idealized claims to legitimacy and the facts of experience have come to be accepted as a normal part of the Tanzanian political scene" (Moore 1988, 171).

Disjunction in Tanzanian politics, rhetoric, and practice has not resulted in political crisis of the variety seen in neighboring countries because Tanzanians pursue a policy of withdrawal and disengagement from the state when it acts in a particularly offensive manner. This, the "problem" of the "elusive leaver" (Hyden and Williams 1994), exemplified by a cultural officer choosing to use her office time to knit, characterizes a significant portion of Tanzanian state-society relations. Tanzanians

> chose to use their exit option rather than engaging the system with a view to changing it. There was little alternative, given the fact that individual rights were downplayed while individual duty was stressed under the terms of the communitarian idiom embodied in Ujamaa. . . . For the most part, this was only possible because most Tanzanians have access to their own means of subsistence, independent of the state-controlled market. It was not necessary to become a free-rider on the socialist bandwagon when people could survive well enough in its shadow. (Hyden and Williams 1994, 93–94)

The Transition to Multipartyism

On July 1, 1992, the Tanzanian government formally instituted multipartyism. Multiparty local government elections were set for October 1994 on the mainland, with presidential elections and Zanzibari civic elections to be held in October 1995. The Tanzanian Parliament had voted in April 1992 to repeal the section of the Constitution that prohibited the formation of political parties other than CCM, and simultaneously amended the Constitution to prescribe new terms, conditions, and procedures for the registration of political parties, and provisions to facilitate the transition to the new multiparty system (Msekwa 1995). On July 1, 1992, the Parliamentary Standing Orders and Rules were amended to accommodate multiple parties, and CCM's financial ties to the government were officially severed. Previously, in May, CCM had initiated its own internal restructuring to fit its new relationship to a multiparty government. It abolished its affiliations with the army, the police, the Prison Authority, the National Service and the Civil Service (all of which had previously supported CCM branches), and declared its intent to downsize the party.

In the interests of "removing the impediments to democracy" (Msekwa 1995, 8), the Constitution was again amended in December 1992 to restrict presidential power, and address the marginalization of women in the political process. For the very first time, Parliament was endowed with the powers to impeach the president "in the event of his being accused of breaching the Constitution, or of behaving in a manner which is incompatible with the authority and dignity of the President" (ibid.) and move a motion of no confidence in the prime minister. The Constitution was also amended to withdraw the power of the president to dissolve Parliament at any time (a power he had previously held) and withdraw his ability to nominate up to fifteen members of Parliament. In addition, the twenty-five regional commissioners, appointees of the president, were removed from Parliament in order that Parliament be composed only of popularly elected members.

To ameliorate gender inequity, the Constitution was altered to require that 15 percent of members of Parliament be women nominated by their respective parties in proportion to the electoral strength of each party. Secondly, the Local Government Laws were amended to require that 25 percent of all councilors in each Local Government Council be women, again nominated by their respective political parties in proportion to their parties' electoral strength. The rationale provided for these amendments was phrased in terms of the stability offered by women to the household and, by extension, to the nation: "These new provisions were made in appreciation of the fact that women are not only economic producers, but they also provide strong stability for the household at family level. The amendments were therefore intended to give them encouragement in their political participation so that they can bring to the political process the same kind of stability which they so ably provide at the household level" (Msekwa 1995, 9). Herzfeld identifies this idiom of "cultural intimacy"—the deployment of domestic images in the furtherance of state power—as a common strategy used by state agents in their efforts to inculcate loyalty from their citizens (Herzfeld 1997).

In accordance with Nyerere's goal to create an egalitarian plural society, the conditions for registering new political parties explicitly excluded parties based on "tribal, ethnic or religious" affiliations. Moreover, the registrar of political parties was required to deny registration to any political party advocating the break-up of the Union of Tanganyika and Zanzibar. The requirements for registration included having not less than two hundred registered members representing at least ten regions of the United Republic, of which one must be from Zanzibar and one from Pemba. Furthermore, the party's leadership must include members "from both Tanzania Mainland and Tanzania Zanzibar" (Msekwa 1995, 8).

With the assistance of grants from donor countries, the government offered campaign funds to would-be election candidates. These funds, allocated by the registrar of political parties in the amounts of Tsh. 5,000,000 to presidential candidates ($10,000 in 1993) and Tsh. 1,000,000 to Parliamentary candidates ($2,000),[14] constituted a resource

Figure 7.1   CUF (Civic United Front) rally, Tanga, November 7, 1994. The sign in the middle reads, "We want political change, not revolution." Photo by author.

Figure 7.2 CUF youths carrying a balloon bearing another popular CUF slogan: "Equal rights for all" at the Tanga rally, November 7, 1994. Photo by author.

eliciting much contest and controversy. It is said that within months after July 1, 1992, when registration was officially initiated, some forty parties placed bids of registration with the registrar of political parties in attempts to claim campaign funding. Stories filled the press with charges of theft and corruption. One party leader made headlines after purportedly losing Tsh. 5,000,000 in party funds, his claim being that it was stolen out of the trunk of his car.[15] Yet by the time of the 1995 elections, a total of thirteen political parties passed all the requirements for registration and participated in the elections; four of them presented candidates for the presidential race. The thirteen parties are listed below, with an asterisk marking those contending for the presidency:

Chama cha Demokrasia na Maendeleo (CHADEMA; "Party of Democracy and Development")
Chama cha Mapinduzi (CCM; "Party of the Revolution")*
Civic United Front (CUF)*
National Committee for Constitutional Reform (NCCR–Mageuzi)*
National League for Democracy (NLD)
National Resistance Alliance (NRA)
Popular National Party (PONA)

Tanzania Democratic Alliance (TADEA)
Tanzania Labour Party (TLP)
Tanzania Peoples' Party (TPP)
Union for Multiparty Democracy (UMD)
United Democratic Party (UDP)*
United People's Democratic Party (UPDP)

During the intervening three years between the institution of multi-partyism in July 1992 and the national elections in October 1995, a vigorous debate was waged in the press on the nature of politics, specifically the nature of Tanzanian politics. Some twenty newspapers (published by various organizations, including the government but also the Organization of Tanzanian Trade Unions [OTTU] and private corporations such as the IPP investment group) were filled with daily editorials and letters to the editor on the elections and the costs and benefits of multiparty democracy, in addition to profiles on candidates, political platforms, and volleying accusations. People debated whether multipartyism would suit a multi-ethnic context like Tanzania where, despite government regulations to the contrary, ethnic and religious difference could be manipulated and reinvigorated. The conflicts in neighboring Rwanda and Burundi incited much self-reflection—could Tanzania devolve into a similar situation? Two political cartoons included here reflect upon the consequences of the change in Tanzania's politics. Figure 7.3 depicts a man bearing the label "Peace" (*amani*), suffering under the weight of a large black bomb (*bomu*) and being tickled on one side by

Figure 7.3   Political cartoon: The Bomb Threatening Peace. Courtesy of Sammi Mwamkinga.

Figure 7.4 Political cartoon: CCM's Broken House. Courtesy of Sammi Mwamkinga.

CCM and on the other by *upinzani* (opposition parties). It warns that the contest between CCM and opposition parties threatens Tanzania's peace. In the second cartoon (figure 7.4), the same artist depicts President Mwinyi, in the midst of a crumbling building labeled Tanzania and CCM, on his knees before bemused and angry citizens asking them, "What do you think, my friends, this is a great house, eh?"

As has happened in more than one recently pluralized political situation, opposition parties found little to unite them beyond laying blame for Tanzania's dire economic situation on CCM. CCM, with its superior financial resources, superior communication networks, superior access to transport, and decades of experience in the arts of campaigning and governance, developed a very successful retaliatory response. Its candidates asked citizens to look at the faces in the opposition and the faces in CCM and discover which party had new faces. The apparently contradictory answer was CCM. There was no denying that CCM had brought the country to the brink of economic disaster. It was pointed out, however, that the old vanguard responsible for the poor economic policies of the past had taken advantage of international (e.g., IMF and World Bank) support for multipartyism and established parties of their own, whereas CCM, now cleansed of the old vanguard, hosted new talent, new faces, new ideas, and new policies. CCM, the incumbent, ran a campaign based on the supposition that it offered a complementary mix of experience and new blood appropriate for a new era of Tanzanian politics.

Of Prostitutes and Pestles: The Birth of Tanzania One Theatre

As a newly reborn party, CCM developed a new cultural policy. Coinciding with the formal installation of multipartyism, CCM established on August 18, 1992,[16] a new cultural troupe named Tanzania One Theatre, soon to be famous by its acronym TOT. Tanzania One Theatre exploded onto the Tanzanian music scene with their song "Ngwinji." *Ngwinji* is a slang term that translates as "high-class prostitute" (track 10 on the accompanying CD).

Ngwinji ("High-Class Prostitute")
Othman Soud, Tanzania One Theatre (TOT), Dar es Salaam

Eti Ngwinji atambe, Atambie kitu gani?
Eti nae ajigambe, Ajigambe ana nini?
Hata ajiremberembe, Ngwinji amtake nani?
Eee Ngwinji eee, Usijitie kundini

A prostitute puts on airs! For what does she put on airs?
She also boasts! Of what can she boast?
Even if she puts on makeup, who will want her?
You prostitute, don't include yourself in the group.

- - -

Ngwinji nae hujisifu, Kammiliki fulani
Hujidai maarufu, Mzuri hapa mjini
Kumbe anajikashifu, Ngwinji apendeze nini?
Eee Ngwinji eee, Hata aibu huoni?

- - -

The prostitute even praises herself for controlling someone.
She acts as though she were famous, the beauty of the town.
In reality, she denigrates herself. In what lies her beauty?
You prostitute, you feel no shame?

- - -

Hukaa kwenye vikundi, Kudanganya ighiwani
Eti kila wikiendi, Anajimwaga mjini
Husema anaspendi, Dola za kimarekani
Eee Ngwinji eee, Hundi atakupa nani?

- - -

She sits in some groups, telling people lies
That every weekend she parades around town.
She says that she spends US dollars.
You prostitute, who will give you the check?

- - -

Kwenye watu wapendwao, Ngwinji humo hesabuni
Hebu punguza hashuo, Kwani umezidi nini?
Ni zamani sio leo, Umeshashuka thamani
Eee Ngwinji eee, Uombwe unacho nini?

- - -

You are not included among those who are loved.
Better you reduce your strutting. What is so special about you?
It was long ago, not now. You have dropped in value.
You prostitute, what do you have that someone would want?

- - -

Chorus
Eti Ngwinji atambe, Atambie kitu gani?
Eti nae ajigambe, Ajigambe ana nini?

A prostitute puts on airs! For what does she put on airs?
She also boasts! Of what can she boast?

The song became an enormous hit. It catapulted TOT to the position of the most talked about group in *taarab* circles. This was not a group that worked its way up into the public's consciousness in the normal progression followed by most *taarab* groups. Black Star, Lucky Star, Golden Star, Babloom, and the various Mombasa groups such as Juma Bhalo, Malika, and Zuhura did not "make it" in a matter of months. Years of hard work with little to show for it have characterized the careers of most *taarab* performers. When attained, success bestows largely intangible rewards (audience appreciation, public recognition) and little material improvement in the domain of everyday life. Thus, one commonly finds famous singers and instrumentalists whose voices and music are recognized throughout the country living in extremely modest if not impoverished conditions.

TOT, on the other hand, conquered the *taarab* world in less than three months and had much to show for it. Rumors were planted and allowed to circulate months in advance that CCM was hiding something new and exciting in the army camp in Bagamoyo (despite having formally severed its ties to the army). For two months prior to their August 18, 1992, debut, TOT's performers were sequestered on the army base for intensive training in not-so-secret secrecy. TOT, it was announced on August 18, was CCM's latest weapon for the propagation and dissemination of the CCM message, as well as for a "CCM campaign to promote Tanzanian Culture to an elevated status."[17] CCM timed TOT's release for the period marked on one end by the announcement of multipartyism and on the other by the 1995 elections. Local knowledge held that the Chinese government supplied TOT's instruments, while CCM provided start-up funding in the amount of Tsh. 20,000,000 (US $50,000) to cover performer salaries, housing, and whatever equipment was missing from the Chinese donations. Later articles in the press confirmed that CCM funded TOT, although exact amounts were not divulged.[18]

Strangely enough, however, CCM's secret weapon did not launch overtly political missiles. The song "Ngwinji" proved only the first of a long and continuing repertoire of songs unequivocally embedded in the *taarab* orientation toward social relations and social commentary. TOT ostensibly aimed to bring Tanzanian culture to new heights, and it certainly did so by exploiting the traditional motifs of insult, challenge, and sexual innuendo to an unprecedented degree of explicitness. And so the party's new cultural troupe sang about prostitutes, adept ("foreign-trained") lovers, and sex. The following are two more examples of TOT hit songs in 1992–93, both in keeping with the *taarab* traditions of *mafumbo* and *mipasho*:

TX Mpenzi ("Expatriate Lover")—excerpt
Othman Soud, Tanzania One Theatre, Dar es Salaam

TX Mpenzi,[19] *Dakta wangu zamani*
Ameispeshalaizi, Digrii yake Sir John
Ananipasua tezi, Siku nyingi tumboni
TX nipasue, Toa maradhi ya ndani

Expatriate lover, my doctor from long
ago.
He is specialized, his degree from Sir
John.
He has been removing tumors from my
abdomen since long ago.
TX, cut me open. Remove my inner
illness.

- - -

- - -

TX ana cheti, Kapasi Ujerumani
Hunipanusu kaputi, Nazimia kitandani
Na fahamu sipati, Nangoja operesheni
TX nipasue, Taja vyote sikughini

TX has a certificate. He graduated in
Germany.
He anesthetizes me and I pass out on the
bed.
I remain unconscious, waiting for the
operation.
TX, cut me open. Mention anything and
I won't refuse you.

- - -

- - -

Mimi ndo mgonjwa wake, Bibi jiweke
pembeni
Napenda sindano zake, Haziumi mwilini
Aminyapo dawa zake, Ganzi tele maungoni
TX nipasue, Mi nawe hatunyimani

I am his only patient. Lady, step aside.
I love his injections, they do not hurt my
body.
He applies his medicine, and my body
goes numb.
TX, cut me open. You and I do not refuse
each other.

- - -

- - -

Chorus
Nipasue daktari nipasue, Toa maradhi ya
ndani
Nipasue TX nipasue, Nangoja operesheni

Cut me open, doctor, cleave me. Remove
my inner illness.
Cut me open, TX, cleave me. I await your
operation.

Mtwangio ("Pestle")
Tanzania One Theatre, Dar es Salaam

Yategeni masikio, Mpate kunisikia
Kubwa langu kusudio, Leo nnawaambia
Nausifu mtwangio, Nnao twangia

Pay attention with your ears so that you
hear me.
My primary aim—today I am telling you,
I praise this pestle with which I pound

- - -

- - -

Kwa kutwanga namba wani, Sifa ninautolea
Sithubutu asilani, Mwengine kuutumia
Wa mwengine sitamani, Huu nimeuzowea

For pounding, it is number one. I give it
praise.
I will never try to use another.
I do not desire someone else's. I am
accustomed to this one.

- - -

- - -

Ukweli nawambieni, Si utani ndugu zangu

I tell you the truth, it is no joke, my
relatives,

Uingiapo kinuni, Huu mtwangio wangu
Unatwanga kwa makini, Kwenye hiki kinu
changu

- - -

Nakamilisha usemi, Nilosema ya hakika
Mtwangio wangu mimi, Kweli umekamilika
Hata kwa masaa kumi, Hutwanga bila
kuchoka

- - -

Chorus
Mtwangio twanga, Usichoke mtwangio
Twanga bila wasiwasi, Ewe mtwangio
wangu
Kinu kimeniridhia

When it enters the mortar, this pestle of
mine,
It pounds perfectly in my mortar.

- - -

I have completed what I want to say and
it is the truth.
I am sure of my pestle.
Even for ten hours, it can pound without
tiring.

- - -

Pestle, pound and do not tire, oh pestle.
Pound without worries, you my pestle,
The mortar accepts you.

The singer of the song "Ngwinji" was Khadija Kopa, formerly a singer with the CCM-sponsored *taarab* orchestra on Zanzibar named Culture Musical Club (see figure 4.2). Her musical associate and life partner, Othman Soud, composed the song and was himself a noted and much-admired singer also formerly with Culture Musical Club. When I was in Zanzibar during the summer of 1990, the two had just begun their ascent in the *taarab* world and were much talked about as Culture's newest talents. In 1992, they were recruited to join the new CCM-sponsored Tanzania One Theatre. This occurred much to the dismay and anger of the Zanzibari CCM apparatus that as late as February 1994 was complaining to the press that Kopa and Soud had deserted their posts with Culture without having acquired the proper permit to leave (yet another example of the omnipresent cultural apparatus at work—permits to join, permits to leave, etc., etc.).[20]

Prior to the establishment of TOT, its director, Captain John Komba, had directed the *kwaya* group of the Tanzania People's Defense Forces, or JWTZ (Jeshi la Wananchi Tanzania). Born in Songea in the southern part of the country, he rose quickly up the army ranks by exploiting his musical talent to sing the country's praises. That the Tanzanian government saw fit to implement a music program in its armed forces may relate to another exchange of cultural policy ideology with China, for in China,

[t]he army had long been a major cultural center through its massive General Political Department. Radicalized before 1966, the army looked like a steady hand for the arts. . . . The army looked good, not only because of its radical politics, but also because it was a safe haven in a turbulent time and provided good housing, food, and facilities. Lesser artists then also pressed to be absorbed into the army's revolutionary and protective embrace. (Kraus 1991, 228)

Even today, well-noted bands remain attached to JWTZ, as well as JKT (National Service Army, or Jeshi la Kujenga Taifa), the police force, and various prisons, especially Magereza Kiwira in Mbeya and Magereza Ukonga in Dar es Salaam. While directing the *kwaya* group of JWTZ, Captain Komba composed several songs that became theme songs for CCM, the most famous one being "CCM Nambari One" ("CCM Is Number One"). This garnered him favored status in the CCM hierarchy, and he was later elected to the CCM National Executive Committee.

CCM Nambari Wani ("CCM Is Number One")
Captain John Komba, JWTZ Kwaya, (then) Tanzania One Theatre Kwaya

Watanzania napo, Watanzania twapendeza	Tanzanians also, Tanzanians are beautiful
Nambari wani eee, Nambari wani ni CCM	CCM is number one
Tieni Mwinyi, Tieni kwa moyo mmoja	Support Mwinyi with one heart
Nambari wani ni CCM	CCM is number one
Malecela tieni, Salmini tieni	Support Malecela, support Salmin[21]
Tieni tieni kwa moyo mmoja	Support [them] with one heart
Nambari wani eee, Nambari wani ni CCM	CCM is number one
Dar es Salaam tieni	Support Dar es Salaam
Tieni kwa moyo mmoja, Nambari wani ni CCM	Support with one heart, CCM is number one
Tanga tieni, Nambari wani ni CCM	Support Tanga, CCM is number one
Kilimanjaro tieni, Nambari wani ni CCM	Support Kilimanjaro, CCM is number one
Pemba tieni, Nambari wani ni CCM	Support Pemba, CCM is number one
Tieni tieni kwa moyo mmoja	Support with one heart
Nambari wani eee, Nambari wani ni CCM	CCM is number one

Captain Komba explained to me that in July 1992, CCM decided to create a new cultural troupe, the cornerstone of which would be *taarab*. When I asked why *taarab*, he responded, "Inapendwa na watu" ("It is loved by the people").[22] This constituted quite a shift in official thought on culture. The CCM mainland government up until this point had always excluded *taarab* from its official cultural policy, including it in the categories of "nontraditional" or "nonindigenous" music. This distinguished the cultural policy of the mainland from that of Zanzibar, where *taarab* constitutes an indisputable national tradition, the island being its official birthplace. On the mainland, however, cultural policy documents lamented Arab-influenced traditions like *taarab* to the same extent that they lamented Western traditions like the foxtrot or waltz.

> The foreigners who came into our country since the [eleventh] century such as the Arabs and Europeans were the major cause of the denigration of our original culture. Arabic influence developed more in areas where Arabs stayed longer. European influences developed in areas where Europeans stayed longer. Faith, games and other activities in the community were spoiled to some extent.[23]

These foreign influences were to be the object of cultural cleansing, a weeding process that would enable the growth and development of "indigenous African traditions."

With associations to Arab colonialism, or worse yet Arab slave raiding and trading, *taarab* occupied a marginalized position within the national culture schema as plotted and defined by Tanzanian culture producers. It was not included as a competitive event in the National Arts and Language Competitions, even though the equally foreign genre of *kwaya* was included. *Kwaya* was adequately cleansed of foreign connotations via the twin processes of politicization and secularization. Although originally derived from Western church music, *kwaya* in the context of national events consists of songs sung in multi-part vocal harmony with secular, political lyrics, often in praise of the government or party. Thus it was on the basis of *kwaya* that Captain Komba made his way up the CCM ladder of power.

Similarly, theater (*tamthiliya* or *maigizo*) is arguably an imported genre, and yet is not only included in the National Arts and Language Competitions, but positioned as the grand finale. This apparent contradiction, as with *kwaya,* is resolved by means of politics. In the realm of policy, no art form received greater emphasis than drama. Drama was privileged in Tanzania as in other socialist settings for its perceived revolutionary subscripts. According to Brazilian educator Paulo Freire, Argentinian theater activist Augusto Boal, and German playwright Bertolt Brecht, theater constitutes an ideological tool through which politics can be taught and social action rehearsed (Desai 1990, 81). It can be used "to discuss issues, to educate, to create awareness and often to mobilise people for specific action including liberation struggles" (Mlama 1991, 20; see also Desai 1990; Barber 1987; Songoyi 1988a; Lihamba 1985; and Etherton 1982). The Popular Theater movement, born in Latin America, was spearheaded in Africa by the University of Dar es Salaam that, in keeping with the city's reputation as Africa's revolutionary mecca, established the first Theater Arts department in East Africa (Etherton 1982, 325). Those who promoted it saw it as a medium for effecting change, not an art for placid consumption by elites. According to Mlama, popular theater in Africa

has been a conscious attempt not only to bring to the fore the voice of the dominated classes but also to involve them in the process of bettering their way of life. In Popular Theatre, people research into their problems of life, discuss and analyse them, bringing out their root causes and suggesting their possible solutions. The problems are also concretised in theatrical portrayals incorporating the people's viewpoints and expressions, followed by collective strategising and mobilisation for action to solve the problems in question. (Mlama 1991, 20)

And if the European socialist/Latin American activist elements seemed at odds with official goals of rediscovering and promoting *indigenous* arts, such concerns were challenged by Tanzanian Popular Theater advocates who viewed *ngoma* and other traditional African performing arts as proto-theatrical genres (Mlama 1991; Lihamba 1985).

Theater, as a didactic and mobilizing medium assumed a central position in Tanzanian cultural policy because it best fit the government's proclaimed goal of promoting art that "will help us to better understand our environment and transform it according to our needs" (Mbughuni and Ruhumbika 1974, 280). It is for this reason that it was reserved as the final event at the National Arts and Language Competitions, preceded by *ngoma* as the other heavily promoted, often politicized, indigenous art form. *Taarab,* on the other hand, did not figure into such conceptions of art and national culture, for it was neither "traditional" enough (like *ngoma*) nor "political" enough (like *kwaya* and theater).

That all changed, however, with the establishment of TOT in August 1992. For the first time, *taarab* was given not only official government mandate but significant financial resources. Captain Komba was entrusted with the task of amassing the best *taarab* talent on the mainland and in the islands to create an unrivaled *taarab* performance group that would also, in keeping with standard cultural troupe performance practices, perform other genres such as *ngoma, kwaya,* and theater. In interviews, Captain Komba reiterated that *taarab* was the troupe's strength and attraction, and went so far as to deny its Arab overtones. Instead, he called it *"muziki wa mwambao"* (coastal music), which would not be accepted as Arab music by Arabs, and which had garnered nationwide popularity. He then went on to describe to me the tremendous effort he put into traveling throughout the country to places like Tanga and Mbeya (where the popular prison troupe Magereza-Kiwira constituted an outpost of *taarab* talent), and of course to Zanzibar to woo the best *taarab* singers, composers, and instrumentalists away from their respective home groups with promises of wealth and fame in this new CCM-sponsored cultural troupe. He said that "TOT was a response to the introduction of multipartyism for the purpose of promoting CCM."[24]

Further support for the dominance and prominence of *taarab* in TOT's *raison d'être* emerge from TOT's performance practice. A typical show begins with *ngoma* and ends with *taarab*—a format followed by most other private as well as government-supported performance troupes throughout the country. When I asked Captain Komba and musicians from both TOT and other troupes why this was so, the answer never varied: I was told that if they performed *taarab* first, the audience would leave immediately afterwards, since it was *taarab* that they came to see and hear.[25] In descriptions of troupe shows that appear in the "Entertainment" sections of Tanzania's many newspapers, one finds statements such as, "But it was . . . the much-awaited taarab category that really made—and almost spoilt the memorable evening,"[26] and

"While both [troupes] have powerful ngoma presentations, it is the *taarab* shows with their poetically social intrigues that many people love to listen [*sic*], watch the singers and sometimes dance to the tunes of *taarab*."[27]

Unraveling TOT's Success

TOT employs fifty performers. For the three shows they performed in Tanga in September 1993 (see table 7.3), TOT made gross profits of Tsh. 2,400,000 (roughly $4,800).

To give a true sense of how these figures compare, let me offer some

Figure 7.5 Tanzania One Theatre advertisement, 1994. Photo of actual advertisement supplied by Captain Komba of TOT; University of Michigan Photo Services.

Table 7.3 Proceeds from TOT Shows September 3–5, 1993, Tanga

Date	Venue	Ticket Price	Total Income
3 Sept 1993	Mkonge Hotel Swimming Pool	Tsh. 1,000	Tsh. 500,000
4 Sept 1993	Splendid View Hotel	Tsh. 700	Tsh. 400,000
5 Sept 1993	Mkwakwani Stadium	Tsh. 500	Tsh. 1,500,000

SOURCE: Interview with Captain John Komba, September 6, 1993, Tanga.

information on the regular incomes of some Tanga bands. During this same time period, Tanga's two most popular bands, Babloom Modern Taarab and the Watangatanga Band played regular weekly performances at the Mkonge Hotel (Watangatanga on Saturday nights, Babloom on Sunday evenings) and Splendid View Hotel (Watangatanga on Sunday nights). Babloom was paid a weekly flat rate of Tsh. 17,000 by the Mkonge Hotel, and no entrance fee was charged; it was free entertainment offered by the hotel, the costs of which they easily recouped in the sale of food and beverages to *taarab* patrons. Babloom derived the bulk of its income from wedding performances. Weddings, however, offer seasonal work for musicians because there are certain months of the Swahili Islamic calendar that are considered propitious for weddings and others when weddings are discouraged or explicitly proscribed, as in the case of Ramadan.[28] At this time (1993–94), Babloom charged Tsh. 30,000 to perform for a wedding in Tanga.[29] TOT, however, charged Tsh. 300,000 for an exclusive *taarab* performance (i.e., minus the other genres that comprised the total cultural troupe performance) and, according to Captain Komba, performed for 3–4 weddings per month in addition to its regular weekend cultural troupe shows.[30] Watangatanga, on the other hand, charged entrance fees of Tsh. 800 at Mkonge and Tsh. 500 at Splendid View. They then split the proceeds with the hotels, giving Mkonge Hotel 35 percent of the Saturday night income and Splendid View 30 percent of the Sunday night income. They averaged Tsh. 40,000–60,000 for their 65 percent of Mkonge show revenues and Tsh. 25,000–30,000 for their 70 percent of the proceeds at Splendid View[31]— again a marked difference from the revenues commanded by TOT.

Captain Komba did not reveal the costs he incurred in bringing TOT to Tanga, housing and feeding the performers, advertising the shows, the deals he cut with Mkonge and Splendid View Hotels, and the rental fee for Mkwakwani Stadium. The operating costs accompanying such a large troupe must correspondingly be quite high. Other bands lose much of their income to transport costs when they tour outside their home districts—a major disincentive to touring (in addition to the hassles of applying for permits to leave and enter, etc.). Some of the initial capital used to establish TOT, however, was earmarked for the purchase of buses, vans, and a car for the director. The stated goal of TOT was to spread the CCM message, and spread it throughout the country. For that, transport was absolutely necessary. Thus, we can presume that TOT's transport costs were kept to a minimum.

No matter what their net profits, however, the ability of TOT consistently to command six and seven-digit figures attests to its tremendous popularity. TOT presents a dazzling show, with their fancy and clearly expensive costumes, multiple costume changes, high-tech equipment, and an innovative *taarab* sound blending the classical orchestra style of Zanzibar with the modern style of Tanga. Moreover, it still bore the mantle of its newness when it came to Tanga, having just celebrated its first anniversary. The people of Tanga came out in large numbers to see with their own eyes and hear with their own ears this new troupe that boasted such tremendous talent and whose songs were broadcast incessantly on the government-run radio station.

In a review of TOT's first year of existence, one journalist explained that TOT's popularity was a direct result of its strategy of accumulating experienced and recognized talent—artists whose names, faces, and voices were already widely known in Tanzania. This advantage, however, also constitutes the troupe's major drawback because it requires great diplomacy to treat the stars with the appropriate respect and status to which they feel entitled. By the Tanga performances, TOT had lost its two biggest *taarab* stars, Khadija Kopa and Othman Soud, the singer and composer of its first hit, "Ngwinji," and it was soon to lose another celebrated singer named Ally Star. The three all left to join the privately run Muungano Cultural Troupe that consequently developed into TOT's arch rival. TOT's secretary Gasper Tumaini attributed the loss of these musicians to the difficulties in balancing egos and privileges.[32]

One final factor in TOT's success that cannot be overlooked is radio broadcast time. Strict government censorship determines what music is played on the government-run radio station, RTD (Radio Tanzania Dar es Salaam)—until 1994 the only station broadcasting in Tanzania.[33] RTD's censorship committee bears a reputation for frequently prohibiting songs interpreted as containing insidious antiparty sentiment or somehow opposing (socially or otherwise) "national interests." Musicians frequently complain of the apparent lack of logic that determines whether a song will pass or not. The committee actively searches for songs that contain *mafunzo* ("teachings, lessons"); for example, if a love song is under review, a determining factor for its approval will be whether or not it includes reference to marriage as the desired outcome.

Songs missing the reference to marriage have been interpreted by the committee as advancing promiscuity and banned. Also, the committee rarely passes songs sung in local languages other than Swahili. One music administrator explained, "At RTD, they refuse to record traditional songs because they are afraid of traditional languages—you can tell secrets that others will not understand."[34]

The relationship between the censorship committee and *taarab* groups is a contradictory one. On the one hand, everyone recognizes the potential for underscored subtexts in *taarab* songs. Like traditional songs in local languages, therefore, *taarab* songs could contain potentially subversive elements. But if a song's meaning was well hidden, it could pass without much trouble. And so *taarab* songs about a welcoming mat on which many guests rest (i.e., a promiscuous spouse),[35] a rifle devoid of bullets (i.e., an impotent man),[36] and a tasty curry spoiled by lime juice (i.e., an attractive woman spoiled by a certain man)[37] passed and are still aired today. In fact, according to one insider, more *taarab* songs than *dansi* songs have been passed by the committee. Finally, bands are well aware that the committee's membership constitutes another determining factor in the process. If a song is rejected, a common strategy is to wait several months before presenting it to the committee again. A song would often pass on the second or third round.

TOT, however, does not face these obstacles to success. It seems exempt from RTD restrictions on either song content or amount of broadcast time. "TX Mpenzi" ("Expatriate Lover"), and "Mtwangio" ("Pestle"), as we have seen, are far from subtle in meaning and yet received and continue to receive significant broadcast time—despite letters to the editor denouncing such inconsistency in policy. TOT also receives an inordinate percentage of broadcast time. While this can be justified in part on the basis of TOT's tremendous popularity ("It should be played because it is what the people want to hear"), it is also true that TOT's tremendous popularity can in part be attributed to the large amount of broadcast time it receives.

TOT continues to compose songs that stretch the boundaries of *taarab* convention in the amount and degree of sexual innuendo, while continuing an outright refusal to compose political songs. There is a clear delineation of where TOT's politics resound and where they are muted. In a typical TOT performance such as one I attended on April 29, 1994, at the inauguration of a new CCM branch in Vingunguti, Ilala (an outlying area of Dar es Salaam), they began by performing three *ngoma* (Makonde, Zanzibari, and one from Musoma of an ethnic group called the Gita),[38] the last one of which had the following lyrics: "Utamaduni Tanzania" ("Tanzanian culture"). A play followed entitled "Ufukara Hatabiriki"

("Troubles Never Cease") about a father with three children—two daughters and one son. His two daughters married well, but his son is a source of shame to him for being poor and unemployed. The father ingratiates himself to his two rich sons-in-law while despising his son, only to have his world turned upside-down when one son-in-law is completely robbed of his wealth, the other killed in a car accident, and his son returns triumphant and enormously wealthy from an adventure in gold mining. The moral of the story, of course, is that wealth should not determine social relations, for it is fleeting.

Kwaya followed the play, and here TOT fulfilled the musical standards espoused by government censors, for a number of their songs taught *mafunzo*, or "lessons"—imbued, however, with CCM politics and rhetoric. They performed a total of four songs (see appendix A for lyrics). The first song, "Muongo Afadhali ya Mchawi" (Better a sorcerer than a liar), warns that liars and gossips disrupt the peace and should be avoided at all costs. The least overtly political of the four, it nevertheless bore political meaning in this context of emergent multipartyism with opposition parties implicitly cast as "liars" and "gossips." The second song, "Tuombe" (Let us pray), describes a world gone mad with violence and oppression. In pointing out the conflicts in Somalia and Mozambique, a comparison is implied with the reigning peace in Tanzania, a situation for which CCM has widely and loudly claimed responsibility. When the 1994 crisis broke out in Rwanda, for example, the Tanzanian press was filled as much with praise for CCM that such a terrible thing did not happen in Tanzania as with breaking news on the conflict.[39] The third song, "Nyumba ya Jirani Yaungua Moto" (The neighbor's house is on fire), could similarly be interpreted as discussing conflicts in neighboring countries, but some people suggested to me that it warns instead against the potential dangers of multipartyism, the "fire" resulting from internal disunity. With the final song, Komba's hit, "Nambari Wani" (now a CCM standard), a CCM flag was raised on high, and the audience sang along in a display of CCM solidarity.

After the *kwaya* performance, there were some political speeches peppered throughout with CCM slogans and chants such as "CCM Oyee!" and "CCM ah, ah! Ina wenyewe!" ("CCM, ah, ah! It has its people!"). With each of the "ah, ah," the audience and speakers would raise high their right fists, punching the air to drive the point home. The chairman of the CCM branch that sponsored the show wore a Mao suit and gave a prolonged speech. The conclusion of the speeches signified the conclusion of TOT's formal politics and the start of *taarab*. Before the performers even appeared on stage, however, members of the audience rushed the stage and confiscated the microphone to shout disparaging slogans about TOT's rival Muungano, a rivalry, as mentioned above, located primarily in *taarab* performance. Clearly, this is what the audience had come to hear, and the show did not disappoint them, filled as it was with crowd-pleasers, such as "TX Mpenzi."

I once asked Captain Komba why TOT did not sing political *taarab* songs. He responded by saying, "If we only sang CCM, people would run away."[40] He then explained that he made the conscious decision to have only one *fani* (genre) used for propaganda, that being *kwaya*. The contradictions dissolve, then, between past and present cultural policy on *taarab*, between TOT's politically motivated birth and its highly apolitical (in the conventional sense) use of *taarab*, and between TOT's role as an agent of the ruling party and the purveyor of highly suggestive, if not outrightly lewd, *taarab* songs.[41] TOT's *taarab* performance, in part because of its transgression of government-enforced standards, attracts crowds of people and their entrance fees. It is the end result of an effective CCM/TOT strategy to amass audiences with the lure of *taarab*, but then withhold it until the very end of the performance, subjecting the audience in the interim to political speeches and songs they might not otherwise come to hear.

I have already argued that *taarab* constitutes an inherently political genre. The politics for which it is utilized in local settings, however, do not easily adapt to the politics promoted by CCM via TOT. Swahili women adroitly manipulate meanings in *taarab* songs to forward their personal political agendas in the realm of social relations. It is my opinion that TOT and other state agents who would seek to capture the same communicative potency in *taarab* for their own purposes do not succeed in doing so. They exploit its relevance for local social relations wherever they perform, hence the large crowds, but, as Captain Komba's statement indicates, are unable to translate it to the realm of CCM and multiparty politics. In the final section of this chapter, I return to Babloom and Tanga to present a case of local politicians attempting to capture *taarab's* communicative potency and falling short of their goal.

Of *Mwanyas* and Multipartyism: The Rebirth of Babloom Modern Taarab

Seif Kisauji came to my home on the morning of September 29, 1993, to tell me that he had composed a new song—would I like to hear it? He alternately sang for me the bass line, lead guitar sectors, and vocal melody, and beat out the accompanying drum rhythm on my desk. Then he produced the poem that constitutes the song lyrics, its text. To my surprise, I read the following from the torn piece of paper he handed me (track 7 on the accompanying CD):

Mwanya ("Attractive Gap between the Front Teeth")
Seif Kassim Kisauji, Babloom Modern Taarab, Tanga

Mwanya ulikuwa nao, Hukuwaza ya
    mbeleni
Ukaiondoa ngao, Wakakugonga kichwani
Kalie na hao hao, Walokutia jangani

- - -

Sivizuri nikutete, Kama u papo sikia
Tena nakutema mate, "Ptuka chaka!"
    yakwelea
Pengo linavuja ute, Matandiko wachafua

- - -

Ukiweka atifisho, Bure unajisumbua
Domo litanuka jasho, Huwezi kukurubiwa
Huna tena ubishoo, Roho utatuchafua

- - -

Pengo lina mkoromo, Unamuudhi mwandani
Ngurumo mumo kwa mumo, Haipati
    burudani
Haupati msimamo, Budi hana afanyeni?
- - -

Chorus
Mwanya umeufuja, Pengo linanguruma
Wasiwasi wasiwasi unao, Wasaalam!

You had a mwanya, but you did not
    think ahead.
You removed your shield, and they hit
    you in the head.
Go cry to those who put you in trouble.
- - -
It is not good for me to speak behind
    your back, so if you are there, listen:
I spit on you, "Ptuka chaka!" that you
    understand.
Your gaping hole leaks saliva, soiling the
    bedding.
- - -
If you get an artificial tooth, you trouble
    yourself needlessly.
Your mouth emits a terrible odor. No one
    can come near you.
You no longer have anything over which
    to boast. You defile our souls.
- - -
Your hole snores disturbing your partner.
Such a terrible racket—he gets no relief.
It does not cease. There is no escape—
    what is he to do?
- - -

You destroyed your mwanya. Your hole
    snores.
You are worried. It's all over!

On its surface, the song spoke of the loss of physical beauty. A *mwanya*, a small yet noticeable gap between the two front teeth, is considered a highly desirable mark of beauty in East Africa. The singer berates a woman who once had this distinguished and enviable characteristic, but who, through her own foolish disregard ("you did not think ahead [and] removed your shield") allowed herself to be hit in the head. Now, instead of a beautiful small gap, she is left with an ugly, gaping hole where once a tooth had been. The song goes on to describe in explicit detail the unpleasant ramifications of this offensive hole: it leaks saliva, releases a bad odor, and creates such a racket of snoring at night that the woman's partner gets no sleep. There had to be another meaning. Yet when I asked, Kisauji merely smiled enigmatically and left me to ponder it on my own, reminding me that I was, after all, the *mtafiti*, the researcher.

Over the course of the next several months, I watched and listened as this song grew in popularity from its initial debut into one of the most commonly requested songs at weddings. Along the way, I collected interpretations of its meanings from a variety of sources. The common denominator was loss of something good, something of value. Babloom's chairman, Kisauji's older brother, explained that the song rebuked someone who had lost a good job through drunkenness, tardiness, or laziness. A wedding guest explained that the metaphor referred to the loss of a good marriage, most likely through unfaithfulness. But it wasn't long before I discovered the meaning that most female listeners brought to the text. The song speaks to a woman who used to be respectable—the *mwanya*, in this case, being significant now for its small size, not so much its rare beauty—but who lost her *mwanya* to have it replaced by a large *pengo* ("gaping hole") due to association with many different men. *Mwanya* signifies a chaste woman, whereas *pengo* signifies a prostitute. It is easy to see how the metaphor plays itself out in the subsequent verses.

Leading into 1994, then, "Mwanya" developed into a hit song in Tanga's wedding circuit. As with many popular *taarab* songs, this song played right into local politics of the personal. Its popularity stemmed in large part from its sharp metaphoric edge, a weapon to be used by skillful *taarab* participants to charge someone publicly yet obliquely with promiscuous behavior. Moreover, local linguistic practice absorbed and appropriated the song's poetry in particular with the adoption of the term *pengo* ("hole") as a slang term for a loose woman. I once overheard a comment made in response to inquiries about the whereabouts of a man who had left the area without saying good-bye. "Oh, he's off in search of a *pengo*" ("Anatafuta pengo") was the reply.

As the city prepared for the upcoming multiparty civic elections in October 1994 (that would precede the national multiparty elections by a year), the local CCM apparatus met to decide upon a campaign strategy. The CCM candidate for the Northern Ngamiani (Ngamiani Kaskazini) council seat was Salim Kassim Kisauji, the older brother of Seif Kisauji and the official chairman of Babloom. Salim Kisauji trained as an aeronautical engineer in the UK and worked for many years in Kenya's airline industry before returning to Tanzania to assume his place as head of the Kisauji household upon his father's death. This was his first attempt to break into the local political scene, in which he had only participated as an interested observer and critic previously. When asked why, with his critical view of CCM governance, he chose to stand with CCM rather than join an opposition party, he explained that for all the party had done wrong in administering the country, it nevertheless had succeeded in uniting it. Moreover, he believed that CCM was the party for change, contrary though that may seem, since the old guard had deserted CCM in the hope of securing for themselves more power as heads of opposition parties. He himself was one example of a newcomer to politics welcomed to represent CCM.

With his obvious ties to Babloom, it was suggested that Salim Kisauji entice Babloom, by this time the most popular band in Tanga, to perform for CCM. Some, remembering the 1991 presidential visit, objected, arguing that the band could not be trusted to represent CCM properly. But Salim Kisauji defended Babloom's loyalty and simultaneously worked out a deal whereby the band would be appropriately reimbursed for its services, paid an amount nearly equivalent to its normal fee. For the band, this was a great improvement over the standard pittances offered for government functions, and the campaign period in the two months prior to the elections happened to fall during a low point of the wedding calendar when other engagements would be rare. The CCM campaign offered steady work, so in the end, the band agreed.

The song "Mwanya" somewhat ironically was adopted as one of the CCM theme songs during the campaign. The message of "You had something good, but you've lost it. Now you are worried," was now directed to opposition parties who struggled to find a position next to CCM supremacy. That they "had something good" referred to the international support from donor countries and institutions like the World Bank and the IMF that lobbied hard for the reintroduction of multipartyism in Tanzania. That they "lost it" projected a (future) electoral loss in the (present) campaign in spite of all the outside support. The song's refrain, "Wasiwasi unao. Waasalam!" ("You are worried. It is finished!") projected a state of concern amongst the opposition parties in recognition of CCM's dominant position.

Throughout the month of October 1994, campaign rallies for the elder Kisauji featured Babloom as the entertainment. As with TOT, Babloom succeeded in drawing a crowd on the basis of its popularity. With a captive crowd eager for the chance to hear Babloom perform for free right there in the neighborhood, Salim Kisauji and his fellow CCM vanguard were able to disseminate their political platform and ideas, dispute the claims of his two opponents (one representing the Civic United Front, CUF, and the other representing the Tanzania Labour Party, TLP), and generate dialogue with ordinary citizens. The local setting, the fact that most people in the crowds drawn from this select area (the Northern Ngamiani ward) knew each other, enabled dialogue somewhat. Salim Kisauji always reserved time for questions and answers from the crowd. But the discursive space more often than not provided a site for contestation exploited by opposition party members who sought to disrupt the event by asking probing, sometimes insulting, questions.

The program of these rallies resembled TOT performances but for one thing: *taarab* both opened and closed the rally, thus drawing people in as well as providing them with a reward for having stayed, but Babloom only launched into its own *taarab* repertoire after first performing the JWTZ/TOT hit, "CCM Nambari Wani." In fact, some of the politicians referred to Babloom as the "TOT of Tanga"—what a shift from having been blacklisted as recently as the 1993 presidential visit, when Babloom significantly was not invited to perform! Oftentimes, the rally would end with the song "Mwanya," a song that became the campaign theme song, with Salim Kisauji appropriating the microphone from Babloom's star female lead Fatuma Kisauji (his sister) to sing the song's refrain himself.

I was often struck by the great incongruity between the meanings brought to the song by local women, on the one hand, and Salim Kisauji and his CCM colleagues on the other. As close as Salim Kisauji was to the band, it was inconceivable that he was simply unaware of the song's other meanings. As self-proclaimed defenders of the social and political order, these politicians surely would not have condoned the song in its popular interpretation, even though the message celebrated *mwanyas* and denigrated *pengos*. By local standards the song was too explicit, which lent even more significance to the TOT comparison than mere identification with CCM. That *taarab* songs are by nature multivalent, however, is commonly accepted by all. So it was enough that the politicians had their interpretation, whether or not it coincided with other interpretations. The existence of alternative interpretations did not make their interpretation any less valid.

Examination of audience reactions during the performances, however, reveals whose interpretation held sway. The fact that these were CCM-sponsored events notwithstanding, audience members tipped according to their politics of the personal and did not, by and large, get swept up in a wave of anti-opposition sentiment. The majority of people tipping, even in these CCM contexts, continued to be women, and they clearly tipped with their own agendas and not those of the CCM apparatus that had convened the occasion. Yet, although it occurred, tipping did not take place on the same scale as at typical weddings. This indicated to me a tacit recognition of the different context, even if not complete concession to it. I understand this to be the case as well with TOT performances, in which personal politics still dominate, in spite of the overarching CCM performance frame. With TOT, however, the high degree of tipping—by women, and increasingly by men—appears unaffected by overtly political contexts, because it was that to which TOT was born.[42] Babloom was not, on the other hand, born to this setting and purpose (to attract crowds of listeners to government/party-organized functions). It has merely accepted the role out of allegiance to its chairman, an allegiance strengthened by Salim Kisauji's ability to negotiate Babloom adequate compensation.

By the same token, however, perhaps it is not fair to write CCM loyalties out of the picture entirely. The elections, both at the civic level in 1994 and the national level in 1995, resulted in CCM victories. Salim Kisauji handily won his the Northern Ngamiani ward, receiving 619 votes, compared with 138 for the CUF candidate and 12 for the TLP candidate. An additional 101 spoiled votes brought the total number of votes cast to 870. The number of registered voters for the Northern Ngamiani ward was 1,291; thus, the voter turnout for the ward measured 67 percent. Similarly, the CCM presidential candidate, Benjamin Mkapa, one year later won by an overwhelming margin in an election proclaimed fair by international observers though marred by massive administrative failures in some areas and repeat elections in Dar es Salaam one week later. Interestingly, Tanga Region was one of five regions nationwide that experienced a complete CCM sweep: in every contest between CCM and opposition-party candidates, CCM won. Thus, CCM sentiment must figure in to some extent. The crowds at Salim Kisauji's campaign rallies responded well to the CCM chants and slogans. They may have come primarily to hear Babloom, but they nonetheless experienced familiar political ritual, routine, and rhetoric that had characterized everyday life since 1965 when CCM (then TANU) was installed as the sole legitimate political party. A generation has been born into the era of CCM. Shaking them of its primacy into a multiparty frame of mind will take time.

The Nationalization of Taarab

In his analysis of the differing relations between two singers, Kalikali and Mwinamila, and the Tanzanian state, Elias Songoyi concludes that "the state's reaction to the artist is not determined by the form and content of the artist's work alone; other factors—time, place, audience and personal relationships—are involved" (Songoyi 1988b, v). In his two case studies, "Coercion by the state . . . turned Kalikali to a praise-singer, while Mwinamila has increasingly become a relentless critic of the Party and Government in spite of the honours and privileges given him" (vi). Babloom Modern Taarab similarly underwent a conflicted yet shifting relationship with the Tanzanian bureaucracy. The 1991 presidential visit was the apex of its critical phase. Performance presented a site for contestation and resistance, a site protected in the name of "art." Yet the shift to multipartyism paradoxically witnessed a strengthening rather than weakening of Babloom's allegiance to CCM.

The incorporation of Babloom into the Tanga CCM apparatus parallels the incorporation of its genre, *taarab*, into CCM cultural policy. Originally excluded (except when needed) on account of its foreignness, *taarab* experienced a sudden show of support from a ruling party in need of something to assist the overhauling of its image as old and failed, like its program of Ujamaa. To the bitter dismay of groups such as Lucky Star Musical Club that had sung the party's praises for years, money was finally made available for *taarab* performers but not for those who had already given of their talents. The money—considerable amounts of it, along with new equipment and instruments from purportedly Chinese sources—was instead spent on the creation of something new that in turn would help CCM invent itself as something new: Tanzania One Theater.

TOT's tremendous popularity relates to its grounding in *taarab* traditions of *mafumbo* (hidden meanings), *mipasho* (messages), and *vishindo* (challenges). TOT added a heavy dose of *matusi* (profanity) to the tradition, eliciting both denunciation and excitement in its audiences. After taking over Tanzania's musical world by storm, TOT was decried as an unfair CCM advantage by opposition parties. In 1995, the year of the national elections, CCM began distancing itself from TOT. It publicly declared TOT an independent organization that, despite some standing ties to CCM in its leadership (likely a reference to Captain Komba's position as a member of the CCM Executive Committee), neither received funding from CCM nor was required to report to CCM on its activities.[43] I learned, however, that although the majority share of TOT was held by its own performers, it was only a majority of two percentage points, with the artists holding 51 percent of TOT's shares and CCM holding the remaining 49 percent. Also, TOT continues to rehearse at a CCM compound and benefit from CCM-purchased vehicles. Easy access to transportation enables it to leave Dar es Salaam whenever there is a hint of its popularity subsiding and tour throughout the country at minimal cost to spread the CCM message.

CCM, in the creation of TOT and the incorporation of Babloom, may have successfully appropriated the art of *taarab* from Swahili women, but I argue that it has yet to acquire the same command of its communicative potency. Although TOT has recruited great talents, acquired the latest in musical equipment, and designed fancy and expensive uniforms, it has not succeeded in producing *taarab* songs that support the politics for which it was created. Through *taarab* performance, Swahili women negotiate their disputes, contest their identities, and confront all the issues that arise in their politics of the personal. Communicative potency draws its effectiveness largely from the intimacies of social knowledge that accompany life in local communities. TOT, however, as a purported vehicle of government propaganda with the entire nation of 28 million as its target audience, is constrained against using *taarab* to sing the party's message and deride the party's opponents. According to Captain Komba, TOT cannot sing about national politics because nobody wants to hear *taarab* of that nature—they would "run away." So instead, TOT successfully derides its rival performance troupe Muungano and performs songs that accommodate local personal politics, thus

MEMBERS of the Tanzania One Theatre (TOT) dancing troupe in action on Saturday at the Vijana Social Hall.

Figure 7.6 Newspaper coverage of a competition between TOT and Muungano Cultural Troupe. *Daily News,* March 28, 1994. Courtesy of M. I. Michuzi.

continuing a long-standing *taarab* tradition of challenges, insults and affirmations.

Coda: The 1995 Presidential Visit

On January 20, 1995, President Mwinyi returned to Tanga to preside over the annual meeting of the CCM Youth League. By that point, Babloom Modern Taarab had led its CCM candidate to victory in the October 1994 civic elections and firmly established itself in the CCM fold. Once again, the Municipal Council met to decide upon the presidential program. The Regional Commissioner was Azan al-Jabry, another fan of *taarab* music, who helped promote the Magereza-Kiwira *taarab* band when he was regional commissioner of Mbeya. He requested that Babloom be included in the program and specifically asked that the song, "Kumanya Mdigo" ("To Know the Digo"; track 9 on the accompanying CD) be sung. This is a song not in Kiswahili but in Kidigo, the language of the Digo ethnic group, who are found along the Tanzanian and Kenyan coast. I was the one who sang this song, and it had become a well-known and quite popular song, a favorite of the regional commissioner.

The same disgruntled cultural officer, still smarting from the reprimands he had received the last time he was in this position, protested and tried to remind everyone of Babloom's checkered past, but the civic elections were far more memorable, and his arguments were silenced. It was decided that Babloom should sing a song in praise of the CCM Youth League first, then the Digo song. Following the *taarab* would be some praise poetry and then the opening speeches of the conference.

The day arrived, and I was filled with apprehension and excitement at the thought of singing for a head of state. My fellow band members were less than enthused, one saying that, "When the big men call, you must go." For me, this was a tremendous honor. For them, it was another low-paying government gig. In comparing our reactions, band members pointed to the example of Lucky Star Musical Club that had had many such "honors," many presidential performances, but now was a defunct band reliant on borrowed instruments for the few performances it gets. When I then asked why they were doing it, someone responded, "Shauri ya shida. Tutafanyaje?" (Because of hardship. What else can we do?). "Don't you Americans say, 'If you can't beat them, join them?'"

The band set up and tested the instruments; then we all waited for the presidential arrival. When he entered the hall, the band played "CCM Nambari Wani" as everyone stood and applauded. Then when everyone had settled in his or her seat, including President Mwinyi, the band sang

its newly composed song praising the CCM Youth League—my apprehension growing with each passing verse. Finally, the song ended, and
I prepared myself for what was to come. As I stood to walk over to the
microphone, the disgruntled cultural officer performed his long-awaited
revenge. He ran over to the microphone, beat me to it, and to the surprise of everyone aware of the planned program, announced the start
of the poetry. It was an effective *coup d'état*. This was a very important
performance, and he knew too well that no one would dare introduce
an embarrassing break in the president's presence to contradict him. The
show had to go on, my song having been successfully eliminated.

Defeated in the Municipal Council meeting and having suffered the
veto of his opinion by the regional commissioner himself, this cultural
officer stole what measure of self-importance he could by cutting the
song from the approved program. In his actions, he reasserted his jurisdiction over culture and arts in defiance of the City Council and regional
commissioner (also denying me my once-in-a-lifetime opportunity to
sing for a head of state). He provides one final example of the contested
imaginary of Tanzania, of the competing interests within and between
the many constituencies that together constitute this nation-state.

8

CONCLUSION: CULTURAL POLICY
BY AND FOR THE PEOPLE

The major change I have made is to set up an entirely new Ministry: the Ministry of National Culture and Youth. I have done this
because I believe that its culture is the essence and spirit of any
nation. A country which lacks its own culture is no more than a
collection of people without the spirit which makes them a nation. Of the crimes of colonialism there is none worse than the
attempt to make us believe we had no indigenous culture of our
own, or that what we did have was worthless—something of
which we should be ashamed, instead of a source of pride.
—Julius Nyerere to Parliament, December 10, 1962

Setting aside the stated objectives that Culture is the backbone
and Spirit of the Nation, the lack of cultural direction in the Nation is the source of these problems.
—"Cultural Policy Recommendations," Workshop on Cultural
Policy, 1995, Morogoro

It was my sixth attempt to interview Mr. Godwin Kaduma, the director
of arts and national language in the Ministry of Education and Culture
and highest-ranking official in the Culture Division of the ministry. He
was often away, traveling around the country and abroad, and I had
consistently missed him during my previous visits to Dar es Salaam. But
this time I had hope. Just last week, the office staff had informed me
that he was expected back in the office earlier this week. As I made my
way up the stairwell in the tired old building sorely in need of paint and
repair that serves as Culture's headquarters, I ran into a man in the hallway who, in answer to my question, confirmed that the director was
indeed in that day. He directed me to Mr. Kaduma's office and told me
to enter and wait; he would inform the director of my presence. I found
the office, door ajar, empty. Hesitantly, I entered and took a seat opposite the director's desk. After ten minutes, the man I had met in the

hallway reappeared and stood in the doorway. I queried, "Did you find the director?" "Yes," he responded. I thanked him and asked, "Is he willing to meet with me?" "Yes," he responded. We then contemplated each other in silence for several minutes—a silence that stretched on and on until finally I asked, "Will he be coming soon?" "He is here now," was the response, and Mr. Kaduma then took his seat opposite me on the other side of the desk.

Godwin Kaduma is an actor by training. Before accepting his position at the ministry, he taught on the faculty of Theatre Arts at the University of Dar es Salaam and among his many credits appeared as the male lead in *Harusi ya Mariamu*, which won the award for best short film at the 1985 Pan-African Film Festival (FESPACO). Perhaps he withheld his identity and assumed another role at first in order to evaluate me—an easy enough strategy for an actor. Whatever the case may be, after I had recovered from my initial confusion, we proceeded with the interview. I prefaced it by explaining the nature of my research, emphasizing my interest and background reading in Tanzanian cultural policy. In answer to my question of what cultural vision he held for the country and how that might differ from those advanced by his predecessors, he replied: "Tanzanian national culture is whatever Tanzanians want it to be." Again confused by this man, I tried to reconcile this statement with the many policy documents I had read outlining very precise cultural engineering goals and objectives. I referred to one of them, yet Mr. Kaduma merely repeated once again (in a tone of resignation?): "Tanzanian national culture is whatever Tanzanians want it to be."[1]

* * *

In his 1995 article entitled "Blurred Boundaries," Akhil Gupta makes the following observation:

> Research on the state, with its focus on large-scale structures, epochal events, major politics, and "important" people, . . . has failed to illuminate the quotidian practices . . . of bureaucrats that tell us about the effects of the state on the everyday lives of rural people. Surprisingly little research has been conducted in the small towns . . . where a large number of state officials, constituting the broad base of the bureaucratic pyramid, live and work—the village-level workers, land record keepers, elementary school teachers, agricultural extension agents, the staff of the civil hospital, and others. This is the site where the majority of people in a rural and agricultural country such as India come into contact with "the state," and this is where many of their images of the state are forged. (Gupta 1995, 376)

Although problematic for perpetuating clear distinctions between "the state" and "the people," Gupta nevertheless makes the important point that for all the theoretical advances recently made in the study of nationalism, remarkably little attention has been paid to the lived practices involved in the construction or "imagining" (Anderson 1989) of nation-states. We require not a shift in focus from official discourse to local actions, but a widening of focus that can accommodate the interplay between the two. Attention to the daily interactions of state agents—who may or may not always align themselves with state interests—with the local citizens they ostensibly serve offers at least two theoretical advantages. First, it can alleviate reigning tendencies to view a state as omnipotent and coherent by showing the tremendous amount of negotiation that occurs on a regular basis and the contradiction inherent in its nature. Second, it can highlight methods and strategies utilized by government and nongovernment agents alike in these negotiations.

In this book, I have examined official and unofficial renderings of Tanzanian national culture and how its ideological underpinnings are multiple, shifting, and always subject to negotiation. State-sponsored musicians and local-level cultural officers, like the agricultural extension workers and land record keepers described by Gupta, exist at the lowest level of the governmental bureaucratic pyramid in Tanzania. Yet they have been charged with the rhetorically significant task of shaping the cultural imaginary of the nation, of developing a national culture. Intrigued by processes of selecting and defining what constitutes "Tanzanian National Culture," I went to Tanzania to compare and contrast local theories and practices of musical performance with those of state agents/agencies invested with the authority to create and, when necessary, invent, Tanzanian Culture, the rhetorical cornerstone for the imagined Tanzanian nation-state. This road of inquiry unearthed a profoundly dialectical process quite distinct from that proposed by Hobsbawm, Ranger, and Anderson, who restrict the power and inspiration for invention to elites (be they political, cultural, or socioeconomic elites) and trace exclusively top-down impositions of invented tradition that substantiate, legitimize, and reinforce the social order. In Tanzania, on the contrary, top-down articulations and presentations met only mild public reception and proved ineffectual in legitimizing the state.

Over the course of my three years working with regional and district cultural officers and musicians from both private and state-sponsored bands in Tanga, I witnessed the negotiation and selective application of principles deemed nationalist by cultural officers and the negotiation and selective adoption—in some cases outright rejection—of these principles by musicians. Immediately apparent was the intensely permeable and constantly elusive boundary between supposed state agents and local citizens. Cultural officers and state-sponsored musicians do not always see themselves as agents of "the state" just as private musicians do not always define themselves in opposition to "the state." Also obvious was the dialogic nature of these interactions, the constant give-and-take, and the absence of clear power differentials between those involved.

My purposes in bringing this ethnography to a close are fourfold: first, to propose an understanding of national identities as rooted in shifting imaginaries—a fundamentally fluid and fundamentally dialogic take on national identity formation not unlike identity formation in individuals who are constantly at work to define themselves; second, to call attention to media other than print media—in this case, musical performance—as crucial to the process of imagining a nation; third, to further the critique voiced by other scholars (Nugent 1994; Gupta 1995; Herzfeld 1997; Shore and Wright 1997; Mitchell 1999) of the theoretical distinction between state and society perpetuated in the literature on nationalism; and, finally, to advance a performative understanding of power. I do so by way of a focus on *taarab,* the genre of sung Swahili poetry that inserted itself into Tanzanian cultural policy through popular force and interrupted a nationalist discourse that continually tripped and fell over its unruly citizenry.

It was not without reason that Mr. Kaduma insisted, "Tanzanian national culture is whatever Tanzanians want it to be."

Tanzania as Postcolony and Postsocialist State

Identifying the "postcolony" as both a specific historical trajectory and a system of signs, Achille Mbembe posits that "the postcolonial relationship [between state power and target populations] is not primarily a relationship of resistance or collaboration but can best be characterised as illicit cohabitation" (Mbembe 1992, 4). A postcolony, Tanzania reflects many of the characteristics delineated by Mbembe. It is also, however, a postsocialist state still racked by the all-encompassing, parasitic bureaucracy to which some theorists attribute the failure of its experiment with socialism.

As reviewed in chapter 1, reigning theories of nationalism and nation-building shed little light on heterogeneous modern states and postcolonies. Gellner, Hobsbawm, and Anderson share theoretical grounding in European-derived assumptions about the homogeneous nature of nation-states. Such assumptions do not find resonance in cases like Tanzania's, where political boundaries were arbitrarily defined and where more than 120 ethnic groups maintain their respective identities. Nor do they apply to less obviously diverse nations, for cultural homogeneity is by and large a theoretical delusion. In Tanzania, moreover, the experience of socialism has lent added layers of ideology and practice (some borrowed from fellow socialist nations like China, others generated from within) that transmuted its nationalizing agenda. Anderson's model assumes capitalism as essential to the universal nationalism he describes, thus striking yet another chord of dissonance with the case presented here. The combination of being both postcolonial and postsocialist forces new theoretical renderings of nation-states, of which this book is but a beginning.

I selected cultural production as my entry into the theories and practices involved in constructing the nation because of the richness of the material, the intensity of involvement at both local and national levels, and its rhetorical importance. When Julius Nyerere inaugurated the Ministry of Culture, he declared culture as "the essence and spirit of any nation. A country which lacks its own culture is no more than a collection of people without the spirit which makes them a nation" (Ministry of National Culture and Youth, n.d., 3). With this statement, he initiated a movement that would span the following two decades.

This movement, an attempted cultural revolution, was directed by an ostensibly new cultural apparatus that, upon closer inspection, proved to be the scion of colonialism glossed in new socialist labels. Colonialism bequeathed both ideological and structural components to the "new" ministry. Concern with *selectivity* and concern with *control* via an extensive and extractive network of fees, licenses, permits, levies, and taxes— to be later reinforced with stamp duties, mandatory contributions to various committees, and group constitutions— constitute the links that traverse colonial and postcolonial histories into the present. Nevertheless, despite these elements of continuity, changing external and internal conditions forced shifts in conceptualizations of the nation that consequently forced shifts in the practices of cultural production.

A Shifting Imaginary

In her analysis of Swiss political ritual, Regina Bendix comments that "Anderson examines the spread of nationalist thinking but does not fully explore how, for how long, and by whom such thinking is experienced" (Bendix 1992, 768). By virtue of their choice of terms, Hobsbawm and Ranger denude "invented traditions" of the possibility—nay, inevitability—of change, as does Anderson of "imagined communities." Their use of the past tense evokes a sense of finality, a sense of completed products and processes. Benefit could be derived from the processual turn in anthropology, which forced recognition of the constancy of change and the fallacy of assuming stasis as the norm, as well as from the critical rejection of viewing social constructions as bounded, both in time and space. Liisa Malkki's (1995) work among Hutu refugees, for example, demonstrates all too clearly how Hutu national consciousness spills across borders and time periods, and how it can be nurtured and sustained even in the absence of a state structure. Moreover, the conception of something being invented/imagined at the upper echelons of the power structure to be summarily handed down for absorption and adoption by lower ranks denies the extent of contestation, contradiction, and negotiation that certainly occurs. It refuses recognition of power held in other-than-elite quarters, power that exists even if constrained by structural factors. Transmission models such as these turn a blind eye and deaf ear to the dialectics of inventing traditions and imagining nations.

These points are clearly demonstrated in the data from Tanzania. Official imaginings of the nation have fluctuated dramatically over time *in response to* public reaction or lack thereof. In analyzing the political derision underlying vulgar humor directed toward the state in Cameroon and Togo, Mbembe explores the dialectics of interaction between state and state subjects in the postcolony but—like Bourdieu and the state-centric theorists surveyed in chapter 1—attributes more power to the state than I suggest is the case in Tanzania. Mbembe writes, "The signs, vocabulary and narratives that it produces are not meant merely to be symbols; they are officially invested with a surplus of meanings which are not negotiable and which one is officially forbidden to depart from or challenge" (1992, 4). In the same vein, Bourdieu asserts, "It is in the realm of symbolic production that the grip of the state is felt most powerfully" (1999, 55). Symbolic/cultural hegemony may have been an objective to which Tanzanian bureaucrats aspired, but if so, it is one they failed to achieve.

I therefore propose a change in theoretical focus and terminology. Rather than furthering our fascination with "imagined communities" or "imagined nations," phrases that betray a finality not reflected in real life, I suggest we concern ourselves instead with "national imaginaries": the multiple and often contradictory layers and fragments of ideology that underlie continually shifting conceptions of any given nation. In reviewing the shifts that occurred in Tanzanian cultural production (specifically in the realm of musical practice), we see quite clearly how the Tanzanian national imaginary is a living, breathing entity that rejects codification, universalism, and essentialism. It is multivalent, multivocal, polyphonic—perhaps even cacophonous.

Polyphonic Politics: Different Musics for Different Nationalisms

Musical performance proves to be a dominant domain of cultural production and contestation in Tanzania—one rarely, if ever, divorced from politics. In chapters 3 and 4, we explored the Tanzanian soundscape getting but a taste of the tremendous variety of musical practices actively pursued by different communities and social strata and how they invariably are related to political processes of one kind or another. Analysis of any one of these many genres—*ngoma, dansi, kwaya, taarab*—could result in a separate book. My coverage here has been necessarily incomplete because of my concern to evaluate how the genres jointly constitute multiple layers of musical discourse and action that are exploited differentially by agents in various social and political contexts.

All too often music is ignored or deemed insubstantial by analysts seeking to understand the internal dynamics of nationalism and the maintenance of state power. One notable exception is Thomas Turino's ethnography on musical nationalism in Zimbabwe. Turino's analysis highlights how Zimbabwean musical forms articulate with ideologies of cosmopolitanism, global economic flows, and transnational movements, and how black elites have pursued a version of nationalism embedded in these same modernist-capitalist cosmopolitan concerns (Turino 2000). Official nationalism in Zimbabwe, in keeping with the cosmopolitan agenda, has sought inspiration primarily from external forces (Anderson defines "official nationalism" as "something emanating from the state, and serving the interests of the state first and foremost" [1989, 145]). The orientation, timing (Zimbabwe acquired its independence in 1980), and historical circumstances (independence was achieved only after a fourteen-year guerrilla war) surrounding cultural production in that case present several interesting points of comparison with Tanzania. For one, it developed a cultural apparatus (Ministry of Culture, National Arts Council, National Dance Company, licenses and fees) almost identical to that of Tanzania (raising the question of how programmatic this structure has become among postcolonial states). But Zimbabwean music, unlike Tanzanian music, has entered a global worldbeat market, and thus furthered the modernist-capitalist cosmopolitan objectives of elite culture producers.

The Tanzanian case demonstrates the high degree to which musical performance is implicated in nationalist endeavors. Indeed, in musical performance one locates the efforts of agents across the Tanzanian social spectrum—elite and non-elite alike—to negotiate, define, and contest that which constitutes their nation. Examination of when and how musical practices coincide with or interrupt official ideologies reveals the strategic shifts that characterize nationalist projects. *Ngoma* associations proved essential to pre-independence nationalist projects in distributing and disseminating political ideas and actions. *Ngoma* songs—widely used for the purposes of communicating criticism, insults, and ulterior messages—could communicate political messages, sometimes overtly yet more commonly camouflaged in the subtle wordplay and metaphors typical of the genre. Moreover, because dance groups nurtured and maintained close affiliations with groups in other cities, *ngoma* networks offered ready pools of members for the emerging Tanganyika African National Union and a highly effective vehicle for spreading nationalist consciousness throughout the territory.

Dansi, the "urban jazz" pulsing in city bars and dance halls, offered a cultural route to social parity with colonizers for Tanganyikans and Zanzibaris making a determined bid for independence. It represented (in both popular and scholarly discourse) a genre of change and modernity in contrast to purportedly frozen-in-tradition *ngoma.* One can see why the heavily amplified montage of musical elements as far-ranging as Western ballroom dancing, Afro-Cuban rhythms, and Congolese guitar style that jointly constitute *dansi* when juxtaposed with the more acoustic, drum-dominated, ritually oriented *ngoma* might lend itself to such interpretations at first glance and listening, but further investigation reveals that the mutability, adaptability, and innovative borrowing of *dansi* prove equally characteristic of *ngoma. Ngoma* and *dansi,* both born of a mutual aesthetic for intertextuality, incessant borrowing, and continual innovation, represent not two poles but two neighboring points on the spectrum of Tanzanian musical practice. More important for our purposes here, these two genres share distinction as potent resources for articulating political sentiment and enacting political activity in colonial and postcolonial Tanzania. To sum up, pre-independence nationalism relied on *ngoma* and *dansi* in multiple ways: by voicing anticolonial sentiment through song, by providing preexisting networks for the dissemination of political ideas and strategies, by attracting new members for the movement, by offering covert venues for political organization and education, and by symbolic appropriation of the trappings of rule and "civilization."

Ngoma, as we saw in chapter 6, continued to carry great political significance in the context of independent Tanzania. Perhaps because of the important role music played in the context of the struggle for freedom, post-independence official discourse privileged music and dance in its nationalist project from very early on. President Nyerere established the Ministry of National Culture and Youth with the words, "When we were at school we were taught to sing the songs of the European. How many of us were taught the songs of the Wanyamwezi or the Wahehe? Many of us have learnt to dance the 'rumba' or the 'chachacha' to rock-and-roll and to 'twist' and even to dance the 'waltz' and the 'foxtrot.' . . . How many Africans in Tanganyika, particularly among the educated, can play the African drums?" (Nyerere 1962, 20–21).

In a conscious attempt, therefore, to revive and recuperate local African culture, *ngoma* was selected as the musical form of nationalist choice. Although *ngoma* and *dansi* both had played significant roles in the pre-independence nationalist movement, they were valued differently after independence by culture-brokers who, taking Nyerere's cue, now viewed *dansi* as tainted and corrupted by Western influences. Early policy documents overtly privileged *ngoma* over all other musical forms. It was essentialized as "authentic" and as "tradition"—a safe musical refuge in what was suddenly deemed an unwelcome onslaught of foreign musical influences. One ministry document argued that "[t]he indiscriminate spread of European musical values brought striking alterations and deformations to the character of indigenous music in Tanzania" (Ministry of National Culture and Youth, n.d., 14–15). These stated concerns with authenticity, with preservation, and with the rejection of foreign influence resulted in the objectification of culture (Handler 1988) in Tanzania, an effect common to nationalist projects around the world.

Ngoma thus suited post-independence nationalism in a way that both *dansi* and *taarab* did not. Although pre-independence nationalism had positively evaluated *dansi* as representative of modernity, this very modernity and attendant Westernization made it undesirable in the newly independent Tanzania. *Taarab,* a genre that played a less obvious political role on the mainland in the years leading up to independence, met a similar assessment. Although heralded as the national music of Zanzibar, on the mainland *taarab* fell subject to the same negative "foreign" categorization—in this case Arab rather than European—as *dansi.* Since the Ministry's inception, *taarab* had been relegated to the *muziki wa nje* ("foreign music") category in cultural policy documents alongside brass bands, choirs, and *dansi.* Even though *taarab* is a wholly indigenous, uniquely coastal East African musical form, and is no less Swahili and no more polyglot than the national language of Kiswahili, *taarab* failed to measure up to nationalists' conceptions of Tanzanian Culture. Thus, *taarab* and *dansi* were both categorically excluded from mainland cultural policy—this despite their continued popularity and performance in cities and communities throughout the country for state-sponsored events and by state-sponsored as well as private bands. The famous *taarab* bands Black Star Musical Club and Lucky Star Musical Club from Tanga, for instance, were regularly called upon to perform for visiting dignitaries and official dinners. Lucky Star, with its famous singer Shakila Said, especially served in this capacity during the 1970s and 1980s, performing for foreign presidents and dignitaries, as well as countless state functions. Performance troupes associated with the National Service Army (JKT) and Prison Authority have performed *taarab* for decades, while the Organization of Tanzanian Trade Unions (OTTU), the

Dar es Salaam Development Corporation (DDC), the CCM Youth League (Umoja wa Vijana), the National Army (JWTZ), and Dar es Salaam Police Force are but a few of the government arms that established *dansi* bands, some of which remain hugely popular today. Thus we find another of the many layers of contradiction between official discourse and cultural practice and between different sectors of "the state": its theoreticians and its practitioners.

Clearly sacrificed in practice, official concern with authenticity and tradition was not wholly consistent at the ideological level either. The key symbolic markers of national identity encompassed a national language (Kiswahili), national anthem ("Mungu Ibariki Africa"), national holidays, national monuments, a national *ngoma* troupe, and national arts and language competitions—all of these overseen and organized by the Ministry of Culture. The national anthem, however, hailed from South Africa, the national *ngoma* troupe performed acrobatics learned in China, and the national arts competitions included a *kwaya* competition—*kwaya* being the musical consequence of interaction with Western Christianity. Thus despite considerable rhetoric to the contrary, it was not the perceived "indigenousness" of something that rendered it acceptable to official post-independent nationalism, but how well it fit with reigning political paradigms and objectives. Alignment with China, one of Tanzania's most generous patrons, and with the continued fight against colonialism in South Africa, allowed for some bending of the authenticity mandate that otherwise dominated Tanzanian cultural policy at the time.

Traditionalism was soon replaced, however, with a new ideological template: socialism. In 1967, when the Arusha Declaration inaugurated Ujamaa socialism, the national imaginary shifted dramatically to adopt a socialist tone and taint. Culture producers in the ministry found increasing resonance in socialist cultural philosophy as articulated by Frantz Fanon, Bertolt Brecht, and Ernst Fischer. A new standard was applied to customs under consideration for inclusion in the National Culture: did they support and reinforce the development of socialist society? Art steeped in capitalist logic was spurned as contaminating and antithetical to the national project. By 1974, the original vision of national culture as a collection of authentic customs was abandoned and replaced by the idea that "the indigenous culture of the peoples of Tanzania has meaning only if it has place in the Tanzanian reality [i.e., socialist reality] of today and . . . tomorrow" (Mbughuni and Ruhumbika 1974, 280). *Ngoma,* cultural officers explained to me, were essentially communal, participatory, authentic, and populist, and therefore an ideal form of indigenous socialist art. This process of recasting indigenous Tanzanian music as inherently socialist music paralleled Nyerere's economic and political programs, which sought a return to a theorized authentic, indigenous communalism, the proto-socialism of Ujamaa. Once again, *dansi* and *taarab,* being associated with elites (Western and Arab respectively), fell short of official approval.

Yet even the celebrated *ngoma* fell subject to official tinkering. While it was now privileged not so much for its perceived indigenousness as for its perceived innate socialist qualities, some *ngoma* were nevertheless deemed more socialist than others. So cultural officers, state-sponsored musicians, and teachers at the National College of Arts began altering *ngoma* performance to better fulfill, embody, and enact socialist objectives. Song lyrics about harvesting and puberty rituals were replaced with lyrics praising the party, its leaders, and socialism more generally. The majority of lyrics were translated from their original languages into the national language of Kiswahili—a notable process of standardization and cultural centralization in a country with more than a hundred languages. Moreover, in keeping with the state's gender-equity objectives, many gender-specific *ngoma* were re-choreographed to include both genders. As described in chapter 6, uniformity of movement, uniformity of dress, synchronization, linear formations, and the repression of improvisation all contributed to a new aesthetic premised upon Tanzanian socialism.

The Nationalization of Taarab

As with other socialist experiments elsewhere in the world, however, Tanzania's Ujamaa program could not sustain itself. President Julius Nyerere's villagization program failed to produce the anticipated agricultural revolution that would make Tanzania self-reliant. Instead, the program unleashed a decade of economic crisis and spiraling decline (see chapters 2 and 7) and, after a drawn-out battle in the early 1980s with the IMF and World Bank over structural adjustment and conditional aid, Nyerere conceded that change was inevitable. The Second Phase government under Ali Hassan Mwinyi began liberalizing the economy and in July 1992 inaugurated political pluralism, officially ending Tanzania's engagement with socialism.

This shift in official economic and political paradigms not surprisingly evoked a parallel shift in cultural ones. This is no better exemplified than in the sudden incorporation of *taarab* into mainland cultural policy the same year—1992—and same month—July—that political liberalization went into effect. Originally excluded on account of its misconstrued foreignness, *taarab* experienced a sudden show of support from CCM when, in the transition toward multiparty democracy, it found itself in need of a new image, and the popularity of the genre was impossible to deny. To the bitterness of *taarab* bands like Lucky Star that had sung the party's praises for years, money rumored to have Chinese origins was lavishly spent in 1992 on the creation of TOT (Tanzania One Theatre), the CCM-sponsored cultural troupe whose chief attraction would be *taarab* performance. As revealed in chapter 7, TOT was billed as "CCM's secret weapon" for the upcoming 1995 multiparty elections and publicly launched in August 1992. Although TOT would later distance itself from CCM (partly in response to cries of favoritism and unfair distribution of cultural resources from opposition parties), it has retained links—sometimes acknowledged, sometimes unacknowledged—to the ruling party.

Gellner, Anderson, Hobsbawm and Ranger, Bourdieu, and Mbembe have all assumed the success of state constructions with little regard to the extent of their acceptance by the citizenry. Their models discount the dialogic nature of nationalism exposed so plainly here. For *taarab* moved from being a cultural outsider (in theory but not in practice) to center stage (in both theory and practice). Its history illuminates the intimate relations between culture and politics in Tanzania and confirms a legacy of music in the service of nationalist endeavors. Yet its ultimate incorporation speaks more importantly to the dialogic nature of nationalism, for it was integrated largely as an official response to its no longer deniable popularity. By the time the government embraced *taarab,* this musical genre had spread from coastal points of origin throughout the Tanzanian mainland and beyond to Kenya, Burundi, the Comoros, Oman, and the United Arab Emirates.

Moreover, the possibility that this form of music—a known vehicle for alternate discourses—could easily turn a critical eye or voice on party politics surely was not lost on mainland party officials. The government radio station RTD, which for years had played all varieties of music, including *ngoma, dansi, kwaya,* and *taarab,* frequently censured *taarab* songs for perceived disloyalty to the state, whether imagined or real. The following excerpt from a song by Babloom, for example, was barred from radio broadcast in 1991 when rumors of impending political liberalization were circulating with increased intensity. One former Ministry official speculated that the censorship committee interpreted it as a rejection of President Mwinyi and an acceptance of opposition parties:

Mkomesheni ("Make Him Stop Harassing Me")—excerpt
Khalid Akida and Seif Kassim Kisauji, Babloom Modern Taarab, Tanga

Mkomesheni akome, Mie sinijuejue	Make him stop harassing me. He should forget about me.
Sababu yani niseme, Walimwengu atambue	Why should I give my reasons for the world to know?

Mwengine naatazame, Atayewezana naye	Let him look for someone else who can suffer his behavior.
- - -	- - -
Iwapo nilikosea, Kumfanya wangu yeye	Even though I erred to make him mine,
Nimekwisha jikosoa, Kheri niwe mbali naye	I have already corrected my mistake.
Mapenzi hajayajua, Mwuacheni ajishaue	Better I be far away from him.
	He doesn't understand love. Let him boast all he wants.

If subversive readings could be found within this love song, what then of songs such as "Nahodha" ("Captain"), performed by the National Service Army *taarab* band, that questions why captains of sea vessels sit at the back (track 11 on the accompanying CD). Like the song "Mwanya" ("Attractive Gap between the Front Teeth"), "Nahodha" can bear multiple meanings, from a critique of political leaders who are not taking an active role in leading their citizens to a critique of sodomy.

Nahodha ("Captain")—excerpt
Ali Mtoto Seif and Elizabeth Sijila, Jeshi la Kujenga Taifa (JKT) Taarab, Dar es Salaam

Hayupo asoyajua, Haya ntayoyasema	There isn't anyone who doesn't know what I am about to say.
Vyombo vya kusafiria, Huenda mbele daima	Vehicles for travel always move forward.
Nahodha twategemea, Awe mbele akinema	We hope that the captain will be in front to steer.
Manahodha wa mashua, Kwa nini wakae nyuma?	Captains of boats—why should they sit at the back?
- - -	- - -
Manahodha wa mashua, Na ngarawa mnadhima	Captains of boats and sailboats cause us trouble.
Sukani mwashikilia, Na hali mkiwa nyuma	You hold the tiller while you are at the back.
Ajali ikitokea, Nani ajibu lawama?	If an accident occurs, who will respond to the blame?
- - -	- - -
Nahodha nakushauri, Uwe mbele sio nyuma	Captain, I advise you to be in front, not at the back.
Ndipo mimi nitakiri, Kuwa safari salama	Only there will I agree that the journey will be safe.
Bila hivyo sisafiri, Naichelea zahama	Without this, I will not travel. I am afraid of distress.

Thus, while in chapter 2 I discuss the conflation of Swahilization and Tanzanian state formation, I later reveal how selective and arbitrary this process proved to be. Some aspects of Swahili culture were deemed "national" while others were scorned and rejected for their foreignness. It may have been officially desirable to embrace the Swahili language, Swa-

hili poetry, and certain other things Swahili in the early years of independence, but not the genre of music most identified with Swahili
coastal regions, namely, *taarab*. One can only suspect that the obvious
musical influences from Middle Eastern and Indian sources struck a
sharp dissonance with the Afrocentrism of post-independence nationalism. When large numbers of Tanzanians expressed their musical taste
for *taarab*, however, raising the genre's popularity to a previously un-
imagined degree, the national imaginary shifted—if uncomfortably and
belatedly—to incorporate it.

Tanzanian National Culture in the Age of Privatization and Political Pluralism

As entrant after entrant in the 1992 National Arts and Language Competitions performed their collective visions of Tanzanian national culture, they brought the nation into being. Their performances materialized the ideologies espoused by government officials. Yet, as revealed in
chapter 6, the nation they brought into being was disjunctive, fragmented, and internally contradictory. This is not surprising, given that
its ideological underpinnings are also disjunctive, fragmented, and internally contradictory. Ethnic identities that in any other context would
have evoked official disapproval were given free reign, heightened, and
ultimately essentialized through certain performative choices (e.g., costumes, props, rhythms, dance movements, and language utilized in song
lyrics). The Union, extolled and jealously guarded in official rhetoric,
received scant attention here: only one out of eighteen *ngoma* performed
in competition hailed from the islands. Mainland identities thus were
consolidated at the expense of a superseding national identity—Tanzanian—while Zanzibar identities were temporarily allowed to disappear
from cultural view. In short, however much Culture officials may have
wished to reinforce key tenets of 1990s Tanzanian nationalism, such as
its lingering commitment to socialism (in a social and philosophical if
no longer economic or political sense), its commitment to the Union,
its commitment to national solidarity through Tanzanian identification
over subnational, ethnic identifications, and its rejection of foreign cultural imperialism, the final outcome fell considerably short of these
goals.

Ideological warfare between capitalism and socialism continues in the
domain of culture despite supposedly clear capitalist/democratic victories elsewhere. It is waged over the creative acts of artists and musicians
who are castigated for falling prey to profit motives yet abused by a parasitic bureaucracy that demands art and music without compensation be-

yond rhetorical praise. Although Songoyi, Mlama, Halimoja, and other local observers continue to lament the prostitution of the arts to capitalist profit, it is in fact the private sector that supports the arts in the wake of dying parastatal organizations. The Tanzanian soundscape has undergone a major move toward privatization. In the past, most if not all bands were supported by one government agency or another: OTTU (Organization of Tanzanian Trade Unions), Vijana Jazz (CCM Youth League), DDC Mlimani Park (Dar es Salaam Development Corporation), JKT (National Service Army), BIMA (National Insurance Company), Urafiki (a nationalized textile mill). Some of these bands no longer exist, having suffered extinction along with the demise of the economy in general and the demise of government parastatals in particular. Those that have survived, however, have just barely done so. Some bands have been told by their government sponsors that they must now become self-reliant (a new use of an old rhetorical argument) and cease to rely on government assistance.[2] With the notable exception of TOT, government bands have fallen into disrepair: their equipment is outdated, and they find it difficult to compete with the increasing number of private bands that now fill the nightclubs of Dar es Salaam. Table 8.1 presents a list of the major government-sponsored and private bands in the Dar es Salaam area from the 1970s to the 1990s, categorized according to genre and marked with an asterisk if no longer in existence. (Note how the greater number of *ngoma* groups, as compared to *dansi* and *taarab*, continue to be sponsored by the government.)[3]

Swahilization, traditionalism, socialism, and privatization constitute four processes that have influenced renderings of Tanzanian National Culture. A fifth process forced yet another shift in the national imaginary: the emergence of political pluralism. Whereas national identity previously had been commensurate with allegiance to CCM, after 1992 it suddenly became necessary to redefine national identity (at least os-

Table 8.1 Musical Groups in Dar es Salaam—An Incomplete List Covering the 1970s–1992

Genre	Government-Sponsored (Sponsoring Agency)	Private
Dansi	DDC Mlimani Park (Dar es Salaam Development Corp.)	Afro-70 Band
	JKT Kimbunga (National Service Army)	Bantu Group
	JWTZ (Tanzania People's Defense Forces)	Bicco Stars Band
	Magereza Jazz Band (Prison Authority)	Dar International
	National Service Band	Diamond Sound
	OTTU Jazz (Organization of Tanzanian Trade Unions; originally NUTA until 1977, then JUWATA before becoming OTTU)	Kilimanjaro Band
		Kilimanjaro Connection
		King Kiki Double O
	Polisi Jazz (Dar es Salaam Police Force)	Mawenzi Stars

Table 8.1 *(continued)*

Genre	Government-Sponsored (Sponsoring Agency)	Private
Dansi (cont'd)	Vijana Jazz Band (*Umoja wa Vijana,* CCM Youth League) *Bandari (Dar es Salaam Port Authority) *BIMA (National Insurance Corporation) *Dar International Airport (Dar International Airport) *Kimulimuli Band (JWTZ) *Mwenge Jazz Band also (also JWTZ) *Reli (Tanzania Railway Authority) *UDA Jazz Band (Usafiri Dar es Salaam, the Dar es Salaam Transport Authority) *Urafiki Jazz Band (Urafiki Textile Mill) *Washirika TZ Stars (Cooperative Union of Tanzania)	Orchestra Maquis Original Orchestra Matimila Shikamoo Jazz Band Tanzanite Band Tatu Nane Zaita Muzika *Chezimba Jazz Band *Dar es Salaam Jazz Band *Kilwa Jazz Band *Lego Stars *M.C.A. International Band *MK Beats *MK Group *MK Sounds *National Panasonic Sounds *Ngorongoro Heroes Band *Orchestra Continental *Orchestra Benebene *Orchestra Makassy *Orchestra Safari Sound *Orchestra Toma Toma *Njohole Jazz Band *Sambulumaa Band *UK Revolution *Western Jazz Band
Taarab	JKT (National Service Army) JWTZ (Tanzania People's Defense Forces) Magereza (Prison Authority) Tanzania One Theatre (CCM) *BIMA (National Insurance Corporation) *DDC-Kibisa (Dar es Salaam Development Corporation) *Dar Nyota Theatre Troup (CCM)	All Stars Modern *Taarab* Al-Watan Musical Club Babloom Modern Taarab Dhamira Egyptian Musical Club: Mamesh Mandela Theatre Troupe Muungano Cultural Troupe Nia Njema *New Extra *Yemen *Young Stars *Makutano Cultural Troupe
Ngoma	Amana Cultural Troupe (CCM, Amana Branch) DDC-Kibisa Ngoma Troup (Dar es Salaam Development Corp.) JKT National Service (National Service Army) National Ngoma Troupe (Ministry of Education and Culture) Tanzania One Theatre (CCM) Village Museum (Ministry of Education and Culture) Wazazi Cultural Troupe (CCM Parents Association)	Mandela Theatre Troupe Mask Dancing Troupe Muungano Cultural Troupe Pachoto Group *Makutano Cultural Troupe

* The asterisk indicates the band no longer exists.

tensibly) as something broader and more inclusive. It remains to be seen how this new process will be accommodated in a multiparty Tanzania still ruled by CCM. The continued strength and dominance of CCM makes it unlikely that the imaginary will need to undergo serious modifications until opposition parties have succeeded in building for themselves greater positions of strength. As illustrated in the material from KIUBATA's preparations for the national competitions, however, public sensitivity to pluralism has already taken root, as evidenced by the choice to sing "Culture builds the nation" in lieu of "CCM builds the nation."

Music and Politics

Equal to my concern with the Tanzanian imaginary is my concern to document the role of musical performance in the service of politics. From its role in parodying colonial authority in Beni, disseminating political consciousness through *ngoma* networks, supporting the powers that be through praise-songs, or fomenting dissent through songs of criticism, music is undeniably and irrevocably implicated in the practice of politics. On another level of politics, namely, Swahili women's politics of the personal, *taarab* provides a mode of political maneuvering that enables subtle and nuanced plays of power. Chapter 4 highlighted the use of *taarab* poetry and performance as a forum for political action, for the construction and contestation of social identities, and for communicating the otherwise incommunicable. This latent power in *taarab* would be misconstrued if interpreted as relating exclusively to the realm of coastal women's wedding celebrations. Its communicative potency and capacity to mask intentions, hide ulterior messages, and hold multiple meanings for different agents in different contexts makes it a powerful vehicle that has been exploited, to varying degrees of success, by government bodies as well. The establishment of Tanzania One Theatre and the use of *taarab* in the CCM campaigns of the Tanga civic elections constitute attempts by government agents (at the extreme upper stratum of government leadership—the CCM National Executive Committee— and at the level of a city council) to harness *taarab's* potency for their own ends. It is a potency employed in the name of resistance (e.g., Babloom's complaint to President Mwinyi concerning local government officials) as well as collaboration (e.g., praise songs) recalling, once again, Mbembe's depiction of postcoloniality as relations of neither pure resistance nor pure collaboration but the "illicit cohabitation" of the two (Mbembe 1992, 4) .

It cannot be denied, however, that music, poetry, and art in general constitute particularly powerful media for the articulation of resistance. Anyone with even a passing interest in African performance could not fail to notice the frequency with which these art forms are employed for registering discontent, voicing resistance, and drawing public attention to the foibles and follies of the powers that be (Tracey 1948; Mitchell 1956; Finnegan 1970; Songoyi 1988b; Gunner 1994; Coplan 1994). As noted by Leroy Vail and Landeg White,

> There have, in fact, been many writers who have noted the phenomenon that the various forms of oral poetry in sub-Saharan Africa are licensed by a freedom of expression which violates normal conventions—that chiefs and headmen may be criticized by their followers, husbands by their wives, fathers by their sons, employers or overseers by their workers, officials and politicians by their underlings, and even Life Presidents by their subjects, in ways that the prevailing social and political codes would not normally permit, so long as it is done through poetry. (Vail and White 1991, 43)

Poetic license combined with the vast social networks engaged in musical performance generated valid concern among colonial and postcolonial authorities in Tanzania—hence the convoluted apparatus of fees, permits, licenses, and so on. This apparatus, justified and legitimized in the name of cultural promotion, was in fact designed to control as much as possible the power intrinsic in such practices.

A New Mode of Cultural Production

In February 1995, the Ministry of Education and Culture convened a three-day workshop on cultural policy. The stated goal was to deliberate upon new directions for Tanzanian cultural policy in the age of multipartyism. In fact, however, participants reiterated long-standing positions lamenting the demise of "traditional arts" (*burudani za asili*), which instill desirable morals and values, in the face of foreign-influenced "modern arts" (*burudani za kisasa*), which evoke desire for material goods and foreign products. Socialist thought lives on at least in this domain of Tanzanian life.

In evaluating the weak condition not only of their own ministry but of the arts in general (lack of infrastructure, low social position of artists and musicians, competition with increasingly attractive cultural productions from abroad, especially in films and music), those attending the workshop found fault with the increased commercialization of culture and lack of government initiative in confronting this problem. They also decried the lack of overall government support for the ministry, arguing as follows:

> In recognizing the importance of Culture in our Nation and to build for us national status among other Nations, the committee would like to say that the Government should see the importance of giving the Culture Division the respect, support, and authority to fulfill and oversee its responsibilities just like any other government division for the purposes of building, strengthening, developing and exploring

new and proper directions for our Nation to develop our national status for our current and future benefit. ("Cultural Policy Recommendations," presented at the Workshop on Cultural Policy, February 15–17, 1995, Morogoro, 5)

So alienated are ministry personnel from the activities and funding of cultural development that they complain openly against "the government" for ignoring the importance of Culture when they themselves are members of that same government! One need not look any further than the establishment of Tanzania One Theatre—the most significant government cultural intervention in recent years—for evidence of the ministry's profound marginalization within the state apparatus. Although established for the express purpose of directing the nation's cultural development, it was significantly not the Culture Division but the CCM National Executive Committee that initiated, planned, organized, and funded TOT's creation. Thus, the main driving force behind cultural policy in Tanzania has been and continues to be the party, which admitted as much in the fifteenth Party Congress in 1971: "Because the Party has the responsibility of ensuring that the people govern their everyday life, the congress resolves that from now on the Party must participate in all cultural activities,"[4] a message repeated in the sixteenth Party Congress and by the Party Executive Committee in 1976.[5] The multiple layers of Tanzania's government alternately clash and pass each other by unnoticed.

Gupta (1995) and Nugent (1994) draw upon similar examples of the multilayered nature of the Indian and Peruvian states, respectively, to deconstruct the "state versus society" dichotomy. Just as society is stratified and fractured into opposing constituencies, so too is the state—as a product of society—a disaggregated, multilayered bureaucracy fraught with competing internal units. The conceptual distinction between the two, argues Herzfeld, is a symbolic construct (Herzfeld 1997, 5) that mystifies, essentializes, and requires deconstruction. Because of official and popular tendencies to reify "the state," as well as the concerted attempts by state practitioners to establish "cultural intimacy" with citizens (Herzfeld 1997), it is difficult to see through the rhetoric and recognize its internal divisions and conflicts. By contrast, "society" is much more clearly seen for its fragmentation and factionalism. Societal factions differ in the degree of support they lend to state enterprises, and this support (or lack of) varies according to the historical moment and the enterprise for which support is sought. Babloom Modern Taarab is a private group of citizens that converted from a critical position vis-à-vis the government to a position of public allegiance and alliance: new categorization as CCM praise-singers.[6] Contrast that with the history of Lucky Star Taarab, another private band whose strong support for and original identification with the government waned for lack of recognition.[7] The lines, therefore, between state and society are necessarily blurred and indistinct, and the domain in which they consistently clash is the field of cultural production, for it is there that the state comes to be imagined, constructed, and contested.

> [T]here is no position strictly outside or inside the state because what is being contested is the terrain of the ideological field. Any struggle against currently hegemonic configurations of power and domination involves a *cultural* struggle, what Gramsci has called the "war of position." What is at stake is nothing less than a transformation in the manner in which the state comes to be constructed. It is a struggle that problematizes the historical divide between those who choose to do political work "within" the state and those who work "outside" it, because the cultural constructions of the state in public culture can result from, and affect, both in equal measure. (Gupta 1995, 393–94)

In assessing Tanzania's cultural state of affairs, authors of the 1995 Cultural Policy report, in an oblique and somewhat ironic reference to Nyerere's foundational speech, claim, "Setting aside the stated objectives that Culture is the backbone and life of the Nation, the lack of cultural direction in the Nation is the source of these problems."[8] This is not an insignificant admission, given the government's thirty-two year rhetorical investment in "Tanzanian National Culture." What we find is the government's designated cultural overseers throwing up their hands in frustration with the perceived lack of substantive action behind the many words of state officials—state officials who simultaneously pay homage to Culture (requiring its presence at state banquets, airport receptions, and the like) but who do little to maintain and promote it. The workshop report concludes with the following statement, fully capitalized for added effect:

> LET US AGREE *BY ACTIONS* THAT CULTURE IS THE FACE AND SPIRIT OF OUR NATION [my emphasis].

Thus, participants in the 1995 workshop voiced extreme dissatisfaction with the state of Tanzanian cultural production. I would contend, however, that if a problem can be said to exist, it lies neither in a lack of cultural direction nor in a lack of government action. The ethnographic data presented in the preceding pages indicates time and again how rich and endlessly inventive cultural practitioners in Tanzania are. Despite all hyperbolic rhetoric to the contrary, foreign art forms rarely, if ever, get adopted wholesale. As demonstrated by the histories of *ngoma, dansi,* and *taarab* (as well as the more recent cases of Swahili rap and Swahili reggae), foreign genres are always ultimately subject to local aesthetic principles. And as for the accusation of government inaction, the history of cultural production in Tanzania illustrates how government action systematically served to stifle rather than encourage creativity, creating endless obstacles and imposing undue and unnecessary hardships on musicians and artists.

I would propose instead that the problem in Tanzania (if, indeed, one exists) is that governing elites have been misguided in their conception of and approach to cultural development. Trouble arises in the persistent refusal to recognize that the nation's cultural direction is not determined solely by intellectuals and government bureaucrats who assume that cultural development is their exclusive responsibility. Failure to take the roles and activities of citizens into account results in a defective plan of action (as exemplified by the slew of ineffective Culture Division initiatives). A new mode of cultural production is thus required: one that posits new relations of production between producers and consumers of culture whereby the means of cultural production are not exclusively "owned" by elites; one that does not locate productive power always and only on one side of a two-sided "state/society" equation; one that accommodates the interplay and exchange of ideas and practices among all members of a given principality.

One could fruitfully extend this argument to the nation's economic and political domains. The flourishing literature on the purportedly "informal" economy that in effect constitutes the majority of economic activity in Tanzania (Tripp 1997) is but one reflection of how relations between and among state agents and citizens require rethinking. While notable strides have been made toward critically reframing "state-society" relations in the realm of economics, in matters of culture and symbolism the tendency among academic observers is still to attribute more power to the state than is warranted. Even if the relative youth and inexperience of the Tanzanian state coupled with the debilitating aftereffects of colonialism and socialism make it a weaker state than others, arguments that unilaterally deposit symbolic and cultural productive power in the hands of state-makers and other elite sectors lead us astray.

And this only exacerbates matters, for, as Handler and others have noted, the line between state discourse and academic discourse is often difficult to determine. Earlier I criticized Bourdieu's assertion that "saying what the state is, caused the state to come into being by stating what it should be" (Bourdieu 1999, 71). In attributing undue vigor to state cultural and symbolic enterprises, we unwittingly justify state abuses in those realms. And in constructing the state as all-powerful in our analyses, we risk bringing such authoritarian states into being.

Toward a Performative Understanding of Power

Gramsci tells us that "[i]n the phase of struggle for hegemony it is the science of politics which is developed" (Gramsci 1971, 404). Tanzanian state officials are struggling for hegemony and in the process are developing their skills in the art and science of politics. They are trying to create national subjects. After the preceding chapters, we now know without doubt that the arts can successfully engage desires and build from those desires new thoughts and actions. Rulers and revolutionaries both know this and wield art forms as tools in their respective struggles to maintain or obtain political power.

According to Ugandan intellectual Okot p'Bitek, there are two kinds of rulers: one skilled in the employment of political and economic force, the other skilled in the arts of persuasion, politics, and philosophy. Out of respect for his eloquence, I quote him at length:

> I am insisting that in any society, anywhere, in any age, there are two types of rulers: namely the artist who provides and sustains the fundamental ideals, the foundation of society; and the political chieftain, who comes to power with the aid of his soldier and rich business brethren, who merely puts these ideas into practice in ruling or misruling society. At times, as was the case with Moses, Mohammed and Mao-Tse-Tung, the two types are fused in one person. The chief, with or without his council, makes his laws or proclaims his decrees, all neatly arranged in chapters, sections and sub-sections for easy reference. Why do men obey these laws? There are the "security forces," some in uniform, others in plain clothes. Then there are "courts of law" manned by judges and magistrates of many ranks. Lawyers argue about points of law and of fact; and if found guilty the prisoner is sent to jail, under the charge of a whole army called warders or gaolers who ensure that the prisoner does not escape. For some crimes he is hanged.
>
> The chieftain and the rich impress society with their instruments of coercion and wealth. Men and women are forced, tortured, threatened, bribed, bought, killed, to obey. Most times these so-called laws do not make sense.
>
> The artist uses his voice, he sings his laws to the accompaniment of the *nanga*, the harp; he twists his body to the rhythm of the drums, to proclaim his rules. He carves his moral standards on wood and stone, and paints his colourful "dos and don'ts" on walls, and canvas. In these and other ways, the artist expresses the joys and sorrows of the people. What is joy? What is sorrow? These questions are meaningless if the philosophy of life, as created and celebrated in arts, is not clear. What is happiness? What is sadness? Surely, these questions do not make sense unless the human situation is what it should be.
>
> It is creative works of the artist that constitute the mental pictures which guide men's lives, which make them human. It is also these works of art that sustain and promote the laws. "The imagination," wrote Shelley, "is the great instrument of moral good, and poetry administers to the effect by acting upon the causes." And commenting on the thin influence of moral philosophers on morality, John Dewey judged, "The sum total of the effect of all reflective treatises on morals is insignificant in comparison with the influence of architecture, the novel, drama, on life, becoming important when "intellectual" products formulate the tendencies of these arts and provide them with an intellectual base."
>
> If there are two types of rulers in every society, that is, those who use physical force to subdue men, and those that employ beautiful things, sweet songs and

funny stories, rhythm, shape and colour, to keep individuals and society sane and flourishing, then in my view, it is the artist who is the greater ruler. (p'Bitek 1986, 39–40)

P'Bitek thus argues for appreciation of art both as a vehicle for societal values and as an effective mode of power. The latter is a point not commonly held. When "power" is mentioned, especially in relation to states, the typical evocations are Marxist and Gramscian concepts of domination or the disciplining power of state institutions from schools to prisons to mental asylums forwarded by Foucault. But modern states, more so perhaps than other power-holders now and in times past, are ultimately beholden to their citizens and thus must publicly demonstrate time and again their "stateliness." They must construct nations where none can be firmly identified and encourage through the development of nationalist sentiment the emergence of national subjects. Art serves this purpose well. Barbara Kirshenblatt-Gimblett writes,

> There is a sort of slippage in what we mean by "nation," "state," and "culture." In order for a state to have any kind of stake in the world, it has had to constitute, at least historically, what we call a "nation." For the nation to have any kind of palpable presence on the international scene, it must construct its own definitive culture. The reclassification of ethnographic material as art has been instrumental to this process. One of the very first things that one can observe in new states is the imperative to create museums of ethnography and national heritage and to form national folkloric ensembles, ballets, symphonies and theater companies. In a sense, these institutions dramatically enact the nation through performing its "culture.". . . Rhetorically speaking, a nation without art is not a nation. (1991, 81)

Returning to the idea of "governance" introduced at the start of this book, it is perhaps easier to exercise "action upon action," as Foucault defined the term (Foucault 1984, 427–28), through musical, poetic, and artistic means than through force. Toward this end, then, state officials employ the arts and strive to become artists themselves (of a sort) so as to rule with greater degrees of ease and success. It is no coincidence that TANU's early ranks overflowed with poets and dancers, musicians and artists. Nor is it coincidence that Tanzania—even with its many contradictions and challenges—has succeeded as a nation where many surrounding states have failed.

Power admittedly comes in many guises—some visible, others invisible, some more performative than others.[9] Where states are concerned, however, emphasis tends toward the visible (even flamboyant) and the performative. Why? Because state officials can perform their allegiance and loyalty to their constituents and citizens can perform their allegiance and loyalty to their rulers when other forms of communication prove inconvenient or ineffective. Singing a national anthem, standing at attention during a state procession, rising to one's feet to acknowledge the arrival of a dignitary, chanting "CCM Number One!" at a political rally, and wearing identical dresses with political portraits emblazoned on the fabric all constitute condensed, symbolically laden, and highly demonstrative strategies for engaging and asserting membership in the nation. Refusal to sing the anthem or stand at attention, chanting the slogan of an opposition party during a CCM rally, having one's dress sewn in such a way that the political portrait falls squarely on the buttocks all constitute equally demonstrative strategies for contesting membership in or posing alternate conceptualizations of the nation. Through their shared performances, the citizens of a state congeal and bring the nation—however variegated—into being.

Foucault's assertion that "power is neither given, nor exchanged, nor recovered, but rather exercised, and that it only exists in action" (Foucault 1980, 89) lays the foundation for a performative understanding of power. In chapter 1, I traced a genealogy of theories of performance and highlighted how performance by definition is emergent, ephemeral, and contingent. Performance, like power, is not a product that can be given, exchanged, or recovered. It always necessarily is a process that is subject to on-the-spot improvisation, varying expectations, the vagaries of history and context, multiple associations and connotations, and remembered or projected meanings. Just as power is a diffuse resource accessible—albeit to varying degrees—to everyone, so too is performance engaged in by everyone present, be they audience members seated before performers on a proscenium stage or guests at a Swahili wedding in a coastal East African town.

The parallels in how both "performance" and "power" (à la Foucault) have been theorized are striking and beg consideration. Eric Wolf, another noted theorist of power, delineates four modes of power: personal, interpersonal, organizational, and structural (Wolf 1990). In discussing the role of power in signification, he argues that "symbolic work is never done, achieves no final solution. The cultural assertion that the world is shaped in this way and not in some other has to be repeated and enacted, lest it be questioned and denied" (Wolf 1990, 593). In other words, the power entailed in trumpeting one version of reality (e.g., the existence of a Tanzanian nation) over others (e.g., the existence of not one but two nations in Tanzania) requires work, continual reenactment, unremitting performance. Power breeds performance, just as performance breeds power.

A performative approach thus has much to offer. According to Schieffelin, "Performance embodies the *expressive dimension of the strategic articulation of practice*" (Schieffelin 1998, 199; emphasis in original). Attention to musical practices and their imbrication with or disenfran-

chisement from state projects reveals the fluctuations in power and intent that are characteristic of national imaginaries. It also, however,
illuminates how differentially positioned agents can be convinced to
align themselves with or alternatively oppose objectives delineated by
state officials depending upon how, when, and under what conditions
those relationships are negotiated. And most importantly, to my mind,
it can expose the continual performance not only required *by* states but
required *of* states that, just like individuals, must continually reinvent
themselves to accommodate the flux and flow of social, political, ideological, and economic change. Bourdieu was only half right. Saying and,
notably, *performing* the nation brings it into being. Words alone are insufficient.

Performing the Nation

In conclusion, I return to Benedict Anderson. "What . . . made the new
communities imaginable was a half-fortuitous, but explosive, interaction between a system of production and productive relations (capitalism), a technology of communications (print), and the fatality of human
linguistic diversity" (Anderson 1989, 46). Were one to apply these three
measures to the case of Tanzanian nationalism, credit would have to be
given to the successful establishment of Kiswahili hegemony throughout the country, but the prerequisite of capitalism would have to be discarded, and the emphasis on print-media minimized. Instead, socialism
defined Tanzanian nationalism in the 1970s and 1980s just as economic
liberalization and political pluralism defined it in the 1990s, and musical
performance more than print media proves to be the dominant vehicle
for its elaboration from colonial times to the present.

The many contradictions that lie at the heart of Tanzania do not iso-
late it among nation-states, for other writers have shown how intrinsically contradictory states are by their very nature. No clear consensus
on what constitutes "Tanzania" exists nor, given the split personality of
the state, should be anticipated any time soon. Having two purportedly
national museums, two national arts competitions, two national archives, and two ministries of national culture raises the question of
what constitutes the Tanzanian nation. From the continuing debates
waged in newspapers, in poetry, in Parliament, and in song, we can see
that it remains an open-ended question. Tanzania is a state engaged in
an ongoing search for a national identity. The active process of continually renegotiating the nation is a commonly articulated concern and a
conversation engaged in by people throughout the country. Negotiation
occurs between competing and conflicting nationalist objectives, be-

tween differentially valued performances, and between differentially positioned performing agents. The unity of purpose presumed of both the
object and objectives of a national imaginary is all too obviously lacking
in Tanzania.

Competing representations of the nation are performed in everyday
practice by musicians, cultural officers, local politicians, coastal wedding
guests, high-ranking politicians, poets, traffic police, Swahili language
experts, and a host of constituencies that jointly comprise the sociopolitical entity of Tanzania. It is a situation wherein cultural policy is
neither the invention of an elite minority, a dominant party, nor of a
bankrupt and marginalized cultural ministry; rather it is a continuous
stream of negotiations among citizens—citizens who may prefer *taarab*
to the officially sanctioned *ngoma* or prefer working their own fields to
those of a public cooperative. Absent are the neat, unilineal, top-down
transmissions posited by some theorists. In their stead lies a national
imaginary in constant and continual flux, always and ever subject to the
approval of those who constitute its members.

Appendix A

SONG TEXTS AND TRANSLATIONS
(PRESENTED IN THE ORDER THEY APPEAR IN THE TEXT)

Chapter 1

Leo Ni Leo ("Today Is the Day")
Women's *ngoma* song, Mombasa

Leo ni leo, leo ni leo
Mtauona mpambano kweli si uongo
- - -
Jamali wa umbo, Na wajihi mwema
Mwingi wa urembo, Nawacha kusema
Wanitenda mambo, Bila ya huruma

Today is the day, today is the day.
You will see a contest, and that's no lie.
- - -
Exquisite in body and in appearance,
Beautiful throughout—I'll stop talking.
You treat me without mercy.

Hasidi ("Envious Person")
Juma Bhalo, Mombasa

Hasidi si mwema, Rabi tunusuru
Akikitizama, Kitu hukidhuru
Jito la huruma, Kwake ni kufuru

A *hasidi* (envious person) is not a good
    person. God help us.
When she looks at something, it spoils.
A merciful eye for her is sacrilege.

- - -
Hasidi ni nyoka, Wa nduma kuwili
Japo wamuweka, Pazuri mahali
Na kukugeuka, Hasidi hajali

- - -
A *hasidi* is a snake that bites with both
    ends.
Even if you care for it in a nice place,
To turn against you, a *hasidi* does not
    care.

- - -
Hasidi ni sumu, Haachi kukuuwa
Ungamkarimu, Haiwi ni dawa
Yeye na laimu, Hali zao sawa

- - -
A *hasidi* is poison. It does not stop killing
    you.
If you would welcome her, it still would
    not be her medicine.
She and a lime are the same.
- - -

- - -
Hasidi hataki, Uwe na neema
Na wivu na chuki, Haachi daima
Wala hatosheki, Chake angachuma

- - -

A *hasidi* does not want you to enjoy
    happiness.
Envy and hatred she cannot ever leave,
Nor is what she has ever enough, even if
    acquired by herself.
- - -

Chorus

Hasidi fisadi, Ni adui nyoka
Nae angazidi, Husuda kutaka
Hasidi hasudi, Ela kulanika

A *hasidi* is a corrupter, an enemy snake,
And she continues to desire envy.
A *hasidi* only succeeds at being cursed.

Chapter 3

Msanja Song
Women's *ngoma* song, Tanga

Kwa mafuta, Mimi natumia ya uto
Ukitaka ya uzuri, utakuja chapwa na fimbo
Fimbo—fimbo spesheli
Bakora ya babu, eeh—bakora spesheli
Kijaluba cha babu jinga—kijaluba spesheli
Mkwaju wa babu, eeh—mkwaju spesheli

For body oil, I use low-grade coconut oil.
If you desire better quality, you will be
	hit with a stick.
A stick—a special stick;
Grandfather's cane—a special cane;
The idiot's tobacco tin—a special tobacco
	tin;
Grandfather's tamarind paddle—a special
	paddle.

Punda wa Tanga ("Donkey of Tanga" [Track 6 on CD])
Mwinshehe Zongo, Gita Musical Club, Tanga

Punda wa Tanga
Mwaka uno waringa kuota pembe
Na pembe nzakubandika

Donkey of Tanga,
You are proud of having grown horns
	this year,
While the horns are artificial.

- - -

Mkulima mwenye moyo
Akikosa mwaka huno anangoja mwakani
Na jembe halitupi mtu

- - -

A determined farmer,
If he suffers loss this year, he waits for
	the next year.
A hoe will not let one down.

- - -

Larawarawa goma laingia mkongwe
Larawarawa Gita laingia mkongwe naja

With a slow motion the big dance is
	coming (to you) old man.
With a slow motion Gita is coming, old
	man, I am coming.

- - -

- - -

Chorus
Hazina uaminifu
Zitaanguka njiani
Nasema punda wa Tanga

They are not reliable.
They will fall along the way.
I am telling you, Donkey of Tanga.

Tanzania Yetu ("Our Tanzania" [Track 5 on CD])
Stephen Hizza and Hassan Ngoma, Atomic Jazz Band, Tanga

Tanzania yetu ndio nchi ya kusifiwa

Our Tanzania is a country worthy of
	praise.

Popote ulimwenguni watu wote watambua
Tanzania yetu ndio nchi ya furaha
Naye Baba Nyerere ndiye wetu muhisani
Naye ndiye aliyeleta uhuru
Tanzania yetu ndio nchi ya furaha

Throughout the world everyone
   recognizes this.
Our Tanzania is indeed a country of
   happiness,
And Father Nyerere is indeed our patron.
It was he who brought us independence.
Tanzania is indeed a country of happiness.

Nimezama ("I Am Drowning" [Track 1 on CD])
Hamza Ali and Mussa Majengo, Golden Star Musical Club, Tanga

Wenzangu nawauliza, Nini dawa ya
   mapenzi?
Waganga nimemaliza, Wa makombe na
   hirizi
Bilahi Mola Muweza, Ataniafu Mwenyezi
- - -
Nimezama kwa mapenzi, Sijui kama tazuka
Kujikwamua siwezi, Taabani nateseka
Bilahi Mola Mwenyezi, Ataniafu Rabuka

- - -

Nimezama nimezama, Kwenye bahari ya
   huba
Moyo wangu walalama, Nalia kitia toba
Bilahi Mola Karima, Taniepushi adhaba

- - -

Nimezama nimezama, Mwenzenu katika
   kina
Nimebaki natazama, La kutenda sina tena
Bilahi Mola Karima, Ataniafu Rabana
- - -

My friends I ask you: what is the
   medicine for love?
I've tried all shamans with their potions
   and talismans.
Oh Almighty God, deliver me.
- - -
I am drowning in love. I don't know if
   I'll emerge safely.
I cannot free myself. I am in great
   distress.
Oh All-Powerful God, deliver me.
- - -
I am drowning, drowning in a sea of
   love.
My heart complains. I plead for mercy.
Oh Beneficent God, relieve me of this
   punishment.
- - -
I am drowning. Your friend is in deep
   waters.
I am left gazing, unable to act.
Oh Gracious God, deliver me.
- - -

Chorus
Nimezama kwa mapenzi, Sijui kama tazuka
Naiona yangu hali, Mimi nimedhoofika

I am drowning in love. I don't know if
   I'll emerge safely.
I see my condition. I have lost all
   strength.

Aliyejaliwa ("The Favored One" [Track 8 on CD])
Ally Star, BIMA Modern Taarab, Dar es Salaam

Tachukia kila siku, Mimi siko sawa nawe
Fanya mchana usiku, Bidii ufanikiwe
Hilo lako dukuduku, Utajishinda mwenyewe

Every day you'll despise the fact that you
   and I are not alike.
Keep persevering day and night so that
   you succeed.
This bitterness of yours will be your
   downfall.

- - -

Wasema kama kasuku, Mengi watu wakujue

- - -

You talk incessantly like a parrot so that
   people know you.

Ulipiga marufuku, Nilipo niondolewe
Hilo ni dua la kuku, Juwa halimpati mwewe

You demanded that I be removed from
    where I was.
Know that the prayer of the chicken does
    not affect the hawk.

- - -

- - -

Wanipangia tuhuma, Wataka uthaminiwe
Kunipachika lawama, Unataka usifiwe
Mtoaji ni Karima, Kipi upatacho wewe?

You accuse me hoping you will be
    believed.
In laying the blame on me, you seek
    praise.
Only God can save. What have you
    achieved?

- - -

- - -

Si kama nakukashifu, Tulia nikuzindue
Panapo maji marefu, Nataka upaelewe
Nawe ni hali dhaifu, Utajitosa mwenyewe

It's not as though I am slandering you.
    Calm down. Let me set you straight.
I want you to understand where deep
    waters lie.
You are in desperate straits, yet you will
    plunge further into this yourself.

- - -

- - -

Chorus
Aliyejaliwa, Wewe usishindane naye
Utajisumbua, Mola ndiye ajuaye

Don't try to compete with the favored
    one.
You'll only trouble yourself. Only God
    knows.

Pendo Raha Yake ("The Joy of Love" [Track 2 on CD])
Salehe Kiroboto and Kamal Basha, Young Novelty Musical Club, Tanga

Sitovumulia, Pendo la hiyana
Pendo ni tabia, Zenye kufanana
Nakutia nia, Hamtogombana
- - -

I refuse to suffer a mean-spirited love.
Love blooms between similar personalities,
And elicits a determination never to fight.
- - -

Pendo raha yake, Mfano hapana
Si tabia yake, Kufanya hiyana
Na uzuri wake, Raha kupeana

The joy of love has no equal.
It does not breed ill will.
Moreover, its goodness lies in giving each
    other joy.

- - -

- - -

Tahadhari sana, Chukua wasia
Si jambo la maana, Lengo kujitia
Utajuta sana, Hutovumilia

Beware, take my warning.
This is not important, not a matter worth
    pursuing.
You will sorely regret it. You will not en-
    dure.

Wajigamba ("You Boast")
Rama Hamadi, Babloom Modern Taarab, Tanga

Wajigamba, Na kudharau wenzio
Wajipamba, Kutaka mafanikio
Jua kwamba, Mwanzo una mwishilio
- - -

You show off and insult others.
You beautify yourself in order to succeed.
Know that every beginning has an end.
- - -

Unatamba, Hakuna wakuwezao
Umefumba, Humshukuru Molao
Kukuumba, Na kukujalia hayo

You boast that no one can beat you.
You have closed your eyes. You do not
    thank your God
For creating you and giving you all you
    have.

- - -

- - -

Usiambe, Kuwa wewe ni hodari	Do not say that you are so brave.
Usivimbe, Mjini kutakabari	Do not be conceited putting on airs
Nawe kumbe, Huwezi ishi dahari	around town.
	For truly you cannot live forever.

- - -

Ufahamu, Mtu hajui la kesho	Understand that no human knows what
Hutadumu, Ungatumia vitisho	tomorrow brings.
Maadamu, Lenye mwanzo lina mwisho	You will not last forever even if you
	resort to scare tactics.
	Because every beginning has an end.

- - -

Chorus

Aaaaa, Punguza kiburi	Reduce your arrogance.
Aaaaa, Mola ni muweza	Only God has the power.

Kidogo Menirambisha ("You Gave Me a Little Taste")
Rama Hamadi, Babloom Modern Taarab, Tanga

Fahamu haijanisha, Hamu ya kilicho chema	Know that my desire for this beautiful
Ambacho menionjesha, Muadhama	thing has not ended
Kidogo menirambisha, Kishae unaninyima	That you gave me to taste, my love.
	You gave me but a taste and then
	withheld it from me.

- - -

Sasa unanitabisha, Moyo wataka lazima	Now you aggravate me, yet still my heart
Hamu haijanitosha, Naungama	insists.
Mbona wanibabisha, Nataka nawe wagoma	Desire has not satisfied me, I confess.
	Why do you tease me? I want, but you
	hold back.

- - -

Kitu cha kuburudisha, Kizuri cha taadhima	Something entertaining, beautiful, and
Mimi kimenilewesha, Nalalama	respectful,
Kiasi ungebakisha, Mwenzio nikajinoma	It intoxicated me. Now I lament.
	If you left me with but a portion of it, I
	would be so proud.

- - -

Nia kuibadilisha, Sio uamuzi mwema	To change your will is not a good decision.
Kutoa na kurudisha, Ni dhuluma	To give and then take it back is torture.
Mja kunidhalilisha, Hunionei huruma	To humiliate me like this—can't you take
	pity on me?

The following is a *mafumbo* song that can be interpreted in multiple ways. The most common interpretation, however, understands *asali* (honey) as a veiled reference to sodomy. Understood in this manner, the composer relates the practice to both excrement and tremendous pleasure (sweetness).

Nyuki ("Bee")
Issa Matona, JKT Taarab, Dar es Salaam

Nyuki wanisikitisha, Ukweli nakueleza	Bee, you cause me regret, truly I tell you.
Asali ulozalisha, Viumbe yatupendeza	We people have come to love the honey
	you produced.

Kumbe waitayarisha, Kwa vitu vilivyooza
Ungelinifahamisha, Kuila nisingeweza

- - -

Nyuki waenda porini, Mizoga kuitundua
Hata mzoga wa nyani, Nyuki wajichukulia
Waja na chumo kinywani, Asali kutengezea
Ukiiona dukani, Viumbe twaigombea

- - -

Utamu wake asali, Hakika umezidia
Ni tamu kushinda wali, Au nyama ya
ngamia
Kaitunuki jalali, Halali kuitumia
Ukiila kwa kikiri, waweza ukazimia
- - -
Viko vingi duniani, Vikioza ni haramu
Na vitoke ugenini, Nchini viwe adimu
Ukila u hatiani, Watu watakushutumu
Hii asali kwa nini, Ihalalishwe dawamu

- - -

Chorus
Awauliza mashekhe, Pamwe na wana
vyuoni
Asali halali yake, Aomba mjulisheni
Asije ipiga teke, Akaitoa thamani

Muhibaka ("Darling")
Rashid Hamadi, Babloom Modern Taarab, Tanga

Ewe muhibaka, Usinitese mwenzio
- - -
Nateseka duniani, Sinapo pakushika
Tafadhali niauni, Ujuwe naadhirika

- - -

Nakupenda si dhihaka, Umo mwangu
moyoni
Huba zako nazitaka, Wangu mwana
sinikhini
- - -
Kutengana nawe siwezi, Ninapata mashaka
Ujuwe nina majonzi, Kwa wewe kunitoroka

- - -

Truth is, you prepare it from rotten
things.
Had you informed me, I would not have
been able to eat it.
- - -
Bee, you go to the forest to look for dead
bodies.
You even take from a dead gorilla's body,
Bee.
You come with your finds in your mouth
to make honey.
If you see it in the shop, we fight for it.
- - -
The sweetness of honey, it certainly is
too much.
It is sweeter than rice, or camel meat.
God blessed it, it is fine to use it.
If you eat it too quickly, you might faint.
- - -
There are many things in the world that
rot and become sinful,
Even if imported and unobtainable in the
country.
If convicted of eating it, people will
abuse you.
Why is it legal for honey?
- - -

He is asking the sheikhs and Islamic
teachers.
He asks to be informed of why honey is
not forbidden.
So as not to kick it away and make it
worthless.

You, my darling, please do not hurt me.
- - -
I suffer much in this world and have
nowhere to go.
Please tend to my needs. Know that I
embarrass myself.
- - -
I love you—it is no joke. You are in my
heart.
I want your love, my dear, do not refuse.

- - -

I cannot be apart from you. I get worried.
Know that I am full of sorrow since you
left me.
- - -

Nakusihi rudi mwana, Unifute machozi
Nipate penzi mwanana, Lako wewe mwenye
* enzi*

I advise you to return, my dear, and wipe
  away my tears.
Give me your true love, you with the
  power to make me happy.

- - -

- - -

Chorus
Aaaaa, Usinitese mwenzio
Hali mimi nakupenda nawe, Usinidhulumu

Aaaaa, don't hurt me.
I am in love with you. Do not treat me
  unjustly.

Chapter 4

Tamu Ya Chai ("The Sweetness of Tea")
Rama Hamadi, Babloom Modern Taarab, Tanga

Japo wamejaa tele, wazuri wa kusifika
Wa rangi hizi na zile, ambao wameumbika
Mimi wangu yule yule. Siwezi kumuepuka

Although there are many praised for their
  beauty,
Of these colors and those, who are nicely
  shaped,
Mine is the same one. I cannot resist her.

- - -

- - -

Siweki tamaa mbele, wala sitoshawishika
Nampenda kama vile, yeye alivyonishika
Kwa furaha na upole, na imani kuiweka

I will not place lust first, nor will I be
  tempted [by others].
I love her dearly the way she loves me,
  she has captured me.
For all happiness and joy, I want to be
  with her forever.

- - -

- - -

Sishiki huku na kule, hapa nimekwishafika
Ingawa wazuri tele, mimi sitofazaika
Penzi langu lile lile, haliwezi malizika

I will not take from there or there. I have
  arrived here.
Even if there are many beautiful ones, I
  will not be attracted.
This is my love. It will never cease.

- - -

- - -

Metua sina kelele, kwake sitobadilika
Taishi nae milele, katu hatonichujuka
Ninampa yule yule, moyoni aloniweka

I have settled, I have no troubles. Toward
  her, I will not change.
I will live with her forever. She will never
  lose her allure.
I give my love only to her. She has
  placed me in her heart.

- - -

- - -

Chorus
Tamu ya chai sukari, Sihadaike na rangi
Hata iwe ya maziwa

The sweetness of tea is the sugar. Do not
  be attracted by the color,
Even if it has milk.

Hawara ("Live-in Lover")
Khalid Akida, Babloom Modern Taarab, Tanga

Kwani utune mafunda, Na maneno
* kuropoka*

Why is it that your cheeks are puffed out
  and you rant and rave?

Mimi wewe kukupenda, Mwenyewe ulinitaka	I only loved you after you loved me first.
Kama umeshindwa nenda, Hawara hana talaka	If you can't take it anymore, go. A lover doesn't need a divorce.
- - -	- - -
Moyoni hayanichomi, Ondoka sina udhia	My heart does not pain me. Leave, I am not bothered,
Na wala sikutazami, Njia unayoendea	Nor will I watch which way you go.
Haiwi nipende mimi, Huku vyangu wanilia	How can I love you when you only love the gifts I give you?
- - -	- - -
Sipendi ya kubishana, Wako wengi kama wewe	I do not like to quarrel. There are many others like you
Wajuao pendo sana, Wafuatao wenyewe	Who understand love and who pursue me themselves.
Hidaya ni kupeana, Si peke nikupe wewe	Real love is shared by two—not given only by me to you.
- - -	- - -
Heshima kuwekeana, Ndio utu na usawa	To respect each other is both human and right.
Kuropoka yaso maana, Ni lipi la kushauwa	To babble nonsense—what makes you do this?
Kama umepata bwana, Nenda usije chelewa	If you've found another man, go. Don't delay.
- - -	- - -

Chorus

Wewe acha kuropoka, Kama menichoka nenda	You—stop babbling! If you are tired of me, go.
Hawara hana talaka, Nenda mwana kwenda	A lover does not need a divorce. Go, woman, go.

Semeni Semeni ("Talk All You Want")
Khalid Akida, Babloom Modern Taarab, Tanga

Semeni semeni, Wala hayatonikera	You can talk, talk all you want but it will never disturb me.
Huyo muhisani, Kwangu mimi ndie bora	He, my lover, is perfect for me.
Nitamthamini, Mpaka kesho akhera	I will cherish him till tomorrow in Heaven.
- - -	- - -
Lilo la maudhi, Yeye sitom tendea	I will never offend him.
Taichunga hadhi, Yake kwa kunyenyekea	I will give him honor, show him reverence,
Sipate maradhi, Au jambo la udhia	So that he will not suffer illness or vexation.
- - -	- - -
Na analotaka, Naahidi nitampa	And whatever he wants, I promise to give him.
Simweki na shaka, Bure katoka mafupa	I won't give him reason to doubt me or grow thin with worry.
Kwangu amefika, Muhibu sitomtupa	He has settled with me, my lover. I will never throw him away.
- - -	- - -
Kweli nampenda, hadharani nabaini	I love him truly. Publicly I make it known.

Penzi talilinda, Sitolitoa thamani
Litaponishinda, Nami siwi duniani

I will cherish this love. I will never
    consider it worthless.
When it overcomes me, it will be when I
    am no longer of this world.

- - -

- - -

Chorus
Semeni, Mchokapo acheni
Muhisani, Simwachi asilani

Talk until you tire then stop.
I will never leave my lover.

Mwana wa Mwenzio ("Someone's Child")
Khalid Akida, Babloom Modern Taarab, Tanga

Jamani isiwe tabu, Kufanya mapenzi nae
Mkatafuta sababu, Ili nimuache yeye
Kwani mwendo taratibu, Atazowea mjue

People, it shouldn't cause trouble that I
    am in love with him.
You search for reasons for me to leave
    him.
Yet he will grow accustomed to my
    love—you should know this.

- - -

- - -

Udogo ni lake umbo, Ni mazito mambo yake
Lipi utafanya jambo, Hata yeye asumbuke
Lolote kwake ni pambo, Jueni msighulike

He may be small in stature, but he is
    great in other things.
What can you do to cause him worry?
Anything I do for him is great. You will
    not confuse him.

- - -

- - -

Kama mwamona hafai, Awakera nini nyie
Huba zangu za kurai, Zitamfanya apowe
Na ikiwa hatambui, Nitamfunza mwenyewe

Even if you don't consider him suitable,
    why does it concern you?
My satisfying love will make him settle,
And if he isn't very experienced in love, I
    will teach him myself.

- - -

- - -

Acheni jama acheni, Maneno mnayosema
Mwajitia shughulini, Kutafutana hasama
Mdogo takuwa lini, Nacheni nikuze jama

Stop it, you people. Stop saying these
    things.
You keep yourselves so busy looking for
    trouble.
For how long will he be too young?
Leave it to me to mature him.

- - -

- - -

Chorus
Nasema yenye ukweli, Walimwengu
    watambue
Mwana wa mwenzio, Mkubwa mwenzio
Mwana wa mwenzio, Chako kitoweo

What I say contains the truth. People of
    the world, recognize this.
Someone's child is suitable for another.
Someone's child is savory for you.

Kubwa Lao ("The Toughest One")
Seif Kassim Kisauji, Babloom Modern Taarab, Tanga

Nimesha ji-prepare, Kwenye shughuli ya leo
Tena niko so sure, Vishindo hapa ni kwao

I have already prepared myself for today's
    event,
And I'm sure all challenges end here with
    me.

Uwanja umetulia, Ainuke kubwa lao

The floor has cleared. Let the toughest one stand up.

\- - -

Hatutaki muamuzi, Nasema leo ni leo
Watangaza sikuwezi, Tutaona mwishilio
Ukishindwa hukatazwi, Waweza timura
mbio

\- - -

We do not want a referee. I say today is the day.
You announced that I cannot beat you—we'll see in the end.
And if you lose, there's nothing to stop you from running away.

\- - -

Si kama nakushitua, Kukweleza ya bayana
Nataka kulichimbua, Lile zizi la fitina
Kibwebwe nakufungia, Tena wasiwasi sina

It's not as if I shock you to tell you openly
I want to dig up the roots of discord.
I tie on *kibwebwe** because of you and am not at all worried.

\- - -

Asonijua ni nani? Ni bora akatulia
Tena nawapa ilani, Mimi siwakuchezea
Kacheza na hayawani, Kiwango uliopangiwa

\- - -

Who doesn't know who I am? Better that person keep quiet.
And I'm giving you a warning: I'm not someone to play with.
Go play with animals—that's more your grade.

\- - -

\- - -

Chorus
Kwa utulivu sipati kifani
Na kwa uovu mimi namba wani

For calmness, I have no match.
And for evil, I am number one.

*Kibwebwe is a *kanga* (cloth) twisted and tied around the hips. It is the female equivalent in this culture to the Western rolling up of the sleeves in preparation for a fight.

Television ("Television")
Shabaan Amour, Babloom Modern Taarab, Tanga

Nimekuja mdhamini, Kumtoa wasiwasi
Afurahi nafusini, Asizishike tetesi
Ndiye wangu duniani, Mwengine hana
nafasi

I have come as guarantor, to dispel her worries,
That she be happy deep in her heart. She should not listen to rumors.
In all the world, she is the one for me. No one else has even a chance.

\- - -

Apendwa hajiamini, Katika yake nafusi
Atue awe makini, Kumuacha si rahisi
Nimemuweka moyoni, Aelewe hanikosi

\- - -

She is loved but does not believe it deep in her heart.
She ought to be calm in spirit. To leave her would not be easy.
I have placed her in my heart. She should understand that she will not lose me.

\- - -

Atulie muimani, Simuweki mashakani
Nitamuenzi yakini, Aone yuko peponi

\- - -

She should be calm, confident. I will not cause her to doubt.
I will honor her faithfully such that she feels she is in Heaven.

Simtwishi ya huzuni, Akaona yu motoni

I will not burden her with sorrow such that she feels she is in Hell.

- - -

- - -

Lau moyo ungekuwa, Ni kama televisheni
Ningalimfungulia, Akaona yalo ndani
Ili apate ridhia, Mwenzie aniamini

If only a heart could be like a television.
Then I would turn mine on so that she see what is inside.
In order that she be content and believe me.

- - -

- - -

Chorus
Apendwa hajiamini, Haniamini mwenzake
Kuwa nnamthamini, Sinae zaidi yake

She is loved but is not sure of it. She does not believe me
That I cherish her and have no other.

Jamvi la Wageni ("The Visitor's Mat")
Rama Hamadi, Babloom Modern Taarab, Tanga

Hakika nimeamini, Mtu ni yake tabia
Sikujua asilani, Mwenzenu nikarukia
Kumbe jamvi la wageni, wanalo pumzikia

Truly I believe a person's character is revealed through their behavior.
I never would have believed it. I, your friend, was taken by surprise.
In fact he is a visitor's mat on which many have taken rest.

- - -

- - -

Nilitia maanani, Moyoni kuniingia
Nikamuweka nyumbani, Yote kumtimizia
Ametoka barazani, Ndani hakuvumilia

I reflected on this, pondered it in my heart.
I cherished him at home, taking care of his every need,
But he wandered outside. He couldn't endure staying inside.

- - -

- - -

Kaniona hayawani, Na mjinga wa dunia
Hakuzoea ya ndani, Kwani anayachukia
Hutokea barazani, Wapate kumkalia

He considered me a dupe, the world's biggest fool.
He could not get used to being inside since he hated it so.
He went out seeking others to sit on him.

- - -

- - -

Amenishinda jamani, Sio nnamchukia
Ni kwamba hawezekani, Kwa mmoja kutulia
Yeye jamvi la wageni, Nnje wanalokalia

I've had enough of him, my friends. It's not that I hate him.
It's that it's not right for just one person to remain true.
He is a visitor's mat on which outsiders sit.

- - -

- - -

Chorus
Sasa naliweka kando
Nimeliacha hilo jamvi la wageni, nimeliacha
Kanichochea karaha
Nimeliacha hilo jamvi la wageni, nimeliacha
Laniudhi moyo wangu
Nimeliacha hilo jamvi la wageni, nimeliacha

So I am putting it aside.
I have left this visitor's mat, I have left it,
Which stirs up feelings of disgust.
I have left this visitor's mat, I have left it.
It pains my heart.
I have left this visitor's mat, I have left it.

Kanioa Siri ("He Married Me Secretly")
Seif Kisauji, Babloom Modern Taarab, Tanga

Mimi sina kosa, Ni ukware wake *Uliza mikasa, Usifedheheke* *Kwangu haji sasa, Tangu zama zake*	It is not my fault—it was his lust. Ask for the reasons. Don't disgrace yourself. He came to me not recently but long ago.
- - -	- - -

Nilimpa penzi, Likamuingia
Humtoshelezi, Akakukimbia
Na angebarizi, Katu singejua
	I gave him love and it entered his blood.
	You are not enough for him. He has run
	    away from you.
	If he would have kept quiet, you would
	    not have known.

- - -	- - -

Ulonae pia, Mwenyewe ni mwingi
Ulipogundua, Tushatenda mengi
Yaliyobakia, Hayana msingi
	The one whom you have cannot be
	    satisfied with only one.
	By the time you found out, we had
	    already progressed so far.
	Things that we have not yet done do not
	    mean much to us.

- - -	- - -

Kwa chako kiburi, Nakupasulia
Kanioa siri, Bila kukwambia
Watu mashuhuri, Wameshuhudia
	For the sake of your pride, today I tell the
	    truth.
	He married me secretly without
	    informing you
	And influential people witnessed.

- - -	- - -

Chorus

Figa moja haliweki chungu *Alo wako na mimi ni wangu*	A single stone will not support the pot.* The one who is yours is also mine.

*The refrain refers to the common East African cooking arrangement of three stones set in triangle formation around hot coals to support a pot. Stones used for this purpose have the specific name of *mafiga* (pl.; *figa*, sing.). Neither one nor two stones will suffice to support a pot—there must be three.

Utasugua ("You Will Scrub")
Rama and Rashid Hamadi, Babloom Modern Taarab, Tanga

Jua si namna moja, Japo rangi za fanana
Shaba waleta viroja, Kutu imegandiana
Nawe wajipa faraja, Na dhahabu kulingana
	Know that these are not the same even if
	    the colors are similar.
	Copper, you bring surprises. You are
	    layered with tarnish.
	And you console yourself that you are
	    compared with gold.

- - -	- - -

Utafanya tafrija, Mwenyewe umekazana
Na kutoa nyingi hoja, Majibu kujibishana
Lakini wajikungoja, Bure Shaba hukuvuna
	You want to host a celebration and make
	    all the effort yourself.
	You make many claims for cross-
	    questioning.
	But you falter. It is useless, Copper, you
	    failed.

- - -	- - -

Tua siwe mpingaji, Ushike ninayonena	Stop, do not act like a defendant. Listen to what I say.
Wewe simtafutaji, Kheri ungetulizana	You are not a capable prospector—better you give up.
Usiwe mchekeshaji, Uso wako kuchuna	Do not make a fool of yourself, feeling no shame.

- - -

- - -

Kwa dhahabu usihoji, Yapendeza kila kona
There is no argument about gold—it shines in every corner.

Humpamba mvaaji, Endapo anajivuna
It beautifies the one who wears it. She is proud wherever she goes.

Wewe lipi wataraji, Shaba unapoipuna
What do you expect to get when you scrub, Copper?

- - -

- - -

Chorus

Utasugua havifanani kwa kusugua
You will scrub, but they do not match even with all the polishing.

Jua shaba sidhahabu
Know that copper is not gold.

Halua ("Halua")

Hussein Kibao, Black Star Musical Club, Tanga

Ukiona vyangu vyaliwa, Usioshe vyombo
When you see that my food is eaten, do not wash the dishes.

Utambue hiyo ni haluwa, Haina makombo
Know that it is *halua,** there are no leftovers to be thrown out.

Ni udugu usokataliwa, Ushoga ni pambo
Kinship cannot be denied, but friendship is mere ornamentation.

- - -

- - -

Ana mengi anayo yafanya, Je? Nipasue
He is doing many things—should I tell them?

Namuona jicho alifinya, Nisiyatobowe
I see him wink at me warning me not to tell.

Basi leo awache kusengenya, Kuwateta wenziwe
Then today he must stop talking about others.

- - -

- - -

Na leo nakupasha tuwa, Uyaone mambo
Today I am telling you so that you feel the pain.

Wanisengenya najuwa, Hunifichi jambo
I know you talk behind my back and hide nothing about me.

Na yako nitayafichua, Ya muuza urembo
Thus today I will reveal the truth about the traveling salesman.

- - -

- - -

Kaditama navunja baraza, Tuyawache yapite
I end here, let us allow them to pass.

Akome kunichunguza, Sinifatefate
He should stop interfering with me.

Akirudiya nitamtangaza, Aipatepate
If he starts again, I will disclose [his shame] so he feels the pain.

- - -

- - -

Chorus

Mwambieni, Awache fitina
Tell him to stop meddling.

Halua is a sweet, gelatinous confection, the main ingredients of which are fat, sugar, and cardamom. The etiquette surrounding its consumption breaks normal Swahili procedure in that whereas food touched by one person cannot generally be consumed by another, *halua* is served on a broad platter from which everyone pulls pieces. The singer's girlfriend (a divorced woman) has been metaphorically tasted by another, yet in comparing her to *halua*, she remains sweet and good to eat. He tells his friend to stop badmouthing his girlfriend, warning him that friendship is easily broken (unlike kinship). The singer is also privy to the knowledge that the friend's wife/girlfriend is having an affair with a traveling salesman of beauty items and that if angered further, he will publicly reveal it to generate in the friend similar feelings of pain.

Sahani Moja ("One Plate")
Shabaan Amour, Babloom Modern Taarab, Tanga

Waliwao vitu vyao, Wenyewe bila kujua
Si vipofu peke yao, Wao nao hufanyiwa
Nasi tunakula nao, Kwa raha pasi kukerwa

Your belongings are being eaten without your knowledge.
It is not only the blind to whom this happens.
And we are eating with them with happiness and no cares.

- - -

Ujanja huzidiana, Atendae hutendewa
Si kipofu unaona, Ni vipi chako chaliwa
Na wala habari huna, Kukicha wajifutuwa

The amount of trickiness has increased: he who tricks is also tricked.
You are not blind. You see. How can yours be eaten?
Moreover you don't even know. Every morning you brag.

- - -

Ukitenda utatendwa, Ukuingie ukiwa
Kama hujui tambua, Mnyoaji hunyolewa
Cha mwenzio kichukua, Na chako chachukuliwa

What you do will be done unto you and you will be sorry.
If you don't know, know now: he who shaves has been shaved.
You took someone's, now yours has been taken.

- - -

Wengi tumejifunza, Wivu tumeshaondoa
Tukitendwa hulipiza, Twajilia kwa murua
Subira nyingi huponza, Uamualo amua

We have learned much and eliminated our jealousy.
If it happens to us, we'd take revenge and be jubilant.
If you wait too long, you'll be crushed. Whatever you'll decide, just decide.

- - -

Chorus
Twala nao sahani moja
Hawajijui, hawajitambui

We all eat from one plate.
They don't know themselves, they don't recognize themselves.

Mnazi Mkinda ("Young Coconut Palm")
Kibwana Said, Black Star Musical Club, Tanga

Zindukana mwenye shida, Usoweza jizuwia

Wake up and take care, needy one who cannot give up.

Hujatimia mda, Ubaya umetokea
Umeandama husuda, Werevu wakuchezea

- - -

Walinda wewe walinda, Mali inateketea
Mnazi wako mkinda, Werevu wauchezea
Kwa hila wamekushinda, Wevi hao
  wamezea

- - -

Kuwa mtu wa busara, Wewe mja
  nakwambia
Punguza zako harara, Kula kitu kutapia
Tajakupata hasara, Mali itateketea

- - -

Chorus
Usijitie mikogo, Ukavitapia vingi
Mwanzo awali ni gogo, Ndio mwendo wa
  msingi
Ukikinai kidogo, Mola atakupa kingi

You haven't reached the proper time,
  something bad has happened.
You pursue spitefulness, wily people toy
  with you.

- - -

You protect yourself, yet your wealth is
  destroyed.
Your young coconut palm—wily people
  toy with it.
They beat you in cunning, those thieves
  who desire it.

- - -

Be prudent, you human being, I am
  telling you.
Reduce your rashness to greedily
  consume everything.
You will end up suffering loss, your
  wealth will be destroyed.

- - -

Stop putting on airs, you consumed
  much.
A trunk is the beginning, the source of a
  good foundation.
If you are content with little, God will
  give you plenty.

Kitumbiri ("Monkey" [Track 3 on CD])
A. S. Jinamizi and Hatibu Akida, Lucky Star Musical Club, Tanga

Hata nawe kitumbiri, Kitumbiri majaliwa
Umejifanya hodari, Miti kutaka nyanyuwa
Hali tawi na tambiri, La kushinda kupasua

- - -

Nia yako na dhamiri, Mwisho itakusumbua
Tendwa bila kufikiri, Ni kutaka jiumbua
Kung'oa miti hatari, Utaitoka dunia

- - -

Kaditamati kwa heri, Kitumbiri majaliwa
Kama ujile kwa shari, Naona umeghumiwa
Utaipata athari, Jiti likikwangukia

- - -

Chorus
Kitumbiri majaliwa
Wala kwenu na kwetu wajajaliza

Even you, monkey, favored monkey,
You thought yourself so great, wanting to
  uproot trees,
When you are incapable of breaking
  branches.

- - -

Your aim and intention will ultimately
  cause you trouble.
Doing without thinking is to invite
  embarrassment.
It is dangerous to uproot trees. You will
  die.

- - -

Good-bye, favored monkey.
I think you are confused if you come
  looking for a fight.
If the mighty tree falls on you, you will
  be injured.

- - -

Favored monkey.
You eat at your home and then come to
  eat again at ours.

Mbweha ("Fox")
Kibwana Said, Black Star Musical Club, Tanga

Mbweha nakupa hakika, Sinitafute undani
Ovyo ovyo kuropoka, Kama mtu afukani
Kamba uliyotamka, Na wewe imo shingoni

Fox, let me assure you, do not test my anger,
Babbling nonsense like a fool.
The rope you mentioned encircles your own neck.

- - -

Usisahau watani, Kwenu ulikozalika
Si mtu mwenye thamani, Wala mwenye kusifika
Sinitafute undani, Kesha wajakasirika

- - -

Do not forget joking relations from your birthplace.
You are someone of no value worthy of no praise.
Do not test my anger. Tomorrow you will be angry.

- - -

Kuumbua ukitaka, Ukashifu mshindani
Uwe umekamilika, Hunalo doa mwilini
Hayo uliyotamka, Mbona nawe ukundini

If you want to embarrass or insult your competitor,
You had better be perfect, your body free of defect.
Are you not a member of the very group you criticize?

- - -

Mbweha ninakuusia, Maovu usiyaombe
Utahadhari dunia, Ina hatari kiumbe
Ajabu ni ya ngamia, Kucheka nundu ya ng'ombe

- - -

Fox, I warn you. Do not ask for evil.
Be careful of the world. It is full of danger, human being.
It is a wonder that the camel laughs at the cow's hump.

Kisebusebu ("Pretensions")
Seif Kassim Kisauji, Babloom Modern Taarab, Tanga

Nimekutoa Sahare, Nikakuleta mjini
Sikukutoa kwa ndere, Ni hiari ya moyoni
Leo wanicheza shere, Ulitarajia nini?

I took you from Sahare (a rural area) and brought you to the city.
It was not with a love charm but your own heart's desire.
Today you mock me. What was your original aim?

- - -

Walikuonea gere, Jinsi ulivyonawiri
Chakula hukula pure, Samaka kwa mahamri
Leo mekuwa mwerere, Kula bada wa hiyari

- - -

They were jealous of you, of how you became so attractive.
You did not eat bean porridge. You ate fish and doughnuts.
Today you have become worthless. Eat your cassava porridge.

- - -

Wa wapi walosifika, Kwa huba na taadhima
Wamebaki wazunguka, Wanaposhika wakwama
Huko ni kuadhirika, Hebu kumbuka ya nyuma

- - -

Where are those who became famous for love and honor?
They are wandering around. Wherever they settle they lose out.
What you do is shameful. Just remember the past.

- - -

Checheku checheko hizo, Ujuwe wachekwa wewe

- - -

The laughter you hear—know that they are laughing at you.

Sio kwa zako pambizo, Tuwa usijifutuwe
Wakuona hamnazo, Kwa hicho chako
   kiwewe

Not for your good looks so do not think
   highly of yourself.
To them you seem crazy because of this
   confusion of yours.

- - -

- - -

Chorus
Kisebusebu, Kiroho papo
Wajionea adhabu, Kila ushikapo sipo

You pretend you don't want me, your
   heart's secret desire.
You feel punished. Whatever you grasp
   escapes you.

Shoga ("Friend")
Khalid Akida, Babloom Modern Taarab, Tanga

Shoga yangu nakupasha, Usinifanye mjinga
Cheko na bashasha, leo hii nazipinga
Ambayo wanionyesha, Yananitia uwoga

My friend, I'm informing you: don't
   make a fool of me.
Today I will put a stop to the laughter
   and charm
That you display in order to intimidate me.

- - -

- - -

Checheki na shemegio, Naona zimezidi
Mejua niayo, Wataka kuhusudi
Nimegutuka mwenzio, Haiwi yako juhudi

Your laughter with your brother-in-law I
   see has increased.
I know your intention—you envy and
   begrudge me my good fortune.
I'm wary of you, pal. Your efforts won't
   succeed.

- - -

- - -

Njama yako meijua, Ni kufanya mageuzi
Ilani natoa, Ukaapo maizi
Nitakuja kuumbua, Yakuingie majonzi

I know your goal is to upset things and
   bring change.
I'm issuing you a warning to consider.
I'll come to disgrace you and make you
   sad.

- - -

- - -

Shoga leo nakukanya, Uwache mwenendo
   huo
Tamaa kuifanya, Kwa aliye wa mwenzio
Jua mimi nakuonya, Mwengine haridhi hilo

Friend, today I'm warning you: stop this
   habit
Of coveting one who belongs to your
   friend.
Know that I'm warning you, but another
   would not be satisfied with this.

- - -

- - -

Chorus
Shoga leo nakwambia
Ukome kumzoea shemejio

Friend, today I'm telling you,
Stop flirting with your brother-in-law.

Chapter 5

Mungu Ibariki Afrika ("God Bless Africa")
Tanzanian National Anthem

Mungu ibariki Afrika
Wabariki viongozi wake
Hekima Umoja na Amani

God bless Africa
Bless its leaders
Wisdom, Unity, and Peace

Hizi ni ngao zetu — These are our shields
Afrika na watu wake — Africa and its people
   Ibariki Afrika — Bless Africa
   Ibariki Afrika — Bless Africa
   Tubariki watoto wa — Africa Bless us children of Africa

- - -

Mungu ibariki Tanzania — God bless Tanzania
Dumisha Uhuru na Umoja — Grant eternal Freedom and Unity
Wake kwa waume na watoto — To its women, men and children
Mungu ibariki — God bless
Tanzania na watu wake — Tanzania and its people
   Ibariki Tanzania — Bless Tanzania
   Ibariki Tanzania — Bless Tanzania
   Tubariki watoto wa Tanzania — Bless us children of Tanzania

Chapter 7

Mrema ("Mrema")
Seif Kassim Kisauji, Babloom Modern Taarab, Tanga

Kwa sote Watanzania, Kusema tuna uhuru — All we citizens of Tanzania are free to say what we want.
Twaona na twasikia, Wapo wanaotudhuru — We hear and see that there are people who are not good to us.
Mbele tayahadithia, Msiseme nakufuru — I am about to tell you, and don't say that I am blaspheming.

- - -

Sahare kubwa mfano, Viwanja tumeuziwa — Sahare is a good example; we were sold many plots,
Huu ni mwaka wa tano, Njia hatujachongewa — But it is now more than five years and roads have not been paved.
Tatizo kama hilono, Nani wakulaumiwa? — For problems like this, who is to blame?

- - -

Ukipanda mshahara, Na forodha kadhalika — If you raise salaries, the taxes and duties also increase,
Kwa sisi tulofukara, Twaona twadhalilika — For we the poor, we find ourselves even more oppressed.
Twaomba uwe imara, Tuweze kunufaika — We ask that you be strong so that we may benefit.

- - -

Jukumu la sungusungu, Wengi tumejitolea — Many of us uphold our *Sungusungu* responsibility.
Kubwa nikuomba Mungu, Lipate kuendelea — We ask God that this continue.
Jigeuze nungu nungu, Choma wanozembea — Transform yourself into a porcupine and attack those who evade it.

- - -

Chorus
Fichu fichu, fichua wazi, Mrema twakuombea — Reveal them for what they are, Mrema, we pray for you.
Pumu zimepata mkohozi,* Wahujumu wanalia — The job has found the right person. Corrupt leaders are crying.

**"Pumu zimepata mkohozi"* is a proverb that translates as "Asthma has found one who coughs," meaning that asthma found a good home in someone who already coughs a lot. In the context of this song, it means that the job of cleaning up corruption in the government has found the right person in Mrema; that is, he is the right man for the job.

Ubaya Hauna Kwao ("Evil Has No Home")
Seif Kassim Kisauji, Babloom Modern Taarab, Tanga

Ukialikwa ziara, Njia zinateuliwa	When you come for a visit, certain roads are selected;
Zinachongwa barabara, Ambazo utapitia	They are paved, the ones on which you will pass.
Nyingine zimedorora, Mashimo yameenea	The rest are left as they are ridden with potholes.
- - -	- - -
Usipite njia hizo, Walizokuchagulia	Do not travel those roads they chose for you.
Chagua uzitakazo, Upate kujionea	Choose your own that you may see their condition.
Mengi ni malimbikizo, Nchi inateketea	Many things have been delayed. Meanwhile the country rots.
- - -	- - -
Hebu amua ziara, Ya ghafula kuvamia	You should make a surprise visit.
Wananchi tutakerwa, Hawakuitegemea	The citizens will be distressed, not expecting it.
Utayaona madhara, Nchi inavyodhuria	You will see the damage, how the country has been ruined.
- - -	- - -
Wao haswa ndio chanzo, Vyama vingi kuliliwa	They are the original reason for the cries for multipartyism.
Hasira wengi tunazo, Kwa nini mali yaliwa	Many of us are filled with anger: Why is our wealth eaten?
Hawatovipa mkazo, Tumeshawagutukia	They will not support multipartyism, but we already know them for what they are.
- - -	- - -
CCM Msimamo, Vyama vingi hatuhofu	CCM prevails, opposition parties do not frighten us.
Wasanii nasi tumo, Tuimara mara dufu	Even we performers belong to CCM, we support it twice as much,
Bali kuna milalamo, Ya watu waharibifu	Yet there are complaints about the corrupt ones in the Party.
- - -	- - -
Mkutano meamua, Sisi twaukubalia	At the meeting you decided upon multipartyism; we accept that.
Hao wanaotumiwa, Kwa hamu twawangojea	We wait for those to come to determine their true intentions.
CCM imetua, Wasiwasi imetoa	CCM has settled upon this, we are not worried.
- - -	- - -

Chorus

Ali Mwinyi, Ubaya hauna kwao	Ali Mwinyi, evil has no home.
Waondoe watu hao, washindwe tena kutamba	Remove those people, stop their boasting.

Manufaa yao, Kwetu sisi ni msiba
Viongozi hao, Twendeni nao sambamba
Watatudhuru

They benefit themselves while we are in mourning.
Those leaders need to be followed step by step.
They will destroy us.

Ngwinji ("High-Class Prostitute" [Track 10 on CD])
Othman Soud, Tanzania One Theatre, Dar es Salaam

Eti ngwinji atambe, Atambie kitu gani?
Eti nae ajigambe, Ajigambe ana nini?
Hata ajiremberembe, Ngwinji amtake nani?
Eee ngwinji eee, Usijitie kundini

A prostitute puts on airs! For what does she put on airs?
She also boasts! Of what can she boast?
Even if she puts on makeup, who will want her?
You prostitute, don't include yourself in the group.

- - -

Ngwinji nae hujisifu, Kammiliki fulani
Hujidai maarufu, Mzuri hapa mjini
Kumbe anajikashifu, Ngwinji apendeze nini?
Eee ngwinji eee, Hata aibu huoni?

The prostitute even praises herself for controlling someone.
She acts as though she were famous, the beauty of the town.
In reality, she denigrates herself. In what lies her beauty?
You prostitute, you feel no shame?

- - -

Hukaa kwenye vikundi, Kudanganya ighiwani
Eti kila wikiendi, Anajimwaga mjini
Husema anaspendi, Dola za kimarekani
Eee ngwinji eee, Hundi atakupa nani?

She sits in some groups, telling people lies,
That every weekend she parades around town.
She says that she spends U.S. dollars.
You prostitute, who will give you the check?

- - -

Kwenye watu wapendwao, Ngwinji humo hesabuni
Hebu punguza hashuo, Kwani umezidi nini?
Ni zamani sio leo, Umeshashuka thamani
Eee ngwinji eee, Uombwe unacho nini?

You are not included among those who are loved.
Better you reduce your strutting. What is so special about you?
It was long ago, not now. You have dropped in value.
You prostitute, what do you have that someone would want?

- - -

Chorus
Eti ngwinji atambe, Atambie kitu gani?
Eti nae ajigambe, Ajigambe ana nini?

A prostitute puts on airs! For what does she put on airs?
She also boasts! Of what can she boast?

TX Mpenzi ("Expatriate Lover")
Othman Soud, Tanzania One Theatre, Dar es Salaam

TX Mpenzi,* Dakta wangu zamani
Ameispeshalaizi, Digrii yake Sir John

Expatriate lover, my doctor from long ago.
He is specialized, his degree from Sir John.

Ananipasua tezi, Siku nyingi tumboni
TX nipasue. Toa maradhi ya ndani

He has been removing tumors from my
abdomen since long ago.
TX, cut me open. Remove my inner illness.

- - -

TX ana cheti, Kapasi Ujerumani
Hunipa nusu kaputi, Nazimia kitandani
Na fahamu sipati, Nangoja operesheni
TX nipasue. Taja vyote sikughini

TX has a certificate. He graduated in
Germany.
He gives me anesthesia and I pass out on
the bed.
I remain unconscious, waiting for the
operation.
TX, cut me open. Mention anything and I
won't refuse you.

- - -

Mimi ndo mgonjwa wake, Bibi jiweke pembeni
Napenda sindano zake, Haziumi mwilini
Aminyapo dawa zake, Ganzi tele maungoni
TX nipasue. Mi nawe hatunyimani

I am his only patient. Lady, step aside.
I love his injections, they do not hurt my
body.
When he applies medicine, my body goes
numb.
TX, cut me open. You and I do not refuse
each other.

- - -

TX akipasua, Raha hupanda kichwani
Kisu anachotumia, Kimoja si thineni
Hafanyi kwa kuripua, Apasua kwa makini
TX nipasue. Mwengine simthamini

When TX lacerates me, my head fills with
happiness.
He uses only one knife, not two.
He does not "hit and run." He cuts very
gently.
TX, cut me open. I do not cherish anyone
else.

- - -

TX hasiti, Kufanya operesheni
Anapenda katikati, Hanipasui pembeni
*Kwa nyuzi za katikati, Ashona ndani kwa
ndani*
TX nipasue. Niipate afueni

TX does not hesitate to operate.
He likes the middle. He does not incise the
ends.
He sews up my middle with thread deep
inside.
TX, cut me open that I may recover.

- - -

Chorus
*Nipasue daktari nipasue, Toa maradhi ya
ndani*
Nipasue TX nipasue, Nangoja operesheni

Cut me open, doctor, cleave me. Remove
my inner illness.
Cut me open, TX, cleave me. I await your
operation.

*"TX" was once the prefix on all car license plates belonging to foreign nationals resid-
ing in Tanzania. It identified the driver/owner as an expatriate. In 1992, the prefix was
dropped from official usage, but nonetheless remained in common parlance as a term for an
expatriate or, as in this case, something akin in quality to "expatriateness" (which is thought
of in largely positive terms).

Mtwangio ("Pestle")
Tanzania One Theatre, Dar es Salaam

Yategeni masikio, Mpate kunisikia
Kubwa langu kusudio, Leo nnawaambia

Pay attention with your ears so that you
hear me.
My primary aim—today I am telling you,

Nausifu mtwangio, Nnao twangia	I praise this pestle with which I pound.
- - -	- - -
Kwa kutwanga namba wani, Sifa ninautolea	For pounding it is number one. I give it praise.
Sithubutu asilani, Mwengine kuutumia	I will never try to use another one.
Wa mwengine sitamani, Huu nimeuzowea	I do not desire someone else's. I am accustomed to this.
- - -	- - -
Ukweli nawambieni, Si utani ndugu zangu	I tell you the truth, it is no joke, my relatives,
Uingiapo kinuni, Huu mtwangio wangu	When it enters the mortar, this pestle of mine,
Unatwanga kwa makini, Kwenye hiki kinu changu	It pounds perfectly in my mortar.
- - -	- - -
Nakamilisha usemi, Nilosema ya hakika	I have completed what I want to say, and it is the truth.
Mtwangio wangu mimi, Kweli umekamilika	I am sure of my pestle.
Hata kwa masaa kumi, Hutwanga bila kuchoka	Even for ten hours, it can pound without tiring.
- - -	- - -

Chorus

Mtwangio twanga, Usichoke mtwangio	Pestle, pound and do not tire, oh pestle.
Twanga bila wasiwasi, Ewe mtwangio wangu	Pound without worries, you my pestle.
Kinu kimeniridhia	The mortar accepts you.

CCM Nambari Wani ("CCM Is Number One")
Captain John Komba, JWTZ Kwaya, (then) Tanzania One Theatre Kwaya

Watanzania napo, Watanzania twapendeza	Tanzanians also, Tanzanians are beautiful.
Nambari wani eee, Nambari wani niCCM	CCM is number one.
Tieni Mwinyi, Tieni kwa moyo mmoja	Support Mwinyi with one heart.
Nambari wani ni CCM	CCM is number one.
Malecela tieni, Salmini tieni	Support Malecela, support Salmin.*
Tieni tieni kwa moyo mmoja	Support [them] with one heart.
Nambari wani eee, Nambari wani ni CCM	CCM is number one.
Dar es Salaam tieni	Support Dar es Salaam.
Tieni kwa moyo mmoja, Nambari wani ni CCM	Support with one heart, CCM is number one.
Tanga tieni, Nambari wani ni CCM	Support Tanga, CCM is number one.
Kilimanjaro tieni, Nambari wani ni CCM	Support Kilimanjaro, CCM is number one.
Pemba tieni, Nambari wani ni CCM	Support Pemba, CCM is number one.
Tieni tieni kwa moyo mmoja	Support with one heart.
Nambari wani eee, Nambari wani ni CCM	CCM is number one.

*These references are to John Malecela, former Tanzanian prime minister and vice president; Salmin Amour, president of Zanzibar.

Bunduki ("Rifle")
Kibwana Said, Black Star Musical Club, Tanga

Bunduki naidadisi, Mliopo sikizeni	Listen you who are here while I analyze the rifle.

Hayo si kama nahisi, Ya ukweli yashikeni
Bunduki bila risasi, Yaua namna gani?

I am not merely guessing, keep this truth in mind.
A rifle without bullets—how can it kill?

- - -

- - -

Bunduki yajulikana, Kama chombo cha thamani
Nakuwinda yatakana, Muwe na risasi ndani
Lakini mwako hamna, Atakae hofu ni nani

A rifle is well known as an expensive item.
In order to hunt it requires bullets inside,
But in yours, there aren't any. Who will fear you?

- - -

- - -

Somo acha utukutu, Msitu kuuchezea
Hivyo si vyema mwenzetu, Mabaya kujitakia
Bunduki isiyo kitu, Huwezi kujivunia

Namesake, stop joking, stop playing with a jungle.
It is not good, friend, you are inviting trouble.
An empty rifle is not something of which to be proud.

- - -

- - -

Chorus
Yaua namna gani, Bunduki bila risasi?

How does a rifle without bullets kill?

Sore Mpishi ("Sorry, Chef")
Mohamed Mrisho, Black Star Musical Club, Tanga

Limao limeharibu, Mchuzi umechachuka
Mlaji aamejaribu, Na ladha imetoweka
Sasa imebidi taabu, Mchuzi hautolika

A lime caused the sauce to ferment.
The one eating it tried but its taste was gone.
Now this has become a problem—the sauce will never be eaten.

- - -

- - -

Mpishi nipe sababu, Mchuzi kuharibika
Nani aliyeharibu, Uliyempa kupika
Kama ni wewe swahibu, Kama ni wewe tamka

The chef gave me the reason for why the sauce spoiled.
Whom did you put in charge of cooking it that spoiled it?
If it is you, my friend, speak out.

- - -

- - -

Vijana na kina babu, Chakula walikitaka
Walisogea karibu, Majanvini kujiweka
Maji hayakuwa taabu, Mikono ikaosheka

Young men and old men wanted the food.
They moved close to it and sat down on mats ready to eat.
Water was not a problem, and hands were washed.

- - -

- - -

Nikisema taratibu, Nielewe kwa hakika
Mmoja alinijibu, Kwa siri akatamka
Limao ndio sababu, Mchuzi kuharibika

Even if I speak slowly, you have to understand me for sure.
One of them answered me, secretly spoke to me.
A lime is the reason why the sauce spoiled.

- - -

- - -

Chorus
Sore mpishi sore, Mchuzi umechachuka

Sorry, chef, sorry. The sauce fermented.

Muongo Afadhali ya Mchawi ("Better a Sorcerer Than a Liar")
Tanzania One Theatre Kwaya, Dar es Salaam

Muongo, mbea, afadhali mchawi	Better a sorcerer than a liar or gossip.
Muongo akipita muepuke	When a liar passes, beware.
Muongo, mbea, anavuruga amani	A liar, a gossip, disrupts the peace.
Muongo, mbea, anaua	A liar, a gossip, kills.
- - -	- - -
Akishapita muongo,	When a liar passes,
Amani, upendo vyote viwili hakuna	Peace and love are both absent.
Muongo, mbea, akishakupa mgongo	When a liar, a gossip, shows you his
Ujue ameeneza hasama	back,
Muongo, mbea, sawasawa na tapeli	Know that he has spread strife.
Muongo, rafiki yake shetani	A liar, a gossip, is the same as a swindler.
Muongo, huyo mbea, ufisadi na fedhuli	A liar's friend is the devil.
	A liar, a gossip, only wants to abuse and
	brag.
- - -	- - -
Muongo hakaribishwi mbinguni	A liar is not welcome in Heaven.
Muongo, mbea, anaua pale penye utulivu	A liar, a gossip, destroys the peace.
Muongo akija ataitia hiyana	When a liar comes, he will inject mean-
	spiritedness.
- - -	- - -
Muongo, mbea, akisha imwaga sumu	When a liar or gossip spreads poison,
Wallahi litazuka sokomoko	I swear it will cause a big problem.
Muongo, mbea, akishafika kundini tegemea	When a liar, a gossip joins the crowd,
mfarakano	discord results.
- - -	- - -
Muongo, mbea, akisha kuwafitini	A liar, a gossip, after causing trouble,
Mjue hamtapeana mikono	Will not shake hands—know this.
Muongo, mbea, anaua hapendi maendeleo	A liar, a gossip, kills and does not like
	development.
- - -	- - -
Muongo, mbea, hadi atayavuruga	A liar, a gossip, until he stirs everything
Muongo, mbea, ukishamuona	up,
Muongo, mbea, adui azomewe mara moja	When you see a liar, a gossip,
muungo	Taunt him right away.

Tuombe ("Let Us Pray")
Tanzania One Theatre (Kwaya), Dar es Salaam

Shime shime wote, shime shime jamani	Come on, everyone, come on people,
Tukazane kuomba	Let us pray hard.
Dunia nayo sasa imekua tambara	The world now has become a torn sheet.
Dunia sasa uwanja wa mapambano	The world now is a demolition derby.
- - -	- - -
Hakuna kufatana, hakuna kupendana,	No more mutual support, no more love,
tuombe	let us pray.
Ulimwengu wote umejaa dhuluma	The whole world has filled with
Binadamu wachinjana kama wanyama	oppression.
Tazama Somali	People are slaughtering each other like
	animals.
	Look at Somalia.

Tazama Msumbiji	Look at Mozambique.
Tuombe	Let us pray.
- - -	- - -
Dunia kwa sasa imani imetoweka	In this world, peace has vanished.
Wengine wanaleta visingizi vya dini	Some produce religious reasons.
Tazama Ulaya,	Look at Europe.
Tazama Afrika	Look at Africa.
Tuombe	Let us pray.

Nyumba ya Jirani Yaungua Moto ("The Neighbor's House Is on Fire")
Tanzania One Theatre Kwaya, Dar es Salaam

Nyumba ya jirani yetu sasa yaungua moto	Our neighbor's house is now on fire.
Wewe, bwana, fanya hima, twende tukazime	You, man, hurry up, let's go put it out.
Tukiachia nyumba itateketea	If we leave it, the house will be destroyed.
Madhara yake sote yatatukumba	The damage will affect us all.
Tushirikiane, mwenzangu, twende tukazime	Let us unite, my friend, let's go put it out.
- - -	- - -
Mwenye nyumba amebaki ameduwaa	The owner of the house remained surprised.
Na chanzo chake ameshindwa kutueleza	He was not able to tell us the cause,
Lakini kuna jambo mwenzangu, twende tukazime	But there should be something, my friend, let's go put it out.
Mimi nimeshachunguza chanzo cha tatizo lile wewe bwana	I have discovered the cause of that problem, my friend.
Sasa fanya hima, twende tukazime	So hurry up, let's go put it out.
Ukorofi umeanza ndani mwake	The trouble started in his own house.
Wapangaji wamekosa kuelewana	The tenants are fighting amongst themselves.
Kila mtu anajifanya anajua	Each one acts as if he knows everything.
- - -	- - -
Mwenye nyumba punguza huruma	Owner of the house, be strict.
Twende tukazime	Let's go put out the fire.

Mwanya ("Attractive Gap between the Front Teeth")
Seif Kassim Kisauji, Babloom Modern Taarab, Tanga

Mwanya ulikuwa nao, Hukuwaza ya mbeleni	You had a *mwanya*, but you did not think ahead.
Ukaiondoa ngao, Wakakugonga kichwani	You removed your shield and they hit you in the head.
Kalie na hao hao, Walokutia jangani	Go cry to those who put you in trouble.
- - -	- - -
Sivizuri nikutete, Kama u papo sikia	It is not good for me to speak behind your back, so if you are there, listen:
Tena nakutema mate, 'Ptuka chaka!' yakwelea	I spit on you, "Ptuka chaka!" so that you understand.
Pengo linavuja ute, Matandiko wachafua	Your gaping hole leaks saliva, soiling the bedding.
- - -	- - -

Ukiweka atifisho, Bure unajisumbua
Domo litanuka jasho, Huwezi kukurubiwa
Huna tena ubishoo, Roho utatuchafua

If you get an artificial tooth, you trouble
  yourself needlessly.
Your mouth emits a terrible odor—no
  one can come near you.
You no longer have cause to boast. You
  defile our souls.

- - -

Pengo lina mkoromo, Unamuudhi mwandani
Ngurumo mumo kwa mumo, Haipati
  burudani
Haupati msimamo, Budi hana afanyeni?
- - -

- - -

Your hole snores disturbing your partner.
Such a terrible racket—he gets no relief,
It does not cease. There is no escape—
  what is he to do?

- - -

Chorus
Mwanya umeufuja, Pengo linanguruma
Wasiwasi wasiwasi unao, Wasaalam!

You destroyed your *mwanya*. Your hole
  snores.
You are worried. It's all over!

Kumanya Mdigo ("To Know a Digo" [Track 9 on CD])
Waziri Kapalata, Babloom Modern Taarab, Tanga

Usimuone kuranda, Mdigo ukambera
Uchimuona kuonda, Kwa ajili ya njara
Neno asirorironda, Kusudi kumuendera

When you see a Digo going about, don't
  look down on him.
When you see him grow thin, it is due to
  hardship.
Don't do to him things he doesn't like.

- - -

Njakara vonda muona, Arivyo kagunguara
Achimia pewe kana, Kwa mwiri kumsakara
Hiye muogove sana, Mriche kumvumbira

- - -

Despite his appearance, he is hard as
  nails.
When he walks, he looks weak because
  his body is aged.
But be frightened of him. Don't play
  around with him.

- - -

Mdigo kana msena, Msenawe ni gongoro
Njakaro vonda muona, Zigida kumenda
  bara
Usizieke nae sana, Manono kumdhanira

- - -

The Digo has no friends. His friend is the
  millipede.
Even though you see him marked with a
  *zigida**
Do not laugh at him nor think well of
  him.

- - -

Asikwambe niva pesa, Nawe uchimwamba
  gwira
Uumanye nawe sasa, Ndio bai ukaera
Ayaziendera pesa, Urikose hata gwara

- - -

When he says, "Give me money," and
  you give him,
You should know that the matter is
  finished.
He will use many ruses to avoid
  returning even five shillings.

- - -

Chorus
Kama kumanya Mdigo, Haya uza
  ndambirwa
Hiye muogove sana, Mriche kumvumbira

If you don't know the Digo, ask and you
  will be told.
Be afraid of him. Don't play around with
  him.

*A *zigida* is a mark on a person's forehead acquired from frequent praying in the Islamic way, which requires the supplicant to touch his/her forehead to the ground. It is considered a sign of great devotion.

Chapter 8

Mkomesheni ("Make Him Stop Harassing Me")
Khalid Akida and Seif Kassim Kisauji, Babloom Modern Taarab, Tanga

Ninataka niwatume, Mwendapo
    mkamwambie
Sitomwacha alalame, Bora la kweli ajue
Mwelezeni anikome, Pendo langu alivue
	I want to send you to go tell him
	I won't leave him to complain. Better he
	    know the truth.
	Tell him to stop harassing me, to shed
	    his love for me.

- - -	- - -

Mkomesheni akome, Mie sinijuejue
Sababu yani niseme, Walimwengu atambue
Mwengine naatazame, Atayewezana naye
	Make him stop harassing me. He should
	    forget about me.
	Why should I give my reasons for the
	    world to know?
	Let him look for someone else who can
	    suffer his behavior.

- - -	- - -

Iwapo nilikosea, Kumfanya wangu yeye
Nimekwisha jikosoa, Kheri niwe mbali naye
Mapenzi hajayajua, Mwuacheni ajishaue
	Even though I erred to make him mine.
	I have already corrected my mistake.
	    Better I be far away from him.
	He doesn't understand love. Let him
	    boast all he wants.

- - -	- - -

Sababu sitotamka, Yeye yote ayajua
Sipendi akaumbuka, Mradi kamvunjia
Hubaze mezitapika, Akome kunizoea
	I will never explain my reasons—he
	    knows them all.
	I do not wish to publicly shame him for
	    failing to stay true.
	He should forget about me. I have
	    vomited his love.

Nahodha ("Captain" [Track 11 on CD])
Ali Mtoto Seif and Elizabeth Sijila, Jeshi la Kujenga Taifa (JKT) Taarab, Dar es Salaam

Hayupo asoyajua, Haya ntayoyasema
Vyombo vya kusafiria, Huenda mbele daima
Nahodha twategemea, Awe mbele akinema
Manahodha wa mashua, Kwa nini wakae
    nyuma?
	There isn't anyone who doesn't know
	    what I am about to say.
	Vehicles for travel normally move
	    forward.
	We hope that the captain will be in front
	    to steer.
	Captains of boats—why should they sit
	    at the back?

- - -	- - -

Manahodha wa mashua, Na ngarawa
    mnadhima
Sukani mwashikilia, Na hali mkiwa nyuma
	Captains of boats and sailboats cause us
	    trouble.
	You hold the tiller while you are at the
	    back.

Ajali ikitokea, Nani ajibu lawama?

\- \- \-

Kuwa mbele abiria, Nahodha akawa nyuma
Ni kinyume cha sheria, Kimwendo na
*   usalama*
Nawaomba kuchungua, Ingawa ya tangu
*   zama*

\- \- \-

Nahodha nakushauri, Uwe mbele sio nyuma
Ndipo mimi nitakiri, Kuwa safari salama
Bila hivyo sisafiri, Naichelewa zahama

\- \- \-

Chorus
Nahodha kakae mbele, Abiria tuwe nyuma
Uvikwepe vipengele, Chombo kisende mrama
Tupige vigelegele, Tukishafika salama

If an accident occurs, who will respond
to the blame?

\- \- \-

Passengers in front, captains at the back.
This mode of travel goes against the law
and is unsafe.
I ask you to investigate, even though it is
from long ago.

\- \- \-

Captain, I advise you to be in front, not
at the back.
Only there will I agree that the journey
will be safe.
Minus this, I will not travel. I am afraid
of distress.

\- \- \-

Captain, go sit in front. We passengers
should be at the back.
Avoid side-paths that our vessel should
not pitch and roll.
So that we can shout with joy when we
have arrived safely.

Appendix B

POEM FROM TANGA TECHNICAL SCHOOL

National Arts and Language Competition, Tanga Region, Northern Zone Entrant
Fani ya Mashairi (Poetry Competition) Performed November 6, 1992, Arusha
Written by Joseph Mayala K. IV, 1989 (Tanga Technical School)

NGUZO NI SISI VIJANA ("We, the Youth, Are the Pillar")

1. *Wasanii twaingia, shairi kuwaimbia,*
   Na ujumbe maridhia, machache kuwaambia,
   Yafaayo kutumia, katika zetu kadhia,
   Nguzo nisisi vijana, katika Taifa letu.

   We artists have come to sing you a poem
   with a message, a few things to tell you
   that are good for you in these circumstances.
   We, the youth, are the pillar in our nation

2. *Taifa linapumua, katika hii dunia,*
   Lenye haja kuinua, raia kuwaokoa,
   Na kiupata shufaa, uchumi kuuinua,
   Nguzo nisisi vijana, katika Taifa letu.

   The nation breathes in this world
   with a need to stand up, rescue the citizenry,
   and to attain fulfillment, improve our economy.
   We, the youth, are the pillar in our nation.

3. *Taifa letu mwajua, lahitaji ujamaa,*
   Na ngao ya ujamaa, vijana wenye kufaa,
   Wazee wajivunia, vijana walo shujaa,
   Nguzo nisisi vijana, katika Taifa letu.

   We know our nation needs socialism,
   and we able youths are the shield of socialism.
   Elders boast that the youth are heroes.
   We, the youth, are the pillar in our nation

4. *Hasha kujiropokea, na neno yasomurua*
   Au kujizururia, bilashi kwenye majia,
   Nchi inadidimia, na sisi tunasinzia,
   Nguzo nisisi vijana, katika Taifa letu.

   Don't speak out with words which are not
   *   good,*
   or roam aimlessly around.
   The country is declining, and we are sleepy.
   We, the youth, are the pillar in our nation

5. *Vijana twawausia, mazuri kujifanyia,*
   Ni chungu sana dunia, acha kiuparamia,
   Itakwacha unalia, na tabu kukuachia,
   Nguzo nisisi vijana, katika Taifa letu.

   We youths have the promise to do good.
   The world is full of bitterness—stop wasting
   *   time.*
   You will be left crying and with troubles.
   We, the youth, are the pillar in our nation.

6. *Taifa lategemea, kilimo cha manufaa,*
   Uchumi kujijengea, faida kujichumia,
   Na viwanda ni sawia, kutoa nyingi bidhaa
   Nguzo nisisi vijana, katika Taifa letu.

   The nation depends on profitable agriculture.
   A self-building economy reaps profit,
   And factories should produce many goods.
   We, the youth, are the pillar in our nation

7. *Uchumi wategemea, vijana kuuinua,*
   Vibaya kututegea, peke yetu kutwachia,
   Bure ukajikalia, kazi ukaisusia,
   Nguzo nisisi vijana, katika Taifa letu.

   We depend on youth to raise the economy.
   It's bad for you to leave us out, by ourselves.
   It's useless to just sit and stop working.
   We, the youth, are the pillar in our nation.

8. *Nguzo ukiichimbia, yabidi kushindilia,*
   Vijana mkikimbia, nani atatujengea?
   Mwisho itaangukia, NI AIBU YA MADOA!!
   Nguzo nisisi vijana, katika Taifa letu.

   To build a pillar you must firmly pack the earth.
   If youth run away, who will build for us?
   In the end it will fall and cause shameful stains.
   We, the youth, are the pillar in our nation.

9. *Nasema haya kwa nia, na sauti ya kupaa,*
   Vijana mnasinzia, uchumi wadidimia,
   Nani atauinua, sisi tukipuuzia,
   Nguzo nisisi vijana, katika Taifa letu.

   I say this with intent and a loud voice.
   Youths, you are sleeping. The economy declines.
   Who will raise the economy if we neglect it?
   We, the youth, are the pillar in our nation.

10. *Nchi yetu changa pia, hakuna asiyejua,*
    Nyuma nyuma kubakia , ili waje kutwinua,
    Hili sisi twachukia latuliza latuua,
    Nguzo nisisi vijana, katika Taifa letu.

    Our nation is young, everyone knows this.
    Backwards we remain for them to come raise us.
    This we hate. It makes us cry and will kill us.
    We, the youth, are the pillar in our nation.

11. *Wapo madui pia, wapingao ujamaa,*
    Hawataki kusikia, neno kujitegemea,
    Wadiriki kutengua, uchumi kuuchafua,
    Nguzo nisisi vijana, katika Taifa letu.

    There also are enemies who hate socialism.
    They don't like to hear about self-reliance.
    They wait to divide us and destroy our economy.
    We, the youth, are the pillar in our nation.

12. *Uchumi kautifua, hitilafu kuutia,*
    Na mno kutusumbua, na hila kutufanyia,
    Mengi kutupakazia, ya ufyoi wa kufyoa,
    Nguzo nisisi vijana, katika Taifa letu.

    Messing with the economy, bringing discord,
    And causing us great trouble, employing deceit,
    Leveling much slander, and insulting us.
    We, the youth, are the pillar in our nation.

13. *Elimu tutie nia, hasa tekinolojia,*
    Sayansi kujisomea, Tukitaka kusogea,
    Bila sayansi kataa, hakuna kuendelea,
    Nguzo nisisi vijana, katika Taifa letu.

    We should strive for education, especially technology.
    Study science if we want to progress.
    If we reject science, we cannot develop.
    We, the youth, are the pillar in our nation.

14. *Ndugu tunawaapia, waziwazi twatongoa,*
    Wageni wanaingia, makwao wakitokea,
    Nchi bora Tanzania, ndivyo wanavyosifia,
    Nguzo nisisi vijana, katika Taifa letu.

    Comrades, we swear openly we tell the truth.
    Foreigners are entering from their countries.
    "Tanzania is a great country," is what they say.
    We, the youth, are the pillar in our nation.

15. *Mengi tulokusudia, mipango kujiwekea,*
    Budi kuyakazania, katu tusije kulia,
    Wa Tanga hadi Songea, Arusha na Kaliua,
    Nguzo nisisi vijana, katika Taifa letu.

    We have many objectives and many plans.
    Better we exert ourselves to avoid crying later.
    From Tanga to Songea, Arusha to Kaliua,
    We, the youth, are the pillar in our nation.

16. *Katu hatujasinzia, hadhara kuiachia,*
    Ulinzi wa Tanzania, ni jukumu letu pia,
    Wa kando hatatokea, hilo kuja tufanyia,
    Nguzo nisisi vijana, katika Taifa letu.

    We should never allow ourselves to appear sleepy in public.
    The defense of Tanzania is also our responsibility,
    So outsiders can't come to harm us.
    We, the youth, are the pillar in our nation.

17. *Taifa lategemea, vijana walotulia,*
    Umuhimu kutambua, na adui kuwajua,
    Macho twapaswa kodoa, pande zote kuyatoa,
    Nguzo nisisi vijana, katika Taifa letu.

    The nation depends on respectable youth.
    It's important to know this and our enemies too.
    We must aim our eyes in every direction.
    We, the youth, are the pillar in our nation.

18. *Mijini kukimbilia, kwa makundi ya mamia,*
    Nini wanachofatia, kuranda hovyo na njia,
    Kazi wakizikimbia, vijijini zimejaa,
    Nguzo nisisi vijana, katika Taifa letu.

To run to the cities in groups of hundreds,
What are you seeking, loitering in the streets?
You run from work, there's plenty in the
    villages.
    We, the youth, are the pillar in our nation.

19. *Kipato cha kuvamia, mno twakipendelea,*
    Huzuni zimekimbia, nyuso zimetuchupaa,
    Tumekuwa haramia, magwiji wa kukwapua,
    Nguzo nisisi vijana, katika Taifa letu.

Sudden wealth is what we like.
Compassion has run away, faces lack shame.
We have become thieves, prostitutes who steal.
    We, the youth, are the pillar in our nation.

20. *Shughuli za kuchomoa, na zile za kuvizia,*
    Hili tunalikemea, bure tunajiumbua,
    Katika hii dunia, kipimo cha kazi ni nia,
    Nguzo nisisi vijana, katika Taifa letu.

Pickpockets and criminals,
This we rebuke; foolishly we destroy ourselves.
In this world, the measure of work is intention.
    We, the youth, are the pillar in our nation.

21. *Wengi wetu twadhania, starehe sio njia,*
    Muziki kujichezea, na ukahaba sawia,
    Mwili kuusabilia, hovyo watu kuchezea,
    Nguzo nisisi vijana, katika Taifa letu.

We think about many of us, pleasure is not the
    way.
Playing music and promiscuity are the same.
Giving your body away for others to enjoy.
    We, the youth, are the pillar in our nation.

22. *Fagio limewadia, hodi limetupigia,*
    Mno linatufagia, laifagia dunia,
    Hili twapaswa kujua, ukimwi unatuua,
    Nguzo nisisi vijana, katika Taifa letu.

The broom has arrived and asks to enter.
It sweeps steadily the entire world.
It's important to know: AIDS is killing us.
    We, the youth, are the pillar in our nation.

23. *Aibu tumeivaa, kama vile sidiria,*
    Vijana tunapungua, kila uchao wa jua,
    Gonjwa limetukitia, ile nanga ya udhia,
    Nguzo nisisi vijana, katika Taifa letu.

We wear shame like a bra.
Youths decrease with every sunset.
This illness sits with us, an anchor of hardship.
    We, the youth, are the pillar in our nation.

24. *Gharika imetujia, Mungu ametuletea,*
    Macho kimeyakodoa, kifo kinatutishia,
    Ukimwi umeenea, dawa hatujagundua,
    Nguzo nisisi vijana, katika Taifa letu.

A terrible storm has arrived brought by God.
Eyes wide open, death frightens us.
AIDS has spread, no cure has been discovered.
    We, the youth, are the pillar in our nation.

25. *Vijana twawaombea, maghufira kwa Jalia,*
    Pia kutupunguzia, adhabu hiyo ni baa,
    Vijana tumepungua, upupu umetwinia,
    Nguzo nisisi vijana, katika Taifa letu.

We youths pray earnestly to God.
It reduces us, this punishment is terrible.
We youths are fewer, poison ivy has besieged
    us.
    We, the youth, are the pillar in our nation.

26. *Yote tulowatajia, na yote tulogusia,*
    Vyema kuyazingatia, kwa matendo twakazia,
    Sio maneno umbea, huku tunateketea,
    Nguzo nisisi vijana, katika Taifa letu.

All this that we mention and hint at,
It is good to take to heart and follow with
    action.
It is not mere gossip. We are dying.
    We, the youth, are the pillar in our nation.

27. *Heshima jambo murua, wazazi kuwapatia,*
    Na wakubwa wote pia, sharti kuwasalimia,
    Hilo tukiliachia, soni tutajipatia,
    Nguzo nisisi vijana, katika Taifa letu.

Respect is a good thing to give your parents
and all elders; you must greet them.
If we leave that, we will bring shame on
    ourselves.
    We, the youth, are the pillar in our nation.

28. *Umoja twamalizia, sijambo la kuachia,*
    Tushikamane jamaa, amani kiutetea,
    Amani kitokomea, vurugu itabakia,
    Nguzo nisisi vijana, katika Taifa letu.

    Unity we relinquish—it's not something to give
    up.
    Let us join together, people, to defend peace.
    If peace disappears, chaos will remain.
    We, the youth, are the pillar in our nation.

29. *Hongera twawatolea, viongozi wote pia,*
    Kuongoza Tanzania, kwa amani na murua,
    Sifa tumejipatia, pande zote za dunia,
    Nguzo nisisi vijana, katika Taifa letu.

    Congratulations we offer to all our leaders
    For leading Tanzania with peace and elegance.
    We have received praise from all parts of the
    world.
    We, the youth, are the pillar in our nation.

30. *Hapa nanga tunatia, tama tunatamatia,*
    Hatuna kuongezea, mwisho tumeufikia,
    Heri tunawatakia, taifa kujijengea,
    Nguzo nisisi vijana, katika Taifa letu.

    Here we set the anchor, we have finished.
    We have no more to say, we have reached the
    end.
    We wish blessings for all that our nation
    rebuild itself.
    We, the youth, are the pillar in our nation.

Appendix C

NOTES ON THE ACCOMPANYING CD

The *Performing the Nation* CD is included for two reasons. First, it is intended to provide examples of the varieties of music discussed in the book for readers' fuller comprehension of the material. Printed text does poor justice to aural arts. Thus my editor, David Brent, and I agreed that, especially given the scarcity of currently available commercial recordings of Tanzanian music, the book could convey a much better sense (an appropriately aural sense) of *taarab, ngoma,* and *dansi* if accompanied by an audio CD. Second, on the advice of my colleague Werner Graebner, owner of Dizim Records, friend, and a fellow anthropologist, we have approached the production of this CD with the intent of creating a high-quality recording that is worthy of listening in its own right, independent of the book. For this reason, the songs appear in the order that makes the most musical sense, rather than following their order in the book. Full song texts with translations for all the songs on the CD are given in appendix A, and the chapters in which they are discussed in the text are identified at the end of each description below. Werner mastered the CD in Germany and did a wonderful job, so enjoy!

Track 1 **"Nimezama" ("I Am Drowning"), poetry by Hamza Ali, music by Mussa Majengo, performed by Mwanahela Salum with Golden Star Musical Club, Tanga.** Golden Star Musical Club is one of the few remaining Tanga *taarab* clubs as of this writing. It is identified with the more Indian-influenced *taarab* style so admired in Mombasa. Golden Star thus performs frequently in Mombasa and is as popular there as in Tanga. This song describes the overwhelming feelings of love and the risk involved in opening your heart to someone who has yet to prove himself or herself. "I am drowning in love," says the singer. "I don't know if I'll emerge safely. I cannot free myself. I am in great distress." (Chapter 3)

Track 2 **"Pendo Raha Yake" ("The Joy of Love"), poetry by Salehe Kiroboto, music by Kamal Basha, performed by Saidi Mohamed with Young Novelty Musical Club, Tanga.** This song extols the joy of love: the desire to give to each other and not fight. Young Novelty, as described in the text, is one of the earlier *taarab* groups in Tanga. This is thus a recording dating probably to 1973 or 1974. (Chapter 3)

Track 3   "Kitumbiri" ("Monkey"), poetry by A. S. Jinamizi, music by Hatibu Akida, performed by Shakila Said with Lucky Star Musical Club, Tanga. Lucky Star Musical Club, one of the most famous clubs in Tanzania, is featured here with its most famous voice: Shakila. This is another recording dating to the early 1970s. This was one in a series of *mafumbo* songs in the rivalry between Lucky Star and Black Star Musical Club. It is performed to the *chakacha* rhythm, the rhythm most suited to insults. "Even you, monkey, favored monkey. You thought yourself so great, wanting to uproot trees when you are incapable of breaking branches." (Chapter 4)

Track 4   Mbuji *ngoma,* performed by KIUBATA at the National Arts and Language Competition, Sheikh Amri Abeid Stadium, November 7, 1992, Arusha. This is a live recording of KIUBATA's performance of the Mbuji *ngoma* at the 1992 National Arts and Languages Competition. The full description of its evolution from rehearsal to this long-awaited and long-prepared-for performance appears in chapter 6.

Track 5   "Tanzania Yetu" ("Our Tanzania"), composed by Stephen Hizza and Hassan Ngoma, performed by Atomic Jazz Band, Tanga. As the sole *dansi* track on this CD (an unfortunate result of limited space), "Tanzania Yetu" is an appropriate choice, given its widespread popularity and frequent usage even today at political events. This recording likely dates to the mid-1960s and extols the praises of Tanzania and its first president Julius Nyerere: "Our Tanzania is a country worthy of praise. Throughout the world everyone recognizes this." (Chapter 3)

Track 6   "Punda wa Tanga" ("Donkey of Tanga"), composed and performed by Mwinshehe Zongo with Gita Musical Club, Tanga. "Punda wa Tanga" is likely directed at Gita's chief competition: the Chera *ngoma*. Although the popularity of these two clubs has faded considerably, their rivalry and concerns remain through songs such as this. A true *mafumbo* song, Gita derides its rival for boasting about artificial horns that are sure to fall off and bring great shame and embarrassment to the wearer. (Chapter 3)

Track 7   "Mwanya" ("Attractive Gap between the Front Teeth"), poetry and music by Seif Kassim Kisauji, performed by Fatuma Kisauji with Babloom Modern Taarab, Tanga. Described at great length in chapter 7, this *mafumbo* song became a huge hit in the Tanga wedding circuit in 1994. Its popularity was subsequently tapped for the city councilman campaign of Babloom's chairman Salim Kisauji. Although the more popular interpretation equates a *mwanya* with a chaste, respectable woman, and a *pengo* (ugly gaping hole) with a loose woman, the campaign relied on the multivocality of *mafumbo* to imbue the song with a new meaning directed against emerging opposition parties. "You destroyed your *mwanya*. Your hole snores. You are worried. It's all over!"

Track 8   "Aliyejaliwa" ("The Favored One"), poetry and music by Ally Star, performed by Ally Star with BIMA Modern Taarab, Dar es Salaam. Like "Kitumbiri" and "Mwanya," "Aliyejaliwa" is a song in the driving *chakacha* beat. As the preferred rhythm for insult songs, it musically assists the singer in saying, "You talk incessantly like a parrot so that people know you. You demanded that I be removed from where I was. Know that the prayer of the chicken does not affect the hawk." (Chapter 3)

Track 9   **"Kumanya Mdigo" ("To Know the Digo"), poetry and music by Waziri Kapalata, performed by Kelly Askew and Waziri Kapalata with Babloom Modern Taarab, Tanga.** This is a somewhat unusual *taarab* song in that it is composed not in Swahili but in Kidigo, the language of the Wadigo ethnic group. Wadigo live in around Mombasa and Tanga, and this song, composed by Waziri Kapalata, who is himself a Digo, warns others not to be misled by the Digo's frail appearance. He is not one to be trifled with. "If you don't know the Digo, ask and you will be told. Be afraid of him. Don't play around with him." (Chapter 7)

Track 10 **"Ngwinji" ("High-Class Prostitute"), poetry and music by Othman Soud, performed by Khadija Kopa with Tanzania One Theatre, Dar es Salaam.** This is the song that catapulted TOT to national fame virtually overnight. TOT mixed Zanzibar classical orchestral sound with the *chakacha* beat popular in Tanga and Mombasa, and added a heavy layer of electronic instruments and Western drum kit (they were the first *taarab* band to my knowledge to introduce the drum kit) to produce this, their signature TOT sound. "A prostitute puts on airs! For what does she put on airs? She also boasts! Of what can she boast?" (Chapter 7)

Track 11 **"Nahodha" ("Captain"), poetry by Ali Mtoto Seif, music by Elizabeth Sijila, performed by Elizabeth Sijila with JKT Taarab, Dar es Salaam.** As befits a book on Tanzanian national culture, we end this CD with the Tanzanian National Service Army *taarab* orchestra: JKT Taarab. This song, composed and performed by Elizabeth Chidila, reflects in subtle musical ways her Gogo ethnic background. The Gogo have a rich musical tradition that has attracted international acclaim (see the Huwe Zawose CDs listed in the Discography). This song, one of my all-time favorites, urges captains of boats to take a lead role in guiding the vehicle and leading their passengers to safety. Would that all political leaders would hear and take to heart its message: "There isn't anyone who doesn't know what I am about to say—vehicles for travel normally move forward. We hope that the captain will be in front to steer. Captains of boats—why should they sit at the back?" (Chapter 8)

Notes

Chapter 1

1. In the context of Africa, the term *Asian* refers to someone from the Indian subcontinent.

2. Every major city in Tanzania has an Ikulu, a State House, built to accommodate the president and other important dignitaries. Tanga's Ikulu saw only very infrequent use. My friends in Tanzania used to dismiss me when I explained that there was only one presidential White House in America. They assumed that since their president had a White House in every city, surely the American president must as well.

3. I thank Mugsy Spiegel for this encapsulating phrase that emerged from a discussion we had in Cape Town, South Africa, May 2000.

4. Interview with Hamad B. Mshindo, principal secretary, Zanzibar Ministry of Information, Culture, Tourism, and Youth, August 16, 1990.

5. Allegations also exist that the mainland government wishes to subsume the Zanzibar government within a single governmental structure. See "Mkapa Dismisses Allegations on One Government: Claims Made by 'Liars,'" *Guardian*, October 18, 2000 (http://www.ippmedia.com/election/election146.htm).

6. Interview with Hamad B. Mshindo.

7. Haroub Othman, "Muungano katika sura ya sasa si wa pekee katika dunia" (The Union in its current stage is not unique in the world), *Mzalendo*, April 23, 1995, 5.

8. Issa Shivji, *Tanzania: The Legal Foundations of the Union* (Dar es Salaam: Dar es Salaam University Press, 1990); Rose Kalemera, "'Union Is Legal,' Says Mwalimu," *Daily News*, August 10, 1990, 1; John Kabudi, "The Union of Tanganyika and Zanzibar: Examination of the Treaty of a Political-Legal Union," *Mawazo* 6, no. 2 (1985):1–17; K. J. Chande, "International Integration: A Case Study of the Union of Tanganyika and Zanzibar" (a dissertation submitted to the Mozambique/Tanzania Centre for Foreign Relations in partial fulfillment of the requirements for the award of the advanced diploma in International Relations, Dar es Salaam, March 1983); Gaston Modest, "Mainland, Zanzibar Constitutions Undemocratic—Legal Expert," *Guardian*, March 29, 1995, 1; "Hakuna mantiki ya kubadili Katiba yote" (There is no reason to change the Constitution), *Uhuru*, April 19, 1995, 9.

9. "Serikali iseme kweli" (The government should tell the truth), *Motomoto*, August 15–31, 1993, 1, 3; "Ni hatari kuanza kuzungumza kuwa 'sisi Watanga-

nyika, wao Wazanzibari'—Nyerere" (It is dangerous to begin speaking of "we Tanganyikans, they Zanzibaris"—says Nyerere), *Uhuru,* August 18, 1993, 5.

10. Although Tanzania did not formally institute a single-party system until 1965, four years after independence, all elections between 1958 and 1965 were essentially single-party elections given the absence of a viable opposition to TANU (Tanganyika African National Union), the party that brokered independence. The only potential rival, the United Tanganyika Party, ceased to exist after it lost hands-down to TANU in the first general elections of 1958.

11. "Consultative Group Meetings: Zanzibar Gets Own Status," *Business Times,* February 24–March 2, 1995, 1.

12. "Ili kupambana na athari za Zanzibar kuwa soko huru: Serikali za Muungano na Visiwani kukutana" (The Union and Zanzibar governments will meet to confront the issue of Zanzibar having a duty-free port), *Majira,* April 28, 1995, 1.

13. Halary Naftal, "Muungano hauna ridhaa ya wananchi" (The Union does not have the acceptance of all citizens), *Heko,* March 16–22, 1995, 6; Haroub Othman, "Muungano katika sura ya sasa si wa pekee katika dunia" (The Union in its current stage is not unique in the world), *Mzalendo,* April 23, 1995, 5; "Wazanzibari wanavyo utumia Muungano kwa faida yao" (How Zanzibaris use the Union for their own benefit), *Rai,* February 23–March 1, 1995, 13; Modest, "Mainland, Zanzibar Constitutions Undemocratic," 1; "Hakuna mantiki ya ku-badili Katiba yote" (There is no reason to change the Constitution), 9.

14. After considerable internal debate on the matter, I have selected "national identity" rather than "national ideology" as my central concern. Although I find the concept of "national ideology" as elaborated by Verdery (1991a) very compelling (e.g., "discursive struggles in which the concept of 'the national' or 'the Romanian people' has formed a central preoccupation" [1991a, 9]), I seek to expose how in a way akin to the fluidity of personal and group identities, national identities also fluctuate with considerable rapidity. Therefore, in order to make a stronger connection between the theoretical advances made in understanding identity issues, I have chosen this term over "ideology," reserving the latter for the implicit and explicit discourses expounded by participants in Tanzanian cultural production. Moreover, definitions of "ideology" are typically restricted to forms of discourse, whereas this book casts the net quite further afield by incorporating music, dance, and other genres that can only problematically be understood as forms of discourse.

15. I use the term *racial* exclusively in respect to racialized discourses originating in colonial policy that stipulated a tripartite racial composition in Tanganyika: European, Asian (from South Asia), and African. Legislative seats and other political, economic, social, and educational benefits were allocated on the basis of this racial hierarchy. See Taylor 1963 for a discussion of how race inflected the political development of Tanzania. I embrace the position that denies the validity of "race" as anything more than a social construct. One might say that Nyerere also championed this view, given that he once argued, "It is said that Tanganyika has 120 tribes. I suggest that the way to democracy is to say we have 123 tribes in Tanganyika, the youngest and relatively the most educated being the European and Asian tribes. Let us then have tribal but not racial problems, if we must have problems at all" (quoted in Taylor 1963, 176).

16. Susan Geiger, *TANU Women: Gender and Culture in the Making of Tangan-yikan Nationalism, 1955–1965* (Portsmouth, NH: Heinemann, 1997); Terence Ranger, *Dance and Society in Eastern Africa, 1890–1970: The Beni Ngoma* (London: Heinemann, 1975); Elias Manandi Songoyi, "The Artist and the State in Tanzania: A Study of Two Singers—Kalikali and Mwinamila," Ph.D. diss., University of Dar es Salaam, 1988.

17. For an examination of the work of culture brokers in the strengthening of ethnic identities, please see Vail 1989.

18. In Swahili, the prefix *ki-* indicates a language (hence Kiswahili means the Swahili language, and Kidigo, the Digo language), the prefix *m-* indicates a person (hence Mswahili means a Swahili person, and Mdigo a Digo person), and the prefix *wa-* indicates a social unit (hence Waswahili means the Swahili ethnic group, and Wadigo means the Digo ethnic group). For clarity, I retain the *ki-* prefix when referring to a language, but forsake the *m-* and *wa-* prefixes.

19. Full texts and translations for all songs cited are included in appendix A.

20. Subsequent preliminary fieldwork occurred during the summers of 1989 and 1990. For my doctoral fieldwork, I lived in Tanzania for three years, from August 1992 to August 1995. Follow-up visits occurred for one month each in 1996 and 1997.

21. Paolo Freire, *Pedagogy of the Oppressed* (New York: Herder & Herder, 1970); see also Penina Muhando Mlama, *Culture and Development: The Popular Theatre Approach in Africa* (Uppsala: Nordiska Afrikainstitutet, 1991).

22. As this book goes to press, Tanga is no longer a site of extensive musical activity. By 1999, the majority of bands I discuss in this book had either disbanded or moved away.

Chapter 2

1. The United Republic of Tanzania, Ministry of Tourism, Natural Resources and Environment, and the Republic of Finland, Ministry for Foreign Affairs, *Project Document: East Usambara Catchment Forestry Project, Phase II: 1995–98, Background and Lessons* (1995).

2. The Tanzanian press was liberated when multipartyism was announced in 1992; private newspapers are now published in unprecedented numbers. At last count, there were 25–30 newpapers covering both Swahili and English—some daily, others weekly, and still others monthly. The government-run newspapers flourish beside private publications.

3. Casson 1989; Huntingford 1980; Stevenson 1932; Gibb 1962. See also Horton and Middleton 2000.

4. Regarding dates of settlement along the coast, Horton writes, "This unified, indigenous seafaring society (the existence of which has been recognized only in the past five years) may have come into existence as early as the first century. By the ninth century it had become an integral component of a large international trading network" (1987, 89). Nurse and Spear (1985, 3) point out that "two market towns (Rhapta and Kanbalu) are known to have existed before 800, but we still do not know where they were located. The first permanent trading settlements that we can identify were established during the ninth cen-

tury in the Lamu Archipelago (at Pate, Shanga, and Manda) and on the southern Tanzanian coast at Mafia and Kilwa." See also the chapter entitled "The Times of Ignorance: A Review of Pre-Islamic and Early Islamic Settlement on the East African Coast," in Freeman-Grenville 1988, 2: 4–17).

5. There are alternate etymologies. Middleton suggests that since "[t]he Arabic word also means 'edge' or 'border' . . . [it] might refer to the people on the borders of Arabic or Islamic civilization" (1992, 201, n. 1). The other is a folk etymology presented to me by a local scholar and poet Sheikh Ahmed Nabhany (interview, Mombasa, Kenya, June 1987), who was born in the Lamu Archipelago on the northern Kenya coast and who, like many from that region, espouses a Lamu-centric worldview. He derives "Swahili" from *siwa hili,* Kiswahili for "this island," referring to Lamu. The word *siwa* more commonly refers to a ceremonial horn symbolizing political power, but in older usage also translates as "a large island" (Johnson 1989, 207, 434); see also Tolmacheva (1976).

6. See Horton and Middleton 2000; Horton 1996, 1987; also LaViolette 1996.

7. See Allen 1993 for a critique of colonial writings.

8. See Freeman-Grenville 1962b for a detailed comparison of the Arabic, Portuguese, and Swahili versions.

9. The "Shirazi question" has generated extensive writings due to changing social, political, and economic connotations (Pouwels 1984, 1987; Nurse and Spear 1985; Spear 1984; Glassman 1995; Fair 2001). To further complicate matters, the label came to serve a bureaucratic purpose several centuries later when "[a]dministrators more prosaically created a 'tribe' which they called 'Swahili-Shirazi,' and used it as a sort of classificatory dustbin into which to sweep all people who, at censuses and in similar contexts, did not fit in anywhere else" (Allen 1993, 4f.).

10. Excerpt from the *Journal of the First Voyage of Vasco da Gama, 1497–1499,* quoted in Freeman-Grenville 1962a, 51.

11. Excerpt from *Vasco da Gama's Return from India, 1499,* quoted in Freeman-Grenville 1962a, 58.

12. One of these towering pillar tombs adorns the frontispiece of Burton's *Zanzibar,* vol. 1.

13. I was told that these are the graves of a Shirazi man and his wife (cause of death unknown) and that from the time of their burial to the present, the tide has never returned at its previously normal level to cover the plain and two graves within. Interview with Rashid Hamadi, November 28, 1993, Ndumi. No mention of the graves appears in the brief archaeological surveys that have been done on the coast, which give some information, if sparse, on Ndumi. The sand is treacherous in places, and I was warned against trying to approach the graves to look for inscriptions.

14. In support of this hypothesis, Burton recorded that on his visit to the now uninhabited Jambe Island opposite Tongoni, he encountered a village of approximately one hundred Wagunya, a Swahili subgroup from the Lamu Archipelago on the northern Kenyan coast.

15. Although the early history of Tanga has never been fully researched, a comprehensive review of existing primary and secondary sources appears in the first two chapters of Chande 1998. The German historian Baumann (1890,

1891) places the establishment of Tanga at the end of the sixteenth century; however, the collection of more than 150 shards of both Islamic pottery and Chinese porcelain dating from the sixteenth to the nineteenth centuries and possibly earlier scattered along the Chumbageni beach of modern Tanga as well as on Toten Island hints at an earlier settlement (Freeman-Grenville 1962b, 158f).

16. *History of Pate* quoted in Freeman-Grenville 1962a, 253. See also Freeman-Grenville 1962b, 113. Yet even archaeologist Freeman-Grenville was compelled to note, "There is no record to illuminate the mention of Tanga, now the second most important town in Tanganyika" (1962b, 116).

17. My interviews with elders in and around Tanga produced this same explanation as for Chande (1998, 15). As Chande points out, however, the explanation is flawed because during Baumann's visit to Tanga in 1890, the hinterland village was called Mkwakwani (a name retained for a certain neighborhood of contemporary Tanga), whereas the island town was still called Tanga. Baumann (1890, 1891) reported that the local people had no explanation for the name Tanga, but perhaps they were disinclined to discuss the matter with him.

18. Project for the Advanced Study of Art and Life in Africa (PASALA) conference, University of Iowa, March 1999.

19. They demanded tribute of 1,500 ounces of gold per year from Kilwa alone.

20. The ruins at Gedi are an important site along the coast, just a few kilometers south of Malindi. The city remains largely intact—an impressive array of ruined stone buildings—but the mystery as to exactly when and for what reasons it was deserted remains unsolved. The Oromo theory is only one of several. Other popular theories focus on natural disasters such as an epidemic or drought.

21. The fate of Mohammad Yusuf bin Hassan is described in a pamphlet on the history of Fort Jesus: "Early in the following year [1632], finding life with his own people as distasteful as it had been with the Portuguese, he sailed away in a captured galleon and became a pirate" (Kirkman 1981, 2).

22. I am indebted to Fred Cooper for sharing this interpretation with me.

23. In 1835, the American consulate was opened in Zanzibar. Salem, Massachusetts was the first American port to begin trading with Zanzibar (Sheriff 1987, 51).

24. These small islands to the east of Madagascar, originally named Ile de France and Bourbon, are known today as Mauritius and Réunion.

25. See Koponen 1994, chap. 2, for a detailed discussion of the possible motivations for Bismarck's change of heart.

26. Lushoto, formerly named Wilhemstal after Kaiser Wilhem II, was the site of the main civilian district office.

27. Interview with Ali Ramadhani, July 11, 1995, Tanga.

28. Sec. 075-186, N.A., Dar es Salaam, quoted in Ranger 1975, 44, n. 3.

29. This is not surprising, given that, with the Tanga School, Tanga was considered the educational center of Tanganyika until the establishment of the University of Dar es Salaam transferred that reputation to the capital; see Ranger 1975, 92, 94; Lonsdale 1968, 131–32.

30. The merger of TANU and ASP into Chama cha Mapinduzi (CCM) occurred on February 5, 1977.

31. Legum 1988 cites the national literacy rate at 85 percent, which surpassed that of any other African country, South Africa included.

32. One notable prisoner was Bibi Titi Mohamed, who played a crucial role in the nationalist movement.

33. At the Magore Street polling station, voters were prohibited from voting for presidential candidates and allowed to vote only for members of Parliament. In another incident, two million shillings ($3,636) were discovered hidden in a ballot box containing votes for the ruling party's candidate Benjamin Mkapa. In the face of these and other problems, the election results from the capital of Dar es Salaam were nullified and fresh elections ordered in all its seven constituencies for November 19.

34. State-owned Radio Tanzania reported that "some polling stations in the capital, Dar es Salaam, opened seven hours late, and others inland were missing ballots and voter lists. In one northern region, 600 election officials had no transportation to voting stations" (quoted in "Multi-party elections suspended," an e-mail report from Msafiri D. Mbaga at the University of Manitoba to Tanzanet@iastate.edu, October 29, 1995).

35. A report issued by the Eastern and Southern Africa Universities Research Programme (ESAURP) noted, "In some cases, either election materials were not at the polling stations, arrived several hours late, were incomplete or never arrived at all," but also commented on the peaceful atmosphere and stated that "the results so far seem to reflect the predictions of most Tanzanians" ("Election Shortfalls Isolated, Local Observer Affirms," *Guardian,* November 7, 1995, 1; see also, "Poll Results Fair, Says ESAURP," *Daily News,* November 7, 1995, 5; "How the National Electoral Commission Fared in Elections," *Daily News,* November 28, 1995, 4).

36. "Café Politics," *BBC Focus on Africa,* October–December 2000, 10.

37. The constituency of Kwahani had 5,235 registered voters, yet 6,840 votes were cast, while Kitope had a total of 6,711 registered voters, and a total of 8,591 votes cast.

38. "The Winning Team," *BBC Focus on Africa,* January-March 2001, 26.

39. "Chaos Erupts as Voter Registration Begins in Zanzibar," *Guardian,* August 9, 2000; "Don't Panic, Police Tell Mainlanders in Isles," *Guardian,* August 10, 2000; "CCM kutawala milele—Dk. Salmin" (CCM will rule forever—Pres. Salmin), *Nipashe,* September 6, 2000; "AI [Amnesty International] Members Appeal to Mkapa, Salmin," *Guardian,* October 24, 2000; "Vote Protested by Opposition in Zanzibar," *New York Times,* October 31, 2000; "32 Die in Zanzibar as Police and Protesters Clash," *New York Times,* January 29, 2001; "Pemba Refugee Trickle Turns to Flood," *Sunday Observer,* February 18, 2001.

40. Nyerere relinquished the party chairmanship in 1990.

41. Interview with Mohamed Athman Majura, regional cultural officer, Tanga, November 7, 1994.

42. Mkapa announced his Cabinet on November 28, 1995.

43. *Pachanga* is the name of a rhythm that greatly resembles the rhythm *bossanova.*

44. Of the newspapers cited here, only the *Daily News* is a government publi-

cation. *Mfanyakazi* is published by the Organization of Tanzania Trade Unions (OTTU). The others are all private.

45. Lowassa, Kolimba, Malecela, and Msuya are well-known vanguards of the previous regimes. All had held some of the highest positions in the government; Malecela and Msuya both served as prime minister. Kikwete, on the other hand, is a relatively new face in CCM, who became known when vying for the CCM presidential candidacy, which he lost to Mkapa.

46. Swahili communities also developed inland, particularly in cities like Tabora, Kijiji, and Mwanza, which were major stops along the caravan routes. For more information on Swahili culture in Kijiji and Mwanza, see McCurdy 2000.

47. "Hamad Says CUF Not Used by Arabs," *Guardian,* August 7, 2000; "Hamad's Promise to Restore Slavery in Zanzibar—Karume," *Guardian,* September 4, 1900.

48. For more on this topic, see Askew 1999.

49. Interview, March 1, 1995, Ngamiani. Bi Abidjani herself has a name rich in local history. The two most prominent football teams in Tanga are African Sports and Coastal Union. Bi Abidjani is a notorious fan of Coastal Union. The team takes its name from the Ivory Coast, the capital of which is Abidjan. Its teammates and club members thus over time gave the name "Bi Abidjani" to this esteemed fan of the club.

50. Glassman 1994 (45) makes reference to camel-driven mills for pressing sesame seed in Pangani, which may also have been found in Tanga.

51. The nationalization of housing helped considerably in this respect by doling out previously white-owned or Asian-owned homes to African applicants.

52. The following story was told to me by Bakari Kajasoro on May 18, 1995. Bakari lives in Kiomoni, the village closest to the Amboni Caves; as a young boy he was befriended by Osale.

53. Interview with Chief Mohamed Ali Kiparisi, April 16, 2001, Ngamiani; interview with Salim Kassim Salim, November 16, 1993, Ngamiani. I have tried to identify as many musical groups as possible on map 2.4, but because some of these *ngoma* have long since died out, people's memories could not always firmly locate them. See Fair 2001, 22–23, for a similar description of Zanzibar.

54. Statistics taken from the *Report on Social and Economic Conditions in the Tanga Province* by E. C. Baker (1934, Annexure 2, 108 ff.).

55. Letter from secretary, Abugusii Sawyers Union, to permanent secretary, Ministry of Home Affairs, August 4, 1964. Tanzania National Archives, Tanga Region, accession 304, file A6/68 vol. 1, "Registration of Societies, Tanga District, vol. 2."

56. Letter from the registrar to the Tanga Area commisioner dated August 14, 1964. Tanzania National Archives, Tanga Region, accession 304, file A6/68 vol. 1, "Registration of Societies, Tanga District, vol. 2."

57. See also Fabian 1986 for a discussion of the role of Kiswahili in the emergence of the Democratic Republic of Congo.

58. "Khanga as a Medium of Communication," *Express,* October 1–4, 1995, 11.

59. The event was sponsored by the Tanzania Media Women's Association (TAMWA); see Ronda Ansted, "In Search of a National Dress," *Sauti ya Siti,* no.

19 (April–June 1993): 2–4; "Why a National Dress?" *Sauti ya Siti,* no. 19 (April–June 1993): 4–5; "Umuhimu wa kuwa na vazi la taifa" (The importance of having a national dress), *Africa Sports and Lifestyle* 3, no. 3 (April/May 1993): 23–27, special issue entitled, "TAMWA Inatafuta Vazi la Kitaifa" (TAMWA searches for a national dress).

60. Chapter 6 examines *ngoma* performance as the one state-endorsed forum for celebrating ethnic particularity.

61. Chapter 7 describes the use of music in his campaign for the council seat he ultimately won. He was named mayor of Tanga in 1998 following the death of the previous mayor.

62. During times of food-rationing in World War II, rice was only allocated to Arabs and Indians, since it was deemed their staple food, whereas everyone else was given maize flour to make *ugali* (a thick porridge) considered the African staple (interview, Salim Kassim Salim, May 6, 1995, Ngamiani).

Chapter 3

1. Kanada utilized Swahili rules of spelling by replacing the initial *C* with a *K,* as evidenced in various government documents. See the communication from the Mtimbwani divisional executive officer to the Tanga Area secretary dated January 17, 1966, ref. no. MTB/A2/66/4 in the Tanga Archives, accession no. 5, box 6, file C1/12, "Ceremonial 1948–1971," document 78A.

2. *Ngoma* also translates as "drum" and "music in general" (Johnson 1989, 336).

3. Secular *kwaya* is most closely identified with the JWTZ army choir and Tanzanian One Theatre (TOT) choir, both affiliated with Captain John Komba (more on TOT and Captain Komba in chapter 7).

4. I reserve analysis of the genres of *kwaya, mchiriku,* rap, and reggae for another project.

5. The extent to which marching was essential to colonial performance is evident from the colonial circular entitled "Orders for King's Birthday Parade—3rd June 1927," containing detailed marching orders. National Archives, accession no. 4, file 602 "Queen's Birthday, 1920–55."

6. Interviews with Fatuma Nassoro Bukhet, Amina Ridhwa Seif, Mwakema Komboza, Migombani Ali, Salima Mwinyinsi, Fatuma Mohamedi, and Mwana Aisha Ismail, August 2, 1995, Tanga.

7. Four years earlier in 1952, the crown passed to Princess Elizabeth, thereafter Queen Elizabeth II, while she was on a royal visit to East Africa that did not include Tanga. Although only a princess, Margaret is memorialized in Tanga *ngoma* performance as *kwini* (a queen), suggesting that the two royal visits have been conflated in local memory.

8. For a description of women's *ngoma* reenactment of the 1952 royal visit of Princess Elizabeth to Kenya, see Farrell 1980, 78–79.

9. See especially Mitchell 1956; Lienhardt 1968; Ranger 1975; Strobel 1979; Farrell 1980; Campbell 1983; Franken 1986; Willis 1993; Fair 1994; Glassman 1995; and Chande 1988.

10. Interviews with Salim Kassim and Waziri Kapalata, November 16, 1993, Tanga. Laura Fair notes a similar environment in Ng'ambo, the African quarter of Zanzibar town during the 1930s: "Archival records also indicate that every

night someone danced. In 1931, there were 2,500 licensed *ngoma,* or roughly seven different *ngoma* each night, in urban Zanzibar. Many elderly Zanzibaris related how, as youth in the 1930s, they would wander around at night watching the numberous *ngoma* and reflecting on the diversity of cultures which came together in Ng'ambo" (Fair 1994, 280).

11. Multiple permutations on the label "Swahili" contribute added complexity to the debate. It has been used variously to refer to Muslims, to people who have "lost tribal feelings" (Madoshi 1971, 91), to cultured or diplomatic individuals, to stingy people or cheaters, to people habitually late or otherwise unreliable, to Kiswahili-speakers, to urban town dwellers, to traders, and finally, to "any Tanzanian . . . who is a full-blooded African . . . often heard in political circles" (Madoshi 1971, 92).

12. Many of the concerns and viewpoints that have marked the evolution and refinement of theories of ethnicity surfaced in the debate over Swahili identity; see Allen 1972; Amory 1990; Arens 1975, 1976; Constantin 1987; Eastman 1971, 1975, 1984, 1988; Janmohamed 1976; Nurse and Spear 1985; Salim 1976, 1985; Shariff 1973; Swartz 1979.

13. See Chande 1991 for a complementary analysis of the competitive rivalry between two mosques in Tanga.

14. Bans on *ngoma* performance were imposed throughout the coastal region at various points in history by various authorities (Songoyi 1988; Fair 2001).

15. Farrell, making a similar case for the subversion of male hierarchy by female *ngoma* groups in Vanga, places more emphasis on the ideological battle fought and sustained through the medium of performance.

16. For a more detailed analysis of the shifts that have occurred in both *ngoma* practice and Swahili gender relations more generally, see Askew 1999.

17. Interview with Fatuma Nassoro Bukhet, August 27, 1995, Tanga.

18. The national competitions constituted the fourth and final round in a two-year-long competition process that began with contests at the district, then regional, then zonal level. Tanzania is subdivided into six zones of which Tanga, together with Moshi (Kilimanjaro) and Arusha, compose the Northern Zone. The zones are further subdivided into twenty regions, Tanga constituting its own region.

19. For a fascinating analysis of the Amboni Company in particular and the Tanzanian sisal industry in general, see Sabea 2000.

20. Interview with Mzee Lucas, Amboni School gardener, February 20, 1993, Amboni.

21. More than thieves and the dwarflike supernatural inhabitants of the forest known as *vibwengu,* I feared army ants and snakes; a python measuring three and a half meters was found in our neighbor's back yard during our time there, and pythons are the least dangerous of the many varieties around.

22. Tanzanian National Archives, accession no. 4, file 602, "Queen's Birthday, 1920–55."

23. One finds that the boundaries between genres of Swahili poetic arts were and still are quite fluid. The more famous poets often were actively engaged in *ngoma* performance or came from areas particularly noted for *ngoma* performance, and, according to a recent survey of Swahili poetry completed by scholars at the University of Dar es Salaam, Swahili poetry traces its roots to

ngoma (Sengo and Mulokozi 1994, 22). Moreover, in public performance, poetry (*mashairi*) is *sung*, thus confirming the intertwined relationships between these expressive arts.

24. Those knowledgeable about Swahili poetry may feel that I should have included several other prominent political poets such as Hemed bin Abdallah el-Buhry (c.1850–1928), the composer of a famous epic poem *(utenzi)* about the nineteenth-century coastal rebellion led by Abushiri bin Salim against the Germans, and Mwinyihatibu Mohamed Amiri (b.1920), composer of another famous epic poem entitled *Utenzi wa Uhuru wa Tanganyika (Poem of Tanganyikan Independence),* but I am attempting to distinguish those holding political posts from those who did not, à la Gramsci, who writes, "The mode of being of the new intellectual can no longer consist in eloquence, which is an exterior and momentary mover of feelings and passions, but in active participation in practical life, as constructor, organiser, 'permanent persuader' and not just a simple orator" (1971, 10). Much of this information on Tanganyika poets is drawn from the Sengo and Mulokozi 1994 report.

25. The text is taken from Mulokozi 1975, 59–60, but the translation was modified by Seif Kassim Kisauji.

26. A note regarding honorific prefixes: *bi* is the short form for *bibi,* literally meaning "grandmother," used to indicate respect. Common usage determines whether 'Bi' or 'Bibi' is used in a name.

27. Bibi Titi Mohamed passed away on November 6, 2000. Thousands of mourners came to pay their respects at her funeral (*Guardian,* November 11, 2000).

28. One cannot apply Gramsci's theory on political parties any further to Tanzania, however, because he opposes the political party (representing civil society) to the state (representing "political society"), which clearly cannot hold true for single-party states like Tanzania from 1964 to 1995.

29. Two very popular *dansi* bands in Dar es Salaam, International Orchestra Safari Sound (IOSS, not to be confused with the Zairean band Orchestra Safari Sound) and Mlimani Park Orchestra, are notorious rivals, in part because IOSS was formed with six leading musicians from Mlimani Park, including singer Muhiddin Maalim Gurumo. A popular song entitled "Chatu Mkali" ("Beware, a Snake Is Dangerous") was composed and performed by IOSS. According to Graebner, "The public heard this as referring to the rivalry between Mlimani and its former members leading IOSS. In fact, in IOSS newspaper advertisements of the time, an elephant is seen tugging a motor vessel out of the sea while a snake (i.e., IOSS) waits dangerously at the shore. A ship, *M.V. Mapenzi* (meaning *Motor Vessel Love),* featured prominently in one of Mlimani's songs of that period, a song that teased Muhiddin for abandoning his *M.V. Mapenzi* (read, Mlimani Park) and throwing himself into the sea only to be eaten by the sharks" (Graebner 1995, 4).

30. The band itself was equally divided into Muslim and Christian believers.

31. This was the song "Malaika" ("Angel") that became an internationally recognized African hit sung by the revered South African vocalist Miriam Makeba as well as Béninoise Afropop star Angélique Kidjo.

32. Dr. Virgina Danielson, personal communication, March 16, 1997, Cambridge, MA.

33. As my friend and colleague Werner Graebner pointed out to me, poetry

is not the sole domain of *taarab*. There are some coastal *ngoma* forms (e.g., *kidumbak*—see Topp 1992) that also follow strict poetic formats, generally identical to those of *taarab*. I would still maintain, however, that these *ngoma* forms occur in strong *taarab* areas and are linked historically and musically to *taarab*. *Taarab* emerged within a cultural domain predisposed to a poetic aesthetic. That poetry is found elsewhere does not undermine as much as support my claim. Beyond the coastal areas of *taarab*'s birth, *ngoma* forms tend not to exhibit the propensity for elaborate, multiverse poetry of *taarab* and *kidumbak*.

34. Excerpt from "Nimezama," poetry by Hamza Ali and music by Mussa Majengo, Golden Star Musical Club, Tanga. In these and all other examples, I separate the two hemistichs with a comma and initial capitalization of the second hemistich. Full texts and translations for all songs cited in this text appear in appendix A.

35. Excerpt from "Wajigamba," poetry and music by Rama Hamadi, Babloom Modern Taarab, Tanga.

36. Excerpt from "Kidogo Menirambisha," poetry and music by Rama Hamadi, Babloom Modern Taarab, Tanga.

37. This is a list of the *maqamat* used by Mombasa *udi* player Zein al'Labdin (interview, Zein al'Labdin, June 1987, Mombasa). Harries also includes a list of *maqamat* which, according to his Swahili informants, were used in Mombasa, Malindi, and Lamu: Rasit, Bayat, Sika, Nawandi, Hijaz, Duka, Jirka, Hijaz Kar, Swaba, Rasidi, and Duka (Harries 1962, 11).

38. I discuss my training in *taarab* performance later, but it is relevant to note that on many occasions when someone announced a key for the next song, I would find myself in a different key from the one everyone else was in. Our understandings of what constituted the key of G major, for example, proved quite different.

39. See Fair 2001, 1994; Graebner 1999, 1994a, 1991; Fargion 1993; Farhan 1992; Jahadhmy et al. 1996; Khatib 1992; Mgana 1991; Saleh 1988a&b, 1980; Suleiman 1969.

40. See Fair 1994 and 2001 for Siti binti Saad's life history.

41. The following information was collected in interviews with Mr. Basakutta during the summers of 1987 and 1989 in Mombasa.

42. Interview with Hamisi Akida Mimi, February 2, 2001, Ilala Buguruni, Dar es Salaam.

43. There is some disagreement on this point. Many Tanga musicians, who admittedly lack Hamisi Akida's extended historical perspective, given his advanced age, identified Shabaab al-Watan as the first *taarab* group to emerge in Tanga.

44. Willi Apel, ed., *Harvard Dictionary of Music,* 2d ed. (Cambridge, MA: Harvard University Press, 1972), 203.

45. Literally, "Mother of Akida"; it is customary to identify adults by their firstborn and call them "Mother of X" and "Father of Y."

46. I am indebted to my friend and colleague Amandina Lihamba, chair of the Theatre Arts department at the University of Dar es Salaam and a noted expert on Tanzanian cultural policy and cultural affairs, for her insights on the incorporation of *taarab* into Dar es Salaam performance practice.

47. As this book was going to press, I received word that Dar performance

practice has now changed: *taarab* constitutes the penultimate act and *dansi* the final event of cultural troupe shows. Presumably, this reflects the typical pattern of musical forms coming in and out of fashion.

48. Usually, the instrument is specified, such as *mpigaji bass* (bass player) or *mpigaji udi* (*udi* player).

49. I have to specify Tanga here because in my observations of *taarab* performed by Mombasan and Zanzibari groups, I noticed much clearer differentiation of musical labor, with the same individuals playing the same instruments, taking the same roles in the music production process again and again.

Chapter 4

1. All names in this chapter are pseudonyms with the exception of identified members of Babloom.

2. The Mkonge Hotel in Ras Kazone.

3. From 1993 to 1996, the resident band at Mkonge was Babloom Modern Taarab, at that time Tanga's most popular *taarab* band. The position originally had been filled by Black Star Musical Club until their instruments proved to be in too bad a condition to ensure an uninterrupted performance (a power surge in February 1993 blew out their only two amplifiers, effectively shutting down the band altogether). After Black Star, Golden Star Musical Club served briefly as resident band, stopping only because their popularity in Mombasa had increased to the point where they were hired to perform there on most weekends. After Golden Star, Babloom was hired. In 1996, Babloom moved to Dar es Salaam and was never replaced.

4. *Kibwebwe* is a *kanga* (cloth) twisted and tied around the hips. Putting it on is the female equivalent in this culture to the Western rolling up of the sleeves in preparation for a fight.

5. From the song "Television," poetry and music by Shaban Amour, Babloom Modern Taarab, Tanga.

6. "Jamvi la Wageni," poetry and music by Rama Hamadi, Babloom Modern Taarab, Tanga. There is another song by the same name composed by Issa Matona of JKT Taarab, Dar es Salaam.

7. Excerpt from "Kanioa Siri," poetry and music by Seif Kisauji, Babloom Modern Taarab, Tanga.

8. From "Utasugua," poetry and music by Rama Hamadi, Babloom Modern Taarab, Tanga.

9. Black Star rose to fame in the late 1960s and remained popular until a few years before it disbanded in February 1993 after the loss of its two amplifiers. The belief was widely circulated among its members that the power surge which destroyed its amplifiers was supernatural intervention invoked by rival bands.

10. From "Halua," poetry and music by Hussein Kibao, Black Star Musical Club, Tanga.

11. Euphemistic references to "eating" as a way of discussing love-making are found the world over. In Swahili, one may refer to a rendezvous with a lover as "Naenda kumla," "I am going to eat her/him."

12. Aside from the government radio station, RTD, no professional recording facilities existed in Tanzania until a year or two ago. Musicians, therefore,

had to travel to Nairobi or Mombasa to record with Philips and Polydor (a unit of Polygram) and the local Mzuri and Saba Saba labels.

13. This is my translation of the following entry: "-pa zawadi mtu baada ya kufanya jambo vizuri k.v. kucheza ngoma, kuimba, n.k." From the *Kamusi ya Kiswahili Sanifu* (Dar es Salaam: Taasisi ya Uchunguzi wa Kiswahili and Oxford University Press, 1981), 287. Alternate definitions of the term are "treat with care or affection; (1) guard, protect, care for, tend, keep safe; (2) attend to, observe, examine, keep an eye on," from Frederick Johnson, *A Standard Swahili-English Dictionary* (Nairobi and Dar es Salaam: Oxford University Press, 1939), 481.

14. It was incomprehensible to many Tanga residents that I would drive a vehicle so unbefitting my status as foreigner.

15. I was told that in the capital, Dar es Salaam, the sergeant in charge of assigning duties was well supported by bribes from underling *trafiki* who vied for assignment to the poorer, congested sections of the city such as Kariakoo. In such neighborhoods, *trafiki* were sure to amass a substantial amount of fines, thanks to the large number of cars in varying degrees of disrepair. Should one fail to negotiate a good relationship with the presiding sergeant, however, one would be assigned to wealthy expatriate neighborhoods where cars pass only two to three times an hour and then only Landcruisers or Pajeros in impeccable, violation-free condition.

Chapter 5

1. The five members of the delegation were Joseph Kasella Bantu (minister of Parliament and leader of the delegation), Mr. F. J. Mchauru (chief secretary, Ministry of Community Development and National Culture), Mr. D. K. Bishota (lawyer and advisor to the delegation), Mr. Mwakambaya (whose title was "officer of explanations" [information officer?]), and Ms. B. Mwankemwa (cultural officer).

2. My translation from a report entitled, "Cultural Delegation to the People's Republic of China," dated August 8, 1966, written by Ms. B. Mwankemwa, a cultural officer from the Ministry of Community Development and National Culture, document 51, file C1/23 "National Culture 1965–1972," box 2, unnumbered accession, Regional Archives, Tanga (9 pp.), 2–3.

3. Clearly, the Indian Ocean trade networks and similar trans-Saharan networks existed long before the advent of colonialism. I mean only to point out how dramatically global economic relations were transformed and reconfigured so as to exploit Africans and their products.

4. Leroy Vail, lectures entitled, "The Technology of Imperialism," "West Africa before Formal Colonialism: 'Westernization' and Political Instability," and "East Africa before Formal Colonialism: Political Turmoil," presented on September 19, 24, and 26, 1996, at Harvard University, Cambridge, MA. See also Colson 1969; Weiskel 1980; Cooper and Stoler 1989.

5. This is likely due in part to the popularity of certain songs lauding German victories—in particular, the British defeat in Tanga (Ranger 1975, 54).

6. Political officer, Lushoto, to political officer, Same, September 15, 1948, saving no. 44/1/115, document 1, file C1/12 "Ceremonial, 1948–71," box 6, accession 5, Regional Archives, Tanga.

344 NOTES TO PAGES 163-172

7. District commissioner, Pare (Same), to district commissioner, Lushoto, September 21, 1948, ref. no. 11/6/67, document 2, file C1/12 "Ceremonial, 1948–71," box 6, accession 5, Regional Archives, Tanga.

8. H. A. Fosbrooke, senior sociologist, October 1951, document nos. 5–6, file C1/12 "Ceremonial, 1948–71," box 6, accession 5, Regional Archives, Tanga.

9. *Jando* is a term for male initiation ceremonies along the East African coast.

10. Fosbrooke, "Ceremonial."

11. Fosbrooke, "Ceremonial."

12. District commissioner, Pare (Same), to provincial commissioner, Tanga, February 5, 1952, ref. no. 11/6/108, documents 7–8, file C1/12 "Ceremonial, 1948–71," box 6, accession 5, Regional Archives, Tanga.

13. Acting provincial commissioner, Tanga, to district commissioner, Same, April 25, 1953, ref. no. 153/14, document 14, file C1/12 "Ceremonial, 1948–71," box 6, accession 5, Regional Archives, Tanga.

14. Acting provincial commissioner, Zanzibar, to chief secretary, July 23, 1936, file AK 14/10, "Ngomas, 1936–69," Provincial Administration, National Archives, Zanzibar.

15. *The Laws of Zanzibar,* n.d., chapter 178, "Ngoma Regulation," 2.

16. For more instances of *ngoma* performance as rebellion, see Glassman 1995.

17. District commissioner, Zanzibar, to provincial commissioner, February 25, 1937, file AK 14/10, "Ngomas, 1936–69," Provincial Administration, National Archives, Zanzibar.

18. Commissioner of police, October 19, 1959, ref. no. PHQ/299/130, C2639/1, as cited in M. H. B. to acting chief secretary, June 18, 1960, file AK 14/10, "Ngomas, 1936–69," Provincial Administration, National Archives, Zanzibar.

19. Permanent secretary to senior district commissioner, February 17, 1962, ref. no. CM/P.40/1/10; acting senior district commissioner to permanent secretary, February 21, 1962; acting attorney general, "A Bill entitled 'A Decree to Amend the Ngoma Regulation Decree,'" March 21, 1962, ref. no. CM/P40/1/10; chief minister, "Draft: The Ngoma Regulation Decree—Cap.178," 1962, ref. no. CM/P.40/1/10; permanent secretary (CM) to senior district commissioner, "The Ngoma Regulation Decree—Cap.178," May 4, 1962, ref. no. CM/P40/1/10; P.N.D. attorney general to permanent secretary (CM), 2 May 1962, ref. no. L.D.613; senior district commissioner to permanent secretary, June 6, 1962, "The Ngoma Regulation Decree—Cap.178," documents 46–53, file AK 14/10, "Ngomas, 1936–69," Provincial Administration, National Archives, Zanzibar.

20. District commissioner (Urban), Zanzibar, to senior commissioner, Zanzibar, February 16, 1956, ref. no. N/4, document 27, file AK 14/10, "Ngomas, 1936–69," Provincial Administration, National Archives, Zanzibar.

21. See also Afigbo et al. 1986, 2: 65.

22. Ali Mazrui, address at Harvard University, Cambridge, MA, April 16, 1992.

23. R. M. Kawawa to Regional Commissioners' Conference, "Memorandum: Promotion of Cultural Activities in Tanzania," February 26–27, 1965, document 1A, file C1/23 "National Culture, 1965–1972," box 2, unnumbered accession, Regional Archives, Tanga, 1.

24. Kawawa, "Memorandum, 2."

25. Kawawa, "Memorandum, 2."

26. R. M. Kawawa to all regional commissioners, "Administration Instructions on Duties of Cultural Committees," June 18, 1965, document 1, file C1/23 "National Culture, 1965–1972," box 2, unnumbered accession, Regional Archives, Tanga, 4.

27. Area commissioner, Handeni, to regional commissioner, Tanga, January 21, 1966, ref. no. S.1/12/I/10, document 21, file C1/23 "National Culture, 1965–1972," box 2, unnumbered accession, Regional Archives, Tanga.

28. Area commissioner, Pangani, to regional commissioner, Tanga, January 21, 1966, ref. no. M.7/3/43, document 22/23, file C1/23 "National Culture, 1965–1972," box 2, unnumbered accession, Regional Archives, Tanga; area commissioner, Korogwe, to regional commissioner, Tanga, March 1, 1966, ref. no. C.1/12/11, document 25, file C1/23 "National Culture, 1965–1972," box 2, unnumbered accession, Regional Archives, Tanga.

29. Administrative secretary, Tanga Region, to commissioner for culture, November 12, 1965, ref. no. C.1/23/12, document 12, file C1/23 "National Culture, 1965–1972," box 2, unnumbered accession, Regional Archives, Tanga.

30. Principal secretary, Ministry of Community Development and National Culture, to all regional commissioners, June 2, 1966, ref. no. CDNC/S.9/4/12, document 36, file C1/23 "National Culture, 1965–1972," box 2, unnumbered accession, Regional Archives, Tanga. For those regions that could prove some progress, the sum of Tsh. 1,000 ($2) was distributed in 1966, and 500 ($1) in 1967 and 1968.

31. Area secretary, Korogwe, to administrative secretary, Tanga Region, October 21, 1966, ref. no. C.1/12/23, document 57, file C1/23 "National Culture, 1965–1972," box 2, unnumbered accession, Regional Archives, Tanga.

32. Minutes of the District Cultural Committee meeting, Handeni, December 12, 1966, document 73A, file C1/23 "National Culture: 1965–72," box 2, unnumbered Accession, Regional Archives, Tanga.

33. Ibid.

34. E. R. Munseri, n.d., attached to letter from principal secretary, Ministry of Community Development and National Culture to all regional and district offices, August 31, 1966, ref. no. CDNC/C.13, document 54, file C1/23 "National Culture: 1965–72," box 2, unnumbered accession, Regional Archives, Tanga.

35. Ibid.

36. Recorded on Gallotone GB 2251, quoted in Whiteley 1969, 63–64.

37. BAKITA objectives as cited in Halimoja 1981, 43–45 and in Ministry of National Culture and Youth, n.d. (1975?), 8–9; BAKIZA objectives as cited in Dept. of Customs and Arts, Zanzibar n.d., 15–16.

38. Commissioner for culture to all district commissioners, February 12, 1969, ref. no. UT/M.5/1/68, document 120, file C1/23 "National Culture, 1965–1972," box 2, unnumbered accession, Regional Archives, Tanga.

39. Information used to create this chart was drawn from multiple sources, including Mbughuni 1974, Lihamba 1985, various policy documents, and interviews with Culture personnel.

40. From *Historia Fupi ya Maisha Yangu* by Ernest Musa Kongola (Dodoma:

n.p., 1989), pages 25–27, translated by Gregory Maddox. My deep thanks go to Greg for sharing this passage with me.

41. Kongola, Historia.

42. Kongola, Historia.

43. Ministry of Community Development, Culture, Youth, and Sports, *Rasimu ya Sera ya Taifa ya Utamaduni* (National cultural policy guidelines), 1988.

44. In 1980, the National Dance Troupe was disbanded and the Bagamoyo College for the Arts established. The discovery that the youths trained in China had missed out on their education embarrassed the government. Under the direction of Director of Arts Louis Mbughuni, the artists were recast as teachers at Bagamoyo entrusted with the goal of training cultural officers and performers who could spread national culture throughout the regions and districts (telephone interview with Louis Mbughuni, April 18, 1997).

45. BASATA was formed in 1987, the result of an amalgamation of the former Baraza la Sanaa la Taifa (National Arts Council, previously focused exclusively on visual arts) and BAMUTA (Baraza la Muziki la Taifa, the National Music Council) that subsequently ceased to exist. Both BAMUTA and the old BASATA were formed in 1974 under the National Arts Council Act. The proposal to create the new BASATA was drafted in 1984 but not passed by Parliament until 1987 (*Sanaa za Taifa, Jamhuri ya Muungano wa Tanzania*, no. 23, 1984).

46. Many thanks to Fred Cooper for this and many more observations and insights that greatly enriched this chapter.

Chapter 6

1. In good economic times, this was a successful strategy for attracting workers, one also employed in neighboring Zambia by copper-mining companies that competed with South African mines for migrant labor (Chauncy 1981). Few companies these days can afford to provide such benefits.

2. By the end of my fieldwork in 1995, the three components were fully united into the new KIUBATA that included all the genres. This was a decision made by the THA administration that affected performers' salaries by standardizing them, whereas before KIUBATA (*ngoma, sarakasi, tamthiliya*) performers had a significantly lower salary than the *taarab* performers, who were paid less than the *dansi* performers.

3. This being a government-owned and operated parastatal, I was limited in what questions I could ask. The issue of salaries proved to be a sensitive topic, making it impossible for me to collect accurate figures, but I was able to ascertain that the rehearsal allowance paid to each performer for every rehearsal attended was a mere Tsh. 150, which at that time converted to U.S. $0.30.

4. What follows is my translation of the original Kiswahili texts. Similar subsequent descriptions are also my own translations.

5. Interview with Lamek Tandika (chairman) and Mzigo wa Ndevu (poetry teacher), October 3, 1992.

6. Interview, L. Tandika and Mzigo wa Ndevu, October 1, 1992.

7. Interview with Mzigo wa Ndevu, October 8, 1992: "Baada ya wakati wa

utawala, tuliacha utamaduni wao wakoloni na tulirudi utamaduni wetu Watanzania. Ilikuwa kwa bidii ya CCM."

8. Letter from area secretary, Handeni to Tanga regional commissioner dated
June 27, 1966, ref. no. P.4/13/II/227, in the Tanga Archives, accession no. 5,
box 6, file C1/12 "Ceremonial 1948–1971," document 80.

9. Other references to an *ngoma* named Mbugi that may or may not be the
same as Mbuji were included in district reports from Pangani, Lushoto and
Muheza Districts. See documents 41, 64, and 75A in file C1/12 "Ceremonial
1948–1971," accession no. 5, box 6, in the Tanga Archives. Also, Mbuji and
Selo were the representative Zigua ngoma performed at the Tanga Region Festival held in July 1964. See file C1/20/B "Tanga Region Festival," accession no.
304, Tanga Region, in the Tanzanian National Archives.

10. Interview with Mzigo wa Ndevu, October 8, 1992, Tanga.

11. For more information on Swahili spirit possession cults, see Giles 1987.

12. For reasons not explained in the accompanying text, no figure is included for the Swahili/Shirazi populations.

13. Interview with Yahaya Bushiri and Mbaraka of Watangatanga, November 18, 1993, Tanga.

14. Interview with Godwin Kaduma, commissioner of culture, Ministry of
Education and Culture, Dar es Salaam, July 26, 1993.

15. Interview, G. Kaduma.

16. The *msondo* drum is associated with many puberty/initiation ceremonies. It is a long, narrow, single-headed drum played straddled between two legs.
A possible linguistic connection emerges from the Sena language in which
nsondo translates as "penis" (personal correspondence, Leroy Vail, June 1997,
Cambridge, MA).

17. Interview with Mr. K. M. Simba, THA chief secretary, October 7, 1992.

18. Interview with Mobali L. Muba, cultural officer, Tanga Region, December
21, 1992.

19. For more information on the conflict-ridden relationship between
nomadic pastoralists and the Tanzanian and Kenyan states, see M. L. ole Parkipuny, "Some Crucial Aspects of the Maasai Predicament," in *African Socialism in Practice: The Tanzanian Experience,* ed. Andrew Coulson (Nottingham:
Spokesman, 1979); Thomas Spear and Richard Waller, eds., *Being Maasai*
(London and Nairobi: James Currrey, 1993); and George Monbiot, *No Man's
Land: An Investigative Journey through Kenya and Tanzania* (London: Macmillan,
1994).

20. Interview with Nestory Mweta, chief officer for the performing arts, Ministry of Education and Culture office, Tanga Region, November 17, 1992.

21. Arguably the most internationally known Tanzanian artist is Hukwe Zawose, a Gogo, who has released several CDs on international labels in collaboration with the National Ngoma Troupe.

22. Two years later, I was in the company of a group of thirty Samburu (a
peripheral group within the Maasai ethnic category) and was able to play for
them my video recording of this performance. I did not introduce it with any
information, but simply played it for them and asked for their opinion. At
first there was only silence. They did not quite know what to make of it. They
recognized the song as Maasai, but clearly were having difficulty reconciling

the song with the performers. When I finally explained that these were Gogo and not Maasai, there was a sense of relief accompanied by laughter. No, they exclaimed, those are certainly not Maasai. And then they proceeded to point out all the inconsistencies that identified the non-Maasai-ness of these artists.

Chapter 7

1. Although we do not know the current state of *taarab* in Burundi, given the recent turmoil, there were at least three *taarab* bands in the 1980s, all established by former members of Tanga's own Lucky Star Musical Club. They were Jasmin, Shani, and New Stars Musical Clubs. For more on the spread of *taarab* throughout Tanzania and beyond, see Askew 2000.

2. For in-depth analyses of the economic and political ramifications of the transitions to a liberal market economy and multiparty democracy, see Tripp 1997; Msekwa 1995; and McHenry 1994.

3. Salim Ahmed Salim was, most recently, the secretary-general of the Organization of African Unity (OAU).

4. The final blow to Black Star was the formation of THA's Bandari Taarab in 1992, to which Sharmila and many other Black Star performers defected, lured by the prospect of regular salaries. But that was yet to come.

5. Interview with Mohamed Omari Shariff and Muhina Hassan of Black Star Musical Club, June 8, 1993, Tanga.

6. *Sungusungu* is the name of a variety of black ant famous for the staunch protection of their queen.

7. "Pumu zimepata mkohozi" is a *methali* (proverb, saying) that literally translates as, "Asthma has found one who coughs," meaning that asthma found a good home in having found someone who already coughs a lot. In the context of this song, it means that the job of cleaning up corruption in the government has found the right person in Mrema (i.e., he is the right man for the job).

8. Interview with Yahaya Bushiri and Mbaraka, November 18, 1993, Tanga.

9. They specify that the balance be paid at the beginning and not the end of the wedding because they have suffered too often from wedding organizers who withhold payment and demand that the band continue playing beyond the acceptable four-hour standard.

10. Interview with Seif Kassim Kisauji, May 9, 1995, Tanga.

11. A news brief issued on June 3, 1997, by the Tanzanian representative in the United Kingdom, reads, "The World Food Programme has warned that food supply in Tanzania 'is extremely precarious,' and that urgent access to food in many of the affected regions was badly needed. 'Many of the poorest are now reduced to living on daily food intake substantially below minimum requirements,' a WFP statement issued in Dar es Salaam yesterday said, adding that the UN agency was ready to move 5,000 tonnes of maize and 480 tonnes of pulses to drought affected regions of the country. The government recently released 20,000 tonnes of food from the Strategic Grain Reserve (SGR) for relief distribution. The Tanzania Crop Monitoring and Early Warning Unit has predicted that the country may have to import over 500,000 tonnes of food this year to cover deficits." Downloaded from "tanzanrep.uk"; <tanzareptanzarep.demon.co.uk>.

12. "Dar Teachers Not Paid Salaries," *Guardian,* October 17, 1995, 1.

13. Operation Rufiji (1968), Operation Handeni (1968), Operation Mtwara (1969?), Operation Dodoma (1971), Operation Kigoma (1972); see Abrahams 1985; Miti 1982; Hyden 1980; McHenry 1979; and Ingle 1972.

14. "Parties Fail to Start Campaigns for Lack of Money," *Daily News,* September 4, 1995, 5; "Election Subsidies Diverted to Administration Costs," *Daily News,* September 27, 1995, 5; "Government to Spend 35.6 Billion on Elections," *Sunday News* October 1,1995, 1.

15. The controversy surrounded James Mapalala, former chairman of the Civic United Front (CUF). See also "Baada ya kunusa kushindwa, wagombea wa upinzani watoweka na ruzuku" (After sensing upcoming loss, opposition candidates vanish with campaign funds) *Uhuru,* October 21, 1995, 1.

16. Interview with Captain John Komba, May 21, 1995, Tanga.

17. "'Cheche' za TOT zatimiza mwaka" (TOT's popularity reaches one year), *Uhuru,* August 14, 1993, 15.

18. Ibid.

19. "TX" was once the prefix on all car license plates belonging to foreign nationals residing in Tanzania. It identified the driver/owner as an expatriate. In 1992, the prefix was dropped from official usage, but nonetheless remained in common parlance as a term for an expatriate or, as in this case, something akin in quality to "expatriate-ness" (which is thought of in largely positive terms).

20. "Soud Othman atimuliwa uanachama Culture" (Othman Soud destroys his membership with Culture), *Dimba* March 27–April 2, 1994, 2.

21. These references are to John Malecela, former Tanzanian prime minister and vice president; Salmin Amour, former president of Zanzibar.

22. Interview with Captain John Komba, May 21, 1995, Tanga.

23. Nestory M. Mweta, "Tanzanian Culture," paper presented at the district seminar of the Ministry of Education and Culture, Art and Language Department (1991), trans. Michael D. Nyangusi.

24. Interview with Captain John Komba, May 21, 1995, Tanga.

25. On my most recent trip to Tanzania in January and February 2001, Captain Komba informed me that *taarab* has fallen in popularity and that now the TOT *dansi* band ends every TOT show. This is not surprising, given the historical pattern of rising and falling musical fashions.

26. "Singers Thrill Fans in Dar" *Daily News,* March 28, 1994.

27. "Muungano, TOT Compete Today," *Daily News,* March 26, 1994.

28. Of the twelve months of the Islamic calendar, the fourth, fifth, eighth and twelfth ("Ramadan") months are inauspicious for weddings. The months considered most popular for weddings are the sixth, seventh, ninth, tenth (Rajabu), and eleventh (Shabani) months. In the remaining three months (first, second, and third), weddings occasionally take place, but generally not many at all. Interview with Mzee Pera Ridhiwani, December 12, 1993, Tanga.

29. Interview with Seif Kisauji, director of Babloom, December 27, 1993, Tanga.

30. Interview with Captain John Komba, September 4, 1993, Tanga.

31. Interviews with Margaret (codirector) and Yahaya Bushiri (secretary) of Watangatanga, September 3, 1993, September 28, 1993, and January 23, 1994, Tanga.

32. "'Cheche' za TOT zatimiza mwaka" (TOT's popularity reaches one year), *Uhuru,* August 14, 1993, 15.

33. I believe that there were a couple of other transmitting stations, one in Dodoma and another in Mwanza, but they were owned and operated by the same government agency and broadcast almost the same materials. In 1994, Radio One the first private radio station hit the airwaves and since then many more have emerged.

34. Interview with John Kitime, chairman of CHAMUDATA (*Cha*ma cha *Mu*ziki wa *Da*nsi cha *Ta*ifa, the National Dansi Music Association), February 1, 1996, Dar es Salaam.

35. "Jamvi la Wageni," Rama Hamadi, Babloom Modern Taarab, Tanga.

36. "Bunduki," Kibwana Said, Black Star Musical Club, Tanga.

37. "Sore Mpishi," Mohamed Mrisho, Black Star Musical Club, Tanga.

38. Not to be confused with the Gita dance society in Tanga.

39. One example comes from an article entitled "Mwinyi Awarded for Role in Rwanda," *Daily News,* May 30, 1994, 1: "President Mwinyi has been awarded a golden medal by the Pan-African Youth Movement (PYM) for his tireless efforts to end senseless massacres in the neighbouring Rwanda. The medal was pinned on Ndugu Mwinyi on Saturday by the PYM Deputy Secretary General Ndugu Mohamd Mahrez amid chants of CCM Juu . . . CCM Juu . . . [Up with CCM]."

40. Interview with Captain John Komba, May 21, 1995, Tanga.

41. TOT's lewdness of lyrics is so famous and known that it sometimes gets top billing as in the advertisement, "'Matusi' ya TOT Kuanza Tandika Ijumaa" (The profanity of TOT to begin in Tandika on Friday), *Mfanyakazi* January 18, 1995, 9.

42. Although not having the local knowledge of social relations for Dar es Salaam that I acquired for Tanga, I cannot say this with the same degree of certainty. There was no mistaking, however, the significant glances and veiled gestures that marked the TOT performances I attended—even if I did not understand how they were used.

43. "TOT haidhibitiwi na CCM—Taarifa" (TOT is not managed by CCM—announcement) *Uhuru,* April 18, 1995, 15.

Chapter 8

1. Interview with Godwin Kaduma, July 26, 1993, Dar es Salaam.

2. OTTU the organization recently divorced itself from the administration of OTTU the band, according to Seif Kisauji (interview, June 18, 1997.

3. The information included in table 8.1 was culled from a variety of sources and is incomplete, but hopefully provides a sense of the disparities in emphasis in government funding across the genres. Data drawn from Lange 1994; interviews with Yahaya Bushiri, Rashid Makunganya, and Majuto Mbugani, August 17, 1993, Tanga; interview with Rashid Hamadi, December 1993, Tanga; interview with Mabrook "Babu Njenje" Hamisi, October 1, 2000, Dar es Salaam; consultations with Werner Graebner, August 2000; and data culled from newspaper articles.

4. "Azimio la 3 la Mkutano Mkuu wa 15 wa TANU," 1971, quoted in Lihamba 1985, 361.

5. "Tamko la Chama Juu ya Utamaduni wa Taifa," Dodoma, 1976, CCM Headquarters, quoted in Lihamba 1985, 361.

6. After Babloom became affiliated with the CCM campaign of Salim Kisauji, they were referred to in the streets of Tanga as "Baby TOT."

7. Recall also Songoyi's (1988b) analysis of the two singers Kalikali and Mwinamila and their contrasting relationships to the Tanzanian state.

8. "Cultural Policy Recommendations," presented at the Workshop on Cultural Policy, February 15–17, 1995, Morogoro, 6.

9. I am indebted to Katherine Verdery for helping me think this through with greater clarity.

Glossary of Swahili Terms

What follows is a limited glossary of key Swahili terms. Not every Swahili word that appears in the text is included, only those that appear more than once or hold particular ethnographic or theoretical significance. Although not every musical form is included here, they all appear in the index. As a rough guide to pronunciation, vowels are generally pronounced as in Spanish or Italian, consonants are generally pronounced as in English, and stress falls on the penultimate syllable.

aibu (n). Shame.
bandari (n). Port, harbor.
bara (n). Hinterland.
bashraf (n). Purely instrumental orchestral piece played at the beginning of classical *taarab* concerts.
Beni (n). Former men's *ngoma.*
beti (n). Verse of a song or poem.
bibi (n). Term of address for a lady or older woman; also, grandmother.
bongos (n). Two attached, single-headed drums introduced from Cuban music.
buibui (n). Full-length black veil worn by Swahili women.
burudani (n). Entertainment, arts.
bwana (n). Term of address for man; in former usage, "master."
chai (n). Tea.
chakacha (n). A women's *ngoma* from Mombasa and Lamu; also, a popular rhythm in *ngoma, taarab,* and *dansi.*
chama; pl. vyama (n). Party or association; applies to both political parties and dance societies, among other things.
-cheza (v). To dance.
daku (n). The midnight meal taken during Ramadan.
dansi (n). A genre of Tanzanian popular music, a.k.a. "jazz."
desturi (n). Customs.
dumbak (n). Arabic, hour-glass-shaped, single-head drum.
fani (n). Genre, art form.
fidla (n). Violin.
fujo (n). Trouble, violence.

gambusi (n). Stringed instrument resembling a mandolin.

gari (n). Car, vehicle.

harusi (n). Wedding.

hawara (n). Live-in lover.

heshima (n). Respect; respectful behavior.

-imba (v). To sing.

-imbia (n). To sing to/about someone.

jamhuri (n). Republic.

jando (n). Male initiation ritual.

kadhi (n). Islamic judge.

kanda (n). Audio cassette.

Kanda (n). Zone; an administrative unit of Tanzanian governance.

kanzu (n). Full-length, typically white, garment worn by Swahili men.

-kata kiuno (v). A style of dance characterized by an intricate circular hip movement.

katibu (n). Secretary.

kesha (n). An all-night wedding celebration.

khanga (n). Two-piece printed cloths worn by women in East Africa.

kibwagizo (n). Refrain to a song or poem; see also *kiitikio*.

kiitikio (n). Refrain to a song or poem; see also *kibwagizo*.

kinyago; pl. *vinyago* (n). Masked dancer; also, carving, statue.

kishindo; pl. *vishindo* (n). Challenge, boast, threatening behavior.

kiuno (n). Hips, waist.

kofia (n). Embroidered hat worn by Swahili men.

kumbwaya (n). A popular coastal *ngoma* rhythm also used in *taarab*.

kungwi; pl. *makungwi* (n). Female instructor in matters relating to initiation and marriage; see also *somo*.

kwaya (n). "choir" music.

Lelemama (n). Former Swahili women's *ngoma* popular throughout the coastal region.

maana (n). Meaning.

-maanisha (v). To imbue with meaning.

mafumbo (n). Metaphorical references.

mafunzo (n). Teachings, lessons.

mageuzi (n). Change; current usage emphasizes political change.

maigizo (n). Acting; also, short form of *michezo ya maigizo*.

matusi (n). Foul or explicit language, profanity.

maulid (n). Devotional form of Swahili poetry often detailing the Prophet Muhammad's life.

mazingaombwe (n). Magical acts.

mchiriku (n). Genre of urban youth music.

mgeni; pl. wageni (n). Stranger.

mhuni; pl. wahuni (n). Hooligans.

michezo ya maigizo (n). Theatrical plays; also, tamthiliya.

mila (n). Traditions.

mipasho (n). Messages.

mizani (n). Poetic meter.

mke; pl. *wanawake* (n). Woman.

Mkoa; pl. *Mikoa* (n). Region; an administrative unit of Tanzanian governance.

mkonge (n). Sisal.

motomoto (n). Excitement; lit. "extreme heat."

mpigaji; pl. *wapigaji* (n). Instrumentalist.

msanii; pl. *wasanii* (n). Artist.

Msanja (n). Women's *ngoma* in Tanga; formerly a mixed-sex *ngoma.*

msondo (n). A tall, single-head drum often played in female initiation ceremonies as well as in Makonde *ngoma;* also the name of the OTTU Jazz Band's *mtindo.*

mtaa; pl. *mitaa* (n). Street; also, neighborhood.

mtafiti; pl. *watafiti* (n). Researcher.

mtindo; pl. *mitindo* (n). Style, especially a musical or dance style.

mtu ; pl. *watu* (n). Person.

mume; pl. *waume* (n). Husband.

muungano (n). Union.

muziki (n). The instrumental interlude between verses of a taarab song; also a general term for music.

muziki wa ala (n). Traditional instrumental music.

mwalimu (n). Teacher.

mwanachama; pl. *wanachama* (n). Member of an association or club.

mwanaume; pl. *wanaume* (n). Man.

mwari; pl. *wari* (n). Initiate.

mwenyeji; pl. *wenyeji* (n). "native-owner of the town," that is, established residents.

mwimbaji; pl. *waimbaji* (n). Singer.

mzungu; pl. *wazungu* (n). White person.

nai (n). Side-blown Arabic flute.

nakshi (n). Decoration, ornamentation; in music used to refer to vocal ornamentation such as slides, trills, and turns.

nchi (n). Country.

ndani (adv). Inside.

ngamia (n). Camel.

ngoma (n). Dance, drum, musical event.

ngonjera (n). A genre of dramatized Swahili poetry, usually with political themes.

nyota (n). Star.

-pasha (v). To send someone a message.

pwani (n). Coast.

raha (n). Happiness, joy.

rais (n). President.

Ramadan (n). The Islamic month of fasting.

rika (n). Tambourine.

sambusa (n). Meat-filled pastry.

sanaa (n). Arts.

sanaa za maonyesho (n). Performing arts.

sarakasi (n). Acrobatics (from "circus").

saruji (n). Cement.

sera (n). Policy/policies.

shairi; pl. *mashairi* (n). Poetry; *mshairi* (n). Poet; *washairi* (n). Poets.

sheria (n). Laws.

shetani; pl. *mashetani* (n). Spirit; also, devil.

siasa (n). Politics.

siwa (n). A carved wood or ivory horn associated with chieftaincy.

somo; pl. *masomo* (n). Female instructress especially in matters relating to wifely duties, marriage, and love-making.

taarab (n). A genre of sung Swahili poetry.

tabla (n). Detached, two-piece drum set from India.

taifa, pl. *mataifa* (n). Nation.

tamthiliya (n). Theatrical plays; also michezo ya maigizo.

tanga (n). Sail of a vessel.

-tangatanga (v). To wander.

Tanzania Bara (n). Mainland Tanzania.

Tanzania Visiwani (n). The islands of Zanzibar and Pemba.

tashkota (n). Hand-picked string instrument.

timing (n). Clave; abbreviated form of "timing sticks."

trafiki (n). Traffic police.

-tunga (v). To compose. -tunza (v). To tip.

udi (n). (1) Incense of aloe wood. (2) Lute.

Ujamaa (n). The economic, social, and political program of "African socialism" designed and implemented by Tanzanian's first president Julius Nyerere.

umoja (n). Unity.

unyago (n). Female initiation ritual.

upinzani (n). Rivalry.

ustaarabu (n). Gentility, civility.

utamaduni (n). Culture.

vina (n). Rhyme.

Vugo (n). A women's *ngoma* in Mombasa; similar to *msanja.*

vyama vingi (n). Multipartyism.

Wilaya (n). District; an administrative unit of Tanzanian governance.

References

Abdulaziz, M. H. 1972 [1968]. "Tanzania national language policy and the rise of Swahili political culture." Pp. 155–64 in *Socialism in Tanzania: An Interdisciplinary Reader,* vol. 1, ed. Lionel Cliffe and John S. Saul. Nairobi: East African Publishing House.

———. 1979. *Muyaka: Nineteenth-Century Swahili Popular Poetry.* Nairobi: Kenya Literature Bureau.

Abrahams, R. G., ed. 1985. *Villagers, Villages, and the State in Modern Tanzania.* Cambridge African Monographs, no. 4. Cambridge: African Studies Centre.

Abu-Lughod, Lila. 1986. *Veiled Sentiments: Honor and Poetry in a Bedouin Society.* Berkeley and Los Angeles: University of California Press.

———. 1990. "Shifting politics in Bedouin love poetry." Pp. 24–45 in *Language and the Politics of Emotion,* ed. C. Lutz and L. Abu-Lughod. New York: Cambridge University Press.

Afigbo, A. E.; E. A. Ayandele; R. J. Gavin; J. D. Omer-Cooper; and R. Palmer. 1986. *The Making of Modern Africa.* Vols. 1 and 2. Essex, England: Longman.

Aldington, T. J. 1975. "Tanzania agriculture: A decade of progress in crop production." *Tanzania Notes and Records* no. 76 (special issue entitled *A Decade of Progress, 1961–1971*): 57–66.

al-Faruqi, Lois Ibsen. 1978. "Ornamentation in Arabian improvisational music." *World of Music* 20, no. 1: 17–32.

———. 1981. "The status of music in Muslim nations: Evidence from the Arab world." *Asian Music* 12, no. 1: 56–85.

Allen, James de Vere. 1972. *Lamu.* Nairobi: Regal Press.

———. 1993. *Swahili Origins: Swahili Culture and the Shungwaya Phenomenon.* Athens: Ohio University Press.

Allen, J. W. T., ed. 1981. *The Customs of the Swahili People: The Desturi za Waswahili of Mtoro bin Mwinyi Bakari and Other Swahili Persons.* Berkeley: University of California Press.

Amankulor. 1989. "The condition of ritual in theatre: An intercultural perspective." *Performing Arts Journal* 33/34 11, no. 3/12, no. 1: 45–58.

Amory, Deborah P. 1990. "*Swahili ni nani?* The politics of Swahili identity and culture." Paper presented at the African Studies Association Meetings, Baltimore, November 1–4, 1990.

———. 1994. "The politics of identity on Zanzibar." Ph.D. diss. Department of Anthropology, Stanford University.

Anderson, Benedict. 1989 [1983]. *Imagined Communities: Reflections on the Origin and Spread of Nationalism.* London and New York: Verso.

Appadurai, Arjun. 1988. "How to make a national cuisine: Cookbooks in contemporary India." *Comparative Studies in Society and History* 30, no. 1: 3–24.

Apter, Andrew. 1999. "The subvention of tradition: A genealogy of the Nigerian durbar." Pp. 213–52 in Steinmetz, ed. 1999.

Arens, W. 1975. "The Waswahili: The social history of an ethnic group." *Africa* 45, no. 4: 426–38.

———. 1976. "Changing patterns of ethnic identity and prestige in East Africa." Pp. 65–75 in *A Century of Change in Eastern Africa,* ed. W. Arens. The Hague: Mouton.

Askew, Kelly M. 1997. "Performing the nation: Swahili musical performance and the production of Tanzanian national culture." Ph.D. diss. Department of Anthropology, Harvard University.

———. 1999. "Female circles and male lines: Gender dynamics along the Swahili coast." *Africa Today* 46, nos. 3 and 4: 67–102.

———. 2000. "Following in the tracks of *Beni:* The diffusion of the Tanga *taarab* tradition." Pp. 21–38 in *Mashindano! Competitive Music Performance in East Africa,* ed. Frank Gunderson and Gregory F. Barz. Dar es Salaam: Mkuki na Nyota Publishers.

Austin, John L. 1965 [1962]. *How to Do Things with Words.* Oxford: Oxford University Press.

Bai, Liu. 1983. *Cultural Policy in the People's Republic of China: Letting a Hundred Flowers Blossom.* Paris: UNESCO.

Bakari, Mtoro bin Mwinyi. 1981. *Desturi za Waswahili.* Ed. J. W. T. Allen. Berkeley: University of California Press.

Baker, E. C. 1934. *Report on Social and Economic Conditions in the Tanga Province.* Dar es Salaam: Government Printer.

Barber, Karin. 1987. "Popular arts in Africa." *African Studies Review* 30, no. 3: 1–78.

Barber, Karin, and Christopher Waterman. 1995. "Traversing the global and the local: *Fújì* music and praise poetry in the production of contemporary Yorùbá popular culture." Pp. 241–62 in *Worlds Apart: Modernity through the Prism of the Local,* ed. Daniel Miller. London and New York: Routledge.

Barber, Karin; John Collins; and Alain Ricard. 1997. *West African Popular Theater.* Bloomington: Indiana University Press; Oxford: James Currey.

Bauman, Richard. 1977. *Verbal Art as Performance.* Prospect Heights, IL: Waveland Press.

Bauman, Richard, and Charles L. Briggs. 1990. "Poetics and performance as critical perspectives on language and social life." *Annual Review of Anthropology* 19: 59–88.

Baumann, Max Peter, ed. 1991. *Music in the Dialogue of Cultures: Traditional Music and Cultural Policy.* Wilhelmshaven: Florian Noetzel Verlag.

Baumann, Oscar. 1890. *In Deutsch-Ostafrika während des Aufstandes.* Wien: Eduard Holzel.

———. 1891. *Usambara und seine Nachbargebiete.* Berlin: D. Reimer.

Bender, Wolfgang. 1991. *Sweet Mother: Modern African Music*. Chicago: University of Chicago Press.

Bendix, Regina. 1992. "National sentiment in the enactment and discourse of Swiss political ritual." *American Ethnologist* 19, no. 4: 768–90.

Bennett, Norman R. 1978. *A History of the Arab State of Zanzibar*. London: Methuen.

Bentley, G. Carter. 1987. "Ethnicity and practice." *Comparative Studies in Society and History* 29, no. 1: 24–55.

———. 1991. "Response to Yelvington." *Comparative Studies in Society and History* 33, no. 1: 169–75.

Berg, F. J. 1968. "The Swahili community of Mombasa, 1500–1900." *Journal of African History* 9, no. 1: 35–56.

Bienen, Henry. 1967. *Tanzania: Party Transformation and Economic Development*. Princeton, NJ: Princeton University Press.

Biersteker, Ann. 1991. "Language, poetry and power: A reconsideration of 'Utendi wa Mwana Kupona." In *Faces of Islam in African Literature*, ed. Kenneth W. Harrow. Portsmouth, NH: Heinemann.

———. 1996. *Kujibizana: Questions of Language and Power in Nineteenth- and Twentieth-Century Poetry in Kiswahili*. Lansing: Michigan State University Press.

Bloch, Maurice. 1974. "Symbols, song, dance, and features of articulation." *European Journal of Sociology* 15: 55–81.

———. 1989. *Ritual, History, and Power: Selected Papers in Anthropology*. London and Atlantic Highlands, NJ: Athlone Press.

Bloch, Maurice, ed. 1975. *Political Language and Oratory in Traditional Society*. London and New York: Academic Press.

Bourdieu, Pierre. 1977. *Outline of a Theory of Practice*. Trans. Richard Nice. Cambridge: Cambridge University Press.

———. 1984. *Distinction: A Social Critique of the Judgment of Taste*. Trans. Richard Nice. Cambridge, MA: Harvard University Press.

———. 1999. "Rethinking the state: Genesis and structure of the bureaucratic field." Pp. 53–75 in Steinmetz, ed. 1999.

Brett, E. A. 1973. *Colonialism and Underdevelopment in East Africa: The Politics of Economic Change, 1919–1939*. New York: NOK Publishers.

Burton, Richard F. 1872. *Zanzibar: City, Island , and Coast*. Vols. 1 and 2. London: Tinsley Brothers.

Butler, Judith. 1990. *Gender Trouble*. New York: Routledge.

———. 1993. *Bodies That Matter*. New York: Routledge.

———. 1997. *Excitable Speech: A Politics of the Performative*. New York: Routledge.

Campbell, Carol A. 1976. "An introduction to the music of Swahili Women." Nairobi: Institute of African Studies, University of Nairobi.

———. 1983. "Nyimbo za Kiswahili: A socio-ethnomusicological study of a Swahili poetic form." Ph.D. diss. Department of Music, University of Washington.

Campbell, Carol A., and Carol M. Eastman. 1984. "Ngoma: Swahili adult song performance in context." *Ethnomusicology* 28, no. 3: 467–93.

Caplan, Patricia. 1975. *Choice and Constraint in a Swahili Community: Property,*

Hierarchy, and Cognatic Descent on the East African Coast. London: Oxford University Press.

———. 1978. "The Swahili of Chole Island, Tanzania." Pp. 141–75 in *Face Values: Some Anthropological Themes,* ed. Anne Sutherland. London: British Broadcasting Corp.

———. 1982. "Gender, ideology, and modes of production on the coast of East Africa." *Paideuma* 28: 29–43.

———. 1995. "'Law' and 'custom': Marital disputes on Northern Mafia Island, Tanzania." Pp. 203–22 in Caplan, ed. 1995.

Caplan, Pat, ed. 1995. *Understanding Disputes: The Politics of Argument.* Oxford and Providence: Berg.

Carlson, Marvin. 1996. *Performance: A Critical Introduction.* New York: Routledge.

Casson, L. 1989. *The Periplus Maris Erythrae: Text with Introduction, Translation, and Commentary.* Princeton, NJ: Princeton University Press.

Chande, Abdin Noor. 1991. "Islam, Islamic leadership, and community development in Tanga, Tanzania." Ph.D. diss. McGill University, Montreal.

———. 1998. *Islam, Ulamaa, and Community Development in Tanzania: A Case Study of Religious Currents in East Africa.* San Francisco: Austin & Winfield.

Chanock, Martin. 1985. *Law, Custom, and Social Order: The Colonial Experience in Malawi and Zambia.* Cambridge: Cambridge University Press.

Chatterjee, Partha. 1986. *Nationalist Thought and the Colonial World: A Derivative Discourse?* Minneapolis: University of Minnesota Press.

———. 1993. *The Nation and Its Fragments: Colonial and Postcolonial Histories.* Princeton, NJ: Princeton University Press.

Chauncy, George. 1981. "The locus of reproduction: Women's labour on the Zambian Copperbelt, 1927–1953." *Journal of Southern African Studies* 7, no. 2: 135–64.

Chittick, H. Neville. 1965. "The 'Shirazi' colonization of East Africa." *Journal of African History* 6: 275–94.

Cliffe, Lionel, and John Saul, eds. 1973–74. *Socialism in Tanzania.* Vols. 1 and 2. Nairobi: East Africa Publishing House.

Colson, Elizabeth. 1969. "African society at the time of the Scramble." Pp. 27–65 in *Colonialism in Africa,* vol. 1, ed. L. I. Gann and P. Duignan. Cambridge: Cambridge University Press.

———. 1995. "The contentiousness of disputes." Pp. 65–82 in Caplan, ed. 1995.

Comaroff, Jean, and John Comaroff, eds. 1993. *Modernity and Its Malcontents: Ritual and Power in Postcolonial Africa.* Chicago and London: University of Chicago Press.

Constantin, François. 1987. "Condition Swahili et identite politique." *Africa* 57, no. 2: 219–33.

Cooper, Frederick. 1977. *Plantation Slavery on the East Coast of Africa.* New Haven, CT: Yale University Press.

———. 1980. *From Slaves to Squatters: Plantation Labour and Agriculture in Zanzibar and Coastal Kenya 1890–1925.* New Haven, CT: Yale University Press.

———. 1987. *On the African Waterfront: Urban Disorder and the Transformation of Work in Colonial Mombasa.* New Haven, CT: Yale University Press.

Cooper, Frederick, and Ann L. Stoler. 1989. "Tensions of empire: Colonial control and visions of rule." *American Ethnologist* 16, no. 4: 609–21.

Coplan, David. 1987. "The power of oral poetry: Narrative songs of the Basotho migrants." *Research in African Literatures* 18, no. 1: 1–35.

————. 1994. *In the Time of Cannibals: The Word Music of South Africa's Basotho Migrants*. Chicago and London: University of Chicago Press.

Corfield, F. D. 1960. *The Origins and Growth of Mau Mau: An Historical Survey*. Sessional Paper no. 5 of 1959–60. Nairobi: Colony and Protectorate of Kenya, Government Printer.

Coronil, Fernando. 1997. *The Magical State: Nature, Money, and Modernity in Venezuela*. Chicago: University of Chicago Press.

Corrigan, Philip, and Derek Sayer. 1985. *The Great Arch: English State Formation as Cultural Revolution*. Oxford: Basil Blackwell.

Coulson, Andrew. 1979. "Introduction." Pp. 1–15 in *African Socialism in Practice: The Tanzanian Experience*. Nottingham: Spokesman.

————. 1982. *Tanzania: A Political Economy*. Oxford: Clarendon Press.

Cowan, Jane K. 1990. *Dance and the Body Politic in Northern Greece*. Princeton, NJ: Princeton University Press.

Daniels, Douglas Henry. 1996. "*Taarab* clubs and Swahili music culture." *Social Identities* 2, no. 3: 413–38.

Desai, Gaurav. 1990. "Theater as praxis: Discursive strategies in African popular theater." *African Studies Review* 33, no. 1: 65–92.

Domínguez, Virginia R., and David Y. H. Wu, eds. 1998. *From Beijing to Port Moresby: The Politics of National Identity in Cultural Policies*. Amsterdam: Gordon and Breach.

Donner, Philip. 1980. "Music forms in Tanzania and their socio-economic base." *Jipemoyo* 3: 88–98.

Drewal, Margaret Thompson. 1991. "The state of research on performance in Africa." *African Studies Review* 34, no. 3: 1–64.

————. 1992. *Yoruba Ritual: Performers, Play, Agency*. Bloomington: Indiana University Press.

Duggan, William Redman, and John R. Civille. 1976. *Tanzania and Nyerere: A Study of Ujamaa and Nationhood*. Maryknoll, NY: Orbis Books.

Eastman, Carol M. 1971. "Who are the Waswahili?" *Africa* 41, no. 3: 228–36.

————. 1975. "Ethnicity and the social scientist: Phonemes and distinctive features." *African Studies Review* 18, no. 1: 29–38.

————. 1984a. "An ethnography of Swahili expressive culture." *Research in African Literatures* 15, no. 3: 313–40.

————. 1984b. "Waungwana na wanawake: Muslim ethnicity and sexual segregation in coastal Kenya." *Journal of Multilingual and Multicultural Development* 5, no. 2: 97–112.

————. 1988. "Women, slaves and foreigners: African cultural influences and group processes in the formation of northern Swahili coastal society." *International Journal of African Historical Studies* 21, no. 1: 1–20.

Erlmann, Veit. 1996. *Nightsong: Performance, Power, and Practice in South Africa*. Chicago and London: University of Chicago Press.

Etherton, Michael. 1982. *The Development of African Drama*. London: Hutchinson University Library for Africa.

Evans, Peter B.; Dietrich Rueschemeyer; and Theda Skocpol, eds. 1985. *Bringing the State Back In.* Cambridge and New York: Cambridge University Press.

Ewens, Graeme. 1994a. "Heart of danceness: The music of Zaire." Pp. 313–23 in *World Music: The Rough Guide,* ed. Simon Broughton, Mark Ellingham, David Muddyman, and Richard Trillo. London: The Rough Guides.

———. 1994b. *Congo Colossus: The Life and Legacy of Franco and OK Jazz.* Norfolk, U.K.: BUKU Press.

Fabian, Johannes. 1986. *Language and Colonial Power: The Appropriation of Swahili in the Former Belgian Congo 1880–1938.* Berkeley: University of California Press.

———. 1990. *Power and Performance: Ethnographic Explorations through Proverbial Wisdom and Theater in Shaba, Zaire.* Madison: University of Wisconsin Press.

Fair, Laura. 1994. "Pastimes and politics: A social history of Zanzibar's Ng'ambo community, 1890–1950." Ph.D. diss. University of Minnesota.

———. 1996. "Identity, difference, and dance: Female initiation in Zanzibar, 1890–1930. *Frontiers* 17, no. 3: 147–72.

———. 1998. "Dressing up: Clothing, class, and gender in post-abolition Zanzibar." *Journal of African History* 39: 63–94.

———. 2001. *Pastimes and Politics: Culture, Community, and Identity in Post-Revolution Urban Zanzibar, 1890–1945.* Athens: Ohio University Press.

Fanon, Frantz. 1963. "On national culture." Pp. 206–48 in *The Wretched of the Earth.* New York: Grove Press.

Fargion, Janet Topp. 1993. "The role of women in *taarab* in Zanzibar: An historical examination of a process of 'Africanisation.'" *The World of Music* 35, no. 2: 109–25.

Farhan, Idi. 1992. "Introduction of *taarab* to Zanzibar in the nineteenth century." Paper presented to the International Conference on the History and Culture of Zanzibar, Zanzibar, December 14–16, 1992.

Farmer, Henry George. 1957. "The music of Islam." *New Oxford History of Music.* Vol. 1. London: Oxford University Press.

Farrell, Eileen Ruth. 1980. "*Ngoma ya ushindani:* Competitive song exchange and the subversion of hierarchy in a Swahili Muslim town on the Kenya coast." Ph.D. diss. Department of Anthropology, Harvard University.

Feld, Steven. 1994. "Communication, music, and speech about music." Pp. 77–95 in *Music Grooves: Essays and Dialogues,* by Charles Keil and Steven Feld. Chicago and London: University of Chicago Press.

Finnegan, Ruth. 1970. *Oral Literature in Africa.* Nairobi and Dar es Salaam: Oxford University Press.

Fischer, Ernst. 1963. *The Necessity of Art: A Marxist Approach.* Trans. Anna Bostock. Middlesex, England: Penguin Books.

———. 1969. *Art against Ideology.* Trans. Anna Bostock. New York: George Braziller.

Foucault, Michel. 1980. *Power/Knowledge: Selected Interviews and Other Writings, 1972–1977.* Ed. Colin Gordon. New York: Pantheon Books.

———. 1991. "Governmentality." Pp. 87–104 in *The Foucault Effect: Studies in Governmentality,* ed. Graham Burchell, Colin Gordon, and Peter Miller. Chicago: University of Chicago Press.

Fox, Richard G. 1990a. "Introduction." Pp. 1–14 in Fox 1990b.

Fox, Richard G., ed. 1990b. *Nationalist Ideologies and the Production of National Cultures*. American Ethnological Society Monograph Series, no. 2. Washington, DC: American Anthropological Association.

Franken, Marjorie Ann. 1986. "Anyone can dance: A survey and analysis of Swahili *ngoma*, past and present." Ph.D. diss. University of California, Riverside.

———. 1987. "Women's dances on the Swahili coast." *UCLA Journal of Dance Ethnology* 11: 30–38.

———. 1994. "Dance and status in Swahili society." *Visual Anthropology* 7, no. 2: 99–113.

Freeman-Grenville, G. S. P. 1962a. *The East African Coast: Select Documents from the First to the Earlier Nineteenth Century*. Oxford: Clarendon Press.

———. 1962b. *The Medieval History of the Coast of Tanganyika*. London: Oxford University Press.

———. 1988. *The Swahili Coast, Second to Nineteenth Centuries: Islam, Christianity, and Commerce in Eastern Africa*. London: Variorum Reprints.

Freire, Paolo. 1970. *Pedagogy of the Oppressed*. New York: Herder & Herder.

———. 1972. *Cultural Action for Freedom*. Harmondsworth, England: Penguin.

Freyhold, Michaela von. 1979. *Ujamaa Villages in Tanzania: Analysis of a Social Experiment*. New York and London: Monthly Review Press.

Fuglesang, Minou. 1994. *Veils and Videos: Female Youth Culture on the Kenyan Coast*. Stockholm: Department of Anthropology, Stockholm University.

Geertz, Clifford. 1973. "Ideology as a cultural system." Pp. 193–233 in *The Interpretation of Cultures*. New York: Basic Books.

Geiger, Susan. 1987. "Women in nationalist struggle: TANU activists in Dar es Salaam." *International Journal of African Historical Studies* 20, no. 1: 1–26.

———. 1997. *TANU Women: Gender and Culture in the Making of Tanganyikan Nationalism, 1955–1965*. Portsmouth, NH: Heinemann.

Gellner, Ernest. 1983. *Nations and Nationalism*. Ithaca, NY: Cornell University Press.

Gibb, H. A. R. 1962. *The Travels of Ibn Battuta, 1325–54*. Vol. 2. London: Hakluyt Society Series, vol. 110.

Gibbe, A. G. 1983. "Tanzania's language policy with special reference to Kiswahili as an educational medium." *Kiswahili* 50, no. 1: 46–50.

Gibbon, Peter. 1995. "Merchantisation of production and privatisation of development in post-*Ujamaa* Tanzania." Pp. 9–36 in Gibbon, ed. 1995.

Gibbon, Peter, ed. 1995. *Liberalised Development in Tanzania*. Uppsala: Nordiska Afrikainstitutet.

Giles, Linda. 1987. "Possession cults on the Swahili coast: A re-examination of theories of marginality." *Africa* 57, no. 2: 234–58.

Glassman, Jonathon. 1995. *Feasts and Riot: Revelry, Rebellion, and Popular Consciousness on the Swahili Coast, 1856–1888*. Social History of Africa Series. Portsmouth, NH: Heinemann.

Gluckman, Max. 1942. "Analysis of a social situation in modern Zululand." *Bantu Studies* 14: 1–30, 147–74.

Gnielinski, Anneliese von. n.d. "Traditional music instruments of Tanzania in the National Museum." National Museums of Tanzania Occasional Paper no. 6. Dar es Salaam: National Museum of Tanzania.

Goffman, Erving. 1959. *The Presentation of Self in Everyday Life.* Garden City, NY: Doubleday.

———. 1974. *Frame Analysis.* New York: Harper & Row.

———. 1980. *Forms of Talk.* Philadelphia: University of Pennsylvania Press.

Graebner, Werner. 1991. "Tarabu—populäre Musik am indischen Ozean." Pp. 181–201 in *Populäre Musik in Afrika,* ed. Veit Erlmann. Berlin: Museum für Völkerkunde.

———. 1992a. "Music, politics, and the media in East Africa." Pp. 223–33 in *1789–1989 Musique, Histoire, Démocratie,* vol. 1. Proceedings of the International Conference of Vibrations (Musiques médias sociétés) and IASPM (International Association for the Studies of Popular Music), Paris, France, 17–20 juillet 1989. Recherche, musique et danse 6. Paris: Edition de la Maison des sciences de l'homme.

———. 1994a. "Swahili musical party: Islamic taarab music of East Africa." Pp. 349–55 in *World Music: The Rough Guide,* ed. Simon Broughton et al. London: The Rough Guides.

———. 1994b. "Marashi ya Dar es Salaam: Dance with style: the flavour of Dar es Salaam." Pp. 355–62 in *World Music: The Rough Guide,* ed. Simon Broughton et al. London: The Rough Guides.

———. 1995. *Muziki wa dansi: Afropop hits from Tanzania.* CD liner notes. Detroit, MI: Africassette.

———. 1999. "Tanzania/Kenya—Taarab: The Swahili coastal sound." Pp. 690–97 in *World Music: The Rough Guide, Vol. 1: Africa, Europe and the Middle East,* ed. Simon Broughton et al. New edition. London: The Rough Guides/Penguin.

———, ed. 1992b. *Sokomoko: Popular Culture in East Africa.* Matatu, no. 9. Amsterdam and Atlanta: Rodopi.

Graham, Ronnie. 1992. *The World of African Music: Stern's Guide to Contemporary African Music.* Vol. 2. London: Pluto Press.

Gramsci, Antonio. 1971. *Selections from the Prison Notebooks.* Ed. and trans. Quintin Hoare and Geoffrey Nowell Smith. New York: International Publishers.

Gulliver, P. H. 1979. *Disputes and Negotiations: A Cross-Cultural Perspective.* New York: Academic Press.

Gunner, Liz, ed. 1994. *Politics and Performance: Theatre, Poetry, and Song in Southern Africa.* Johannesburg: Witwatersrand University Press.

Gupta, Akhil. 1995. "Blurred boundaries: The discourse of corruption, the culture of politics, and the imagined state." *American Ethnologist* 22, no. 2: 375–402.

Halimoja, Yusuf. 1981. *Utamaduni wa Taifa (National Culture).* Tanzania Inavyojitawala (How Tanzania rules itself), series no. 12. Dar es Salaam: Mwangazi Publishers.

Hamilton, Genesta. 1957. *Princes of Zinj: The Rulers of Zanzibar.* London: Hutchinson.

Handler, Richard. 1988. *Nationalism and the Politics of Culture in Quebec.* Madison: University of Wisconsin Press.

Harries, Lyndon. 1962. *Swahili Poetry*. Oxford: Oxford University Press.

———. 1964. "The Arabs and Swahili culture." *Africa* 34, no. 3: 224–29.

Havnevik, Kjell J. 1993. *Tanzania: The Limits to Development from Above*. Uppsala: Nordiska Afrikainstitutet.

Heath, Deborah. 1994. "The politics of appropriateness and appropriation: Recontextualizing women's dance in Senegal." *American Ethnologist* 21, no. 1: 88–103.

Herzfeld, Michael. 1982. *Ours Once More: Folklore, Ideology, and the Making of Modern Greece*. Austin: University of Texas Press.

———. 1987. *Anthropology through the Looking-Glass: Critical Ethnography in the Margins of Europe*. Cambridge: Cambridge University Press.

———. 1988. "Rhetoric and the constitution of social relations." *Working Papers and Proceedings of the Center for Psychosocial Studies*, no. 22.

———. 1991. *A Place in History: Social and Monumental Time in a Cretan Town*. Princeton, NJ: Princeton University Press.

———. 1997. *Cultural Intimacy: Social Poetics in the Nation-State*. New York and London: Routledge.

Hirsch, Susan F. 1998. *Pronouncing and Persevering: Gender and the Discourses of Disputing in an African Islamic Court*. Chicago: University of Chicago Press.

Hitchcock, Sir Eldred. 1959. "The sisal industry of East Africa." *Tanganyika Notes and Records*, no. 52: 4–17.

Hobsbawm, Eric J. 1990. *Nations and Nationalism Since 1780: Programme, Myth, Reality*. Cambridge: Cambridge University Press.

Hobsbawm, Eric, and Terence Ranger, eds. 1983. *The Invention of Tradition*. Cambridge: Cambridge University Press.

Hornsby, G. 1962. "A brief history of Tanga School up to 1914." *Tanganyika Notes and Records* nos. 58 and 59: 148–50.

Horton, Mark. 1987. "The Swahili Corridor." *Scientific American* 257, no. 3 (Sept. 1987): 86–93.

———. 1996. *Shanga: The Archaeology of a Muslim Trading Community on the Coast of East Africa*. London: The British Institute in Eastern Africa.

Horton, Mark, and John Middleton. 2000. *The Swahili: The Social Landscape of a Mercantile Society*. Oxford and Malden, MA: Blackwell.

Hughes-Freeland, Felicia, ed. 1998. *Ritual, Performance, Media*. ASA Monographs no. 35. New York: Routledge.

Huntingford, G. W. B., ed. 1980. *The Periplus of the Erythraean Sea*. London: Hakluyt Society.

Hussein, Ebrahim N. 1974. "On the development of theatre in East Africa." Ph.D. diss. Humboldt-Universität zu Berlin.

Hyden, Goran. 1980. *Beyond Ujamaa in Tanzania: Underdevelopment and an Uncaptured Peasantry*. Berkeley: University of California Press.

Hyden, Goran, and Donald C. Williams. 1994. "A community model of African politics: Illustrations from Nigeria and Tanzania." *Comparative Studies in Society and History* 36, no. 1: 68–96.

Hymes, Dell. 1964. *Language in Culture and Society*. New York: Harper & Row.

Ihonvbere, Julius O. 1994. "The 'irrelevant' state, ethnicity, and the quest for nationhood in Africa." *Ethnic and Racial Studies* 17, no. 1: 42–60.

Iliffe, John. 1979. *A Modern History of Tanganyika*. Cambridge: Cambridge University Press.

Ingle, Clyde R. 1972. *From Village to State in Tanzania: The Politics of Rural Development*. Ithaca and London: Cornell University Press.

Jahadhmy, A. A.; S. Matola; Mwalim Shabaan; and W. H. Whiteley. 1966. *Waimbaji wa Juzi*. Dar es Salaam: Chuo cha Uchunguzi wa Lugha ya Kiswahili.

Janmohamed, Karim K. 1976. "Ethnicity in an urban setting: A case study of Mombasa." Pp. 186–206 in *History and Social Change in East Africa*, ed. B. Ogot. Nairobi: East African Literature Bureau.

Jengo, Elias; Louis A. Mbughuni; and Saadani Abdu Kandoro. 1982. *Falsafa ya Sanaa Tanzania*. Dar es Salaam: Baraza la Sanaa la Taifa, Tanzania.

Joel, Lawi. 1996. "Tanzania's woes worsen." *Daily Nation,* January 16, 1996.

Johnson, Frederick. 1989 [1939]. *A Standard Swahili-English Dictionary*. Nairobi and Dar es Salaam: Oxford University Press.

Kaba, Lansiné. 1976. "The Cultural Revolution, artistic creativity, and freedom of expression in Guinea." *Journal of Modern African Studies* 14, no. 2: 201–18.

Kaduma, Godwin Z. 1971. "They dance to progress." *Africa Report* 16, no. 9: 15–17.

Kaeppler, Adrienne L. 1993. "Poetics and politics of Tangan laments and eulogies." American Ethnologist 20, no. 3: 474–501.

Kapferer, Bruce. 1988. *Legends of People, Myths of State: Violence, Intolerance, and Political Culture in Sri Lanka and Australia*. Washington: Smithsonian Institution Press.

Kertzer, David I. 1988. *Ritual, Politics, and Power*. New Haven, CT, and London: Yale University Press.

Khatib, M. S. 1992. *Taarab Zanzibar*. Dar es Salaam: Tanzanian Publishing House.

Kimambo, I. N., and A. J. Temu, eds. 1969. *A History of Tanzania*. Nairobi: East African Publishing House.

Kirshenblatt-Gimblett, Barbara, et al. 1991. "Art and national identity: A critics' symposium." *Art in America* (September 1991): 80–83, 142–43.

Kirkman, James. 1981. *Fort Jesus, Mombasa*. 9th ed. Mombasa: National Museum of Kenya.

Kligman, Gail. 1988. *The Wedding of the Dead: Ritual, Poetics, and Popular Culture in Transylvania*. Berkeley: University of California Press.

Knappert, Jan. 1967. *Traditional Swahili Poetry: An Investigation into the Concepts of East African Islam as Reflected in the Utenzi Literature*. Leiden: Brill.

———. 1977. "Swahili *tarabu* songs." *Afrika und Übersee* 60, nos. 1 and 2: 116–55.

———. 1979. *Four Centuries of Swahili Verse: A Literary History and Anthology*. London: Heinemann.

———. 1983. "Swahili songs with double entendre." *Afrika und Übersee* 66, no. 1: 67–76.

———. 1991. "Swahili songs." Pp. 92–128 in *A Different Kind of Journey: Essays in Honor of Marja-Liisa Swantz*, ed. Jeremy Gould. Transactions of the Finnish Anthropological Society, no. 28. Helsinki.

Knappert, Jan, ed. and trans. 1972. *A Choice of Flowers, Chaguo la Maua: An Anthology of Swahili Love Poetry.* London: Heinemann.

Kondo, Dorinne. 1990. *Crafting Selves: Power, Gender, and Discourses of Identity in a Japanese Workplace.* Chicago: University of Chicago Press.

Koponen, Juhani. 1988. *People and Production in Late Precolonial Tanzania: History and Structures.* Transactions of the Finnish Anthropological Society, no. 23. Helsinki.

———. 1994. *Development for Exploitation: German Colonial Policies in Mainland Tanzania, 1884–1914.* Finnish Historical Society Studia Historica, no. 49. Helsinki/Hamburg.

Krapf, Rev. Dr. J. Lewis. 1860. *Travels, Researches, and Missionary Labours During an Eighteen Years' Residence in Eastern Africa.* London: Trübner.

Kraus, Richard. 1991. "Arts policies of the Cultural Revolution: The rise and fall of Culture Minister Yu Huiyong." Pp. 219–41 in *New Perspectives on the Cultural Revolution,* ed. William A. Joseph, Christine P. W. Wong, and David Zweig. Cambridge, MA : The Council on East Asian Studies/ Harvard University.

Landberg, Pamela. 1977. "Kinship and community in a Tanzanian coastal village." Ph.D. diss. Department of Anthropology, University of California, Davis.

Lange, Siri. 1994. "From nationbuilding to popular culture: The modernization of performance in Tanzania." Cand. Polit. degree diss. University of Bergen.

LaViolette, Adria. 1996. "Report on excavations at the Swahili site of Pujini, Pemba Island, Tanzania." *Nyame Akuma* 46: 72–83.

Lears, T. J. Jackson. 1985. "The concept of cultural hegemony: Problems and possibilities." *American Historical Review* 90, no. 3: 567–93.

Le Guennec-Coppens. 1981. "Stratification sociale et division sexuelle dans la communauté Swahili de Lamu." *L'Ethnographie* 77, no. 85: 37–150.

Legum, Colin. 1988. "The Nyerere years: A preliminary balance sheet." In *Tanzania after Nyerere,* ed. Michael Hodd. London: Pinter.

Lewis, G. W., and E. G. Makala. 1990. *The Traditional Musical Instruments of Tanzania.* Dar es Salaam: Music Conservatoire of Tanzania.

Lienhardt, Peter. 1968. *The Medicine Man: "Swifa ya Nguvumali," by Hasani bin Ismael.* Oxford: Clarendon Press.

Lihamba, Amandina. 1985. "Politics and theatre in Tanzania after the Arusha Declaration, 1967–1984." Ph.D. diss. School of English, University of Leeds.

———. 1991. "The role of culture." Pp. 270–76 in *Re-Thinking the Arusha Declaration,* ed. Jeannette Hartmann. Copenhagen, 1991.

Lonsdale, John. 1968. "Some origins of nationalism in East Africa." *Journal of African History* 9, no. 1: 119–46.

———. 1981. "States and social processes in Africa: A historiographical survey." *African Studies Review* 24, nos. 2 and 3: 139–225.

Lonsdale, John, and Bruce Berman. 1979. "Coping with the contradictions: The development of the colonial state in Kenya, 1895–1914." *Journal of African History* 20, no. 4: 487–505.

Lucas, Stephen, and Gerard Philippson. 1973. "Ethnic characteristics." Pp. 156–75 in *The Population of Tanzania: An Analysis of the 1967 Population Cen-*

sus, ed. Bertil Egero and Roushdi A. Henin. Census vol. 6. Dar es Salaam: BRALUP and Bureau of Statistics.

Machiavelli, Niccoló. 1961. *The Prince.* Trans. George Bull. Harmondsworth, England: Penguin Books.

Mackey, Eva. 1997. "The cultural politics of populism: Celebrating Canadian national identity." Pp. 136–64 in Shore and Wright, eds. 1997.

Maguluko, Frank R. C. 1991. "Continuity and change in traditional dances: A case study of *Mdumange* and *Ukala* dance." B.A. diss. University of Dar es Salaam.

Malkki, Liisa H. 1995. *Purity and Exile: Violence, Memory, and National Cosmology among Hutu Refugees in Tanzania.* Chicago: University of Chicago Press.

Marcus, George E. 1997. "Introduction." Pp. 1–17 in *Cultural Producers in Perilous States: Editing Events, Documenting Change,* ed. George E. Marcus. Late Editions 4. Chicago and London: University of Chicago Press.

Martin, Stephen H. 1980. "Music in urban East Africa: A study of the development of urban jazz in Dar es Salaam." Ph.D. diss. University of Washington.

———. 1982. "Music in urban East Africa: Five genres in Dar es Salaam." *Journal of African Studies* 9, no. 3: 155–63.

———. 1991. "Brass bands and the *beni* phenomenon in urban East Africa." *Journal of the International Library of African Music* 7, no. 1: 72–81.

Max, John A. O. 1991. *The Development of Local Government in Tanzania.* Dar es Salaam: Educational Publishers and Distributors.

Mazrui, Alamin M., and Ibrahim Noor Shariff. 1994. *The Swahili: Idiom and Identity of an African People.* Trenton, NJ: Africa World Press.

Mbembe, Maryon. 1992. "Provisional notes on the postcolony." *Africa* 62: 3–37.

Mbughuni, L. A. 1974. *The Cultural Policy of the United Republic of Tanzania.* Paris: The UNESCO Press.

Mbughuni, L. A., and G. Ruhumbika. 1974. "TANU and national culture." Pp. 275–87 in *Towards Ujamaa: Twenty Years of TANU Leadership,* ed. G. Ruhumbika. Nairobi: East African Literature Bureau.

McCurdy, Sheryl. 2000. "Transforming associations: Fertility, therapy, and the Manyema diaspora in urban Kigoma, Tanzania, c. 1850–1993." Ph.D. diss. Columbia University.

McHenry, Dean E., Jr. 1979. "The struggle for rural socialism in Tanzania." In *Socialism in Sub-Saharan Africa: A New Assessment,* ed. Carl G. Rosberg and Thomas M. Callaghy. Berkeley: Institute of International Studies/ University of California, Berkeley.

———. 1994. *Limited Choices: The Political Struggle for Socialism in Tanzania.* Boulder and London: Lynne Reiner.

Meienberg, Hildebrand. 1966. *Tanzanian Citizen: A Civics Textbook.* Nairobi: Oxford University Press.

Meisner, Maurice. 1985. "Iconoclasm and Cultural Revolution in China and Russia." Pp. 279–93 in *Bolshevik Culture,* ed. Abbott Gleason, Peter Kenez, and Richard Stites. Bloomington: Indiana University Press.

Mekacha, Rugatiri. 1992. "Are women devils? The portrayal of women in Tanzanian popular music." Pp. 99–113 in *Sokomoko: Popular Culture in East*

Africa, ed. Werner Graebner. Matatu, no. 9. Amsterdam and Atlanta: Rodopi.

Mfoulou, Jean. 1974. "Ethnic pluralism and national unity in Africa." Pp. 110–32 in *Symposium Leo Frobenius: Perspectives of Contemporary African Studies.* Final report of an international symposium organized by the German and Cameroon Commissions for UNESCO, December 3–7, 1973, in Youndé. Pullach/München: UNESCO.

Mgana, Issa. 1991. *Jukwaa la Taarab Zanzibar.* Helsinki: Mediafrica.

Middleton, John. 1992. *The World of the Swahili: An African Mercantile Civilization.* New Haven, CT, and London: Yale University Press.

Ministry of National Culture and Youth. n.d. (possibly 1975). *Cultural Revolution in Tanzania.* Dar es Salaam: Ministry of National Culture and Youth.

———. 1979. *Utamaduni Chombo cha Maendeleo* (Culture: instrument of development). Dar es Salaam: Ministry of National Culture and Youth.

Mirza, Sarah, and Margaret Strobel. 1989. *Three Swahili Women: Life Histories from Mombasa, Kenya.* Bloomington: Indiana University Press.

Mitchell, J. Clyde. 1956. *The Kalela Dance: Aspects of Social Relationships among Urban Africans in Northern Rhodesia.* Manchester: Manchester University Press.

Mitchell, Timothy. 1999. "Society, economy, and the state effect." Pp. 76–97 in Steinmetz, ed. 1999.

Miti, Katabaro. 1982. "Ujamaa vijijini: Policy and implementation." *Taamuli* 12: 47–61.

Mkabarah, Jumaa R. R. 1975. *Mwanamuziki wa Tanzania Salum Abdallah.* Dar es Salaam: Taasisi ya Uchunguzi wa Kiswahili, Chuo Kikuu cha Dar es Salaam.

Mlama, Penina Muhando. 1980. "Sanaa za maonyesho katika jamii za asili" (The performing arts in traditional society). Pp. 150–71 in Omari and Mvungi, eds. 1980.

———. 1991. *Culture and Development: The Popular Theatre Approach in Africa.* Uppsala: Nordiska Afrikainstitutet .

Mohiddin, Ahmed. 1981. *African Socialism in Two Countries.* London: Croom Helm.

Moore, Sally Falk. 1985. *Social Facts and Fabrications: "Customary" Law on Kilimanjaro, 1880–1980.* Cambridge: Cambridge University Press.

———. 1988. "Legitimation as a process: The expansion of government and party in Tanzania." Pp. 155–72 in *State Formation and Political Legitimacy,* ed. Ronald Cohen and Judith D. Toland. Vol. 6 of *Political Anthropology.* New Brunswick and Oxford: Transaction Books.

———. 1995. "Imperfect communications." Pp. 11–38 in Caplan, ed. 1995.

Moore, Sally Falk, and Barbara Meyerhoff, eds. 1977. *Secular Ritual.* Assen, Netherlands: Van Gorcum.

Msekwa, Pius. 1995. *The Transition to Multiparty Democracy.* Dar es Salaam: Tema Publishers and Tanzania Publishing House.

Mtobwa, Ben R. 1988. *Remmy Ongala: Bob Marley wa Tanzania* (Remmy Ongala: the Bob Marley of Tanzania). Dar es Salaam: Heko Publishers.

Mturi, A. A. 1975. *A Guide to Tongoni Ruins.* Dar es Salaam: Division of Antiquities, Ministry of National Culture and Youth.

Mulokozi, M. M. 1975. "Revolution and reaction in Swahili poetry." *Kiswahili* 45, no. 2: 46–65.

———. 1982. "Protest and resistance in Swahili poetry: 1600–1885." *Kiswahili* 49, no. 1: 25–51.

Mulokozi, M. M., and T. S. Y. Sengo. 1995. *History of Kiswahili Poetry* (A.D. 1000–2000). Dar es Salaam: Institute of Kiswahili Research, University of Dar es Salaam.

Mvungi, M. V. 1980. "Lugha ya Kiswahili na jamii" (Swahili language and society). Pp. 61–71 in Omari and Mvungi, eds. 1980.

Ngugi wa Thiong'o. 1983. *Barrel of a Pen: Resistance to Repression in Neo-Colonial Kenya*. London: New Beacon Books.

———. 1986. *Decolonising the Mind*. London: James Currey.

———. 1993. *Moving the Centre: The Struggle for Cultural Freedoms*. London: James Currey.

Nicholls, C. S. 1971. *The Swahili Coast: Politics, Diplomacy, and Trade on the East African Littoral, 1798–1856*. London: George Allen & Unwin.

Nugent, David. 1994. "Building the state, making the nation: The bases and limits of state centralization in 'modern' Peru." *American Anthropologist* 96, no. 2: 333–69.

Nurse, Derek, and Thomas Spear. 1985. *The Swahili: Reconstructing the History and Language of an African Society, 800–1500*. Philadelphia: University of Pennsylvania Press.

Nyerere, Julius K. 1968. "Socialism and rural development." In *Ujamaa: Essays on Socialism*. Dar es Salaam: Oxford University Press.

ole Parkipuny, M. L. 1979. "Some crucial aspects of the Maasai predicament." Pp. 136–57 in *African Socialism in Practice: The Tanzanian Experience*, ed. Andrew Coulson. Nottingham: Spokesman.

Omari, C. K. 1980. "Utamaduni na jamii" (Culture and society). Pp. 1–27 in Omari and Mvungi, eds. 1980.

Omari, C. K., and M. Mvungi, eds. 1980. *Urithi wa Utamaduni Wetu* (Our cultural heritage). Mitaala ya Lugha na Fasihi Na. 9. Dar es Salaam: Tanzania Publishing House.

Osaghae, Eghosa E. 1990. "The crisis of national identity in Africa: Clearing the conceptual underbush." *Plural Societies* 19, no. 2: 116–32.

Parkin, David. 1985. "Being and selfhood among intermediary Swahili." In *Swahili Language and Society*, ed. Joan Maw and David Parkin. Beiträge zur Afrikanistik, Band 23. Vienna: Institute für Afrikanistik und Aegyptologie der Universität Wien, 247–60.

———. 1989. "Swahili Mijikenda: Facing both ways in Kenya." *Africa* 59: 161–75.

———. 1991. *Sacred Void: Spatial Images of Work and Ritual among the Giriama of Kenya*. Cambridge: Cambridge University Press.

———. 1996. "Introduction: The power of the bizarre." Pp. xv–xl in Parkin, Caplan, and Fisher, eds. 1996.

Parkin, David, ed. 1994. *Continuity and Autonomy in Swahili Communities: Inland Influences and Strategies of Self-Determination*. Beiträge zur Afrikanistik, Band 48. London: School of Oriental and African Studies.

Parkin, David; Lionel Caplan; and Humphrey Fisher, eds. 1996. *The Politics of Cultural Performance*. Providence and Oxford: Berghahn Books.

p'Bitek, Okot. 1973. *Africa's Cultural Revolution.* Nairobi: Macmillan Books for Africa.

———. 1986. *Artist, the Ruler: Essays on Art, Culture, and Values.* Nairobi: Heinemann.

Pouwels, Randall. 1984. "Oral historiography and the Shirazi of the East African coast." *History in Africa* 11: 237–67.

———. 1987. *Horn and Crescent: Cultural Change and Traditional Islam on the East African Coast, 800–1900.* Cambridge: Cambridge University Press.

Pratt, Cranford. 1976. *The Critical Phase in Tanzania, 1945–1968: Nyerere and the Emergence of a Socialist Strategy.* Cambridge: Cambridge University Press.

Prins, A. H. J. 1961. *The Swahili-Speaking Peoples of Zanzibar and the East African Coast (Arabs, Shirazi, and Swahili).* Ethnographic Survey of Africa: East-Central Africa, part 12. London: International African Institute.

Qureshi, Regula Burckhardt. 1995 (1986). *Sufi Music of India and Pakistan: Sound, Context, and Meaning in Qawwali.* 2d ed. Chicago and London: University of Chicago Press.

Racy, Jihad. 1983. "Music in nineteenth-century Egypt: An historical sketch." *Selected Reports in Ethnomusicology,* 4: 157–79.

———. 1984. "Arab music—An overview." Pp. 9–13 in *Maqam: Music of the Islamic World and Its Influences,* ed. Robert H. Browning. New York: Alternative Museum.

Ranger, Terence O. 1969. "The movement of ideas, 1850–1939." Pp. 161–88 in Kimambo and Temu, eds. 1969.

———. 1975. *Dance and Society in Eastern Africa, 1890–1970: The Beni Ngoma.* London: Heinemann.

———. 1983. "The invention of tradition in colonial Africa." Pp. 211–62 in Hobsbawm and Ranger, eds. 1983.

Rigby, Peter. 1996. *African Images: Racism and the End of Anthropology.* Oxford and Washington, DC: Berg.

Robert, Shabaan bin. 1967. *Wasifu wa Siti binti Saad: Mwimbaji wa Unguja* (Praises of Siti binti Saad: singer of Zanzibar. Nairobi: Thomas Nelson and Sons.

Royce, Anya Peterson. 1977. *The Anthropology of Dance.* Bloomington: Indiana University Press.

———. 1984. *Movement and Meaning: Creativity and Interpretation in Ballet and Mime.* Bloomington: Indiana University Press.

Ruete, Emily (born Sayyida, Princess of Zanzibar). 1996 [1888]. *Memoirs of an Arabian Princess from Zanzibar.* 2d printing, 1989 ed. Princeton, NJ: Markus Wiener.

Sabea, Hanan. 2000. "Moments and processes: Redefining the building of 'A New Society' in Tanzania." Ph.D. diss. Department of Anthropology, Johns Hopkins University.

Said, Mohamed. 1998. *The Life and Times of Abdulwahid Sykes (1924–1968): The Untold Story of the Muslim Struggle against British Colonialism in Tanganyika.* London: Minerva Press.

Saleh, S. S. 1980. "Nyimbo za taarab Unguja" (Zanzibari taarab songs). *Lugha Yetu,* no. 37: 35–46.

———. 1988a. "Historia na muundo wa taarab." *Lugha na Utamaduni* 1: 8–11.

————. 1988b. "Historia na muundo wa taarab. Sehemu ya pili." *Lugha na Utamaduni* 2: 9–11, 24.

Salim, Ahmed Idha. 1973. *The Swahili-Speaking Peoples of Kenya's Coast, 1895–1965*. Nairobi: East African Publishing House.

————. 1976. "'Native or non-native?' The problem of identity and the social stratification of the Arab-Swahili of Kenya." Pp. 65–85 in *History and Social Change in East Africa*, ed. Bethwell A. Ogot. Nairobi: East African Literature Bureau.

————. 1985. "The elusive 'Mswahili'—Some reflections on his identity and culture." Pp. 215–27 in *Swahili Language and Society*, ed. Joan Maw and David Parkin. Beiträge zur Afrikanistik, Band 23. Wien.

Saul, John S. 1979. *The State and Revolution in Eastern Africa*. New York and London: Monthly Review Press.

Sawa, George D. 1981. "The survival of some aspects of medieval Arabic performance practice." *Ethnomusicology* 25, no. 1: 73–86.

Schechner, Richard. 1985. *Between Theater and Anthropology*. Philadelphia: University of Pennsylvania Press.

————. 1988. *Performance Theory* (2d rev. ed. of *Essays on Performance Theory*). London and New York: Routledge.

Schechner, Richard, and Willa Appel. 1990. "Introduction." Pp. 1–7 in Schechner and Appel, eds. 1990.

Schechner, Richard, and Willa Appel, eds. 1990. *By Means of Performance: Intercultural Studies of Theatre and Ritual*. Cambridge: Cambridge University Press.

Schieffelin, Edward L. 1996. "On failure and performance: Throwing the medium out of the séance." Pp. 59–89 in *The Performance of Healing*, ed. Carol Laderman and Marina Roseman. New York and London: Routledge.

————. 1998. "Problematizing performance." Pp. 194–207 in *Ritual, Performance, Media*, ed. Felicia Hughes-Freeland. London and New York: Routledge.

Schjeldahl, Peter, et al. 1991. "Art and national identity: A critics' symposium." *Art in America* (September 1991): 80–83, 142–143.

Searle, J. R. 1969. *Speech Acts*. Cambridge: Cambridge University Press.

Sengo, T. S. Y., and M. M. Mulokozi. 1994. *Research on the History of Kiswahili Poetry*, A.D. 1000–2000: Final Report. Dar es Salaam: OSSREA/IKR.

Shao, Ibrahim F. 1982. "A neo-colony and its problems during the process of attempting to bring about socialist rural transformation—The case of Tanzania." *Taamuli* 12: 29–46.

Shariff, Ibrahim Noor. 1973. "*Waswahili* and their language: some misconceptions." *Kiswahili* 43, no. 2: 67–75.

————. 1988. *Tungo Zetu: Msingi wa Mashairi na Tungo Nyinginezo*. Trenton, NJ: Red Sea Press.

Shelemay, Kay Kaufman. 1989. *Music, Ritual, and Falasha History*. East Lansing: Michigan State University Press.

————. 1991. *A Song of Longing: An Ethiopian Journey*. Urbana and Chicago: University of Illinois Press.

Sheriff, Abdul. 1987. *Slaves, Spices, and Ivory in Zanzibar: Integration of an East*

African Commercial Empire into the World Economy, 1770–1873. Athens: Ohio University Press.

Shivji, Issa. 1976. *Class Struggles in Tanzania.* New York and London: Monthly Review Press.

———. 1990. *Tanzania: The Legal Foundations of the Union.* Dar es Salaam: Dar es Salaam University Press.

Shore, Cris, and Susan Wright. 1997. "Policy: A new field of anthropology." Pp. 3–39 in Shore and Wright, eds. 1997.

Shore, Cris, and Susan Wright, eds. 1997. *Anthropology of Policy: Critical Perspectives on Governance and Power.* New York: Routledge.

Skene, R. 1917. "Arab and Swahili dances and ceremonies," *Journal of the Royal Anthropological Institute of Great Britain and Ireland* 47: 413–34.

Songoyi, Elias Manandi. 1988a [1983]. "Commercialization and its impact on traditional dances." Trondheim: Radet for folkemusikk og folkedans.

———. 1988b. "The artist and the state in Tanzania. A study of two singers: Kalikali and Mwinamila." Ph.D. diss. University of Dar es Salaam.

Soyinka, Wole. 1991. "Africa's cultural producers." *Society* 28, no. 2: 32–40.

Spear, Thomas. 1978. *The Kaya Complex: The History of the Mijikenda Peoples of the Kenya Coast to 1900.* Nairobi: Kenya Literature Bureau.

———. 1984. "The Shirazi in Swahili traditions, culture, and history." *History in Africa* 11: 291–305.

Steinmetz, George. 1999. "Introduction: Culture and the state." Pp. 1–49 in Steinmetz, ed. 1999.

Steinmetz, George, ed. 1999. *State/Culture: State-Formation after the Cultural Turn.* Ithaca, NY: Cornell University Press.

Stern, Carol Simpson, and Bruce Henderson. 1993. *Performance: Texts and Contexts.* London: Longman.

Stevenson, E. L. 1932. *The Geography of Claudius Ptolemy.* New York: New York Public Library.

Stokes, Martin, ed. 1994a. *Ethnicity, Identity, and Music: The Musical Construction of Place.* Oxford and Providence: Berg.

———. 1994b. "Introduction: ethnicity, identity and music." Pp. 1–27 in *Ethnicity, Identity and Music: The Musical Construction of Place.* Oxford and Providence: Berg.

Strobel, Margaret. 1979. *Muslim Women in Mombasa: 1890–1975.* New Haven, CT, and London: Yale University Press.

Suleiman, A. A. 1969. "The Swahili singing star Siti binti Saad and the *taarab* tradition in Zanzibar." *Swahili* 39: 87–90.

Swartz, Marc J. 1979. "Religious courts, community, and ethnicity among the Swahili of Mombasa: An historical study of social boundaries." *Africa* 49, no. 1: 29–41.

Taasisi ya Uchunguzi wa Kiswahili (Swahili Research Institute). 1981. *Kamusi ya Kiswahili Sanifu* (Standard Swahili dictionary). Dar es Salaam: Taasisi ya Uchunguzi wa Kiswahili and Oxford University Press.

Tambiah, Stanley. 1988. "Foreword." Pp. 1–6 in *Ethnicities and Nations: Processes of Interethnic Relations in Latin America, Southeast Asia, and the Pacific,* ed. Remo Guidieri, Francesco Pellizzi and Stanley Tambiah. Houston: Rothko Chapel.

Tanzania Library Services. 1977. *A List of Tanzanian Ministries from Independence to 1977.* Mimeo. Dar es Salaam: Tanzania Library Services.

Taylor, J. Clagett. 1963. *The Political Development of Tanganyika.* Stanford, CA: Stanford University Press.

Tolmacheva, Marina. 1976. "The origin of the name 'Swahili.'" *Tanzania Notes and Records* 77/78: 27–37.

Topp, Janet. 1992. "Women and the Africanisation of *taarab* in Zanzibar." Ph.D. diss. School of Oriental and African Studies, London.

Tracey, Hugh. 1948. *Chopi Musicians, Their Music, Poetry, and Instruments.* London and New York: Oxford University Press.

Tripp, Aili Mari. 1997. *Changing the Rules: The Politics of Liberalization and the Urban Informal Economy in Tanzania.* Berkeley: University of California Press.

Turner, Victor. 1974. *Dramas, Fields, and Metaphors: Symbolic Action in Human Society.* Ithaca, NY: Cornell University Press.

———. 1986. *The Anthropology of Performance.* New York: PAJ Publications.

———. 1990. "Are there universals of performance in myth, ritual, and drama?" Pp. 8–18 in Schechner and Appel, eds. 1990.

Turino, Thomas. 2000. *Nationalists, Cosmopolitans, and Popular Music in Zimbabwe.* Chicago: University of Chicago Press.

United Republic of Tanzania, Ministry of Tourism, Natural Resources and Environment, and the Republic of Finland, Ministry for Foreign Affairs. 1995. *Project Document: East Usambara Catchment Forestry Project, Phase II: 1995–98, Background and Lessons.* Tanga, Tanzania: Government Printer.

Vail, Leroy. 1989. "Introduction: Ethnicity in Southern African history." Pp. 1–19 in *The Creation of Tribalism in Southern Africa,* ed. Leroy Vail. Berkeley and Los Angeles: University of California Press.

Vail, Leroy, and Landeg White. 1991. *Power and the Praise Poem: Southern African Voices in History.* Charlottesville: University Press of Virginia.

Verdery, Katherine. 1990. "The production and defense of 'The Romanian Nation,' 1900 to World War II." Pp. 81–111 in Fox, ed. 1990b.

———. 1991a. *National Ideology under Socialism: Identity and Cultural Politics in Ceaușescu's Romania.* Berkeley: University of California Press.

———. 1991b. "Theorizing socialism: A prologue to the 'transition'." *American Ethnologist* 18, no. 3: 419–39.

———. 1993. "Whither 'nation' and 'nationalism'?" *Daedalus* 122, no. 3: 37–46.

———. 1996. *What Was Socialism and What Comes Next?* Princeton, NJ: Princeton University Press.

Wehr, H. 1976. *Dictionary of Modern Written Arabic.* Wiesbaden: Otto Harrassowitz.

Weiskel, Timothy. 1980. *French Colonial Rule and the Baule Peoples: Resistance and Collaboration, 1889–1911.* Oxford: Clarendon Press.

Whiteley, Wilfred. 1969. *Swahili: The Rise of a National Language.* Studies in African History 3. London: Methuen.

Wilk, Richard. 1995. "Learning to be local in Belize: Global systems of common difference." Pp. 110–33 in *Worlds Apart: Modernity through the Prism of the Local,* ed. Daniel Miller. London and New York: Routledge.

Williams, Brackette F. 1990. "Nationalism, traditionalism, and the problem of cultural inauthenticity." Pp. 112–29 in Fox, ed. 1990b.

———. 1991. *Stains on My Name, War in My Veins: Guyana and the Politics of Cultural Struggle.* Durham and London: Duke University Press.

Willis, Justin. 1993. *Mombasa, the Swahili, and the Making of the Mijikenda.* Oxford: Clarendon Press.

Wraith, Ronald E. 1959. *East African Citizen.* London: Oxford University Press.

Wolf, Eric. 1990. "Distinguished lecture: Facing power—old insights, new questions." *American Anthropologist* 92, no. 3: 586–96.

———. 1999. *Envisioning Power: Ideologies of Dominance and Crisis.* Berkeley: University of California Press.

Yelvington, Kevin A. 1991. "Ethnicity as practice? A comment on Bentley." *Comparative Studies in Society and History* 33, no. 1: 158–68.

Discography

The following discography is not intended to be a comprehensive inventory of recordings of East African music. Various genres such as Swahili rap, reggae, *kwaya, mchiriku,* and Kenyan *benga* that are highly significant but fall outside the stated purview of this book are not included. The genres of *taarab, dansi,* and *ngoma* are represented for the purposes of (1) informing interested readers of currently available recordings, (2) offering a sense of the breadth and depth of band repertoires, and (3) providing some historical coverage of both the local and international East African recording industries. To give readers a sense of the diversity in lyrical content, I have translated all but a few titles into English. The few that have been left untranslated are either names, dance styles, or in languages other than Kiswahili.

A variety of sources and persons were consulted in compiling this discography. The collection of Leo Sarkisian ("The Music Man of Africa") at the Voice of America provided the bulk of the 45s included here. In compiling the lists of LPs and CDs, I consulted Douglas Paterson, Werner Graebner, and Matthew Lavoie, each of whom has an encyclopedic knowledge and extensive collection of African music recordings. Ronnie Graham's *Stern's Guide to Contemporary African Music,* vols. 1 and 2, were additional sources of valuable information. The inventory of local cassettes largely reflects my own collection, acquired over the past fourteen years. I restricted coverage here primarily to bands and musical groups in Tanga, Zanzibar, and Dar es Salaam, although Morogoro is included for its significance to the history of *dansi.* Numerous *dansi* bands existed in other parts of the country (e.g., Tabora and Arusha) but for reasons of space could not be included here. Similar decisions were made with regard to *taarab.* The flourishing cassette industry in Mombasa, Kenya, which is dominated by *taarab* recordings, regrettably is not represented here. I tried, however, to be comprehensive with regard to *ngoma,* relying heavily on information from Radio Tanzania Dar es Salaam (RTD). As the primary government station commissioned with the responsibility for preserving for posterity the nation's musical culture, RTD made (and currently sells) recordings of *ngoma* from more than fifty-three ethnic groups. Due to the importance of *ngoma* to early articulations of nationalist rhetoric, all of the RTD *ngoma* recordings on which I could obtain information are included here. Finally, for purposes of clarification, whenever a cassette recording lacked a title (a common occurrence in pre-1995 cassette production, which rarely included cassette covers), I used the title of the first song on the tape as the cassette title.

The discography is organized first by genre and then by available format in the following sequence:

T.1a   *Taarab—Tanga—CDs*
T.1b   *Taarab—Tanga—45s*
T.1c   *Taarab—Tanga—Cassettes*
T.2a   *Taarab—Zanzibar—CDs*
T.2b   *Taarab—Zanzibar—Cassettes*
T.3a   *Taarab—Dar es Salaam—Cassettes*
T.4a   *Taarab—Mombasa—CDs*
T.4b   *Taarab—Mombasa—45s*
T.5a   *Taarab—Comoro Islands—CDs*
D.Xa   *Dansi—Tanzania (all varieties)—CDs*
D.Xb   *Dansi—Tanzania (all varieties)—LPs*
D.1a   *Dansi—Tanga—45s*
D.1b   *Dansi—Tanga—Cassettes*
D.2a   *Dansi—Dar es Salaam—45s*
D.2b   *Dansi—Dar es Salaam—Cassettes*
D.3a   *Dansi—Morogoro—45s*
D.3b   *Dansi—Morogoro—Cassettes*
D.4a   *Dansi—Kenya—CDs*
D.4b   *Dansi—Kenya—LPs*
N.1a   *Ngoma—Tanzania—CDs*
N.1b   *Ngoma—Tanzania—LPs*
N.1c   *Ngoma—Tanzania—Cassettes*
N.2a   *Ngoma—Kenya—LPs*
N.3a   *Ngoma—Comoro Islands—CDs*

I wish to thank all the people mentioned above for their invaluable assistance and advice, and additionally Aisha Diwani Mabrook for her willingness to check and double check all my translations. Responsibility for all gaps and omissions, however, remains solely with me.

Taarab
T.1a Tanga: CDs
Black Star Musical Club/Lucky Star Musical Club. 1989. *Nyota: Classic Taarab from Tanga*. GlobeStyle Records, CDORBD 044.

T.1b Tanga: 45s
Black Star Musical Club (Amina). n.d. "Pili Pili" (Pepper"). Philips, HL 7-210A.
———. (Amina). n.d. "Nilikupenda" (I loved you). Philips, HL 7-210B.
———. (Sharmila). n.d. "Enyi Wanaadamu" (You humans). Philips, HL 7-240A.
———. (Sharmila). n.d. "Mnazi Mkinda" (The short coconut tree). Philips, HL 7-240B.
———. (Kibwana). n.d. "Amana" (Peace). Philips, HL 7-259A.

————. n.d. "Ukuu Kuu" (The biggest honor). Philips, HL 7-259B.

————. 1976. "Uache Masikitiko" (Stop regretting). Uhuru Stars, US 7-47A.

————. 1976. "Maskini Punda" (Poor donkey). Uhuru Stars, US 7-47B.

Lucky Star Musical Club (Shakila). 1972. "Kupe" (Tick). Polydor, POL 7-096A.

————. (Asmahan). 1972. "Nakupenda" (I love you). Polydor, POL 7-096B.

————. (Shakila and Tahir). N.d. "Saba Saba" (July 7th). Polydor, POL 7-207A.

————. (Asmahan). n.d. "Nimebaki Ng'onda" (I remain dried out). Polydor, POL 7-207B.

————. (Asmahan). n.d. "Kiumbe Mkosa Ari" (A living being without a conscience). Saba Saba, SABA 7-73A.

————. (Shakila). n.d. "Fikira Moyoni" (Thoughts in my heart). Saba Saba, SABA 7-73B.

————. (Shakila). n.d. "Mapenzi Yamepungua" (Love has diminished). Saba Saba, SABA 7-74A.

————. (Asmahan). n.d. "Udugu wa Dhati" (A very close relative). Saba Saba, SABA 7-74B.

————. (Shakila). n.d. "Macho Yanacheka" (The eyes laugh). Saba Saba, SABA 7-75A.

————. (Asmahan). n.d. "Mwiba wa Mahaba" (Thorn of love). Saba Saba, SABA 7-75B.

————. (Tahiri Aliy). n.d. "Pendo Lanipa" (Love gives me).

————. (Asmahan). n.d. "Mimi na Wewe" (Me and you).

————. (Asmahan). n.d. "Nawauliza Wenzangu" (I ask you my friends).

————. (Shakila). n.d. "Mapenzi Asali" (Love is honey).

————. (Shakila). n.d. "Mapenzi ni Kama Donda" (Love is like a wound).

————. (Iddi Ramadhani). n.d. "Mola Ulie wa Haki" (God you are just).

Young Novelty Club (Fatuma Mohamed). n.d. "Ilahi" (God). Mzuri, ASM 037A.

————. (Saleh Kiroboto). n.d. "Pokea Salamu" (Receive greetings). Mzuri, ASM 037B.

————. (Fatuma Mohamed). n.d. "Shukurani" (Thanks). Mzuri.

————. (Saidi Mohamed). n.d. "Pendo Raha Yake" (The joy of love). Mzuri.

————. (Saleh Kiroboto). n.d. "Ahadi ni Deni" (A promise is a debt). Mzuri.

————. (Mohamed Abdallah). n.d. "Unapitapita" (You are just passing through). Mzuri.

T.1c Tanga: Cassettes

Babloom Modern Taarab. 1991? Vol. 1: *Wape Wape* (Give them). Top Music House, Tanga.

————. 1991? Vol. 2: *Malimwengu* (Troubles of the world). Top Music House, Tanga.

————. 1992? Vol. 3A: *Duku Duku* (Confusion). Top Music House, Tanga.

————. 1992? Vol. 3B: *Kidonda cha Penzi* (Wound of love). Top Music House, Tanga.

————. 1993. Vol. 4: *Jitoto* (Beautiful baby). Mbwana Radio Service, Mombasa.

————. 1994. Vol. 5: *Yawapi Mash* (It's too late). Top Music House, Tanga.

————. 1995. Vol. 7: *Shuka* (Bedsheet). Top Music House, Tanga.

Babloom Modern Taarab with Kelly. 1995. *Kipaji Changu* (My talent). Top Music House, Tanga.

Black Star Musical Club/Lucky Star Musical Club. n.d. *Kifo cha Mahaba* (Death of love). Radio Tanzania DSM, No. 2.

Freedom Modern Taarab. 1995. Vol. 1: *Chura* (Frog). Top Music House, Tanga.

———. 1997? Vol. 2: *Pumbazo* (Consolation). Top Music House, Tanga.

Golden Star Taarab. n.d. Vol. 1: *Mtu Asiyekupenda* (The one who doesn't love you). Top Music House, Tanga.

———. n.d. Vol. 2: *Halina Thamani* (It's worthless). Top Music House, Tanga.

———. n.d. Vol. 3: *Katu Sina Mwenginewe* (I'll never have anyone else). Top Music House, Tanga.

———. n.d. Vol. 4: *Japo Wanitesa* (Even though you hurt me). Top Music House, Tanga.

———. n.d. Vol. 5: *Japo Mwakereka* (Even though they are annoyed). Top Music House, Tanga.

———. n.d. Vol. 6: *Mtumishi* (Messenger). Top Music House, Tanga.

———. n.d. Vol. 7: *Sema Utakacho* (Say what you want). Top Music House, Tanga.

———. n.d. Vol. 8A: *Nimezama kwa Mapenzi* (I'm drowning in love).

———. n.d. Vol. 8B: *Nakupenda Wewe Tu* (I love only you).

———. n.d. Vol. 9: *Nimezama* (I'm drowning).

———. 1994. Vol. 9A: *Nimekujia Mganga* (I, your healer, have come to you).

———. 1994. Vol. 9B: *Furaha* (Happiness).

———. n.d. Vol. 10. *Unganihadaa Kupenda Kwako* (Even if you deceived me with your love).

———. n.d. Vol. 11. *Wasemao na Waseme* (Let them talk). Dar es Salaam?

———. 1997. *Buzi* (Boyfriend/lover). FM Music Bank, Dar es Salaam.

———. 1999? Vol. 13A: *Buzi No. 2*. Mitha and Sons et al., Dar es Salaam.

———. 1999? Vol. 13B: *Mwiko* (Taboo). Mitha and Sons et al., Dar es Salaam.

———. 2000. Vol. 14A: *Kajisunde* (He went to enjoy life). Dar es Salaam.

———. 2000. Vol. 14B: *Hukutaka Uambiwe* (You didn't want to be told). Dar es Salaam.

Lucky Star Musical Club. n.d. *Mkono Inuka* (Raise your hand).

Lucky Star Musical Club/Black Star Musical Club. n.d. *Kifo cha Mahaba* (Death of love). Radio Tanzania DSM, No. 2.

Mrisho, Mohamed. 1995. Vol. 1: *Ni Wangu* (S/he is mine). Mamu et al., Dar es Salaam.

Mrisho, Mohamed. 1995. Vol. 2: *Napendeza* (Attractive). Mamu et al., Dar es Salaam.

Shomanga, Issa. 1995. *Kakojoa Kilingeni* (S/he urinated on stage). Top Music House, Tanga.

T.2a Zanzibar: CDs

Bi Kidude. 1998. *Bi Kidude: Zanzibar*. RetroAfric,12 CD.

Culture Musical Club. 1989. *Taarab 4: The Music of Zanzibar*. GlobeStyle Records, CDORBD 041.

———. 1996. *Mila na Utamaduni—Spices of Zanzibar*. Network Medien, LC 6759.

———. 2000. *Bashraf: Taarab Instrumentals from Zanzibar*. Dizim Records, dizim 4509.

Ikhwani Safaa Musical Club. 1988. *Taarab 2: The Music of Zanzibar*. GlobeStyle Records, CDORBD 033.

Saleh, Seif Salim, and Abdullah Mussa Ahmed. 1988. *Taarab 1: The Music of Zanzibar*. GlobeStyle Records, CDORBD 032.

Various: Music Clubs of the Island. 1990. *Taarab 3: The Music of Zanzibar*. GlobeStyle Records, ORBD 040.

Various. 2000. *Zanzibar: Music of Celebration*. Topic Records, TSCD917.

T.2b Zanzibar: Cassettes

Culture Musical Club. n.d. Vol. 1A: *Usiniige Huniwezi* (Don't imitate me, you'll fail). Alakeifak Music House, Zanzibar.

———. n.d. Vol. 1B: *Haya Maumbile Yangu* (This is my nature). Alakeifak Music House, Zanzibar.

———. n.d. *Changu Chako* (Mine, yours). Alakeifak Music House, Zanzibar.

———. 1996. *Eddy El Fitry 96*. Alakeifak Music House, Zanzibar.

———. 1990? *Kadandie* (Jump on). Alakeifak Music House, Zanzibar.

———. n.d. *Khadija Kopa*. Alakeifak Music House, Zanzibar.

———. n.d., *Tumewatia Kizani* (We kept you in the dark). Alakeifak Music House, Zanzibar.

East African Melody Modern Taarab. 1994? Vol. 1: *Mavituzy na Majambos* (Events and news). Alakeifak Music House, Zanzibar.

———. n.d. Vol. 2: *Mimi Si Mgomvi Wako* (I'm not your enemy). Zanzibar.

———. n.d. Vol. 13: *Mambo Bam Bam* (Everything is great). Zanzibar.

———. n.d. Vol. 14: *Mbona Watakereka Sana* (They'll be sorry). Zanzibar.

———. n.d. Vol. 16: *Nawaseme Wasemao* (Let them say whatever). Alakeifak Music House, Zanzibar.

———. n.d. *Choko Choko* (Gossip). Zanzibar.

———. n.d. *Nani Zaidi* (Who is better?). Zanzibar.

———. n.d. *Sakina Dahal Jimbo in Dubai*. Zanzibar.

———. n.d. *Ngoma Iko Huku (Live)* (The action is here). Mitha and Sons, Dar es Salaam.

———. n.d. *Hakuna "Tenda" Hakuna Buzi "Paparazi"* (For you, no tenderness, no boyfriend; you're like a paparazzi). Mitha and Sons, Dar es Salaam.

———. 1997? *Iddi El-Haj Taarab Show*. Zanzibar.

———. 1997. *Melody's Safarini Gulf Tour 1997*. EAM-9700 1. Zanzibar.

———. 1997. *Summer Time Holiday—Powa Utuwe* (Stay cool). Zanzibar.

———. 1998. *Kumbe Kweli Huyawezi* (Truly you can't do it). Mitha and Sons, Dar es Salaam.

———. 1999. *Sakata Lako*. Mamu et al., Dar es Salaam.

———. 1999. *Kufa na Tai Shingoni!* (Die with a tie around your neck) Mitha and Sons, Dar es Salaam.

———. 1999. *Kwa Raha Zangu . . . Nikigombwa* (With my pleasure). Mitha and Sons, Dar es Salaam.

———. 1999. *Zuhura Shaabani: Kimasomaso*. Zanzibar.

———. 2000. Vol. 21: *Mimi wa Karne* (I'm the one this century). Mitha and Sons, Dar es Salaam.

———. 2000. *Kinyago cha Mpapure: Nyamaza Nikustiri* (Keep quiet, masked dancer, I hold your secrets). Zanzibar.

———. 2000. *Mimi wa Karne 21* (I'm the one in the twenty-first century). Mitha and Sons, Dar es Salaam.

———. 2000. *Mkoko Unalika Maua* (Flowers of the mangrove tree are being eaten). Mitha and Sons, Dar es Salaam.

Ikhwani Safaa Musical Club. n.d. Vol. 1. Alakeifak Music House, Zanzibar.

———. n.d. Vol. 1B: *Pendo La Ndondondo* (Slow love). Alakeifak Music House, Zanzibar.

———. *Nishani.* Alakeifak Music House, Zanzibar.

Kangagani Musical Club, Pemba. n.d. Vol. 3: *Vida Sina.* Alakeifak Music House, Zanzibar.

———. n.d. *Mtakoma.* Alakeifak Music House, Zanzibar.

Kikundi cha Taifa cha Taarab, Zanzibar. 1991. *Wahoi* (They are tired). Mediafrica, Helsinki.

Royal Air Force. 1991. *Fasten Your Seat Belts!* Mediafrica, MIA 5, Helsinki.

Various. 1992. *Taarab de Zanzibar.* Credo.

T.3 Dar es Salaam: Cassettes

Abassi Mzee with Egyptian Musical Club. n.d. Vol. 1: *Fitina Mbaya* (Quarreling is bad). Alakeifak Music House, Zanzibar.

African Musical Taarab. n.d. *Kitatange Najigamba* (Boasting sea porcupine). Mamu et al.

Al Watan Musical Club/Egyptian Musical Club. n.d. Vol. 1: *Alianza Pekepeke* (S/he started causing trouble). Radio Tanzania DSM, No. 7.

———. n.d. Vol. 2: *Umeumbika* (You are beautiful). Radio Tanzania DSM, No. 174.

All Stars Modern Taarab. n.d. *Nnatamba Nae* (I show off with him/her). Alakeifak Music House, Zanzibar.

———. n.d. *Chakubimbi* (Inquisitive). Alakeifak Music House, Zanzibar.

———. n.d. *Sabahi Muchacho,* Vol. 1. Alakeifak Music House, Zanzibar.

———. n.d. *Sabahi Muchacho,* Vol. 2. Alakeifak Music House, Zanzibar.

———. n.d. Vol. 1: *Chakubimbi.* Mamu Stores et al., Dar es Salaam.

———. n.d. Vol. 2: *Utulize Moyo Wako* (Calm your heart). Mamu Stores et al., Dar es Salaam.

———. n.d. Vol. 3: *Choko Choko* (Annoyance). Mamu Stores et al., Dar es Salaam.

———. n.d. Vol. 7: *Kilio Changu* (My cry). Dar es Salaam.

———. n.d. Vol. 8: *Wamefeli Mbinu Zao* (Their plan failed). Dar es Salaam.

———. 1998. Vol. 10: *Si Hirizi Si Sisimizi* (Neither an amulet nor a root). Dar es Salaam.

———. 2000. Vol. 12: *Si Testi Yangu* (Not my type). Mitha and Sons, Dar es Salaam.

———. 2000. Vol. 13: *Mtu Mzima Dawa* (A mature person is the cure). Mitha and Sons et al., Dar es Salaam.

Babloom Modern Taarab. 1995. Vol. 8: *Kimbweru* (Harlot). RetroTan, Dar es Salaam.

———. 1996. *Best of Babloom Modern Taarab.* Mitha and Sons et al., Dar es Salaam.

———. 1997. Vol. 10: *Utapendaje Wawili* (How can you love two?). Dar es Salaam.

———. 1997. Vol. 11: *Chombeza Time* (Time to rest). Dar es Salaam.

———. 1999? Vol. 12: *Kanisabilia* (S/he gave of her/himself completely). Dar es Salaam.

———. 2000. Vol. 13: *Jimama* (Big Mama). Dar es Salaam.

———. 2001. Vol. 14: *Kigego* (A child whose upper teeth emerge first). Dar es Salaam.

BIMA Modern Taarab. n.d. *Kijiba cha Moyo* (Thorn in the heart). Dar es Salaam.

———. 1992. *Nimemdhibiti* (I guarded him/her). Dar es Salaam.

BIMA Taarab/New Extra Musical Club. n.d. *Tupendane kwa dhati*. Radio Tanzania DSM, No. 156.

Dar Nyota Theatre Taarab. n.d. Vol. 3: *Pendo* (Love). Dar es Salaam.

Egyptian Musical Club/Alwatan Musical Club. n.d. Vol. 1: *Alianza Pekepeke* (S/he started to investigate). Radio Tanzania DSM, No. 7.

———. n.d. Vol. 2: *Umeumbika* (You are beautiful). Radio Tanzania DSM, No. 174.

JKT Taarab. n.d. Vol. 1: *Umevamia Karata* (You crashed the card game). Mamu et al., Dar es Salaam.

———. 1991. *Jamani Mapenzi* (Oh! Oh! Love!). Mediafrica, MIA 6. Helsinki.

———. 1994. Vol. 2: *Muongo* (Liar). Mamu et al., Dar es Salaam.

———. 1998. Vol. 8: *Mpishi* (Cook). Mamu et al., Dar es Salaam.

Mandela Theatre Troupe Taarab. n.d. Vol. 1: *Uvuvi* (Fishing). Mamu et al., Dar es Salaam.

———. 1994. *Ukuni Mmoja* (A piece of firewood). Dar es Salaam.

———. n.d. Vol. 4: *Chaumbea* (Meddler). Dar es Salaam.

Mandela Theatre Troupe with Mwanachia. 1996. *Shoga Si Shoga* (A friend who is not a friend). Dar es Salaam.

Matona, Issa. n.d. *Uliyenae Umzuie* (Restrain your lover). Tanzania Film Company, TFCLP 004. Dar es Salaam.

———. n.d. *Bwana Anakula Solo* (Husband is eating the wedding feast). Dar es Salaam.

———. n.d. *Issa Matona*. Dar es Salaam.

———. 1985. *Kimasomaso*. Tanzania Film Company, TFCLP 003. Dar es Salaam.

———. n.d. Vol. 2: *Kimasomaso: Hekima za Ndoa na Maisha*. Dar es Salaam.

Matona, Issa and Mridu. 1999. *Sambusa*. Dar es Salaam.

Muungano Cultural Troupe. n.d. Vol. 1: *Donge la Nini* (Why the lump in your heart?). Mamu et al., Dar es Salaam.

———. 1993? Vol. 2: *Limbukeni* (Fool). Mamu et al., Dar es Salaam.

———. 1994. Vol. 3: *Hutowahi* (You won't make it in time). Mamu et al., Dar es Salaam.

———. 1994. Vol. 4: *Hatuachani* (We won't break up). Mamu et al., Dar es Salaam.

———. 1995. Vol. 5: *Kiduhushi* (Inquisitive person). Dar es Salaam.

———. 1995. Vol. 6: *Staharuki* (Not to be shocked). Mamu et al., Dar es Salaam.

———. 1995. Vol. 7: *Salaam za Mtwangaji* (Greetings of the pestle-bearer). Dar es Salaam.

———. 1996. Vol. 8: *Homa ya Jiji* (Fever in the city). Dar es Salaam.

———. 1996. Vol. 9: *Sijui Nikuambie?* (I don't know what to tell you). Mamu et al., Dar es Salaam.

———. 1996. Vol. 10: *Yasiyokuhusu* (It doesn't concern you). Mamu et al., Dar es Salaam.

———. 1997. Vol. 11: *Utayaweza?* (Can you do it?). Mamu et al., Dar es Salaam.

———. 1997. Vol. 12: *Wakuchacha Wana Mambo* (Those who have nothing have something). Mamu et al., Dar es Salaam.

———. 1998. Vol. 13: *Mtambaji Katambiwa* (The braggart now is cause for another's bragging). Mamu et al., Dar es Salaam.

———. 1998. Vol. 14: *Kwa Jeuri Hiyo Huna* (Because of your rudeness you're left with nothing). Mamu et al., Dar es Salaam.

———. n.d. Vol. 15: *Kisonoko Umechemsha* (Imbecile, you are ruined). Mamu et al., Dar es Salaam.

———. n.d. Vol. 16: *Si Ulisusa! Wenzio Twala* (You refused, now we are eating). Mamu et al., Dar es Salaam.

———. n.d. Vol. 17: *Mambo Yapo Huku* (Everything is here). Mamu et al., Dar es Salaam.

———. n.d. Vol. 18: *Mambo Bado* (Not yet). Mamu et al., Dar es Salaam.

———. n.d. Vol. 19: *Sanamu la Michelini* (The Michelin tire man). Mamu et al., Dar es Salaam.

———. 1999. *Kilio cha Afrika: Nyimbo za Maombolezo* (Africa in mourning). Dar es Salaam.

———. n.d. Vol. 2: *Tusifanye Taklifu* (Let's not trouble ourselves). Alakeifak Music House, Zanzibar.

TOT Taarab. 1992. Vols. 1/2: *Ngwinji* (High-class prostitute). Dar es Salaam.

———. 1993. Vol. 3: *TX Mpenzi* (Foreign-trained lover). Dar es Salaam.

———. 1993. Vol. 4: *Zumbu Kuku* (Fool). Dar es Salaam.

———. 1993. Vol. 5: *Koroboi* (Kerosene lamp). Space Original, Dar es Salaam.

———. 1994. Vol. 6: *Mtwangio* (Pestle). Dar es Salaam.

———. 1994. Vol. 7: *Tamu Tamu* (Sweet sweet). Top Music House, TMH 001. Tanga.

———. 1994? Vol. 8: *Kasheshe* (Problems). Dar es Salaam.

———. 1995? Vol. 9: *Kidudu Mtu* (Backbiter). Dar es Salaam.

———. 1995. Vol. 10: *Natanga na Njia* (Roaming the path). Dar es Salaam.

———. 1995. Vol. 11: *Kimburumatari*. Mamu et al., Dar es Salaam.

———. 1996. Vol. 12: *Kimbaumbau* (Skinny). Mamu et al., Dar es Salaam.

———. 1996. Vol. 13: *Kisonoko* (Imbecile). Mamu et al., Dar es Salaam.

———. 1996. Vol. 14: *Manamba* (Sisal plantation worker). Dar es Salaam.

———. 1996. Vol. 15: *Ukikereka* (If you get angry). Dar es Salaam.

———. 1997. Vol. 16: *Huna Chako, Talaka Ina Mambo* (You don't have yours, divorce has something). Dar es Salaam.

———. 1997? Vol. 17: *Quinine*. Dar es Salaam.

———. 1997? Vol. 18: *Dunia* (The world). Dar es Salaam.

———. 1997? Vol. 19: *Sheshi Beshi* (Beautiful girl). Mamu et al., Dar es Salaam.

———. 1998. Vol. 20: *Utaishia Kunawa* (You'll be left washing your hands). Mamu et al., Dar es Salaam.

———. 1998. Vol. 21: *Umechokoza El Ninyo* (Teasing el Niño). Mamu et al., Dar es Salaam.

———. 1999? Vol. 22: *Mambo Iko Huku* (Everything is here). TOT-561, Dar es Salaam.

————. 1999? Vol. 23: *Zoba* (Idiot). Dar es Salaam.

————. 2000. Vol. 24: *Mtie Kamba Mumeo* (Tie up your husband). TOT-563, Dar es Salaam.

————. 2000. Vol. 25: *New Milenia 2000 Y2K* (New millennium). TOT-565. Dar es Salaam.

T.4a Mombasa: CDs
Malika. 1996. *Tarabu Music from the Swahili of Kenya*. Haus der Kulturen der Welt, SM 1520-2.
Maulidi Musical Party. 1990. *Mombasa Wedding Special*. GlobeStyle Records, ORBD 058.
Zein l'Abdin (a.k.a., Zein Musical Party). 1990. *Mtindo wa Mombasa: The Style of Mombasa*. GlobeStyle Records, CDORBD 066.
————. 1999. *The Swahili Song Book*. Dizim Records, dizim 4502.
Zuhura Swaleh, with Maulidi Musical Party. 1992. *Jino la Pembe*. GlobeStyle Records. ORBD 075.

T.4b Mombasa: 45s
Bhalo, Juma and Party. n.d. "Malimwengu" (Troubles of the world). Philips, HL 7-251A.
————. n.d. "Usighilibiwe" (Do not be confused). Philips, HL 7-251B.
Malika. 1970. "Peleleza" (Investigate). Polydor, POL 7-046A.
————. 1970. "Amin" (Amen). Polydor, POL 7-046B.
Morning Star (Matano Juma). 1973. "Pokea Salamu" (Receive greetings). Pwani, PIN 7-101A.
————. (Matano Juma). 1973. "Roho Yangu" (My spirit). Pwani, PIN 7-101B.
————. (Zuhuru Swaleh). 1973. "Sultwana." Pwani, PIN 7-102A.
————. (Zuhuru Swaleh). 1973. "Janatu Naimu." Pwani, PIN 7-102B.
————. (Zuhuru Swaleh). 1973. "Mfano Wako Hapana" (There is none like you). Pwani, PIN 7-107A.
————. (Zuhuru Swaleh). 1973. "Karama Zijiri." Pwani, PIN 7-107B.
————. (Matano Juma). 1973. "Wakati" (Time). Pwani, PIN 7-108A.
————. (Matano Juma). 1973. "Safina." Pwani, PIN 7-108B.
————. (Matano Juma). 1974. "Mpenzi Mtaratibu" (A careful lover). Pwani, PIN 7-115A.
————. (Matano Juma). 1974. "Nyongo Mkalia Ini." Pwani, PIN 7-115B.

T.5 Comoro Islands: CDs
Hassan, Mohamed. 2000. *Duniya: Twarab Legend from Grande Comore*. Dizim Records, dizim 4507.
Sambe-Comores. 2000. *Modern Traditions from Ngazija, Grande Comore*. Dizim Records, dizim 4508.

Dansi
D.Xa Tanzania (all varieties): CDs
Abdallah, Salum and Cuban Marimba. 2000. *Ngoma Iko Huko: Vintage Tanzanian Dance Music, 1955*
1965. Dizim Records, dizim 4701.

Bana Maquis. 1995. *Leila*. Dakar Sound, DKS 009.

DDC Mlimani Park Orchestra. 1994a. *Sikinde*. Africassette, AC 9402.

——. 1994b. *Sungi*. Popular African Music, pam 403.

Kilimanjaro Band. 1997. *Maua* (Flowers).

——. 2000. *Kinyaunyau* (Kitten).

Mwinshehe, Mbaraka, and the Morogoro Jazz Band. 2000. *Masimango: Best of Tanzania, 1969*

1972. Dizim Records, dizim 4702.

Ongala, Remmy and Super Matimila. 1996. *Sema*. WOMAD SELECT, WS 002.

——. 1989. *Songs for the Poor Man*. Real World, CDRW 06.

——. 1991. *Mambo*. Real World, CDRW 22.

TatuNane. 1995. *Bongoland*. Amanda Music, MC AMA 9504.

——. 1997. *Tanzanian Beat (World Music Library)*. King Record Co., KICC 5221.

Various. 1995. *Dada Kidawa* (Sister Kidawa). Original Music, OMCD032.

Various. 1995. *Muziki wa Dansi* (Dansi music). Africassette, AC 9403.

Various. n.d. *The Tanzania Sound*. Original Music, OMCD 018.

D.Xb Tanzania (all varieties): LPs

Abdalla, Salim, and Kiko Kids. n.d. *Zilizopendwa from TZ* (Old favorites from Tanzania). Polygram Archives, CPOLP 1021.

Dar International and Vijana Jazz. 1982. *Ni Sababu ya Mapendo*. Polydor, POLP 534.

DDC Mlimani Park Orchestra. 1983. *Taxi Driver*. Polydor, POLP 523?

——. 1982. *Dunia Kuna Mambo*. Polydor, POLP 530.

——. 1986. *The Best of DDC Mlimani Park Orchestra*. Ahadi (Kenya), AHDLP 6002.

——. 1988. *The Best of Volume 2*. Ahadi (Kenya), AHDLP 6006.

——. 1988. *Maisha Ni Kuona Mbele* (Life is about looking ahead). Polydor, POLP 579.

——. 1989. *Dua La Kuku* (Sign of the chicken). Polydor, POLP 589.

Morogoro Jazz Band. 1970s. *Mtaa Wasaba* (7th Street). Polydor, POLP 002.

——. 1984. *Morogoro*. Polydor, POLP 500.

——. n.d. *Mfululrowa*. Polydor, POLP 502.

Mwinshehe, Mbaraka. 1983. *Ukumbusho* (Memories), Vol. 1: *Nisalimie Wanazaire* (Greet the people of Zaire for me). Polydor, POLP 536.

——. 1983. *Ukumbusho*, Vol. 2: *Urafiki Mwisho wa Mwezi* (Friendship at the end of the month). Polydor, POLP 537.

——. 1983. *Ukumbusho*, Vol. 3: *Nirudie Mama* (Return to me, Mother). Polydor, POLP 542.

——. 1984. *Ukumbusho: Pesa* (Money) No. 1. Polydor, POLP 544.

——. 1985. *Ukumbusho*, Vol. 4: *Bibi wa Watu* (People's grandmother). Polydor, POLP 550.

——. 1986. *Ukumbusho*, Vol. 5: *Matamko ya Viongozi Wetu* (Our leaders' pronunciation). Polydor, POLP 553.

——. 1987. *Ukumbusho*, Vol. 6: *Kifo cha Pesa* (The death of money). Polydor, POLP 564.

——. 1988. *Ukumbusho*, Vol. 7: *Penzi Lako Hatari* (Your love is dangerous). Polydor, POLP 566.

NUTA Jazz Band. 1987. *Zilizopendwa* (Golden Hits). Polydor, POLP 557.

Ongala, Remmy, and Super Matimila. 1987. *Kifo* (Death). MC 507.

————. 1988. *Nalilia Mwana* (I cry for my child). WOMAD, WOMAD010.

————. 1988. *On Stage With*. Ahadi (Kenya), AHDLP 6007.

————. 1989. *Songs for the Poor Man*. Real World, RWLP 6.

Orchestre Makassy. 1982. *Agwaya*. Virgin (UK), V 2236.

————. 1984. *Muziki Orchestre Makassy*. ZEMKC 1.

Orchestre Maquis Original du Zaire. 1986. *Karubandika*. Ahadi (Kenya), AHDLP 6001.

————. 1987. *Angelu*. Ahadi (Kenya), AHDMC 005.

————. n.d. *Clara*. Ahadi (Kenya), AHDMC 007.

————. 1988. *Ngalula*. Ahadi (Kenya), AHDMC 011.

Orchestre Safari Sound. 1984. *Dunia Msongamano* (So much is happening in the world). Tanzania Film Company, TFCLP 001.

Orchestre Volcano (Mbaraka Mwinshehe). 1979. *Shida* (Hardship).

————. 1979. *The Last Recordings*. Polydor, POLP 512.

————. 1979. *The Very Last Recordings*. Polydor.

————. 1982. *Baniani* (Hindu)

Mwinshehe Mwaruka. Polydor, POLP 517.

Tanzania Police Band. 1977. *Tanzania Police Band: The United Republic of Tanzania*. AIT 502.

Various. n.d. *Hits of the 60's*, Vol. 1 *(Morogoro Jazz, NUTA Jazz Band, Dar-es-Salaam Jazz Band, Atomic Jazz Band, Jamhuri Jazz Band)*. Polydor, POLP 508.

————. 1980? *Hit Parade Number 1 (Les Wanyika, Maroon Commandos, Simba Wanyika, Mlimani Park)*. Polydor, POLP 516.

————. 1988. *Tanzania Hit Parade 88 (Vijana, Maquis, Safari, etc.)*. Ahadi (Kenya), AHDLP 6005.

Vijana Jazz. 1986. *Mary Maria*. Ahadi (Kenya), AHDLP 6004.

D.1a Tanga: 45s

Atomic Jazz Band. n.d. "Sarafu Zetu" (Our coins). Philips, HL 7-73A. Mzuri Recording. [Cha Cha]

————. n.d. "We Zaina" (Hey, Zaina). Philips, HL 7-73B. Mzuri Recording. [Pachanga]

————. n.d. "Siku ya Jumamozi" (Saturday). Philips, HL 7-94A. Mzuri Recording. [Pachanga]

————. n.d. "Twendeni Jamaa" (Let's go, guys). Philips, HL 7-94B. Mzuri Recording. [Cha Cha Cha]

————. 1968. "Usitamani Kitu" (Don't hope for anything). Polydor, POL 7-005A. ASL Recording. [Rumba]

————. 1968. "Fika Uwone Mwenyewe" (Go and see for yourself). Polydor, POL 7-005B. ASL Recording. [Cha Cha]

————. 1969. "Atomic Tumetimia" (Atomic has arrived). Polydor, POL 7-024A. ASL Recording. [Cha Cha]

————. 1969. "Hata Mkisema Sana" (Even if you gossip a lot). Polydor, POL 7-024B. ASL Recording. [Rumba]

————. 1971. "Ewe Nikupendaye" (Let me love you). Polydor, POL 7-054A. [Rumba]

———. 1971. "Vijana wa Atomic" (The youths of Atomic). Polydor, POL 7-054B. [Rumba]

———. (John Kijiko and Roger Isaac). n.d. "Shemeji Usimpige Dada-1" (Stop beating my sister). Saba Saba, SABA 7-36A. A. P. Chandarana Recording. [Kiweke]

———. (John Kijiko and Roger Isaac). n.d. "Mpenzi Stela" (Stella my love). Saba Saba, SABA 7-36B. A. P. Chandarana Recording. [Kiweke]

———. (John Kijiko and Roger Isaac). n.d. "Nakujutiya Salima" (I feel sorry for you Salima). Saba Saba, SABA 7-37A. A. P. Chandarana Recording. [Kiweke]

———. (John Kijiko and Roger Isaac). n.d. "Tangu Umesafiri" (Since you went away). Saba Saba, SABA 7-37B. A. P. Chandarana Recording. [Kiweke]

———. (John Kijiko and Roger Isaac). n.d. "Mpenzi Joisi" (Joyce my love). Saba Saba, SABA 7-38A. A. P. Chandarana Recording. [Kiweke]

———. (John Kijiko and Roger Isaac). n.d. "Mpenzi Selina" (Selina my love). Saba Saba, SABA 7-38B. A. P. Chandarana Recording. [Kiweke]

———. (John Kijiko and Roger Isaac). n.d. "Dunia Ina Tabu" (The world has troubles). Saba Saba, SABA 7-39A. A. P. Chandarana Recording. [Kiweke]

———. (John Kijiko and Roger Isaac). n.d. "Dada Tabiya Zako Mbaya" (Sister, your behavior is bad). Saba Saba, SABA 7-39B. A. P. Chandarana Recording. [Kiweke]

———. (John Kijiko and Roger Isaac). 1971. "Mpenzi Sisiliya" (Cecelia, my love). Saba Saba, SABA 7-41A. A. P. Chandarana Recording. [Kiweke]

———. (John Kijiko and Roger Isaac). 1971. "Ufukara Umezidi" (Sorrows have increased). Saba Saba, SABA 7-41B. A. P. Chandarana Recording. [Kiweke]

———. (John Kijiko and Roger Isaac). 1971. "Madoo Mpenzi Wangu" (Madoo my love). Saba Saba, SABA 7-42A. A. P. Chandarana Recording. [Kiweke]

———. (John Kijiko and Roger Isaac). 1971. "Naona Waleta Tabu" (I see you are bringing trouble). Saba Saba, SABA 7-42B. A. P. Chandarana Recording. [Kiweke]

———. (John Kijiko and Roger Isaac). 1971. "Katerina Nakupenda Sana" (Katerina I love you). Saba Saba, SABA 7-43A. A. P. Chandarana Recording. [Kiweke]

———. (John Kijiko and Roger Isaac). 1971. "Mume Wangu Mbaya" (My husband is bad). Saba Saba, SABA 7-43B. A. P. Chandarana Recording. [Kiweke]

———. (John Kijiko and Roger Isaac). n.d. "Tineja Masikini" (Poor teenager). Saba Saba, SABA 7-101A. A. P. Chandarana Recording. [Kiweke]

———. (John Kijiko and Roger Isaac). n.d. "Monica Dada" (Sister Monica). Saba Saba, SABA 7-101B. A. P. Chandarana Recording. [Kiweke]

———. (John Kijiko and Roger Isaac). n.d. "Mama wa Kambo" (Stepmother). Saba Saba, SABA 7-102A. A. P. Chandarana Recording. [Kiweke]

———. (John Kijiko and Roger Isaac). n.d. "Mpenzi Wadanganyika" (My love, you are deceived). Saba Saba, SABA 7-102A. A. P. Chandarana Recording. [Kiweke]

———. (John Kijiko and Roger Isaac). n.d. "Pongezi Baba Nyerere" (Congratulations Nyerere). Saba Saba, SABA 7-103A. A. P. Chandarana Recording. [Kiweke]

———. (John Kijiko and Roger Isaac). n.d. "Mariamu." Saba Saba, SABA 7-103B. A. P. Chandarana Recording. [Kiweke]

————. (Kijiko and Stevens). 1974. "Maria Usibadilike" (Don't change, Maria). Saba Saba, SABA 7-222A. A. P. Chandarana Recording. [Kiweke-Latin]

————. (Kijiko and Roger). 1974. "Zuhura Mwanangu" (My dear Zuhura). Saba Saba, SABA 7-222B. A. P. Chandarana Recording. [Kiweke]

Jamhuri Jazz Band. 1969. "Twamuomba Mola" (We pray to God). Philips, PK 7-9046A. [Soukous]

————. 1969. "Kiboko" (Hippopotamus). Philips, PK 7-9046B. [Soukous]

————. 1969. "Ahadi Yako" (Your promise). Philips, PK 7-9052A. [Soukous]

————. 1969. "Maria Cha Cha." Philips, PK 7-9052B. [Cha Cha]

————. 1970. "Bibi Mwenye Chongo" (Grandma with a blind eye). Philips, PK 7-9061A. [Rumba-Kiri Kiri]

————. 1970. "Ewe Wangu Mpenzi" (You, my love). Philips, PK 7-9061B. [Rumba-Kiri Kiri]

————. 1970. "Shingo ya Upanga" (The neck of the sword). Philips, PK 7-9070A. [Apollo]

————. 1970. "Kipande cha Papa" (A piece of shark). Philips, PK 7-9070B. [Dondora]

————. 1970. "Simba Mwituni" (A lion in the forest). Philips, PK 7-9072A. [Apollo]

————. 1970. "Wasiwasi Ondoa" (Remove your doubts). Philips, PK 7-9072B. [Dondora]

————. 1970. "Ooh Masikini" (Poverty). Philips, PK 7-9077A. [Dondora]

————. 1970. "Ulisema Sina Pesa" (You said you have no money). Philips, PK 7-9077B. [Dondora]

————. 1971. "Kibodi" (A small body). Philips, PK 7-9090A. [Apollo]

————. 1971. "Fadhili Iwapi" (Where is a sponsor). Philips, PK 7-9090B. [Dondora]

————. 1971. "Susana." Philips, PK 7-9092A. [Dondora]

————. 1971. "Sophia Amerika" (American Sophia). Philips, PK 7-9092B. [Dondora]

————. 1971. "Kwa Mapenzi" (For love). Philips, PK 7-9096A. [Dondora]

————. 1971. "Ewe Mwana Usipayuke" (Hey girl, don't curse). Philips, PK 7-9096B. [Dondora]

D.1b Tanga: Cassettes

Atomic Jazz Band. n.d. *John Kijiko and Atomic Jazz Band.*

Atomic Jazz Band/Jamhuri Jazz Band. n.d. *Atomic Jazz Band and Jamhuri Jazz Band:* Vol. 1. Radio Tanzania DSM, No. 5.

————. n.d. *Atomic Jazz Band and Jamhuri Jazz Band:* Vol. 2. Radio Tanzania DSM, No. 29.

The Watangatanga Band. n.d. Vol. 1: *Igembe Nsambhow.*

————. 1995. Vol. 2: *Shemahonge.* Top Music House.

D.2a Dar es Salaam: 45s

Afro 70 Band (Patrick Balisidya). 1973. "Safari ya Nairobi" (Trip to Nairobi). Saba Saba, SABA 7-207A. A. P. Chandarana Recording.

————. 1973. "Kufaulu" (To succeed). Saba Saba, SABA 7-207B. A. P. Chandarana Recording.

———. 1973. "Shangwe" (Happiness). Saba Saba, SABA 7-208A. A. P. Chandarana Recording.

———. 1973. "Florence." Saba Saba, SABA 7-208B. A. P. Chandarana Recording.

———. 1974. "Unavyo Fikiria" (What you think). Saba Saba, SABA 7-219A. A. P. Chandarana Recording. [Afrousa]

———. 1974. "Mwenzangu Nakupenda" (My dear, I love you). Saba Saba, SABA 7-219B. A. P. Chandarana Recording. [Afrousa]

———. 1974. "Nakupenda kama Lulu" (I love you like Lulu). Moto Moto, MOTO 7-904A. E.I.T. Pub. [Afrousa]

———. (Didi Musecken). 1974. "Kabla Hujafa" (Before you die). Moto Moto, MOTO 7-904B. E.I.T. Pub. [Afrousa]

Dar es Salaam Jazz Band. 1968. "Sivizuri Rukya" (It's not good, Rukia). Polydor, POL 7-009A. ASL Recording. [Mata Dar]

———. 1968. "Mahindi ya Amerika" (American corn). Polydor, POL 7-009B. ASL Recording. [ChaChiCho]

———. 1969. "Mpenzi Umeniachia Huzuni" (You left me with sorrow). Polydor, POL 7-011A. [Dar Sengo]

———. 1969. "Siku Tutaonana Dada" (We'll see each other again). Polydor, POL 7-011B. [Mata Dar]

———. 1969. "Siyo Tunatorokana" (We're not running away from each other). Polydor, POL 7-030A. [Rumba]

———. 1969. "Mpenzi Usemayo" (Whatever you say, my love). Polydor, POL 7-030B. [Rumba]

Kilwa Jazz 73 (Samos). 1973. "Malaika" (Angel). Saba Saba, SABA 7-203A. A. P. Chandarana Recording.

———. (A. Kipande). 1973. "Jeni Nateseka" (Jane, you're in trouble). Saba Saba, SABA 7-203B. A. P. Chandarana Recording.

———. 1973. "Nikuonyeshapo Pesa" (When I show you the money). Saba Saba, SABA 7-204A. A. P. Chandarana Recording.

———. 1973. "Uwache Kuruka" (Stop jumping). Saba Saba, SABA 7-204B. A. P. Chandarana Recording.

———. 1974. "Matatizo ya Africa" (Problems of Africa). Saba Saba, SABA 7-221A. A. P. Chandarana Recording.

———. 1974. "Wakulima" (Farmers). Saba Saba, SABA 7-221B. A. P. Chandarana Recording.

Magereza Jazz Band (Billy Mbwana). n.d. "Rudi Nyumbani Mke Wangu" (Return home, my wife). Saba Saba, SABA 7-96A. A. P. Chandarana Recording.

———. n.d. "Selina Mama." Saba Saba, SABA 7-96B. A. P. Chandarana Recording.

———. n.d. "Suzana." Saba Saba, SABA 7-97A. A. P. Chandarana Recording.

———. n.d. "Dina Mama." Saba Saba, SABA 7-97B. A. P. Chandarana Recording.

National Service Band. 1968. "Nalia Lia Mama" (Mother, I am crying). Philips, PK 7-9038A. [Rumba]

———. 1968. "Salaam Baba na Mama" (Greetings father and mother). Philips, PK 7-9038B. [Rumba]

Njohole Jazz Band. 1969. "Nyerere Baba wa Tanzania" (Nyerere father of Tanzania). African Beat, AB 7-5068A. [Rumba-Pachanga]

————. 1969. "Ubaya Wako Mwana Helena" (Helena, evil exists). African Beat, AB 7-5068B. [Rumba]

————. 1971. "Elina Mpenzi" (Elina my love). Polydor, POL 7-055A. [Rumba]

————. 1971. "Furaha Yako" (Your happiness). Polydor, POL 7-055B. [Rumba]

————. (Edmond Kazingoma). n.d. "Mwatusema na Kutuadhiri" (You gossip about and embarrass us). Bonanza, BZ 7-2004A. Lamore Recording. [Rumba]

————. (Edmond Kazingoma). n.d. "Tanzania Iko Macho" (Tanzania is alert). Bonanza, BZ 7-2004B. Lamore Recording. [Rumba]

NUTA Jazz Band. 1969. "Amina." African Beat, AB 7-5069A. Associated Sounds Recording. [Rumba]

————. 1969. "Bwana Mwizi" (Mister thief). African Beat, AB 7-5069B. Associated Sounds Recording. [Sekusi]

————. 1969. "Ninapo Kuona" (Where I see you). African Beat, AB 7-5076A. Associated Sounds Recording. [Rumba]

————. 1969. "Gomiyangu." African Beat, AB 7-5076B. Associated Sounds. [Segele]

————. 1970. "Ae Sipendi Tena" (I don't want any more). Philips, PK 7-9074A. [Msondo]

————. 1970. "Ndugu Zangu Leo" (Today, my relative). Philips, PK 7-9074B. [Msondo]

Safari Trippers (Marijani). 1973. "Nenda Shule Rosa" (Go to school, Rosa). Saba Saba, SABA 7-152A. A. P. Chandarana Recording.

————. 1973. "Arusi" (Wedding). Saba Saba, SABA 7-152B. A. P. Chandarana Recording.

Urafiki Jazz Band (Juma Mrisho). n.d. "Papara Zako Acha" (Stop your haste). Saba Saba, SABA 7-52A. A. P. Chandarana Recording. [Mchaka-Mchaka]

————. (Juma Mrisho). n.d. "Eva Umeumbika" (Eva, you are beautiful). Saba Saba, SABA 7-52B. A. P. Chandarana Recording. [Mchaka-Mchaka]

————. (Juma Mrisho). n.d. "Tucheze Mchakamchaka" (Let's dance at high speed). Saba Saba, SABA 7-54A. A. P. Chandarana Recording. [Mchaka-Mchaka]

————. (Juma Mrisho). n.d. "Mpenzi Acha Kunitesa" (Love, stop harassing me). Saba Saba, SABA 7-54B. A. P. Chandarana Recording. [Mchaka-Mchaka]

————. (Michael Vincent). n.d. "Tutachekwa Jenny" (Jenny, we'll be ridiculed). Saba Saba, SABA 7-104A. A. P. Chandarana Recording. [Mchaka-Mchaka]

————. (Michael Vincent). n.d. "Pole Kwa Njohole Jazz" (Condolences to Njohole Jazz). Saba Saba, SABA 7-104B. A. P. Chandarana Recording. [Mchaka-Mchaka]

Vijana Jazz Band (Chiriku H. Manet and H. Z. Kalala). 1975. "Magdalina No. 2." Moto Moto, MOTO 7-918A. Oluoch Kanindo/E.I.T. Pub.

————. 1975. "Miaka Mingi" (Many years). Moto Moto, MOTO 7-918B. Oluoch Kanindo/E.I.T. Pub.

————. (C. H. Manet and Pascal Pius). 1975. "Ujirani Mwema" (Being good neighbors). Moto Moto, MOTO 7-922A. S. P. Kanindo/E.I.T. Pub.

————. (H. S. Kalala). 1975. "Koka-Koka No. 1." Moto Moto, MOTO 7-922B. S.P. Kanindo/E.I.T. Pub.

——. (C. H. Manet and Pascal Pius). 1975. "Shangazi" (Aunt). Moto Moto, MOTO 7-923A. S. P. Kanindo/E.I.T. Pub.

——. (C. H. Manet and I. Chikupele). 1975. "Gwe Manetu Fii." Moto Moto, MOTO 7-923B. S. P. Kanindo/E.I.T. Pub.

——. (C. H. Manety). 1976. "Pili Nihurumie" (Pili, take pity on me). Moto Moto, MOTO 7-928A. E.I.T. Pub.

——. (C. H. Manety). 1976. "Zuhura Naondoka" (Zuhura, I'm leaving). Moto Moto, MOTO 7-928B. E.I.T. Pub.

Western Jazz Band. 1967. "Nitafurahi Ukitumwa Tena" (I'll be happy if you are sent back). Philips, PK 7-9007A. ASL Recording. [Cha Cha Cha]

——. 1967. "Tangu Umeondoka" (Since you left). Philips, PK 7-9007B. ASL Recording. [Mila]

——. 1967. "Tuliya Mama" (Calm down, Mama). Philips, PK 7-9019A. ASL Recording. [Boucher]

——. 1967. "Sasa Tucheza Cha Cha" (Let's dance the Cha Cha). Philips, PK 7-9019B. ASL Recording. [Cha Cha]

——. (H. Tosha). 1974. "Amina Maliza Masomo" (Amina, finish your studies). Africa, AFR 7-900A. E.I.T. Pub.

——. (Shamba and H. Tosha). 1974. "Balaa Limeni Andama" (Bad luck pursues me). Africa, AFR 7-900B. E.I.T. Pub.

——. (Cosmas Thobias). 1974. "Mke Mlevi" (Drunken wife). Africa, AFR 7-901A. E.I.T. Pub.

——. (Wema Abdala). 1974. "Aza." Africa, AFR 7-901B. E.I.T. Pub.

——. (Wema Abdala). 1974. "Asante" (Thank you). Africa, AFR 7-903A. E.I.T. Pub.

——. (Wema Abdala). 1974. "Pokea Salaam" (Receive greetings). Africa, AFR 7-903B. E.I.T. Pub.

——. (Shamba Ramadhan). 1974. "Buibui Mkononi" (Veil in the hand). Africa, AFR 7-904A. E.I.T. Pub.

——. (Mikidadi Abdala). 1974. "Mwali" (A virgin). Africa, AFR 7-904B. E.I.T. Pub.

——. (Wema Abdala). 1974. "Shemeji" (Brother-in-law). Africa, AFR 7-905A. E.I.T. Pub.

——. (Shamba). 1974. "Mpenzi Rukia" (Rukia my love). Africa, AFR 7-905B. E.I.T. Pub.

——. (S. A. Kabanga). 1974. "Eliza Mpenzi" (Eliza my love). Africa, AFR 7-906A. E.I.T. Pub.

——. (Shamba). 1974. "Usiamini Binadamu" (Don't trust humans). Africa, AFR 7-906B. E.I.T. Pub.

——. (H. Thosha). 1974. "Nashindwa na Tabia Yako" (I've had it with your behavior). Africa, AFR 7-907A. E.I.T. Pub.

——. (Wema Abdala). 1974. "Simuachi Mpenzi Wangu" (I won't leave my lover). Africa, AFR 7-907B. E.I.T. Pub.

D.2b Dar es Salaam: Cassettes

African Stars Band. n.d. *Twanga Pepeta: Jirani* (Neighbor).

——. n.d. Twanga Pepeta: *Kisa cha Mpemba* (Story of the person from Pemba).

Afro 70 Band/National Service. n.d. *Weekend.* Radio Tanzania DSM, No. 34.

Assosa, Tshimanga with Orchestra Maquis Original. n.d. *Sendema ya Moto.*

Beta Musica. 2000? *Caterpillar.* Mamu et al.

Bichuka and Ngurumo with Orchestra Ndekule. n.d. *Siwazuri Binadamu* (It's not good, humans).

Bushoke, Max. n.d. Vol. 2 *Mesenja* (Messenger).

Chu-Chu Sound. 2000? *Kombora Ndani na Nje ya Jiji* (A missile is inside and outside the city). FKW Production.

Dandu's Planet Cool James. n.d. *Rafiki Yangu* (My friend).

Dar International/Safari Trippers. n.d. *Zuwena.* Radio Tanzania DSM, No. 61.

Dar International/Alfa Group. n.d. *Rufaa ya kifo* (Appeal to death). Radio Tanzania DSM, No. 175.

Dar es Salaam Jazz Band/Toma Toma Jazz Band. n.d. *Hayo yote ni ya dunia* (All this is of the world). Radio Tanzania DSM, No. 18.

Dar es Salaam Jazz Band/Polisi Jazz Band. n.d. *Nimekwisha Kutupa* (I've already thrown it away). Radio Tanzania DSM, No. 19.

Dar es Salaam Jazz Band/UDA Jazz. n.d. *Yamewafika Wenzetu* (It has happened to our friends). Radio Tanzania DSM, No. 21.

Dar es Salaam Jazz Band/Western Jazz Band. n.d. *Mtoto Wacha Kupiga Mayowe* (Child, stop shouting). Radio Tanzania DSM, No. 12.

DDC Mlimani Park Orchestra. 1997. *Kauli Mali* (Advice is wealth). Mamu et al.

———. n.d. *Maisha ni Kuona Mbele* (Life is about looking ahead).

———. 1993. Vol. 1 *Mawifi* (Sisters-in-law). Mamu et al.

———. n.d. *Ubaya* (Evil). Mitha and Sons.

———. n.d. *Nawashukuru Wazazi* (I thank parents). Mitha and Sons.

———. n.d. *Pata Potea* (Gambling). Mitha and Sons.

———. n.d. *Barua Toka kwa Mama* (Letter from Mama).

———. n.d. *Kassimu.*

———. n.d. *Nelson Mandela.*

———. n.d. *Kupenda Sio Ndoto* (To love is not a dream).

———. n.d. *Nalala kwa Tabu* (I sleep with difficulty).

———. n.d. *Dua la Kuku* (Prayer of the chicken).

———. n.d. *The Best of Orchestra DDC Mlimani Park.*

———. n.d. *Dawa ya Pendo* (Love medicine).

———. n.d. *Hapendeki* (S/he cannot be loved).

———. n.d. *Asha Bora.*

DDC Mlimani Park Orchestra/Urafiki Jazz Band. n.d. *Barua Toka kwa Mama* (Letter from Mama). Radio Tanzania DSM, No. 28.

DDC Mlimani Park Orchestra/Butiama Jazz Band. n.d. *Talaka ya hasira* (A divorce in anger). Radio Tanzania DSM, No. 163.

F. M. Musica Academia. 2000. *New Look.* FKW Production.

———. 2000. *Adija.* FKW Production.

———. 2000. *Sitoweza* (I won't be able). FKW Production.

Halilali, Zege and Washirika Tanzania Stars Band. n.d. *Penzi la Kusuasua* (Love full of worries).

———. n.d. *Kidudu Mtu* (Backbiter).

JUWATA Jazz Band. n.d. *JUWATA Jazz Band.*

———. n.d. *Queen Kase.*

————. n.d. *Mpenzi Zarina* (Zarina, my love).

————. n.d. *Solemba* (Abandoned)

————. n.d. *Hasira Hasara* (Anger brings loss).

JUWATA Jazz Band/BIMA Jazz Band. n.d. *Rudi mpenzi Zarina* (Come back, Zarina my love). Radio Tanzania DSM, No. 154.

Kalala, Hamza. n.d. Vol. 7: *Kisimbago Kaabhuka.*

Kalala, Hamza and Bantu Group Band. 2000. *Manamba* (Sisal laborers).

Kilwa Jazz Band/NUTA Jazz Band. n.d. Vol. 1. Radio Tanzania DSM, No. 6.

————. n.d. Vol. 2. Radio Tanzania DSM, No. 31.

Marijani Rajabu and Dar International. n.d. Vol. 1: *Pesa Sabuni ya Roho* (Money is soap for the soul). MSK CAS 515.

————. n.d. Vol. 2: *Masudi.* MSK CAS 516.

————. n.d. Vol. 3: *Mwanameka.* MSK CAS 517.

————. n.d. Vol. 4: *Paulina.* MSK CAS 518.

————. n.d. Vol. 5: *Kifo ya Rufaa* (Appeal to death). MSK CAS 519.

————. n.d. Vol. 6: *Carolina.* MSK CAS 520.

————. n.d. Vol. 7: *Zuwena.* MSK CAS 521.

————. n.d. Vol. 8: *Pendo* (Love). MSK CAS 522.

————. n.d. *Mwanameka.* Radio Tanzania DSM, No. 16.

Mchinga Sound Band. n.d. *Kisiki cha Mpingo* (Blackwood stump). Mamu et al.

National Service/Afro 70 Band. n.d. *Weekend.* Radio Tanzania DSM, No. 34.

NUTA Jazz Band/Kilwa Jazz Band. n.d. Vol. 1. Radio Tanzania DSM, No. 6.

————. n.d. Vol. 2. Radio Tanzania DSM, No. 31.

Ongala, Remmy and Orchestra Super Matimila. 1994? *Kilio cha Samaki* (Cries of a fish). RetroTan, RC 002.

————. n.d. *Mambo* (News).

————. n.d. *Kilio cha Samaki* (Cries of a fish). Mamu et al.

————. n.d. *Kifo* (Death). Mamu et al.

————. n.d. *Pesa* (Money). Radio Tanzania DSM, No. 126.

Orchestra Bima Lee. n.d. *Visa vya Messanger* (Story of the Messenger).

————. n.d. *Super BIMA.*

————. n.d. *Magnet Tingisha* (Shake the magnet).

Orchestra Maquis Original. n.d. *Kiongo* (A small lie).

————. n.d. *Baba Wile* (Father of Willy).

Orchestra Quelado. n.d. *Mume Kachala* (Indigent husband). Radio Tanzania DSM, No. 20.

OTTU Jazz Band. n.d. *OTTU Jazz Band.*

————. 1994. *Kauka Nikuvae* (Dry out so I can wear you). Mamu et al.

————. n.d. *Don't Cry Jane.* Mamu et al.

————. 1995. *Mama Kanitupa* (Mother has abandoned me).

————. 1998. *Kimanzichana.*

————. 1998. *Gangamala* (To be tough). Mamu et al.

————. 2000. *Demokrasia ya Mapenzi (Democracy of love).* Mitha and Sons.

Polisi Jazz Band/Dar Jazz Band. n.d. *Nimekwisha Kutupa* (I've already thrown it away). Radio Tanzania DSM, No. 19.

Safari Trippers. n.d. *Sauti Yako Nyororo* (Your voice is beautiful). Radio Tanzania DSM, No. 17.

Safari Trippers/Dar International. n.d. *Zuwena.* Radio Tanzania DSM, No. 61.

Shikamoo Jazz Band. n.d. Vol. 1: *Chela Chela*. RetroTan.

———. n.d. Vol. 2: *Wazee wa Safari* (Traveling elders). RetroTan, RC 005.

Super Matimila Orchestra. 1998. *Mama*. Radio Tanzania DSM, No. 113.

Tancut Almasi. n.d. *Samahani ya Uongo* (False apology).

Tancut Almasi with Dingituka Molay. n.d. *Vituko vya Neto*.

TOT Jazz Band. 2000. Vol. 1: *Achimenengule: Mtaji wa Masikini* (Poverty's capital). TOT 567.

———. 2001? *Achiminingule*.

UDA Jazz Band/Dar Jazz Band. n.d. *Yamewafika Wenzetu* (It has happened to our friends). Radio Tanzania DSM, No. 21.

Urafiki Jazz Band/DDC Mlimani Park Orchestra. n.d. *Barua Toka kwa Mama* (Letter from Mama). Radio Tanzania DSM, No. 28.

Vijana Jazz Band. n.d. *Ngoma*. Radio Tanzania DSM, No. 23.

———. 1980s. *Mundinde*. MSK 509.

———. n.d. Vol. 1: *Wifi* (Sister-in-law).

———. 1993-94. *Top Queen*. Mamu et al.

———. 1995. *Chivalavala*.

———. n.d. *Ngapulila*.

———. 1997. Vol. 3: *Mwanamke Salo* (A shapely woman).

———. n.d. *Penzi Haligawanyiki* (Love cannot be divided).

———. n.d. Vol. 4: *VIP*.

———. n.d. *Ogopa Tapeli* (Beware of con artists).

———. n.d. *Mzinga* (Salute). C 4860.

Vijana Jazz/ Morogoro Jazz/Super Volcano. n.d. *Gubu la Mume* (A husband's moodiness). Radio Tanzania DSM, No. 62.

Wazee wa Kazi. n.d. *Embe Dodo* (a variety of mango). Mushroom Records, MRC008R.

Western Jazz Band. n.d. Vol. 1. Radio Tanzania DSM, No. 14.

Western Jazz Band/Dar es Salaam Jazz Band. n.d. *Mtoto Wacha Kupiga Mayowe* (Child, stop shouting). Radio Tanzania DSM, No. 12.

Zilipendwa. n.d. Vol. 1. Radio Tanzania DSM, No. 8.

———. n.d. Vol. 2. Radio Tanzania DSM, No. 9.

———. n.d. Vol. 3. Radio Tanzania DSM, No. 10.

———. n.d. Vol. 4. Radio Tanzania DSM, No. 22.

———. n.d. Vol. 5. Radio Tanzania DSM, No. 24.

———. n.d. Vol. 6. Radio Tanzania DSM, No. 25.

———. n.d. Vol. 7. Radio Tanzania DSM, No. 26.

———. n.d. Vol. 10. Radio Tanzania DSM, No. 112.

———. n.d. Vol. 11. Radio Tanzania DSM, No. 171.

———. n.d. Vol. 12. Radio Tanzania DSM, No. 172.

———. n.d. Vol. 13. Radio Tanzania DSM, No. 173.

D.3a Morogoro: 45s

Cuban Marimba Band. n.d. "Shirikisho-Chechembo." Philips, HL 7-80A. Mzuri Recording.

———. n.d. "Wetu Katutoka" (S/he left us). Philips, HL 7-80B. Mzuri Recording.

———. n.d. "Kusema Si Kutenda" (To say is not to do). Philips, HL 7-130A. Mzuri Recording.

————. n.d. "Uluguru." Philips, HL 7-130B. Mzuri Recording.

————. n.d. "Njoo Mpenzi Wangu" (Come, my love). Philips, HL 7-131A. Mzuri Recording.

————. n.d. "Kioo Kinadanganya" (The mirror deceives). Philips, HL 7-131B. Mzuri Recording.

Cuban Marimba Band (Juma Kilaza). n.d. "Kibibi" (The little old lady). Saba Saba, SABA 7-26A. A. P. Chandarana Recording. [Ambiyansey]

————. n.d. "Nyerere-Kaunda". Saba Saba, SABA 7-26B A. P. Chandarana Recording. [Ambiyansey-Sikisa]

————. 1971? "Nakupa Pongezi" (I congratulate you). Saba Saba, SABA 7-46A. A. P. Chandarana Recording. [Mikambo-71]

————. 1971? "Maggie." Saba Saba, SABA 7-46B. A. P. Chandarana Recording. [Tanifey]

————. 1971. "Heko Wanadinga" (Congratulations Wanadinga). Saba Saba, SABA 7-47A. A. P. Chandarana Recording. [Mikambo-71]

————. 1971. "Muke Wangu" (My wife). Saba Saba, SABA 7-47B. A. P. Chandarana Recording. [Tanifey]

————. 1971? "Hongera Nyerere" (Congratulations Nyerere). Saba Saba, SABA 7-76A. A. P. Chandarana Recording. [Mikambo-71]

————. 1971? "Moshi" (Smoke). Saba Saba, SABA 7-76B. A. P. Chandarana Recording. [Tanifey]

————. 1971? "Ajali Yangu" (My accident). Saba Saba, SABA 7-77A. A. P. Chandarana Recording. [Mikambo-71]

————. 1971? "Emma." Saba Saba, SABA 7-77B. A. P. Chandarana Recording. [Mikambo-71]

————. 1972? "Uhuru na Maendeleo" (Freedom and development). Saba Saba, SABA 7-119A. A. P. Chandarana Recording. [Lyiipika-72]

————. 1972? "Kifo cha Karume" (The death of Karume). Saba Saba, SABA 7-119B. A. P. Chandarana Recording. [Lyiipika-72]

————. 1972? "One Kaunda-One Nation." Saba Saba, SABA 7-120A. A. P. Chandarana Recording. [Subi Subi]

————. 1972? "Kilimo" (Agriculture). Saba Saba, SABA 7-120B. A. P. Chandarana Recording. [Mikambo]

————. 1972? "Kucha Kulangala." Saba Saba, SABA 7-121A. A. P. Chandarana Recording. [Mikambo-72]

————. 1972? "Pole Wana Moro" (Condolences, people of Moro). Saba Saba, SABA 7-121B. A. P. Chandarana Recording. [Subi Subi]

Kilombero Sugar Jazz Band. n.d. "Jamani Nipeni Pole" (Give me your condolences). Saba Saba, SABA 7-8A. A. P. Chandarana Recording.

————. n.d. Paulina "Wileke Dance." Saba Saba, SABA 7-8B. A. P. Chandarana Recording.

Morogoro Jazz Band. 1969. "Nalilia Raha" (I cry for lost happiness). Polydor, POL 7-019A. ASL Recording. [Likembe-Kiri Kiri]

————. 1969. "Penzi la Mashaka" (A love full of doubts). Polydor, POL 7-019B. ASL Recording. [Likembe-Kiri Kiri]

————. n.d. "Kula Hoteli" (Go eat in a restaurant). Philips, HL 7-132A. Mzuri Recording.

————. n.d. "Dunia" (The world). Philips, HL 7-132B. Mzuri Recording.

Morogoro "Jazz Band" (Mbarak Mwinshehe). 1970. Watalii (Tourists). Polydor, POL 7-050A. [Likembe-Mahoka]
———. 1970. "Regina." Polydor, POL 7-050B. [Likembe-Mahoka]
———. 1970. "Choyo Uache" (Leave your bitterness). Polydor, POL 7-051A. [Likembe-Mahoka]
———. 1970. "Pole Dada" (Sorry, sister). Polydor, POL 7-051B. [Likembe-Mahoka]
———. 1971. "Mkatae" (Stop him/her). Polydor, POL 7-052A. [Likembe-Mahoka]
———. 1971. "Waandishi wa Magazeti" (Journalists). Polydor, POL 7-052B. [Likembe-Mahoka]
———. 1971. "Expo -70 No. 1." Polydor, POL 7-061A. [Mizuka]
———. 1971. "Expo -70 No. 2." Polydor, POL 7-061B. [Mizuka]
Morogoro Jazz Band (Mbaraka mwi Mwaruka). n.d. "Dawa ya Mapenzi" (The medicine for love). Saba Saba, SABA 7-16A. [Likembe]
———. n.d. "Niliota Ndoto" (I had a dream). Saba Saba, SABA 7-16B. [Rumba]
Morogoro Jazz Band (Mbaraka Mwinshehe and Nyamwela). n.d. "Morogoro Yapendeza" (Morogoro is a beautiful place). Philips, HL 7-117A. Mzuri Recording. [Rumba]
———. n.d. "Mobutu Baba Congo" (Mobuto, Father of Congo). Philips, HL 7-117B. Mzuri Recording. [Rumba-Pachanga]
Morogoro Jazz Band (Kulwa Salum). n.d. "Wema" (Goodness). Philips, HL 7-123A. Mzuri Recording.
———. n.d. "Tabu Nyingi Sana" (So many troubles). Philips, HL 7-123B. Mzuri Recording.
Super Volcano (Mbarak Mwinshehe and Bonzo). 1974. "Masika No. 2." Polydor, POL 7-265A. [Masika]
———. 1974. "Masika Zole-Zole." Polydor, POL 7-265B. [Zole-Zole]

D.3b Morogoro: Cassettes
Morogoro Jazz Band/Cuban Marimba. n.d. *Morogoro Jazz Band and Cuban Marimba:* Vol. 1. Radio Tanzania DSM, No. 1.
———. n.d. *Morogoro Jazz Band and Cuban Marimba:* Vol. 2. Radio Tanzania DSM, No. 4.
———. n.d. *Morogoro Jazz Band and Cuban Marimba:* Vol. 3. Radio Tanzania DSM, No. 176.
Morogoro Jazz/Vijana Jazz/Super Volcano. n.d. *Gubu la Mume* (A husband's moodiness). Radio Tanzania DSM, No. 62.

D.4a Kenya: CDs
Konde, Fundi. 1994. *Retrospective* Vol. 1 (1947
56). RetroAfric, RETRO 8CD.
Them Mushrooms. 1994. *Songs from Kenya*. Rags Music, RPM 002-2.
———. 1985. *New Horizon*. Polygram, POLP 548.
———. 1989. *Going Places*. Polygram, POLP 573.
Various. 1989. *The Nairobi Beat: Kenyan Pop Music Today*. Rounder, 5030 1989.
Various. 1996. *The Rough Guide To Kenya and Tanzania*. World Music Network, RGNET 1007.

Various. 1991. *Kenya Dance Mania*. Earthworks, 3-1024-2.
Various. 1990. *Guitar Paradise of East Africa*. Earthworks, 3-1021-2.

D.4b Kenya: LPs
Les Wanyika. 1980s. *New Dance*. Polygram, POLP 513.
————. 1980. *Sina Makossa* (I didn't do anything wrong). 12-inch single. MEA 716.
————. 1981. *Pamela*. Polygram, POLP 513. Same as *New Dance Les Les*.
————. 1988. *Nilipi La Ajabu* (Is there anything strange?). Polygram, POLP 582.
————. 1989. *Nimaru*. Polygram, POLP 598.
————. 1990. *Les Les Non Stop*. Polygram, POLP 606.
————. 1991. *Kabibi*. Polygram, POLP 626.
————. 1998. *Amigo*. Cliff Lugard Productions, CLP 001.
Maroon Commandos. 1984. *Kusema Na Kufanya* (To say and to do). Polygram, POLP 514.
————. n.d. *Riziki Haivatu*. Polygram, POLP 518.
————. n.d. *Dawa Nimuone "Hani"* (Medicine to see my Honey). Polygram, POLP 532.
————. 1981. *Usiniambie Unaende* (Don't tell me you're leaving). Ken-Tanza (CBS), KTLP 003.
————. 1986. *And Daudi Kabaka*. Polygram, POLP 554.
————. 1986. *Hasira na Hasara* (Anger and loss). Polygram, POLP 555.
————. 1990. *Mwakaribishwa Na Maroon* (You are welcomed by Maroon). Polygram, POLP 600.
————. 1991. *Bonya Kuche*. Polygram, POLP 608.
————. 1991. *Shikamoo*. Polygram, POLP 628.
Simba Wanyika. 1980s. *Jiburudisheni na Simba Wanyika* (Relax with Simba Wanyika). Polygram, POLP 506.
————. 1980s. *Jiburudisheni*, Vol. 2. Polygram, POLP 510.
————. 1984. *Shillingi* (Shillings). Polygram, POLP 540.
————. 1985. *Halleluya*. Polygram, POLP 552.
————. 1988. *Dunia Haina Wema* (The world lacks goodness). Polygram, POLP 565.
————. n.d. *Baba Asiya*. African Music Gallery (USA), AMG 003.
————. 1988. *Mapenzi Ni Damu* (Love is blood). Polygram, POLP 572.
————. n.d. *Maisha Si Nguvu* (Life is not strength). Polygram, POLP 574.
————. 1989. *Live in Europe*.
Simba Wanyika Stars. 1984. *Sigalame*. ANAC 15.
————. 1984? *Mpita Njia* (Passer-by). Editions FrancAfrique (AIT), NYIKALP 01.
————. 1984. *Pole Pole* (Slowly). Editions FrancAfrique (AIT), NYIKALP 02.
————. 1985. *Bwana Musa*. NYIKALP 03.
————. 1985? *Sigalame II*. Editions FrancAfrique (AIT), NYIKALP 04.
————. 1986. *Mwana wa Ifwe*. ANAC 19.
————. 1986. *Safari*. ANAC 18.
————. 1990. *Sigalame*. Disque Afrique, AFRILP 008.
————. 1989. *Issa Juma and Super Wanyika*. SER 131.
————. 1983. *Matatizo Nimeyazoea* (I am accustomed to problems). POLELP 001.

Various. 1980? *Hit Parade Number 1 (Les Wanyika, Maroon Commandos, Simba Wanyika, Mlimani Park)*. Polydor, POLP 516.
Various. 1983. Swahili Special Hit Parade 1983 (Simba Wanyika, Kurugenzi Jazz, Vijana Jazz, Maroon Commandos). Polydor, POLP 539.

Ngoma
N.1a Tanzania: CDs
The Secret Museum of Mankind. 1998. *Music of East Africa. Ethnic Music Classics: 1925–48*. Yazoo 7015.
Various. n.d. *Maisha: Musiques de Tanzanie*. Buda Records, 92546-2.
Various. 1997. *Music from Tanzania and Zanzibar 1*. Caprice Records, CAP 21554.
Various. 1997. *Music from Tanzania and Zanzibar 2*. Caprice Records, CAP 21573.
Various. 2000. *Music from Tanzania and Zanzibar 3*. Caprice Records, CAP 21577.
Various. 1987. *Music of Tanzania (World Music Library)*. King Record Co., KICC 5150.
Various. 1991. *Witchcraft and Ritual Music: Kenya and Tanzania*. Elektra-Nonesuch, 7559-72066-2.
Various. 1997. *Tanzania: Music of the Farmer Composers of Sukumaland*. Multicultural Media, MCM 3013.
Various. 1997/98. *Tanzanie-Tanzania*. Air Mail Music-Sunset SA, 141007.
Various. 2000. *Wagogo Songs*. Ocora, C560155.
Zawose, Hukwe. 1996. *Chibite*. Real World, CDRW 57.
Zawose, Hukwe, and Master Musicians of Tanzania. 1989. *Mateso* (Suffering). Triple Earth Music, Terracd 104.
Zawose, Hukwe, and Charles Zawose. n.d. *Mkuki Wa Roho* (Spear of the spirit). WOMAD SELECT, WSCD 107.

N.1b Tanzania: LPs
Bagamoyo College of Arts. 1984. *Tanzania Yetu* (Our Tanzania). Triple Earth, TERRA 101.
Various. 1974. *Musik fran Tanzania*. Caprice Records, CAP 1089.
Various. 1955. *Tanganyika*, Vol. 1, No. 25. Gallo, GALP 1320.
Zawose, Hukwe. 1987. *The Art of Hukwe Zawose*. JVC Ethnic Series, VID 25011.

N.1c Tanzania: Cassettes
Gita Musical Club. 1995. Vol. 1: *Mgunga Umemchachia* (Confusion has spoiled him). Top Music House.
———. 1995. Vol. 2: *Mpende Akupendae* (Love the one who loves you). Top Music House.
Ngoma kutoka Kigoma. n.d. *Sungura* (Rabbit). Radio Tanzania DSM, No. 72.
Ngoma kutoka Zanzibar. n.d. *Wimbo* (Song). Radio Tanzania DSM, No. 73.
Ngoma ya Chioda. n.d. *Mtu ni afya* (A human is health). Radio Tanzania DSM, No. 130.
Ngoma ya Daku. n.d. *Hodi hodi wafungaji* (Hello, you-who-fast). Radio Tanzania DSM, No. 106.

Ngoma ya Hiari ya Moyo (TYL)-Nyamwezi. n.d. *Ndandike kabarua ka siri* (S/he wrote a secret letter). Radio Tanzania DSM, No. 76.

Ngoma ya Maneva na Tokomile. n.d. *Nimekuja na mwanangu* (I came with my child). Radio Tanzania DSM, No. 147.

Ngoma za Masewe na Selesya. n.d. *Achimwene*. Radio Tanzania DSM, No. 133.

Ngoma ya Todi na Kitoto. n.d. *Nyerere kawasha Mwenge* (Nyerere lit the Independence Torch). Radio Tanzania DSM, No. 146.

Ngoma za Wa-Arusha/Wakwavi/Watindiga. n.d. *Eskabai*. Radio Tanzania DSM, No. 90.

Ngoma ya Wabena. n.d. *Mama pagatu mwana paiyemba*. Radio Tanzania DSM, No. 141.

Ngoma ya Wabena na Wamahanje. n.d. *Kangalage*. Radio Tanzania DSM, No. 144.

Ngoma ya Wabondei. n.d. *Mnyanyuo/Kimbungumbungu*. Radio Tanzania DSM, No. 88.

Ngoma ya Wachagga. n.d. *Msumi ochilaki*. Radio Tanzania DSM, No. 87.

Ngoma ya Wadigo. n.d. *Kiringingo/Gita*. Radio Tanzania DSM, No. 93.

———. n.d. *Chera: Idumu siasa ya CCM*. Radio Tanzania DSM, No. 110.

Ngoma ya Wafipa. n.d. *Nalukila mayi*. Radio Tanzania DSM, No. 104.

———. n.d. *Vol. 2*. Radio Tanzania DSM, No. 162.

Ngoma ya Wagogo. n.d. *Vol. 1*. Radio Tanzania DSM, No. 74.

———. n.d. *Vol. 2*. Radio Tanzania DSM, No. 114.

Ngoma ya Waha. n.d. *Mahori mwaheke*. Radio Tanzania DSM, No. 138.

Ngoma ya Wahaya. n.d. *Kwiki basi*. Radio Tanzania DSM, No. 77.

———. n.d. *Vol. 2*. Radio Tanzania DSM, No. 120.

Ngoma ya Wahehe. n.d. *Sapula madulu na mapilipili*. Radio Tanzania DSM, No. 140.

Ngoma za Wahehe na Wabena. n.d. *Sapula madulu na mapilipili*. Radio Tanzania DSM, No. 69.

Ngoma ya Wajita. n.d. *TANU yajenga nchi* (TANU builds the nation). Radio Tanzania DSM, No. 94.

———. n.d. *Vol. 2*. Radio Tanzania DSM, No. 153.

Ngoma ya Wakaguru. n.d. *Vijana tunaimba* (We youth sing). Radio Tanzania DSM, No. 117.

Ngoma ya Wakerewe. n.d. *Pole pole wanachalo*. Radio Tanzania DSM, No. 136.

Ngoma ya Wakinga. n.d. *Wilima kyenyeji wapa sidebe*. Radio Tanzania DSM, No. 92.

Ngoma ya Wakurya. n.d. *Wimbo wa kutukuzana* (Praise songs). Radio Tanzania DSM, No. 83.

———. n.d. *Vol. 2*. Radio Tanzania DSM, No. 151.

Ngoma ya Wakutu (Kudauhimbe). n.d. *Pongezi Mwenyekiti Nyerere* (Congratulations, Chairman Nyerere). Radio Tanzania DSM, No. 180.

Ngoma ya Wakwere. n.d. *Budi na bigililo*. Radio Tanzania DSM, No. 116.

Ngoma ya Waluguru. n.d. *Vol. 1*. Radio Tanzania DSM, No. 58.

———. n.d. *Vol. 2*. Radio Tanzania DSM, No. 135.

Ngoma ya Wamakonde. n.d. *Nimezaliwa Litaya* (I was born in Litaya). Radio Tanzania DSM, No. 64.

Ngoma ya Wamakonde. n.d. *Deda*. Radio Tanzania DSM, No. 118.

Ngoma ya Wamanda. n.d. *Mganda*. Radio Tanzania DSM, No. 75.
———. n.d. *Vol. 2*. Radio Tanzania DSM, No. 142.
Ngoma ya Wamasai. n.d. *Oloparo*. Radio Tanzania DSM, No. 78.
Ngoma ya Wamatambwe. n.d. *Yowe yowe rundenda*. Radio Tanzania DSM, No. 109.
Ngoma ya Wamatumbi. n.d. *Kilio* (Mourning). Radio Tanzania DSM, No. 80.
———. n.d. *Vol. 2*. Radio Tanzania DSM, No. 128.
Ngoma ya Wambugwe. n.d. *Jinalongondo*. Radio Tanzania DSM, No. 137.
Ngoma ya Wameru. n.d. *Mwinyi waria kura tapo*. Radio Tanzania DSM, No. 89.
Ngoma ya Wamwera/Wayao. n.d. *Njoo dada tucheze* (Come, sister, let's dance). Radio Tanzania DSM, No. 79.
Ngoma ya Wandamba. n.d. *Lindenda*. Radio Tanzania DSM, No. 149.
———. n.d. *Vol. 2*. Radio Tanzania DSM, No. 170.
Ngoma ya Wandengereko. n.d. *Nombe*. Radio Tanzania DSM, No. 96.
———. n.d. *Mchunje*. Radio Tanzania DSM, No. 148.
Ngoma ya Wandwewe. n.d. *Bangasela na lindenda*. Radio Tanzania DSM, No. 169.
Ngoma ya Wangindo. n.d. *Byagile byagile rabanja*. Radio Tanzania DSM, No. 115.
———. n.d. *Vol. 2*. Radio Tanzania DSM, No. 165.
Ngoma ya Wangoni. n.d. *Kitoto*. Radio Tanzania DSM, No. 65.
Ngoma ya Wanyakusa. n.d. *Chezeni bendera*. Radio Tanzania DSM, No. 82.
Ngoma ya Wanyanja. n.d. *Malipenga*. Radio Tanzania DSM, No. 119.
Ngoma ya Wanyaturu. n.d. *Habari njija*. Radio Tanzania DSM, No. 81.
Ngoma ya Wanyiramba. n.d. *Simba limandende*. Radio Tanzania DSM, No. 95.
Ngoma ya Wapangwa. n.d. *Tujenge wilaya ya Ludewa* (Let's build Ludewa District). Radio Tanzania DSM, No. 143.
Ngoma ya Wapare. n.d. *Wimbo* (Song). Radio Tanzania DSM, No. 86.
Ngoma ya Wapogoro. n.d. *Vol. 1*. Radio Tanzania DSM, No. 59.
———. n.d. *Vol. 2*. Radio Tanzania DSM, No. 129.
Ngoma ya Warangi. n.d. *Hodo hodi warum* (Hello men). Radio Tanzania DSM, No. 85.
Ngoma za Warua, Wabisa na Wamanyema. n.d. *Luomba wetu na kalampe*. Radio Tanzania DSM, No. 131.
Ngoma ya Wasafwa. n.d. *Simwayongo*. Radio Tanzania DSM, No. 145.
Ngoma za Wasagara na Wakaguru. n.d. *Ne mdudu*. Radio Tanzania DSM, No. 132.
Ngoma ya Wasambaa. n.d. *Wanamdumange*. Radio Tanzania DSM, No. 65.
———. n.d. *Vol. 2 (Mdumange)*. Radio Tanzania DSM, No. 127.
Ngoma ya Wasandawe. n.d. *Michango tuko*. Radio Tanzania DSM, No. 101.
Ngoma ya Wasukuma. n.d. *Vol. 1*. Radio Tanzania DSM, No. 60.
———. n.d. *Vol. 3*. Radio Tanzania DSM, No. 152.
Ngoma ya Wayao na Amakua. n.d. *Nthari unawana*. Radio Tanzania DSM, No. 105.
Ngoma ya Wazanaki. n.d. *Wimbo* (Song). Radio Tanzania DSM, No. 134.
Ngoma ya Wazaramo. n.d. *Katikati ya bahari nimwokoe nani* (Whom will I rescue from the middle of the ocean?). Radio Tanzania DSM, No. 57.
———. n.d. *Vol. 2*. Radio Tanzania DSM, No. 108.

Ngoma ya Wazigua. n.d. *Kafuluma kwa majembe*. Radio Tanzania DSM, No. 91.

Nyimbo kwa Lugha ya Kimakonde. n.d. *Kila munu ave na kwao*. Radio Tanzania DSM, No. 111.

Nyimbo za Harusi. n.d. *Vol. 1*. Radio Tanzania DSM, No. 48.

———. n.d. *Vol. 2*. Radio Tanzania DSM, No. 49.

Nyimbo za Wali wa Jando. n.d. *Dada Amina*. Radio Tanzania DSM, No. 166.

N.2 Kenya
LPs
Various. 1980. *Kenya: Musique de marriage a Lamu*. SELAF-ORSTOM, CETO 791.

Various. 1985. *Music of the Waswahili of Lamu:* Vol. 1 *Maulidi*. Ethnic Folkways, FE 4093.

Various. 1985. *Music of the Waswahili of Lamu*. Vol. 2. *Other Sacred Music*. Ethnic Folkways, FE 4094.

Various. 1985. *Music of the Waswahili of Lamu*. Vol. 3. *Secular Music*. Ethnic Folkways, FE 4095.

Various. n.d. *Songs the Swahili Sing*. Original Music, OMA 103.

Various. n.d. *Muziki wa Kiasili* (Folk Music of Kenya). AIR.ZAIT 503.

N.3 Comoro Islands: CDs
Boina Riziki and Soubi. 1999. *Chamsi na Mwezi: Gabusi and Ndzendze from Moheli, Comoros*. Dizim Records, dizim 4503.

Alphabetical Song Index

Index

Page numbers for figures are in italics.

Abu-Lughod, Lila, 128, 156
Abrahams, R. G., 236
academic discourse, 288
acrobatics, 116, 190, 193, 197, 277
aesthetics, 107, 134–5, 275, 278, 287
African-Arab dichotomies, 54–5, 79–81, 225
African National Congress (ANC), 94
African Socialism, 47, 160, 178, 235–40
Afro-Cuban rhythms, 90, 98, 115
Afro-Shirazi Party, 47, 64, 189, 336n. 30
agriculture, 36–8, 47, 218, 235–8, 240. *See also* plantation agriculture
Akida Jumbe, 112
al-Faruqi, Lois Ibsen, 108
al-Jabry, Azan, 266
Al Watan, 111
All Stars Modern Taarab, 115, 148–9
Allen, James de Vere, 35, 39, 334n. 9
Ally Star, 104, 255
Amboni caves, 57
Amboni Company, 57, 87–9, 100, 213, 339n. 19
Amnesty International, 49
Amour, Salmin, 49, 250, 349n. 21
Anderson, Benedict, 9–10, 12, 270, 271–2, 274, 279, 292
Angola, 45
animism, 2, 51
anticolonialism, 179, 190, 275
Appadurai, Arjun, 10
Appel, Willa, 15, 18
Arab. *See* African-Arab dichotomies; Hadrami Arabs; Omani Arabs
Arabian Peninsula, 2, 32, 54
Arabian musical styles, 15, 107–10, 114, 281
Arinoti, 45, 75

army. *See* Jeshi la Kujenga Taifa; Jeshi la Wananchi Tanzania
Arusha, 89, 197, 206, 217, 218
Arusha Declaration, 47, 178, 184, 190, 277
Asians, 1, 37, 43, 54, 55, 331n. 1
Atomic Jazz Band, 92, *93*
audience. *See* performers, and audience
Austin, John, 18
Australia, 9
Authenticité, 170
authenticity, concern with, 202–8, 221, 222, 276–8
authority, competing forms of, 5, 83, 162–9, 206–7, 235. *See also* state

Babloom Modern Taarab, 106, 112, 115, 116–21, 124, 125, 129, 130, 135, 148–53, 227–35, 247, 254, 258–64, 266–7, 284, 286, 341nn. 35, 36, 342n. 3, 348n. 9, 351n. 6
Bagamoyo, 95, 247
Bajuni, 81
Bakari, Mtoro bin Mwinyi, 82–3, 139, 141
Baker, E. C., 91
ballroom dancing. *See* Western ballroom musical styles
Bandari Orchestra, 101, 196–8
Bandari Taarab, 196–8, 348n. 4
Barawa, 34
Baraza la Kiswahili la Taifa (BAKITA—National Swahili Council), 183
Baraza la Kiswahili la Zanzibar (BAKIZA—Zanzibar Swahili Council), 183
Baraza la Muziki la Taifa (BAMUTA—National Music Council), 346n. 46
Baraza la Sanaa la Taifa (BASATA–National Arts Council), 194, 227, 274, 346n. 46

ujamaa villages, 236–8
Ukala, 198, 203–9, 211, 213
Umoja wa Vijana (CCM Youth League),
4, 266–7, 277, 282
Umoja wa Wanawake wa Tanganyika
(UWT—National Women's Organiza-
tion), 172–4
underdevelopment, 144, 161
Unguja, 81
uniformity, as an aesthetic principle,
213–15, 217, 278
uniforms, 2–3, 5, 72, 118–19, 200, 220,
255
Union government, 6, 53–4
Union, of Tanganyika and Zanzibar, 5–
6, 47, 242, 281, 331nn. 8, 9, 332nn.
11, 12, 13; legality of, 7, 331nn. 8
Union for Multiparty Democracy
(UMD), 95, 244
unions. *See* trade unions
United Arab Emirates, 279
United Democratic Party (UDP), 48, 244
United Peoples' Democratic Party
(UPDP), 244
United States of America, 41, 335n. 23
University of Dar es Salaam, 251, 269,
335n. 29
unyago, 75
Urafiki Textile Mill, 282
urban migration, 235
urbanism, 36, 90, 99
Usagara Secondary School, 86, 216, 219
Usambara Mountains, 27–8, 34, 37, 43,
58, 123, 333n. 1
Usambara Railway, 44, 55, 71, 197

Vail, Leroy, 127, 285, 333n. 17
Vasco da Gama, 34, 39
Verdery, Katherine, 8, 10, 11, 12, 127,
235, 238–9, 332n. 14, 351n. 9
Vijana Jazz Band, 282, 283
villagization, 47, 175, 236–8, 278
vishindo, 133, 148, 264
Vugo, 78, 83, 107, 110

Wasin Island, 36, 40
Watangatanga Band, 101–2, *103*, 116,
120, 226–9, 231, 233, 254, 340n. 30
Waterman, Christopher, 90, 99–100,
203, 222
weddings, 15–18, 75, 83, 89, 99, 106,
110, 115, 126, 144, 145, 152, 227,

233–4, 254, 260, 262, 284, 291, 349n.
28
Western ballroom musical styles, 90–4,
98–9, 275
White, Landeg, 127, 285
Whiteley, Wilfred, 181–2
White Star Taarab, 112, 226
Wilk, Richard, 93–4
Williams, Brackette, 10
Williams, Donald, 238, 240
Willis, Justin, 39, 80–1, 83, 97
Wolf, Eric, 14, 291
women, 68–9, 73–5, 99–100, 110, 112,
180, 225, 258, 262, 264, 284
World Bank, 7, 48, 238, 245, 261, 278
World War I, 43, 45
World War II, 168
Wright, Susan, 271

Yao, 59
Yelvington, Kevin A., 80
Yoruba, 99–100, 203
Young Novelty Musical Club, 105, 112
Youth League. *See* Umoja wa Vijana

Zaire. *See* Democratic Republic of the
Congo
Zambia, 45, 191
Zanaki, 66
Zanzibar, 6, 30, 36, 48, 53–4, 64, 70, 72,
81, 120, 165–9, 189, 193, 223, 226,
242, 256, 275; cultural policy in, 165–
9, 189, 250; history of, 39–47; taarab
in, 69, 109–10, 113–15, 224, 226,
252, 255, 276, 281, 342n. 49; violence
in, 47, 49, 336n. 39
Zanzibar Arts Council. *See* Baraza la Sa-
naa la Zanzibar
Zanzibar government, 6, 54
Zanzibar Revolution, 6, 47
Zanzibar Swahili Council. *See* Baraza la
Kiswahili la Zanzibar
Zaramo, 51
Zein l'Abdin Musical Party, 115–16,
341n. 37
Zelewski, Emil von, 42–3
Zigua, 59, 63, 198–211, 221
Zimba, 39
Zimbabwe, 34, 45, 191, 274
Zimbabwe African National Union
(ZANU), 94, 191
Zuhura Swaleh, 116, 247